Judging the Law of the Sea

Judging the Law of the Sea

Judicial Contributions to the UN Convention on the Law of the Sea

NATALIE KLEIN
UNSW Sydney

and

KATE PARLETT
Twenty Essex, London

OXFORD
UNIVERSITY PRESS

OXFORD
UNIVERSITY PRESS

Great Clarendon Street, Oxford, OX2 6DP,
United Kingdom

Oxford University Press is a department of the University of Oxford.
It furthers the University's objective of excellence in research, scholarship,
and education by publishing worldwide. Oxford is a registered trade mark of
Oxford University Press in the UK and in certain other countries

First Edition published in 2022

Impression: 1

Published in the United States of America by Oxford University Press
198 Madison Avenue, New York, NY 10016, United States of America

British Library Cataloguing in Publication Data

Data available

Library of Congress Control Number: 2022937833

ISBN 978–0–19–885335–0

DOI: 10.1093/law/9780198853350.001.0001

Printed and bound in the UK by
TJ Books Limited

Acknowledgements

The idea of this book was first discussed over a breakfast at an American Society of International Law meeting some years ago, and then over cocktails in London. The global pandemic prevented the authors from further in-person discussions and also resulted in some delays. Needless to say, Natalie is very grateful to Kate for sticking with the project despite the demands of a busy practice, life with Covid and family commitments, and Kate is very grateful to Natalie for her endless patience with extensions to deadlines.

Natalie warmly acknowledges the wonderful research environment provided by the University of Edinburgh during her MacCormick Fellowship while on sabbatical from Macquarie University in 2017. Early drafts of some chapters were written during this time and Natalie thanks Emeritus Professor Alan Boyle, Professor James Harrison, and other colleagues in the Faculty of Law at the University of Edinburgh for their support. An early version of Chapter 2 was presented as the annual lecture for the Scottish Centre of International Law and feedback from participants is gratefully acknowledged. Natalie also acknowledges the financial support provided by the SHARP scheme at UNSW Sydney that facilitated the research and writing of this book.

Kate acknowledges support from her colleagues at Twenty Essex in London, as well as useful discussions with Sir Michael Wood KCMG, Sam Wordsworth KC, Coalter Lathrop, and Amy Sander.[1] Kate's work on dispute settlement in the law of the sea was encouraged by discussions at a workshop at the K.G. Jebsen Centre for the Law of the Sea at the Arctic University of Norway in Tromsø, Norway, in 2016, as well as through discussions at the University of Oxford Public International Law Interest Group.

We have benefited from excellent research and editorial assistance throughout the writing of this book. Natalie is very thankful for the excellent work of UNSW Sydney students Caleb O'Brien and Crystal Xiaojing Ji. Kate thanks Andrew Brown from King's College London for his invaluable assistance with research. This book would not have made it to the finish line without the extraordinary efforts of UNSW Sydney student Jack McNally. We are both extremely grateful to Jack for his painstaking attention to detail across all editorial matters and helpful comments on the drafts. Case law and website addresses were all current as of January 2022.

Some parts of Chapters 2, 3, and 4 have drawn on our earlier publications and we acknowledge that those publications are reproduced with varying degrees of modification with the kind permission of the publishers:

- Kate Parlett, 'Beyond the Four Corners of the Convention: Expanding the Scope of Jurisdiction of Law of the Sea Tribunals' (2017) 48 ODIL 284;
- Natalie Klein, 'The Vicissitudes of Dispute Settlement under the Law of the Sea Convention' (2017) 32 IJMCL 332;

[1] Any views expressed herein are not to be attributed to members of Twenty Essex, nor to any of the authors' clients.

- Natalie Klein, 'Stakeholders in Dispute Settlement under the UN Convention on the Law of the Sea' in Marta Chantal Ribeiro, Fernando Loureiro Bastos, and Tore Henriksen (eds), *Global Challenges and the Law of the Sea* (Springer 2020) 239.

We further note that permission was granted from the United Nations to reprint the full text of Articles 61 and 62 from the UN Convnetion on the Law of the Sea, by Division of Ocean Affairs and the Law of the Sea, © (2018) United Nations: <https://www.un.org/depts/los/convention_agreements/texts/unclos/closindx.htm>. This text appears in Chapter 8.

Finally, we are very grateful for the love and support from our families. Natalie thanks Matthew, Dulcie, Tessa, and Joshua for their understanding and occasional interest in the law of the sea or at least things ocean-related. Kate thanks Tommy for his encouragement, and Laurence, Arthur and James for providing welcome (and perhaps too frequent) distractions from all things international law-related.

Contents

List of Cases

List of Treaties and Other International Instruments

TREATIES

OTHER INTERNATIONAL INSTRUMENTS

List of Case Name Abbreviations

Abbreviation	Full Citation
2013 SPRFMO Review Panel	*Review Panel Established Under the Convention on the Conservation and Management of High Seas Fishery Resources in the South Pacific Ocean* (Findings and Recommendations of the Review Panel of 5 July 2013) PCA Case No 2013-14
2018 SPRFMO Review Panel	*Review Panel established under the Convention on the Conservation and Management of High Seas Fishery Resources in the South Pacific Ocean* (Findings and Recommendations of the Review Panel of 5 June 2018) PCA Case No 2018-3
Anglo-Norwegian Fisheries	*Anglo-Norwegian Fisheries (United Kingdom v Norway)* (Judgment) [1951] ICJ Rep 116
Aegean Sea Continental Shelf	*Aegean Sea Continental Shelf (Greece v Turkey)* (Judgment) [1978] ICJ Rep 3
ARA Libertad	*ARA Libertad (Argentina v Ghana)* (Provisional Measures, Order of 15 December 2012) ITLOS Reports 2012, 332
ARA Libertad, Annex VII Arbitration	*ARA Libertad (Argentina v Ghana)* (Termination Order of 11 November 2013) PCA Case No 2013-11
Arctic Sunrise, Compensation	*Arctic Sunrise (Netherlands v Russia)* (Award on Compensation of 10 July 2017) PCA Case No 2014-02
Arctic Sunrise, Jurisdiction	*Arctic Sunrise (Netherlands v Russia)* (Award on Jurisdiction of 26 November 2014) PCA Case No 2014-02
Arctic Sunrise, Merits	*Arctic Sunrise (Netherlands v Russia)* (Award on the Merits of 14 August 2015) PCA Case No 2014-02
Arctic Sunrise, Provisional Measures	*Arctic Sunrise (Netherlands v Russia)* (Provisional Measures, Order of 22 November 2013) ITLOS Reports 2013, 230
Atlanto-Scandian Herring	*Atlanto-Scandian Herring Arbitration (Denmark in respect of the Faroe Islands v the European Union)* (Termination Order of 23 September 2014) PCA Case No 2013-30

Abbreviation	Full Citation
Barbados v Trinidad and Tobago	*Barbados v Trinidad and Tobago* (Award of the Arbitral Tribunal of 11 April 2006) PCA Case No 2004-02
Bay of Bengal Arbitration	*Bay of Bengal Maritime Boundary Arbitration (Bangladesh v India)* (Award of 7 July 2014) PCA Case No 2010-16
Bay of Bengal Delimitation	*Delimitation of the Maritime Boundary in the Bay of Bengal (Bangladesh/Myanmar)* (Judgment) ITLOS Reports 2012, 4
Beagle Channel	*Beagle Channel Arbitration (Argentina/Chile)* (Report and Decision of the Court of Arbitration dated 18 February 1977) 21 RIAA 53
Cameroon v Nigeria, Judgment	*Land and Maritime Boundary (Cameroon v Nigeria)* (Judgment) [2002] ICJ Rep 303
Cameroon v Nigeria, Preliminary Objections	*Land and Maritime (Cameroon v Nigeria)* (Preliminary Objections) [1998] ICJ Rep 275
Camouco	*Camouco (Panama v France)* (Prompt Release, Judgment) ITLOS Reports 2000, 10
Certain Phosphate Lands in Nauru	*Certain Phosphate Lands in Nauru (Nauru v Australia)* (Preliminary Objections) [1992] ICJ Rep 240
Chagos Advisory Opinion	*Legal Consequences of the Separation of the Chagos Archipelago from Mauritius in 1965* (Advisory Opinion) [2019] ICJ Rep 95
Chagos MPA	*Chagos Marine Protected Area Arbitration (Mauritius v United Kingdom)* (Award of 18 March 2015) PCA Case No 2011-03
Chaisiri Reefer 2	*Chaisiri Reefer 2 (Panama v Yemen)* (Prompt Release) ITLOS Case No 9
Coastal State Rights in the Black Sea	*Dispute Concerning Coastal State Rights in the Black Sea, Sea of Azov, and Kerch Strait (Ukraine v Russia)* (Preliminary Objections Award of 21 February 2020) PCA Case No 2017-06
Conservation of Swordfish Stocks	*Conservation and Sustainable Exploitation of Swordfish Stocks (Chile/European Community)* (Order of 16 December 2009) ITLOS Reports 2008–2010, 13
Construction of a Road	*Certain Activities Carried Out by Nicaragua in the Border Area (Costa Rica v Nicaragua), Construction of a Road in Costa Rica along the San Juan River (Nicaragua v Costa Rica)* (Judgment) [2015] ICJ Rep 665

Abbreviation	Full Citation
Corfu Channel	*Corfu Channel (United Kingdom v Albania)* [1949] ICJ Rep 4
Croatia-Slovenia Arbitration, Final Award	*Arbitration between the Republic of Croatia and the Republic of Slovenia* (Final Award of 29 June 2017) PCA Case No 2012-04
Croatia-Slovenia Arbitration, Partial Award	*Arbitration between the Republic of Croatia and the Republic of Slovenia* (Partial Award of 30 June 2016) PCA Case No 2012-04
Delimitation of the Continental Shelf	*Delimitation of the Continental Shelf between Nicaragua and Colombia beyond 200 Nautical Miles from the Nicaraguan Coast (Nicaragua v Colombia)* (Preliminary Objections) [2016] ICJ Rep 100
Detention of Three Ukrainian Naval Vessels, Provisional Measures	*Detention of Three Ukrainian Naval Vessels (Ukraine v Russia)* (Provisional Measures Order of 25 May 2019) ITLOS Case No 26
Detention of Ukrainian Naval Vessels and Servicemen	*Detention of Ukrainian Naval Vessels and Servicemen (Ukraine v Russia)* PCA Case No 2019-28
Duzgit Integrity	*Duzgit Integrity Arbitration (Malta v São Tomé and Príncipe)* (Award of 5 September 2016) PCA Case No 2014-07
East Timor	*East Timor (Portugal v Australia)* (Judgment) [1995] ICJ Rep 90
Enrica Lexie, Annex VII Provisional Measures	*Enrica Lexie (Italy v India)* (Request for the Prescription of Provisional Measures, Order of 29 April 2016) PCA Case No 2015-28
Enrica Lexie, Award	*Enrica Lexie (Italy v India)* (Award of 21 May 2020) PCA Case No 2015-28
Enrica Lexie, ITLOS Provisional Measures	*Enrica Lexie (Italy v India)* (Provisional Measures, Order of 24 August 2015) ITLOS Reports 2015, 182
Eritrea/Yemen, First Stage	*Sovereignty and Maritime Delimitation in the Red Sea (Eritrea/Yemen)* (Award of the Arbitral Tribunal in the First Stage of 3 October 1996: Territorial Sovereignty and Scope of the Dispute) PCA Case No 1996-04
Eritrea/Yemen, Second Stage	*Sovereignty and Maritime Delimitation in the Red Sea (Eritrea/Yemen)* (Award of the Arbitral Tribunal in the Second Stage of 17 December 1999: Maritime Delimitation) PCA Case No 1996-04

Abbreviation	Full Citation
Filleting Award	*Filleting within the Gulf of St Lawrence between Canada and France* (Decision of 17 July 1986) (1990) 82 ILR 591
Spain v Canada	*Fisheries Jurisdiction (Spain v Canada)* (Jurisdiction) [1998] ICJ Rep 432
Ghana/Côte d'Ivoire, Judgment	*Delimitation of the Maritime Boundary between Ghana and Côte d'Ivoire in the Atlantic Ocean (Ghana/Côte d'Ivoire)* (Judgment of 23 September 2017) ITLOS Case No 23
Ghana/Côte d'Ivoire, Provisional Measures	*Delimitation of the Maritime Boundary between Ghana and Côte d'Ivoire in the Atlantic Ocean (Ghana/Côte d'Ivoire)* (Provisional Measures Order of 25 April 2015) ITLOS Reports 2015, 146
Grand Prince	*Grand Prince (Belize v France)* (Prompt Release, Judgment) ITLOS Reports 2001, 17
Gulf of Maine	*Delimitation of the Maritime Boundary in the Gulf of Maine Area (Canada v United States)* (Merits) [1984] ICJ Rep 246
Guinea v Guinea-Bissau	*Delimitation of the Maritime Boundary (Guinea/Guinea-Bissau)* (Award of 18 February 1985) 25(2) (1986) ILM 251
Guinea-Bissau/Senegal	*Delimitation of Maritime Boundary (Guinea-Bissau/Senegal)* 83 ILR 1
Guyana v Suriname	*Guyana v Suriname* (Award of the Arbitral Tribunal of 17 September 2007) PCA Case No 2004-04
Hoshinmaru	*Hoshinmaru (Japan v Russia)* (Prompt Release, Judgment) ITLOS Reports 2005-2007, 18
Icelandic Fisheries	*Fisheries Jurisdiction (United Kingdom v Iceland)* (Jurisdiction) [1973] ICJ Rep 3
Juno Trader	*Juno Trader (Saint Vincent and the Grenadines v Guinea-Bissau)* (Prompt Release, Judgment) ITLOS Reports 2004, 17
Land Reclamation, Award	*Land Reclamation by Singapore in and around the Straits of Johor (Malaysia v Singapore)* (Award on Agreed Terms of 1 September 2005) PCA Case No 2004-05
Land Reclamation, Provisional Measures	*Land Reclamation by Singapore in and around the Straits of Johor (Malaysia v Singapore)* (Provisional Measures, Order of 8 October 2003) ITLOS Reports 2003, 10

Abbreviation	Full Citation
Land, Island and Maritime Frontier, Judgment	*Land, Island and Maritime Frontier Dispute (El Salvador/Honduras: Nicaragua Intervening)* (Judgment) [1992] ICJ Rep 351
Libya/Malta	*Continental Shelf (Libya/Malta)* (Judgment) [1985] ICJ Rep 13
Louisa, Judgment	*M/V Louisa (Saint Vincent and the Grenadines v Spain)* (Judgment) ITLOS Reports 2013, 4
Louisa, Provisional Measures	*M/V Louisa (Saint Vincent and the Grenadines v Spain)* (Provisional Measures, Order of 23 December 2010) ITLOS Reports 2008–2010, 58
Maritime Delimitation between Greenland and Jan Mayen	*Maritime Delimitation in the Area between Greenland and Jan Mayen (Denmark v Norway)* (Judgment) [1993] ICJ Rep 38
Maritime Delimitation in the Black Sea	*Maritime Delimitation in the Black Sea (Romania v Ukraine)* (Judgment) [2009] ICJ Rep 61
Maritime Delimitation in the Caribbean Sea and the Pacific Ocean	*Maritime Delimitation in the Caribbean Sea and the Pacific Ocean (Costa Rica v Nicaragua)* and *Land Boundary in the Northern Part of Isla Portillos (Costa Rica v Nicaragua)* (Judgment) [2019] ICJ Rep 139
Maritime Delimitation in the Indian Ocean, Preliminary Objections	*Maritime Delimitation in the Indian Ocean (Somalia v Kenya)* (Preliminary Objections) [2017] ICJ Rep 3
Maritime Delimitation in the Indian Ocean, Judgment	*Maritime Delimitation in the Indian Ocean (Somalia v Kenya)* (Judgment of 12 October 2021) General List No 161
Marshall Islands Cases	*Obligations concerning Negotiations relating to Cessation of the Nuclear Arms Race and to Nuclear Disarmament (Marshall Islands v India)* (Preliminary Objections) [2016] ICJ Rep 255; *Obligations concerning Negotiations relating to Cessation of the Nuclear Arms Race and to Nuclear Disarmament (Marshall Islands v Pakistan)* (Preliminary Objections) [2016] ICJ Rep 552; *Obligations concerning Negotiations relating to Cessation of the Nuclear Arms Race and to Nuclear Disarmament (Marshall Islands v United Kingdom)* (Preliminary Objections) [2016] ICJ Rep 833
Mauritius/Maldives, Preliminary Objections	*Delimitation of the Maritime Boundary between Mauritius and Maldives in the Indian Ocean (Mauritius/Maldives)* (Preliminary Objections Judgment of 28 January 2021) ITLOS Case No 28

Abbreviation	Full Citation
Mauritius/Maldives, Merits	*Delimitation of the Maritime Boundary between Mauritius and Maldives in the Indian Ocean (Mauritius/Maldives)* (Merits) ITLOS Case No 28
Monte Confurco	*Monte Confurco (Seychelles v France)* (Prompt Release, Judgment) ITLOS Reports 2000, 86
MOX Plant, Order No 3	*MOX Plant (Ireland v United Kingdom)* (Order No 3 on Suspension of Proceedings on Jurisdiction and Merits, and Request for Further Provisional Measures, Order of 24 June 2003) PCA Case No 2002-01
MOX Plant, Provisional Measures	*MOX Plant (Ireland v United Kingdom)* (Provisional Measures, Order of 3 December 2001) ITLOS Reports 2001, 95
MOX Plant, Termination	*MOX Plant (Ireland v United Kingdom)* (Order No 6 on Termination of Proceedings, Order of 6 June 2008) PCA Case No 2002-01
Nicaragua v Honduras	*Territorial and Maritime Dispute between Nicaragua and Honduras in the Caribbean Sea (Nicaragua v Honduras)* (Preliminary Objections) [2007] ICJ Rep 659
Norstar, Judgment	*M/V Norstar (Panama v Italy)* (Judgment of 10 April 2019) ITLOS Case No 25
Norstar, Preliminary Objections	*M/V Norstar (Panama v Italy)* (Preliminary Objections Judgment of 4 November 2016) ITLOS Case No 25
North Atlantic Coast Fisheries	*North Atlantic Coast Fisheries (United Kingdom v United States of America)*, Award of 7 September 1910, XI UNRIAA 167
North Sea, Judgment	*North Sea Continental Shelf (Federal Republic of Germany/Denmark; Federal Republic of Germany/Netherlands)* (Judgment) [1969] ICJ Rep 3
Pedra Branca/Pulau Batu Puteh, Middle Rocks and South Ledge	*Sovereignty over Pedra Branca/Pulau Batu Puteh, Middle Rocks and South Ledge (Malaysia/Singapore)* (Judgment) [2008] ICJ Rep 12
Peru v Chile	*Maritime Dispute (Peru v Chile)* (Judgment) [2014] ICJ Rep 3
Pulp Mills, Merits	*Pulp Mills on the River Uruguay (Argentina v Uruguay)* (Merits) [2010] ICJ Rep 14
Pulp Mills, Provisional Measures	*Pulp Mills on the River Uruguay (Argentina v Uruguay)* (Provisional Measures) [2006] ICJ Rep 113

Abbreviation	Full Citation
Qatar v Bahrain, Merits	*Maritime Delimitation and Territorial Questions between Qatar and Bahrain (Qatar v Bahrain)* (Merits) [2001] ICJ Rep 40
Saiga No 2, Judgment	*M/V Saiga (No 2) (Saint Vincent and the Grenadines v Guinea)* (Judgment) ITLOS Reports 1999, 10
Saiga No 2, Provisional Measures	*M/V Saiga (No 2) (Saint Vincent and the Grenadines v Guinea)* (Provisional Measures, Order of 11 March 1998) ITLOS Reports 1998, 24
Saiga, Prompt Release	*M/V Saiga (Saint Vincent and the Grenadines v Guinea)* (Prompt Release, Judgment) ITLOS Reports 1997, 16
San Padre Pio, Provisional Measures	*M/T San Padre Pio (Switzerland v Nigeria)* (Provisional Measures, Order of 6 July 2019) ITLOS Case No 27
Seabed Advisory Opinion	*Responsibilities and Obligations of States with Respect to Activities in the Area* (Advisory Opinion) ITLOS Reports 2011, 10
South China Sea, Award	*South China Sea Arbitration (Philippines v China)* (Award of 12 July 2016) PCA Case No 2013-19
South China Sea, Jurisdiction and Admissibility	*South China Sea Arbitration (Philippines v China)* (Award on Jurisdiction and Admissibility of 29 October 2015) PCA Case No 2013-19
Southern Bluefin Tuna, Jurisdiction and Admissibility	*Southern Bluefin Tuna (New Zealand v Japan; Australia v Japan)* (Jurisdiction and Admissibility) (2000) 23 RIAA 1
Southern Bluefin Tuna, Provisional Measures	*Southern Bluefin Tuna (New Zealand v Japan; Australia v Japan)* (Provisional Measures, Order of 27 August 1999) ITLOS Reports 1999, 280
SRFC Advisory Opinion	*Request for Advisory Opinion Submitted by the Sub-Regional Fisheries Commission* (Advisory Opinion) ITLOS Reports 2015, 4
St Pierre and Miquelon	*Delimitation of Maritime Areas (St Pierre and Miquelon) (Canada/France)* (Decision of 10 June 1992) 31 (1992) ILM 1145
Territorial and Maritime Dispute, Preliminary Objections	*Territorial and Maritime Dispute (Nicaragua v Colombia)* (Preliminary Objections) [2007] ICJ Rep 832
Territorial and Maritime Dispute, Judgment	*Territorial and Maritime Dispute (Nicaragua v Colombia)* (Judgment) [2012] ICJ Rep 624

Abbreviation	Full Citation
Timor Sea Conciliation, Decision on Competence	*Conciliation between The Democratic Republic of Timor-Leste and the Commonwealth of Australia* (Decision on Australia's Objections to Competence of 19 September 2016) PCA Case No 2016-10
Timor Sea Conciliation, Report	*Conciliation between The Democratic Republic of Timor-Leste and the Commonwealth of Australia* (Report and Recommendations of the Compulsory Conciliation Commission, 9 May 2018) PCA Case No 2016-10
Tomimaru	*Tomimaru (Japan v Russia)* (Prompt Release, Judgment) ITLOS Reports 2005–2007, 74
Tunisia/Libya	*Continental Shelf (Tunisia/Libya)* (Judgment) [1982] ICJ Rep 18
UK/France	*Delimitation of the Continental Shelf* (United Kingdom/France) (Decision of 30 June 1977) 18 RIAA 3
Virginia G	*M/V Virginia G (Panama/Guinea-Bissau)* (Judgment) ITLOS Reports 2014, 4
Virginia G, Order of 2 November	*M/V 'Virginia G' (Panama/Guinea-Bissau)* (Order of 2 November 2012) ITLOS Reports 2012, 309
Volga	*Volga (Russia v Australia)* (Prompt Release, Judgment) ITLOS Reports 2002, 10

List of Other Abbreviations

Please note that abbreviated journal names are not provided here. Full references may be found in the Bibliography.

1994 Agreement	Agreement Relating to the Implementation of Part XI of the United Nations Convention on the Law of the Sea 10 December 1982 (adopted 28 July 1994, entered into force 16 November 1994) 1836 UNTS 3
Auckland Convention	Convention on the Conservation and Management of High Seas Fishery Resources in the South Pacific Ocean (adopted 14 November 2009 entered into force 24 August 2012) ATS 28
CBD	Convention on Biological Diversity (adopted 5 June 1992, entered into force 29 December 1993) 1760 UNTS 79
CITES	Convention on the International Trade in Endangered Species of Wild Fauna and Flora (adopted 3 March 1973, entered into force 1 July 1975) 993 UNTS 243
CLCS	Commission on the Limits of the Continental Shelf
CMATS Treaty	Treaty between Australia and the Democratic Republic of Timor-Leste on Certain Maritime Arrangements in the Timor Sea (adopted 12 January 2006, entered into force 23 February 2007) 2483 UNTS 359
COLREGS	Convention on the International Regulations for Preventing Collisions at Sea (adopted 20 October 1972, entered into force 15 July 1977) 1050 UNTS 1976
Continental Shelf Convention	Convention on the Continental Shelf (opened for signature 29 April 1958, entered into force 10 June 1964) 499 UNTS 311
Declaration of Conduct	2002 China-ASEAN Declaration on the Conduct of Parties in the South China Sea
ECJ	European Court of Justice
EEZ	Exclusive economic zone
EIA	Environmental impact assessment

FAO	Food and Agriculture Organization of the United Nations
Fish Stocks Agreement	United Nations Agreement for the Implementation of the Provisions of the United Nations Convention on the Law of the Sea of 10 December 1982 relating to the Conservation and Management of Straddling Fish Stocks and Highly Migratory Fish Stocks (adopted 4 August 1995, entered into force 11 December 2001) 2167 UNTS 3
ICCPR	International Covenant on Civil and Political Rights (adopted 16 December 1966, entered into force 23 March 1976) 999 UNTS 171
ICJ	International Court of Justice
ICJ Rules	International Court of Justice, Rules of Court (adopted 14 April 1978, entered into force 1 July 1978)
ICJ Statute	Statute of the International Court of Justice
ILC	International Law Commission
IMO	International Maritime Organization
ISA	International Seabed Authority
ITLOS	International Tribunal for the Law of the Sea
ITLOS Rules	International Tribunal for the Law of the Sea, Rules of the Tribunal, Doc No ITLOS/8 (adopted 28 October 1997, amended 25 March 2021)
ITLOS Statute	Statute of the International Tribunal for the Law of the Sea (UNCLOS Annex VI)
IUCN	International Union for Conservation of Nature
IUU fishing	Illegal, Unregulated and Unreported Fishing
Klein, *Dispute Settlement*	Natalie Klein, *Dispute Settlement in the UN Convention on the Law of the Sea* (CUP 2005)
MARPOL Convention	International Convention for the Prevention of Pollution from Ships (adopted 2 November 1973, entered into force 2 October 1983) 1340 UNTS 62
MCA Convention	Convention on the Determination of the Minimal Conditions for Access and Exploitation of Marine Resources within the Maritime Areas under Jurisdiction of the Member States of the Sub-Regional Fisheries Commission (adopted 8 June 2012, entered into force 16 September 2012)
MPA	Marine protected area
NM	Nautical miles

Nodules Regulations	International Seabed Authority, 'Regulations on Prospecting and Exploration for Polymetallic Nodules in the Area' (22 July 2013) UN Doc ISBA/19/C/17
OSPAR Convention	Convention for the Protection of the Marine Environment of the North-East Atlantic (opened for signature 22 September 1992, entered into force 25 March 1998) 2354 UNTS 67
PCIJ	Permanent Court of International Justice
Proelss Commentary	Alexander Proelss (ed), *United Nations Convention on the Law of the Sea: A Commentary* (CH Beck, Hart and Nomos 2017)
RFMO	Regional Fisheries Management Organisation
Rio Declaration	'Rio Declaration on Environment and Development' (adopted 13 June 1992) UN Doc A/Conf.151/26 (Vol I)
SBT Convention	Convention for the Conservation of Southern Bluefin Tuna (adopted 10 May 1993, entered into force 20 May 1994) 1819 UNTS 359
SOLAS Convention	International Convention for the Safety of Life at Sea (adopted 1 November 1974, entered into force 25 May 1980) 1184 UNTS 278
SPRFMO	South Pacific Regional Fisheries Management Organisation
SRFC	Sub-Regional Fisheries Commission
Stockholm Declaration	'Declaration of the United Nations Conference on the Human Environment' (adopted 16 June 1972) UN Doc A/Conf.48/14/Rev.1 (Stockholm Declaration)
STS	Ship-to-ship
Sulphides Regulations	International Seabed Authority, 'Regulations on Prospecting and Exploration for Polymetallic Sulphides in the Area' (15 November 2010) UN Doc ISBA/16/A/12/Rev.1
Territorial Sea Convention	Convention on the Territorial Sea and Contiguous Zone (opened for signature 29 April 1958, entered into force 10 September 1964) 516 UNTS 205
Timor Sea Treaty	Timor Sea Treaty between the Government of East Timor and the Government of Australia (adopted 20 May 2002, entered into force 2 April 2003) [2003] ATS 13

UN	United Nations
UNCLOS	United Nations Convention on the Law of the Sea (adopted 10 December 1982, entered into force 16 November 1994) 1833 UNTS 397
VCLT	Vienna Convention on the Law of Treaties (adopted 23 May 1969, entered into force 27 January 1980) 1155 UNTS 331
Virginia Commentary	Myron H Nordquist (ed), *United Nations Convention on the Law of the Sea 1982: A Commentary* (Martinus Nijhoff 1985–2012)
WTO	World Trade Organization

1
Introduction

I. The UN Convention on the Law of the Sea: Background and Overview

As Hersch Lauterpacht noted when writing about the International Court of Justice (ICJ), 'Institutions set up for the achievement of definite purposes grow to fulfil tasks not wholly identical with those which were in the minds of their authors at the time of their creation'.[1] This book explores this idea in relation to ongoing judicial interpretations of the UN Convention on the Law of the Sea (UNCLOS or Convention)[2] pursuant to the dispute settlement regime established under that Convention. Our examination begins in this section with a background and overview of the law of the sea. The chapter then provides an overview of the UNCLOS dispute settlement procedures and reflections on the role of this dispute settlement regime and its inherent importance for ocean governance.

The international law of the sea has developed over time to encompass some of the most detailed rules and norms, which interact with a broad range of other areas of international law. Initially focused on the questions of status and control of maritime space, modern rules of law of the sea address the extent of coastal State sovereignty and jurisdiction alongside a broad range of other issues, including fisheries, marine environmental protection, marine scientific research, military uses of the oceans, and the interests of non-coastal States and the international community in the high seas and the deep seabed.

One of the earliest and most influential contributions to the development of the law of the sea was made by the Dutch scholar Hugo Grotius, through the publication of *Mare Liberum* in 1608.[3] He suggested that the sea cannot be appropriated because: '[T]hat which cannot be occupied, or which has never been occupied, cannot be the property of any one, because all property has arisen from occupation'.[4] He argued that: '[T]he sea is common to all, because it is so limitless that it cannot become a possession of any one, and because it is adapted for the use of all, whether we consider it from the point of view of navigation or fisheries'.[5]

The rule of absolute freedom of the seas was generally accepted from the seventeenth to the nineteenth centuries. However, the ability of foreign naval powers to launch attacks from waters adjacent to coastal States' coasts eventually led to coastal States claiming a right

[1] Hersch Lauterpacht, *The Development of International Law by the International Court* (CUP 1958) 5.

[2] United Nations Convention on the Law of the Sea (adopted 10 December 1982, entered into force 16 November 1994) 1833 UNTS 397 (UNCLOS).

[3] Hugo Grotius, *The Freedom of the Seas or the Right which Belongs to the Dutch to Take Part in the East Indian Trade* (Ralph Van Deman Magoffin tr, OUP 1913).

[4] ibid 27.

[5] ibid 28.

to control the adjacent waters, so that by the end of the nineteenth century claims over a territorial sea began to emerge.

In the 1920s, there were various initiatives to codify the law of the sea: through a Committee of Experts of the League of Nations, as well as by the Institut de Droit International, the International Law Association, the German and Japanese Societies of International Law, the American Institute of International Law, and Harvard Law School.[6] At the Hague Codification Conference in 1930, the law of the sea was considered, but the regime of the territorial sea was contentious and no treaty was proposed. Nonetheless, State practice continued to develop, with various claims made by coastal States to territorial sea zones. After the Second World War, the United States made the first substantive claim to an offshore resources zone, through the so-called Truman Proclamation.[7] Similar claims were made by other coastal States throughout the late 1940s, 1950s, and 1960s. In parallel, the ICJ began to decide law of the sea disputes, starting with its first judgment, the 1949 *Corfu Channel* case, which allowed the Court to address the emerging regime of the territorial sea and navigational rights and freedoms through international straits.[8] Soon after, the Court addressed the territorial sea regime and the use of straight baselines to measure the territorial sea in the 1951 *Fisheries* case.[9] Around the same time, the UN General Assembly recommended that the International Law Commission (ILC) address the regime of the high seas and later, territorial seas, and in 1956 the ILC adopted articles on the law of the sea, with commentaries.[10]

The ILC's work was highly influential at the First United Nations Conference on the Law of the Sea (UNCLOS I) held in Geneva in 1958. It resulted in the conclusion of four conventions: the Convention on the Territorial Sea and Contiguous Zone;[11] the Convention on the Continental Shelf;[12] the Convention on the High Seas;[13] and the Convention on Fishing and Conservation of the Living Resources of the High Seas.[14] While UNCLOS I was highly productive, especially considering that the negotiations took place over only nine weeks, aspects of customary international law remained uncodified.

A Second United Nations Conference on the Law of the Sea (UNCLOS II) was convened in Geneva just two years later, with the intention of focusing on two issues, namely the breadth of the territorial sea and fishery limits. However, the six-week conference was split between those favouring a six nautical mile (NM) territorial sea and those favouring a breadth of twelve NM.[15] Ultimately, UNCLOS II failed to reach any agreement on modifications or additions to the 1958 Geneva Conventions.

[6] DP O'Connell, *The International Law of the Sea*, vol 1 (Clarendon Press 1982) 20–21.

[7] 'Policy of the United States with Respect to the Natural Resources of the Subsoil and Seabed of the Continental Shelf' (Presidential Proclamation 2667 of 28 September 1945, 10 Fed Reg 12303); 'Policy of the United States with Respect to Coastal Fisheries in Certain Areas of the High Seas' (Presidential Proclamation 2668 of 28 September 1945, 10 Fed. Reg. 12304).

[8] *Corfu Channel (United Kingdom v Albania)* [1949] ICJ Rep 4.

[9] *Fisheries (United Kingdom v Norway)* [1951] ICJ Rep 116.

[10] International Law Commission, Articles concerning the Law of the Sea with Commentaries [1956] 2 UNYBILC 265.

[11] Convention on the Territorial Sea and Contiguous Zone (opened for signature 29 April 1958, entered into force 10 September 1964) 516 UNTS 205.

[12] Convention on the Continental Shelf (opened for signature 29 April 1958, entered into force 10 June 1964) 499 UNTS 311.

[13] Convention on the High Seas (adopted 29 April 1958, entered into force 30 September 1962) 450 UNTS 1.

[14] Convention on Fishing and Conservation of the Living Resources of the High Seas (adopted 29 April 1958, entered into force 26 September 1968) 599 UNTS 285.

[15] DW Bowett, 'The Second United Nations Conference on the Law of the Sea' (1960) 9(3) ICLQ 415, 416–21.

The Third United Nations Conference on the Law of the Sea (UNCLOS III) was held over a nine-year period between 1973 and 1982, with eleven negotiating sessions held in three countries. As there were no ILC draft articles on which to base a convention, it was a very different negotiation than the earlier Conferences. It was attended by a much larger number of States, with 151 attending the final session in 1982. As the Conference developed, the 'Group of 77' emerged as a significant negotiating bloc, promoting initiatives that reflected the concerns of developing countries. The UN Convention on the Law of the Sea (UNCLOS), which emerged from the UNCLOS III negotiations, was adopted in 1982.

By the time of UNCLOS III, there was a high level of momentum for the recognition of an expanded offshore resources zone, and the debates in respect of that zone eventually formed the basis of the recognition of the exclusive economic zone (EEZ). In parallel to the negotiations, a significant number of coastal States unilaterally proclaimed expanded fisheries zones or an EEZ, so even before the conclusion of UNCLOS III there was considerable acceptance of the concept in State practice.[16]

There was a high level of consensus during UNCLOS III on many aspects of the law of the sea. At an early stage, agreement was reached on the breadth of the territorial sea at twelve NM. This agreement facilitated the creation of the regime of transit passage through international straits. In addition to the consensus on the EEZ, there was also general consensus on the need to address the deep seabed. With regard to the deep seabed, there was significant support for the concept of the common heritage of humankind, originating in the declaration of Ambassador Pardo for Malta, who had proclaimed before the UN General Assembly in 1967 that the seabed and ocean floor form part of the common heritage of humankind. In 1970, the General Assembly had adopted Resolution 2749 (XXV) 'Declaration of Principles Governing the Sea-bed and Ocean Floor, and the Subsoil Thereof, beyond the Limits of National Jurisdiction'. That resolution paved the way for the matter to be discussed at UNCLOS III, resulting in Part XI of UNCLOS on the deep seabed (or 'Area').

Given the wide range of issues addressed at the Conference, it was recognised that the outcome would have to be a 'package deal' if it were to gain wide acceptance. Consistent with that objective, Article 309 of UNCLOS provides that no reservations or exceptions may be made unless expressly permitted. Under Article 310, States may make declarations and statements, provided that they are not in effect reservations.

When UNCLOS was concluded, there was initially a high level of response from participating States. However, towards the end of the negotiations, in 1981, the United States had expressed significant reservations about the deep seabed mining regime and the common heritage principles in Part XI of UNCLOS. Although it was unable to achieve any modifications to the text at that stage, it forced the Convention to a vote, and voted against, together with Israel, Turkey, and Venezuela; 130 States were in favour, with 17 abstentions. Soon after the Convention opened for signature, it became clear that the reservations expressed by the United States over Part XI were gaining support among other States. A solution to this impasse was only reached in 1994, when the UN Secretary-General negotiated a resolution resulting in modifications to Part XI prior to its entry into force. The resolution contained an Agreement Relating to the Implementation of Part XI of UNCLOS (the 1994 Agreement).[17]

[16] See *Delimitation of the Maritime Boundary in the Gulf of Maine Area (Canada v United States)* (Merits) [1984] ICJ Rep 246, para 94.

[17] Agreement Relating to the Implementation of Part XI of the United Nations Convention on the Law of the Sea 10 December 1982 (adopted 28 July 1994, entered into force 16 November 1994) 1836 UNTS 3.

UNCLOS finally entered into force on 16 November 1994, a year after sixty States had ratified it. As at 2021, it has 168 parties. Given its broad coverage and large number of parties, UNCLOS has long been described as the 'constitution of the oceans'.[18]

UNCLOS is one of the most comprehensive international treaties addressing a general subject matter. It is comprised of 320 articles in 17 parts, together with nine annexes. Its objectives are emphasised in the preamble, which records, inter alia:

- that 'the problems of ocean space are closely interrelated and need to be considered as a whole';
- the desirability of establishing 'a legal order for the seas and oceans' to facilitate international communication, 'promote the peaceful uses of the seas and oceans, the equitable and efficient utilization of their resources, the conservation of their living resources and the study, protection and preservation of the marine environment';
- the desire to develop the principles embodied in UN General Assembly Resolution 2749 (XXV)[19] with respect to the common heritage of humankind; and
- the belief that the codification and progressive development of the law of the sea 'will contribute to the strengthening of peace, security, cooperation and friendly relations' and 'will promote the economic and social advancement of all peoples of the world'.

Part I of UNCLOS is comprised of the single Article 1 containing definitions. Part II sets out the regime of the territorial sea and the contiguous zone. Part III creates a regime of transit passage through straits used for international navigation. Part IV recognises archipelagic States and makes special provision for these States and navigation in their waters. Parts V and VI deal with the EEZ and continental shelf, respectively. Part VII addresses the high seas regime. Part VIII deals with the regime of islands including their maritime entitlements. Part IX defines and contains provisions addressing enclosed or semi-enclosed seas. Landlocked and geographically disadvantaged States are addressed in Part X. Part XI addresses the regime of the deep seabed, based on the principle of the common heritage of humankind. Part XII addresses the protection and preservation of the marine environment. Part XIII deals with marine scientific research, and Part XIV deals with the development and transfer of marine technology. Part XV contains the Convention's regime for the settlement of disputes. Parts XVI and XVII contain general provisions with respect to good faith in exercising UNCLOS rights, and the use of the oceans for peaceful purposes, together with procedural provisions relating to signature, ratification, and entry into force.

[18] See eg Elisabeth Mann Borgese, 'A Constitution for the Oceans' in Elisabeth Mann Borgese and David Krieger (eds), *The Tides of Change: Peace, Pollution and the Potential of the* Oceans (Mason/Charter 1975); Tommy TB Koh, 'A Constitution for the Oceans: Remarks of the President of the Third United Nations Conference on the Law of the Sea' (Statements Given at the Final Session of the Conference at Montego Bay, 5 and 11 December 1982) https://www.un.org/depts/los/convention_agreements/texts/koh_english.pdf; Jin-Hyun Paik, 'How Healthy is the Ocean's Constitution? 25 Years of the United Nations Convention on the Law of the Sea' (UNCLOS Conference, 17 October 2019) https://www.itlos.org/fileadmin/itlos/documents/statements_of_president/paik/UNCLOS_25_171019_en.pdf.

[19] 'Declaration of Principles Governing the Sea-Bed and the Ocean Floor, and the Subsoil Thereof, beyond the Limits of National Jurisdiction', UNGA Res 2749(XXV) (17 December 1970) UN Doc A/RES/2749(XXV).

II. Overview of the UNCLOS Dispute Settlement Process

The compulsory dispute provisions in Part XV of UNCLOS are widely considered to be one of the great achievements of UNCLOS III, because they are comprehensive and compulsory, subject only to limited exceptions.[20] The first President of UNCLOS III, Hamilton Shirley Amerasinghe, asserted that the 'the provision of effective dispute settlement procedures is essential for stabilizing and maintaining the compromises necessary for the attainment of agreement', and that the '[d]ispute settlement procedures will be the pivot upon which the delicate equilibrium of the compromise must be balanced'.[21] By providing for compulsory dispute settlement, UNCLOS was a significant step forward when compared to the 1958 Geneva Conventions: as Treves remarked, 'a major achievement of [UNCLOS] is that it has brought the law of the sea under the jurisdiction of international courts and tribunals'.[22]

The settlement of disputes is addressed in Part XV of UNCLOS in three sections. Section 1 contains general provisions involving voluntary dispute settlement procedures: for example, through procedures chosen by the parties (Article 280) or by conciliation (Article 284). Section 2 addresses the compulsory procedures for dispute settlement.[23] Section 3 sets out the limitations and optional exceptions to the compulsory procedures.[24] Provisions in other parts of UNCLOS address specific aspects of dispute settlement: Section 5 of Part XI addresses dispute settlement and advisory opinions by the Seabed Chamber of ITLOS; Annex V deals with conciliation; Annex VI with the International Tribunal for the Law of the Sea (ITLOS); Annex VII with arbitration; and Annex VIII with special arbitration.

A choice of forum for compulsory dispute settlement procedures is set out in Article 287. Negotiations at UNCLOS III on the question of forum were difficult. While a significant number of developing States supported the creation of a new international tribunal, many European and some Latin American States were supportive of recourse to the ICJ, while the former socialist States of Eastern Europe pushed for arbitration. Ultimately, the compromise that was reached incorporates all these options. Article 287 sets out the so-called 'Montreux formula' (so named because it was suggested by the Working Group's meeting in Montreux at the 1975 session),[25] which provides four options for dispute settlement:

- ITLOS;
- ICJ;
- an arbitral tribunal constituted in accordance with Annex VII; and
- a special arbitral tribunal constituted in accordance with Annex VIII.

20 See eg Donald R Rothwell and Tim Stephens, *The Law of the Sea* (2nd edn, Bloomsbury 2016) 473; Bernard Oxman, 'Courts and Tribunals: The ICJ, ITLOS, and Arbitral Tribunals' in Donald R Rothwell and others (eds), *The Oxford Handbook of the Law of the Sea* (OUP 2015); Michael Wood, 'The International Tribunal for the Law of the Sea and General International Law' (2007) 22(3) IJMCL 351, 353.

21 'Memorandum by the President of the Conference' (31 March 1976) UN Doc A/CONF.62/WP.9, Add.1*, para 6. See also Dinah Shelton, 'Form, Function, and the Powers of International Courts' (2009) 9 Chi J Intl L 537, 559–60.

22 Tulio Treves, 'The Development of the Law of the Sea Since the Adoption of the UN Convention on the Law of the Sea: Achievements and Challenges for the Future' in Davor Vidas (ed), *Law, Technology and Science for Oceans in Globalisation: IUU Fishing, Oil Pollution, Bioprospecting, Outer Continental Shelf* (Martinus Nijhoff 2010) 47.

23 Establishing jurisdiction under art 288 and questions as to the admissibility of disputes for compulsory procedures entailing binding decisions are discussed in ch 3(II) and (III).

24 See UNCLOS (n 2) arts 297 and 298. These provisions are discussed in detail in ch 4.

25 See AO Adede, *The System of Settlement of Disputes under the United Nations Convention on the Law the Sea: A Drafting History and Commentary* (Martinus Nijhoff 1987) 243.

ITLOS has twenty-one members,[26] elected for nine-year terms,[27] and may also sit as a special chamber with a smaller number of judges at the request of the parties. An Annex VII tribunal consists of five members: two of those are appointed by each of the parties to the dispute; the remaining three (including the President) are appointed with the agreement of the parties, or by the President of ITLOS if no agreement is reached.[28] A special Annex VIII tribunal also consists of five members, who are to be experts in the fields of fisheries; protection and preservation of the marine environment; marine scientific research; and navigation, including pollution from vessels and dumping. The jurisdiction of Annex VIII tribunals is limited to disputes in those particular areas.[29] The composition of ITLOS and Annex VII tribunals is discussed further in Chapter 2;[30] so far no Annex VIII tribunals have been formed as no disputes have been referred to Annex VIII arbitration.

Article 287(1) provides that, when signing, ratifying, or acceding to UNCLOS or at any time thereafter, a State is free to choose one or more of the four means for dispute settlement set out above. However, ITLOS has compulsory jurisdiction over a request for the prompt release of vessels and crews[31] and a request for provisional measures,[32] unless the parties otherwise agree. If no Article 287 declaration is made, the State is deemed to have accepted Annex VII arbitration.[33] If the parties to a dispute accept the same procedure, it may be submitted to that procedure only, unless the parties agree.[34] If the parties to a dispute have not accepted the same procedure, it may be submitted only to Annex VII arbitration, unless the parties agree otherwise.[35] Thus, Article VII arbitration is in effect the default forum for disputes, and in practice a significant number of disputes have been submitted to Annex VII tribunals. Although ITLOS initially had very few cases, the number of disputes referred to it has increased over time, as will be clear from the case analyses that follow in the chapters below.

So far, as noted above, there have been no Annex VIII arbitrations under UNCLOS. In *Coastal State Rights in the Black Sea*, a question emerged as to the jurisdiction of an Annex VII tribunal in light of the selection of Annex VIII special arbitration by each of the parties under Article 287.[36] Russia argued that the Ukrainian claims relating to fisheries and marine scientific research should be submitted to Annex VIII arbitration. Ukraine rightly pointed out that the dispute existing between the States relating to the interpretation of UNCLOS was much broader than fisheries or marine scientific research, and argued that the resolution of the dispute should not be artificially divided among different tribunals.[37] The Tribunal agreed with Ukraine that there was not a 'single, unified dispute',[38] and thus

[26] See UNCLOS (n 2) Annex VI, art 2(1).
[27] ibid Annex VI, art 5(1).
[28] ibid Annex VII, art 3.
[29] ibid Annex VII, art 5.
[30] See ch 2(II).
[31] UNCLOS (n 2) art 292.
[32] ibid art 290(5).
[33] ibid art 287(3).
[34] ibid art 287(4).
[35] ibid art 287(5).
[36] *Dispute Concerning Coastal State Rights in the Black Sea, Sea of Azov, and Kerch Strait (Ukraine v Russia)* PCA Case No 2017-06 (Preliminary Objections Award of 21 February 2020) para 404 (*Coastal State Rights in the Black Sea*).
[37] ibid para 442.
[38] ibid para 441.

sought to avoid fragmentation of the dispute across the fora available under Part XV of UNCLOS in rejecting Russia's submission.[39]

III. Reflections on the Role of Dispute Settlement under UNCLOS

At the time UNCLOS was adopted, the dispute settlement regime in Part XV was widely lauded for its inclusion of compulsory procedures entailing binding decisions for all States parties. Commentary hailing its significance at the time of adoption included statements that '[t]he world community's interest in the peaceful settlement of disputes and the prevention of use of force in the settlement of disputes between States have been advanced by the mandatory system of dispute settlement in the Convention'.[40] As noted above, Part XV of UNCLOS was to be 'the pivot upon which the delicate equilibrium of the compromise must be balanced'.[41] As Boyle has suggested, UNCLOS dispute settlement is 'the cement which should hold the whole structure together and guarantee its continued acceptability and endurance for all parties'.[42]

There are a number of ways that the dispute settlement regime in UNCLOS was to be viewed as indispensable to the overall operation of many facets of the Convention.[43] For example, the dispute settlement regime was requisite for those parts of UNCLOS where a particularly delicate balance of interests had been achieved in the text and third-party adjudication or arbitration could be used to safeguard that balance. The most common balance of interests in this regard is between the exclusive interests of coastal States and the inclusive interests of all other States, often flag States, in seeking to protect their respective rights.[44] This sort of balance is manifest, for example, in the transit passage regime,[45] as well as in Articles 56 and 58 pertaining to different State interests within the EEZ.

Another reason that the UNCLOS dispute settlement regime was needed was to flesh out some of the very broad or general obligations included in the Convention.[46] Judicial decision-making would not of course be the only avenue available for this purpose, as UNCLOS anticipated further developments in organisations like the International Maritime Organization (IMO),[47] or among concerned States under separate agreements, such as with regional fisheries management organisations or arrangements.[48] However, if a

[39] ibid para 443.

[40] 'Statement by the President' (6 December 1982) UN Doc A/CONF.62/SR.185.

[41] 'Memorandum by the President of the Conference on Document A/CONF.62/WP.9' (31 March 1976) UN Doc A/CONF.62/WP.9/Add.1, para 6 (the President explaining his initiative in preparing an informal single negotiating text on the Settlement of Disputes).

[42] Alan E Boyle, 'Dispute Settlement and the Law of the Sea Convention: Problems of Fragmentation and Jurisdiction' (1997) 46 ICLQ 37, 38.

[43] In Natalie Klein, *Dispute Settlement and the UN Convention on the Law of the Sea* (CUP 2005), Klein considered the role of dispute settlement in the overall operation of the Convention, focusing on what dispute settlement procedures were needed for different substantive areas covered in UNCLOS and how well aligned was Part XV with the other Parts of the Convention.

[44] Among the cases that most clearly demonstrate this point are *Volga (Russia v Australia)* (Prompt Release, Judgment) ITLOS Reports 2002, 10; *Camouco (Panama v France)* (Prompt Release, Judgment) ITLOS Reports 2000, 10; *Monte Confurco (Seychelles v France)* (Prompt Release, Judgment) ITLOS Reports 2000, 86. See also 109.

[45] See UNCLOS (n 2) arts 38, 39, 42, 44.

[46] Klein (n 43) 362–63.

[47] See eg UNCLOS (n 2) art 204 and other provisions in Part XII relating to the protection and preservation of the marine environment from different forms of pollution.

[48] A practice reflected in the adoption of the 1995 Fish Stocks Agreement. United Nations Agreement for the Implementation of the Provisions of the United Nations Convention on the Law of the Sea of 10 December

dispute could not be resolved between States concerning the interpretation and application of provisions setting out general standards of conduct, it would inevitably be left to a court or tribunal to determine what would fall within those particular standards in the circumstances of the case.

Yet procedures entailing binding decisions were only compulsory in some, not all, instances. Importantly, there are situations where mandatory procedures entailing binding decisions were not considered necessary by the drafters of UNCLOS. As such, Articles 297 and 298 of Part XV set out limitations and optional exceptions in this regard. The limitations primarily insulate the decision-making powers of the coastal State in its EEZ in relation to fisheries and marine scientific research, potentially including its related law enforcement activities. Other disputes that could be excluded from compulsory procedures entailing binding decisions include those concerning military activities, disputes over which the Security Council is exercising its functions and the delimitation of maritime boundaries pursuant to Articles 15, 74, and 83 of UNCLOS.[49] In addition, UNCLOS anticipates that States will seek to resolve disputes through procedures other than those available in the Convention and this flexibility is reflected in various provisions of Section 1 of Part XV, most notably Articles 281 and 282.[50] As such, it could rightly be expected that some disputes would not be resolved under Part XV of UNCLOS. Instead, creating a dispute settlement regime that accommodated alternative dispute settlement procedures and incorporated many limitations and exceptions was politically realistic and would not necessarily thwart the operation of the substantive provisions of the treaty.[51]

Commentators, including Oxman and Tanaka,[52] have observed competing views as to the purpose of the UNCLOS dispute settlement regime. Oxman identifies the 'substantive' model as follows:

> According to what might be called a substantive model, influenced in some measure by a regime-building conception, the LOS Convention stands at the heart of the public order of the oceans, and compulsory jurisdiction is integral to that public order. The primary function of the Convention is to lay down basic substantive principles and rules regarding the rights and duties of states concerning the sea. From this perspective, compulsory jurisdiction under the LOS Convention is designed to ensure both authoritative articulation of the meaning of the public order established by the Convention and compliance with its substantive principles and rules.[53]

The other is described by Oxman as the 'procedural' model:

1982 relating to the Conservation and Management of Straddling Fish Stocks and Highly Migratory Fish Stocks (adopted 4 August 1995, entered into force 11 December 2001) 2167 UNTS 3.

[49] UNCLOS (n 2) art 298.

[50] Discussed further in ch 3(II)(B).

[51] A notable sceptic at the time UNCLOS was adopted was former ICJ President, Shigeru Oda. See eg Shigeru Oda, 'Some Reflections on the Dispute Settlement Clauses in the United Nations Convention on the Law of the Sea' in Jerzy Makarczyk (ed), *Essays in International Law in Honour of Judge Manfred Lachs* (Brill 1984) 645, 655.

[52] Yoshifumi Tanaka, 'Reflections on the Philippines/China Arbitration Award on Jurisdiction and Admissibility' (2016) 15 LPICT 305; Bernard H Oxman, 'Complementary Agreements and Compulsory Jurisdiction' (2001) 95 AJIL 277.

[53] Oxman (n 52) 279 (citations omitted).

> According to what might be called a procedural model, influenced in some measure by a Westphalian conception, the LOS Convention is to be implemented by political arrangements that translate its general principles into precise legal measures, and compulsory jurisdiction is ancillary to the system of political institutions established to implement those principles.[54]

Which model is followed may depend on the circumstances, or emphases, of particular cases,[55] and may be reflected in the arguments of the parties or the judgments dealing with the interpretation of varied UNCLOS provisions.

These descriptions of the UNCLOS dispute settlement regime reflect in some measure a broader debate in the literature about the role of international courts in the international legal system and within international relations more generally. International courts have been described as critical in the development and evolution of international law as well as in enforcing law. Guzman, for example, argued that there are 'two functions of courts: to assist states to come to a common understanding on disputed law and facts, and to sanction a party that has violated its legal obligations'.[56] The Handbook of the ICJ has similarly recognised these core roles: '[A] judgment of the Court does not simply decide a particular dispute but inevitably also contributes to the development of international law. Fully aware of this, the Court takes account of these two objectives in the substance and wording of its judgments.'[57]

These are undoubtedly core functions, but the role of international courts arguably goes beyond these tasks.'[58]

Shelton has identified four different functions of international courts as dispute settlement, compliance assessment, enforcement and legal advice.[59] She considers that one of those functions might be dominant even if all are performed by the court. To this end, Shelton considers the ICJ and ITLOS as primarily concerned with dispute settlement, whereas the human rights courts have a key function of compliance assessment, and the international criminal courts are primarily concerned with enforcement in finding individuals guilty of violations of international law obligations.[60] While it might be true to say that ITLOS is primarily concerned with dispute settlement, the tribunals constituted under the

[54] ibid (citations omitted). This contrast could also be described as a 'constructivist' perspective as opposed to a 'rationalist' perspective in legal realism, where the former is 'substantive' and the latter is 'procedural' in Oxman's terms. See Gregory C Shaffer and Mark A Pollack, 'Hard vs Soft Law: Alternatives, Complements, and Antagonists in International Governance' (2010) 94(3) Minn L Rev 706, 751.

[55] Oxman (n 52) 280, 312: 'The Westphalian and regime-building models do not necessarily and inevitably contradict one another if the role of compulsory jurisdiction in relation to both is carefully considered. At least for the time being, one of the most significant contributions courts can make may be to find areas of confluence and accommodation between the two conceptions of the international order during the foreseeably substantial period in which neither can be ignored. Reconciliation of the tensions between the values that guide us is one of the important things we ask of law and legal process.'

[56] Cited in Geir Ulfstein, 'International Courts and Judges: Independence, Interaction, and Legitimacy' (2014) 46 NYU J Intl L & Pol 849, 851.

[57] ICJ, *The International Court of Justice: Handbook* (5th edn, 2004) 77. The ICJ Statute refers more simply to the function of the Court as 'to decide in accordance with international law such disputes as are submitted to it': Statute of the International Court of Justice, art 38(1).

[58] See, eg, David D Caron, 'Towards a Political Theory of International Courts and Tribunals' (2006) 24 Berk J Intl L 401, 410; Armin von Bogdandy and Ingo Venzke, 'On the Functions of International Courts: An Appraisal in Light of Their Burgeoning Public Authority' (2013) 26 LJIL 49, 50.

[59] Shelton (n 21) 539.

[60] ibid 557–58.

UNCLOS dispute settlement regime are expected to perform all these functions. Oxman's substantive model is especially relevant for the compliance assessment tasks of UNCLOS tribunals. As discussed above, the compulsory nature of UNCLOS dispute settlement is essential to the enforcement of the rules set out within the Convention.

Some scholars have considered that international courts hold positions as 'trustees' in relation to the legal regime in which they operate. Stone Sweet and Brunell describe the traits of a 'trustee' court as follows:

> In the international context, a trustee court can be identified on the basis of three criteria: (1) the court is recognized as the authoritative interpreter of the regime's law, which it applies to resolve disputes concerning state compliance; (2) the court's jurisdiction, with regard to state compliance, is compulsory; and (3) it is virtually impossible, in practice, for contracting states to reverse the court's important rulings on treaty law.[61]

The tribunals under UNCLOS could be argued to have some of these traits. First, in relation to the 'authoritative interpreter', it must be noted that the diverse fora available for dispute resolution under UNCLOS means that there are different bodies with responsibility for resolving disputes relating to the interpretation or application of UNCLOS. This position may be contrasted to the role of the Appellate Body within the World Trade Organization's (WTO) dispute settlement regime. Secondly, there is compulsory jurisdiction, albeit with exceptions, under UNCLOS. Thirdly, it remains to be seen if there is an avenue for States to reverse a ruling. Arguably, a separate agreement might be needed to re-interpret a holding, or subsequent State practice may be relevant in the context of treaty interpretation.[62] Certainly we have examples of different tribunals adopting alternative positions in separate cases.[63] The trustee perspective may align with Oxman's substantive model, as it allows the courts to operate with a degree of autonomy rather than under threat of state sanction.[64]

An alternative model considers international courts as 'agents', simply providing useful information to State parties and as focal points for action; this model anticipates an authoritative role for States in decision-making.[65] In this setting, international courts are perceived as having little influence over international law.[66] There are possible weaknesses within the UNCLOS dispute settlement regime inasmuch as States are not compelled to appear in cases, a path chosen by Russia and China in recent disputes,[67] although non-appearance

[61] Cited in Ulfstein (n 56) 852.

[62] See Vienna Convention on the Law of Treaties (adopted 23 May 1969, entered into force 27 January 1980) 1155 UNTS 331, arts 31(3)(a) and (b).

[63] As occurred in relation to the interpretation of art 281. These contradictory views are discussed in ch 3(II)(B)(1).

[64] See Karen J Alter, 'Agents or Trustees? International Courts in Their Political Context' (2008) 14 Eur J Intl Rel 33; Alec Stone Sweet, 'Constitutional Courts and Parliamentary Democracy' (2002) 25 W Eur Pol 77; Karen J Alter, 'The Multiple Roles of International Courts and Tribunals: Enforcement, Dispute Settlement, Constitutional and Administrative Review' in Jeffrey L Dunoff and Mark A Pollack (eds), *International Law and International Relations: Synthesizing Insights from Interdisciplinary Scholarship* (CUP 2013) (Alter, 'Multiple Roles').

[65] Discussed in Alter, 'Multiple Roles' (n 64). See also Shelton (n 21) 543–44.

[66] See eg Jack L Goldsmith and Eric A Posner, *The Limits of International Law* (OUP 2005); Eric A Posner and John C Yoo, 'Judicial Independence in International Tribunals' (2005) 93 Cal L Rev 1.

[67] Russia did not participate in *Arctic Sunrise (Netherlands v Russia)* (Award on the Merits of 14 August 2015) PCA Case No 2014-02, but it is participating in Annex VII cases brought by Ukraine: *Coastal State Rights in the Black Sea* (n 36); and *Detention of Ukrainian Naval Vessels and Servicemen (Ukraine v Russia)* PCA Case No 2019-28. Russia also participated in the proceedings relating to a regional fisheries panel, which is discussed in ch 8(VI): *Review Panel Established Under the Convention on the Conservation and Management of High Seas Fishery Resources in the South Pacific Ocean* (Findings and Recommendations of the Review Panel of 5 July 2013) PCA

does not prevent a case from being decided.[68] Moreover, enforcement options to ensure compliance with decisions are more limited under UNCLOS dispute settlement than is the situation for cases before the ICJ,[69] or under the WTO's dispute settlement system.[70] Yet the widespread shared interest in regulating ocean space and activities for mutual benefit ensures that statements about the meaning of UNCLOS requirements will be considered significant by State actors, especially in the context of the entitlement to and division of maritime space in maritime boundary delimitation cases.[71]

The different roles conceived of for international courts generally, and in the context of UNCLOS specifically, further need to be reconciled in a broader frame that is concerned with promoting the peaceful settlement of disputes, upholding the rule of law,[72] and supporting the public order of the oceans. These fundamental objectives are all critical elements to international society as a whole, and find voice throughout the international legal system. These elements are all to be found in the Preamble to UNCLOS,[73] as well as being reflected in arguments and judgments in the UNCLOS dispute settlement regime.

An example is seen in discussions as to whether certain features within the South China Sea should be considered as rocks in accordance with Article 121(3) of UNCLOS in the *South China Sea* arbitration. The Philippines explicitly argued that the land features should only be considered rocks as it would 'reduce the incentive to "flex muscles and demonstrate sovereignty over miniscule features" that generate a maximum entitlement of 12 nm, and thus contribute to the "legal order and the maintenance of peace in the South China Sea"'.[74] There was further an appeal to the Tribunal's 'mandate to "promote the maintenance of legal order in respect of the relevant maritime areas, and the avoidance or reduction of threats to international peace and security that inevitably would emanate from a situation of such legal uncertainty", in accordance with the UN Charter and the Preamble of the Convention'.[75]

Case No 2013-14 China did not directly appear in the *South China Sea* arbitration, although it communicated and engaged in the process external to the actual proceedings: *South China Sea Arbitration (Philippines v China)* (Award of 12 July 2016) PCA Case No 2013-19 (*South China Sea*, Award).

[68] See UNCLOS (n 2) Annex VI, art 28; Annex VII, art 9.

[69] Under art 94(2) of the UN Charter, there is the possibility that the Security Council will take measures or make recommendations in the event a State does not comply with a judgment, but the option has rarely ever been used.

[70] See WTO Agreement: Marrakesh Agreement Establishing the World Trade Organization (opened for signature 15 April 1994, entered into force 1 January 1995) 1867 UNTS 154, Annex 2, art 3(7).

[71] See Lea Brilmayer and Natalie Klein, 'Land and Sea: Two Sovereignty Regimes in Search of a Common Denominator' (2001) 33 NYU J Intl L & Pol 703 (discussing importance of marketable title and reliance on norms in the law of the sea as compared to territorial sovereignty regime).

[72] Follesdal comments that international courts must show their commitment to 'the international rule of law; to the particular [international court] to help maintain or increase its reputation; and to ensure that justice is done and seen to be done in the case at hand, according to the express objectives of the regime': Andreas Follesdal, 'To Guide and Guard International Judges' (2014) 46 NYU J Intl L & Pol 793, 800–801. Shelton similarly notes: 'Independent courts also monitor the principle of the rule of law that all conduct, including that go governments and their agents, is subject to the law': Shelton (n 21) 541.

[73] The preamble refers to: 'desire to settle, in a spirit of mutual understanding and cooperation, all issues relating to the law of the sea'; 'codification and progressive development of the law of the sea achieved in this Convention will contribute to the strengthening of peace, security, cooperation and friendly relations among all nations in conformity with the principles of justice and equal rights'; 'desirability of establishing through this Convention... a legal order for the seas and oceans': UNCLOS (n 2) Preamble.

[74] *South China Sea*, Award (n 67) para 421.

[75] ibid.

Reference to the rule of law has also been explicitly endorsed by judges within ITLOS in the context of interpreting terms in the Convention.[76] Six of the dissenting judges in the *Virginia G* case stated: 'There is no provision of the Convention which is immune from interpretation by the competent judicial body. Therefore, when the occasion arises, the Tribunal is competent to interpret every word and expression in the Convention. Any other view will be contrary to the rule of law.'[77] A former President of ITLOS promised that 'it shall be the constant endeavour of the Tribunal to promote the rule of law in matters relating to the oceans in accordance with' the Convention.[78] As will be evident throughout the discussions in this work, the judges deciding cases within the UNCLOS dispute settlement regime address to varying degrees their perceived role in settling cases between the parties.[79]

IV. Outline of Book

In this chapter, we have highlighted the different frames that are being used at present to explain the purpose of international dispute settlement in UNCLOS and the role of international courts in international relations more generally. The role of the judges in relation to UNCLOS dispute settlement is the focus of our next chapter. While observing the fundamental objectives that drive international dispute settlement in the law of the sea—peaceful settlement of disputes, the rule of law, public order of the oceans—the discussion seeks to delve deeper into what judges are doing when they decide cases, and what they should be doing in order to meet the grand objectives of the UNCLOS dispute settlement regime. Given the increasing amount of case law developing under UNCLOS in the decades since its entry into force, it is timely to reflect on how the law is evolving as a result of judicial interpretation and to contemplate why it is evolving the way it is. We consider the role of the judges to be critical in this regard, but, as we will discuss, it is not an exclusive role. The law of the sea is a complex and changing system and our efforts in this work seek to capture aspects of that process and contribute to its future development.

Chapters 3 to 9 comprehensively analyse the cases where UNCLOS has been interpreted and applied by international tribunals. In addition to considering the way in which provisions of UNCLOS have been elucidated and interpreted by these tribunals, each chapter considers what goals the judges are seeking to achieve through their decision-making.

[76] Judge Gao, for example, in dissent in the provisional measures stage of *San Padre Pio* considered that 'the proceedings of the present case should strive to make a contribution to the rule of law in promoting stability and security in the Gulf of Guinea, and support Nigeria's efforts to combat maritime crime': *M/T San Padre Pio (Switzerland v Nigeria)* (Provisional Measures, Order of 6 July 2019) ITLOS Case No 27 (Dissenting Opinion of Judge Gao) para 92.

[77] *M/V Virginia G (Panama/Guinea-Bissau)* (Judgment) ITLOS Reports 2014, 4, para 46 (Joint Dissenting Opinion of Vice-President Hoffmann and Judges Marotta Rangel, Chandrasekhara Rao, Kateka, Gao, and Bouguetaia). Also cited in *Duzgit Integrity Arbitration (Malta v São Tomé and Príncipe)* (Award of 5 September 2016) PCA Case No 2014-07, para 132.

[78] ITLOS, 'Press Release: Thirteenth Session of the Tribunal' ITLOS/Press 64 (27 March 2002) https://www.itlos.org/fileadmin/itlos/documents/press_releases_english/PR_No.64.pdf.

[79] See eg *Responsibilities and Obligations of States with Respect to Activities in the Area* (Advisory Opinion) ITLOS Reports 2011, 10, para 30: 'The Chamber is mindful of the fact that by answering the questions it will assist the Council in the performance of its activities and contribute to the implementation of the Convention's regime.'

Chapters 3 and 4 focus on issues that are central to jurisdiction in relation to UNCLOS dispute settlement.

- Chapter 3 addresses how jurisdiction is established under UNCLOS, and the most common objections to admissibility, including standing, estoppel, indispensable third parties, exhaustion of local remedies, and clean hands. Chapter 3 also examines the main incidental and other proceedings that have arisen in UNCLOS dispute settlement to date, including provisional measures, counter-claims, and proceedings to secure the prompt release of vessels under Article 292 of UNCLOS.
- Chapter 4 examines cases where issues of subject matter jurisdiction under UNCLOS have arisen, including the question of territorial sovereignty disputes which are interrelated to maritime boundary disputes, incidental jurisdiction, jurisdictional limitations in disputes concerning fishing and the maritime environment, and the optional exceptions to compulsory jurisdiction under UNCLOS, which include maritime boundary delimitation disputes, historic bays, and historic title disputes, as well as disputes concerning military activities and certain law enforcement activities. Chapter 4 also examines the difference between applicable law and subject matter jurisdiction, and the relevance of renvoi and rules of reference in UNCLOS for jurisdiction.

Each of the subsequent chapters is focused on a particular substantive area of the law of the sea.

- Chapter 5 considers cases that have been concerned with the different maritime spaces. It examines definitions of low-tide elevations, rocks and islands, the drawing of baselines, and the different maritime zones: internal waters, territorial sea, EEZ, and continental shelf.
- Chapter 6 addresses and analyses the significant number of maritime boundary delimitation disputes that have been decided by UNCLOS tribunals. It first explains common methods of delimitation, before examining the way in which tribunals have interpreted and applied the delimitation provisions of UNCLOS in the delimitation of the territorial sea, EEZ and continental shelf, and the extended continental shelf. It also covers cases that have assessed the provisions of UNCLOS concerning provisional arrangements pending delimitation of boundary disputes.
- Chapter 7 discusses the aspects of navigation that have been considered by UNCLOS tribunals, including the status of vessels, the scope of the freedom of navigation, and cases that have addressed interference with navigation and navigational safety matters. The final part of the chapter examines different aspects of law enforcement by coastal States, as well as limits on the use of force and the right of hot pursuit.
- Chapter 8 addresses decisions that have considered international fisheries and their regulation under UNCLOS. It assesses decisions relating to traditional fishing and then turns to fishing in the territorial sea, and in the EEZ. The chapter also addresses the few cases on straddling stocks and highly migratory species, as well as fisheries disputes on the high seas: in particular focusing on the UNCLOS provisions dealing with the conservation and management of high seas fisheries.
- Chapter 9 is centred on cases relating to the marine environment, assessing judicial considerations of the core obligation to protect and preserve the marine environment

and its application to all maritime zones and the types of activities that are implicated in that obligation. It also addresses cases concerned with obligations to protect the marine environment from pollution, the conservation of marine living resources and the protection of the deep seabed (Area), as well as cases examining the duty to co-operate, environmental impact assessments, the precautionary approach, safeguards against the enforcement of environmental requirements and due diligence standards.

Taking account of the assessments contained in the earlier chapters, Chapter 10 concludes, summarising the main findings on jurisdiction for the compulsory resolution of disputes under UNCLOS, together with the central conclusions that have emerged from judicial consideration of maritime space, maritime boundary delimitation, navigation, fisheries and the protection of the marine environments. It also revisits the role of the judge, acknowledging the significant roles played by judges but noting that they are one of many actors that make decisions contributing to the public order of the oceans. It concludes that UNCLOS dispute settlement continues to play an important role in elaborating on international obligations in UNCLOS and setting future expectations on ocean governance.

2

The Role of Judges

I. Introduction

There are many actors, interests, rules, and processes encompassed in the peaceful resolution of disputes under the United Nations Convention on the Law of the Sea (UNCLOS or Convention).[1] This chapter focuses on the key actors involved in UNCLOS dispute settlement. Obviously, the States that are claimants are central actors and they will have a variety of motivations as to why proceedings are instituted against another State under UNCLOS.[2] Yet once a State commences arbitration or adjudication under UNCLOS, that State is ceding decision-making authority to the judges on the particular court or tribunal to make binding determinations as to the State's rights and responsibilities in relation to the Convention. For this reason, the role of the judges becomes critical.

We acknowledge that the titles of the individuals acting as decision-maker (judges, arbitrators, experts) will vary depending on the forum in which they operate within the UNCLOS dispute settlement regime and that the title usually reflects the degree of permanence of the role and the scope of functions. Similar distinctions exist as between the different institutions: courts, tribunals, commissions, or chambers. There are important differences, and these will be identified where relevant to the discussion. Otherwise, purely for ease of reading, we will use the term 'judges' to encompass all of these individuals. When we are discussing decisions of specific institutions, they will be identified as a particular chamber, commission, tribunal, the International Tribunal for the Law of the Sea (ITLOS), or the International Court of Justice (ICJ). Where we need a more generic label to discuss these institutions collectively, we will use 'tribunal', as it captures the most active fora engaged in UNCLOS dispute settlement: ITLOS and ad hoc Annex VII arbitral tribunals.

This chapter discusses the role of the judge through different lenses. First, we consider an empirical assessment of who has been appointed to the different fora available for resolving disputes under UNCLOS. We provide some data on the backgrounds and traits of those individuals involved in making decisions under the UNCLOS dispute settlement regime. Perhaps because of its complex structure, the UNCLOS dispute settlement system is not commonly studied in empirical analyses of international courts. The characteristics of UNCLOS judges are relevant to the extent that any observer should acknowledge subjective choices, or perhaps subconscious biases, in the way that the various questions that are put to tribunals are answered.

Second, we track some of the key judicial functions that are performed during UNCLOS dispute settlement proceedings. These functions are what judges actually do. One such task

[1] United Nations Convention on the Law of the Sea (adopted 10 December 1982, entered into force 16 November 1994) 1833 UNTS 397 (UNCLOS).

[2] For reasons as to why States might litigate see Shirley V Scott, 'Litigation Versus Dispute Resolution Through Political Processes' in Natalie Klein (ed), *Litigating International Law Disputes* (CUP 2014) 24.

is setting the procedure of the case, and may involve decisions over the appointment of the judges, the timing of the proceedings and whether and which other actors may be involved and in what capacity (such as experts on specific topics, or amicus briefs from interested organisations, or witness participation). One of the most important tasks for judges deciding cases under UNCLOS is treaty interpretation. This task will be revisited throughout this book in assessing the work of UNCLOS judges thus far, and in this chapter we simply highlight what is involved in treaty interpretation as a judicial function. Fact-finding and resolving claims are other key functions, along with settling the actual dispute or contributing to the resolution of a larger dispute of which the UNCLOS dispute is one part. Advisory opinions may additionally contribute to the resolution of disputes in a broader setting. These latter tasks feed back more directly into the core objectives of the dispute settlement process.

Finally in this chapter, having considered who the judges are and what they do, we examine further what the purposes of their roles might or should be. In this regard, we seek to acknowledge the complex factors that are inherent to the judicial decision-making process as well as recognise the importance of engaging with these diverse facets. To capture the complex decision matrix, we explore the possible application of stakeholder identification theory as a way to explain who and what counts in the decision-making process. The judges' identification of and response to different stakeholders is essential to meet the fundamental objectives of UNCLOS dispute settlement, in terms of pacific settlement of disputes, the rule of law, and public order of the oceans. These elements go some way to answering the question of what the role of the judge should be. Ultimately, we argue that an analysis of the judicial interpretation of UNCLOS requires consideration of how the decisions are contributing to the overall good order of the oceans both for the present purpose of resolving the immediate dispute and influencing the future conduct of all stakeholders in ocean governance.

II. Who Are the Judges?

Article 287 of UNCLOS provides States with a choice of fora for the resolution of disputes arising under the Convention.[3] As a result, the decision-makers may be extremely varied. Those deciding cases under UNCLOS may be judges of permanent institutions, such as the ICJ or the ITLOS, or may be ad hoc arbitrators selected under the requirements of Annex VII or experts appointed pursuant to Annex VIII of UNCLOS. Annex VII anticipates that each State party will nominate up to four individuals as potential arbitrators.[4] Under Annex VIII, each State party may nominate up to two experts in each field of fisheries, marine environment, marine scientific research, and navigation, including pollution from vessels and dumping.[5] If proceedings are instituted under Annex VII or Annex VIII, there is no requirement that individuals nominated on the respective lists must be selected, even though it is preferable under the terms of each Annex.[6] The ad

[3] See ch 1(II)(C).
[4] UNCLOS (n 1) Annex VII, art 2.
[5] ibid.
[6] See ibid Annex VII, art 3 and Annex VIII, art 3.

hoc arbitrators selected for Annex VII arbitrations are less typically those included on the lists.[7]

As a result of the different fora available, the sheer number of individuals who may be involved in the resolution of disputes under UNCLOS at any one time is considerable:

- the ICJ has fifteen judges, potentially more if ad hoc judges are appointed;
- the ITLOS has twenty-one judges, also with the possibility of ad hoc judges being appointed by a party;
- with 168 State parties to UNCLOS, there may be 672 arbitrators listed for Annex VII arbitrators;[8] and
- there is a further possibility of 1,344 experts being listed for Annex VIII tribunals.

Beyond these more than 2,000 individuals are those persons appointed by States as specific disputes arise, and account could further be taken of the individuals who may be involved in conciliations.[9]

Ensuring clarity around the role of judges deciding cases under UNCLOS is therefore critical given the range of people potentially engaged in the process. The reality, however, is that not every State has nominated as many arbitrators as it could under Annex VII. So far, as of November 2021, only 127 arbitrators have been nominated.[10] Moreover, there is yet to be an Annex VIII special arbitration and hence none of the possible 1,344 experts has thus far been involved. In fact, only 291 experts have been nominated as of November 2021.[11]

We must also account for the cross-over in practice whereby ITLOS and ICJ judges will also be appointed as ad hoc arbitrators under Annex VII. For example, the *South China Sea* Tribunal was comprised of President Mensah, Judge Cot, Judge Pawlak, Professor Soons, and Judge Wolfrum.[12] President Mensah had been on ITLOS, and Judges Cot, Pawlak, and Wolfrum were members of ITLOS at the time the case was decided. Both President Mensah and Judge Cot had served as judges ad hoc at the ICJ as well. As another example, the Tribunal in the *Bay of Bengal Arbitration* consisted of President Wolfrum, Judge Mensah, Dr Pemmaraju Sreenivasa Rao, Professor Shearer, and Judge Cot.[13] This composition reflects that past and present ITLOS judges may serve on more than one arbitral tribunal, and

[7] Only seventeen of those arbitrators who have been appointed to Annex VII arbitrations are also nominated on the list under art 2 of Annex VII.

[8] As of November 2021, there are 127 arbitrators nominated. This number includes the listings of at least two nominated arbitrators who have passed away.

[9] Similar to the other Annexes, Annex V also anticipates a list of conciliators, comprising up to four individuals from each State party. UNCLOS (n 1), Annex V, art 2. A majority of the individuals nominated as arbitrators are also listed as available as conciliators (68 of 127). There are 31 distinct nominations of conciliators as of November 2021.

[10] United Nations (UN), 'Status of Treaties: United Nations Convention on the Law of the Sea' (*United Nations Treaty Collection*) https://treaties.un.org/Pages/ViewDetailsIII.aspx?src=TREATY&mtdsg_no=XXI-6&chapter=21&Temp=mtdsg3&clang=_en.

[11] See Division for Ocean Affairs and the Law of the Sea, 'List of Experts for the Purposes of Article 2 of Annex VIII (Special Arbitration) to the Convention' *Oceans and Law of the Sea* (20 September 2019) www.un.org/depts/los/settlement_of_disputes/experts_special_arb.htm. There have been 126 navigation experts nominated; thirty-five marine scientific research experts nominated; fifty-seven fisheries experts nominated, and seventy-nine marine environment experts nominated as of February 2020.

[12] *South China Sea Arbitration (Philippines v China)* (Award of 12 July 2016) PCA Case No 2013-19 (*South China Sea*, Award).

[13] *Bay of Bengal Maritime Boundary Arbitration (Bangladesh v India)* (Award of 7 July 2014) PCA Case No 2010-16.

that ad hoc judges of ITLOS and the ICJ may also serve as arbitrators under Annex VII.[14] The movement of judges that may occur between the permanent and ad hoc institutions may be important for the cross-fertilisation of ideas and allow for consideration of broader systemic consequences of a decision in an Annex VII tribunal in relation to the permanent institution.[15]

As of 1 November 2021, we can consider the fourteen ad hoc Annex VII arbitrations instituted under UNCLOS, which have involved a total of sixty-nine arbitrators.[16] Of those arbitrators, some judges have been involved in more than one arbitration. Once duplicates are removed, there are forty-five specific individuals who have acted as arbitrators.[17] Among those arbitrators, twenty also have served on ITLOS as permanent or ad hoc judges (without distinguishing as to whether their ITLOS affiliation was concurrent with their arbitral work).[18]

The relationship of judges to particular tribunals may have some background importance for emphases or explanations of specific decisions. It may also be relevant whether a judge was involved in the negotiations of UNCLOS. The first-hand knowledge of the drafting process may influence perceptions as to the object and purpose of the language, or its context. In reviewing the biographies of the current ITLOS judges, it may be noted that the balance of judges at ITLOS has now moved to the point that UNCLOS negotiators are in the minority.[19] Given the vagaries of memories of a process that occurred over forty years ago, obviously written resources will be more reliable. Yet in the absence of a verbatim record and given the extent of informal consultations and deliberations that occurred across the years of drafting, the usefulness of existing *travaux préparatoires* undoubtedly varies and it is possible that personal recollections may be given some emphasis by those judges who were involved in the negotiations.

From the universe of Annex VII arbitrators identified above, we can also observe other characteristics. The oldest was born in 1927,[20] and the youngest born in 1958;[21] only five were born in 1950 or later.[22] There was only one woman arbitrator appointed, in a case that never proceeded to any substantive decision.[23] Twenty-seven were from developed

[14] See further Appendix A. In November 2018, the then President of the ICJ, Judge Yusuf, announced that sitting ICJ judges would only be permitted to sit in one inter-State arbitration at any given time, with prior authorisation in accordance with a mechanism put in place by the Court, and that judges would not accept appointments by States in any pending case before the Court. See Abdulqawi A Yusuf, 'Speech by H.E. Mr Abdulqawi A Yusuf, President of the International Court of Justice, on the Occasion of the Seventy-Third Session of the United Nations General Assembly' (25 October 2018) 12 www.icj-cij.org/public/files/press-releases/0/000-20181025-PRE-02-00-EN.pdf.

[15] See Douglas Guilfoyle, 'Governing the Oceans and Dispute Resolution: An Evolving Legal Order?' in Danielle Ireland-Piper and Leon Wolff (eds), *Global Governance and Regulation: Order and Disorder in the 21st Century* (Routledge 2018) 185–86.

[16] This data is set out in Appendix A at the end of this work. Data is based on open-source, English-language materials, and was as accurate as possible at time of publication but some errors may remain. The list provided is limited to the ad hoc arbitrations instituted under UNCLOS, rather than all arbitrations that have interpreted and applied provisions of UNCLOS.

[17] See UNCLOS (n 1) App A.

[18] ibid.

[19] In 2002, the President of ITLOS commented that 'almost all the judges of the Tribunal took part in drafting the Convention on the Law of the Sea, that, being draftsmen of the Convention, they were uniquely situated to interpret the Convention': ITLOS, 'Press Release: Thirteenth Session of the Tribunal' ITLOS/Press 64 (27 March 2002) www.itlos.org/fileadmin/itlos/documents/press_releases_english/PR_No.64.pdf.

[20] Professor Hans Smit.

[21] Judge Paik.

[22] Judges Al-Khasawneh, Hoffman, and Paik, as well as Sir Christopher Greenwood and Professor Vaughan Lowe. We were not able to locate the birth date of Professor Francesco Francioni.

[23] Judge Elsa Kelly was appointed for the *ARA Libertad* case, which was terminated before any written or oral proceedings.

economies.[24] Among the forty-five arbitrators, only six of them did not have any formal education at a university based in either Western Europe or the United States.[25] In terms of legal backgrounds, the arbitrators were evenly divided between common law and civil law systems (with five from jurisdictions that might be described as mixed).[26]

If we compare the composition of ITLOS in the period 2017–2020 and to date,[27] there is immediately more geographic diversity than observed in relation to Annex VII arbitrators because of the requirements of Annex VI relating to the election of judges.[28] Of the twenty-one judges on ITLOS in February 2020, three were women (the first being elected in 2011).[29] This number increased slightly to five following the June 2020 elections.[30] Among all twenty-one judges, their ages range from those born in 1933 to 1970, with less than half born in the 1930s or 1940s.[31] While the nationalities vary more compared to Annex VII arbitrators, we can see educational background does not change much: all but four of the judges received formal education in Western Europe or the United States.[32] Only seven judges come from non-civil law jurisdictions, which could potentially influence approaches taken on procedural questions and in assessing the relevance of previous decisions.[33] In terms of prior professional experience, the vast majority have previously served as legal advisers to their governments.

The situation of UNCLOS tribunals is not necessarily unique when considering international dispute settlement more broadly. A 2012 study by Swigart and Terris observed that '[t]he modal profile of an international judge ... featured the following characteristics: citizenship in a European state; male; between 58 and 67 years old; and significant past work experience in the public sector as a judge, civil servant, and/or member of one or more national or international bodies'.[34] The overall expansion of the international judiciary, with the creation of an increasing number of international courts, has led to increased diversity among those serving as international judges.[35] However, more recent studies have indicated that there is room for significant progress across a range of metrics and courts in improving

[24] Using the list of developed economies provided by the UN: UN, 'World Economic Situation and Prospects' (Report 2021) 125–26.

[25] Judges Golitsyn, Pawlak, P Chandrasekhara Rao, and Tresselt, as well as Professors Donald M McRae,and Janusz Symonides. Professor McRae and Judge Tresselt both received their educations at institutions in high-income countries (the Universities of Otago and Canterbury, and Oslo respectively).

[26] Algeria, Jordan, the Philippines, South Africa, and Sri Lanka. There may, however, be different views as to what counts as a mixed system of law.

[27] As of November 2021. This data provides a snapshot rather than a holistic examination of the composition of ITLOS since its creation. It is set out in Appendix B at the end of the volume.

[28] UNCLOS (n 1) Annex VI, art 2(2).

[29] Judge Kelly was elected in 2011, followed by Judges Chadha and Lijnzaad, who were both elected in 2017. Professor Anna Petrig was the first woman to be appointed as an ad hoc judge of ITLOS in 2019 for *San Padre Pio (Switzerland v Nigeria)* (Provisional Measures, Order of 6 July 2019) ITLOS Case No 27 (*San Padre Pio*, Provisional Measures).

[30] Judges Infante Caffi, Brown, and Caracciolo joined Judges Chadha and Lijnzaad. Judge Kelly retired.

[31] This number dropped from nine to seven following the June 2020 elections.

[32] The exceptions again being the Eastern European judges, and also Judge Yanai from Japan. See Appendix B.

[33] Some of the jurisdictions could be described as mixed jurisdictions, as common law does feature in these legal systems. Following the June 2020 elections, three judges come from common law jurisdictions (India, Jamaica, and Tanzania), whereas four are from mixed jurisdictions (Cameroon, Malta, South Africa, and Thailand).

[34] Leigh Swigart and Daniel Terris, 'Who are International Judges?' in Cesare PR Romano, Karen J Alter, and Chrisanthi Avgerou (eds), *The Oxford Handbook of International Adjudication* (OUP 2013) 621. The study surveyed '304 judges ... serving on 21 of the most significant international judicial bodies'.

[35] ibid 633.

diversity among judges on international courts,[36] and that steps are needed to enhance both the reality and perception of judicial independence.[37]

The consequences of the particular characteristics of UNCLOS judges may not be readily apparent to all, and may explain why the all-male composition of ITLOS went largely unchallenged for its first fifteen years of operation.[38] It has been suggested that there is 'little scholarly evidence to support the idea that more women judges make a substantial difference in how international courts conduct their work' in the context of inter-State disputes, as opposed to human rights courts or courts that address gender-sensitive issues.[39] Yet this cuts against arguments that international institutions should reflect the composition of half of the world's population,[40] and is essential for the legitimacy of international courts.[41] Certainly in the area of international investment arbitration and international commercial arbitration, there is increasing recognition that greater gender diversity would be beneficial even though these tribunals do not typically address gender-sensitive issues.[42] In relation to age, youth may bring fresh ideas and perspectives, but Swigart and Terris suggest that a younger judge who has to contemplate a long career beyond the immediate judicial appointment may prompt concerns about judicial independence.[43] An alternative perspective is that a judge at the start of his or her career may be more concerned about reputational risk around conduct and bias and so adhere to high standards, as compared to judges approaching the end of their working lives. Representativeness across a range of characteristics—gender, age, religion, national origin—all potentially contribute to the decisions of a court,[44] and the perceived legitimacy of those decisions.[45]

Yet there are overarching traits that are expected to be common to all judges. Most particularly in this regard are the requirements as to impartiality and integrity, which are encapsulated in the oaths sworn by judges at the start of their duties.[46] As lawyers, each judge should also adhere to the ethical standards associated with their domestic jurisdiction and

[36] See eg Nienke Grossman, 'Shattering the Glass Ceiling in International Adjudication' (2016) 56 Va J Intl L 213. Grossman has suggested that reforming the election process and aspirational statements or quotas for gender balance may assist in this regard. See also Nienke Grossman, 'Sex-Representative International Court Benches' (2016) 110 AJIL 82, 86, 92–94; Cecily Rose, 'Justifying Arguments about Selection Procedures for Judges at International Courts and Tribunals: A Response to Nienke Grossman' (2016) 110 AJIL Unbound 86.

[37] See eg Malcolm Langford, Daniel Behn, and Runar Lie, 'The Revolving Door in International Investment Arbitration' (2017) 20 J Intl Econ L 301; Marie Davoise, 'Can't Fight the Moonlight? Actually, You Can: ICJ Judges to Stop Acting as Arbitrators in Investor-State Disputes' *EJIL: Talk!* (18 November 2019) www.ejiltalk.org/cant-fight-the-moonlight-actually-you-can-icj-judges-to-stop-acting-as-arbitrators-in-investor-state-disputes/.

[38] Nienke Grossman, 'Sex on the Bench: Do Women Judges Matter to the Legitimacy of International Courts' (2012) 12 Chi J Intl L 647, 674.

[39] Swigart and Terris (n 34) 624.

[40] Hilary Charlesworth, Christine Chinkin, and Shelley Wright, 'Feminist Approaches to International Law' (1991) 85 AJIL 613, 624.

[41] See generally Grossman (n 38) (arguing that equal sex representation matters for both normative legitimacy and sociological legitimacy).

[42] See eg Lucy Greenwood, 'Tipping the Balance: Diversity and Inclusion in International Arbitration' (2017) 33 Arb Intl 99; Susan D Franck and others, 'The Diversity Challenge: Exploring the "Invisible College" of International Arbitration' (2015) 53 Colum J Transnatl L 429.

[43] Swigart and Terris (n 34) 625.

[44] Meron has observed that a 'diversity in backgrounds also means that the judicial decisions must be reached in the context of the interplay between different legal cultures and legal systems.' Remarks by Theodor Meron, 'Decision-making in International Courts and Tribunals: A Conversation with Leading Judges and Arbitrators' (2011) ASIL Proc 224.

[45] Grossman (n 38) 668–75; Rose (n 36).

[46] The International Criminal Court has its own Code of Judicial Ethics. International Criminal Court, 'Code of Judicial Ethics' (adopted 9 March 2005) www.icc-cpi.int/NR/rdonlyres/A62EBC0F-D534-438F-A128-D3AC4CFDD644/140141/ICCBD020105_En.pdf.

reflected at the international level.[47] Judicial independence is critical to the rule of law. As Dunoff and Pollack have noted, '[s]ince independent courts can detect, identify, and publicize violations, they tend to increase the cost of violations and therefore increase the probability that states will comply with their obligations'.[48] Judicial independence may thus be seen as a safeguard against injustice.[49] In exercising discretion, judges should adhere to professional legal norms and publicity about their reasoning should be encouraged.[50] There may be accountability for judges through renomination by their governments and re-election to ITLOS,[51] or reappointment to the ad hoc tribunals under Annex VII of UNCLOS.[52]

Justice Florentino Feliciano, a member of the WTO Appellate Body and judge on the *Southern Bluefin Tuna* arbitration,[53] described the essential qualities of judges in his extra-judicial writings.[54] He emphasised the importance of learning as one such quality, and that this learning was not just to come from a detailed and incisive knowledge of the law,[55] but had to be about the community in which the judge lives, the community's social concerns, its politics and economics, and its notions of moral rectitude.[56] Judges must further be aware that their 'decisions have consequences for human values'.[57] So a judge is not to choose an outcome that might suit their own personal conception of what might be a desirable consequence but must look to the community. Another quality of a judge highlighted by Justice Feliciano was that of humility. He wrote:

[47] These international ethical standards include the International Bar Association's International Principles on Conduct for the Legal Profession and the International Law Association's Hague Principles on Ethical Standards for Counsel Appearing before International Courts and Tribunals. See International Bar Association, 'International Principles on Conduct for the Legal Profession' (25 May 2019) https://acica.org.au/wp-content/uploads/IBA_Guidelines/IBA-Guidelines-on-Conflict-of-Interest.pdf; Study Group of the International Law Association on the Practice and Procedure of International Courts and Tribunals, 'The Hague Principles on Ethical Standards for Counsel Appearing before International Courts and Tribunals' (27 September 2010) www.ucl.ac.uk/international-courts/sites/international-courts/files/hague_sept2010.pdf. See also International Commission of Jurists, 'International Principles on the Independence and Accountability of Judges, Lawyers and Prosecutors: Practitioners Guide No 1' (2nd edn 2007) www.refworld.org/pdfid/4a7837af2.pdf; 'Bologna and Milan Global Code of Judicial Ethics' (approved at the International Conference of Judicial Independence held at the University of Bologna and at Bocconi University of Milano, June 2015) www.icj.org/wp-content/uploads/2016/02/Bologna-and-Milan-Global-Code-of-Judicial-Ethics.pdf; International Bar Association, 'IBA Guidelines on Conflicts of Interest in International Arbitration' (adopted by resolution of the IBA Council, 23 October 2014) https://www.icj.org/wp-content/uploads/2014/10/IBA_International_Principles_on_Conduct_for_the_legal_prof.pdf.

[48] Jeffrey L Dunoff and Mark A Pollack, 'The Judicial Trilemma' (2017) 111 AJIL 225, 233.

[49] See Dinah Shelton, 'Form, Function, and the Powers of International Courts' (2009) 9 Chi J Intl L 537, 545 (referring to the maxim *nemo index in causa sua*). See also CF Amerasinghe, 'Reflections on the Judicial Function in International Law' in Tafsir Malick Ndiaye and Rüdiger Wolfrum (eds), *Law of the Sea, Environmental Law and Settlement of Disputes:* Liber Amicorum *Judge Thomas A Mensah* (Martinus Nijhoff 2007) 123.

[50] Andreas Follesdal, 'To Guide and Guard International Judges' (2014) 46 NYU J Intl L & Pol 793, 803–805. Follesdal also suggests that the use of precedents and persuasive past decisions may also assist in this regard, but this tradition is more associated with common law jurisdictions.

[51] Gleider Hernández, 'Interpretative Authority and the International Judiciary' in Andrea Bianchi, Daniel Peat, and Matthew Windsor (eds), *Interpretation in International Law* (OUP 2015) 180.

[52] See Anthea Roberts, 'Power and Persuasion in Investment Treaty Interpretation: The Dual Role of States' (2010) 104 AJIL 179, 197–98 (referring to motivations to support the regime mean that judges have accountability). See also Dunoff and Pollack (n 48) 234–35.

[53] *Southern Bluefin Tuna (New Zealand v Japan; Australia v Japan)* (Jurisdiction and Admissibility) (2000) 23 RIAA 1 (*Southern Bluefin Tuna*, Jurisdiction and Admissibility).

[54] Florentino P Feliciano, 'Qualities of a Good Judge' (1994) 3 The Lawyers Rev 68. See also W Michael Reisman, 'A Judge's Judge: Justice Florentino P Feliciano's Philosophy of the Judicial Function' in Steve Charnovitz, Debra P Steger, and Peter Van den Bossche (eds), *Law in the Service of Human Dignity: Essays in Honour of Florentino Feliciano* (CUP 2005) 5.

[55] Feliciano (n 54).

[56] ibid.

[57] ibid 69.

> The judge should have a clear understanding not only of his [or her] own personal limitations but also of the limitations of professional competence of the judicial process itself. A truly humble judge should be able to resist the shimmering vision of an 'imperial judiciary' and should come to realize that [s]he has neither the commission nor the competence to solve all the problems of the nation and that there are other 'workers in the vineyard'.[58]

This observation seems especially insightful because it explicitly recognises the limits of the judicial role. Understanding and accepting the parameters of the judicial role is critical in a legal system that is predicated on State consent for its operation.

The attributes and characteristics of individual judges are important as a widely representative group with different political and cultural representation is more likely to be perceived as producing credible and authoritative judgments.[59] Ultimately, these complex features of an individual judge all have to be considered alongside the actual tasks that a judge performs within a particular tribunal. These activities are considered in the next section of the chapter.

III. Diverse Roles in Exercising Judicial Functions

The core function for any UNCLOS judge in any of the fora listed under Article 287 is the settlement of disputes.[60] This core function requires the performance of different tasks, as necessitated by the circumstances of a particular case, but generally involving: settling the procedure, treaty interpretation, fact-finding, deciding on claims and, where warranted, assessing remedies.[61] Yet the function of settling disputes may resound more broadly than these tasks when account is taken of the setting in which specific UNCLOS disputes may arise. The dispute relating to the interpretation or application of UNCLOS may be one dimension of a larger conflict or situation of tension between the States concerned. Depending on the circumstances of the case, there may be regional or even global interest in the bilateral dispute that has emerged within the UNCLOS dispute settlement procedures. The dispute settlement function may therefore encompass consideration of this broader setting in order to contribute both to the peaceful resolution of the dispute and the public order of the oceans. Judicial contribution to broader disputes is also manifest in the issuance of advisory opinions. These opinions by their nature are not intended to resolve specific claims between parties but can elucidate the law and facilitate ongoing interactions between States. These different judicial roles are considered immediately below.

[58] ibid 68.

[59] Oscar Schachter, 'The Invisible College of International Lawyers' (1977) 2 Northwest U L Rev 217, 222.

[60] Shelton (n 49) 559–60.

[61] The ICJ referred to the characteristics of judicial institutions as 'considering the arguments of the parties, appraising the evidence produced by them, establishing the facts and declaring the law applicable to them': *Effect of Awards of Compensation Made by the United Nations Administrative Tribunal* (Advisory Opinion) [1954] ICJ Rep 47, 56.

A. Settling the Procedure

When a case is instituted under UNCLOS, procedural issues for the running of the case must be determined. Depending on the forum involved, the procedural matters may concern the appointment of the judges or ad hoc judges, appointing a secretariat, determining the timetable for written and oral arguments as well as whether there are preliminary questions to address before turning to the merits. Many of these procedural dimensions will be addressed under the Statute of ITLOS or of the ICJ,[62] and their accompanying rules.[63] Annex VII arbitration and Annex VIII special arbitration also have basic requirements set out within UNCLOS. Annex VII arbitrations have predominantly relied on the Permanent Court of Arbitration to provide secretariat services.[64]

Some of the key procedural questions to have been addressed under UNCLOS dispute settlement thus far include the appointment of arbitrators, non-participation of State parties, and non-State actor participation. Decisions on procedure may relate predominantly to the smooth progress of the dispute settlement proceedings, such as the deadlines for submitting pleadings and documents, but may also have implications for decisions on jurisdiction and on the merits. For example, when Panama and Guinea Bissau opted to move their dispute from arbitration to ITLOS for resolution,[65] a question arose as to whether admissibility challenges could still be raised before ITLOS.[66] How procedural matters are resolved can thus be important to parties' litigation strategies and further reflect the important level of control that judges exercise throughout the dispute settlement proceedings.

In relation to the appointment of arbitrators for Annex VII arbitrations, Article 3 of Annex VII sets out the requirements for constituting a tribunal. In particular, each party is able to select one member of a five-member tribunal. The three other members are to be appointed by agreement between the parties,[67] and the president of the tribunal selected from among those three members.[68] In the absence of agreement between the parties on appointments, the President of ITLOS has the authority to make the necessary appointments (or the next senior member of ITLOS shall do so if the President of ITLOS is of the same nationality of one of the parties).[69] When China refused to participate in the *South China Sea* arbitration, President Yanai of Japan exercised his appointing authority in selecting the remaining four arbitrators.[70] A change was made to the initial appointment of Dr Pinto as President because of concerns about impartiality due to his wife being a national of the

[62] Statute of the International Court of Justice (ICJ Statute); Statute of the International Tribunal for the Law of the Sea, UNCLOS (n 1) Annex VI (ITLOS Statute).

[63] International Court of Justice (adopted 14 April 1978, entered into force 1 July 1978) (ICJ Rules); Rules of Court International Tribunal for the Law of the Sea, Rules of the Tribunal, Doc No ITLOS/8 (adopted 28 October 1997, amended 25 March 2021) (ITLOS Rules).

[64] All but one Annex VII arbitration has been administered through the Permanent Court of Arbitration; the one exception being *Southern Bluefin Tuna*, Jurisdiction and Admissibility (n 53), which used the International Centre for the Settlement of Investment Disputes (ICSID) as its registry.

[65] *M/V Virginia G (Panama/Guinea-Bissau)* (Judgment) [2014] ITLOS Rep 4, paras 3, 4, 6, and 85–92 (*Virginia G*).

[66] *Southern Bluefin Tuna*, Jurisdiction and Admissibility (n 53) paras 93–98.

[67] UNCLOS (n 1) Annex VII, art 3(d).

[68] ibid.

[69] ibid art 3(d), (e).

[70] See ITLOS, 'New Arbitrator and President Appointed in the Arbitral Proceedings Instituted by the Republic of the Philippines Against the People's Republic of China' ITLOS/Press 197 (24 June 2013) www.itlos.org/filead min/itlos/documents/press_releases_english/PR_197_E.pdf.

Philippines.[71] The process followed the requirements of Article 3 of Annex VII and, although Chinese media criticised the perceived bias in the exercise of appointing powers by a Japanese judge,[72] China chose not to avail itself of the rights available to it under UNCLOS. A similar process was followed in relation to the *Arctic Sunrise* arbitration.[73]

The non-participation of a party in proceedings before an UNCLOS tribunal prompts further procedural questions beyond appointment of arbitrators in relation to the presentation of evidence (discussed further below) and providing opportunities to each side to submit its case. To ensure the equality of the parties given the non-appearance of Russia in the *Arctic Sunrise* arbitration, the Tribunal adopted a specific rule on default appearance, building on Article 9 of Annex VII in UNCLOS. This article in the Rules of Procedure set out a process for the tribunal to request written arguments from the appearing party, as well as timeframes for submitting pleadings after the communication of the appearing party's submissions.[74] At the merits stage of the *Arctic Sunrise* arbitration, although Russia did not participate, after the close of hearings and the Netherlands' final written submission, Russia sent a 'position paper' to the Tribunal. Russia advised that the position paper was not to be interpreted as an acceptance of jurisdiction or as participation in the proceedings.[75] As such, because of that statement and because it was submitted at such a late stage of the proceedings, the Tribunal opted not to take any formal action in relation to that position paper.[76]

Participation of diverse actors in UNCLOS proceedings may be managed through procedural decisions of tribunals. Both Annex VII tribunals and ITLOS have managed the examination of witnesses in cases involving the seizure of vessels.[77] In its advisory proceedings, ITLOS and the Seabed Chamber contemplated the involvement of non-governmental organisations and opted to include their written submissions, not to allow oral presentations, and to post their pleadings online without making them part of the official file of the proceedings.[78] In contrast, the International Union for the Conservation of Nature, which has both States and civil society as members, was treated as an inter-governmental organisation and presented both written and oral arguments in relation to the advisory opinions sought from ITLOS[79] and the Seabed

[71] Bing Jia and Stefan Talmon, 'Introduction' in Stefan Talmon and Bing Bing Jia (eds), *The South China Sea Arbitration: A Chinese Perspective* (Hart Publishing 2014) 12.

[72] Bethany Allen-Ebrahimian, 'Beijing: Japanese Judges Means South China Sea Tribunal is Biased' *Foreign Policy* (21 June 2016) https://foreignpolicy.com/2016/06/21/beijing-japanese-judge-means-south-china-sea-tribunal-is-biased-china-philippines-maritime-claims/.

[73] See ITLOS, 'Arbitrators Appointed in the Arbitral Proceedings Instituted by the Kingdom of the Netherlands against the Russian Federation in Respect of the Dispute Regarding the *Arctic Sunrise*' ITLOS/Press 207 (13 January 2014) www.itlos.org/fileadmin/itlos/documents/press_releases_english/PR_207_E.pdf.

[74] *Arctic Sunrise (Netherlands v Russia)* (Procedural Order No 2 of 17 March 2014) PCA Case No 2014-02.

[75] *Arctic Sunrise (Netherlands v Russia)* (Award on the Merits of 14 August 2015) PCA Case No 2014-02, para 68 (*Arctic Sunrise*, Merits).

[76] ibid.

[77] See eg ibid paras 58–60; *Virginia G* (n 65) paras 35–37; *M/V Norstar (Panama v Italy)* (Judgment of 10 April 2019) ITLOS Case No 25, paras 55–57.

[78] See *Responsibilities and Obligations of States with Respect to Activities in the Area* (Advisory Opinion) ITLOS Reports 2011, 10, paras 13–14 (*Seabed Advisory Opinion*); *Request for Advisory Opinion Submitted by the Sub-Regional Fisheries Commission* (Advisory Opinion) ITLOS Reports 2015, 4, paras 13, 15, and 23 (*SRFC Advisory Opinion*).

[79] *SRFC Advisory Opinion* (n 78) paras 17, 26. Also submitting written proceedings beyond IUCN and the SRFC were the Forum Fisheries Agency, the Caribbean Regional Fisheries Mechanism, the United Nations, the Food and Agriculture Organization, and the Central American Fisheries and Aquaculture Organization: see para 17. The Caribbean Regional Fisheries Mechanism and the SRFC also presented oral arguments: see para 26.

Chamber.[80] Advocate participation is arguably more varied before ITLOS than before the ICJ when regard is had to prompt release proceedings before ITLOS where lawyers representing shipping companies are able to present their claims on behalf of a State.[81]

Procedural decisions clearly influence the way that claims are presented to the judges. The extent that any one procedural decision influences the final settlement of a dispute may only be a matter of speculation. What matters for present purposes is acknowledging this dimension of the judicial function and how this task is part of an overall complex of decision-making that contributes to the ultimate resolution of any dispute.

B. Treaty Interpretation

The task of treaty interpretation has long been recognised as the cornerstone of international judicial functions.[82] For UNCLOS judges settling disputes, this task concerns the interpretation and application of UNCLOS.[83] This authoritative role is accorded to them in the grant of jurisdiction under Article 288 of UNCLOS. In becoming parties to UNCLOS, States consent to a tribunal having power to resolve disputes concerning the interpretation or application of UNCLOS under the terms of Article 286.[84]

An initial important role for judges is the determination of whether they have jurisdiction to resolve the dispute submitted to them. They are empowered to make this decision by virtue of the *compétence de la compétence* principle, enshrined in Article 288(4) of UNCLOS. Interpreting and applying UNCLOS is not limited to the provisions of the dispute settlement regime, but of course extends to determining the substantive claims and whether the requirements of UNCLOS have been violated. While judges hold a privileged position in the interpretation and application of UNCLOS by dint of the compulsory dispute settlement process, all actors engaging in ocean use also undertake their own interpretations and applications of UNCLOS, from which a cognisable practice may emerge. These activities may be relevant for the judicial task of treaty interpretation,[85] and in assessing the normative authority of decisions emanating from UNCLOS dispute settlement procedures.

[80] *Seabed Advisory Opinion* (n 78) paras 11 and 17. The Interoceanmetal Joint Organization also presented a written statement: see para 11. The Intergovernmental Oceanographic Commission of UNESCO also presented oral arguments: see para 17.

[81] Under the ITLOS Rules (n 63), a prompt release application may be made 'by or on behalf of' the flag State of the detained vessel: art 110(1). See eg *Juno Trader (Saint Vincent and the Grenadines v Guinea-Bissau)* (Prompt Release) (Application on Behalf of Saint Vincent and the Grenadines of 18 November 2004) ITLOS Case No 13; *Chaisiri Reefer 2 (Panama v Yemen)* (Prompt Release) (Application Submitted on Behalf of Panama of 2 July 2001) ITLOS Case No 9; *Grand Prince (Belize v France)* (Application Submitted on Behalf of Belize of 21 March 2001) ITLOS Case No 21 March 2001.

[82] Sir Hersch Lauterpacht wrote that 'almost the entire history of the work of the Permanent Court of International Justice could be given in terms of cases arising out of the interpretation of treaties': Hersch Lauterpacht, *The Function of Law in the International Community* (Clarendon Press 1933) 108. Hernández cites this proposition and observes it holds true in relation to modern courts, including the ICJ, WTO dispute settlement panels and ITLOS: Hernández (n 51) 167.

[83] 'Interpretation is the process of determining the meaning of a text; application is the process of determining the consequences which, according to the text, should follow in a given situation': Hernández (n 51) 176.

[84] 'Subject to section 3, any dispute concerning the interpretation or application of this Convention shall, where no settlement has been reached by recourse to section 1, be submitted at the request of any party to the dispute to the court or tribunal have jurisdiction under this section.' UNCLOS (n 1) art 286.

[85] For example, as possible state practice in the application of the treaty: Vienna Convention on the Law of Treaties (adopted 23 May 1969, entered into force 27 January 1980) 1155 UNTS 331, art 31(3)(b) (VCLT).

In undertaking treaty interpretation during UNCLOS dispute resolution, tribunals will commonly follow the rules of treaty interpretation enshrined in Articles 31 and 32 of the Vienna Convention on the Law of Treaties (VCLT). Article 31 provides:

1. A treaty shall be interpreted in good faith in accordance with the ordinary meaning to be given to the terms of the treaty in their context and in the light of its object and purpose.
2. The context for the purpose of the interpretation of a treaty shall comprise, in addition to the text, including its preamble and annexes:
   (a) Any agreement relating to the treaty which was made between all the parties in connexion with the conclusion of the treaty;
   (b) Any instrument which was made by one or more parties in connexion with the conclusion of the treaty and accepted by the other parties as an instrument related to the treaty.
3. There shall be taken into account, together with the context:
   (a) Any subsequent agreement between the parties regarding the interpretation of the treaty or the application of its provisions;
   (b) Any subsequent practice in the application of the treaty which establishes the agreement of the parties regarding its interpretation;
   (c) Any relevant rules of international law applicable in the relations between the parties.
4. A special meaning shall be given to a term if it is established that the parties so intended.

Article 32 of the VCLT provides for reference to the *travaux préparatoires* to confirm an interpretation reached under Article 31. Otherwise, reference to the *travaux préparatoires* may be determinative if the means under Article 31 produce a result that is 'manifestly absurd or unreasonable' or a meaning that is 'ambiguous or obscure'.[86] The Seabed Chamber in the *Seabed Advisory Opinion* explicitly stated that the rules in the Vienna Convention on the interpretation of treaties apply to the interpretation of provisions of UNCLOS and the Agreement Relating to the Implementation of Part XI of UNCLOS (1994 Agreement).[87]

The rules of treaty interpretation allow for some '"dynamic" or "evolutive" interpretations of a treaty—"in the light of its object and purpose"'.[88] Judge Lucky of ITLOS described the function in the following terms: 'It is accepted that judges do not make law, but they can point out deficiencies or ambiguities in the law or give a wide interpretation to an article or section of a treaty or convention to assist in the development of the jurisprudence of international law.'[89] Examples of such an approach may be discerned in the judicial decisions emerging from UNCLOS dispute settlement, as will be discussed in the chapters that follow.

[86] ibid art 32.

[87] *Seabed Advisory Opinion* (n 78) para 58. Anton and others have further noted that this view 'applied to agreements, such as the regulations, that did not have treaty status but treaty-like status, consistent with the ICJ's approach to Security Council resolutions': Donald K Anton, Robert A Makgill, and Cymie R Payne, 'Seabed Mining: Advisory Opinion on Responsibility and Liability' (2011) 41 Env Poly & L 60, 61.

[88] Follesdal (n 50) 798.

[89] *SRFC Advisory Opinion* (n 78) 92 [10] (Separate Opinion of Judge Lucky).

Yet this very process, both under UNCLOS and in other international courts, has prompted discussions about the role of judges as law-makers.[90] In this regard, judges may be viewed as the 'guardians of the very coherence of these rules themselves'.[91] Judges thus need some discretion where modifications of a treaty would otherwise be difficult to achieve.[92] An alternative perspective is to ask if judges are 'cloaking themselves in the formalism of classical legal positivism so as to abdicate political responsibility for the constitutive role of their interpretations?'[93] These varied theories align to some extent with the discussions set out in Chapter 1 about the role of courts more generally in the international legal system.[94] Hernández captures both elements in writing:

> Yet with power comes responsibility: interpretation cannot just be reduced to the recognition of a norm's meaning, nor by omnipresent and all-pervasive structures. The interpretative act, when undertaken by certain law-applying actors (and in particular judicial institutions), involves not only a considerable degree of freedom, but amounts to a claim to authority . . . Lest we forget that judges are also human beings, not only acting to perpetuate their own power (although in fact, often very concerned with their prestige), but also *normative* actors conditioned by their legal upbringing and the career that brought them to the international bench in the first place.[95]

So while interpretation is a central task for judges, it is inherently complex and multifaceted. Judicial interpretations may need to account for the consequences of that action as well as contemplate coherency with the existing legal order.[96] Treaty interpretation thus has far-reaching outcomes when considering the role of dispute settlement in the overall good order of the oceans.

C. Fact-finding

Another distinct legal task for judges beyond treaty interpretation is deciding questions of fact based on the evidence presented.[97] In determining whether a claim of an UNCLOS violation is established or not, the judges will have to draw on particular facts. In international judicial proceedings, the burden of proof typically rests on the party making the claim,[98]

[90] Literature on the role of judges in law-making processes is extensive and form significant parts of key debates in legal jurisprudence. See eg Hans Kelsen, *Pure Theory of Law* (2nd edn, University of California Press 1970); HLA Hart, *The Concept of Law* (2nd edn, Clarendon Press 1994); Ronald Dworkin, *Taking Rights Seriously* (Harv UP 1977); Jürgen Habermas, *Between Facts and Norms: Contributions to a Discourse Theory of Law and Democracy* (MIT Press 1998); Martii Koskenniemi, *From Apology to Utopia: The Structure of International Legal Argument* (CUP 2005).

[91] Hernández (n 51) 167–68.

[92] Follesdal (n 50) 798; Guilfoyle (n 15) 174–75.

[93] Hernández (n 51) 168.

[94] See ch 1(III).

[95] Hernández (n 51) 183–84.

[96] Neil MacCormick considered the consequences and coherency aspects as 'second-order justifications' for legal interpretations that went beyond deductive justifications and required a choice between possible views: Neil MacCormick, *Legal Reasoning and Legal Theory* (1994 OUP) chs 5–7.

[97] 'Good fact-finding is important to the credibility and legitimacy of the court': Shelton (n 49) 550.

[98] In the *Pulp Mills* case, the ICJ referred to the well-established principle of *onus probandi incumbit actori*, which is the duty of the party which asserts certain facts to establish the existence of such facts: *Pulp Mills on the River Uruguay (Argentina v Uruguay)* (Merits) [2010] ICJ Rep 14, para 162.

but the standard of proof may be varied.[99] UNCLOS tribunals have not always explicitly articulated this burden and standard,[100] but do frequently engage in an assessment of facts in order to ascertain if a particular claim has been established.[101]

These factual determinations have been all the more important in cases where one of the parties refuses to appear.[102] There is no automatic default judgment in favour of the party that appears, as might occur in domestic jurisdictions. The tribunal still has jurisdiction to make binding determinations, but must be satisfied that it has jurisdiction and ensure that any claim is well founded in fact and law.[103] This requirement aligns with the dispute settlement function of tribunals; the dispute would probably be exacerbated rather than resolved if default judgments were used.[104]

In the *Arctic Sunrise* arbitration, in the default of Russia's appearance, the Tribunal was left to procure Russian laws and regulations that were considered useful beyond relying on the Netherlands' documentation and witnesses.[105] In the *South China Sea* arbitration, the Tribunal requested additional information from the Philippines and undertook its own archival research.[106] Spijkers has observed that a strategy of non-participation effectively forces the appearing party and the tribunal to 'do all the work', but may be disadvantageous in that the appearing party will not necessarily produce evidence directly contrary to its own position.[107]

Fact-finding may be facilitated by reliance on expert reports, either prepared and presented by the parties to the case or separately sought by the tribunals.[108] Tribunals constituted under UNCLOS have developed rules to address the involvement of these experts, including that expert witnesses should present written reports in addition to being heard during the oral proceedings.[109] Judges have considered party-appointed experts more

[99] See Chester Brown, *A Common Law of International Adjudication* (OUP 2007) 97–101; Yoshifumi Tanaka, *The Peaceful Settlement of International Disputes* (CUP 2018) 182.

[100] In the *MV Saiga*, ITLOS considered whether allegations were 'of a sufficiently plausible character' in the context of prompt release proceedings: *M/V Saiga (Saint Vincent and the Grenadines v Guinea)* (Prompt Release, Judgment) ITLOS Reports 1997, 16, para 51. The ITLOS Rules (n 63) require that an allegation be 'well-founded'. See Natalie Klein, *Dispute Settlement in the UN Convention on the Law of the Sea* (CUP 2005) 91–93.

[101] See eg *Grand Prince (Belize v France)* (Prompt Release, Judgment) ITLOS Reports 2001, 17, paras 85–89 (determining nationality of the vessel); *San Padre Pio*, Provisional Measures (n 29) (Dissenting Opinion of Judge Lucky) paras 46–60.

[102] As observed in the *Arctic Sunrise*, Merits (n 25) the Tribunal noted that it 'appreciates that the evidence before it may not include all of the evidence that would have been put before it had both parties participated in the proceedings': see para 73.

[103] UNCLOS (n 1) Annex VII, art 9; Annex VI, art 28. The Netherlands referred to a 'three-pronged' test in the *Arctic Sunrise*. See 'Verbatim Record' *Arctic Sunrise (Netherlands v Russia)* (Provisional Measures) (ITLOS Case No 22, 6 November 2013) 6.

[104] Shelton (n 49) 562. But see Otto Spijkers, 'Non-Participation in Arbitral Proceedings Under Annex VII United Nations Convention on the Law of the Sea: *Arctic Sunrise* and *South China Sea* Compared' in Angela Del Vecchio and Roberto Virzo (eds), *Interpretations of the United Nations Convention on the Law of the Sea by International Courts and Tribunals* (Springer 2019) 188 (arguing that an outcome more strongly resembling a default judgment may influence state decision-making on non-participation and render participation more likely).

[105] *Arctic Sunrise*, Merits (n 25) para 66.

[106] The Tribunal sets out in detail the efforts it took to address China's non-appearance to meet the requirements of art 9 of Annex VII of UNCLOS (n 1). See *South China Sea*, Award (n 12) paras 131–42.

[107] Spijkers (n 104) 186–87.

[108] For discussion see Lucas Carlos Lima, 'The Use of Experts by the International Tribunal for the Law of the Sea and Annex VII Arbitral Tribunals' in Angela Del Vecchio and Roberto Virzo (eds), *Interpretations of the United Nations Convention on the Law of the Sea by International Courts and Tribunals* (Springer 2019) 407. For discussion in relation to the practice of the ICJ, including in relation to maritime boundary cases see Yusuf (n 14).

[109] Lima (n 108) 409–410.

reliable when they can discern agreement between each side's experts,[110] or the expert evidence presented is uncontested.[111] The latter situation arose in the maritime delimitation between Nicaragua and Costa Rica (where the Court had appointed experts).[112]

Tribunal-appointed experts are anticipated under Article 289 of UNCLOS,[113] or may be independently appointed by the ICJ, ITLOS or Annex VII tribunals in accordance with their respective rules.[114] For example, in the *South China Sea* arbitration, an expert hydrographer was appointed by the Tribunal.[115] The Tribunal described the role played by this hydrographer as assisting it

> in 'reviewing and analysing geographic and hydrographic information, photographs, satellite imagery and other technical data in order to enable the Arbitral Tribunal to assess the status (as a submerged feature, low-tide elevation, or island)' of the features named in the Philippines' Submissions or any other such feature determined to be relevant during the course of the reference. While the appointment of hydrographic experts is common practice in Annex VII arbitrations, in light of China's non-participation, [the expert hydrographer] was also tasked with assisting with a 'critical assessment of relevant expert advice and opinions submitted by the Philippines'.[116]

The nature of the role of the expert would typically be one that does not allow the expert to impose their will (at least not overtly) on the decision-maker.

The judges' role as fact-finder is certainly a critical one. The findings create a historical, political or scientific record, as well as being relevant to the decision on specific claims. It raises the question as to the relevance of this record outside the immediate proceedings. In *South China Sea*, for example, it is noticeable that the assessment of island or rock status ultimately drew on information also relevant to determinations of territorial sovereignty. A variety of evidence was used in determining whether various features were rocks or islands. The arbitrators looked to satellite images, historical data about usage, survey maps and information, naval charts, sailing directions, and conditions on the features, such as presence and quantity of potable water, vegetation, agriculture potential, and commercial operations.[117] Does this mean that if there was ever a case on territorial sovereignty that any of the factual findings in the *South China Sea* arbitration would have to be taken into consideration? Do those findings constitute a 'decision' under Article 296 that is final and binding, but only between the Philippines and China? It might be expected at least that

[110] See eg *Barbados v Trinidad and Tobago* (Award of the Arbitral Tribunal of 11 April 2006) PCA Case No 2004-02, para 307.

[111] *Delimitation of the Maritime Boundary in the Bay of Bengal (Bangladesh/Myanmar)* (Judgment) ITLOS Reports 2012, 4, para 444 (*Bay of Bengal Delimitation*). See also Lima (n 108) 410.

[112] *Maritime Delimitation in the Caribbean Sea and the Pacific Ocean (Costa Rica v Nicaragua)* and *Land Boundary in the Northern Part of Isla Portillos (Costa Rica v Nicaragua)* (Judgment) [2019] ICJ Rep 139, para 71.

[113] UNCLOS (n 1) art 289 provides: 'In any dispute involving scientific or technical matters, a court or tribunal exercising jurisdiction under this section may, at the request of a party or *proprio motu*, select in consultation with the parties no fewer than two scientific or technical experts chosen preferably from the relevant list prepared in accordance with Annex VIII, article 2, to sit with the court or tribunal but without the right to vote.'

[114] Lima (n 108) 414–15.

[115] *South China Sea*, Award (n 12) para 58.

[116] ibid para 133 (citations omitted).

[117] See ibid paras 577–626.

third-party proceedings may look to the factual determinations in one case to draw analogies to other fact patterns leading to similar legal conclusions.

D. Settling the Dispute Presented

Each party to a case will present a series of claims that the tribunal must judge as substantiated or not. The culmination of the above activities, namely settling the procedure, fact-finding, and interpreting UNCLOS, should be a judicial decision as to whether UNCLOS has been violated or not. In the context of maritime boundary cases, the outcome should be a judicial determination of where the boundary lies consistent with UNCLOS. The claims and prayers for relief put forward by the parties should thus be formulated in such a way that the dispute is resolved by virtue of these decisions.

The judicial settlement of an international dispute may be considered as the enforcement of international law. Alter describes the 'enforcement' role of international courts in this regard as follows:

> The enforcement role involves [international courts] reviewing the actions of states, public bodies and in some cases individuals to see if they cohere with the requirements of international law. [International courts] primarily name a state practice as legal or illegal, and secondarily authorize remedies designed to compensate victims and create costs associated with illegal behavior.[118]

Alter's observation that the primary task of international courts is assessing legality and that determining remedies is a secondary task is consonant with the experience of tribunals constituted under UNCLOS. Declarations have commonly been issued in determining the claims of States in judgments on the merits.

In the *South China Sea* arbitration, the Philippines sought declarations from the Tribunal that essentially required China to adhere to its treaty obligations under UNCLOS in the future.[119] The Tribunal did not consider such a declaration to be necessary,[120] but stated 'the purpose of dispute resolution proceedings is to clarify the Parties' respective rights and obligations and thereby to facilitate their future relations in accordance with the general obligations of good faith that both governments unequivocally recognise'.[121] As the Tribunal had sought to clear up the 'fundamentally different understandings' of each State of its rights and obligations under UNCLOS,[122] these determinations were expected to apply in the relations between the States going forward.[123]

[118] Karen J Alter, 'The Multiple Roles of International Courts and Tribunals: Enforcement, Dispute Settlement, Constitutional and Administrative Review' in Jeffrey L Dunoff and Mark A Pollack (eds), *International Law and International Relations: Synthesizing Insights from Interdisciplinary Scholarship* (CUP 2013) 345, 350.

[119] *South China Sea*, Award (n 12) paras 1192–95.

[120] ibid para 1201.

[121] ibid para 1198.

[122] ibid.

[123] UNCLOS (n 1) art 296(1).

E. Role in Broader Dispute Settlement

It would be quite common for any international proceeding to represent one dimension of a broader dispute—or at least a tense relationship—that might exist between the parties concerned.[124] Any judge in this situation would be aware that their decision would have implications for this larger relationship and so their role encompasses a contribution to the overall settlement of the dispute. The *Southern Bluefin Tuna* arbitration may be seen within this frame, for example. While the decision that the tribunal lacked jurisdiction proved highly controversial among many commentators,[125] one of the lawyers acting for New Zealand acknowledged that the Tribunal's decision was extremely useful for resolving the underlying dispute within the Southern Bluefin Tuna Commission, which necessitated returning the Commission to functionality and expanding its membership.[126] To this end, Mansfield has commented:

> A ruling on whether Japan's previous [experimental fishing programmes] were or were not contrary to their legal obligations (the relief Australia and New Zealand were seeking) was not going to restore functionality to the Commission. In fact the adversarial mindset and effort involved in preparation for the merits phase might well have had the reverse effect.[127]

In other instances, a judge may proceed on the basis that the resolution of a specific legal dispute must occur irrespective of the wider ramifications. The *South China Sea* Tribunal adopted this position,[128] consistent with the ICJ, which has observed that there are no grounds to 'decline to take cognisance of one aspect of a dispute merely because that dispute has other aspects, however important'.[129] ITLOS appeared willing to proceed on this basis too when Ukraine sought provisional measures following Russia's seizure of three Ukrainian naval vessels and their crew,[130] even though the incident in question is part of a greater dispute between Ukraine and Russia relating to sovereignty over Crimea and associated territorial and maritime rights.[131] Yet one might speculate that international judicial

[124] The ICJ has observed that '[l]egal disputes between sovereign States by their very nature are likely to occur in political contexts, and often form only one element in a wider and long-standing political dispute between the States concerned': *United States Diplomatic and Consular Staff in Tehran (United States v Iran)* (Judgment) [1980] ICJ Rep 3, 19 [37].

[125] See eg Bernard H Oxman, 'Complementary Agreements and Compulsory Jurisdiction' (2001) 95 AJIL 277; David A Colson and Peggy Hoyle, 'Satisfying the Procedural Prerequisites to the Compulsory Dispute Settlement Mechanisms of the 1982 Law of the Sea Convention: Did the Southern Bluefin Tuna Tribunal Get it Right?' (2003) 34 ODIL 59.

[126] See Bill Mansfield, 'Peaceful Settlement of International Disputes: Litigation or Negotiation: Some Practical Considerations' (2016) 14 Otago L Rev 329.

[127] ibid 332.

[128] *South China Sea Arbitration (Philippines v China)* (Award on Jurisdiction and Admissibility of 29 October 2015) PCA Case No 2013-19, para 152. See also Gregory L Rose, 'Arbitration Jurisdiction in *Philippines v PRC*: Quixotic Judicialisation and Sovereign Resistance in Law of the Sea' (2018) 15 Soochow LJ 11, 32 ('Arbitration Jurisdiction').

[129] *United States Diplomatic and Consular Staff in Tehran* (n 124) 19–20 [36].

[130] *Case Concerning the Detention of Three Ukrainian Naval Vessels (Ukraine v Russia)* (Provisional Measures Order of 25 May 2019) ITLOS Case No 26.

[131] The latter issue had been separately submitted to Annex VII arbitration. See *Dispute Concerning Coastal State Rights in the Black Sea, Sea of Azov, and Kerch Strait (Ukraine v Russia)* PCA Case No 2017-06. Ukraine also instituted proceedings against Russia at the ICJ. *Application of the International Convention for the Suppression of the Financing of Terrorism and of the International Convention on the Elimination of All Forms of Racial Discrimination (Ukraine v Russia)* (Preliminary Objections) [2019] ICJ Rep 558.

decision-making is not siloed and that judges acknowledge, to varying degrees, some of the policy elements of their decisions.[132]

An example of policy influence that may be seen in the *South China Sea* arbitration was the discussion on rocks and islands. State practice was dismissed in one paragraph with the assertion it aligned with the Tribunal's interpretation.[133] The judges explicitly endorsed the policy they considered at play during UNCLOS negotiations, namely that tiny areas of land should not be used to claim exclusive rights over large expanses of ocean space that would otherwise be high seas.[134] Yet commentators, and probably government advisers, were quick to note how the Tribunal's approach would apply in other situations.[135]

The broader consequences of judges' decisions also tie into the question of the normative relevance of judgments under UNCLOS for all other State parties.[136] Most notably, it can be asked to what extent any interpretation is to be regarded as authoritative?[137] This authoritative nature of judgments has two key possible outlets.[138] First, the authoritative position of a judgment may be borne out in future cases. While there is no binding system of precedent, predictability and stability are valued in the public order of the oceans, just as they are in other areas of international law. As such, earlier interpretations may be subsequently followed, or used as a basis for further reasoning, and judges have observed the need for *jurisprudence constante*.[139] Judge Wolfrum has reflected on the role of international tribunals developing in particular the law relating to maritime delimitation in what he terms as an '*acquis judiciaire*'. In this regard, he has observed:

> It is the feature of this law not to be static but to be open to progressive development by the international courts and tribunals concerned. It is the responsibility of these international courts and tribunals not only to decide delimitation cases while remaining within the framework of such *acquis judiciaire* but also to provide for the progressive development of the latter. They are called upon in further developing this *acquis judiciaire* to take into account new scientific findings.[140]

As discussed further in Chapter 6, the maritime delimitation case law has significantly developed understandings of Articles 74 and 83 of UNCLOS, which address the delimitation

[132] Ulfstein has observed that there is no evidence that judges work as if diplomats, but there is evidence to show that they 'are acutely aware of the political context in which they operate': Geir Ulfstein, 'International Courts and Judges: Independence, Interaction, and Legitimacy' (2014) 46 NYU J Intl L & Pol 849, 853.

[133] *South China Sea*, Award (n 12) para 553.

[134] ibid paras 512–20.

[135] Notably, Japan and the United States would potentially use more maritime space than China if their claimed maritime zones over features such as Okinotorishima and Johnston Atoll were reassessed on the basis that these islands are rocks for the purposes of UNCLOS (n 1) art 121(3). See Natalie Klein, 'Agora Contribution, Rocks and Islands after the South China Sea Arbitration' (2016) 34 Aust YBIL 21, 27–29.

[136] Higgins observed that 'a common discussion [at the ICJ] is: Are we merely deciding the case in front of us, or is there a pedagogical function for the Court to perform?'. Remarks by Rosalyn Higgins, 'Decision-making in International Courts and Tribunals: A Conversation with Leading Judges and Arbitrators' (2011) 105 ASIL Proc 217.

[137] Hernández (n 51) 174.

[138] Zarbiyev has noted that legal academics also serve to legitimate judicial activism: Fuad Zarbiyev, 'Judicial Activism in International Law: A Conceptual Framework for Analysis' (2012) 3 JIDS 247, 267–71.

[139] See eg *Bay of Bengal Delimitation* (n 111) para 238. India also referred to *jurisprudence constante* in its arguments in *Enrica Lexie (Italy v India)* (Award of 21 May 2020) PCA Case No 2015-28, para 285.

[140] *Bay of Bengal Delimitation* (n 111) 137 (Declaration of Judge Wolfrum).

of overlapping exclusive economic zones (EEZs) and continental shelves between States with opposite or adjacent coasts.

The second outlet for assessing the authoritative nature of judgments is in the reception of the judgment beyond the parties to the dispute and its influence on State practice. For the parties, the decision is final and binding.[141] Other State parties to UNCLOS may take account (or not) of a judgment interpreting a provision in the Convention in their internal decision-making and policies or in interactions with other States. Even States that are not parties to UNCLOS may have regard to a judgment to the extent the provisions interpreted are considered to reflect customary international law, or for the purpose of better understanding obligations in the Convention should they become parties to UNCLOS.

F. Advisory Opinions

In some instances, judges may not be deciding on specific claims presented by parties in contentious proceedings but asked to offer legal answers to questions that will facilitate understanding and potentially clarify positions of interest to States (and other stakeholders). Strictly, advisory opinions are not to settle disputes, but their purpose is to furnish legal advice to those requesting the opinion.[142] Those opinions are not legally binding, although the Special Chamber in *Mauritius/Maldives* found an ICJ advisory opinion could have legal effect.[143] Similar to the discussion in the preceding section, an advisory opinion may still contribute to broader dispute resolution where the legal opinion is relevant as one dimension among many in efforts to resolve differences between States.

Under UNCLOS, the Seabed Disputes Chamber shall issue advisory opinions at the request of the International Seabed Authority's Assembly when the request is sponsored by at least one quarter of the Authority's members and the request relates to a proposal before the Assembly.[144] The Council of the Authority may also request advisory opinions from the Seabed Disputes Chamber.[145] The requests are to relate to 'legal questions arising within the scope of [the Assembly or the Council's] activities'.[146] To date, only one such request has been presented to the Seabed Disputes Chamber, which was issued in 2011 and related to the responsibilities and obligations of States that sponsor entities conducting activities in the Area.

In the *Seabed Advisory Opinion*, the Chamber described itself as having the 'exclusive function of interpreting Part XI of the Convention and the relevant annexes and regulations that are the legal basis for the organization and management of activities in the Area'.[147] Further, it was tasked as acting as 'an independent and impartial body' within the organisational structure for the Authority.[148] Although the Seabed Chamber affirmed its 'exclusive function', there was also appreciation within the Chamber of its broader role in issuing an

[141] UNCLOS (n 1) art 296(1).

[142] See *Legality of the Threat or Use of Nuclear Weapons* (Advisory Opinion) [1996] ICJ Rep 226, para 15.

[143] *Dispute Concerning Delimitation of the Maritime Boundary between Mauritius and Maldives in the Indian Ocean (Mauritius/Maldives)* (Merits) ITLOS Case No 28, para 205. See further discussion in ch 4(II).

[144] UNCLOS (n 1) art 159(10).

[145] ibid art 191.

[146] ibid.

[147] *Seabed Advisory Opinion* (n 78) para 25.

[148] ibid para 26.

advisory opinion. To this end, the Chamber noted that it was 'mindful of the fact that by answering the questions it will assist the Council in the performance of its activities and contribute to the implementation of the Convention's regime'.[149] The Chamber further endorsed the view of the Authority's Secretary-General about the Chamber's contribution to the good governance of the Area.[150]

To issue an advisory opinion, Article 191 of UNCLOS sets out three criteria to establish jurisdiction, namely, that the request is from either the Council or the Assembly and the request is adopted consistently with that organ's rules of procedure; the request concerns legal questions; and, the legal questions have arisen within the scope of the activities of the requesting organ.[151] In the *Seabed Advisory Opinion*, the Seabed Chamber determined that the questions posed concerned the interpretation of Convention provisions and raised questions of general international law so that a response was susceptible to a reply based on law.[152] Further, after setting out the powers and function of the Council, the Chamber decided the questions posed were within the Council's scope of activities as they related to the Council's power to approve plans of work. The Seabed Chamber did not resolve an issue raised before it as to whether a discretion existed to refuse to provide an advisory opinion in light of Article 191's provision that the Chamber 'shall give' advisory opinions, which is contrasted to Article 65(1) of the ICJ Statute, which notes that Court 'may give' advisory opinions.[153] It would seem arguable that the difference in language should hold relevance, especially when the language of Article 159(10) of UNCLOS is predicated on an assumption that an opinion for the Chamber will be forthcoming for the Assembly to be able to proceed with its work.

While the jurisdiction and admissibility dimensions of the Seabed Disputes Chamber are relatively straightforward, more controversial has been the question as to whether ITLOS, sitting as a full tribunal, may also provide advisory opinions when requested. This power is not set out expressly in Article 21 of the ITLOS Statute, although there is a general reference to its jurisdiction over 'all matters specifically provided for in any other agreement which confers jurisdiction on the Tribunal'. By contrast, the ITLOS Rules do explicitly anticipate ITLOS performing this function in certain situations. Article 138 of the ITLOS Rules provides in relevant part:

> 1. The Tribunal may give an advisory opinion on a legal question if an international agreement related to the purposes of the Convention specifically provides for the submission to the Tribunal of a request for such an opinion.
> 2. A request for an advisory opinion shall be transmitted to the Tribunal by whatever body is authorized by or in accordance with the agreement to make the request to the Tribunal.

[149] ibid para 30.
[150] ibid para 29.
[151] ibid paras 32–35.
[152] ibid para 39.
[153] ibid paras 47–49. It should also be noted that art 138 of the ITLOS Rules (n 63) also considers that ITLOS 'may give' an advisory opinion. This provision in the Rules would presumably not override the express terms of art 191 of the Convention.

The scope of these powers came under scrutiny in the *SRFC Advisory Opinion* when the Sub-Regional Fisheries Commission (SRFC) requested an advisory opinion under Article 33 of the Convention on the Determination of the Minimal Conditions for Access (MCA Convention).[154]

Some State parties challenged the jurisdiction of ITLOS on the basis that there were no express or implied powers set out in the Convention granting the full Tribunal authority to issue an advisory opinion, and that ITLOS should not grant itself such a power.[155] Those challenging the Tribunal's jurisdiction considered that the reference to 'all matters' in Article 21 of the ITLOS Statute should not be read so as to arrogate power to ITLOS that was inconsistent with the grant of jurisdiction set out in Article 288 of UNCLOS.[156] Contrary arguments included the position that the purpose of Article 21 of the ITLOS Statute was partly 'to shape the Tribunal as a living institution'.[157]

The Tribunal did not consider that Article 21 of the ITLOS Statute was subordinate to Article 288 of UNCLOS, as the ITLOS Statute is an integral part of the Convention.[158] Rather, it accepted the view that 'all matters' should be understood more broadly than the words 'disputes' and 'applications', which are also referenced in Article 21 of the ITLOS Statute,[159] and that what counts as the 'matter' will be whatever is specifically provided in the other international agreement.[160] As such, Article 21 of the ITLOS Statute in its own right does not provide for advisory jurisdiction.[161] Article 138 of the ITLOS Rules provided the criteria to be met for the issuance of an advisory opinion and was not to be relied upon as a head of jurisdiction.[162]

A goal for the SRFC in seeking an advisory opinion was for 'enlightenment' on the course of action it should take in relation to illegal, unregulated and unreported (IUU) fishing.[163] The Tribunal thus perceived its role in giving the advisory opinion as assisting the SRFC

[154] Convention on the Determination of the Minimal Conditions for Access and Exploitation of Marine Resources within the Maritime Areas under Jurisdiction of the Member States of the Sub-Regional Fisheries Commission (adopted 8 June 2012, entered into force 16 September 2012).

[155] *SRFC Advisory Opinion* (n 78) paras 40–41. Tanaka has observed that ten of the twenty-two states submitting written statements opposed jurisdiction. See Yoshifumi Tanaka, 'Reflections on the Advisory Jurisdiction of ITLOS as a Full Court: The ITLOS Advisory Opinion of 2015' (2015) 14 LPICT 318, 319.

[156] *SRFC Advisory Opinion* (n 78) para 46. For further discussion on these objections see Tom Ruys and Anemoon Soete, '"Creeping" Advisory Jurisdiction of International Courts and Tribunals? The Case of the International Tribunal for the Law of the Sea' (2016) 29 LJIL 155, 159–60.

[157] *SRFC Advisory Opinion* (n 78), para 49. This vision was shared by Judge Lucky in relation to UNCLOS more generally. He stated: 'The 1982 Convention and the Statute of the Tribunal are "living instruments". This means that they "grow" and adapt to changing circumstances ... The law of the sea is not static. It is dynamic and, therefore, through interpretation and construction of the relevant articles a court or tribunal can adhere and give positive effect to this dynamism.' *SRFC Advisory Opinion* (n 78) para 18 (Separate Opinion of Judge Lucky).

[158] *SRFC Advisory Opinion* (n 78) para 52. Though some commentators have noted that the two provisions should still be read consistently, and the Tribunal's view of art 21 of its Statute was not consistent with art 288 of the Convention. See eg Michael A Becker, 'Request for an Advisory Opinion Submitted by the Sub-Regional Fisheries Commission (SRFC)' (2015) 109 AJIL 851, 855.

[159] The Tribunal's approach to interpretation was criticised for its inconsistency with the rules of treaty interpretation, particularly the failure to consider context and the *travaux préparatoires*. See *SRFC Advisory Opinion* (n 78) 73 [3] (Declaration of Judge Cot). For more detailed discussion on this point see Massimo Lando, 'The Advisory Jurisdiction of the International Tribunal for the Law of the Sea: Comments on the Request for an Advisory Opinion Submitted by the Sub-Regional Fisheries Commission' (2016) 29 LJIL 441, 445–54.

[160] *SRFC Advisory Opinion* (n 78) para 58.

[161] But see ibid paras 2, 13 (Declaration of Judge Cot). See also Jianjun Gao, 'The ITLOS Advisory Opinion for the SRFC' (2015) 14 Chinese JIL 735, 741–42.

[162] *SRFC Advisory Opinion* (n 78) para 59. See further Tanaka (n 155) 323–24 (noting the views of Australia, Ireland, and the United Kingdom on this point).

[163] *SRFC Advisory Opinion* (n 78) para 76.

'in the performance of its activities and contribut[ing] to the implementation' of the MCA Convention.[164] While the reasoning of ITLOS to establish jurisdiction has garnered criticism,[165] it can at least be noted that the thrust of its approach (and that of the Seabed Chamber) is consistent with judicial functions that seek to contribute to the future conduct of varied stakeholders in ocean governance.

* * *

This section has demonstrated the vast array of tasks that judges perform during dispute settlement under UNCLOS. Each task may be closely inter-related, such as when a procedural decision or instance of fact-finding aligns with treaty interpretation or application. What is important to note is that each of these tasks is critical in resolving disputes, even if the importance of the task will vary depending on the circumstances or context of any case. Having considered who the judges are and what they do, we next consider what the purpose of the judge's role is in the resolution of disputes under UNCLOS.

IV. What Should Be the Role of the Judge?

As noted at the outset of this chapter, the role of the judge in UNCLOS dispute settlement is complex because of the range of responsibilities associated with the judicial function and because of the role that dispute settlement performs within the UNCLOS legal regime and the international legal system more broadly. In Chapter 1, we discussed how the law is interpreted and applied within the framework of UNCLOS dispute settlement and how the role of international courts may be perceived within the international legal system. The very availability of compulsory jurisdiction is a significant attribute of the UNCLOS dispute settlement regime and necessarily enhances the ability of State parties to develop and enforce the rules through reference to judicial decision-makers. Even though prospects for enforcement are improved in this regard, challenges remain in terms of limitations in the dispute settlement process and in ensuring compliance.

An assessment of the role of judges in UNCLOS dispute settlement must further be framed in relation to the perceived role of dispute settlement in relationship to the UNCLOS regime overall. As discussed in Chapter 1, there are two models that may be utilised. The first, which is variously described as a procedural model, Westphalian model, or voluntarist approach, stresses State sovereignty and emphasises restrictions on compulsory dispute settlement under UNCLOS. In this model, UNCLOS dispute settlement is ancillary to the political decisions of States.[166] The second model, which is an objectivist approach or substantive or regime-building model, stresses, according to Tanaka, 'the international legal order beyond individual states'.[167] In this second model, greater emphasis is accorded

[164] ibid para 77.

[165] See eg Nuwan Peiris, 'Advisory Opinion on Fisheries in the Exclusive Economic Zone from the International Tribunal for the Law of the Sea: The Birth of Regional Treaty-based Advisory Jurisdiction' (2017) 31 Ocean YB 250; Tanaka (n 155) 325–28; Ruys and Soete (n 156) 162–71.

[166] Yoshifumi Tanaka, 'Reflections on the *Philippines/China* Arbitration' (2016) 15 LPICT 305, 323.

[167] ibid.

to dispute settlement under UNCLOS as integral to the international legal order established in the Convention.[168]

Against these settings, this chapter has so far highlighted the individual traits of the judges as well as the diverse tasks and decisions they undertake in UNCLOS dispute settlement. We therefore have a picture of the multifaceted role of the judge, which requires accounting for (i) the key judicial tasks performed; (ii) the role of dispute settlement in the UNCLOS regime; and (iii) the central objectives of dispute settlement. These roles obviously do not occur in isolation so we must acknowledge the views and actions of other actors in the UNCLOS legal regime. These actors may be vast and include the States that have instituted the proceedings; other State parties; States not party to UNCLOS but ocean users; shipping companies and their employees; shipping unions; intergovernmental organisations; non-governmental organisations; and individuals undertaking diverse activities at sea (such as fishers, migrants, scientists, criminals). Each of these actors have specific interests in ocean use and its regulation. The judges' role is one of privilege among these actors because judges have decision-making authority. Therefore, in resolving disputes under UNCLOS, it is important to discern the parameters within which judges should operate.

One possible explanatory paradigm is stakeholder identification theory, which has been used in the management context for managers to determine who are the salient stakeholders in making decisions in the interests of the organisation.[169] Stakeholder theory seeks to answer the question of who and what counts for managers in their decisions.[170] In utilising this theory, we equate managers with judges, as they are the ultimate decision-makers for disputes resolved by arbitration or adjudication under UNCLOS. The decisions they make are for 'the organisation', which we can understand to be the UNCLOS regime. Judges as the managers must make decisions that are in the best interests of the organisation, that is, the UNCLOS regime. The stakeholders are then the various other actors identified above with interests in dispute settlement. In creating this analogy, we have the opportunity to articulate what factors, including different actors, could or should influence judges. How should judges prioritise these different interests? We can therefore assess the possible applicability of stakeholder theory in the context of UNCLOS dispute settlement.

A stakeholder may be broadly defined as 'any group or individual who can affect or is affected by the achievement of the organization's objectives'.[171] To achieve the organisation's objectives, managers (or, in our case, judges) must pay varying attention to different types of stakeholders.[172] Mitchell, Agle, and Wood propose that we look to the power, legitimacy,

[168] This approach aligns with the trustee/principal model discussed in ch 1. See ch 1(III).

[169] A description of this theory (and its application to the *South China Sea* Tribunal's interpretation of art 121) has been set out in Natalie Klein, 'Stakeholders in Dispute Settlement under the UN Convention on the Law of the Sea' in Marta Chantal Ribeiro, Fernando Loureiro Bastos, and Tore Henrikson (eds), *Global Challenges and the Law of the Sea* (Springer 2020) 239, 245–48. Part of that text is reproduced here with permission.

[170] A seminal work in this area is R Edward Freeman, *Strategic Management: A Stakeholder Approach* (Pitman Publishing 1984). Stakeholder identification theory and how to determine the salience of stakeholders was expounded in an influential piece in 1997 by Mitchell, Agle, and Wood. Ronald K Mitchell, Bradley R Agle, and Donna J Wood, 'Toward a Theory of Stakeholder Identification and Salience: Defining the Principle of Who and What Really Counts' (1997) 22 Academy of Management Rev 853. The 1997 piece remains the key starting point. Ronald K Mitchell, Jae Hwan Lee, and Bradley R Agle, 'Stakeholder Prioritization Work: The Role of Stakeholder Salience in Stakeholder Research' in David M Wasieleski and James Weber (eds), *Stakeholder Management* (Emerald Publishing 2017).

[171] Freeman (n 170) 46.

[172] Mitchell, Agle, and Wood (n 170) 855. This assessment involves determining stakeholder salience, which is 'the degree to which managers give priority to competing stakeholder claims': see 854.

and urgency associated with stakeholders.[173] The *power* held may be coercive ('based on physical resources of force, violence, or restraint'); utilitarian ('based on material or financial resources'); or normative ('based on symbolic resources').[174] Whatever the source of power, the upshot is that it enables the stakeholder to impose its will.[175]

Legitimacy may have different meanings depending on its context, and was given a broad-based definition by Suchman, as follows: 'a generalized perception or assumption that the actions of an entity are desirable, proper, or appropriate within some socially constructed system of norms, values, beliefs and definitions'.[176] Legitimacy has a strong place in international law,[177] and is important in consent-based treaty regimes where State actors can make rational decisions on their level of involvement in the regime.

In applying stakeholder identification theory to UNCLOS dispute settlement, a question emerges as to how we might differentiate normative power from legitimacy? Symbolic power could be ascribed to an actor adhering to the rules of international law and taking steps to uphold or enforce those rules. The key difference would seem to be the ability to impose one's will based on the assertion of legal rules. Some actors are more able to enforce international law than others. Yet the very availability of the UNCLOS dispute settlement regime for all parties to that treaty does open up the possibility of States parties having normative power if they choose to avail themselves of compulsory dispute settlement procedures entailing binding decisions and there are no barriers to doing so.

Urgency assesses the time sensitivity of claims or relationships as well as the importance of the claim or the relationship to the stakeholder.[178] It is the urgency of the claim of the stakeholder rather than the urgency of the stakeholder itself that matters.[179]

These are the factors that must be weighed by the manager in making strategic decisions for the organisation; they determine which stakeholders are salient.[180] As such, the attributes of the manager play their own role—this is where our assessment of the backgrounds of the judges becomes relevant. The attributes of judges inform or influence their decisions around salience.

In assessing stakeholders, a process may be undertaken in determining which stakeholders possess power, legitimacy, and urgency, or perhaps just two of those attributes or only one. A sliding scale applies. As such, a stakeholder exhibiting all three of power, legitimacy, and urgency means that a manager (judge) has 'a clear and immediate mandate

[173] See ibid 859–63 and 865–68.

[174] ibid 865, citing Amitai Etzioni, *Modern Organizations* (Prentice-Hall 1964) 59.

[175] Mitchell, Agle, and Wood (n 170) 865.

[176] Mark C Suchman, 'Managing Legitimacy: Strategic and Institutional Approaches' (1995) 20 Academy of Management Rev 571, 574, cited by Mitchell, Agle, and Wood (n 170) 866.

[177] Epitomised by Thomas Franck's writing in the area. See eg Thomas M Franck, *Fairness in International Law and Institutions* (OUP 1995).

[178] Mitchell, Agle, and Wood (n 170) 867. An additional dimension proposed to the urgency of a claim is the probability of the claim's occurrence. See Cathy Driscoll and Mark Starik, 'The Primordial Stakeholder: Advancing the Conceptual Consideration of Stakeholder Status for the Natural Environment' (2004) 49 J Bus Ethics 55, discussed in Mitchell, Lee, and Agle (n 170) 139, although arguably this dimension could be captured in an assessment of the importance of the claim or relationship.

[179] See Mitchell, Lee, and Agle (n 170) 140, discussing the work of Charles Eesley and Michael J Lennox, 'Firm Responses to Secondary Stakeholder Action' (2006) 27 Strategic Management J 765. Stakeholder urgency would instead be part of the power attribute.

[180] Mitchell, Agle, and Wood (n 170) 870–71.

to attend to and give priority to that stakeholder's claim'.[181] A stakeholder may gain or lose attributes over time so this fluidity must also be taken into account.

While these three categories provide a way to classify the interests of stakeholders, it must also be acknowledged that the attributes of stakeholders may vary over time, might entail subjective determinations, and may or may not be asserted in any given context.[182] Yet even with this possible nuance, the categories allow us to identify the stakeholders and their interests in a decision-making process.

Stakeholder identification theory provides a tool for articulating what should be influencing decision-making and why decision-makers should take heed. There is no consistent set of variables, but we instead have an opportunity to look broadly at the variety of actors in the international system and different forms of communications between those actors and have a means to weight those interactions and assess their salience in the judicial decision-making process. There is therefore an opportunity to account for the complexity of UNCLOS dispute settlement and to engage more transparently in what has influenced outcomes. Inherent difficulties remain of course, as it not usually evident on the face of any judgment how or why a judge has either emphasised, downplayed, or overlooked any specific dimension of a case.[183] It is perhaps in the process of assessing what decisions have been made and why they might have been made that we can then point to how decisions should be made in the future.

What potentially remains elusive is whether the judges all share the same objectives for the organisation. The identification of stakeholders' attributes only makes sense when we have a clear sense of what ends a judge is trying to achieve in making decisions on claims presented. Chapter 1 set out the broad aims: the peaceful settlement of disputes, the rule of law, and the public order (or good governance) of the oceans. Judges are no doubt motivated by these goals.[184] There needs to be a connection between who and what counts in decision-making with the outcome sought to be achieved. Venzke has suggested '[i]n order to succeed, an interpretation of a rule needs to connect to the past in a way that shapes future applications'.[185] This task is obviously easier said than done. What it means for our purposes is that in assessing the judicial development of the law of the sea, we need to consider to what extent the decisions are contributing to the overall good order of the oceans both for the present purpose of resolving the immediate dispute and for future conduct of all stakeholders in ocean governance. In some instances, the reasoning may be deductive because of the facts proven and the clarity of the rule in question. In other instances, the judicial intervention may need to be assessed taking into account the possible consequences beyond the case at hand and the coherency of the decision for the public order of the oceans.[186]

We can use a variety of benchmarks to assess how well the judges are performing their roles in this regard. We could potentially list the following: the immediate reaction of the

[181] ibid 878. As there are three types of power, arguably the more of these types of power attributes exhibited then this would also positively influence the salience of the stakeholder. See Milena M Parent and David L Deephouse, 'A Case Study of Stakeholder Identification and Prioritization by Managers' (2007) 75 J Bus Ethics 1.

[182] Mitchell, Agle, and Wood (n 170) 868.

[183] Context will remain important, including the characteristics of the judges making the decisions. See Mitchell, Lee, and Agle (n 170) 141.

[184] See ch 1(III).

[185] Ingo Venzke, 'The Role of International Courts as Interpreters and Developers of the Law: Working Out the Jurisgenerative Practice of Interpretation' (2011) 34 Loy LA Intl & Comp LJ 99, 121.

[186] Reflecting MacCormick's (n 96) theory on legal interpretation.

parties to the decision; the shorter, medium, and longer term reactions of the parties to the decision; the responses of other relevant States in the immediate aftermath of the decision, taking into account the relative importance of those States; commentators' assessments of the judgment; whether the judges concerned are re-elected or appointed to another court or tribunal again; and, over time, subsequent judicial decision-making or other international law-making activities (such as within the International Law Commission or the work of the International Law Association committees) that reflect the decisions of the judges.

State parties to UNCLOS may find their own ways to influence or respond to the roles that judges play, even if these means are not always readily available. Formal steps might include a State nominating its own judge, amending the constitutive instrument, or withdrawing from the Convention. Less formal ways could also be sought.[187] These options might include 'quasi law-making' (such as through informal agreements); or voicing critique of methods of interpretation or findings of courts.[188] These communications and activities may ultimately feed back into the assessment of stakeholder's interests in future judicial decision-making.

V. Concluding Remarks

In discussing the role of judges, we recall from Chapter 1 that their overarching role is performed in light of the main goals of UNCLOS dispute settlement: pacific settlement of disputes, the rule of law, and public order of the oceans. In any one case, judges may believe they have a mission to construct a global legal order as part of their tasks.[189] Alternatively, the mission may be perceived as something significantly more modest. As Justice Feliciano suggested, 'there are other "workers in the vineyard"',[190] and it may be incumbent on judges to remember as much given that the reverberations of any judicial decision may extend further than initially expected. Reisman has well described the 'proper judicial role' as:

> restricted like any other, with limitations that are accepted and honored by the role player. Within this role, rules are properly seen as communications carrying relevant and authoritative policy information that must be shaped in the idiosyncratic texture of each controversy, to provide a decision that best approximates the minimum order and larger policy objectives of the community.[191]

We have suggested that the judicial decisions under UNCLOS not only contribute to the good order of the oceans in resolving the immediate dispute but also contribute to the future conduct of a larger set of stakeholders. These elements are taken into account in our analyses of the different judgments in the chapters that follow.

The analyses of judicial interpretation and application under UNCLOS in this work are necessarily limited to what information is publicly available about any one case. As such,

[187] Ulfstein (n 132) 855–56.
[188] ibid.
[189] See also Rose, 'Arbitration Jurisdiction' (n 128) 61.
[190] Feliciano (n 54) 68.
[191] W Michael Reisman, 'Judge Shigeru Oda: Reflections on the Formation of a Judge' in Misuke Ando, Edward McWhinney, and Rüdiger Wolfrum (eds), *Liber Amicorum Judge Shigeru Oda* (Kluwer Law 2002) 65.

in this chapter, we have acknowledged the complex matrix of judicial decision-making that occurs in UNCLOS dispute settlement. We have sought to recognise, as Shaffer and Pollock have observed, that '[j]udges are viewed as situated decision makers who respond to disputes in light of particular social, political, and historical contexts which shape their views of the facts of a particular case'.[192] These contexts matter but the degree of influence is speculative and the primary focus must necessarily remain on the judgments themselves.

Nonetheless, we have observed some of the shared traits that may be found among ITLOS judges and judges appointed to Annex VII arbitrations. Consistent with other international courts, there is an imbalance towards older, male judges who are educated in Western Europe or the United States. While the study of ITLOS judges was limited in this chapter to the current and immediate past composition of ITLOS, there is no expectation that this general conclusion would vary in any study that included all judges who had ever been appointed to ITLOS. Diversity has only slightly improved in recent years. Further studies are needed to consider if there is relevance in ITLOS's composition with its weighting in favour of former government legal advisers. To date, critical studies on international courts have not usually examined the law of the sea bodies,[193] or, if they do, tend to consider only ITLOS and not the other fora contemplated under Article 287 of the Convention.[194]

We have explained that judges undertake a number of tasks as part of their judicial function: settling procedure, fact-finding, treaty interpretation, deciding claims, and influencing broader dispute resolution. In setting out some of the varied tasks performed by judges, we have sought to underline further that judicial decision-makers have a complex role. To capture the totality of the decision-making process of the judge, we have suggested that stakeholder identification theory might be a useful tool to account for the claims and relationships of different actors in assessing what decisions judges must take to promote the interests of the organisation. With more transparency and accountability in appreciating the totality of the role of judges within the UNCLOS dispute settlement regime, there is a greater chance of ensuring that decisions promote the good order of the oceans in resolving the present dispute as well as establishing rules of future conduct for all stakeholders. Judges may be seen as acquitting their responsibilities well when the overall 'organisation' flourishes. The extent that the UNCLOS dispute settlement regime is prospering and contributing to the overall good order of the oceans is assessed in the remaining chapters.

[192] Gregory C Shaffer and Mark A Pollock, 'Hard vs Soft Law: Alternatives, Complements and Antagonists in International Governance' (2010) 94 Minn L Rev 706, 749.

[193] See eg Theresa Squatrito, Oran R Young, Andreas Follesdal, and Geir Ulfstein (eds), *The Performance of International Courts and Tribunals* (CUP 2018); Ignacio de la Rasilla and Jorge Viñuales (eds), *Experiments in International Adjudication* (CUP 2018); Daniel Peat, *Comparative Reasoning in International Courts and Tribunals* (CUP 2019); Yuval Shany, *Assessing the Effectiveness of International Courts* (OUP 2014). Some of the general textbooks on international dispute settlement do include chapters on the law of the sea. See eg J G Merrills, *International Dispute Settlement* (6th edn, CUP 2017); Yoshifumi Tanaka, *The Peaceful Settlement of International Disputes* (CUP 2018).

[194] For example, the work of the ILA Study Group on the Content and Evolution of the Rules of Interpretation looks only to ITLOS in its reports on different courts and tribunals. See Valérie Boré Eveno, 'ITLOS Report' (Working Document, ILA Study Group on the Content and Evolution of the Rules of Interpretation, April 2017) www.ila-hq.org/index.php/study-groups?study-groupsID=75. See also Nienke Grossman, Harlan Grant Cohen, Andreas Follesdal, and Geir Ulfstein (eds), *Legitimacy and International Courts* (CUP 2018); Gary Born, 'A New Generation of International Adjudication' (2012) 61 Duke LJ 775; Ruth Mackenzie, Cesare PR Romano, Yuval Shany, and Philippe Sands (eds), *The Manual on International Courts and Tribunals* (2nd edn, OUP 2010).

3

Preliminary, Incidental, and Other Proceedings

I. Introduction

In accordance with Article 286 of the United Nations Convention on the Law of the Sea (UNCLOS or Convention), a State party to UNCLOS can submit a dispute to a court or tribunal constituted under the Convention when that dispute concerns the interpretation or application of UNCLOS, the subject matter of the dispute does not fall within any exception or limitation set out in Article 297 or Article 298, and 'where no settlement has been reached by recourse to section 1'.[1] There are a number of criteria packed into this provision that reflect the jurisdictional limits of tribunals resolving disputes under UNCLOS. These criteria include that there must be a dispute to resolve, that the dispute must concern the interpretation or application of the Convention, and that the dispute must exist at the time of the filing of the application instituting proceedings.[2] For a Part XV tribunal to have personal jurisdiction, *ratione personae*, in contentious proceedings, the States, or other entities,[3] in the case must be parties to UNCLOS when those proceedings are instituted.[4] Subject matter jurisdiction, *ratione materiae*, is discussed in detail in Chapter 4. This chapter is concerned with other preliminary objections that raise questions of jurisdiction and admissibility, as well as dealing with incidental and other discrete proceedings under UNCLOS.

Preliminary objections were described by the Permanent Court of International Justice (PCIJ) in the *Panevezys-Saldutiskis Railway* case as 'any objection of which the effect will be, if the objection is upheld, to interrupt further proceedings in the case, and which it will therefore be appropriate for the Court to deal with before enquiring into the merits'.[5] Preliminary objections may encompass any matter that has to be clarified in the case prior to any further proceedings taking place.[6] Questions of jurisdiction that emerge in the context of UNCLOS

[1] United Nations Convention on the Law of the Sea (adopted 10 December 1982, entered into force 16 November 1994) 1833 UNTS 397, art 286 (UNCLOS).

[2] *M/V Louisa (Saint Vincent and the Grenadines v Spain)* (Judgment) ITLOS Reports 2013, 4, para 151 (*Louisa*, Judgment); *South China Sea Arbitration (Philippines v China)* (Award on Jurisdiction and Admissibility of 29 October 2015) PCA Case No 2013-19, paras 131, 148 (*South China Sea*, Jurisdiction and Admissibility).

[3] Under UNCLOS (n 1) certain international organisations—most particularly the European Union—may participate in the Convention, consistent with UNCLOS annex IX art 4. Under art 305, UNCLOS is also open to self-governing associated States meeting the criteria set out therein as well as prescribed territories enjoying full internal self-government that have the necessary competence. In this respect, it may be noted that Palestine is party to UNCLOS, even though not universally recognised as a State. The Cook Islands and Niue are also parties to UNCLOS pursuant to art 305.

[4] Tribunals routinely refer to the status of the parties as parties to UNCLOS (n 1) at the beginning of discussions on jurisdiction, including when the Convention entered into force as between them. This approach is consistent with *pacta tertiis* and with the requirement that States consent to the exercise of jurisdiction by international courts or tribunals.

[5] *Panevezys-Saldutiskis Railway* (*Estonia v Lithuania*) (Judgment) PCIJ Rep Series A/B No 76, 16.

[6] Shabtai Rosenne, 'International Courts and Tribunals, Jurisdiction and Admissibility of Inter-State Applications' in Anne Peters (ed), *Max Planck Encyclopaedia of Public International Law* (OUP 2006) para 5 (Rosenne, 'Inter-State Applications').

cases, beyond subject matter jurisdiction, concern the existence of a dispute, the requirement under Article 283 of UNCLOS to exchange views prior to resorting to compulsory arbitration or adjudication, and the availability of alternative means of dispute settlement to be used in lieu of arbitration or adjudication under UNCLOS pursuant to Articles 281 and 282. The challenges to admissibility include lack of standing, failure to exhaust local remedies, and indispensable third parties. Other grounds of admissibility that have been argued include estoppel, acquiescence, the application having no object (mootness), and clean hands. The possible role of the Commission on the Limits of the Continental Shelf (CLCS) is also considered in this context as it has implications for the resolution of maritime boundary delimitation disputes and is addressed further in Chapter 6.

Under UNCLOS, any dispute as to the jurisdiction of a tribunal or the admissibility of a dispute is to be resolved by a decision of that tribunal.[7] The application of this *compétence de la compétence* principle is 'essential to prevent the frustration' of any agreement establishing jurisdiction over a particular dispute.[8] Jurisdiction will be ascertained *proprio motu* by a tribunal even if a party has not raised a challenge.[9] While preliminary objections will often be addressed at their own stage of proceedings, those that do not 'possess an exclusively preliminary character' will be addressed together with the merits of the dispute.[10]

The most common incidental proceedings arising in UNCLOS dispute settlement proceedings beyond challenges to jurisdiction and admissibility are requests for provisional measures under Article 295, seeking interim relief pending the final judgment in the case. The prompt release of vessels under Article 292 is another distinct proceeding that is anticipated under Part XV of UNCLOS. Aspects of the latter proceeding are discussed in more detail in Chapter 8 with regard to the question of release and determination of the reasonableness of the bond. Incidental proceedings may also extend to counter-claims, other questions pertinent to the control of the procedure before the tribunal, and intervention. Derivative jurisdiction for controversies concerning the interpretation or manner of implementation of an award is anticipated in UNCLOS dispute settlement procedures but has not yet arisen in disputes concerned with the Convention.[11] This chapter only addresses the incidental and prompt release proceedings that have arisen to date as part of the Part XV procedures.[12]

Whenever a tribunal constituted under UNCLOS is deciding on preliminary objections, there is already a high level of engagement in the resolution of the dispute that has arisen between the parties and the mere fact of the litigation commencing may have its own impetus in dispute settlement efforts beyond the third-party mechanism in play.[13] As such,

[7] UNCLOS (n 1) art 288(4).

[8] Rosenne, 'Inter-State Applications' (n 6) para 23.

[9] See eg *Delimitation of the Maritime Boundary between Ghana and Côte d'Ivoire in the Atlantic Ocean (Ghana/Côte d'Ivoire)* (Judgment of 23 September 2017) ITLOS Case No 23 (*Ghana/Côte d'Ivoire*, Judgment) para 545; *Grand Prince (Belize v France)* (Prompt Release, Judgment) ITLOS Reports 2001 (*Grand Prince*) 17, para 79.

[10] See eg *South China Sea*, Jurisdiction and Admissibility (n 2) para 380; *Guyana v Suriname* (Award of the Arbitral Tribunal of 17 September 2007) PCA Case No 2004-04, para 2 (*Guyana v Suriname*) para 2; *Chagos Marine Protected Area Arbitration (Mauritius v United Kingdom)* (Award of 18 March 2015) PCA Case No 2011-03(*Chagos MPA*) paras 28–31.

[11] UNCLOS (n 1) Annex VI, art 33(3); ibid Annex VII, art 12. Power is accorded to the ICJ to interpret a judgment under art 60 or to revise it if needed in line with article 61 of the Court's Statute: Statute of the International Court of Justice, art 61.

[12] The power to order reparations may be seen as part of derivative jurisdiction. See Rosenne, 'Inter-State Applications' (n 6) para 20.

[13] As evident in *Southern Bluefin Tuna (New Zealand v Japan; Australia v Japan)* (Jurisdiction and Admissibility) (2000) 23 RIAA 1 (*Southern Bluefin Tuna*, Jurisdiction and Admissibility). See ch 2(III)(E).

the decisions on preliminary objections fit within our broader assessment of how UNCLOS dispute settlement has impact in peacefully resolving the current dispute and enlightening the parameters for dispute settlement in the future. Moreover, States must have a keen understanding of the relevant hurdles in UNCLOS dispute settlement if they are to secure a binding decision on the merits from an UNCLOS tribunal. Yet the possible barriers to compulsory jurisdiction entailing a binding decision serve as a reminder that what matters is the peaceful resolution of disputes and maintaining good governance of the oceans. It is perhaps this result that might matter more than the means by which it is achieved (that is, the outcome may still be reached even if a decision on the merits from a tribunal is not ultimately delivered). Nonetheless, as discussed in Chapter 1, another school of thought is that compulsory dispute settlement under UNCLOS is essential for the attainment of these goals and, in this paradigm, prioritising the exercise of jurisdiction is a dominant consideration in the reasoning. At the moment, judges preferring interpretations that facilitate the exercise of jurisdiction appears to be the prevailing approach. This approach may well foster the peaceful resolution of disputes, public order of the oceans, and the rule of law. Yet given the competing interests of stakeholders, attention is still needed regarding Justice Feliciano's view, noted in the previous chapter, that judges are just one of many 'workers in the vineyard'.[14] The ineluctable challenge is getting the balance right. These varied dimensions are addressed in discussing preliminary objections as well as incidental and other proceedings in this chapter.

II. Establishing Jurisdiction under UNCLOS

Jurisdiction will be derived from the constitutive instrument that manifests the consent of the parties to the resolution of specific disputes by particular third-party mechanisms. Where proceedings are instituted under UNCLOS, jurisdiction will be assessed by reference to Article 288(1) of the Convention or to any separate agreement that establishes the consent of the parties in accordance with Article 288(2). It is further possible that the conduct of the parties will indicate their consent to the resolution of aspects of a dispute.[15]

As outlined in Chapter 1, the choice of forum for resolving disputes under UNCLOS is set out in Article 287, which allows for States to declare their preference as between the International Tribunal for the Law of the Sea (ITLOS), the International Court of Justice (ICJ), arbitration under Annex VII or special arbitration under Annex VIII.[16] Where parties to UNCLOS have not declared their preferred forum, or parties have selected different fora, they will be deemed to have accepted arbitration under Annex VII.[17] States will on occasions commence arbitration and then agree to refer their case to ITLOS, at which point the agreement to refer to ITLOS usually becomes the basis of ITLOS jurisdiction by virtue of Article 287(4).[18] Transferring proceedings to ITLOS by special agreement does

[14] Florentino P Feliciano, 'Qualities of a Good Judge' (1994) 3 The Lawyers Rev 68, 68.

[15] See *Ghana/Côte d'Ivoire*, Judgment (n 9) para 552 (referring to jurisprudence of the ICJ that has allowed for the broadening of the Court's jurisdiction by reference to the conduct of the parties).

[16] UNCLOS (n 1) art 287(1).

[17] ibid art 287(5).

[18] See eg *Delimitation of the Maritime Boundary in the Bay of Bengal (Bangladesh/Myanmar)* (Judgment) ITLOS Reports 2012, 4 (*Bay of Bengal Delimitation*). This process was assessed by Judge Treves in his Declaration. See *Bay of Bengal Delimitation* (Declaration of Judge Treves) para 4. See also *M/V Saiga (No 2) (Saint Vincent and the Grenadines v Guinea)* (Judgment) ITLOS Reports 1999, 10, paras 40–43 (*Saiga No 2*, Judgment).

not preclude the possibility of one of the parties raising objections to admissibility.[19] Where a State has narrowly defined its acceptance of jurisdiction, as was the case in relation to St Vincent and the Grenadines in *Louisa*,[20] the designated tribunal may only exercise jurisdiction as agreed in those declarations.[21] The latter approach is consistent with Article 287(4) of UNCLOS. If the dispute falls outside the specific reference accepting jurisdiction of one of the courts or tribunals under Article 287, jurisdiction will still reside in an arbitral tribunal constituted under Annex VII, as that would be consistent with the default procedure under Article 287(3).

This section examines various threshold jurisdictional issues, some of which are unique to UNCLOS dispute settlement and some which are not. The first, existence of a dispute, is a question that has been raised before different international courts and tribunals and relates to whether there is a difference of views between the States even before considering if there is a difference of views relating to the interpretation or application of UNCLOS. It is not typically an argument that has found favour with judges and perhaps the utility in the argument rests more in establishing the factual context of the case than in providing a strong basis for challenging a tribunal's jurisdiction. Secondly, this section considers the alternative means of dispute settlement that are recognised as prevailing over compulsory arbitration or adjudication under UNCLOS. These alternatives are set out in Articles 281 and 282 of UNCLOS. While the wording of each provision has prompted close judicial scrutiny, the examination sits within a broader debate about the availability of compulsory arbitration or adjudication under UNCLOS as opposed to other methods of dispute settlement. To what extent is there an imperative to utilise UNCLOS compulsory procedures as opposed to other peaceful means of dispute settlement? In answering these questions, judicial decision-makers are very much imposing their views on the preferred means to achieve dispute settlement goals. Thirdly, and related to these broad questions, is the threshold requirement of exchanging views in the terms required under Article 283 of UNCLOS. This obligation also sits within a debate as to how much emphasis must be accorded to alternative means of dispute settlement instead of compulsory arbitration or adjudication. Careful decisions are needed in balancing an applicant State's assessment of how well and by what means dispute resolution is progressing with a respondent State's willingness to pursue meaningful efforts to resolve the dispute outside compulsory adjudication or arbitration.

A. Existence of a Dispute

For a contentious case to be pursued under Part XV of UNCLOS, the applicant State must establish that a dispute concerning the interpretation or application of the Convention

[19] *M/V Virginia G (Panama/Guinea-Bissau)* (Judgment) ITLOS Reports 2014, 4, para 98 (*Virginia G*, Judgment). See also *Saiga No 2*, Judgment (n 18) para 51.

[20] *Louisa*, Judgment (n 2) para 81: 'in cases where States Parties have made declarations of differing scope under article 287 of the Convention, its jurisdiction exists only to the extent to which the substance of the declarations of the two parties to a dispute coincides'. See also para 82 (referring to the narrower declaration prevailing consistent with the intention of the State making the declaration).

[21] This position is consistent with the jurisprudence of the ICJ, which has held that the Court only has jurisdiction as defined by the narrower of two declarations accepting jurisdiction. See *Certain Norwegian Loans (France v Norway)* (Preliminary Objections) [1957] ICJ Rep 9, 23.

exists between the parties.[22] There have been occasions where a respondent State has alleged that there is no dispute between the parties, either because the dispute is one of science (as Japan alleged in *Southern Bluefin Tuna*),[23] or because a private lawyer addressing the detention of a vessel was not duly authorised by a State to act (as Italy argued against Panama in relation to the detention of the M/V Norstar).[24] In *Mauritius/Maldives*, the Special Chamber focused on determining whether the dispute existed at the time the case was instituted.[25]

In addressing the existence of a dispute, ITLOS has consistently relied on authority from the ICJ.[26] In *Southern Bluefin Tuna*, for example, the Tribunal noted: '[A] dispute is a "disagreement on a point of law or fact, a conflict of legal views or of interests" … and "[i]t must be shown that the claim of one party is positively opposed by the other".'[27]

Decisions of the ICJ also informed a tribunal's position in holding that whether a dispute exists may be inferred from a failure of a State to respond to claims,[28] and that a disagreement may be established by inference irrespective of expressed views of the parties.[29] While the threshold for establishing the existence of a dispute is thus low, the mere assertion of a dispute is not sufficient.[30] The task of the tribunal is to 'isolate the real issue in the case and to identify the object of the claim'.[31] Within the context of dispute settlement proceedings

[22] 'It is common ground that the existence of a dispute is the primary condition for a court to exercise its judicial functions.' *M/V Norstar (Panama v Italy)* (Preliminary Objections Judgment of 4 November 2016) ITLOS Case No 25 (*Norstar*, Preliminary Objections) (Joint Separate Opinions of Judges Wolfrum and Attard) para 12.

[23] *Southern Bluefin Tuna (New Zealand v Japan; Australia v Japan)* (Provisional Measures, Order of 27 August 1999) ITLOS Reports 1999, 280, para 42 (*Southern Bluefin Tuna*, Provisional Measures); *Southern Bluefin Tuna*, Jurisdiction and Admissibility (n 13) para 41(c).

[24] *Norstar*, Preliminary Objections (n 22) paras 97, 99–102.

[25] Determining that the dispute did so exist at the time the application was filed. See *Delimitation of the Maritime Boundary between Mauritius and Maldives in the Indian Ocean (Mauritius/Maldives)* (Preliminary Objections Judgment of 28 January 2021) ITLOS Case No 28, para 332 (*Mauritius/Maldives*, Preliminary Objections).

[26] ibid paras 322–24. For discussion of ICJ jurisprudence on this point see Juliette McIntyre, 'Put on Notice: The Role of the Dispute Requirement in Assessing Jurisdiction and Admissibility before the International Court' (2018) 19 Melb J Intl L 546.

[27] *Southern Bluefin Tuna*, Provisional Measures (n 23) para 44, citing *Mavrommatis Palestine Concessions (Greece v United Kingdom)* (Jurisdiction) PCIJ Rep Series A No 2, 11, and *South West Africa (Liberia v South Africa; Ethiopia v South Africa)* (Preliminary Objections) [1962] ICJ Rep 319, 328.

[28] *Norstar*, Preliminary Objections (n 22) para 99, citing *Application of the International Convention on the Elimination of All Forms of Racial Discrimination* (*Georgia v Russia*) (Preliminary Objections) [2011] ICJ Rep 70, para 30 and the Marshall Islands Cases: *Obligations concerning Negotiations relating to Cessation of the Nuclear Arms Race and to Nuclear Disarmament* (*Marshall Islands v India*) (Preliminary Objections) [2016] ICJ Rep 255, para 37; *Obligations concerning Negotiations relating to Cessation of the Nuclear Arms Race and to Nuclear Disarmament* (*Marshall Islands v Pakistan*) (Preliminary Objections) [2016] ICJ Rep 552, para 37; *Obligations concerning Negotiations relating to Cessation of the Nuclear Arms Race and to Nuclear Disarmament* (*Marshall Islands v United Kingdom*) (Preliminary Objections) [2016] ICJ Rep 833, para 40 (collectively referred to as the *Marshall Islands* cases).

[29] *Norstar*, Preliminary Objections (n 22) para 100, citing *Land and Maritime Boundary between Cameroon and Nigeria (Cameroon v Nigeria: Equatorial Guinea intervening)* (Preliminary Objections) [1998] ICJ Rep 275, para 89, and the *Marshall Islands* cases (n 28). See also *South China Sea*, Jurisdiction and Admissibility (n 2) para 161.

[30] *Dispute Concerning Coastal State Rights in the Black Sea, Sea of Azov, and Kerch Strait (Ukraine v Russia)* (Preliminary Objections Award of 21 February 2020) PCA Case No 2017-06, para 188 (*Coastal State Rights in the Black Sea*).

[31] *South China Sea*, Jurisdiction and Admissibility (n 2) para 150, citing *Nuclear Tests* (*New Zealand v France*) (Judgment) [1974] ICJ Rep 457, para 30, and *Request for an Examination of the Situation in Accordance with Paragraph 63 of the Court's Judgment of 20 December 1974 in the Nuclear Tests (New Zealand v France) Case* (Order of 22 September 1995) [1995] ICJ Rep 288, para 55.

under UNCLOS, it is important to note that the dispute must be one that relates to the interpretation or application of UNCLOS, rather than an international law dispute more generally.[32]

In considering this argument in *Mauritius/Maldives*, Judge ad hoc Oxman had concerns about whether the maritime boundary dispute had properly crystallised between the parties because of the sovereignty dispute over the Chagos Archipelago. In his Separate and Dissenting Opinion, Judge ad hoc Oxman highlighted the difficult political position of the Maldives in which it was endeavouring to balance the competing interests of two States with which it enjoyed 'important and friendly relations'.[33] In that setting, it was normal for the Maldives not to want to be drawn into negotiations with either of those States and Judge ad hoc Oxman queried whether UNCLOS should effectively compel a State to negotiate a maritime boundary delimitation when such sensitivities exist.[34] Seemingly the answer to this question had already been provided in the *Timor Sea Conciliation*,[35] as the Commission in that instance insisted that it could proceed with the conciliation process notwithstanding an explicit 'agreement not to agree' in the Treaty between Australia and the Democratic Republic of Timor-Leste on Certain Maritime Arrangements in the Timor Sea (CMATS Treaty).[36] Yet Judge ad hoc Oxman emphasised that boundaries may remain undelimited for highly political reasons and in such situations, the requirements on provisional arrangements under Articles 74(3) and 83(3) should then be viewed as applicable so as to live with the unresolved issue.[37] The maritime boundary delimitation was not ripe for resolution in Judge ad hoc Oxman's view:

> The Maldives has made clear that its reluctance to negotiate a maritime boundary is based on its desire not to be drawn into a dispute between other States that is not of its making and to which it is not party. The Maldives has also indicated that it is prepared to proceed with delimitation negotiations once the dispute between the other States is resolved. As previously noted, that position in my view merits respect for important reasons of public order.[38]

This view resounds with judicial restraint and an appreciation of the broader setting of the dispute.

[32] See *M/V Louisa (Saint Vincent and the Grenadines v Spain)* (Provisional Measures, Order of 23 December 2010) ITLOS Reports 2008–2010, 58 (Dissenting Opinion of Judge Treves) para 5 (*Louisa*, Provisional Measures). For further discussion on characterising the dispute under art 288 see ch 4(II).

[33] *Mauritius/Maldives* (n 25) (Separate and Dissenting Opinion of Judge ad hoc Oxman) para 5.

[34] ibid para 8.

[35] *Conciliation between The Democratic Republic of Timor-Leste and the Commonwealth of Australia* (Decision on Australia's Objections to Competence of 19 September 2016) PCA Case No 2016-10 (*Timor Sea Conciliation*, Decision on Competence).

[36] Treaty between Australia and the Democratic Republic of Timor-Leste on Certain Maritime Arrangements in the Timor Sea (adopted 12 January 2006, entered into force 23 February 2007) 2483 UNTS 359 (CMATS Treaty). See discussion further below in section II(B)(1).

[37] *Mauritius/Maldives* (n 25) (Separate and Dissenting Opinion of Judge ad hoc Oxman) para 13.

[38] ibid para 38.

B. Other Dispute Settlement Procedures Available

Article 279 of UNCLOS, consistent with Article 286, requires that States 'shall seek a solution' of any dispute concerning the interpretation or application of UNCLOS. That solution must be sought by peaceful means, and through the means indicated under Article 33(1) of the UN Charter. Article 33(1) anticipates States relying on 'negotiation, enquiry, mediation, conciliation, arbitration, judicial settlement, resort to regional agencies or arrangements, or other peaceful means of their own choice'.[39] The *Barbados v Trinidad and Tobago* Tribunal considered that this requirement necessitated the parties negotiating,[40] but it would seem that the scope is broader than a strict obligation to negotiate.[41] Rather, seeking a solution would align with expectations in Section 1 of Part XV that States are to utilise different peaceful means available to resolve their disputes up until they resort to compulsory arbitration or adjudication; more critical is not resorting to the threat or use of force.[42]

As such, the UNCLOS dispute settlement regime sits within the general requirement to settle disputes peacefully under international law. Section 1 of Part XV recognises that States have a wide choice of means in determining how they will resolve disputes concerning the law of the sea. Consistent with the 'true purpose' of Section 1 of Part XV to settle disputes by peaceful means,[43] States are allowed to settle their disputes by any peaceful means of their own choice,[44] including through procedures other than those set out in Section 2 of Part XV of UNCLOS.[45] Section 1 of Part XV therefore acknowledges the existence of other dispute settlement techniques that States may use, including the dispute settlement choices that may be enshrined in other treaties relating to the law of the sea. Under Section 1 of Part XV, these alternate means as anticipated in Articles 281 and 282 are acceptable as viable alternatives to adjudication or arbitration under Section 2 of Part XV. Each of these Articles is discussed in the two subsections that follow immediately below.

1. Article 281

One provision allowing for alternative dispute settlement mechanisms other than compulsory arbitration or adjudication under Section 2 of Part XV of UNCLOS is Article 281, entitled 'Procedure where no settlement has been reached by the parties'. Article 281(1) provides:

[39] Charter of the United Nations, art 33(1).

[40] *Barbados v Trinidad and Tobago* (Award of the Arbitral Tribunal of 11 April 2006) PCA Case No 2004-02, para 206 (*Barbados v Trinidad and Tobago*).

[41] The *South China Sea* Tribunal suggested as much but was not required to explore this point in light of the facts demonstrating significant negotiation efforts as between the Philippines and China: *South China Sea*, Jurisdiction and Admissibility (n 2) para 347.

[42] *Land Reclamation by Singapore in and around the Straits of Johor (Malaysia v Singapore)* (Provisional Measures, Order of 8 October 2003) ITLOS Reports 2003, 10, 53 (Separate Opinion of Judge Jesus) (*Land Reclamation*, Provisional Measures).

[43] *Land Reclamation*, Provisional Measures (n 42) (Separate Opinion of Judge Lucky) para 3.

[44] UNCLOS (n 1) art 280, which reads: 'Nothing in this Part impairs the right of any States Parties to agree at any time to settle a dispute between them concerning the interpretation or application of this Convention by any peaceful means of their own choice.' Serdy notes that 'Art. 280 reflects the emphasis on the will of the parties to a dispute in determining how they go about settling it'. See Andrew Serdy, 'Article 280' in Alexander Proelss (ed), *United Nations Convention on the Law of the Sea: A Commentary* (CH Beck, Hart and Nomos 2017) 1817, para 1 (*Proelss Commentary*).

[45] *MOX Plant (Ireland v United Kingdom)* (Provisional Measures, Order of 3 December 2001) ITLOS Reports 2001, 95 (*MOX Plant*, Provisional Measures) (Separate Opinion of Vice-President Nelson) para 2. See also Serdy, 'Article 280' (n 44) 1817, para 1.

> If the States Parties which are parties to a dispute concerning the interpretation or application of this Convention have agreed to seek settlement of the dispute by a peaceful means of their own choice, the procedures provided for in this Part apply only where no settlement has been reached by recourse to such means and the agreement between the parties does not exclude any further procedure.[46]

This Article acknowledges the common situation of States accepting alternative methods of dispute settlement over maritime issues in their bilateral and multilateral relations[47] and sets out the circumstances where these methods should prevail over the compulsory procedures available in UNCLOS. Some multilateral maritime agreements have referred disputes to the UNCLOS dispute settlement regime.[48] The most notable example in this regard is the Fish Stocks Agreement.[49] Regional fisheries agreements more commonly have their own dispute settlement regimes,[50] and bilateral agreements may include dispute settlement clauses intended to capture the parties' preferred means of dispute settlement to resolve the law of the sea disputes arising under that treaty. Bankes has observed that Article 281 is 'a significant carve-out from the commitment to compulsory and binding dispute settlement'.[51]

The parameters of Article 281 were first tested in *Southern Bluefin Tuna*, where Australia and New Zealand instituted proceedings against Japan under UNCLOS, challenging the legality of Japan's experimental fishing programme.[52] Although Australia, New Zealand, and Japan were managing the southern bluefin tuna fisheries under what was then a trilateral agreement, the 1993 Convention for the Conservation of Southern Bluefin Tuna (SBT Convention),[53] Australia and New Zealand claimed that Japan's actions instituting the experimental fishing programme also violated provisions of UNCLOS. The Annex VII Tribunal held that Australia and New Zealand were precluded from bringing claims against Japan because the SBT Convention had its own dispute settlement clause that fell within the terms of Article 281.

Relevant to the application of Article 281 was the dispute settlement clause included in the SBT Convention, Article 16. Article 16 of the SBT Convention states:

46 UNCLOS (n 1) art 281(1).

47 Natalie Klein, 'Law of the Sea Dispute Settlement Outside of the United Nations Convention on the Law of the Sea' in Hélène Ruiz Fabri (ed), *Max Planck Encyclopedia of International Procedural Law* (OUP 2021) (Klein, 'Dispute Settlement Outside UNCLOS').

48 ITLOS, 'International Agreements Conferring Jurisdiction on the Tribunal' https://www.itlos.org/en/main/jurisdiction/international-agreements-conferring-jurisdiction-on-the-tribunal/.

49 United Nations Agreement for the Implementation of the Provisions of the United Nations Convention on the Law of the Sea of 10 December 1982 relating to the Conservation and Management of Straddling Fish Stocks and Highly Migratory Fish Stocks (adopted 4 August 1995, entered into force 11 December 2001) 2167 UNTS 3, art 30 (Fish Stocks Agreement).

50 See eg Convention for the Conservation of Southern Bluefin Tuna (adopted 10 May 1993, entered into force 20 May 1994) 1819 UNTS 359, art 16 (SBT Convention); Agreement for the Establishment of the Indian Ocean Tuna Commission (adopted 25 November 1993, entered into force 27 March 1996) 1927 UNTS 329, art 23. For a survey of these provisions see Klein, 'Dispute Settlement Outside UNCLOS' (n 47).

51 Nigel Bankes, 'Precluding the Applicability of Section 2 of Part XV of the Law of the Sea Convention' (2017) 48 ODIL 239, 241.

52 Australia and New Zealand initially sought provisional measures before ITLOS: *Southern Bluefin Tuna*, Provisional Measures (n 23).

53 SBT Convention (n 50).

1. If any dispute arises between two or more of the Parties concerning the interpretation or implementation of this Convention, those Parties shall consult among themselves with a view to having the dispute resolved by negotiation, inquiry, mediation, conciliation, arbitration, judicial settlement or other peaceful means of their own choice.
2. Any dispute of this character not so resolved shall, with the consent in each case of all parties to the dispute, be referred for settlement to the International Court of Justice or to arbitration; but failure to reach agreement on reference to the International Court of Justice or to arbitration shall not absolve parties to the dispute from the responsibility of continuing to seek to resolve it by any of the various peaceful means referred to in paragraph 1 above.
3. In cases where the dispute is referred to arbitration, the arbitral tribunal shall be constituted as provided in the Annex to this Convention. The Annex forms an integral part of this Convention.[54]

In reviewing this provision, the *Southern Bluefin Tuna* Tribunal determined that it fell within the terms and intent of Article 281(1).[55] The Tribunal considered that the parties' prolonged, serious, and intense efforts to negotiate[56] demonstrated compliance with the requirement of Article 281(1) that 'no settlement has been reached by recourse' to the alternative means available.[57]

Also critical to the application of Article 281(1) was whether Article 16 of the SBT Convention 'exclude[d] any further procedure'.[58] In this regard, the Tribunal recognised that 'the absence of an express exclusion of any procedure in Article 16 is not decisive'.[59] Rather, the intent of the provision was to exclude non-consensual modes of dispute settlement, which would thereby include the dispute settlement procedures under Section 2 of Part XV of UNCLOS.[60] This conclusion was reinforced by acknowledging the important exceptions and limitations within UNCLOS that curtail resort to compulsory procedures entailing binding procedures.[61] Further, the *Southern Bluefin Tuna* Tribunal was cognisant of the large number of treaties addressing maritime matters that were concluded subsequent to UNCLOS with their own diverse dispute settlement clauses. The Tribunal observed:

> To hold that disputes implicating obligations under both UNCLOS and an implementing treaty such as the 1993 Convention—as such disputes typically may—must be brought within the reach of section 2 of Part XV of UNCLOS would be effectively to deprive of substantial effect the dispute settlement provisions of those implementing agreements which prescribe dispute resolution by means of the parties' choice.[62]

[54] ibid art 16.

[55] *Southern Bluefin Tuna*, Jurisdiction and Admissibility (n 13) para 55.

[56] Which were noted as satisfying the conditions of UNCLOS (n 1) art 283. See *Southern Bluefin Tuna*, Jurisdiction and Admissibility (n 13) para 55.

[57] *Southern Bluefin Tuna*, Jurisdiction and Admissibility (n 13) para 55.

[58] ibid para 56.

[59] ibid para 57.

[60] ibid paras 57–58.

[61] Namely Section 3 of Part XV of UNCLOS (n 1). See ibid paras 60–62.

[62] *Southern Bluefin Tuna*, Jurisdiction and Admissibility (n 13) para 63. The Tribunal, however, did note a possibility of a different conclusion where the conduct of a State is 'so egregious, and risk[s] consequences of such gravity': see para 64. See also Natalie Klein, *Dispute Settlement in the UN Convention on the Law of the Sea* (CUP 2005) 43 (Klein, *Dispute Settlement*).

The *Southern Bluefin Tuna* Tribunal correctly identified that the UNCLOS dispute settlement system 'falls significantly short of establishing a truly comprehensive regime of compulsory jurisdiction entailing binding decisions'.[63] As Judges Wolfrum and Cot affirmed in their Joint Separate Opinion in *ARA Libertad* when reflecting on the purpose of Part XV of UNCLOS:

> Any attempt to broaden the jurisdictional power of the Tribunal and that of arbitral tribunals under Annex VII going beyond what is prescribed in article 288 of the Convention is not in keeping with the basic philosophy governing the dispute settlement system of the Convention. It undermines the understanding reached at the Third UN Conference on the Law of the Sea, namely that the dispute settlement system under the Convention will be mandatory but limited as far its scope is concerned. This limitation is not only reflected in the wording of article 288 of the Convention but equally in Section 3 of Part XV enumerating various limitations and exceptions.[64]

The *Southern Bluefin Tuna* decision reflects a proper interpretation of the operation and purpose of the UNCLOS dispute settlement regime, particularly as it relates to implementing agreements under UNCLOS.[65] However, the decision was subjected to significant academic criticism,[66] partly because it limits the opportunities for States to rely on compulsory arbitration or adjudication under UNCLOS for law of the sea disputes.[67] The separate opinion of Judge Keith in *Southern Bluefin Tuna* highlighted the need for an explicit exclusion of UNCLOS compulsory dispute settlement procedures for Article 281(1) to exclude jurisdiction.[68]

Commentators suggested that the *Barbados v Trinidad and Tobago* Tribunal moved away from or limited the position espoused in *Southern Bluefin Tuna*,[69] but the wording of the judgment relied on in this regard is far from clear and fails to indicate that alternative dispute settlement means will prevail over the procedure otherwise available in Part XV of UNCLOS. The relevant passage from the judgment reads as follows:

> Article 281 applies where Parties 'have agreed' to seek settlement of their dispute by a peaceful means of their own choice ... it would appear that Article 281 is intended primarily to *cover the situation where the Parties have come to an* ad hoc *agreement* as to the

[63] *Southern Bluefin Tuna*, Jurisdiction and Admissibility (n 13) para 62.

[64] *ARA Libertad (Argentina v Ghana)* (Provisional Measures, Order of 15 December 2012) ITLOS Reports 2012, 332 (*ARA Libertad*) (Joint Separate Opinion of Judges Wolfrum and Cot) para 6.

[65] Klein, *Dispute Settlement* (n 62) 35–43. Kunoy has observed that the holding in relation to an implicit exclusion aligns with the view espoused in Myron H Nordquist (ed), *United Nations Convention on the Law of the Sea 1982: A Commentary* (Martinus Nijhoff 1985–2012) (*Virginia Commentary*). See also Bjørn Kunoy, 'The Scope of Compulsory Jurisdiction and Exceptions Thereto under the United Nations Convention on the Law of the Sea' (2021) 58 Canadian YBIL 78, 88.

[66] See eg Igor V Karaman, *Dispute Resolution in the Law of the Sea* (Martinus Nijhoff 2012) 260; David A Colson and Peggy Hoyle, 'Satisfying the Procedural Prerequisites to the Compulsory Dispute Settlement Mechanisms of the 1982 Law of the Sea Convention: Did the Southern Bluefin Tuna Tribunal Get It Right?' (2003) 34 ODIL 59.

[67] See eg Bernard H Oxman, 'Complementary Agreements and Compulsory Jurisdiction' (2001) 95 AJIL 277.

[68] *Southern Bluefin Tuna*, Jurisdiction and Admissibility (n 13) (Separate Opinion of Justice Sir Kenneth Keith) para 13.

[69] See eg Barbara Kwiatkowska, 'The 2006 Barbados/Trinidad and Tobago Award: A Landmark in Compulsory Jurisdiction and Equitable Maritime Boundary Delimitation' (2007) 22 IJMCL 7, 27. It is, perhaps, notable that Judge Stephen M Schwebel served as president of both the *Southern Bluefin Tuna* (n 13) and the *Barbados v Trinidad and Tobago* (n 40) Tribunals.

> means to be adopted to settle the particular dispute which has arisen. Where they have done so, then their obligation to follow the procedures provided for in Part XV will arise where no settlement has been reached through recourse to the agreed means and where their agreement does not exclude any further procedure.[70]

The reasoning of the *Barbados v Trinidad and Tobago* Tribunal to limit the operation of Article 281 to apply only to ad hoc agreements appears to run against the explicit wording of that provision. Moreover, it is unclear what a tribunal may consider to be an 'ad hoc' dispute settlement agreement. Seemingly any agreement adopted to resolve a specific maritime issue (but only that one issue?) may be classed as 'ad hoc'. There was no detailed discussion in this decision on the meaning and purport of Article 281 and these points of difficulty from *Barbados v Trinidad and Tobago* remain unresolved for the moment.

Instead, the focus from the decision on Article 281 in *Southern Bluefin Tuna* has been on whether there must be an explicit exclusion of other dispute settlement procedures within the alternative dispute settlement regime for Article 281 to apply.[71] In the *South China Sea* arbitration, this issue arose because China had argued that the Philippines was required to negotiate the dispute existing between the parties instead of instituting arbitration, and this obligation arose from different bilateral and multilateral agreements.[72] One of the key instruments on which China relied in this regard was the 2002 China–ASEAN Declaration on the Conduct of Parties in the South China Sea (Declaration of Conduct).[73] An initial consideration was whether this instrument constituted a binding 'agreement' for the purposes of Article 281.[74] The Tribunal considered that it did not constitute a legally binding agreement in relation to dispute resolution, as indicated by its purpose and the circumstances surrounding its adoption.[75] Similarly, a series of joint statements adopted between the parties (separate to the Declaration of Conduct) were political and aspirational rather than legally binding instruments.[76] As such, Article 281 did not need to be further addressed in relation to this argument, but the Tribunal opted to consider the other elements of Article 281 'for completeness and in light of their potential relevance for the other instruments'.[77]

The two other elements of Article 281 the *South China Sea* Tribunal addressed in relation to a purported obligation to negotiate were whether a settlement has been reached by recourse to the agreed means and whether the agreements excluded any further procedure. The first element was easily dispensed with as a matter of fact, as the parties clearly had been unable to reach a settlement of their differences.[78] On the final element of excluding further procedure, it was clear that the Declaration of Conduct did not do so explicitly.[79] The Philippines thus urged the Tribunal to adopt Judge Keith's view from *Southern Bluefin Tuna* and focus on explicit exclusions of the UNCLOS dispute settlement regime.[80] The Tribunal

70 *Barbados v Trinidad and Tobago* (n 40) para 200 (emphasis added).
71 *Southern Bluefin Tuna*, Jurisdiction and Admissibility (n 13) para 57. See also *Southern Bluefin Tuna*, Jurisdiction and Admissibility (n 13) (Separate Opinion of Justice Sir Kenneth Keith) paras 13, 17–19.
72 *South China Sea*, Jurisdiction and Admissibility (n 2) para 196.
73 China-ASEAN Declaration on the Conduct of Parties in the South China Sea (signed 4 November 2002).
74 *South China Sea*, Jurisdiction and Admissibility (n 2) para 212.
75 ibid para 217.
76 ibid paras 242–45.
77 ibid para 219.
78 ibid para 220.
79 ibid para 221.
80 ibid para 210.

considered the majority approach of *Southern Bluefin Tuna* as well as that of Judge Keith, concluding that 'the better view is that Article 281 requires some clear statement of exclusion of further procedures'.[81] The Tribunal remarks that this 'requires an "opting out" of Part XV procedures'.[82]

On this basis, seemingly any treaty relating to ocean matters adopted post-1982, or at least subsequent to the entry into force of UNCLOS in 1994, must have an explicit exclusion of UNCLOS dispute settlement (an 'opt-out') as part of its dispute settlement provisions. If it does not, the parties' preferred choice of dispute settlement under that treaty will not be upheld as the prevailing means of dispute settlement by a tribunal constituted under UNCLOS. The consent to specific dispute settlement procedures in these other treaties thus runs the risk of being negated unless the negotiators had the foresight to exclude resort to UNCLOS in express terms at the time of drafting. If States do not want to find their law of the sea disputes that arise under a bilateral or regional agreement being referred to compulsory procedures entailing binding decisions under UNCLOS, there may now be a need for an additional agreement to clarify the exact preference for dispute settlement beyond what has already been included in a treaty's dispute settlement clause.

How did the Tribunal reach this conclusion, contrary to the finding in *Southern Bluefin Tuna*? The *South China Sea* Tribunal stated that it 'shares the views of ITLOS in its provisional measures orders in the *Southern Bluefin Tuna* and *MOX Plant* cases'.[83] However, ITLOS did not mention Article 281 at all in its provisional measures order in *MOX Plant*, although two of the separate judgments did.[84] ITLOS made a passing reference to Article 281 in listing one of Japan's arguments in its provisional measures order for *Southern Bluefin Tuna*,[85] but the Tribunal's order does not otherwise set out any discussion of the meaning of Article 281. There do not appear to be any views to share with ITLOS in this regard, contrary to what was stated in *South China Sea*.

It must be recalled that the discussion as to an explicit or implicit exclusion of any further procedures was not necessary on the facts before the *South China Sea* Tribunal in assessing any obligation to negotiate as claimed by China. The Tribunal determined that the Declaration of Conduct did not even implicitly exclude further procedures.[86] Similarly, the regional peace agreement, the Treaty of Amity and Cooperation in Southeast Asia,[87] was clear on its face that further procedures were not excluded.[88] The views of the *South China Sea* Tribunal on the need for an explicit exclusion of UNCLOS dispute settlement procedures for the purposes of Article 281 were therefore not at all dispositive in assessing China's submissions regarding an obligation to negotiate, unlike in *Southern Bluefin Tuna*. This

[81] ibid para 223.

[82] ibid para 224. Kunoy (n 65) has aptly observed that 'to attribute such importance to explicit exclusiveness of an alternative procedure is simplistic and appears to disregard matters of substance in regard to the interpretation and application of Article 281': see para 12.

[83] *South China Sea*, Jurisdiction and Admissibility (n 2) para 223, citing *Southern Bluefin Tuna*, Provisional Measures (n 23); and *MOX Plant*, Provisional Measures (n 45).

[84] *MOX Plant*, Provisional Measures (n 45) (Separate Opinion of Vice-President Nelson); *MOX Plant*, Provisional Measures (n 45) (Separate Opinion of Judge Treves).

[85] *Southern Bluefin Tuna*, Jurisdiction and Admissibility (n 13) para 56.

[86] *South China Sea*, Jurisdiction and Admissibility (n 2) para 226.

[87] Treaty of Amity and Cooperation in Southeast Asia (signed 24 February 1976, entered into force 15 July 1976) 1025 UNTS 297.

[88] *South China Sea*, Jurisdiction and Admissibility (n 2) para 268. But see Bing Bing Jia, 'The Curious Case of Article 281: A "Super" Provision within UNCLOS' (2015) 46(4) Ocean Dev & Intl L 268, 272–73 (arguing the Treaty of Amity did preclude the exercise of jurisdiction under art 281(1)).

issue was not revisited in the subsequent decision of *Coastal State Rights in the Black Sea*, as the dispute settlement clause at issue on its face allowed the parties to refer disputes to other procedures.[89]

The *South China Sea* Tribunal also proceeded to consider whether Article 281 of UNCLOS had application in relation to arguments concerning the Convention on Biological Diversity (CBD).[90] The question was whether China and the Philippines—by the dispute settlement procedure under Article 27 of the CBD—had agreed to settle disputes concerning Articles 192 and 194 of UNCLOS by that alternative procedure.[91] Article 27 of the CBD has a detailed dispute settlement regime, requiring:

> 1. In the event of a dispute between Contracting Parties concerning the interpretation or application of this Convention, the parties concerned shall seek solution by negotiation.
> 2. If the parties concerned cannot reach agreement by negotiation, they may jointly seek the good offices of, or request mediation by, a third party.
> 3. When ratifying, accepting, approving or acceding to this Convention, or at any time thereafter, a State or regional economic integration organization may declare in writing to the Depositary that for a dispute not resolved in accordance with paragraph 1 or paragraph 2 above, it accepts one or both of the following means of dispute settlement as compulsory:
>   (a) Arbitration in accordance with the procedure laid down in Part 1 of Annex II;
>   (b) Submission of the dispute to the International Court of Justice.
> 4. If the parties to the dispute have not, in accordance with paragraph 3 above, accepted the same or any procedure, the dispute shall be submitted to conciliation in accordance with Part 2 of Annex II unless the parties otherwise agree.
> 5. The provisions of this Article shall apply with respect to any protocol except as otherwise provided in the protocol concerned.[92]

The *South China Sea* Tribunal concluded that the CBD dispute settlement regime did not trigger Article 281. While there was 'some overlap in the subject matter of Part XII of the Convention and the subject matter of the CBD',[93] such that the two conventions have established 'parallel environmental regimes that overlap in a discrete area', a dispute under UNCLOS does not become a dispute under the CBD merely because of some overlap between the two.[94] The parallel disputes discerned by the *South China Sea*

[89] *Coastal State Rights in the Black Sea* (n 30) para 490. The Agreement between the Russian Federation and Ukraine on Cooperation in the Use of the Sea of Azov and the Kerch Strait (adopted 24 December 2003, entered into force 5 May 2004) https://zakon.rada.gov.ua/laws/show/643_205?lang=en#Text, unofficial English translation available at https://www.jura.uni-hamburg.de/die-fakultaet/professuren/proelss/dateien-valentin/agreement-sea-of-azov (Azov/Kerch Cooperation Treaty) referred to disputes that may be settled by 'any other peaceful/amicable means as may be selected by the parties' and so the Tribunal concluded that Annex VII arbitration was thus not precluded: *Coastal State Rights in the Black Sea* (n 30) para 490.

[90] Convention on Biological Diversity (adopted 5 June 1992, entered into force 29 December 1993) 1760 UNTS 79 (CBD).

[91] *South China Sea*, Jurisdiction and Admissibility (n 2) para 283.

[92] CBD (n 90) art 27.

[93] *South China Sea*, Jurisdiction and Admissibility (n 2) para 284.

[94] ibid para 285.

Tribunal could be viewed differently to the single dispute said to exist in *Southern Bluefin Tuna*.[95]

The *South China Sea* Tribunal reasoned that the CBD covered a broader field than UNCLOS on the basis that it dealt with all biodiversity rather than being uniquely concerned with the marine environment.[96] On this basis, it could have been argued that the CBD was different to the SBT Convention in that the latter was more clearly in the nature of an implementing agreement whereas the CBD creates its own distinct environmental regime with its own broad remit. Yet Article 281 draws no distinction on this basis, although the rationale is stronger for implying that the dispute settlement provisions of an implementing agreement 'exclude[s] any further procedure'.

Apart from this substantive difference, which may have been viewed as dispositive of the issue anyway,[97] there are strong parallels between the position of the CBD and the SBT Convention in considering the possible application of Article 281. The *South China Sea* Tribunal considered that Article 22 of the CBD, which addresses the relationship of the CBD with other international agreements, required consistent implementation of the CBD and other treaties. Article 22 of the CBD provides:

> 1. The provisions of this Convention shall not affect the rights and obligations of any Contracting Party deriving from any existing international agreement, except where the exercise of those rights and obligations would cause a serious damage or threat to biological diversity.
> 2. Contracting Parties shall implement this Convention with respect to the marine environment consistently with the rights and obligations of States under the law of the sea.[98]

The SBT Convention contains a similar 'without prejudice' clause.[99] Consistent implementation allows for the possibility that Article 281 is activated and the dispute settlement regime of the CBD applies unless no settlement is reached through Article 27,[100] and Article 27 does not preclude further procedures. Similar to Article 16 of the SBT Convention, Article 27 is predicated on States evincing their consent for adjudication or arbitration. The *South China Sea* Tribunal nonetheless found 'a clear exclusion of Part XV procedures is required in order for Article 281 to present an obstacle for the tribunal's jurisdiction'.[101]

There are now two conflicting decisions on the interpretation of Article 281.[102] This result may be partly attributable to the engagement of diverse dispute settlement bodies under

[95] Peter Tzeng, 'Ukraine v Russia and Philippines v China: Jurisdiction and Legitimacy' (2017) 46(1) Denv J Intl L & Pol 1, 10.

[96] *South China Sea*, Jurisdiction and Admissibility (n 2) para 285.

[97] Bankes suggests that '[a]t a minimum, one would think that there would have to be substantial coincidence of subject matter as between the two agreements': Bankes (n 51) 243. He notes, however, that the *Timor Sea Conciliation*, Decision on Competence (n 35) did not appear to endorse this view: see 243.

[98] CBD (n 90) art 22.

[99] SBT Convention (n 50) art 4, which provides: 'Nothing in this Convention nor any measures adopted pursuant to it shall be deemed to prejudice the positions or views of any Party with respect to its rights and obligations under treaties and other international agreements to which it is party or its positions or views with respect to the law of the sea.'

[100] This aspect of art 281 is not discussed at all by the Tribunal in relation to the CBD (n 90), presumably because it considered the second element of art 281 was not applicable.

[101] *South China Sea*, Jurisdiction and Admissibility (n 2) para 286.

[102] Churchill has observed that the *Southern Bluefin Tuna* arbitration 'contained no members who were or would become ITLOS judges and only one member who would participate in another Annex VII tribunal'. See Robin Churchill, 'The General Dispute Settlement System of the UN Convention on the Law of the Sea: Overview,

Article 287 of UNCLOS. As Romano has noted, 'ad hoc Tribunals can make ad hoc justice. While this may be useful to preserve international peace, it is not necessarily beneficial to the preservation of the international legal order'.[103] Coherency in approach among the different mechanisms is thus desirable. The *South China Sea* Tribunal's judgment reflects an affirmation of the view that an explicit exclusion of further procedures, indeed perhaps an explicit exclusion of UNCLOS procedures in particular, is necessary for Article 281 to prevent the exercise of jurisdiction. This decision has the effect of broadening the availability and scope of compulsory jurisdiction under UNCLOS in the future.

Further interpretation of Article 281 was undertaken in a decision on jurisdiction and competence by a Conciliation Commission constituted under Annex V of UNCLOS.[104] In 2016, Timor-Leste commenced compulsory conciliation proceedings against Australia in an attempt to resolve their maritime boundary dispute in the Timor Sea.[105] At the time the proceedings were commenced, the CMATS Treaty between Australia and Timor-Leste had placed a moratorium on maritime boundary delimitation. The parties relevantly agreed in the following paragraphs of Article 4 of the CMATS Treaty:

> 4. Notwithstanding any other bilateral or multilateral agreement binding on the Parties, or any declaration made by either Party pursuant to any such agreement, neither Party shall commence or pursue any proceedings against the other Party before any court, tribunal or other dispute settlement mechanism that would raise or result in, either directly or indirectly, issues or findings of relevance to maritime boundaries or delimitation in the Timor Sea.
> 5. Any court, tribunal or other dispute settlement body hearing proceedings involving the Parties shall not consider, make comment on, nor make findings that would raise or result in, either directly or indirectly, issues or findings of relevance to maritime boundaries or delimitation in the Timor Sea. Any such comment or finding shall be of no effect, and shall not be relied upon, or cited, by the Parties at any time.[106]

For dispute settlement, Article 11 of the CMATS Treaty provides: 'Any disputes about the interpretation or application of this Treaty shall be settled by consultation or negotiation.' The validity of the CMATS Treaty was also contested between the parties.[107]

Context, and Use' (2017) 48 ODIL 216, 224 (Churchill, 'General Dispute Settlement System'). This composition provides pause for thought in contrasting the approaches of those steeped in UNCLOS interpretations to those who possibly have broader sensibilities to general international law and the peaceful settlement of international disputes.

[103] Cesare Romano, 'The Southern Bluefin Tuna Dispute: Hints of a World to Come ... Like It or Not' (2001) 32 ODIL 313, 333 (commenting on the use of ad hoc tribunals as opposed to permanent institutions for important constitutional-like decisions).

[104] *Timor Sea Conciliation*, Decision on Competence (n 35).

[105] For discussion, including on the background to this dispute see Natalie Klein, 'Timor Sea Conciliation: A Harbinger for Dispute Settlement under UNCLOS?' in Hélène Ruiz Fabri and others (eds), *A Bridge Over Troubled Waters: Dispute Resolution in the Law of International Watercourses and the Law of the Sea* (Brill Nijhoff 2020) 105 (Klein, 'Timor Sea Conciliation').

[106] CMATS Treaty (n 36).

[107] In a separate arbitration, Timor-Leste alleged the CMATS Treaty was invalid in light of allegations that Australia spied on Timor-Leste during the negotiations. See Donald K Anton, 'The Timor Sea Treaty Arbitration: Timor-Leste Challenges Australian Espionage and Seizure of Documents' (2014) 18 ASIL Insights https://www.asil.org/insights/volume/18/issue/6/timor-sea-treaty-arbitration-timor-leste-challenges-australian-espionage.

Following Australia's challenge to the competence of the Commission, the Commission considered if the CMATS Treaty constituted an agreement under Article 281 'to seek settlement of the dispute by a peaceful means of their own choice'.[108] The Commission characterised the CMATS Treaty as 'an agreement *not* to seek settlement of the Parties' dispute over maritime boundaries for the duration of the moratorium'.[109] As such, an agreement not to pursue dispute settlement for the stated period of time, according to the Commission, was not a dispute settlement means of the parties' own choice. The Commission did not explain why a bilateral agreement choosing very explicitly to resolve the maritime boundary dispute at a later point in time was not a valid choice of dispute settlement for the purposes of Article 281. The curious outcome that resulted was that the engagement of the parties in the conciliation process under UNCLOS placed them in violation of their commitments under the CMATS Treaty.[110] Instead, we are presented with another scenario where Article 281 was held not to apply and the UNCLOS dispute settlement prevailed.

In *Coastal State Rights in the Black Sea*, the Tribunal addressed a Russian argument that there was no jurisdiction on the basis of clauses in two bilateral treaties:[111] the State Border Treaty[112] and the Azov/Kerch Cooperation Treaty.[113] Although the parties differed slightly in their interpretations of the treaty texts,[114] the Tribunal considered that the clauses in question generally referred to settling questions or issues by agreement and the ordinary meaning as well as the context and negotiations indicated that they were not dispute settlement clauses.[115] The Tribunal considered that a dispute settlement clause had to refer to the means by which the parties would be able to resolve disputes,[116] and not just reflect the outcome ('agreement') from discussions.[117] These clauses did not meet the criterion in Article 281 of reflecting 'settlement of the dispute by a peaceful means'. The approach to Article 281 in the *Timor Sea Conciliation* and the *Coastal State Rights in the Black Sea* thus indicates that a dispute settlement provision in another treaty must refer to a method of dispute settlement and that method of dispute settlement must be presently available rather than deferred for a period of time.

The inconsistencies in outcomes as well as the prioritisation of the UNCLOS dispute settlement regime over alternatives selected by the parties in other treaties may be construed as beneficial in situating UNCLOS as the preeminent law of the sea treaty and its dispute settlement regime as the preferred mechanism for all maritime disputes. It is not necessarily apparent that such an approach will ultimately promote the good governance of the oceans when it counters long-standing core interests manifest in the principle that States must consent to the exercise of jurisdiction for adjudication or arbitration. If these

[108] *Timor Sea Conciliation*, Decision on Competence (n 35) para 61.

[109] ibid para 62 (emphasis in original).

[110] This situation was short-lived, however, in light of Timor-Leste's decision to terminate the CMATS Treaty. See *Conciliation between The Democratic Republic of Timor-Leste and the Commonwealth of Australia* (Report and Recommendations of the Compulsory Conciliation Commission, 9 May 2018) PCA Case No 2016-10, paras 103–109 (*Timor Sea Conciliation*, Report).

[111] *Coastal State Rights in the Black Sea* (n 30) para 451.

[112] Treaty between Ukraine and the Russian Federation on the Ukrainian-Russian State Border (adopted 28 January 2003, entered into force 23 April 2004).

[113] Azov/Kerch Cooperation Treaty (n 89).

[114] *Coastal State Rights in the Black Sea* (n 30) paras 477–78.

[115] See ibid paras 485–87.

[116] ibid para 483.

[117] ibid para 482.

sorts of decisions are perceived by stakeholders as the decision-makers operating beyond the bounds of the UNCLOS regime, there is a risk of backlash.[118] Future tribunals constituted under UNCLOS will need to consider these alternative perspectives closely, both in relation to the dispute before that tribunal and in relation to how UNCLOS dispute settlement should operate as part of global ocean governance.

2. Article 282

Article 282 reads:

> If the States Parties which are parties to a dispute concerning the interpretation or application of this Convention have agreed, through a general, regional or bilateral agreement or otherwise, that such dispute shall, at the request of any party to the dispute, be submitted to a procedure that entails a binding decision, that procedure shall apply in lieu of the procedures provided for in this Part, unless the parties to the dispute otherwise agree.[119]

Similar to Article 281, the context of this provision was drawn from the view espoused during UNCLOS negotiations that States would have freedom to utilise a dispute settlement method of their own choosing and where they had selected another method, it should have precedence over the procedures laid out in Part XV.[120] As Kunoy notes, Article 282 'allows autonomous choices of forum notwithstanding the binding nature of section 2 of Part XV'.[121]

The United Kingdom invoked this Article at the provisional measures stage of the *MOX Plant* case, arguing that Ireland's claims were governed by regional agreements and either were, or were about to be, submitted to the dispute settlement regimes of those regional agreements and provided for alternative and binding means of dispute settlement.[122] ITLOS did not consider these agreements to be sufficient to deny prima facie jurisdiction as none of them addressed the interpretation or application of UNCLOS specifically, but rather concerned the clauses of those other pertinent instruments.[123] Moreover, even where there were identical or similar provisions found in UNCLOS and other agreements, each had a separate existence and their interpretation 'may not yield the same results, having regard to, inter alia, differences in the respective contexts, objects and purposes, subsequent practice of parties and *travaux préparatoires*'.[124] In these circumstances, Article 282 would not be applicable to deny the jurisdiction of a Part XV tribunal.

Judge Wolfrum went further in his Separate Opinion in the *MOX Plant* provisional measures proceedings, stating: 'An intention to entrust the settlement of disputes concerning the interpretation and application of the Convention to other institutions must be expressed

[118] As is manifest in the current issues enveloping the World Trade Organization. See eg Amrita Bahri, '"Appellate Body Held Hostage": Is Judicial Activism at Fair Trial?' (2019) 53 JWT 293.

[119] UNCLOS (n 1) art 282.

[120] HS Amerasinghe, 'Memorandum by the President of the Conference on Document A/CONF.62/WP.10' (22 July 1977) UN Doc A/CONF.62/WP.10/Add. 1, 122; '60th Plenary Meeting' (6 April 1976) UN Doc A/CONF.62/SR.60, para 55 (Statement by the Japanese delegation); '59th Plenary Meeting' (5 April 1976) UN Doc A/CONF.62/SR.59, para 46 (Statement by the Argentinian delegation); *Virginia Commentary* (n 65) vol 5, 26. Cited in *MOX Plant*, Provisional Measures (n 45) (Separate Opinion of Vice-President Nelson) para 2.

[121] Kunoy (n 65) 19.

[122] *MOX Plant*, Provisional Measures (n 45) para 39.

[123] ibid para 49.

[124] ibid para 51. See further *MOX Plant*, Provisional Measures (n 45) (Separate Opinion of Judge Wolfrum) 1.

explicitly in respective agreements.'[125] He rejected the argument that an explicit exception would deny Article 282 of its substance.[126] By contrast, in the same case, Vice-President Nelson indicated that ITLOS may have gone too far in its holding on the inapplicability of Article 282 and sounded a caution against an interpretation that would deny the object and purpose of this provision, along with Article 281.[127]

In the *MOX Plant* provisional measures proceedings, Judge Treves analysed Article 282 in the following terms:

> While other provisions of section 1 (such as, in particular, articles 281 and 283) set out obstacles to the possibility of resorting to compulsory adjudication in general, article 282 expresses a preference between different means of compulsory adjudication that would otherwise be applicable. In interpreting article 282, such preference must be balanced not by the general idea that limitations to sovereignty cannot be presumed or that States may not be presumed to accept submission to adjudication without their consent, which may be relevant in interpreting articles 281 and 283, but by the general freedom of States to utilise whichever means of compulsory adjudication are available under treaties in force for them.[128]

While Judge Treves' view indicates how parties are allowed to choose between compulsory dispute settlement procedures, this emphasis on party preference was not borne out in the *MOX Plant* Annex VII proceedings. The Annex VII Tribunal constituted to resolve the *MOX Plant* dispute had regard to the possibility that the European Court of Justice (ECJ) might determine that the issues raised by Ireland would fall within the exclusive competence of the European Community.[129] If that were to be the case, both Ireland and the United Kingdom agreed that Article 282 would preclude the exercise of jurisdiction by the Annex VII Tribunal. The Tribunal thus determined that rather than rely on the parties' views and its own determination as to what may or may not fall within the exclusive competence of the European Community legal order, proceedings under UNCLOS would be suspended.[130] This decision was made 'bearing in mind considerations of mutual respect and comity which should prevail between judicial institutions both of which may be called upon to determine rights and obligations as between two States',[131] as well as a desire to avoid conflicting decisions between the two courts.[132]

The decision of the ECJ,[133] which determined that Ireland had failed to fulfil its European Community obligations in instituting proceedings against the United Kingdom, led to Ireland's termination of the UNCLOS proceedings without further discussion of the relevance of Article 282 to the proceedings. The ECJ invoked Article 282 in its proceedings to

125 *MOX Plant*, Provisional Measures (n 45) (Separate Opinion of Judge Wolfrum) 2.
126 ibid.
127 *MOX Plant*, Provisional Measures (n 45) (Separate Opinion of Vice-President Nelson) para 7. See also *MOX Plant*, Provisional Measures (n 45) (Separate Opinion of Judge Jesus) para 2.
128 *MOX Plant*, Provisional Measures (n 45) (Separate Opinion of Judge Treves) para 4.
129 See *MOX Plant (Ireland v United Kingdom)* (Order No 3 on Suspension of Proceedings on Jurisdiction and Merits, and Request for Further Provisional Measures, Order of 24 June 2003) PCA Case No 2002-01 (*MOX Plant*, Order No 3) para 22.
130 ibid para 26.
131 ibid para 28.
132 ibid.
133 *Commission v Ireland* [2006] ECLI:EU:C:2006:345.

note that the European Community's dispute resolution system resulted in binding decisions and in principle was to take precedence over UNCLOS dispute settlement procedures.[134]

Article 282 was considered briefly at the provisional measures stage of the *Southern Bluefin Tuna* cases. Japan argued that the SBT Convention had its own dispute settlement procedure and recourse to an UNCLOS tribunal was therefore precluded.[135] Australia and New Zealand argued that Article 282 could not be applicable in relation to the dispute settlement regime in the SBT Convention because the latter was not binding.[136] The latter position was accepted by ITLOS without any detailed examination.[137] The issue was briefly raised again before the Annex VII Tribunal in light of the fact that all three States had also accepted the compulsory jurisdiction of the ICJ. However, Japan indicated to the Tribunal that it would similarly object to the ICJ's jurisdiction because of reservations in the respective declarations of each State, if a case was instituted before that forum.[138]

In parsing the elements of Article 282, the *South China Sea* Tribunal highlighted the following factors in determining whether UNCLOS dispute settlement procedures were excluded:

> (a) that the parties must have agreed through a "general, regional or bilateral agreement or otherwise" that, (b) at the request of any party to the dispute, (c) the dispute shall be submitted to a procedure "that entails a binding decision," and (d) that the parties have not otherwise agreed to retain access (i.e., to opt back in) to the Part XV, Section 2 procedures.[139]

Although the Tribunal addressed this provision in relation to the Declaration of Conduct, political statements, the Treaty of Amity and Cooperation in South-East Asia, and the CBD, it rightly concluded that none of these agreements 'entails a binding decision'.[140] The compulsory conciliation under the CBD would only produce recommendations for the parties.[141] Thus, while setting out the key elements, the *South China Sea* Tribunal in this instance did not engage in any further analysis of this provision given its lack of immediate relevance to the case before it.

The key analysis of Article 282 to date has been in an ICJ decision in proceedings brought by Somalia against Kenya for the delimitation of their maritime boundary in the Indian Ocean: *Maritime Delimitation in the Indian Ocean*.[142] This case was instituted on the basis

[134] ibid para 125.

[135] *Southern Bluefin Tuna*, Provisional Measures (n 23) para 53. Japan also appears to have argued the applicability of art 281, but ITLOS folded the requirements of art 281 into a consideration of the requirements for exchanging views in accordance with art 283. See para 56.

[136] ibid para 54.

[137] ibid para 55 (stating 'the fact that the Convention of 1993 applies between the parties does not preclude recourse to the procedures in Part XV, section 2, of the Convention on the Law of the Sea').

[138] *Southern Bluefin Tuna*, Jurisdiction and Admissibility (n 13) para 39. This position arguably foreshadowed what occurred in *Maritime Delimitation in the Indian Ocean (Somalia v Kenya)* (Preliminary Objections) [2017] ICJ Rep 3 (*Maritime Delimitation in the Indian Ocean*, Preliminary Objections), which is discussed further below.

[139] *South China Sea*, Jurisdiction and Admissibility (n 2) para 291. Kunoy (n 65) considers that this interpretation did not align with the views of Judge Treves from *MOX Plant*, Provisional Measures (n 45) as the *South China Sea* Tribunal seemingly imposed stricter requirements that would make it less likely that the alternative forum to UNCLOS would be prioritised: see paras 20–21.

[140] *South China Sea*, Jurisdiction and Admissibility (n 2) paras 299–302, 309, 320.

[141] ibid para 320. Similarly, although the United Kingdom argued in *Chagos MPA* (n 10) that the dispute settlement regime for the Indian Ocean Tuna Commission applied by virtue of art 282, this argument could not hold because that regime provided only for compulsory conciliation and optional referral to the ICJ: *Chagos MPA* (n 10) para 259.

[142] *Maritime Delimitation in the Indian Ocean*, Preliminary Objections (n 138) para 1.

of each State's acceptance of the ICJ's compulsory jurisdiction under Article 36(2) of its Statute rather than under UNCLOS. However, a complicating factor in the application of Article 282 was that Kenya's acceptance of the Court's jurisdiction was subject to an exception that it did not consent where the parties have agreed to have recourse to some other method of dispute settlement.[143] Kenya argued that this reservation was relevant both to a Memorandum of Understanding adopted by the parties and to the parties' consent to compulsory arbitration or adjudication under UNCLOS.[144] In relation to UNCLOS, Somalia argued that the Court's jurisdiction took precedence by virtue of Article 282.[145] Article 282 was potentially at issue because acceptances of the ICJ's compulsory jurisdiction reflect agreement by the parties to submit their dispute to a binding mechanism other than the UNCLOS compulsory procedures.[146]

Kenya took the position that Article 282 could not apply where there was a reservation in the unilateral declaration that excludes the Court's jurisdiction.[147] The reservation, which purported to exclude from the Court's jurisdiction 'disputes in regard to which the parties to the dispute have agreed or shall agree to have recourse to some other method or methods of settlement', meant that the forum selection in Article 287 (in this instance arbitration) was to prevail.[148] Somalia, however, pointed out that on Kenya's argument there would be circularity between the exception in Kenya's acceptance under Article 36(2) and Article 282 whereby the parties in each instance would be pointed to the other dispute settlement procedure.[149] However, if a limitation to the consent provided to the Court under Article 36(2) would deny the Court's jurisdiction then seemingly there are no compulsory procedures actually available in lieu of those under UNCLOS. Kenya denied the circularity argument on the basis that the UNCLOS dispute settlement procedures would apply because they were *lex posterior* and *lex specialis*.[150] The ICJ rejected this argument on the basis that Kenya's acceptance of ICJ jurisdiction did not give any priority to a method of dispute settlement that was *lex posterior* and *lex specialis*.[151]

On the applicability of Article 282 in this setting, the ICJ had regard to the dispute settlement system established under UNCLOS and noted the relevance of Section 1 in preserving the rights of parties to utilise dispute settlement procedures other than the compulsory procedures entailing binding decisions in Section 2 of Part XV of UNCLOS.[152] Notably, the Court emphasised that Article 282 applied to the alternative dispute settlement procedures applying *in lieu* of the UNCLOS procedures.[153] Further, acceptances of the ICJ's jurisdiction

[143] ibid para 31. The existence of a reservation in art 36(2) was not an element that had been considered in commentary on art 282 previously. See *Maritime Delimitation in the Indian Ocean*, Preliminary Objections (n 138) (Dissenting Opinion of Judge Robinson) para 31. See also Kai-chieh Chan, 'The ICJ's Judgement in *Somalia v Kenya* and Its Implications for the Law of the Sea' (2019) 34 Utrecht J Intl & Eur L 195, 199.

[144] *Maritime Delimitation in the Indian Ocean*, Preliminary Objections (n 138) paras 32–33.

[145] ibid para 34.

[146] See Klein, *Dispute Settlement* (n 62) 43–44; *Virginia Commentary* (n 65) vol 5, 26–27. This perspective was, unsurprisingly, accepted by the ICJ. See *Maritime Delimitation in the Indian Ocean*, Preliminary Objections (n 138) paras 128, 130.

[147] ibid para 110.

[148] See Xiaohui Wu, 'Case Note: Maritime Delimitation in the Indian Ocean (*Somalia v Kenya*), Judgment on Preliminary Objections' (2018) 17 Chinese JIL 841, 849–50.

[149] *Maritime Delimitation in the Indian Ocean*, Preliminary Objections (n 138) para 113.

[150] ibid para 114.

[151] ibid para 120.

[152] ibid para 125.

[153] ibid para 125.

under Article 36(2) of its Statute fell within the terms of Article 282, consistent with the ordinary meaning of Article 282, as well as UNCLOS *travaux préparatoires*.[154] This reasoning well reflects the general relationship between jurisdiction under Article 36(2) of the Court's Statute and Article 282.

Yet Kenya's reservation excluding cases subject to another dispute settlement regime added a complicating factor. In this scenario, the ICJ determined that acceptances of the Court's jurisdiction under Article 36(2) of its Statute still apply in lieu of compulsory procedures under UNCLOS even where those acceptances include reservations comparable to those of Kenya's in the case before it.[155] In this respect, the Court considered that the acceptance under Article 36(2) and reservations like Kenya's were to be regarded as a unity, rather than distinguishing the reservation from the act of acceptance in applying Article 282.[156] For the operation of Article 282, what mattered the most to the ICJ was the existence of consent under Article 36(2) of the Court's Statute and less so the limitations placed by States on that consent.[157] As such, the choice of procedure under Article 287 could not operate to deny the effect of Article 282 in this context.[158] In focusing on the simple existence of the Article 36(2) acceptance, rather than the limitations to that acceptance, a further implication is that choices made to exclude binding maritime boundary dispute settlement under Article 298(1)(a) would not be upheld.[159] The ICJ's approach has been seen as prioritising its own jurisdiction over that of the other choices of procedure set out in Article 287,[160] which is inconsistent with the design of UNCLOS dispute settlement.[161]

* * *

The dynamic involved in Article 282 contests of jurisdiction, as evinced in *Maritime Delimitation in the Indian Ocean*, is different to those that may emerge under Article 281, as seen in the *Southern Bluefin Tuna* and *South China Sea* cases. While both concern the inter-relationship of the UNCLOS dispute settlement regime with alternative dispute settlement methods, the focus in Article 282 is on alternative avenues of compulsory jurisdiction before international courts and tribunals. In either setting, the dispute is being subjected to a third-party mechanism that entails a binding decision. The debate thus sits within a

[154] ibid paras 126–27.

[155] ibid para 130. The Court took into account the fact that this reservation would have been well known to the negotiators of UNCLOS as it was already included in many of the optional clause acceptances at the time UNCLOS was drafted: see para 129. Judge Robinson was very critical of this assessment. *Maritime Delimitation in the Indian Ocean*, Preliminary Objections (n 138) (Dissenting Opinion of Judge Robinson) paras 17 ff.

[156] Wu (n 148) 850.

[157] A position that may need to be rethought in future cases when the reservations under art 36(2) relate to the subject matter jurisdiction of a case. States with exclusions for law of the sea-related cases include Australia, Japan, Barbados, Bulgaria and Romania. Young has commented that a different approach to subject matter jurisdiction would be followed. Margaret A Young, 'Maritime Delimitation by the International Court of Justice: Implications of Somalia v Kenya' (ARF Workshop on Dispute Resolution and Law of the Sea, Dili, 27–28 February 2020). It is notable that Australia and Japan also have exclusions in their Declarations under art 36(2) similar to Kenya's on alternative means of dispute settlement.

[158] See Wu (n 148) 854.

[159] Kunoy (n 65) 24.

[160] Wu (n 148) 858. See also Marco Benatar and Erik Franckx, 'The ICJ's Preliminary Objections Judgment in Somalia v Kenya: Causing Ripples in Law of the Sea Dispute Settlement?' *EJIL: Talk!* (22 February 2017) https://www.ejiltalk.org/the-icjs-preliminary-objections-judgment-in-somalia-v-kenya-causing-ripples-in-law-of-the-sea-dispute-settlement/; Christine Gray, 'The 2017 Judicial Activity of the International Court of Justice' (2018) 112 AJIL 254, 259.

[161] Klein, *Dispute Settlement* (n 62) 54–59.

broader frame concerning the interactions of international courts and their respective roles for the international law regimes that they enforce. The Article 281 debate is concerned with the inter-relationship of compulsory adjudication or arbitration with other, possibly non-binding, dispute settlement processes and what the parties sought to achieve in devising the means by which disputes emerging under different international law regimes would be resolved. Judge Treves sought to underline the relevance of parties' decisions for Article 282 in the context of *MOX Plant* but that Tribunal elevated the question to the interaction of courts and not preferencing the parties' choices. Those predilections seem more relevant for Article 281 when the purpose and context of different treaties' dispute settlement regimes is under consideration.

When we consider the broad settings for the operation of Articles 281 and 282, it may then be unreasonable to expect perfect consistency in decision-making under Article 281 when regard must be had to parties' intentions under different treaties. A similar variation may emerge in relation to Article 282 if the Court's 'unity' approach to declarations under Article 36(2) was not subsequently followed because of the varied exclusions from compulsory jurisdiction in those declarations. Where consistency is desirable, albeit elusive, is in relation to these broad settings: Does the existence of ICJ jurisdiction trump the UNCLOS dispute settlement regime? Does UNCLOS dispute settlement trump the dispute settlement choices made in a myriad of other international agreements pertaining to ocean governance? If there is a choice between extending jurisdiction or limiting jurisdiction then which better aligns with the purposes of UNCLOS dispute settlement?[162] At the moment, the judges concerned must grapple with these questions, taking account of the views of the diverse stakeholders. State parties to UNCLOS may eventually take steps to clarify these questions but the heterogeneity of the international legal system may mean that it is not possible to progress further than what is already contained in Articles 281 and 282.

C. Exchange of Views under Article 283

Before States may institute arbitration or adjudication under UNCLOS, Section 1 of Part XV further requires in Article 283 that States proceed to an exchange of views when a dispute concerning the interpretation or application of UNCLOS arises. More precisely, Article 283(1) reads: 'When a dispute arises between States Parties concerning the interpretation or application of this Convention, the parties to the dispute shall proceed expeditiously to an exchange of views regarding its settlement by negotiation or other peaceful means.'[163] The obligation to exchange views is continuous,[164] and extends to the implementation of any settlement agreement under Article 283(2).[165] The inclusion of Article 283 in the Convention was to underline the primary obligation between States in dispute that they make every effort to resolve their differences through negotiation.[166]

Early judicial interpretations of Article 283 had considered what was required in any communication between the parties to meet this obligation, including to what extent the

[162] Oxman (n 67) has considered these questions.
[163] UNCLOS (n 1) art 283(1).
[164] *Virginia Commentary* (n 65) vol 5, 29.
[165] See Klein, *Dispute Settlement* (n 62) 33.
[166] *Virginia Commentary* (n 65) vol 5, 29.

claims of UNCLOS violations were expected to be articulated.[167] As Article 283 specifically references a dispute 'concerning the interpretation or application of' UNCLOS, States parties have sought to argue that UNCLOS must be invoked during the exchange of views for this requirement to be satisfied.[168] The *Guyana v Suriname* Tribunal considered that matters 'incidental to the real dispute' did not have to be raised specifically in an exchange of views for the purposes of satisfying Article 283.[169]

Rather than focus on the subject matter of the dispute, the *Chagos Marine Protected Area* (*Chagos MPA*)[170] Tribunal placed a different emphasis on the interpretation of Article 283. The Tribunal in that case reviewed the wording of Article 283 and concluded the obligation is one to exchange views regarding the means for resolving the dispute, not an obligation to negotiate the substance of the dispute.[171] This approach would not require the parties to specify what dispute concerning the interpretation or application of UNCLOS was at issue but would entail discussion as to how the dispute was to be settled between the parties. No 'undue formalism as to the manner and precision' of the exchange of views was required.[172]

The Annex VII Tribunal in *Arctic Sunrise* also followed this approach,[173] and the *South China Sea* Tribunal reaffirmed the interpretation.[174] ITLOS shared the view of the *Chagos MPA* Tribunal in the *Norstar* case.[175] The *Arctic Sunrise* Tribunal further indicated that 'Article 283(1) does not require the Parties to engage in negotiations regarding the subject matter of the dispute'.[176] The greater emphasis is on the need under UNCLOS for the parties to undertake some effort to determine how the dispute is to be resolved.

In the *Norstar* case, Italy argued that Article 283 'requires the parties to indicate a view on the most appropriate means of settlement in the circumstances existing at the time, which is not the same as announcing the intention to have recourse to litigation'.[177] While acknowledging that the exchange of views only had to address the means of dispute settlement, consistent with the more recent case law on this point, Italy argued that the applicant still had to present the subject matter of the dispute in such a way as to indicate what the dispute concerned and its relevance under the Convention.[178] This effort to resurrect an earlier consideration was not addressed by ITLOS, however, which instead focused on Italy's failures to respond in any way to communications from Panama. ITLOS noted that the absence of a response by a State did not negate the fulfilment of the requirement to exchange views under Article 283.[179]

[167] See Klein, *Dispute Settlement* (n 62) 62–64 (discussing this case law).

[168] See eg *Southern Bluefin Tuna*, Jurisdiction and Admissibility (n 13) para 39(d); *Duzgit Integrity Arbitration (Malta v São Tomé and Príncipe)* (Award of 5 September 2016) PCA Case No 2014-07, para 188 (*Duzgit Integrity*). See also para 64.

[169] *Guyana v Suriname* (n 10) para 410. Although the Tribunal considered this to apply in the particular circumstances before it, which related to a challenged law enforcement incident in a disputed and undelimited maritime area: see para 410.

[170] *Chagos MPA* (n 10).

[171] ibid para 378.

[172] ibid para 382.

[173] *Arctic Sunrise (Netherlands v Russia)* (Award on the Merits of 14 August 2015) PCA Case No 2014-02, paras 149–56 (*Arctic Sunrise*, Merits).

[174] *South China Sea*, Jurisdiction and Admissibility (n 2) para 333.

[175] *Norstar*, Preliminary Objections (n 22) para 208.

[176] ibid para 151.

[177] ibid para 178.

[178] ibid para 179.

[179] ibid para 215: 'The Tribunal considers that the absence of a response from one State Party to an attempt by another State Party to exchange views on the means of settlement of a dispute arising between them does not prevent the Tribunal from finding that the requirements of article 283 have been fulfilled.'

ITLOS has reiterated in its decisions that a State is not obliged to pursue procedures under Part XV, Section 1, including an exchange of views, when that State concludes that the possibilities of settlement have been exhausted.[180] The time that must elapse for an exchange of views to have occurred can be quite small, as demonstrated by the *Arctic Sunrise* proceedings. In that instance, the Netherlands had sent two *notes verbales* to Russia on 23 and 26 September 2013; Russia responded on 1 October 2013; and the Netherlands then raised the spectre of proceeding to arbitration in light of the different viewpoints on 3 October 2013 and instituted proceedings the following day. ITLOS determined that this exchange was sufficient to meet the requirements of Article 283 in assessing prima facie jurisdiction for the prescription of provisional measures. However, the extremely short timeframe raised questions as to how meaningful the exchange must be to meet the purposes of resolving the dispute peacefully without resorting to compulsory arbitration or adjudication.[181] The Annex VII Tribunal in *Arctic Sunrise* again addressed Article 283 and considered that the timeframe was adequate because of the urgency for the Netherlands in securing the release of the vessel and those on board.[182] Such a short amount of time, the Tribunal acknowledged, 'may not suffice in every case'.[183]

In the provisional measures stage of *Detention of Three Ukrainian Naval Vessels*, Ukraine gave Russia a ten-day window to respond to its request to proceed to an exchange of views.[184] ITLOS considered that setting a deadline of ten days was acceptable since Article 283 requires an 'expeditious' exchange of views.[185] However, while Russia did respond within this deadline, its note sought to follow up at some undefined point in time on the exchange of views.[186] Russia subsequently engaged in consultations with Ukraine in accordance with Article 283 but alleged that Ukraine did not do so meaningfully but sought to continue its claim for provisional measures.[187] In the view of the Tribunal, this ambiguity and lack of urgency on behalf of Russia warranted Ukraine determining that its efforts to exchange views were satisfied, at least for the purposes of prescribing provisional measures.[188]

There have also been instances where States have announced in a diplomatic note their intention to commence arbitration or adjudication under the UNCLOS dispute settlement regime.[189] Announcing this intention without any invitation to exchange views would appear to negate the purpose of Article 283 and fall short of meeting its requirements. Nonetheless, these actions have been considered sufficient in the provisional measures proceedings of the *Arctic Sunrise* and *Louisa*, despite reservations from dissenting judges.[190]

[180] See *Southern Bluefin Tuna*, Provisional Measures (n 23) para 60; *MOX Plant*, Provisional Measures (n 45) para 60; *Louisa*, Provisional Measures (n 32) para 63; *Detention of Three Ukrainian Naval Vessels (Ukraine v Russia)* (Provisional Measures Order of 25 May 2019) ITLOS Case No 26 (*Detention of Three Ukrainian Naval Vessels*, Provisional Measures) para 87.

[181] See *Arctic Sunrise (Netherlands v Russia)* (Provisional Measures, Order of 22 November 2013) ITLOS Reports 2013, 230 (*Arctic Sunrise*, Provisional Measures) (Dissenting Opinion of Judge Golitsyn) paras 9–12, 14.

[182] *Arctic Sunrise*, Merits (n 173) para 154.

[183] ibid para 153.

[184] *Detention of Three Ukrainian Naval Vessels*, Provisional Measures (n 180) para 81.

[185] ibid para 86.

[186] ibid para 82.

[187] ibid para 85.

[188] ibid para 89.

[189] See eg *Arctic Sunrise*, Provisional Measures (n 181) (Dissenting Opinion of Judge Golitsyn) para 12; *Louisa*, Provisional Measures (n 32) (Dissenting Opinion of Judge Wolfrum) para 28.

[190] See eg *Louisa*, Provisional Measures (n 32) (Dissenting Opinion of Judge Wolfrum) para 28, (Dissenting Opinion of Judge Treves) para 12 (both voicing concern that art 283 had been rendered meaningless as a result). The issue was not revisited at the merits stage of the proceedings, as ITLOS concluded that it lacked jurisdiction on

Moreover, ITLOS has consistently held that it is for the applicant State to determine when efforts under Article 283 are satisfactory. It has stated, and reiterated, that a party is not required to continue efforts to exchange views when it concludes the possibility of reaching agreement have been exhausted.[191] Thus, in the provisional measures stage of *Land Reclamation by Singapore in and around the Straits of Johor* (*Land Reclamation*), ITLOS determined that Malaysia had met the requirements under Article 283 when 'it concluded that this exchange could not yield a positive result'.[192] Judge Chandrasekhara Rao did question this approach in *Land Reclamation*, noting:

> The requirement of this article regarding exchange of views is not an empty formality, to be dispensed with at the whims of a disputant. The obligation in this regard must be discharged in good faith, and it is the duty of the Tribunal to examine whether this is being done.[193]

There nonetheless appears to have been a steady regression away from holding States to account with regard to efforts to resolve their disputes peacefully prior to the institution of arbitration or adjudication.

The relevance of Article 283 was further minimised when the *Barbados v Trinidad and Tobago* Tribunal considered its application in relation to the requirement on States to seek agreement in the delimitation of their overlapping maritime zones under Articles 74 and 83 of UNCLOS.[194] The Tribunal considered that the obligation to seek agreement 'subsumed' any 'negotiation' requirement in Article 283.[195] No other maritime delimitation case to date under UNCLOS has found that the requirements of Article 283 have not been met, but it could typically be assumed that the requirements of Article 283 have been met if States have fulfilled their obligations under Articles 74 and 83 in seeking agreement on a maritime boundary prior to resorting to compulsory arbitration or adjudication.

Overall, the threshold established under Article 283 is low on any interpretation that we now have of the provision. This situation has emerged despite admonitions on occasions from judges not to devoid the requirements of Article 283 of any content. For example, Judge Wolfrum in *Louisa* considered the application of Article 283 in that case had rendered the requirement 'meaningless' because of the lack of exchange of views on the facts presented.[196] A central purpose associated with Article 283 is to ensure that the other party is aware of the issues in dispute and so not taken by surprise with the institution of

the basis that there was no dispute arising on the facts that related to the interpretation or application of UNCLOS. See *Louisa*, Judgment (n 2) para 152.

[191] *MOX Plant*, Provisional Measures (n 45) para 60; *Land Reclamation*, Provisional Measures (n 42) paras 47–48; *Southern Bluefin Tuna*, Provisional Measures (n 23) para 60; *Louisa*, Provisional Measures (n 32) paras 60–61; *ARA Libertad* (n 64) para 69; *M/T San Padre Pio (Switzerland v Nigeria)* (Provisional Measures, Order of 6 July 2019) ITLOS Case No 27, para 73 (*San Padre Pio*, Provisional Measures).

[192] *Land Reclamation*, Provisional Measures (n 42) para 48. See also *Detention of Three Ukrainian Naval Vessels*, Provisional Measures (n 180) para 87 (and sources cited therein).

[193] *Land Reclamation*, Provisional Measures (n 42) (Separate Opinion of Judge Chandrasekhara Rao) para 11.

[194] *Barbados v Trinidad and Tobago* (n 40) paras 201–205.

[195] ibid para 202.

[196] *Louisa*, Provisional Measures (n 32) (Dissenting Opinion of Judge Wolfrum) para 28. See also *Louisa*, Provisional Measures (n 32) (Dissenting Opinion of Judge Treves) paras 10–13; *Arctic Sunrise*, Provisional Measures (n 181) (Dissenting Opinion of Judge Golitsyn) paras 13–14.

compulsory dispute settlement proceedings.[197] Arguably, the notification of the existence of a dispute and a desire to resolve the dispute could be formulated in diverse ways.[198] As to when or whether specific provisions of UNCLOS must be referenced, the reality of international practice is that UNCLOS will often be cited in the context of affirming a State's legal position. It would normally be expected that States refer to the means of resolving disputes as well as the substance of the dispute when exchanging views on an issue that has arisen between them.[199] The progressive understanding of Article 283 indicates that the requirement to exchange views will not usually prove too difficult for a State to establish once it reaches the point that it decides to institute arbitration or adjudication.[200]

Churchill has observed that Article 286 allows for recourse to compulsory arbitration or adjudication only where 'no settlement has been reached by recourse to section 1' and that the process required under Article 283 is not enough in its own right to determine if this jurisdictional hurdle is met.[201] Instead, judicial bodies are 'to appraise what efforts the parties have made to settle the dispute by using the consensual means set out in section 1 of Part XV, and if no meaningful efforts have been made, to decline jurisdiction'.[202] Churchill's argument thus suggests an assessment at the efforts of peaceful resolution of the dispute through other means is required to establish jurisdiction for arbitration or adjudication. This interpretation is not akin to an obligation to negotiate,[203] but would resonate with Article 300 arguments concerning good faith and not taking action that amounts to an abuse of rights.

With the lowering of the threshold of Article 283 as a barrier to jurisdiction, future respondents that consider disputes submitted prematurely to adjudication or arbitration may instead pursue this line of argument based on Article 286. Judges responding to this argument will need to decide carefully if interests in the peaceful resolution of disputes are best served through prompt adjudication of disputes or if other means of dispute settlement should be equally respected as potentially serving a valid purpose in ocean governance. At present, the emphasis has been on proceeding to arbitration or adjudication rather than trusting other dispute settlement methods to achieve overarching goals related to the peaceful settlement of disputes, public order of the oceans, and the rule of law. Perhaps the perception is that these goals can only be achieved with judicial intervention rather than other stakeholders determining outcomes that they believe meet these objectives.

197 *South China Sea*, Jurisdiction and Admissibility (n 2) para 343; *Arctic Sunrise*, Provisional Measures (n 181) (Declaration of Judge ad hoc Anderson) para 3.

198 For example, Judge Kittichaisaree observed that Ukraine had circulated and eventually ensured the adoption of a General Assembly resolution regarding the Russian detention of its naval vessels and servicemen. As such, Russia was well aware of the dispute between them. See *Detention of Three Ukrainian Naval Vessels*, Provisional Measures (n 180) (Separate Opinion of Judge Kittichaisaree) para 16.

199 *South China Sea*, Jurisdiction and Admissibility (n 2) para 332.

200 Talmon goes so far as to suggest that it seems 'highly unlikely' that art 283 will ever prevent recourse to compulsory dispute settlement procedures. See Stefan Talmon, 'The Chagos Marine Protected Area Arbitration: Expansion of the Jurisdiction of UNCLOS Part XV Courts and Tribunals' (2016) 65 ICLQ 927, 932.

201 Churchill, 'General Dispute Settlement System' (n 102) 222.

202 ibid.

203 Which is not the purport of art 283 of UNCLOS. *Chagos MPA* (n 10) para 378. See also Andrew Serdy, 'Article 283' in *Proelss Commentary* (n 44) 1831, para 10.

III. Admissibility

While questions of jurisdiction address whether a tribunal can entertain a case, questions of admissibility concern whether a tribunal *should* examine the merits of a case.[204] A variety of objections may be presented in this regard and standards have developed in judicial practice to address certain of these claims. Rosenne has described the judicial task of determining objections to admissibility in the following terms:

> It may import an element of discretion that has to be exercised not whimsically but strictly in accordance with legal criteria having regard to the place of judicial settlement of international disputes in the conduct of international affairs, the manner in which an international court or tribunal works, and how it obtains its authority to decide a case.[205]

Issues of admissibility are typically to be assessed at the date that an application is submitted to institute proceedings under UNCLOS. There are some situations, however, where a change in circumstances may prompt a reassessment of the admissibility of an application, especially if it would render the application without object.[206]

A. Standing

Respondent States may challenge whether a claimant State has the authority to present a claim on behalf of a particular vessel. In this context, one State may argue that a flag State may not raise claims in relation to a vessel because of a lack of a 'genuine link'.[207] This challenge prompts the question of whether a State may grant its nationality to a vessel in the absence of a genuine link to that vessel.[208] Once a ship is registered in or flying the flag of a particular State, that State must exercise effective jurisdiction and control over the vessel.[209] The UNCLOS decisions on vessel nationality are discussed further in Chapter 7.

For standing purposes, the question is if a State grants nationality to a vessel without a genuine link or fails to exercise effective jurisdiction and control over its vessel, may it still assert claims of international law violations in relation to that vessel? This question was raised by Guinea Bissau in *Virginia G*, but ITLOS concluded that Panama had a genuine link to the vessel so did not need to answer this question of admissibility.[210] This argument

[204] The ICJ has described admissibility in this regard as follows: 'Objections to admissibility normally take the form of an assertion that, even if the Court has jurisdiction and the facts stated by the applicant State are assumed to be correct, nonetheless there are reasons why the Court should not proceed to an examination of the merits'. See *Oil Platforms* (*Iran v United States*) (Merits) [2003] ICJ Rep 161, para 29. See also Gerald Fitzmaurice, 'The Law and Procedure of the International Court of Justice, 1951-54: Questions of Jurisdiction, Competence and Procedure' (1958) 34 BYIL 1, 12–13.

[205] Rosenne, 'Inter-State Applications' (n 6) para 2.

[206] See *Hoshinmaru (Japan v Russia)* (Prompt Release, Judgment) ITLOS Reports 2005–2007, 18, para 64 (*Hoshinmaru*). An application without object is discussed below. This position is consistent with the jurisprudence of the ICJ. See eg *Nuclear Tests* (*Australia v France*) (Judgment) [1974] ICJ Rep 253, para 62.

[207] UNCLOS (n 1) art 91(1) provides: 'Every State shall fix the conditions for the grant of its nationality to ships, for the registration of ships in its territory, and for the right to fly its flag. Ships have the nationality of the State whose flag they are entitled to fly. There must exist a genuine link between the State and the ship.' See further ch 7. See eg *Virginia G*, Judgment (n 19) para 102; *Saiga No 2*, Judgment (n 18) para 75.

[208] *Virginia G*, Judgment (n 19) para 107.

[209] UNCLOS (n 1) art 94.

[210] *Virginia G*, Judgment (n 19) paras 117–18.

also emerged in the *Norstar* case, where Italy argued that the vessel was neither owned, fitted out, nor rented by any Panamanian national and the criminal proceedings that had prompted the seizure of the M/V Norstar were not directed at a Panamanian national.[211] However, ITLOS rejected that submission.[212] In any event, ITLOS considered in the *M/V Saiga (No 2)* that the criterion of the genuine link was 'not to establish criteria by reference to which the validity of the registration of ships in a flag State may be challenged by other States'.[213] Guinea therefore had no basis for refusing to recognise the right of the M/V Saiga to fly the flag of Saint Vincent and the Grenadines.[214] The prominent place of the flag State has thus been affirmed in these decisions, thereby closing off an avenue to challenge the open registration industry that allows ship owners to select their preferred level of regulation among different States.

The operation of national laws in law enforcement operations may have implications for standing. In particular, if the vessel is confiscated, does its nationality change for the purposes of the flag State instituting proceedings under Part XV of UNCLOS? Confiscation may affect the status of the ownership of the vessel, but ITLOS found in the *Juno Trader* that in the circumstances of that case there had been no change in the nationality of the concerned vessel.[215] In the *Tomimaru* case, Russia argued that the change in ownership of the vessel by virtue of its confiscation rendered the prompt release application without object.[216] The Tribunal considered that confiscation could not prevent the Tribunal from considering a prompt release application under the Convention while the domestic proceedings were still going ahead.[217] However, once the procedures before the domestic courts ended, an order from ITLOS to release the vessel upon payment of a reasonable bond would run contrary to the requirement that the prompt release proceedings not prejudice the merits of those domestic procedures.[218] It would only be in the context that standards of international due process had not been met, or the confiscation was undertaken in such a way as to thwart recourse to seek release of the vessel, that any further consideration could be accorded to the release of the vessel.[219] Neither of those conditions pertained in the *Tomimaru* case and consequently the application was considered to be without object. As the domestic proceedings had concluded, ITLOS has not yet had occasion to consider an Article 292 claim where a vessel's nationality was forcibly changed to the respondent State upon the arrest and detention of the vessel. As such a measure would seemingly frustrate the operation of Article 292, it is unlikely to be recognised as valid by ITLOS.

Standing questions also emerge when a State seeks to act on behalf of crew or other individuals on vessels that are detained. ITLOS has held in the *M/V Saiga (No 2)*, the *Virginia G*,

[211] *Norstar*, Preliminary Objections (n 22) para 224.

[212] ibid para 231.

[213] *Saiga No 2*, Judgment (n 18) para 83.

[214] ibid para 86.

[215] *Juno Trader (Saint Vincent and the Grenadines v Guinea-Bissau)* (Prompt Release, Judgment) ITLOS Reports 2004, 17, para 63 (*Juno Trader*). The Tribunal clearly leaves open the possibility that different facts would demonstrate that the confiscation not only changed ownership but also nationality of the vessel. Seemingly, the requirements for registering or flagging the vessel under the domestic law would have to be met for a definitive change of nationality. See further (Joint Separate Opinions of Judges Mensah and Wolfrum) paras 9–11, (Separate Opinion of Judge Ndiaye) paras 28–29. See also discussion in ch 7.

[216] *Tomimaru (Japan v Russia)* (Prompt Release, Judgment) ITLOS Reports 2005–2007, 74, para 50 (*Tomimaru*). This argument was also made in *Grand Prince* (n 9) para 65.

[217] *Tomimaru* (n 216) para 78.

[218] ibid para 80.

[219] ibid para 79.

and the *Norstar* cases that the flag State must be considered as the representative of the ship as a unit, which includes all persons 'involved or interested in its operations' and all things on the ship.[220] The same holding was made by an Annex VII Tribunal in the *Duzgit Integrity* arbitration.[221] This position pertains irrespective of the nationalities of the various individuals associated with the ship. In this situation, the flag State may take up an international claim on behalf of the ship and all entities connected to the ship.

This view is consistent with the International Law Commission (ILC) Draft Articles on Diplomatic Protection that provide in Article 18:

> The right of the State of nationality of the members of the crew of a ship to exercise diplomatic protection is not affected by the right of the State of nationality of a ship to seek redress on behalf of such crew members, irrespective of their nationality, when they have been injured in connection with an injury to the vessel resulting from an internationally wrongful act.[222]

The ILC recognised that there were strong policy reasons to support such an approach, as had been recognised in *M/V Saiga (No 2)*, including a practical element that on ships that have crew from a number of different countries, it could not be realistically expected that each State of nationality would pursue a claim on behalf of each crew member.[223] This right of the flag State to take up claims on behalf of crew members when there is an injury to the vessel is not diplomatic protection, but the State of nationality of the crew member still holds that right of diplomatic protection. The exercise of the latter right may be important in situations where the flag State has failed to take steps to exercise effective control over its vessels that result in harm, injury, or potentially human rights violations in relation to the individuals on board the vessel.[224]

One difficulty with the ship-as-unit concept emerged in the *Arctic Sunrise* provisional measures order where ITLOS was asked to prescribe a measure releasing all crew of the vessel from detention in Russia, even though some crew members were Russian nationals. The order to release the vessel and all of its crew conformed to the ship-as-unit approach, but some judges queried whether the ship-as-unit theory should override the link of nationality that otherwise exists between the detaining State and its citizens.[225]

A further complication that arose in the *Arctic Sunrise* Annex VII proceedings was that not all persons on board were crew members as would normally be the situation on a fishing or cargo vessel or warship. This situation raised the question as to whether all the individuals would still be part of the ship-as-unit. The Netherlands argued that those on board were all 'interested' and 'involved' in the operation of the vessel.[226] The Annex VII Tribunal accepted this argument, noting that '[e]ven if some did not engage directly in the functioning

[220] *Saiga No 2*, Judgment (n 18) para 106; *Virginia G*, Judgment (n 19) para 126; *Norstar*, Preliminary Objections (n 22) para 230.

[221] *Duzgit Integrity* (n 168) para 150.

[222] International Law Commission, 'Draft Articles on Diplomatic Protection with Commentaries' (2006) 2(2) UNYBILC 26, 52 (Article 18) ('Draft Articles on Diplomatic Protection').

[223] ibid 53 (commentary to art 18, para 7).

[224] ibid 53 (commentary to art 18, para 8).

[225] See eg *Arctic Sunrise*, Provisional Measures (n 181) (Separate Opinion of Judge Jesus) para 20 (describing it as 'over-stretching' the ship-as-unit concept).

[226] *Arctic Sunrise*, Merits (n 173) para 161.

of the vessel as would a crewmember, they were all closely involved or interested in the ship's campaigning operations for Greenpeace through protest at sea'.[227]

To date, the decisions on standing have indicated that a flag State must demonstrate that a vessel is duly registered under its authority and a wide factual investigation may ensue if there are doubts raised in this regard. Once that registration is demonstrated, it may not be challenged by reference to any standard of 'genuine link'. In this respect, judges have indicated that they will not interpose themselves in complex questions relating to shipping registration and the oversight of that system. Due recognition of the position of the flag State is further underlined by the ship-as-unit concept, allowing the flag State to act for individuals on board its vessel. Where the flag State is acting to protect the rights of those on board, this approach aligns with considerations of humanity. So far, there have not been cases under the UNCLOS dispute settlement regime that have challenged the flag State's lack of protection of individuals on board a vessel. Presumably, considerations of humanity should not permit the ship-as-unit construct to shield a flag State from responsibility.[228]

B. Exhaustion of Local Remedies

In accordance with Article 295 of UNCLOS, a dispute may only be subjected to compulsory dispute settlement under Part XV 'after local remedies have been exhausted where this is required by international law'.[229] International law requires local remedies to be exhausted before a State may assert an international claim for injury caused to one of its nationals (or vessels) on the basis of diplomatic protection. This rule does not apply in relation to direct injuries to the State. Where there are injuries to individuals as well as to the State, a tribunal must assess whether the claims are preponderantly based on an injury to a person or preponderantly based on an injury to the State. If the former, local remedies must be exhausted for the claim to be admissible.[230]

An issue that has emerged in relation to the requirement to exhaust local remedies has been where a flag State has sought to challenge the treatment of a vessel flying its flag in arrest, detention, and/or seizure scenarios. In this situation, is the flag State exercising a right of diplomatic protection on behalf of the vessel and all entities associated with the ship-as-unit, or is the flag State preponderantly claiming its own rights have been violated? In determining whether a claim is preponderantly that of the flag State, a tribunal must look to the subject of the dispute, the nature of the dispute and remedy claimed.[231] In some instances, this assessment may necessitate a determination of this plea once the merits of the case have been fully argued.[232]

[227] ibid para 171.

[228] Which would be clear if the State of nationality was making a claim on behalf of individuals on board a ship who had been mistreated in the absence of flag State effective control, but would it be so clear if another State party brought a claim under art 94 of UNCLOS for non-nationals on board a flag State's ship? If there is a direct injury to another State party then standing can be established, but what if the injury is indirect or there is a failure of due diligence? Does the flag State owe obligations *erga omnes* in this situation? These questions are presently speculative.

[229] UNCLOS (n 1) art 295.

[230] See ILC, 'Draft Articles on Diplomatic Protection' (n 222) art 14(3).

[231] ibid 45–46.

[232] *Norstar*, Preliminary Objections (n 22) (Declaration of Judge Cot) para 9.

In *M/V Saiga (No 2)*, the Tribunal had distinguished between breaches of obligations owed in relation to the treatment of aliens as compared to direct violations of obligations owed to the flag State.[233] ITLOS has recognised that where an infringement of the enjoyment of rights on the high seas or in the exclusive economic zone (EEZ) occurs, the claim as a whole is an injury to the flag State.[234] The freedom of the high seas is clearly designated as one belonging to States even though by necessity it is enjoyed by natural or juridical persons.[235] This view was also maintained in *Virginia G*.[236] Individual judges have criticised the assessment of the nature of these claims on the basis that it renders Article 295 devoid of any meaning in excessively relying on the direct injury to the State.[237]

Questions have occasionally emerged as to the intersection between the rule of exhaustion of local remedies and the prompt release proceedings under Article 292.[238] Under Article 292(3), the Tribunal hearing applications under that provision 'shall deal only with the question of release, without prejudice to the merits of any case before the appropriate domestic forum against the vessel, its owner or its crew'. ITLOS has considered this dynamic in its prompt release proceedings, and determined that the domestic proceedings will count as facts and circumstances of which they should take account in assessing the reasonableness of any bond.[239] If an appeal is before a domestic court as to the reasonableness of a bond and the release of the vessel, there has been a perceived risk that the Article 292 proceedings are duplicative and potentially creates a situation of *lis pendens*.[240] However, ITLOS has denied the possibility of reading Article 295 into Article 292 proceedings.[241] Such a requirement would unduly lengthen the prompt release proceedings and undercut their core purpose.[242]

[233] *Saiga No 2*, Judgment (n 18) para 98.

[234] *Virginia G*, Judgment (n 19) para 157; *Norstar*, Preliminary Objections (n 22) para 270.

[235] See *Norstar*, Preliminary Objections (n 22) (Declaration of Judge Heidar) para 7.

[236] *Virginia G*, Judgment (n 19) paras 156–58.

[237] See *Norstar*, Preliminary Objections (n 22) (Declaration of Judge Cot) para 5; *Norstar*, Preliminary Objections (n 22) (Dissenting Opinion of Judge ad hoc Treves) para 20 ('Following this approach, mixed cases to which the preponderance test may apply would never exist. The practical effect would be to eliminate or drastically reduce the relevance of article 295. Such effect would obviously be contrary to the Convention and prejudice the wisely crafted relationship between domestic and international law it represents.') See also *Virginia G*, Judgment (n 19) (Joint Separate Opinions of Judge Cot and Judge Kelly) para 14, (Joint Separate Opinions of Judge Cot and Judge Kelly) para 28.

[238] See Klein, *Dispute Settlement* (n 62) 101–103; see further ch 8(IV)(E). It has further been underlined by ITLOS that art 292 proceedings are not an avenue of appeal but a distinct procedure in their own right. See eg *Camouco (Panama v France)* (Prompt Release, Judgment) ITLOS Reports 2000, 10, para 58 (*Camouco*).

[239] See eg *Monte Confurco (Seychelles v France)* (Prompt Release, Judgment) ITLOS Reports 2000, 86, para 74 (*Monte Confurco*).

[240] *Camouco* (n 238) para 55. See further *Camouco* (n 238) (Dissenting Opinion of Judge Vukas) para 7.

[241] *Camouco* (n 238) para 57. But see *Camouco* (n 238) (Dissenting Opinion of Judge Anderson) 2. Churchill has observed that prompt release proceedings cannot be considered as tantamount to the traditional exercise of diplomatic protection as a result of the inapplicability of the requirement to exhaust local remedies. See Robin Churchill, 'Trends in Dispute Settlement in the Law of the Sea: Towards the Increasing Availability of Compulsory Means' in Duncan French, Matthew Saul and Nigel D White (eds), *International Law and Dispute Settlement: New Problems and Techniques* (Hart Publishing 2010) 153 (Churchill, 'Trends in Dispute Settlement').

[242] Seline Trevisanut, 'Twenty Years of Prompt Release of Vessels: Admissibility, Jurisdiction, and Recent Trends' (2017) 48 ODIL 300, 301. This approach aligns with the views of those drafting UNCLOS. See Karaman (n 66) 70–71.

C. Third Parties as Indispensable Parties

In bilateral disputes before international courts or tribunals, a respondent State may challenge the resolution of a particular claim on the basis that in doing so, the court or tribunal must also assess the international responsibility of another State that is not before that court or tribunal.[243] In that situation, the interests of the third party form the very subject matter of the dispute and cannot be adjudicated upon in the absence of consent of that third party. The ICJ articulated this 'indispensable party' principle in *Monetary Gold*,[244] and further refined its application in *East Timor*.[245] In the latter case, the ICJ clarified that the indispensable party principle would apply where the international responsibility of another State had to be determined prior to any assessment of the lawfulness of the conduct of the respondent State.[246] The underlying rationale for this principle is based on the consent of States to international adjudication or arbitration and that no State should be judged on the lawfulness of its actions in the absence of that consent.[247] Whether the principle is entirely apposite in the setting of UNCLOS Part XV may be questioned as an absent State party to UNCLOS has in fact consented to the exercise of jurisdiction. The situation would be different for a State that was not party to UNCLOS.

This issue arose in *Norstar*, as Italy had issued an order for the seizure of the M/V Norstar in connection with criminal proceedings underway in Italy, which was executed by Spanish authorities in Spain's internal waters at the request of Italy. Italy argued that as Panama challenged the legality of the arrest and detention of the M/V Norstar, any determination would necessarily involve an assessment of the lawfulness of Spain's conduct.[248] However, the Tribunal found that Spain's involvement was limited to the execution of Italy's request for the seizure of the vessel and that it was the interests of Italy that formed the very subject matter of the dispute; no prior determination of the responsibility of Spain was required.[249]

In *Mauritius/Maldives*, the question of indispensable third parties arose when the Maldives argued that the United Kingdom was an indispensable party because of its continued assertion of sovereignty over the Chagos Archipelago. Mauritius and the Maldives only had overlapping maritime entitlements requiring delimitation due to the presence of the Chagos Archipelago. However, at the time of this case, Mauritius argued that the United Kingdom could no longer assert sovereignty over the Chagos Archipelago in light of the ICJ's *Chagos Advisory Opinion*.[250] In that Advisory Opinion, the ICJ stated that the process of decolonisation of Mauritius was not lawfully completed with the separation of the Chagos Archipelago and the United Kingdom was required to bring its administration of the Chagos Archipelago to an end as rapidly as possible.[251] However, the United

[243] This claim is considered in some instances to go to a question of jurisdiction. See eg *Norstar*, Preliminary Objections (n 22).

[244] *Monetary Gold Removed from Rome in 1943* (Judgment) [1954] ICJ Rep 19, 33.

[245] *East Timor* (*Portugal v Australia*) (Judgment) [1995] ICJ Rep 90 (*East Timor*). See also *Certain Phosphate Lands in Nauru (Nauru v Australia)* (Preliminary Objections) [1992] ICJ Rep 240, paras 49–55 (*Certain Phosphate Lands in Nauru*).

[246] *East Timor* (n 245) para 29.

[247] See ibid paras 26, 34.

[248] *Norstar*, Preliminary Objections (n 22) paras 144–46.

[249] ibid para 173.

[250] *Legal Consequences of the Separation of the Chagos Archipelago from Mauritius in 1965* (Advisory Opinion) [2019] ICJ Rep 95 (*Chagos Advisory Opinion*).

[251] ibid para 183.

Kingdom rejected the views of the ICJ and underlined the legally non-binding nature of the opinion.[252] The United Kingdom maintained that it continued to exercise sovereignty over the Chagos Archipelago.[253] In *Mauritius/Maldives*, the key point for the Maldives in relation to indispensable third parties was that the ITLOS Special Chamber constituted to hear the case would be compelled to resolve the ongoing sovereignty dispute between the United Kingdom and Mauritius to be able to proceed to the maritime boundary delimitation,[254] as the sovereignty dispute was clearly ongoing.[255]

Mauritius argued that the *Monetary Gold* principle could not apply in a situation where a third party has no rights,[256] underlining that the ICJ had 'determined' that the United Kingdom did not have any sovereignty or sovereign rights in respect of the Chagos Archipelago.[257] The Special Chamber confirmed the potential applicability of the *Monetary Gold* principles in its jurisprudence.[258] For present purposes, the Special Chamber identified the central issue between the parties to turn on the question as to whether the sovereignty dispute between the Mauritius and the United Kingdom continued to exist or was resolved.[259] The Special Chamber ultimately found that Mauritius' sovereignty over the Chagos Archipelago could be inferred from the ICJ's determinations in the *Chagos Advisory Opinion*.[260] Gaver has noted that '[t]he Special Chamber did not decide on the issue of sovereignty so much as observe that the preceding developments vitiated the UK's claim to the islands'.[261] As such, the United Kingdom could not be considered to have any legal interests when it was engaging in a continuing wrongful act that it had failed to bring to a conclusion as required.[262]

Finally, this challenge to admissibility was briefly considered in the *South China Sea* arbitration in light of the fact that Viet Nam 'and/or others' also claimed territorial sovereignty over some of the maritime features for which the Philippines sought a determination as regards their maritime entitlement.[263] Viet Nam provided a statement to the Tribunal that reflected its views on questions of jurisdiction and raised the spectre of intervening in the arbitration.[264] As the Tribunal did not have to resolve any questions of territorial sovereignty in the case submitted by the Philippines, Viet Nam was not an indispensable third party; its rights and obligations did not have to be ascertained prior to resolving the dispute before the Tribunal.[265] The issue as to whether a State may be allowed to intervene in proceedings before an Annex VII Tribunal remains to be determined, but it would seemingly

[252] UK Foreign and Commonwealth Office, 'Statement and Explanation of Vote on the Resolution on the British Indian Ocean Territory by Ambassador Karen Pierce, UK Permanent Representative to the UN' (21 June 2019) https://www.gov.uk/government/speeches/resolution-on-the-british-indian-ocean-territory.

[253] *Mauritius/Maldives*, Preliminary Objections (n 25) paras 73, 76, 77.

[254] ibid para 83.

[255] ibid paras 85–86.

[256] ibid para 90.

[257] ibid para 93.

[258] ibid para 97.

[259] ibid para 98.

[260] ibid para 246.

[261] Craig D Gaver, 'Dispute Concerning Delimitation of the Maritime Boundary between Mauritius and Maldives in the Indian Ocean (Mauritius/Maldives)' (2021) 115(3) AJIL 519, 524.

[262] *Mauritius/Maldives*, Preliminary Objections (n 25) para 247.

[263] *South China Sea*, Jurisdiction and Admissibility (n 2) para 179.

[264] See ibid paras 182–86. China voiced its opposition to intervention by other States as contrary to the practice of international arbitration: see para 185. Viet Nam did not ultimately seek to intervene, and so no formal decision was necessary as a result: see para 186.

[265] ibid para 180.

be permissible in light of the possibility of intervention before other fora available under Article 287 and could be supported by the implied powers of arbitral tribunals.[266]

D. Other Claims of Inadmissibility

There are diverse claims of inadmissibility that may be presented in any given case. This section focuses on those arguments that have emerged more frequently in UNCLOS jurisprudence and considers estoppel and acquiescence; good faith and clean hands; and mootness. It finally addresses the specific situation of the Commission on the Limits of the Continental Shelf (CLCS), which is discussed further in Chapter 6 in the context of the maritime boundary delimitation case law.

1. Estoppel and Acquiescence

In *Norstar*, Italy alleged that Panama's case was inadmissible on the bases of acquiescence, estoppel, and extinctive prescription, which are all general principles of law.[267] Italy relied particularly on the delays in Panama's institution of proceedings under UNCLOS, as the M/V Norstar had been seized over eighteen years earlier.[268] Panama denied the applicability of these principles to the proceedings, rather than denying them as bars to admissibility.[269] ITLOS examined acquiescence as 'equivalent to tacit recognition manifested by unilateral conduct which the other party may interpret as consent',[270] but considered it was not established on the facts.[271] Similarly, extinctive prescription could not be established on the facts,[272] as the timeframes allowed under international law for the submission of claims to international proceedings are generous,[273] and ITLOS supported the view of the ILC that once a claim has been notified, delay in its prosecution will not usually render the claim inadmissible.[274]

Estoppel has been considered in several UNCLOS cases. The elements are drawn from the case law of the ICJ and are comprised of a representation by one State upon which another State has relied to its detriment.[275] While a potential bar to the admissibility of a claim in the *Norstar* case, the doctrine was not established on the facts.[276] The *South China Sea* Tribunal considered the possibility that a series of political agreements adopted as between

[266] Which led to the Iran–US Claims Tribunal issuing provisional measures: *E-Systems Inc v Iran (Award No ITM 13-388-FT)* (1983) 2 Iran–US CTR 51, 57. See also Chester Brown, 'Inherent Powers in International Adjudication' in Cesare PR Romano, Karen J Alter and Yuval Shany (eds), *The Oxford Handbook of International Adjudication* (OUP 2014) 834–37.

[267] *Norstar*, Preliminary Objections (n 22) para 274.

[268] ibid para 275.

[269] ibid para 302. Panama did raise what appeared to be a passing argument that these principles were relevant to an assessment of the merits of the claim, but ITLOS considered that they had not been adequately substantiated as such and could be determined as objections to the admissibility of the claims: see para 300.

[270] ibid para 303, citing *Delimitation of the Maritime Boundary in the Gulf of Maine Area (Canada v United States)* (Merits) [1984] ICJ Rep 246, para 130.

[271] *Norstar*, Preliminary Objections (n 22) paras 304–305.

[272] ibid para 313.

[273] As seen in *Certain Phosphate Lands in Nauru* (n 245) para 32.

[274] *Norstar*, Preliminary Objections (n 22) para 310, citing International Law Commission, 'Draft Articles on Responsibility of States for Internationally Wrongful Acts with Commentaries' (2001) 2(2) UNYBILC 31, 123 (commentary art 45, para 10).

[275] *Norstar*, Preliminary Objections (n 22) para 307; *Bay of Bengal Delimitation* (n 18) para 124.

[276] *Norstar*, Preliminary Objections (n 22) para 308.

the Philippines and China that referred to the resolution of their differences through negotiations could estop the Philippines from resorting to compulsory arbitration.[277] However, the Philippines had never made any representation that it would not resort to compulsory procedures and estoppel was thus not established.[278] In the *ARA Libertad* provisional measures proceedings, Judges Wolfrum and Cot suggested that estoppel could be the basis for establishing *prima facie* jurisdiction, as Ghana had provided assurances regarding the visit of the Argentine vessel to its port.[279]

In *M/V Saiga (No 2)*, ITLOS not only considered whether the nationality of the vessel could be established on the basis of the facts as Saint Vincent and the Grenadines presented, but also looked to the conduct of Guinea in determining its position vis-à-vis the nationality of the M/V Saiga. In this regard, the Tribunal noted that Guinea had failed to question Saint Vincent and the Grenadines' right to assert the claim 'when it had every reasonable opportunity to do so'.[280] Judge Wolfrum considered in more detail the use of estoppel and acquiescence as bases for denying Guinea's challenge to the right of Saint Vincent and the Grenadines to act as flag State.[281] Although the Tribunal did not explicitly address these doctrines, ITLOS also commented that the consistent behaviour of Saint Vincent and the Grenadines further demonstrated its authority as the flag State.[282] This specific position of the Tribunal was validly criticised in the dissenting opinion of Judge Warioba, who queried the idea that matters of nationality of vessels could be determined on the basis of a State's conduct.[283]

Estoppel has otherwise been addressed as part of the claims of UNCLOS violations.[284] For example, Ghana argued that Côte d'Ivoire was estopped from denying the applicability of a boundary based on an equidistance line in their maritime boundary dispute.[285] In the *Chagos MPA* arbitration, the Tribunal closely examined the requirements of estoppel and determined that the United Kingdom was estopped from denying the binding effect of commitments relating to the return of the Archipelago, the preservation of benefits of mineral resources, and fishing rights being available as far as practicable.[286] Ultimately, for the purposes of admissibility, each of these arguments is highly factual dependent, and the threshold for relying on acquiescence or estoppel to prevent a claim from proceeding is yet to be reached.

2. Good Faith and Clean Hands

Arguments of good faith have arisen in the context of Article 300, which requires State parties to 'fulfil in good faith the obligations assumed' under UNCLOS,[287] but also in the context of admissibility claims. For example, in *Guyana v Suriname*, each party challenged the

[277] *South China Sea*, Jurisdiction and Admissibility (n 2) para 249.
[278] ibid para 251.
[279] *ARA Libertad* (n 64) (Joint Separate Opinion of Judges Wolfrum and Cot) para 68.
[280] *Saiga No 2*, Judgment (n 18) para 73(c).
[281] ibid (Separate Opinion of Judge Wolfrum) paras 40–44. See also (Separate Opinion of Judge Chandrasekhara Rao) para 12.
[282] *Saiga No 2*, Judgment (n 18) para 73(b).
[283] ibid (Dissenting Opinion of Judge Warioba) paras 46–47.
[284] See eg *Bay of Bengal Delimitation* (n 18) paras 124–25.
[285] *Ghana/Côte d'Ivoire*, Judgment (n 9) para 230.
[286] *Chagos MPA* (n 10) para 448.
[287] UNCLOS (n 1) art 300, which also requires rights under the Convention to be exercised in a manner that would not constitute an abuse of right.

good faith and 'clean hands' of the other in relation to a maritime border incident where Surinamese officials threatened a Guyanese licensee undertaking exploratory work in a disputed maritime area. The doctrine of clean hands does not have a widely accepted definition and, although argued before the ICJ, has not yet been applied.[288] The *Guyana v Suriname* Tribunal considered that the doctrine, if it existed, would only be relevant to ongoing violations of reciprocal obligations under international law, which did not present on the facts of the case before it.[289]

3. Mootness

Parties have on occasions argued that the dispute between them has become moot when during the pendency of the proceedings, a change in the circumstances between the parties has, in the view of one of the parties, rendered a claim without object. As discussed in relation to standing to bring prompt release cases, ITLOS determined that the application for the release of the Tomimaru under Article 292 was without object because the domestic court proceedings had concluded and resulted in the confiscation of the vessel as a penalty for its unlawful fishing offences.[290] Russia also argued that a prompt release application became moot in *Hoshinmaru* because at the point the application was filed, no bond had been set but this step was then taken prior to the decision of the Tribunal.[291] Japan maintained, and ITLOS agreed, that there was still a dispute as to the reasonableness of the amount of bond in this case.[292]

In *Southern Bluefin Tuna*, Australia and New Zealand had instituted proceedings against Japan challenging, as noted previously, the institution of its experimental fishing programme in excess of the national allocation agreed between the parties. During the proceedings, Japan agreed to reduce the take to an amount previously proposed by Australia.[293] Japan therefore argued that the case between them was moot.[294] However, Australia and New Zealand advised the Annex VII Tribunal that the earlier proposal was no longer on offer and that they maintained concerns as to the method and design associated with the experimental fishing programme beyond the actual quantity of fish taken.[295] As such, the Tribunal agreed with Australia and New Zealand that their case was not moot given the ongoing differences of views in relation to the experimental fishing programme.[296]

4. Role of the Commission on the Limits of the Continental Shelf

As discussed further in Chapter 6, maritime boundary delimitation cases have addressed whether a Part XV tribunal should delimit the outer continental shelf in light of the role accorded to the CLCS under UNCLOS in assessing the outer limits of the continental shelf.[297] This question has also emerged in maritime boundary delimitation cases at the ICJ. For present purposes, it may be noted that the potentially conflicting roles of the CLCS and a

[288] See *Guyana v Suriname* (n 10) para 418 (referring to ICJ case law on this point). See eg *Certain Iranian Assets (Iran v US)* (Preliminary Objections) [2019] ICJ Rep 7, paras 116–24.
[289] *Guyana v Suriname* (n 10) para 421.
[290] See nn 216–19 and accompanying text.
[291] *Hoshinmaru* (n 206) para 62.
[292] ibid para 65.
[293] *Southern Bluefin Tuna*, Jurisdiction and Admissibility (n 13) para 45.
[294] ibid.
[295] ibid.
[296] ibid para 46.
[297] See UNCLOS (n 1) art 76.

tribunal resolving a maritime boundary case may reflect a challenge as to the scope of jurisdiction or the admissibility of the dispute. For example, in the *Bay of Bengal Delimitation*, Myanmar argued that ITLOS could exercise jurisdiction but did not consider it appropriate to do so.[298] In one of its submissions, Myanmar considered that the Tribunal should not determine a boundary on a hypothetical basis when it was not known what the CLCS would establish as the outer limits of the continental shelf.[299]

ITLOS differentiated between the respective roles of the Tribunal and the CLCS in the *Bay of Bengal Delimitation*, noting:

> Under [Article 76], the Commission is assigned the function of making recommendations to coastal States on matters relating to the establishment of the outer limits of the continental shelf, but it does so without prejudice to the delimitation of maritime boundaries. The function of settling disputes with respect to delimitation of maritime boundaries is entrusted to dispute settlement procedures under article 83 and Part XV of the Convention, which include international courts and tribunals.[300]

The Annex VII Tribunal constituted to resolve the *Bay of Bengal Arbitration* endorsed this position,[301] as did the ITLOS Special Chamber in *Ghana/Côte d'Ivoire*,[302] and the ICJ in *Delimitation of the Continental Shelf*.[303] In *Ghana/Côte d'Ivoire*, the CLCS had already issued recommendations on Ghana's outer continental shelf and Côte d'Ivoire had submitted its claims to the CLCS. For the Special Chamber, the CLCS view that Ghana was entitled to an outer continental shelf meant that Côte d'Ivoire also was because the geological situation was identical.[304] This conclusion was probably correct but still raises questions of possible interference with the work of the CLCS in stating there was 'no doubt' that an outer continental shelf exists.[305] In *Delimitation of the Continental Shelf*, the ICJ rejected Colombia's objection to jurisdiction on the basis that the CLCS had not made any recommendation, noting that the procedure before the CLCS concerns the delineation of the outer limits of the continental shelf, which is distinct from its delimitation.[306] Most recently, in its judgment on the merits in *Maritime Delimitation in the Indian Ocean*, the ICJ proceeded to delimit the outer continental shelf even in the absence of a high degree of certainty as to an entitlement beyond 200 NM.[307] As discussed further in Chapter 6, the ICJ's approach has been criticised by judges and commentators, and it remains to be seen whether its approach is followed in subsequent cases.

The goal for any tribunal in these circumstances must be ensuring that each of the institutions established under UNCLOS work in a coherent and complementary fashion to ensure

[298] *Bay of Bengal Delimitation* (n 18) para 342.

[299] ibid para 345. Myanmar also argued that any judicial pronouncement may prejudice the rights of third parties or rights in relation to the international seabed: see para 344.

[300] ibid para 376.

[301] ibid paras 76, 80–82.

[302] *Ghana/Côte d'Ivoire*, Judgment (n 9) para 493.

[303] *Delimitation of the Continental Shelf between Nicaragua and Colombia beyond 200 Nautical Miles from the Nicaraguan Coast (Nicaragua v Colombia)* (Preliminary Objections) [2016] ICJ Rep 100 (*Delimitation of the Continental Shelf*).

[304] *Ghana/Côte d'Ivoire*, Judgment (n 9) para 491.

[305] ibid.

[306] *Delimitation of the Continental Shelf* (n 303) paras 105–15.

[307] *Maritime Delimitation in the Indian Ocean (Somalia v Kenya)* (Judgment of 12 October 2021) General List No 161, para 194.

the efficient implementation of the Convention.[308] ITLOS in the *Bay of Bengal Delimitation* affirmed that the exercise of functions of ITLOS was to be without prejudice to the CLCS's exercise of functions, and vice versa.[309] Yet ITLOS still had to avoid a situation where the CLCS had deferred the exercise of its functions pending the resolution of the maritime boundary dispute and the Tribunal also refrained from exercising its functions pending the CLCS decision. To resolve this impasse, it was incumbent on ITLOS to resolve the dispute before it as well as thereby ensuring the effective implementation of the Convention.[310] It appears that the ICJ was motivated by similar considerations in reaching the same conclusion in *Delimitation of the Continental Shelf* and *Maritime Delimitation in the Indian Ocean.*

* * *

Consistent with the decisions relating to Section 1 of Part XV, admissibility claims have not been readily accepted to deny cases from proceeding before tribunals constituted under UNCLOS. The decisions on admissibility have often drawn from ICJ jurisprudence, which allows for greater consistency in the application of general principles of law. Questions of standing have held significance for the UNCLOS dispute settlement regime because they go to the relationship of flag States with their vessels and reconciling core rules regarding flag State duties with UNCLOS dispute settlement. While UNCLOS tribunals have not been drawn into any assessment of what constituted a 'genuine link' to determine the admissibility of a dispute, they have been willing to scrutinise adherence to national requirements and systems of registration. This position shows some deference to flag State authority over vessels but has not entirely removed third-party scrutiny from registration when proceedings are instituted under UNCLOS. Critics of deference to flag State authority and the use of open registries may well find this balance too weighted in favour of flag States; ongoing problems in this regard may prompt a shift in future perspectives to enhance future ocean governance.

IV. Incidental and Other Proceedings

Rosenne usefully described incidental jurisdiction in relation to the ICJ in the following way:

> [Incidental jurisdiction] comprises a series of miscellaneous and usually interlocutory matters that can arise during the conduct of a case. These include the power of the Court to decide a dispute as to its own jurisdiction in the case, its general power to control the proceedings, its power to indicate provisional measures of protection, its ability to consider request by third States to intervene in pending proceedings, and its ability to deal with counter-claims and with the discontinuance of a case. Although these different matters appear to have no connection with one another, common to them all is that their

[308] *Bay of Bengal Delimitation* (n 18) para 373.
[309] ibid para 379.
[310] ibid paras 391–92.

> parameters are fixed by the mainline proceedings, and that is what gives them their *incidental* character.[311]

One of the most common incidental proceedings in UNCLOS dispute settlement involves a request for provisional measures to be prescribed pending the result of an arbitration or adjudication. These measures are intended to restrain either or both parties from disrupting the existing situation so as to ensure that the final judgment will be effective.[312] As noted by Rosenne, applications for intervention also constitute incidental proceedings, and are anticipated under the Statute and Rules of ITLOS.[313] To date, no applications to intervene have been submitted, although it was contemplated in relation to indispensable third parties in the *South China Sea* arbitration, raising the question of whether intervention is permissible before an Annex VII tribunal.[314] Other proceedings, which are addressed in this section, are counter-claims and preliminary proceedings in accordance with Article 294 of the Convention.

The other main dispute settlement procedures that have so far arisen under Part XV of UNCLOS are prompt release proceedings. Trevisanut has described prompt release proceedings under Article 292 of the Convention as 'an autonomous procedure' as it is 'neither incidental nor prejudicial to the procedure on the merits before the national courts'.[315] As discussed in this section and in Chapter 7, Article 292 procedures were an important component in balancing coastal State and flag State rights in the EEZ.

Each of the proceedings discussed below form important adjuncts to the resolution of disputes arising under UNCLOS. Indeed, in some instances, the incidental or other proceedings have been enough in their own right to cause the resolution of the dispute. In other ways, it is evident that these procedures have important functions in safeguarding the rights of parties in dispute. As such, the interests at stake may be just as complex in incidental or other proceedings as they are in merits proceedings.

A. Provisional Measures

Article 290(1) of UNCLOS permits a court or tribunal with prima facie jurisdiction to prescribe provisional measures that are 'appropriate under the circumstances to preserve the respective rights of the parties to the dispute or to prevent serious harm to the marine environment, pending the final decision'. Measures may also be sought from ITLOS pending the constitution of an arbitral tribunal under the procedure in paragraph 5 of Article 290,[316] where the 'urgency of the situation' so requires.[317] If a State seeks provisional measures

[311] Shabtai Rosenne, *The World Court: What It Is and How It Works* (5th edn, Martinus Nijhoff 1995) 81 (emphasis in original).

[312] See JG Merrills, *International Dispute Settlement* (5th edn, CUP 2011) 124.

[313] UNCLOS (n 1) Annex VI, art 31; International Tribunal for the Law of the Sea, Rules of the Tribunal, Doc No ITLOS/8 (adopted 28 October 1997, amended 25 March 2021) art 99 (ITLOS Rules).

[314] See n 264 and accompanying text.

[315] Trevisanut (n 242) 301.

[316] Prior to the constitution of an arbitral tribunal, provisional measures can be sought under UNCLOS art 290(5) from 'any court or tribunal agreed upon by the parties or, failing such agreement within two weeks from the date of the request for provisional measures, the International Tribunal for the Law of the Sea or, with respect to activities in the Area, the Seabed Disputes Chamber': UNCLOS (n 1) art 290(5).

[317] *Southern Bluefin Tuna*, Jurisdiction and Admissibility (n 13) (Separate Opinion of Judge Treves) (commenting on the differing application of 'urgency' in paras 1 and 5 of art 290).

before the resolution of a dispute, Article 290 requires certain conditions to be fulfilled prior to the prescription of provisional measures.

The rationale for provisional measures was eloquently explained by a former President of the ICJ as follows:

> [T]he essential justification for the impatience of a tribunal in granting relief before it has reached a final decision on its competence and on the merits is that the action of one party *pendent lite* causes or threatens a damage to the rights of the other of such nature that it would not be possible fully to restore those rights, or remedy the infringements thereof, simply by a judgment in its favor.[318]

Although the language of the ICJ and ITLOS Statutes is different in the grant of authority for the use of provisional measures pending the resolution of a dispute, the criteria considered by each institution have been similarly applied in their cases. Tanaka has identified five elements: 'Prima facie jurisdiction, the plausible character of the alleged rights in the principal request, the link between the alleged rights and the measures requested, urgency and risk of irreparable prejudice.'[319]

In addition, the prescription of provisional measures under UNCLOS specifically references the protection of the marine environment as a consideration for provisional measures.[320] In this regard, the situation is slightly distinct to that before the ICJ. The ICJ could still consider risk of environmental harm as a reason to indicate provisional measures, but its mandate in this regard is not as specific as for the tribunals operating under UNCLOS. This section considers the elements discussed in most detail during provisional measures proceedings: prima facie jurisdiction; protecting rights pending the resolution of the dispute; urgency; protection of the marine environment; and examines the types of provisional measures orders issued in UNCLOS dispute settlement.

1. Prima Facie Jurisdiction

The first basic prerequisite is that the relevant court or tribunal has prima facie jurisdiction.[321] Similar to the ICJ, tribunals constituted under UNCLOS have considered prima facie jurisdiction established where 'there is nothing which manifestly and in terms excludes the tribunal's jurisdiction'.[322] Judge Wolfrum explained this standard in more detail in his dissenting opinion in *Louisa*:

> [I]t is necessary for the adjudicative body to take into account the facts which are known to it at the moment of deciding on provisional measures and to consider whether on this basis,

[318] *Aegean Sea Continental Shelf (Greece v Turkey)* (Judgment) [1978] ICJ Rep 3, 16–17.

[319] Yoshifumi Tanaka, *The Peaceful Settlement of International Disputes* (CUP 2018) 255 (Tanaka, *Peaceful Settlement*).

[320] UNCLOS (n 1) art 290(1).

[321] In respect of art 290(1), the court or tribunal makes this determination on its own account whereas under para 5, the court or tribunal asked to prescribe provisional measures makes this decision for the *ad hoc* arbitral tribunal that is yet to be constituted.

[322] See eg *MOX Plant*, Order No 3 (n 129) para 14. See also Shabtai Rosenne, 'The Case-Law of ITLOS (1997-2001): An Overview' in Myron H Nordquist and John Norton Moore (eds), *Current Marine Environmental Issues and the International Tribunal for the Law of the Sea* (Martinus Nijhoff 2001) 133 (noting that a finding of prima facie jurisdiction is a very low threshold and allows the prescription of provisional measures provided 'the absence of jurisdiction is not manifest').

together with legal basis invoked by the applicant, prima facie jurisdiction on the merits may be established.[323]

In this regard, it is not enough for an applicant merely to invoke various provisions of UNCLOS, but there must also be a sufficient factual record established to support the relevance of those provisions as part of its claims.

Jurisprudence under UNCLOS has so far indicated that bars to a finding that no jurisdiction exists on a prima facie basis include where the requirement in Article 283 to proceed expeditiously to an exchange of views has not been met,[324] the existence of alternative dispute settlement procedures that are to be utilised in lieu of those in UNCLOS,[325] and whether the exclusions and limitations in Section 3 of Part XV apply.[326] In the *Enrica Lexie* provisional measures order under Article 290(5), ITLOS observed that the 'very nature of the dispute' concerned the exercise of jurisdiction and so was not prepared to address a challenge relating to the exhaustion of local remedies.[327] On this basis, it would seem that the potential application of this principle would not prevent prima facie jurisdiction from being established.[328] Exceptions to subject matter jurisdiction under Articles 297 or 298 have not yet formed a basis for denying prima facie jurisdiction.[329]

2. Protecting Rights Pending the Resolution of the Dispute

If there is prima facie jurisdiction, the standard that must be met is whether the circumstances warrant the prescription of measures pending the final decision of the court or tribunal in order to preserve the rights of the parties or whether there is a need to prevent serious harm to the marine environment. The low threshold to be established for prima facie jurisdiction may be balanced by expectations of a party establishing urgency to warrant a tribunal ordering provisional measures.[330]

For the purposes of the provisional measures proceedings, a Special Chamber of ITLOS considered that it did not need to 'determine definitively whether the rights which they each wish to see protected exist'.[331] Rather, the rights claimed to exist must at least be plausible.[332] This standard of plausibility had not previously been applied in the context

[323] *Louisa*, Provisional Measures (n 32) (Dissenting Opinion of Judge Wolfrum) para 12.

[324] See eg *Southern Bluefin Tuna*, Jurisdiction and Admissibility (n 13) paras 60–61; *MOX Plant*, Provisional Measures (n 45) para 68; *Land Reclamation*, Provisional Measures (n 42) para 48; *Enrica Lexie (Italy v India)* (Request for the Prescription of Provisional Measures, Order of 29 April 2016) PCA Case No 2015-28, paras 59–60 (*Enrica Lexie*, Annex VII Provisional Measures). See further Karaman (n 66) 126–30.

[325] Prima facie jurisdiction may be lacking if either arts 281 or 282 clearly bar recourse to the compulsory procedures in Section 2 of Part XV, or if the dispute does not involve the interpretation or application of UNCLOS. See *Southern Bluefin Tuna*, Jurisdiction and Admissibility (n 13) paras 51, 55; *Land Reclamation* (n 42) Provisional Measures, para 57; *MOX Plant*, Provisional Measures (n 45) para 51.

[326] See eg *M/V Saiga (No 2) (Saint Vincent and the Grenadines v Guinea)* (Provisional Measures, Order of 11 March 1998) ITLOS Reports 1998, 24, para 30 (*Saiga No 2*, Provisional Measures).

[327] *Enrica Lexie (Italy v India)* (Provisional Measures, Order of 24 August 2015) ITLOS Reports 2015, 182 para 67 (*Enrica Lexie*, ITLOS Provisional Measures) .

[328] ITLOS similarly determined that the exhaustion of local remedies should be determined at a later stage during the provisional measures proceedings in the *Louisa*. See *Louisa*, Provisional Measures (n 32) para 68.

[329] See *Detention of Three Ukrainian Naval Vessels*, Provisional Measures (n 180) paras 63–77; *Arctic Sunrise*, Provisional Measures (n 181) para 45; *Saiga No 2*, Provisional Measures (n 324) paras 28 and 30.

[330] See *Enrica Lexie*, ITLOS Provisional Measures (n 327) (Dissenting Opinion of Judge Heidar) para 3; *ARA Libertad* (n 64) (Declaration of Judge Paik) para 1.

[331] *Delimitation of the Maritime Boundary between Ghana and Côte d'Ivoire in the Atlantic Ocean (Ghana/Côte d'Ivoire)* (Provisional Measures Order of 25 April 2015) ITLOS Reports 2015, 146, para 57 (*Ghana/Côte d'Ivoire*, Provisional Measures).

[332] ibid para 58. ITLOS utilised this standard subsequently in *Enrica Lexie*, ITLOS Provisional Measures (n 327) paras 84–85.

of provisional measures under UNCLOS, but followed more recent jurisprudence of the ICJ.[333] The standard is to be applied in relation to the claims of the applicant to show that the rights claimed exist and will be applicable in the merits stage.[334] It is separate to an assessment of what rights are to be preserved or protected by the provisional measures order.[335]

The plausibility standard was applied in *Ghana/Côte d'Ivoire*,[336] when Côte d'Ivoire requested an order from the Special Chamber requiring Ghana to suspend all ongoing oil exploration and exploitation activities in the disputed area, as well as refrain from any new permits for such activity in the disputed area.[337] Further, Côte d'Ivoire sought an order that Ghana refrain from using any information relating to any exploration activities in any way that would be to Côte d'Ivoire's detriment.[338] Côte d'Ivoire also requested that all steps be taken to preserve the continental shelf, its superjacent waters, and its subsoil, and that no unilateral actions be taken that would risk prejudicing the rights of Côte d'Ivoire or aggravate the dispute. The Special Chamber considered that Côte d'Ivoire had met the threshold that the rights to be protected were plausible.[339] However, what may be considered 'plausible' is not particularly clear, and there is a risk that this assessment injects an element of uncertainty into provisional measures decisions under UNCLOS.[340]

On the request that Ghana take steps to prevent information from being used to the detriment of Côte d'Ivoire, Ghana had challenged whether such a right to information existed under UNCLOS.[341] The Special Chamber concluded otherwise:

> [t]he Special Chamber considers that the rights of the coastal State over its continental shelf include all rights necessary for and connected with the exploration and exploitation of the natural resources of the continental shelf and that the exclusive right to access to information about the resources of the continental shelf is plausibly among those rights.[342]

The Special Chamber further considered that the risk of prejudice to these rights was imminent pending the decision on the merits. As a result, it prescribed a provisional measure to prevent information that was not already in the public domain being used in any way to the detriment of Côte d'Ivoire. In this regard, Ghana provided an undertaking in the proceedings, which was judicially noted, that it would record information currently being gathered and make it available to Côte d'Ivoire if ordered to do so in the case.[343]

333 Yoshifumi Tanaka, 'Unilateral Exploration and Exploitation of Natural Resources in Disputed Areas: A Note on the Ghana/Côte d'Ivoire Order of 25 April 2015 before the Special Chamber of ITLOS' (2015) 46(4) ODIL 315, 318 (Tanaka, 'Unilateral Exploration'). This requirement was first articulated in *Questions relating to the Obligation to Prosecute or Extradite (Belgium v Senegal)* (Provisional Measures Order of 28 May 2009) [2009] ICJ Rep 139, 151 and applied subsequently.

334 *Enrica Lexie*, ITLOS Provisional Measures (n 327) (Dissenting Opinion of Judge Heidar) paras 18, 20. See also *Detention of Three Ukrainian Naval Vessels*, Provisional Measures (n 180) para 95.

335 *Enrica Lexie*, ITLOS Provisional Measures (n 327) (Dissenting Opinion of Judge Heidar) para 19.

336 Ghana had initially instituted proceedings against Côte d'Ivoire, shortly after removing its declaration under art 298 excluding maritime boundary delimitation disputes from compulsory procedures entailing a binding decision. The dispute would normally have been referred to arbitration, but the parties agreed that the case would instead be referred to a Special Chamber of the ITLOS. The configuration of this case thus became one of special agreement rather than applicant-respondent as initially instituted.

337 *Ghana/Côte d'Ivoire*, Provisional Measures (n 331) para 25.

338 ibid.

339 ibid para 62.

340 Tanaka, 'Unilateral Exploration' (n 333) 319.

341 *Ghana/Côte d'Ivoire*, Provisional Measures (n 331) (Written Statement of Ghana) vol 1, para 107.

342 *Ghana/Côte d'Ivoire*, Provisional Measures (n 331) para 94.

343 ibid paras 92–93.

The plausibility standard has been subsequently applied in *Detention of Three Ukrainian Naval Vessels*,[344] *Enrica Lexie*,[345] and *San Padre Pio*.[346] In the latter case, the Tribunal did not assess the plausibility of one of Switzerland's claims on the basis that it 'would have required the examination of legal and factual issues which were not fully addressed by the Parties'.[347] The Tribunal was instead able to establish the plausibility of two of Switzerland's claims, and provided an indication of a threshold that might need to be reached if certain rights are to be considered plausible to warrant an indication of provisional measures.[348]

A range of factors will be considered in assessing the respective rights of the parties, and judges have occasionally differed on achieving a balance of interests to be protected as between the parties.[349] In *ARA Libertad*, Argentina sought the release of its warship from a Ghanaian port and arguably the release of the vessel might have prejudiced the rights of Ghana if it considered it had a basis for detaining the ship. Nonetheless, the dynamic of the case was that the Ghanaian executive supported the release of the vessel but had been unable to interfere with the judicial processes underway before its national courts.[350] In these circumstances, where Ghana could not rely on its internal law or constitution to excuse a violation of international law and was internationally responsible for the conduct of its judicial officials, ITLOS did not consider that Ghana's rights to retain the vessel for its domestic legal proceedings were to be protected against Argentina's right to have its vessel released.[351]

3. Urgency

When ITLOS is asked to prescribe provisional measures pending the constitution of an Annex VII arbitral tribunal, there must be a temporal urgency for the protection of rights as otherwise the Annex VII tribunal would have authority to issue provisional measures itself. Yet any measures adopted under Article 290(5) do not have to be limited to the time period until the Annex VII tribunal is constituted,[352] and any assessment of urgency can take into account the time that may be available until the arbitral tribunal is able to modify or revoke the provisional measures.[353] The concept of urgency for provisional measures 'is linked to the notion of irreparability'.[354]

[344] *Detention of Three Ukrainian Naval Vessels*, Provisional Measures (n 180) para 95.

[345] *Enrica Lexie*, ITLOS Provisional Measures (n 327) para 84.

[346] *San Padre Pio*, Provisional Measures (n 191) para 105.

[347] ibid para 110.

[348] Switzerland had argued: '[w]hat is required is something more than assertion but less than proof; in other words, the party must show that there is at least a reasonable possibility that the right which it claims exists as a matter of law and will be adjudged [by the tribunal] to apply to that party's case': ibid para 79.

[349] See eg *Enrica Lexie*, ITLOS Provisional Measures (n 327) where judges in their separate and dissenting opinions queried whether the Italian marines should have been released. See further nn 396–401 and accompanying text.

[350] See *ARA Libertad* (n 64) (Separate Opinion of Judges Wolfrum and Cot) para 54, (Separate Opinion of Judge Lucky) para 31, (Separate Opinion of Judge Rao) para 4, (Declaration of Judge Paik) para 4.

[351] See *ARA Libertad* (n 64) (Separate Opinion of Judges Wolfrum and Cot) para 55, (Separate Opinion of Judge Lucky) para 32; (Separate Opinion of Judge Rao) para 7.

[352] See eg *Land Reclamation*, Provisional Measures (n 42) para 67; *Arctic Sunrise*, Provisional Measures (n 181) para 84. Ishii has criticised ITLOS decisions for effectively merging the timing considerations from arts 290(1) and 290(5). Yurika Ishii, 'Introductory Note to Case Concerning the Detention of Three Ukrainian Naval Vessels (Ukraine v Russian Federation): Provisional Measures (ITLOS)' (2019) 58 ILM 1147, 1148.

[353] See eg *Land Reclamation*, Provisional Measures (n 42) para 68. Tanaka refers to broad and narrow readings of arts 290(1) and 290(5) in this regard whereby a broad understanding of the timing renders the urgency frame comparable under both provisions. Yoshifumi Tanaka, 'Release of a Detained Warship and Its Crew through Provisional Measures: A Comparative Analysis of the ARA Libertad and Ukraine v Russia Cases' (2020) 96 ILS 223, 249–51.

[354] Karaman (n 66) 141.

Moreover, in *Ghana/Côte d'Ivoire*, Ghana challenged that there was any urgency in relation to Côte d'Ivoire's requests—commenting that Côte d'Ivoire had not even argued that urgency was a requirement to be met.[355] The Special Chamber confirmed the standard for prescribing provisional measures as requiring 'a real and imminent risk that irreparable prejudice may be caused to the rights of the parties in dispute',[356] and that urgency is thus required.[357] Urgency has thereby emerged as a requirement for the prescription of provisional measures under Article 290(1), as well as Article 290(5), even though it is only explicitly mentioned in the latter.[358]

In the *Enrica Lexie* provisional measures order under Article 290(5), ITLOS ordered that both parties refrain from any legal proceedings in relation to the two Italian marines arrested for shooting two Indian fishermen.[359] Yet during the proceedings both Italy and India advised the Tribunal that no steps were expected within either of their court systems prior to the establishment of the Annex VII Tribunal. Similarly, ITLOS noted a number of commitments made by the parties during the *Land Reclamation* provisional measures proceedings, although still considered there was urgency 'to build on the commitments made to ensure prompt and effective cooperation of the parties in the implementation of their commitments'.[360] Hence, the 'urgency' threshold seemed *de minimis* in these circumstances.[361]

Urgency was also disputed in *Detention of Three Ukrainian Naval Vessels* where Ukraine sought the release of its naval vessels and the accompanying crew, arguing that irreparable harm was ensuing from the vessels being out of service and unavailable for 'important public duties'.[362] Further, the detention of the crew, which had extended beyond five months at the time of the hearing and was ongoing, was also argued to create irreparable prejudice.[363] Russia instead noted that Ukraine had waited four months before instituting proceedings so the risk was not as urgent as Ukraine indicated and that Russia had already positively responded to an order of the European Court of Human Rights to improve the conditions of detention of the servicemen concerned.[364] Nonetheless, the Tribunal agreed with Ukraine that irreparable prejudice to Ukraine's rights was real and ongoing, as well as noting 'the continued deprivation of liberty and freedom of Ukraine's servicemen raises humanitarian concerns'.[365] Tanaka has observed that the 'urgency' element assessed by the Tribunal tends to reflect an interlinkage of past conduct, to what is currently happening and what risks are realistically anticipated for the future.[366]

355 *Ghana/Côte d'Ivoire*, Provisional Measures (n 331) (Written Statement of Ghana) vol 1, para 89.

356 *Ghana/Côte d'Ivoire*, Provisional Measures (n 331) para 41, citing the standard used in *Louisa*, Provisional Measures (n 32) para 72. See also *Enrica Lexie*, ITLOS Provisional Measures (n 327) para 87.

357 *Ghana/Côte d'Ivoire*, Provisional Measures (n 331) para 42.

358 *Enrica Lexie*, Annex VII Provisional Measures (n 322) paras 85, 89. See also *Ghana/Côte d'Ivoire*, Provisional Measures (n 331) para 42.

359 *Enrica Lexie*, ITLOS Provisional Measures (n 327) para 131.

360 *Land Reclamation*, Provisional Measures (n 42) para 98. This standard of urgency was queried by individual judges in that case. See eg *Land Reclamation*, Provisional Measures (n 42) (Separate Opinion of Judge Anderson) para 3.

361 See *Enrica Lexie*, ITLOS Provisional Measures (n 327) (Declaration of Judge Kateka) para 6.

362 *Detention of Three Ukrainian Naval Vessels*, Provisional Measures (n 180) para 102.

363 ibid paras 104–106.

364 ibid paras 107–108.

365 ibid para 112.

366 Yoshifumi Tanaka, 'Release of a Detained Warship and Its Crew through Provisional Measures: A Comparative Analysis of the ARA Libertad and Ukraine v Russia Cases' (2020) 96 ILS 223, 249.

4. Protecting the Marine Environment

Côte d'Ivoire's request for provisional measures in *Ghana/Côte d'Ivoire* also rested on its concerns that serious harm to the marine environment was at stake. Even though the Special Chamber found that Côte d'Ivoire had not discharged its burden of proof to demonstrate that Ghana's activities in the disputed area created an imminent risk of serious harm to the marine environment,[367] the Special Chamber was still minded to address environmental protection pending the resolution of the maritime boundary dispute. The Special Chamber took into account key environmental principles, including the obligation not to cause transboundary harm[368] and the need to act with 'prudence and caution'.[369] Also noted were the core obligations to protect and preserve the marine environment as enshrined in Article 192 of UNCLOS and the duty to cooperate in the prevention of pollution of the marine environment.[370] These factors also motivated ITLOS in the *Land Reclamation* provisional measures proceedings, where it commented:

> [G]iven the possible implications of land reclamation on the marine environment, prudence and caution require that Malaysia and Singapore establish mechanisms for exchanging information and assessing the risks or effects of land reclamation works and devising ways to deal with them in the areas concerned.[371]

The need to protect and preserve the marine environment in the context of provisional measures may hence precipitate a range of procedural requirements in terms of monitoring, exchanging information, and reporting.[372]

In ordering provisional measures that permitted Ghana to continue drilling in *Ghana/Côte d'Ivoire*, a constraint was placed on Ghanaian activity to the extent that Ghana was required to carry out 'strict and continuous monitoring of all activities' in the disputed area to prevent serious harm to the marine environment.[373] ITLOS thus required that both parties take all necessary steps to prevent serious harm to the marine environment.[374] Arguably, such a provisional measure would not change, or add to, the environmental obligations that already bind Ghana. Yet it did at least underline the commitment of the UNCLOS dispute settlement process to environmental protection. Further, the requirements for the parties to report back on the steps taken to conform to the provisional measures order[375] imposed a procedural onus and third-party oversight in relation to adherence to environmental norms.[376]

[367] *Ghana/Côte d'Ivoire*, Provisional Measures (n 331) para 67.
[368] ibid para 71.
[369] ibid para 72.
[370] ibid paras 69, 73.
[371] *Land Reclamation*, Provisional Measures (n 42) para 99. In the *MOX Plant* provisional measures order, ITLOS similarly noted: 'prudence and caution require that Ireland and the United Kingdom cooperate in exchanging information concerning risks or effects of the operation of the MOX plant and in devising ways to deal with them, as appropriate': *MOX Plant*, Provisional Measures (n 45) para 84.
[372] See eg *MOX Plant*, Provisional Measures (n 45) para 89. See further Klein, *Dispute Settlement* (n 62) 81–84.
[373] *Ghana/Côte d'Ivoire*, Provisional Measures (n 331) para 108, Operative [1(b)].
[374] ibid para 108, Operative [1(c)].
[375] ibid para 108, Operative [2].
[376] This oversight allows for the possibility that a State that fails to report, or even fails to undertake the necessary steps, as required by a provisional measures order, could be found to have violated international obligations at the merits stage of the dispute. Such an argument was made by Côte d'Ivoire at the merits stage, but its claim in this regard was not upheld. See *Ghana/Côte d'Ivoire*, Judgment (n 9) paras 652–58.

Fisheries disputes may also prompt the prescription of provisional measures, especially given the view of ITLOS that the conservation of marine living resources is part of the protection and preservation of the marine environment.[377] In the context of the *Southern Bluefin Tuna* cases, all parties were in agreement about the severe decline of the status of this stock,[378] and the Tribunal therefore had a basis to insist on 'prudence and caution to ensure that effective conservation measures are taken to prevent serious harm to the stock of southern bluefin tuna'.[379]

5. Types of Provisional Measures

In assessing what provisional measures to prescribe, ITLOS has commented that it may order 'any provisional measures which it considers appropriate under the circumstances to preserve the respective rights of the parties'.[380] This approach aligns with the permissive language of Article 290(1). An important consideration in this context is that the measures should equally preserve the rights of both parties.[381] If one of the parties provides any assurance as to its conduct during the provisional measures proceedings, these will be judicially noted and placed on record.[382] In that instance, the assurance does not need to be repeated in the prescription of provisional measures orders on the basis that good faith compliance with international undertakings are to be assumed.[383] There is nonetheless flexibility in issuing orders different to what the parties might have requested.[384] Any order is to be without prejudice to decisions on the merits,[385] or indeed in relation to the establishment of jurisdiction.

A Special Chamber of ITLOS considered whether it should prescribe a measure requiring Ghana to stop drilling activities in Ghana's concession areas. Côte d'Ivoire had observed that the unilateral activities deprived it of the right to determine 'when, how and under what conditions the exploitation of these resources will take place, and even *whether* it should take place'.[386] Moreover, Côte d'Ivoire submitted that drilling was an irreversible activity, preventing any possibility of the subsoil being returned to its prior state.[387] This

377 *Southern Bluefin Tuna*, Provisional Measures (n 23) para 70. For further discussion on this holding see ch 9(II)(C).

378 *Southern Bluefin Tuna*, Provisional Measures (n 23) para 71.

379 ibid para 77.

380 *Enrica Lexie*, ITLOS Provisional Measures (n 327) para 87; *Louisa*, Judgment (n 2) para 72. As noted above, this decision is separate to assessing the plausibility of the applicant's rights. See *Enrica Lexie*, ITLOS Provisional Measures (n 327) (Dissenting Opinion of Judge Heidar) paras 18–20.

381 See eg *San Padre Pio*, Provisional Measures (n 191) (Separate Opinion of Judge Heidar) para 2.

382 See eg *Land Reclamation*, Provisional Measures (n 42) para 81. See further para 88 (placing on record 'Commitments' provided by Singapore during the proceedings) para 80. There is, though, a difference between the parties reaching such an agreement and it being recorded within the order compared to the situation where the Tribunal imposes such an assurance or undertaking upon a State party. See *San Padre Pio*, Provisional Measures (n 191) (Dissenting Opinion of Judge Kateka) paras 9–10.

383 See *Land Reclamation*, Provisional Measures (n 42) (Declaration of President Nelson) para 6 (concerned that ITLOS had not properly accounted for this 'cardinal principle' in its order in that case).

384 See eg *Enrica Lexie*, ITLOS Provisional Measures (n 327) para 127. See also Klein, *Dispute Settlement* (n 62) 79. It may be noted that Judge ad hoc Shearer questioned whether this deviation was permissible without providing the parties an opportunity to be heard. The measures could only be a 'partial grant' or 'modified version' of what the parties had requested to be within power. See *Southern Bluefin Tuna*, Provisional Measures (n 23) (Separate Opinion of Judge ad hoc Shearer) para 10.

385 See eg *ARA Libertad* (n 64) para 106. However, arguably there are instances where the orders, particularly requiring the release of vessels, do approach vindication of what the applicant is seeking on the merits, as was especially evident in the *ARA Libertad* and *Detention of Three Ukrainian Naval Vessels*.

386 *Ghana/Côte d'Ivoire*, Provisional Measures (n 331) para 77 (citing Côte d'Ivoire's arguments).

387 ibid para 78.

position was consistent with the approaches taken in *Aegean Sea Continental Shelf* as well as in *Guyana v Suriname*.[388] Ghana resisted any suggestion that it should halt the activities of its concession holders because of the severe financial implications that would flow from such a suspension or cessation of activity.[389] Ghana further considered that Côte d'Ivoire's concerns were ultimately related to financial loss.[390]

The Special Chamber, however, took into account possible modifications to the physical characteristics of the continental shelf that would be significant and permanent and not fully compensable through financial reparations.[391] It therefore unanimously prescribed that 'Ghana shall take all necessary steps to ensure that no new drilling either by Ghana or under its control takes place in the disputed area'.[392] The order is more limited than Côte d'Ivoire had sought.[393] The Special Chamber recognised that *ongoing* activities in respect of which drilling had already taken place would entail considerable financial loss and potentially harm the environment as well.[394] It would therefore fall to the parties to determine what drilling may be construed as new and what was part of an ongoing operation. According to Ghana, the 'activities of exploration and exploitation that it has undertaken or authorized in the disputed areas "are not new"'.[395]

Tanaka has rightly criticised the decision on the basis that the Special Chamber was too deferential to the interests of Ghana, even though those interests were predominantly financial and did not reflect an imminent risk of financial loss.[396] In this respect, the Special Chamber's decision may show a greater tolerance for mining activities in disputed areas than would have been accepted under the previous cases. The threshold for what constitutes a forbidden activity because of the risk of hampering or prejudicing final resolution of the maritime boundary dispute has therefore shifted in *Ghana/Côte d'Ivoire* and opens the door for further manoeuvring by ambitious States in future decisions. It may have been acceptable in the factual context of this case on the basis that both parties had been regulating seabed activity prior to the litigation.[397] There is, therefore, an opening to limit the relevance of this decision in future disputes given its factual setting.

The release of individuals being detained has been sought in the context of provisional measures proceedings, even though the right of detention may be at issue in the merits of the case.[398] The release of Italian marines in *Enrica Lexie* was not granted as a provisional measure by ITLOS, despite recognition of the importance of considerations of humanity,[399] as it would essentially have prejudged the merits.[400] Italy sought the relaxation

[388] See discussion in Natalie Klein, 'Provisional Measures and Provisional Arrangements' in Alex G Oude Elferink, Tore Henriksen and Signe Veierud Busch (eds), *Maritime Boundary Delimitation: The Case Law* (CUP 2018) 117.

[389] *Ghana/Côte d'Ivoire*, Provisional Measures (n 331) paras 82–85.

[390] ibid para 87.

[391] ibid para 89.

[392] ibid para 108.

[393] As noted above, a tribunal acting under art 290 may vary the measures prescribed to what was requested from the applicant State.

[394] *Ghana/Côte d'Ivoire*, Provisional Measures (n 331) para 99.

[395] *Ghana/Côte d'Ivoire*, Provisional Measures (n 331) (Separate Opinion of Judge Mensah) para 6.

[396] Tanaka, 'Unilateral Exploration' (n 333) 325.

[397] *Ghana/Côte d'Ivoire*, Provisional Measures (n 331) paras 51–52.

[398] See eg *Enrica Lexie*, ITLOS Provisional Measures (n 327) para 29; *Arctic Sunrise*, Provisional Measures (n 181) para 95.

[399] *Enrica Lexie*, ITLOS Provisional Measures (n 327) para 133, citing *Saiga No 2*, Judgment (n 18).

[400] See *Enrica Lexie*, ITLOS Provisional Measures (n 327) (Declaration of Judge Paik) para 6. Note, however, that Judge Kelly and Judge Jesus would have allowed the release of the Italian Marines pending the arbitration, provided

of bail conditions allowing its national to return to Italy in provisional measures before the Annex VII Tribunal.[401] This Tribunal ordered that the parties cooperate to allow the relaxation of bail conditions so that the Italian marine could return to Italy in circumstances that would preserve the rights of both parties, but still account for 'considerations of humanity' that focused on the possible social isolation experienced by the marine while staying in India.[402] In return, Italy provided a binding commitment to return the marines to India for trial if required at the closure of the UNCLOS procedures.[403] In *San Padre Pio*, ITLOS indicated that the master and crew be allowed to leave Nigeria but stated that Switzerland had a binding international legal obligation to ensure their return should the Annex VII Tribunal find in favour of Nigeria.[404] While such an obligation could be imposed on Italy in relation to its own marines, it remains more challenging to expect that Switzerland would have the necessary jurisdiction to ensure the return of Ukrainian nationals to Nigeria if those nationals are not in Switzerland at the time.[405]

The length of time that individuals are held in detention, as well as the offences with which they have been charged, may influence whether an order for release is warranted as a provisional measure.[406] In *Arctic Sunrise*, ITLOS required the release of the vessel and its crew upon payment of a bond or other financial security.[407] In *ARA Libertad*, the Argentine warship and its crew were also ordered for release as a provisional measure in light of the immunity enjoyed by that vessel under general international law.[408] Similarly, in *Detention of Three Ukrainian Naval Vessels*, the Tribunal took the view that after four months in detention, 'the continued deprivation of liberty and freedom of Ukraine's servicemen raises humanitarian concerns' and contributed to a situation posing a real and imminent risk of irreparable prejudice to the rights of Ukraine.[409] Even though separate proceedings before the European Court of Human Rights had denied the transfer of the servicemen but sought to ameliorate the conditions of their detention through provision of medical assistance, ITLOS nonetheless ordered the release of the servicemen.[410]

they were returned to India for trial if that was the outcome of the UNCLOS proceedings. India's rights would only have been prejudiced if they were not returned when required. See *Enrica Lexie*, ITLOS Provisional Measures (n 327) (Declaration of Judge Kelly) para 6, (Separate Opinion of Judge Jesus) para 21, (Separate Opinion of Judge ad hoc Francioni) para 9 (also querying the Tribunal's lack of trust in Italy in this regard).

[401] *Enrica Lexie*, Annex VII Provisional Measures (n 324) para 25. The relaxation of bail conditions was intended to recognise India's ongoing interests in the prosecution of the Italian marine, rather than a request to release him entirely, as Italy had sought before ITLOS: see para 75. One of the marines had already returned to Italy for medical reasons.

[402] ibid paras 104, 106–107.

[403] ibid paras 127–31.

[404] *San Padre Pio*, Provisional Measures (n 191) para 141.

[405] ibid (Joint Declaration of Judges Cabello and Chadha) paras 6–9, (Declaration of Judge Kolodkin) para 11, (Separate Opinion of Judge ad hoc Murphy) para 55, (Dissenting Opinion of Judge Gao) para 75, (Dissenting Opinion of Judge Bouguetaia) paras 12–13 (contrasting the position in this case with the situation in *Enrica Lexie*). See also Yurika Ishii, 'Comments on ITLOS, M/T "San Padre Pio" Case (Switzerland v Nigeria), Provisional Measures Order (6 July 2019)' *EJIL: Talk!* (31 July 2019) https://www.ejiltalk.org/comments-on-itlos-m-t-san-padre-pio-case-switzerland-v-nigeria-provisional-measures-order-6-july-2019/.

[406] See eg *Enrica Lexie*, ITLOS Provisional Measures (n 327) (Separate Opinion of Judge Jesus) para 11; *Arctic Sunrise*, Provisional Measures (n 181) para 95.

[407] *Arctic Sunrise*, Provisional Measures (n 181) para 95. As discussed above, the effect of the treatment of the *Arctic Sunrise* under the ship-as-unit concept was that Russia was ordered to allow its own nationals to leave its territory. See *Arctic Sunrise*, Provisional Measures (n 181) (Dissenting Opinion of Judge Golitsyn) para 46. See n 225 and accompanying text.

[408] *ARA Libertad* (n 64) para 98.

[409] *Detention of Three Ukrainian Naval Vessels*, Provisional Measures (n 180) paras 112–13.

[410] ibid para 108.

The Tribunal did not engage with the spectre of two cases presenting different results, but Judge Kittichaisaree observed in his Separate Opinion that the cases each involved distinct claims and the Tribunal could prescribe provisional measures within the limits of its own competence.[411]

The status of individuals detained has not been a factor in orders for release in relation to provisional measures. Arguably, the special status of crew on warships or naval auxiliaries might have been a consideration. The ICJ indication of provisional measures in the *Tehran Hostages* case could hold some analogies in assessing the risk to individuals with special status under international law and their ongoing detention.[412] However, given the release of private individuals in *Arctic Sunrise* and *San Padre Pio*, this distinction does not appear to have been a consideration.

In *San Padre Pio*, the Tribunal considered that the vessel, cargo, and crew had to be addressed as a unit.[413] Why they were considered as a unit is unclear given that the ship-as-unit concept is associated with the standing of Switzerland as flag State. In the same case, the Tribunal did not consider that the rights asserted could be fully repaired by monetary compensation,[414] yet the vessel, cargo, and crew were ordered released on payment of a financial bond.[415] It may have made more sense not to treat the vessel, cargo, and crew as a unit but rather to single out the crew given the associated humanitarian concerns, which ITLOS noted,[416] and consider that damage to the vessel and cargo could have been compensated if needed once a full determination on the merits occurred.[417]

If national proceedings are ongoing in relation to the incident prompting the UNCLOS dispute, an order may be prescribed suspending domestic court proceedings. This step was taken in relation to in *Enrica Lexie*,[418] and in *M/V Saiga (No 2)*,[419] but not in *San Padre Pio* where the proceedings could continue, although the individuals had to be allowed to leave Nigeria.[420] The risk of interference, or the need for interference, in domestic court proceedings was especially pertinent in *ARA Libertad* where Ghana's executive was unable to intervene in the judicial proceedings because of the separation of powers.[421] This approach was open to ITLOS in *Detention of Three Ukrainian Naval Vessels*, and Russia further pointed out that the release of the vessels and servicemen as an order for provisional measures prejudged the merits.[422] Without explanation, ITLOS instead ordered that 'in the circumstances' the vessels and servicemen were to be released.[423] In *San Padre Pio*,

[411] ibid (Separate Opinion Judge Kittichaisaree) para 32.

[412] *United States Diplomatic and Consular Staff in Tehran (United States v Iran)* (Judgment) [1980] ICJ Rep 3.

[413] *San Padre Pio*, Provisional Measures (n 191) para 128.

[414] ibid para 128.

[415] ibid para 138. But see *San Padre Pio*, Provisional Measures (n 191) (Declaration of Judge Kolodkin) para 6.

[416] *San Padre Pio*, Provisional Measures (n 191) para 130.

[417] Although some judges suggested that the humanitarian needs of the crew members concerned would have been met if they had left the vessel and moved to alternative lodgings, given that they were free to go anywhere in Nigeria. See eg *San Padre Pio*, Provisional Measures (n 191) (Joint Declaration of Judges Cabello and Chadha) para 10.

[418] *Enrica Lexie*, ITLOS Provisional Measures (n 327) para 131.

[419] *Saiga No 2*, Provisional Measures (n 326) para 41.

[420] *San Padre Pio*, Provisional Measures (n 191) para 142.

[421] *ARA Libertad* (n 64) (Declaration of Judge Paik) para 4.

[422] *Detention of Three Ukrainian Naval Vessels*, Provisional Measures (n 180) para 117.

[423] ibid para 118. Judge Lucky concurred with this approach in his separate opinion, noting that it would have been wrong for an international court to interfere in national court proceedings when the former was not superior to the latter: *Detention of Three Ukrainian Naval Vessels*, Provisional Measures (n 180) (Separate Opinion of Judge Lucky) para 18.

the Tribunal determined the amount of bond to be paid that seemingly incorporated an amount for the vessel, its cargo, and for the criminal charges against the remaining four crew members.[424]

Some judges have queried whether bonds should be used in provisional measures proceedings, and so outside the context of prompt release proceedings.[425] Given the flexible range of provisional measures open to tribunals under Article 290, this overlap between provisional measures and prompt release proceedings does not seem problematic given that vessels may be arrested and bonded for a bigger range of offences under national laws than exists under UNCLOS. It does, however, still raise the question as to whether a bond indicates that the harm is not irreparable if monetary compensation is envisioned as an adequate alternative.

Tribunals will routinely prescribe that the parties abstain from taking any steps that may aggravate or extend the dispute, without any more specific requirement.[426] In complying with such an order, a party is not to be seen as waiving its rights or an admission of the other party's claims.[427]

Once prescribed, provisional measures may be modified or revoked if the circumstances justifying their prescription have been changed or cease to exist.[428] Consistent with their incidental nature, provisional measures orders are not final and may be revoked, unlike judgments on the merits.[429] An arbitral tribunal constituted under Annex VII may issue provisional measures under Article 290(1) on its own accord after ITLOS has issued provisional measures under Article 290(5).[430] At the jurisdictional stage of *Southern Bluefin Tuna*, the Annex VII Tribunal revoked ITLOS' order but still noted that the revocation did 'not mean that the Parties may disregard the effects of the Order or their own decisions made in conformity with it'.[431] As such, the possibility exists that if a court or tribunal prescribes provisional arrangements, the parties may then use this order as a basis for negotiating their own temporary arrangement and this agreement could be grounds for revoking the order. If a State does not comply with an order for provisional measures, the opposing State may raise this violation as an additional claim at the merits stage of their case. Examples of this argument arising include claims pursued by Côte d'Ivoire in *Ghana/Côte d'Ivoire*,[432] and by the Netherlands in *Arctic Sunrise*.[433] In the latter case, the Tribunal confirmed that a failure to comply with the provisional measures order constituted an internationally wrongful act.[434]

* * *

[424] *San Padre Pio*, Provisional Measures (n 191) paras 138–39.

[425] See *San Padre Pio*, Provisional Measures (n 191) (Dissenting Opinion of Judge Kateka) paras 4–7; *Arctic Sunrise*, Provisional Measures (n 181) (Separate Opinion of Judge Jesus) paras 7(c), 11.

[426] See Klein, *Dispute Settlement* (n 62) 79.

[427] *Louisa*, Provisional Measures (n 32) para 79; *Arctic Sunrise*, Provisional Measures (n 181) para 99.

[428] UNCLOS, art 290(2).

[429] Karaman (n 66) 97.

[430] As occurred in the *Enrica Lexie* and *MOX Plant* cases. See *MOX Plant*, Order No 3 (n 129) para 39; *Enrica Lexie*, Annex VII Provisional Measures (n 324) para 74.

[431] *Southern Bluefin Tuna*, Jurisdiction and Admissibility (n 13) para 67.

[432] See *Ghana/Côte d'Ivoire*, Judgment (n 9) paras 635–58.

[433] *Arctic Sunrise*, Merits (n 173) paras 334–62.

[434] ibid para 337.

As discussed at the outset of this section, incidental proceedings may effectively resolve the dispute between the parties without proceeding to the merits. An order of provisional measures may be an impetus for renewed negotiations or engagement through other fora for resolving the dispute.[435] The earlier jurisprudence demonstrated some creativity and judicial activism in managing how the dispute would move forward.[436] More recent cases have been dominated by claims for the release of vessels and crews following law enforcement proceedings. When vessels and crew are released, as occurred in *ARA Libertad* and *San Padre Pio*, it becomes arguable that key goals of the merits have been achieved at this preliminary stage. Whether such an outcome is desirable in all circumstances must be carefully considered, even in the narrow timeframes available for provisional measures proceedings. Judge Gao, for example, was willing to consider in *San Padre Pio* contributions to the rule of law in the region, as well as ramifications for other States in the region and beyond in deciding on what order to make while criminal proceedings are pending following law enforcement efforts in the Gulf of Guinea.[437] The very nature of provisional measures underlines how judicial decisions on these claims are relevant for the future conduct of the parties specifically, as well as for all stakeholders in ocean governance. Judicial intervention at the provisional measures stage may constitute an important safeguard in relation to law enforcement activities—although at present that safeguard appears to align more with the freedom of navigation and the liberty of individuals rather than reinforcing the efforts of coastal States to enhance efforts at maintaining maritime security.

B. Prompt Release of Vessels under Article 292

The earliest jurisprudence of ITLOS was dominated by prompt release cases arising under Article 292 of the Convention.[438] The provision reads:

> 1. Where the authorities of a State Party have detained a vessel flying the flag of another State Party and it is alleged that the detaining State has not complied with the provisions of this Convention for the prompt release of the vessel or its crew upon the posting of a reasonable bond or other financial security, the question of release from detention may be submitted to any court or tribunal agreed upon by the parties or, failing such agreement within 10 days from the time of detention, to a court or tribunal accepted by the detaining State under article 287 or to the International Tribunal for the Law of the Sea, unless the parties otherwise agree.
> 2. The application for release may be made only by or on behalf of the flag State of the vessel.

[435] These examples may be seen in relation to the *MOX Plant*, Provisional Measures (n 45) and *Land Reclamation*, Provisional Measures (n 42) proceedings. See also Tullio Treves, 'Article 290' in *Proelss Commentary* (n 44) 1866, para 34.

[436] See Klein, *Dispute Settlement* (n 62) 83–85; Karaman (n 66) 167; Churchill, 'Trends in Dispute Settlement' (n 241) 152.

[437] See *San Padre Pio*, Provisional Measures (n 191) (Dissenting Opinion of Judge Gao) paras 92, 95.

[438] ITLOS has residual, compulsory jurisdiction over prompt release proceedings in the event that no other forum is selected by the parties to resolve the claims. See UNCLOS (n 1) art 292(1). Given the timing involved in prompt release proceedings, it is practically unlikely that any forum other than ITLOS will determine these applications.

3. The court or tribunal shall deal without delay with the application for release and shall deal only with the question of release, without prejudice to the merits of any case before the appropriate domestic forum against the vessel, its owner or its crew. The authorities of the detaining State remain competent to release the vessel or its crew at any time.
4. Upon the posting of the bond or other financial security determined by the court or tribunal, the authorities of the detaining State shall comply promptly with the decision of the court or tribunal concerning the release of the vessel or its crew.[439]

Article 292 was included as part of the overall balance created in the institution of the EEZ whereby a mechanism was considered necessary to protect the navigational rights of flag States against the new enforcement rights of the coastal State in relation to fishing and protection of the marine environment.[440] Articles 73, 220, and 226 of the Convention expect that detained or arrested vessels will be promptly released upon payment of a reasonable bond. This requirement anticipated that coastal States would be able to pursue the enforcement of their fisheries and environmental laws and ensure that penalties associated with offences under those laws could be collected where warranted but also protect the ongoing navigational interests of the vessels (and especially their owners) in allowing inter alia the vessel to continue lawful fishing activities.

Article 292 reinforces the requirement for vessels to be promptly released upon payment of a reasonable bond in creating a procedure at the international level in the event that the domestic proceedings had not progressed as anticipated under the Convention. Nonetheless, as noted, Article 292 proceedings are not to prejudice the domestic proceedings relating to the enforcement of relevant coastal State laws. The procedure under Article 292 was initially criticised for 'not mak[ing] any sense' and condemned as 'unworkable'.[441] Nonetheless, nine of the first fifteen cases at ITLOS were prompt release proceedings and, at the time of writing, the last prompt release case was well over ten years ago.[442] To date, all of the prompt release cases have concerned actions taken in relation to Article 73 pertaining to the enforcement of a coastal State's fisheries laws in the EEZ.[443] There have instead been cases on the merits that have otherwise dealt with the detention of vessels in different contexts.[444]

The prompt release jurisprudence has gradually worked through a range of issues in the implementation of Article 292. In Article 292 proceedings, the key points for resolution most commonly relate to jurisdiction, questions of admissibility, whether the allegation of

[439] UNCLOS (n 1) art 292.

[440] See eg *Volga (Russia v Australia)* (Prompt Release, Judgment) ITLOS Reports 2002, 10, para 77 (*Volga*); *Monte Confurco* (n 239) para 70. See also Trevisanut (n 242) 301; David Heywood Anderson, 'Prompt Release of Vessels' in Rüdiger Wolfrum (ed), *Max Planck Encyclopedia of Public International Law* (OUP 2008) para 3 (describing the genesis of art 292 from the negotiations of the Convention).

[441] Shigeru Oda, 'Dispute Settlement Prospects in the Law of the Sea' (1995) 44 ICLQ 863, 866–67.

[442] The *Tomimaru* (n 216) case, which the Tribunal found to be without object given that the domestic proceedings before Russian courts were completed pending the outcome of the art 292 procedure. See nn 218–19 and accompanying text.

[443] In *Virginia G*, Judge Kulyk noted that by including bunkering vessels within the scope of enforcement powers under art 73, the Tribunal has caused art 292 procedures also to be available to bunkering vessels, or other vessels directly supporting fishing activities, and not just fishing vessels: *Virginia G*, Judgment (n 19) (Declaration of Judge Kulyk) paras 14–15.

[444] See eg *Virginia G*, Judgment (n 19); *San Padre Pio*, Provisional Measures (n 191); *Louisa*, Provisional Measures (n 32); *Louisa*, Judgment (n 2).

the applicant is well-founded,[445] and whether the obligation to release the vessel promptly upon payment of a reasonable bond has been breached or not.[446] This section will assess jurisdiction, issues of admissibility that are distinct to Article 292 proceedings (and not addressed in section III above), and considerations as to whether the application is well-founded or not. Given the prompt release cases have all involved Article 73 so far, Chapter 8 considers the obligation of promptly releasing the vessel upon payment of a reasonable bond in the context of enforcement of fisheries laws.[447]

Article 292 raises a number of criteria to be met for ITLOS to entertain an application for the prompt release of a vessel.[448] In terms of temporal jurisdiction, ITLOS has jurisdiction if the parties have not agreed to submit their case to another court or tribunal within ten days of the vessel's detention.[449] There is an emphasis on resolving prompt release cases as quickly as possible and ITLOS has maintained a swift schedule in each instance. In some instances, parties have complained about the slow speed of the respondent State in setting a bond,[450] or in instituting proceedings,[451] or the respondent has opted not to submit written pleadings because of the short timeframe.[452] If anything, these matters may go to admissibility rather than the temporal jurisdiction of the tribunal.

To establish personal jurisdiction for Article 292 proceedings, both States must be parties to UNCLOS, and the applicant State must be the flag State of the detained vessel at the time the application is filed.[453] Questions of personal jurisdiction might arise if there are questions as to whether the applicant State is the flag State of the detained vessel.[454] The latter dimension may further arise in the context of confiscation through domestic law enforcement proceedings and was discussed above.[455] In one of the few instances where vessel owners may access the tribunal,[456] Article 292(2) allows for proceedings to be instituted 'by or on behalf of' the flag State. Allowing applications 'on behalf of' the flag State is implicit

[445] As required under art 113 of the ITLOS Rules (n 313). This element had caused some confusion in the first prompt release case before ITLOS but has subsequently been settled. See Klein, *Dispute Settlement* (n 62) 91–93. See also Thomas A Mensah, 'The Tribunal and the Prompt Release of Vessels' (2007) 22 IJMCL 425, 434–35.

[446] See eg *Tomimaru* (n 216) para 20 (outlining the elements of Japan's application to the Tribunal). Mensah describes the three criteria to be met as follows: 'The first is that it must be shown that there is a "detention" of the vessel (or crew) by the detaining State; the second is that the detention is covered by a provision of the Convention that requires "the prompt release of the vessel upon the posting of a bond or other financial security," and the third condition is that the detaining State must have failed to release the vessel or crew, as required by the relevant provision of the Convention': Mensah (n 443) 435.

[447] For discussion on the calculation of the amount of the bond see Karaman (n 66) 77–89; Michael White, 'Prompt Release Cases in ITLOS' in Tafsir Malick Ndiaye and Rüdiger Wolfrum (eds), *Law of the Sea, Environmental Law and Settlement of Disputes:* Liber Amicorum *Judge Thomas A. Mensah* (Brill 2007) 1050–52; Yoshifumi Tanaka, 'Prompt Release in the United Nations Convention on the Law of the Sea: Some Reflections on the ITLOS Jurisprudence' (2004) 51 NILR 237, 258–68.

[448] The parties must also follow arts 110–114 of the ITLOS Rules (n 313).

[449] More precisely, the application 'may be submitted to any court or tribunal agreed upon by the parties or, failing such agreement within 10 days from the time of detention, to a court or tribunal accepted by the detaining State under article 287 or to the International Tribunal for the Law of the Sea, unless the parties otherwise agree': UNCLOS (n 1) art 292(1).

[450] See eg *Hoshinmaru* (n 206) paras 23, 63.

[451] *Camouco* (n 238) paras 51 (claiming the delay in submitting the application under art 292 created a situation akin to estoppel) and 54 (the Tribunal rejecting this argument).

[452] *Juno Trader* (n 215) para 15. But see *Juno Trader* (n 215) (Separate Opinion of Judge Lucky) paras 11–26 (discussing this issue and the problem with ITLOS Rules (n 311) giving a possible advantage to the respondent).

[453] See *Grand Prince* (n 9) para 93.

[454] See eg ibid paras 77–93.

[455] See section (III)(A).

[456] The other being in relation to disputes before the Seabed Disputes Chamber. See UNCLOS (n 1) art 187.

recognition of the significant financial interests of the shipowner.[457] If the application is 'on behalf of' the flag State, the State must still duly authorise the application and the case is recorded in the name of the flag State as applicant.[458] The level of involvement of the flag State in the proceedings is then a matter for that State to determine.[459]

The applicant State must allege that the respondent State is in violation of its obligation to release the vessel promptly upon payment of a reasonable bond. For subject matter jurisdiction under Article 292, the application can only relate to the question of the release of the vessel and the payment of the bond. Requests for prompt release may only concern the detention of vessels pursuant to Articles 73(2), 220(7), and 226(1)(b) of the Convention,[460] and not any other forms of detention.[461] As such, where questions arise reflecting on other issues concerning the Convention then they may not be determined in prompt release proceedings. For example, Australia's pursuit of the Volga raised questions about the legality of the hot pursuit, but this matter could not be addressed by ITLOS under Article 292.[462] Equally, only Article 73(2) is part of the allegation and not any of the other provisions relating to fisheries law enforcement under Article 73.[463]

Article 292 proceedings account for the importance of the national judicial processes that are engaged in law enforcement against fishing vessels alleged to have violated coastal State laws and regulations. Notably, Article 292(3) requires that the prompt release case be addressed 'without prejudice to the merits of any case before the appropriate domestic forum against the vessel, its owner or its crew'. ITLOS has observed that this restriction does not prevent it from examining the 'facts and circumstances of the case to the extent necessary for a proper appreciation of the reasonableness of the bond'.[464] Nonetheless, once domestic proceedings have been completed and there are no further appeals possible, proceedings under Article 292 are without object.[465] To continue under Article 292 in such an instance would run counter to the requirement that the prompt release proceedings are not to prejudice domestic processes in accordance with Article 292(3);[466] an order to release a vessel upon payment of a reasonable bond would encroach on national competences in this situation.[467] This finding was part of the balance between the interests of the coastal State and the flag State in the prompt release of vessels.[468]

[457] 'Private parties also play an important role in the postadjudication phase since the bond or other financial security fixed by the Tribunal will likely be paid either by the ship owner or by his or her insurance company': Trevisanut (n 242) 303.

[458] See eg *Juno Trader* (n 215) para 1; *Monte Confurco* (n 239) para 1; *Camouco* (n 238) para 46; *M/V Saiga (Saint Vincent and the Grenadines v Guinea)* (Prompt Release, Judgment) ITLOS Reports 1997, paras 43–44 (*Saiga*, Prompt Release) (Guinea challenged the authorisation given by Saint Vincent and the Grenadines but ITLOS rejected this argument). The authorisation must come from an official within the State who has treaty-making power (such as the head of State, the Minister for Foreign Affairs, or the Attorney-General). See Tullio Treves, 'Article 292' in *Proelss Commentary* (n 44) 1881, para 34.

[459] No involvement is possible. See Anderson (n 440) para 5.

[460] *Saiga*, Prompt Release, 16, para 52; *Volga* (n 438) para 77. See further Karaman (n 66) 28–29.

[461] See *Saiga*, Prompt Release (n 458) paras 52–59; *Saiga*, Prompt Release (n 458) (Dissenting Opinion of Judges Park, Nelson, Chandrasekhara Rao, Vukas, and Ndiaye) para 24.

[462] See *Volga* (n 440) para 33.

[463] See *Monte Confurco* (n 239) paras 26, 61–63; *Camouco* (n 238) para 59.

[464] *Monte Confurco* (n 239) para 74.

[465] *Tomimaru* (n 216) para 81. See discussion in Vincent P Cogliati-Bantz, 'International Tribunal for the Law of the Sea, Hoshinmaru (Japan v Russian Federation) and Tomimaru (Japan v Russian Federation), Prompt Release Judgments of 6 August 2007' (2009) 58 ICLQ 241, 253–55.

[466] *Tomimaru* (n 216) para 80.

[467] ibid.

[468] ibid para 74.

The importance of the rule of law has found voice in Article 292 proceedings. For example, the Tribunal observed in *Juno Trader* that the prompt release obligation includes 'elementary considerations of humanity and due process of law'.[469] The value of applying human rights standards in considering the position of a detained crew has been acknowledged by ITLOS, although more commonly expounded in separate opinions.[470] The due process dimension has been especially important in considering the effects of confiscation and what implications the coastal State's actions in this regard have for flag State in seeking to protect their interests under Article 292.[471] Although ultimately limited in scope, the prompt release proceedings in their broader setting allow for judicial consideration of how their decisions implicate diverse relationships in ocean governance.

C. Counter-Claims

As noted at the outset of this section, counter-claims constitute another form of incidental proceedings. The possibility of counter-claims being pursued is not specifically anticipated under the ITLOS Statute, although ITLOS jurisdiction is broad enough to encompass 'all disputes and all applications submitted to it in accordance with this Convention and all matters specifically provided for in any other agreement which confers jurisdiction on the Tribunal'.[472] Rather, Article 98 of the ITLOS Rules anticipates that a counter-claim may be submitted 'provided that it is directly connected with the subject-matter of the claim of the other party and that it comes within the jurisdiction of the Tribunal'.[473] It falls to the Tribunal to determine if the counter-claim is to be joined to the original proceedings once it has heard arguments from the parties.[474]

Counter-claims have not frequently been presented in UNCLOS proceedings, even though they would constitute an important avenue to address related claims and disputes beyond the initial litigation posture of the applicant. It may be the case that a defence to a claim can be presented as a counter-claim. This situation arose in *Virginia G*. However, the question of counter-claims in that case was complicated by the fact that Panama and Guinea-Bissau had entered into a special agreement to transfer their case to ITLOS whereas it would have otherwise been resolved by an Annex VII arbitral tribunal.[475] Panama, as

[469] *Juno Trader* (n 215) para 77. See further Vincent P Bantz, 'Views from Hamburg: The Juno Trader Case or How to Make Sense of the Coastal State's Rights in the Light of Its Duty of Prompt Release' (2005) 24 UQLJ 415, 430–32.

[470] A notable contributor to the development of human rights perspectives on assessment of crew detention is Judge Tullio Treves. See eg *Juno Trader* (n 215) (Separate Opinion of Judge Treves). See further Irini Papinicolopulu, 'International Judges and the Protection of Human Rights at Sea' in Nerina Boschiero and others (eds), *International Courts and the Development of International Law: Essays in Honour of Tullio Treves* (Asser Press 2013).

[471] See eg Abdul Ghafur Hamid and Khin Maung Sein, 'Prompt Release of Vessel and Crew Under Article 292 of the UNCLOS: Is It an Adequate Safeguard Against the Powers of Coastal States?' (2011) 7 J Appl Sci Res 2421, 2430; Cogliati-Bantz (n 465) 256–57.

[472] UNCLOS (n 1) Annex VI, art 21.

[473] ITLOS Rules (n 313) art 98(1). This rule was based on art 80 of the ICJ Rules but has not been updated since adopted to reflect changes that have since been made to the ICJ Rules. See P Chandrasekhara Rao and Philippe Gautier, *The Rules of the International Tribunal for the Law of the Sea: A Commentary* (Martinus Nijhoff 2006) 280–83.

[474] ITLOS Rules (n 313) art 98(3).

[475] *M/V 'Virginia G' (Panama/Guinea-Bissau)* (Order of 2 November 2012) ITLOS Reports 2012, 309, paras 4–5 (*Virginia G*, Order of 2 November).

applicant, was seeking to challenge Guinea-Bissau's detention of one of its vessels. Guinea-Bissau's counter-claim alleged that Panama violated Article 91 by granting nationality to a ship without any genuine link to Panama and that Panama should be responsible for the damage caused to Guinea-Bissau by the vessel.[476] The President of the Tribunal determined that an initial examination of the admissibility of the counter-claim under Article 98 of the Rules was required.[477]

Panama argued in *Virginia G* that the counter-claim was outside the jurisdiction of the Tribunal as set out in the special agreement.[478] Panama further submitted that the counter-claim was not directly connected to the subject matter of Panama's claim or the facts it had presented.[479] The Tribunal rejected both of these arguments without any detailed analysis.[480] Several judges noted that it may have been preferable for the Tribunal to avail itself of the possibility of joining the claim to the original proceedings without prejudging its admissibility.[481] Judge ad hoc Treves, in dissent, highlighted that counter-claims should not be accepted simply because they also allege violations of UNCLOS. Rather, given the constitutive nature of the Convention and the vast coverage of issues, it was necessary to consider the different claims more precisely.[482] In this case, according to Judge Treves, Panama was alleging that Guinea-Bissau had violated its rights as coastal State in the exercise of its authority in the EEZ and so a claim based on the nationality of a ship under Article 91 was 'devoid of direct connection'.[483] Ultimately, the Tribunal determined at the merits stage of the case that Panama did have a genuine link to the Virginia G at the time of the incident,[484] and Guinea-Bissau's counter-claim was dismissed as a result.[485]

While counter-claims have their own distinct procedure under the ITLOS Rules, the respondent State may still raise a claim against the applicant State in an Annex VII arbitration. For example, although the rules of procedure did not anticipate counter-claims in *Guyana v Suriname*, each State raised claims against the other that they had each violated obligations not to hamper or jeopardise the delimitation of their maritime boundary.[486] The authority of an Annex VII Tribunal to determine counter-claims was confirmed in *Enrica Lexie* based on an 'inherent power', consistent with the approaches in *Barbados v Trinidad and Tobago* and *Guyana v Suriname*.[487] Further, in line with a 'general principle of procedural law', an Annex VII tribunal was said to have jurisdiction over a counter-claim if that claim fell within the jurisdiction of the Tribunal and it was directly connected with the subject matter of the claim of the other party.[488] Any Annex VII tribunal may wish to contemplate a rule on counter-claims in adopting their rules of procedure. In doing so, the language of the ITLOS

[476] ibid para 16.
[477] ibid para 20.
[478] ibid para 29.
[479] ibid paras 27–28.
[480] ibid paras 35–39.
[481] *Virginia G*, Order of 2 November 2012 (n 475) (Declaration of Judges Cot and Kulyk), (Declaration of Judge Türk).
[482] ibid (Dissenting Opinion of Judge ad hoc Treves) para 6.
[483] ibid para 5.
[484] *Virginia G*, Judgment (n 19) para 117.
[485] ibid para 407.
[486] As required under UNCLOS (n 1) arts 74(3) and 81(3).
[487] *Enrica Lexie (Italy v India)* (Award of 21 May 2020) PCA Case No 2015-28, para 254, citing *Barbados v Trinidad and Tobago* (n 40), and *Guyana v Suriname* (n 10) (*Enrica Lexie*, Award).
[488] *Enrica Lexie*, Award (n 487) para 256.

Rules could be followed, but it may be desirable to clarify the language to emphasise the 'direct connection', consistent with Judge ad hoc Treves' views in *Virginia G.*[489]

D. Preliminary Proceedings under Article 294

Article 294 anticipates preliminary proceedings when a dispute emerges concerning a coastal State's exercise of sovereign rights under Article 297. Either at the request of a party or *proprio motu*, a court or tribunal constituted under UNCLOS can decide if the institution of proceedings pertaining to that dispute is an abuse of legal process or whether it is prima facie well-founded.[490] Thus far, no specific Article 294 proceedings have been instituted. However, parties have on occasions alleged an abuse of process in the institution of proceedings against them,[491] and tribunals have considered Article 294 in this context. For example, the *South China Sea* Tribunal concluded that there was no abuse of legal process, as potentially anticipated under Article 294 of UNCLOS, as the Philippines was entitled to institute proceedings against China on a unilateral basis pursuant to the dispute settlement regime set out in the Convention.[492] China's objections were to be more properly considered as objections to jurisdiction and were assessed as such.[493]

The interface with domestic court proceedings has prompted reference to Article 294. In the *Camouco* prompt release proceedings, France considered that an application under Article 292 for prompt release while the domestic case was proceeding rendered the prompt release application inadmissible.[494] ITLOS did not specifically address Article 294, considering more the question of local remedies that had to be exhausted prior to prompt release proceedings under UNCLOS.[495] India reserved its rights under Article 294 in the context of Italy's request for provisional measures in *Enrica Lexie* before ITLOS, as India considered that Italy had selected to pursue the claims against detention before Indian courts and international proceedings were thus an abuse of process.[496] Italy characterised India's view in this regard as importing a 'fork in the road' forum selection clause into UNCLOS

[489] A position that would also seemingly align with that of the ICJ. See International Court of Justice, Rules of Court (adopted 14 April 1978, entered into force 1 July 1978) art 80(1). See further Christine Gray, 'The 2017 Judicial Activity of the International Court of Justice' (2018) 112 AJIL 254–73 (discussing *Alleged Violations of Sovereign Rights and Maritime Spaces in the Caribbean Sea (Nicaragua v Colombia)* (Preliminary Objections) [2016] ICJ Rep 3).

[490] UNCLOS (n 1) art 294(1).

[491] In *Mauritius/Maldives*, Preliminary Objections (n 25), the Maldives further bundled its concerns about the resolution of the territorial sovereignty dispute into a complaint that Mauritius was engaged in an abuse of process but did not raise art 294 as at issue. The Maldives submitted that '[u]sing UNCLOS compulsory procedures to obtain a ruling on a territorial dispute with a third State is the very definition of an abuse of process.' Mauritius, however, contended that it was not seeking the resolution of the territorial sovereignty dispute because on its view of the *Chagos Advisory Opinion* (n 250) this question had been resolved in favour of Mauritius. Instead, Mauritius considered the abuse of process lay with the Maldives for failing to cooperate with the UN following the *Chagos Advisory Opinion*. The Special Chamber dealt briefly with the arguments, focusing on the existence of a dispute under arts 74 and 83 of the Convention, which existed at the time the application was filed, and that the proceedings were properly limited to the matters set out in those provisions: *Mauritius/Maldives*, Preliminary Objections (n 25) paras 339–48.

[492] *South China Sea*, Jurisdiction and Admissibility (n 2) para 128.

[493] ibid.

[494] *Camouco* (n 238) para 16.

[495] Pablo Ferrara, 'Article 294' in *Proelss Commentary* (n 44) 1898, para 6.

[496] *Enrica Lexie*, ITLOS Provisional Measures (n 327) paras 69–70.

proceedings and rejected the assertion on this basis.[497] ITLOS agreed that parties were not deprived from instituting international proceedings, including seeking a request for provisional measures, even when they were engaged in domestic court proceedings as well.[498] India did not proceed with an Article 294 challenge, however.

Article 294 has the potential to constitute an additional shield for a respondent State that is concerned about the adversarial tactics of an applicant State. The proceeding may hold more relevance in the future in light of the increasingly expansive approach to jurisdiction in UNCLOS proceedings. Yet as the provision was intended as additional protection for coastal State sovereign rights,[499] it would seem to be most salient in situations where flag States are seeking to assert their rights within the EEZ or on the continental shelf of a coastal State. The connection to Article 297 reduces the circumstances in which a court or tribunal might hear such a claim. Moreover, this proceeding is most likely to be pertinent in the initial stages of a dispute, especially in the context of a request for provisional measures. Otherwise, it would seem that the reasons for an abuse of process might be subsumed within other challenges to jurisdiction and admissibility, as occurred in the *South China Sea* arbitration.

V. Concluding Remarks

Writing extra-judicially, Judge Mensah has observed:

> Article 292 [on prompt release] reflects the fundamental understanding that underpins the dispute settlement regime of the Convention, which is that the parties to a dispute have at all times the right to settle the dispute by any procedure that they may agree upon. Furthermore, any such procedure agreed upon by the parties always takes precedence over the mechanisms and procedures established by the Convention in Section 2 of Part XV. This is spelt out in express terms in Section 1 of Part XV of the Convention where it is stated that the dispute settlement regime in that Part does not in any way impair 'the right of any State Parties to agree at any time to settle a dispute between them concerning the interpretation or application of this Convention by any peaceful means of their choice'.[500]

Preliminary objections and incidental and other proceedings provide mechanisms by which the parties can seek to control what and how disputes are resolved through arbitration and adjudication under UNCLOS.

In this chapter, some of the objections to jurisdiction and to the admissibility of the dispute have been canvassed (noting that subject matter jurisdiction is the focus of the following chapter). In relation to jurisdiction, the tendency thus far is to expand the exercise of compulsory jurisdiction under UNCLOS. In rendering the barriers to compulsory proceedings under UNCLOS close to meaningless, the tribunals concerned risk disengagement of and/or defiance from States parties. Arguments on admissibility have been managed largely

[497] ibid para 72.
[498] ibid para 73.
[499] Ferrara (n 495) 1897.
[500] Mensah (n 445) 429.

consistently with other international jurisprudence and have been chiefly fact dependent. Issues of standing in relation to flag States and their vessels are likely to remain polemic in dispute settlement under UNCLOS because of the open registry system.

Among incidental and other proceedings, one of the main forms of incidental proceedings that emerges in UNCLOS dispute settlement is requests for provisional measures. Consistent with ICJ jurisprudence, these measures are intended 'to preserve the respective rights of the parties pending the decision of the Court, and presupposes that irreparable prejudice should not be caused to rights which are the subject of dispute in judicial proceedings'.[501] Experience in UNCLOS dispute settlement thus far indicates that tribunals will show initiative in seeking to calibrate the interests of both parties, although where the emphasis falls in whose rights to safeguard remains somewhat unpredictable.

Prompt release proceedings under Article 292 have been another key avenue of judicial activity in UNCLOS dispute settlement and are further addressed in Chapter 8 in the context of fisheries law enforcement. The discussion in this chapter has focused on the varied hurdles to consider for applications to be heard and to achieve an order for the prompt release of a vessel upon payment of a reasonable bond. The case law has become more settled over time and it is notable that fewer cases have been instituted under Article 292 in more recent years—the reasons for this shift could prompt a high degree of speculation. Instead, more cases are being instituted on the merits that concern the detention of vessels and crew. Clearly, the exercise of coastal State law enforcement powers as compared to the freedom of navigation enjoyed by the vessels of flag States remains one of the most contentious balances in ocean governance. This tension has also emerged in determining the scope of subject matter jurisdiction and is further examined in the following chapter.

[501] *Passage through the Great Belt (Finland v Denmark)* (Provisional Measures, Order of 29 July 1991) [1991] ICJ Rep 12, para 16.

4
Subject Matter Jurisdiction

I. Introduction

The starting point for defining the scope of subject matter jurisdiction of a Part XV tribunal is Article 286 of the United Nations Convention on the Law of the Sea (UNCLOS), which provides that 'any dispute concerning the interpretation or application of this Convention' may be submitted to the court or tribunal having jurisdiction under Section 2 of Part XV, subject to exceptions and limitations set out in Articles 297 and 298. Article 288(1) replicates that same formulation in defining the jurisdiction of a Part XV tribunal as covering 'any dispute concerning the interpretation or application of the Convention'.[1]

Establishing that a dispute falls within the subject matter jurisdiction of a court or tribunal constituted under UNCLOS entails an assessment of whether the dispute concerns 'the interpretation or application' of UNCLOS, as well as whether it falls within an exception to the UNCLOS dispute settlement procedure. The characterisation of the dispute will naturally depend on the particular aims of the States concerned. That is, does the government want the dispute resolved through arbitration or adjudication under UNCLOS or not? The lawyers engaged in the dispute will then frame the case accordingly. As Boyle rightly noted: '[E]verything turns in practice not on what each case involves but on how the issues are formulated. Formulate them wrongly and the case falls outside compulsory jurisdiction. Formulate the same case differently and it falls inside.'[2]

It necessarily falls to judges to make the determination as to whether there is a dispute concerning the interpretation or application of the Convention.[3] In doing so, the International Tribunal for the Law of the Sea (ITLOS) has indicated that it will 'establish a link between the facts advanced' by the applicant and the UNCLOS provisions relied upon so as to 'show that such provisions can sustain the claims submitted'.[4] Although the mere invocation of a provision of the Convention is insufficient,[5] the standard does not appear to

[1] United Nations Convention on the Law of the Sea (adopted 10 December 1982, entered into force 16 November 1994) 1833 UNTS 397, art 288(1). Article 288(2) provides that an UNCLOS tribunal shall also have jurisdiction over any dispute concerning the interpretation or application of another international agreement related to the purposes of the Convention, submitted to it in accordance with that agreement.

[2] Alan E Boyle, 'Dispute Settlement and the Law of the Sea Convention: Problems of Fragmentation and Jurisdiction' (1997) 46 ICLQ 37, 38.

[3] 'In the event of a dispute as to whether a court or tribunal has jurisdiction, the matter shall be settled by decision of that court or tribunal': UNCLOS (n 1) art 288(4).

[4] *M/V Norstar (Panama v Italy)* (Preliminary Objections Judgment of 4 November 2016) ITLOS Case No 25, para 110 (*Norstar*, Preliminary Objections); *M/V Louisa (Saint Vincent and the Grenadines v Spain)* (Provisional Measures, Order of 23 December 2010) ITLOS Reports 2008–2010, 58, para 99 (*Louisa*, Preliminary Objections).

[5] *Duzgit Integrity Arbitration (Malta v São Tomé and Príncipe)* (Award of 5 September 2016) PCA Case No 2014-07, para 127 (the arguments of Sao Tome, referencing the *Louisa* decision) (*Duzgit Integrity*).

be very high but may be as simple as whether the actions in question 'may be viewed as' an infringement of a relevant provision.[6]

This chapter explores judicial decision-making to date on subject matter jurisdiction in relation to four matters. First, we consider the core requirement that the dispute concerns the interpretation or application of UNCLOS and how this scope of jurisdiction is to be determined in the difficult situation of closely intertwined territorial sovereignty and maritime disputes. Secondly, the limitations on compulsory jurisdiction imposed by Article 297 are assessed, with a focus on the decisions relating to fisheries and marine environment disputes. Thirdly, although not all States have made declarations under Article 298 excluding the specific disputes listed therein, the exclusions have prompted challenges before tribunals constituted under Part XV of UNCLOS. These disputes concern maritime boundary delimitation, historic bays and titles, military activities, and certain law enforcement activities. The precise scope of these exceptions is being elucidated through the jurisprudence, although the decisions also reveal the potential for differing interpretations. Finally, this chapter addresses the intersection that has emerged between subject matter jurisdiction and the applicable law for resolving UNCLOS disputes. Some tribunals have conflated the wide scope of applicable law with subject matter jurisdiction and careful attention is needed to what laws and instruments may be considered in UNCLOS dispute settlement and for what purpose. Similar to the trend discussed in the previous chapter, the jurisdictional decisions in relation to subject matter have tended to favour the inclusion of disputes within the compulsory procedures available under Part XV of UNCLOS. In favouring interpretations that seek to expand the exercise of jurisdiction, some stakeholders may seek alternative means for resolving law of the sea disputes rather than relying on the process in Part XV of UNCLOS—or remain outside the UNCLOS regime altogether. While the exceptions to compulsory jurisdiction have been cast narrowly to allow for judicial engagement in resolving law of the sea disputes, the initial use of Article 293 on applicable law to widen the scope of jurisdiction has progressively lessened.

II. Disputes Concerning the Interpretation or Application of UNCLOS

Article 288(1) of UNCLOS defines the subject matter jurisdiction of a tribunal constituted under it as follows: 'A court or tribunal referred to in article 287 shall have jurisdiction over any dispute *concerning the interpretation or application of the Convention* which is submitted to it in accordance with this Part.'[7]

Article 288(2) provides that an UNCLOS tribunal shall also have jurisdiction over any dispute concerning the interpretation or application of another international agreement related to the purposes of the Convention, submitted to it in accordance with that agreement.[8] No contentious case has been decided on the basis of Article 288(2) to date.

[6] See *Norstar*, Preliminary Objections (n 4) para 122. For criticism of this standard see *Norstar*, Preliminary Objections (n 4) (Joint Separate Opinions of Judges Wolfrum and Attard) para 5; Robin Churchill, 'Dispute Settlement in the Law of the Sea: Survey for 2015, Part II and 2016' (2017) 32 IJMCL 379, 381–85.

[7] UNCLOS (n 1) art 288(1) (emphasis added).

[8] ibid art 288(2).

The subject matter jurisdiction of any tribunal constituted under UNCLOS must therefore fall within the parameters of addressing a 'dispute concerning the interpretation or application' of UNCLOS as a preliminary matter. In *Louisa*, ITLOS concluded that it did not have jurisdiction because the dispute did not ultimately concern the interpretation or application of UNCLOS. In this case, Saint Vincent and the Grenadines challenged Spain's actions in arresting and detaining the M/V Louisa, a vessel flagged to Saint Vincent and the Grenadines. Spain arrested the vessel for criminal proceedings because its alleged activities related to the protection of underwater cultural heritage and 'the possession and handling of weapons of war'.[9] Saint Vincent and the Grenadines alleged that Spain's actions were in violation of Articles 73, 87, 226, 227, and 303 of UNCLOS.[10] Spain challenged the Tribunal's jurisdiction on the basis that none of the provisions related to the particular facts of the case. For this purpose, the Tribunal stated:

> To enable the Tribunal to determine whether it has jurisdiction, it must establish a link between the facts advanced by Saint Vincent and the Grenadines and the provisions of the Convention referred to by it and show that such provisions can sustain the claim or claims submitted by Saint Vincent and the Grenadines.[11]

No further explanation was given as to the standard that must be met for the 'link' to be established.[12] Given the location of the vessel in port at the time it was detained and the activities in which it was alleged to be engaged, ITLOS concluded that none of the provisions supported the claims asserted by Saint Vincent and the Grenadines.[13] Consequently, jurisdiction could not be established.

The most controversial aspect of Article 288(1) thus far has concerned the question of whether territorial sovereignty disputes, which necessarily implicate the maritime rights that follow from that sovereignty, may be resolved through proceedings under UNCLOS.

A. Territorial Sovereignty Disputes in UNCLOS Proceedings

Maritime disputes may well emerge where territorial sovereignty over land is disputed. In this situation, which State is the 'coastal State' may be contentious and result in differing views as to which State has what rights and responsibilities in a given maritime area. In these circumstances, it is essential to establish which State has territorial sovereignty so as to understand the lawful distribution of rights and duties in the adjacent maritime space.[14] The importance of this point is reflected in the principle that land dominates the sea,[15] and

[9] *M/V Louisa (Saint Vincent and the Grenadines v Spain)* (Judgment) ITLOS Reports 2013, 4, para 104 (*Louisa*, Judgment).

[10] ibid para 98.

[11] ibid para 99.

[12] An issue discussed by Judge Paik in his Declaration. See *Louisa*, Judgment (n 9) (Declaration of Judge Paik) para 12.

[13] *Louisa*, Judgment (n 9) para 151. Several judges had reached this conclusion at the provisional measures stage, even where only prima facie jurisdiction had to be established.

[14] The ICJ 'has made clear that maritime rights derive from the coastal State's sovereignty over the land, a principle which can be summarized as "the land dominates the sea"': *North Sea Continental Shelf Cases (Germany/Denmark; Germany/Netherlands)* (Judgment) [1969] ICJ Rep 3, para 96 (*North Sea Continental Shelf*); *Aegean Sea Continental Shelf (Greece v Turkey)* (Judgment) [1978] ICJ Rep 3, 36, para 86.

[15] See eg *Grisbadarna Maritime Frontier (Norway v Sweden)* (1910) 4 AJIL 186, 226.

the International Court of Justice (ICJ) has recognised this proposition on a variety of occasions.[16] As maritime rights and duties often flow from a State's sovereignty over land, it may be necessary to resolve the question of sovereignty so as to resolve competing maritime claims. Four cases have so far prompted consideration of this issue: *Chagos Marine Protected Area Arbitration* (*Chagos MPA*),[17] the *South China Sea* arbitration,[18] *Coastal Rights in the Black Sea*[19] and *Mauritius/Maldives*.[20] For present purposes, the critical issue is whether a tribunal constituted under UNCLOS may resolve the question of disputed territorial sovereignty so as to resolve the disputed maritime claims. Any tribunal in this situation must balance the limits of consent to jurisdiction with responsibilities to exercise jurisdiction fully and effectively.[21]

In *Chagos MPA*, the Mauritian claim centred on a decision of the United Kingdom to establish a Marine Protected Area (MPA) around the Chagos Islands. In the early nineteenth century, Mauritius was ceded by France to the United Kingdom, and the Chagos Archipelago was administered by the United Kingdom as a dependency of Mauritius. In the context of Mauritius' move towards independence, the Chagos Archipelago was detached from Mauritius for the purpose of establishing a strategic US airbase on one of the islands. In the context of that process, there were negotiations between the United Kingdom and the Mauritian Council of Ministers resulting in the 'Lancaster House Undertakings'.[22] These recorded conditions on the agreement to detach the Chagos islands, including that 'if the need for the [US defence] facilities on the islands disappeared the islands should be returned to Mauritius' and that the United Kingdom would ensure that fishing rights would remain available to Mauritius.[23] In 1968, Mauritius became an independent State. From around 1980, the issue of sovereignty over the Chagos Archipelago was raised by Mauritius and there were ongoing negotiations between it and the United Kingdom on this issue. There had also been opposing claims to maritime entitlements of the islands, including in respect of the extended continental shelf.

In December 2010, Mauritius commenced an Annex VII arbitration against the United Kingdom under Article 287 of UNCLOS in response to the United Kingdom's declaration of an MPA for the Chagos Archipelago, under which there was to be a complete ban on fishing once existing licences expired. Two of Mauritius' submissions gave rise to questions of the scope of jurisdiction under Article 288(1). The first submission was that the United Kingdom was not entitled to declare a MPA because it was not a coastal State under UNCLOS. The second submission was that the United Kingdom was prevented from unilaterally declaring the MPA due to Mauritius' rights as a coastal State under UNCLOS.

[16] See eg *Territorial and Maritime Dispute (Nicaragua v Colombia)* (Judgment) [2012] ICJ Rep 624, 674 (*Territorial and Maritime Dispute*, Judgment); *Maritime Delimitation in the Black Sea (Romania v Ukraine)* (Judgment) [2009] ICJ Rep 61, 89.

[17] *Chagos Marine Protected Area Arbitration (Mauritius v United Kingdom)* (Award of 18 March 2015) PCA Case No 2011-03 (*Chagos MPA*).

[18] *South China Sea Arbitration (Philippines v China)* (Award of 12 July 2016) PCA Case No 2013-19 (*South China Sea*, Award).

[19] *Dispute Concerning Coastal State Rights in the Black Sea, Sea of Azov, and Kerch Strait (Ukraine v Russia)* (Preliminary Objections Award of 21 February 2020) PCA Case No 2017-06 (*Coastal State Rights in the Black Sea*).

[20] *Delimitation of the Maritime Boundary between Mauritius and Maldives in the Indian Ocean (Mauritius/Maldives)* (Merits) ITLOS Case No 28 (*Mauritius/Maldives*, Merits).

[21] Robert G Volterra, Giorgio F Mandelli, and Álvaro Nistal, 'The Characterisation of the *Dispute Concerning Coastal State Rights in the Black Sea, Sea of Azov, and Kerch Strait*' (2018) 33 IJMCL 614, 617.

[22] *Chagos MPA* (n 17) paras 74–77.

[23] ibid para 77.

The Tribunal's analysis of its jurisdiction over the first and second submissions addressed Article 288(1) and incidental jurisdiction in some detail. The Tribunal first noted that term 'coastal State' was not defined in UNCLOS, nor did UNCLOS provide guidance on identification of the 'coastal State' in circumstances where land territory fronting a coast is disputed. Thus, 'the identity of the coastal State for the purposes of the Convention would be a matter to be determined through the application of rules of international law lying outside the international law of the sea'.[24] Whether a Part XV tribunal could address such matters and apply exterior sources of law 'raise[d] a question of the scope of jurisdiction under the Convention'.[25]

Referring to Article 288(1), the Tribunal then noted that the question of its jurisdiction 'hinge[d] entirely on whether the issues raised in Mauritius' First Submission represent a dispute "concerning the interpretation or application" of the Convention'.[26] In the Tribunal's view, it raised two questions:

> first, what is the nature of the dispute encompassed in Mauritius' First Submission? Second, to the extent that ... the ... dispute [is], at its core, a matter of territorial sovereignty, to what extent does Article 288(1) permit a tribunal to determine issues of disputed land sovereignty as a necessary precondition to a determination of rights and duties in the adjacent sea?[27]

In relation to the nature of the dispute, it is worth noting that the ICJ had cause to examine the subject matter of disputes before it in order to determine whether a dispute fell within its jurisdiction.[28] The ICJ had summarised its approach from previous cases in the *Obligation to Negotiate Access to the Pacific Ocean*.[29] In that case, Chile argued that the subject matter of Bolivia's claim was 'territorial sovereignty and the character of Bolivia's access to the Pacific Ocean'.[30] Chile considered that Bolivia's Application obfuscated the true subject matter of the claim.[31] Bolivia contended that the case was a distinct matter concerning an obligation to negotiate sovereign access to the sea.[32]

In resolving these claims, the ICJ stated that it must determine the subject matter of the dispute on an objective basis, taking into account the positions and pleadings of both parties, in order to isolate the real issue in the case.[33] Yet in doing so, there was an emphasis on how the applicant had formulated the dispute and what facts the applicant identified as the basis of its claim. The ICJ stated that:

[24] ibid para 203.
[25] ibid.
[26] ibid para 206.
[27] ibid.
[28] The Court's Statute and its Rules require applicants to specify the 'precise nature of the claim' in the applications instituting proceedings: Statute of the International Court of Justice, art 40(1); International Court of Justice, Rules of Court (adopted 14 April 1978, entered into force 1 July 1978) art 38(1).
[29] *Obligation to Negotiate Access to the Pacific Ocean (Bolivia v Chile)* (Preliminary Objections) [2015] ICJ Rep 592.
[30] ibid para 28.
[31] ibid para 32.
[32] ibid para 30.
[33] ibid para 26.

> while it may be assumed that sovereign access to the Pacific Ocean is, in the end, Bolivia's goal, a distinction must be drawn between that goal and the related but distinct dispute presented by the Application, namely, whether Chile has an obligation to negotiate Bolivia's sovereign access to the sea and, if such an obligation exists, whether Chile has breached it. The Application does not ask the Court to adjudge and declare that Bolivia has a right to sovereign access.[34]

The Court was therefore willing to proceed on the narrow and precise question presented by Bolivia irrespective of the wider implications of the dispute.

The *Chagos MPA* Tribunal acknowledged the earlier jurisprudence of the ICJ, but placed less emphasis on the view of the applicant in its approach.[35] Instead, the Tribunal stated:

> For the purpose of characterizing the Parties' dispute, however, the Tribunal must evaluate where the relative weight of the dispute lies. Is the Parties' dispute primarily a matter of the interpretation and application of the term 'coastal State', with the issue of sovereignty forming one aspect of a larger question? Or does the Parties' dispute primarily concern sovereignty, with the United Kingdom's actions as a 'coastal State' merely representing a manifestation of that dispute? In the Tribunal's view, this question all but answers itself.[36]

The Tribunal was quite clear in ascertaining that two of Mauritius' submissions that queried whether the United Kingdom had acted lawfully as a 'coastal State' went to a question of territorial sovereignty.[37] The Tribunal noted that there was a long-standing dispute between the two States as to sovereignty over the Chagos Archipelago, and, in all the circumstances, it concluded that this was the primary dispute underlying the first submission.[38] The Tribunal thus considered that the first submission primarily concerned sovereignty, and not interpretation or application of UNCLOS. Therefore, the majority of the Tribunal held that it was outside its jurisdiction.[39]

Mauritius' second submission was that the United Kingdom was prevented from declaring unilaterally the MPA because Mauritius had rights as a 'coastal State'.[40] The Tribunal found that this was a dispute distinct from Mauritius' first submission, but found that the underlying dispute as to sovereignty was 'predominant',[41] and therefore for the same reasons as the First Submission, was outside its jurisdiction.[42]

[34] ibid para 32.
[35] *Chagos MPA* (n 17) para 229.
[36] ibid para 211.
[37] ibid para 212.
[38] ibid para 211. The Tribunal noted that Mauritius had acknowledged before the Tribunal that the consequences of a finding that the United Kingdom was not the coastal State would extend beyond the validity of the MPA, such that the United Kingdom would be required to leave the Archipelago: see para 211, citing *Chagos Marine Protected Area Arbitration (Mauritius v United Kingdom)* (Final Transcript) PCA Case No 2011-03, 1030:13–21 (*Chagos MPA*, Final Transcript). The Tribunal considered that these kinds of consequences were not ones that follow from a narrow dispute as to the interpretation of the words 'coastal State' for the purposes of certain provisions of UNCLOS. The Tribunal therefore concluded that the dispute was one properly characterized as relating to land sovereignty over the Chagos Archipelago, with an ancillary issue relating to the interpretation and application of UNCLOS: *Chagos MPA* (n 17) para 212.
[39] *Chagos MPA* (n 17) para 221.
[40] ibid para 222.
[41] ibid para 229.
[42] ibid para 230. On this issue, Judges Kateka and Wolfrüm also dissented. They considered that this was a dispute as to whether the United Kingdom had ceded its rights as a coastal State through its commitments in the Lancaster House Undertakings: (Dissenting and Concurring Opinion of Judges Kateka and Wolfrum) para 19. In

The minority in *Chagos MPA* disagreed in relation to the characterisation of the dispute, but instead took the position that the dispute could not be qualified as one about the sovereignty of the Chagos Archipelago.[43] Judges Kateka and Wolfrum adhered more closely to the approach of the ICJ in this regard, and opted to focus on the wording used in Mauritius' submission. On this basis, the minority judges concluded: 'The differing views on the coastal State are the dispute before the Tribunal and the issue of sovereignty over the Chagos Archipelago is merely an element in the reasoning of Mauritius and not to be decided by the Tribunal.'[44] Although the minority judges took the position that the sovereignty issue did not have to be decided, they nonetheless proceeded to assess whether the excision of the Chagos Archipelago at the time of Mauritian independence was lawful and concluded it was not.[45] To reach such a conclusion appears to cut against their initial characterisation of the dispute, including that sovereignty did not have to be decided in the course of resolving Mauritian claims. As such, the approach of the majority is preferable in seeking to characterise the 'predominant' aspect of the dispute as one of territorial sovereignty and hence not concerning the interpretation or application of UNCLOS.

The question of whether the dispute concerned contested territorial sovereignty or was one concerning the interpretation or application of UNCLOS was considered in the *South China Sea* arbitration. China considered that the case submitted by the Philippines fundamentally concerned a question of territorial sovereignty and hence was outside the scope of UNCLOS dispute settlement entirely.[46] The Philippines instead focused one of the core aspects of its case on different provisions of UNCLOS and followed an approach of seeking determinations of maritime entitlements to particular marine features, which the Philippines considered could be done in the absence of knowledge of the ownership of those features. The Philippines dismissed the relevance of sovereignty to any consideration of what the maritime entitlement of some land might be. They did so on the basis that the status of a feature as a rock or island does not alter depending on which State might be sovereign over that feature but is instead an objective determination.[47]

In its decision on jurisdiction, the *South China Sea* Tribunal confirmed that, in accordance with Article 288(1) of UNCLOS, disputes must concern the interpretation and application of the Convention.[48] It was necessary that the Tribunal identify and characterise the dispute on an objective basis.[49] The Tribunal noted that there was an extant dispute over land sovereignty of the relevant maritime features in the South China Sea, but said that

the view of the minority, the Tribunal ought to have considered whether the undertakings in the Lancaster House Undertakings were rights under Article 56(2) of UNCLOS: (Dissenting and Concurring Opinion of Judges Kateka and Wolfrum) para 47.

[43] ibid (Separate Opinion of Judges Kateka and Wolfrum) para 9.
[44] *Chagos MPA* (n 17) para 17.
[45] ibid paras 70–80.
[46] Ministry of Foreign Affairs of the People's Republic of China, 'Position Paper of the Government of the People's Republic of China on the Matter of Jurisdiction in the South China Sea Arbitration Initiated by the Republic of the Philippines' (7 December 2014) http://www.fmprc.gov.cn/mfa_eng/zxxx_662805/t1217147.shtml (China's Position Paper).
[47] *South China Sea Arbitration (Philippines v China)* (Award on Jurisdiction and Admissibility of 29 October 2015) PCA Case No 2013-19, para 144 (*South China Sea*, Jurisdiction and Admissibility).
[48] ibid para 148.
[49] ibid para 150.

it did not automatically follow that it was that dispute that was before the Tribunal.[50] The Tribunal then said that it:

> might consider that the Philippines' Submissions could be understood to relate to sovereignty if it were convinced that either (a) the resolution of the Philippines' claims would require the Tribunal first to render a decision on sovereignty, either expressly or implicitly; or (b) the actual objective of the Philippines' claims was to advance its position in the Parties' dispute over sovereignty.[51]

In applying its two-stage test, the Tribunal:

(a) noted that the Philippines had not asked the Tribunal to rule on sovereignty and repeatedly requested that the Tribunal refrain from doing so;
(b) agreed with the Philippines that it was entirely possible to decide whether the maritime features generated maritime entitlements accepting China's case that it is sovereign over them; and
(c) said that it would ensure, in addressing the merits, not to advance or detract from either Party's claims to land sovereignty in the South China Sea.[52]

The Tribunal then distinguished the *Chagos MPA* arbitration on the basis that Mauritius' first and second submissions would have required an implicit decision on sovereignty, whereas the Philippines' claims could be determined without rendering any decision on sovereignty.[53]

It is apparent that the *South China Sea* Tribunal took an arguably narrower approach to the characterisation of the dispute than the *Chagos MPA* Tribunal, because it acknowledged the broader dispute but then it focused on the specific claims made in the Philippines' submissions. The *Chagos MPA* Tribunal would have asked, what was the primary dispute? Arguably, the primary dispute between the Philippines and China was not whether these individual shoals generate maritime entitlements but who gets those maritime entitlements.[54] Yet the *South China Sea* Tribunal's approach aligned more with that of the ICJ,[55] and was subsequently used in *Coastal State Rights in the Black Sea*.[56]

The background to the *Coastal State Rights in the Black Sea* arbitration concerned Russia's occupation of Crimea and assertion of rights over the adjacent maritime areas from 2014. Russia maintained that a referendum held in the Crimean Peninsula indicated a preference for reunification with Russia at that time.[57] Ukraine instead challenged Russia's views on the validity of the referendum and maintained that Russia had unlawfully used force against the territorial integrity of Ukraine.[58] In the context of the Annex VII arbitration, Russia

[50] ibid para 152.
[51] ibid para 153.
[52] ibid para 153.
[53] ibid.
[54] See Natalie Klein, 'The Vicissitudes of Dispute Settlement under the Law of the Sea Convention' (2017) 32 IJMCL 332, 345–49 (Klein, 'The Vicissitudes').
[55] See nn 28–34 and accompanying text.
[56] '[T]he Arbitral Tribunal needs to examine the positions of the Parties, while giving particular attention to the formulation of the dispute chosen by Ukraine as Applicant: *Coastal State Rights in the Black Sea* (n 19) para 151.
[57] ibid para 4.
[58] ibid para 6.

contested the Tribunal's jurisdiction, arguing that 'a predicate dispute on sovereignty over Crimea exists' and this dispute was at the heart of the dispute, rather than ancillary to the dispute.[59] As such, this dispute was outside the jurisdiction bestowed on the Tribunal under Article 288(1) of the Convention.

Ukraine characterised Russia's annexation of Crimea as an armed aggression against Ukraine.[60] The claims it asserted before the Annex VII Tribunal were largely all founded on Ukraine being sovereign over Crimea.[61] Ukraine argued that Russia's claim of sovereignty over Crime was 'inadmissible' and 'implausible'. Ukraine thus presented its case on the basis that there was no sovereignty dispute over Crimea;[62] presumably because Ukraine considered its sovereignty over Crimea to be manifest in the face of Russian aggression. Ukraine alternatively submitted that if there was a sovereignty dispute, it was ancillary to the determination of the maritime dispute that Ukraine had submitted to the Tribunal.[63]

The Tribunal considered that it had to determine the scope of jurisdiction under Article 288(1) as a means of deciding whether a question of disputed territorial sovereignty could be resolved in the arbitration. To this end, the Tribunal supported the view from *Chagos MPA* that the failure to include territorial sovereignty disputes within the limitations and exceptions of Section 3 of Part XV was indicative of the drafters' intent that these sorts of disputes were not considered to be a 'dispute concerning the interpretation or application of the Convention'.[64] This approach makes sense because territorial sovereignty disputes would be even more important to the national interest of States than maritime boundary or historic title disputes.[65] The Tribunal further endorsed the approach of the *South China Sea* Tribunal in refraining from any explicit or implicit determination of sovereignty or allowing for one party to advance its claim to sovereignty through the UNCLOS proceedings.[66]

The subsequent question to resolve in *Coastal State Rights in the Black Sea* was 'the existence *vel non* of a sovereignty dispute over Crimea'.[67] The Tribunal easily determined that the parties were in disagreement as to which State was sovereign over Crimea and hence which was the 'coastal State' for the purposes of assessing violations of the Convention.[68] Furthermore, 'the question of sovereignty [was] a prerequisite to the Arbitral Tribunal's decision on a number of claims submitted by Ukraine under the Convention'.[69] The resolution of many of the Ukrainian claims would have necessitated the Tribunal determining either explicitly or implicitly the sovereignty of either party over Crimea.[70] Ukraine thus had to reformulate its claims for resolution on the merits that took into account this jurisdictional limitation of the Tribunal.

Contested sovereignty in relation to the Chagos Archipelago again emerged in *Mauritius/ Maldives*. However, at this point, the case was submitted following an advisory opinion of

59 ibid para 161.
60 See eg ibid paras 51 and 52.
61 ibid paras 152, 154.
62 ibid para 161.
63 ibid.
64 ibid para 156. See also Chagos *MPA* (n 17) para 215.
65 Andrew Serdy, 'Article 298' in Alexander Proelss (ed), *United Nations Convention on the Law of the Sea: A Commentary* (CH Beck, Hart Publishing, and Nomos 2017) 1918, para 17 (*Proelss Commentary*).
66 *Coastal State Rights in the Black Sea* (n 19) para 161.
67 ibid para 154.
68 ibid para 165.
69 ibid para 195.
70 ibid para 197.

the ICJ (*Chagos Advisory Opinion*) on the question as to whether the decolonisation of Mauritius was lawful and the consequences of such a finding for the United Kingdom.[71] The ICJ concluded that the decolonisation of Mauritius was unlawful because of the separation of the Chagos Archipelago and that the United Kingdom was required to bring to a rapid end its administration of the Chagos Archipelago.[72] Subsequent to this Opinion, the United Kingdom commented that it 'did not share the approach' of the Court and would continue to exercise its sovereignty over the Chagos Archipelago until it was no longer needed for defence purposes.[73]

Before the Special Chamber, the parties seemingly agreed that a question of territorial sovereignty was outside the scope of jurisdiction available under Article 288(1) of UNCLOS.[74] The Special Chamber stated as much in unequivocal terms: 'The Special Chamber considers that a dispute, which requires the determination of a question of territorial sovereignty, may not be regarded as a dispute concerning the interpretation or application of the Convention under article 288, paragraph 1, of the Convention.'[75] Yet the legal status of the Chagos Archipelago was at the core of the parties' contentions.[76]

In addressing the relevance of the *Chagos Advisory Opinion*, the Maldives argued that if the ICJ had resolved the territorial sovereignty dispute between Mauritius and the United Kingdom then it had gone beyond the questions posed and exceeded its jurisdiction.[77] Mauritius emphasised that the ICJ was aware of the much broader questions at stake, which were the focus of its opinion, even if that examination had the effect of determining the question of Mauritius's sovereignty over the Chagos Archipelago.[78] The Special Chamber considered that there was indeed a close relationship between sovereignty and decolonisation.[79] It further observed that while the principle of consent could not be obviated, the reality was that the advisory opinion could, and did, entail implications for sovereignty.[80] Moreover, the non-binding nature of the advisory opinion did not mean that the views of the Court were without legal effect.[81] The United Kingdom's 'mere assertion' of its continued sovereignty did not demonstrate the existence of a sovereignty dispute over the Chagos Archipelago,[82] but was considered contrary to the ICJ findings in the *Chagos Advisory Opinion*.[83] Instead, the Special Chamber determined that the conclusions of the *Chagos MPA* arbitration, which had recognised that Mauritius held certain rights in relation to the

[71] *Legal Consequences of the Separation of the Chagos Archipelago from Mauritius in 1965* (Advisory Opinion) General List No 169 [2019] ICJ Rep 95, para 1 (setting out the questions posed by the UN General Assembly) (*Chagos Advisory Opinion*).

[72] ibid para 183.

[73] HC Deb 30 April 2019, vol 659, col 4WS.

[74] *Delimitation of the Maritime Boundary between Mauritius and Maldives in the Indian Ocean (Mauritius/Maldives)* (Preliminary Objections Judgment of 28 January 2021) ITLOS Case No 28, para 107 (noting that Mauritius had not contested this point) 111 (*Mauritius/Maldives*, Preliminary Objections).

[75] ibid para 110.

[76] ibid para 115.

[77] ibid para 148.

[78] ibid paras 154–55 and para 157.

[79] ibid para 166.

[80] ibid para 168; see further para 189.

[81] ibid paras 203–205. The Special Chamber appeared to draw a distinction between 'authoritative' and 'binding'. See Thomas Burri and Jamie Trinidad, 'Introductory Note to Dispute Concerning Delimitation of the Maritime Boundary between Mauritius and Maldives in the Indian Ocean, Preliminary Objections (ITLOS)' (2021) 60(6) ILM 969, fns 26–30.

[82] *Mauritius/Maldives*, Preliminary Objections (n 74) para 245.

[83] ibid para 246.

waters of the Chagos Archipelago under the Lancaster House Undertakings, and the ICJ's views in the *Chagos Advisory Opinion* were sufficient to treat Mauritius as the coastal State for the purpose of delimiting the maritime boundary.[84]

In reaching this conclusion, what was previously a legally non-binding determination has become a binding decision of the Special Chamber. The effect of proceeding in such a way is to render a decision on the territorial sovereignty dispute that, at least from the United Kingdom's perspective (and arguably those States that voted against or abstained from the UN General Assembly resolution),[85] continued. Judge ad hoc Oxman did not consider it necessary to risk 'calling into question the coherence of the jurisprudence regarding jurisdiction to determine rights to land territory in proceedings instituted under the compulsory jurisdiction provisions of Section 2 of Part XV of the Convention'.[86] However, the Special Chamber essentially moved away from the determination that there was a territorial sovereignty dispute in the *Chagos MPA* arbitration to a view that there was no longer such a dispute in light of the clarification from the *Chagos Advisory Opinion* and subsequent UN General Assembly resolution.[87]

The case law on this issue to date has thus clarified that a territorial sovereignty dispute does not constitute a 'dispute concerning the interpretation or application of the Convention' for the purposes of Article 288 of UNCLOS. However, Akande has observed that 'if the international tribunal is simply applying a legal finding which is already binding or authoritative with respect to the third state there can be no complaint of an overreach of competence as the tribunal is not really exercising its own competence but simply accepting a reality already determined by a competent body' and that arguably this situation existed in *Mauritius/Maldives*.[88] The extent of authority accorded to advisory opinions may be of some concern given the perceived shift in favour of the legal status of such opinions.[89] The only other means by which a territorial sovereignty dispute might still come before a tribunal constituted under UNCLOS would be in the context of a maritime boundary dispute

[84] ibid para 250.

[85] 'Advisory Opinion of the International Court of Justice on the Legal Consequences of the Separation of the Chagos Archipelago from Mauritius in 1965', UNGA Res 73/295 of (24 May 2019) UN Doc A/RES/73/295. There were 116 States in favour, to six against (Australia, Hungary, Israel, Maldives, United Kingdom, and the United States) with fifty-six abstentions.

[86] *Mauritius/Maldives*, Preliminary Objections (n 74) (Separate and Dissenting Opinion of Judge ad hoc Oxman) para 41. Judge ad hoc Oxman would have instead cast the dispute far more narrowly in focusing only on the requirements for negotiating to reach a maritime boundary delimitation: see paras 38, 40.

[87] See Volker Roeben and Sava Jankovic, 'Unpacking Sovereignty and Self-Determination in ITLOS and the ICC: A Bundle of Rights?' *EJIL: Talk!* (4 March 2021) https://www.ejiltalk.org/unpacking-sovereignty-and-self-determination-in-itlos-and-the-icc-a-bundle-of-rights/. See also Craig D Gaver, 'Dispute Concerning Delimitation of the Maritime Boundary between Mauritius and Maldives in the Indian Ocean (Mauritius/Maldives)' (2021) 115(3) AJIL 519, 520 ('The Special Chamber stitched together a series of legal documents that, considered individually, were either nonbinding or limited in scope to achieve a determination greater than the sum of its parts—one that effectively resolved the disputed sovereignty over the Chagos Archipelago').

[88] Dapo Akande, 'Introduction to the Symposium on Zachary Mollengarden and Noam Zamir "The Monetary Gold Principle: Back to Basics"' (2021) 115 AJIL Unbound 140, 143. See also Sarah Thin, 'The Curious Case of the "Legal Effect" of ICJ Advisory Opinions in the Mauritius/Maldives Maritime Boundary Dispute' *EJIL: Talk!* (5 February 2021) https://www.ejiltalk.org/the-curious-case-of-the-legal-effect-of-icj-advisory-opinions-in-the-mauritius-maldives-maritime-boundary-dispute/> (describing the Special Chamber as deeming the territorial sovereignty dispute as 'already solved'). Kunoy suggests that the factual and legal circumstances of *Mauritius/Maldives* are sufficiently unique that the holding should not disturb the position established under the other cases in placing territorial sovereignty disputes outside the jurisdiction of UNCLOS tribunals, unless a minor and incidental issue: Bjørn Kunoy, 'The Scope of Compulsory Jurisdiction and Exceptions Thereto under the United Nations Convention on the Law of the Sea' (2021) Canadian YBIL 1, 52, 64.

[89] See Thin (n 88).

where the territorial sovereignty question is 'minor' and 'ancillary' to the core dispute before the tribunal. This dimension, which is justified on the existence of incidental jurisdiction, is explored in the next section.

B. Jurisdiction over Ancillary Disputes

The question of the scope of a tribunal's incidental jurisdiction has arisen in other areas of international law. Bin Cheng set out what has been described as the 'classical approach' to incidental jurisdiction, saying: '[w]here a tribunal has jurisdiction in a particular matter, it is also competent in regard to all relevant incidental questions, subject to express provision to the contrary'.[90] He drew upon the decision of the Permanent Court of International Justice (PCIJ) in 1925 in *German Interests in Upper Silesia*,[91] where the Court was deciding whether Poland had breached certain provisions of the Geneva Convention relating to expropriation of properties belonging to German nationals in Upper Silesia. Poland argued that the impugned act was implementing the terms of the Treaty of Versailles, which was outside the jurisdiction of the Court. The Court accepted that the question of breach of the Geneva Convention could not be decided without first exercising jurisdiction in respect of a question arising under the Treaty of Versailles. It held that the exercise of jurisdiction over the Treaty of Versailles was a question merely 'preliminary or incidental to the application of the Geneva Convention', and that 'the interpretation of other international agreements is indisputably within the competence of the Court if such interpretation must be regarded as incidental to a decision on a point in regard to which it has jurisdiction'.[92] Thus, the Permanent Court was satisfied that it was necessary for it to interpret the Treaty of Versailles to exercise its jurisdiction under the Geneva Convention.[93]

In *Chagos MPA*, the Tribunal considered the extent to which it could exercise 'jurisdiction in respect of a dispute over land sovereignty when, as here, that dispute touches in some ancillary manner on matters regulated by the Convention'.[94] The majority considered that the negotiating history of the Convention did not provide any explicit answer to the question of the extent of jurisdiction over issues relating to land sovereignty.[95] It noted

[90] Bin Cheng, *General Principles of International Law as Applied by International Courts and Tribunals* (Stevens 1953) 266.

[91] *Certain German Interests in Polish Upper Silesia (Germany v Poland)* (Preliminary Objections) [1925] PCIJ Rep Series A No 18.

[92] ibid 18.

[93] See also *Legal Consequences for States of the Continued Presence of South Africa in Namibia (South West Africa) notwithstanding Security Council Resolution 276 (1970)* (Advisory Opinion) [1971] ICJ Rep 16, 45. The Court stated in that Opinion: 'It was suggested that though the request was not directed to the question of the validity of the General Assembly resolution and of the related Security Council resolutions, this did not preclude the Court from making such an enquiry. On the other hand it was contended that the Court was not authorized by the terms of the request, in the light of the discussions preceding it, to go into the validity of these resolutions. It was argued that the Court should not assume powers of judicial review of the action taken by the other principal organs of the United Nations without specific request to that effect, nor act as a court of appeal from their decisions. Undoubtedly, the Court does not possess powers of judicial review or appeal in respect of the decisions taken by the United Nations organs concerned. The question of the validity or conformity with the Charter of General Assembly resolution 2145 (XXI) or of related Security Council resolutions does not form the subject of the request for advisory opinion. However, *in the exercise of its judicial function and since objections have been advanced the Court, in the course of its reasoning, will consider these objections before determining any legal consequences arising from those resolutions*' (emphasis added).

[94] *Chagos MPA* (n 17) para 213.

[95] ibid para 215.

that the 'simple explanation for the lack of attention to this question is that none of the Conference participants expected that a long-standing dispute over territorial sovereignty would ever be considered to be a dispute "concerning the interpretation or application of the Convention" '.[96]

As to the scope of its incidental jurisdiction, the Tribunal stated:

> As a general matter, the Tribunal concludes that, where a dispute concerns the interpretation or application of the Convention, the jurisdiction of a court or tribunal pursuant to Article 288(1) extends to making such findings of fact or ancillary determinations of law as are necessary to resolve the dispute presented to it. Where the 'real issue in the case' and the 'object of the claim' do not relate to the interpretation or application of the Convention, however, an incidental connection between the dispute and some matter regulated by the Convention is insufficient to bring the dispute, as a whole, within the ambit of Article 288(1).[97]

The Tribunal stated it did not 'categorically exclude that in some instances a minor issue of territorial sovereignty could indeed be ancillary to a dispute concerning the interpretation or application of the Convention', but held that this was not the case here, 'and the Tribunal therefore has no need to rule upon the issue'.[98]

The *South China Sea* Tribunal did not address whether the territorial sovereignty issues were ancillary or not given the framing of the Philippines' claims. In *Coastal State Rights in the Black Sea*, that Tribunal did address this question in light of Ukraine's alternative submission that even if the question of territorial sovereignty was properly before the Tribunal, it was ancillary to a dispute concerning the interpretation or application of the Convention.[99] The Tribunal accepted the approach from *Chagos MPA* without further discussion, and instead focused on the characterisation of the dispute before it. The Tribunal determined that the 'dispute regarding sovereignty over Crimea is not a minor issue ancillary to the dispute concerning the interpretation or application of the Convention' but instead a 'prerequisite' to determining many of Ukraine's claims.[100]

This decision may suggest that a territorial sovereignty question that is not a 'prerequisite' for the resolution of claims arising under UNCLOS, perhaps similar to the assessment of claims arising under the *Monetary Gold* principle,[101] falls within incidental jurisdiction. An assessment of what is prerequisite makes sense in the context of the land dominates the sea principle—there are instances where sovereignty over the land must be known prior to determining maritime rights and duties. Yet what falls within the category of a minor territorial sovereignty question that is ancillary to a question of interpretation of UNCLOS remains to be determined. Tanaka has suggested that a low-tide elevation may be a case in point.[102] In this situation, the delimitation of a maritime boundary may result in confirming

[96] ibid.
[97] ibid para 220 (citations omitted).
[98] ibid para 221.
[99] *Coastal State Rights in the Black Sea* (n 19) para 194.
[100] ibid para 195.
[101] *Monetary Gold Removed from Rome in 1943 (Italy v France; Italy v United Kingdom; Italy v United States)* (Preliminary Question) [1954] ICJ Rep 19. Particularly as applied in the *East Timor (Portugal v Australia)* (Judgment) [1995] ICJ Rep 90, paras 33–35. See also ch 3(III)(C).
[102] Yoshifumi Tanaka, *The South China Sea Arbitration: Toward an International Legal Order in the Oceans* (Hart 2019) 37 (Tanaka, *Toward an International Legal Order*).

a coastal State's sovereignty over such a feature.[103] The *Chagos MPA* and *Coastal State Rights in the Black Sea* cases should otherwise underline that the UNCLOS dispute settlement regime is not intended to provide compulsory jurisdiction to resolve outstanding territorial sovereignty disputes, which must be resolved through other peaceful means.[104]

The question of incidental jurisdiction was critical in the *Enrica Lexie* arbitration,[105] which focused on whether India could exercise jurisdiction over two Italian marines who were responsible for shooting two Indian fishers on the St Anthony fishing vessel in the Indian EEZ. The Enrica Lexie was an Italian-flagged oil tanker en route to Port Said, Egypt, and had taken onboard a Vessel Protection Detachment from the Italian Navy in Sri Lanka as security against possible pirate attacks. Italy submitted that the crew on the Enrica Lexie believed that the St Anthony was approaching it for the purposes of a pirate attack and after warnings and attempted contact with the St Anthony, shots were fired resulting in the death of two Indian fishers.[106] India requested the Enrica Lexie enter its territorial sea and escorted it to Kochi port to assist in inquiries in relation to the incident.[107] Subsequently, two of the Italian marines were arrested on an allegation of murder.[108] In challenging India's assertion of jurisdiction,[109] Italy argued inter alia that the immunity of its State officials prevented India from prosecuting the Italian marines. A key question for the Annex VII Tribunal was whether the question of immunity fell within its jurisdiction to interpret and apply the Convention under Article 288(1). India argued that immunity was the 'real subject matter' of the dispute and concerned rules extraneous to UNCLOS.[110] The Tribunal considered that the dispute 'may' raise the question of immunity but was not limited to that question, as a range of UNCLOS provisions were at issue between the parties.[111]

While the Tribunal had jurisdiction to assess the application of different UNCLOS provisions in *Enrica Lexie*, whether it could also consider questions relating to the immunity of the Italian marines was not apparent given that no specific provision of UNCLOS deals with the immunity of State personnel.[112] Italy raised a number of bases of jurisdiction to allow for the Tribunal's exercise of jurisdiction over this question. These arguments included that Articles 2(3), 56(2), and 58(2), which have references to international law more generally, 'import[ed] immunity by *renvoi*'.[113] Italy further argued that immunity of the marines was 'sufficiently connected to the real issue in the case' to fall within the scope of Article

[103] As happened in *Maritime Delimitation and Territorial Questions between Qatar and Bahrain (Qatar v Bahrain)* (Merits) [2001] ICJ Rep 40, and in *Territorial and Maritime Dispute*, Judgment (n 16). See also 37–38.

[104] See further Natalie Klein, 'Land and Sea: Resolving Contested Land and Disappearing Land Disputes under the UN Convention on the Law of the Sea' in Chiara Giorgetti and Natalie Klein (eds), *Resolving Conflicts in the Law: Essays in Honour of Lea Brilmayer* (Brill 2019). See also Valentin Schatz, 'The Award concerning Preliminary Objections in *Ukraine v Russia*: Observations regarding the Implicated Status of Crimea and the Sea of Azov' *EJIL: Talk!* (20 March 2020) https://www.ejiltalk.org/the-award-concerning-preliminary-objections-in-ukraine-v-russia-observations-regarding-the-implicated-status-of-crimea-and-the-sea-of-azov/.

[105] *Enrica Lexie (Italy v India)* (Award of 21 May 2020) PCA Case No 2015-28 (*Enrica Lexie*, Award).

[106] Many of the facts were contested during the proceedings. For Italy's account of the incident see ibid paras 87–104. For India's account of the incident see paras 105–17.

[107] The parties disputed as to whether India requested the Enrica Lexie to enter its territorial sea and port or whether there was a ruse or an implicit order requiring its entry: ibid para 391. The Tribunal determined that there was no violation of Italy's freedom of navigation but rather the Enrica Lexie voluntarily entered into India's territorial sea consistent with professional seafaring conduct: see paras 482, 487, 503–505.

[108] ibid para 168.

[109] Italy also conducted an investigation into the marines and the alleged murder of the two fishers: ibid para 211.

[110] ibid para 226.

[111] ibid para 243.

[112] UNCLOS (n 1) instead provides for the immunity of certain vessels: see eg arts 95, 96.

[113] *Enrica Lexie*, Award (n 105) para 734.

288(1).[114] The Tribunal did not accept these views, dismissing the applicability of Articles 2(3), 56(2), 58(2), 95, and 96,[115] and considered that the Convention did not provide for an 'independent immunity claim under general international law'.[116] Instead, the Tribunal relied on incidental jurisdiction, as described by the PCIJ as covering 'questions preliminary or incidental to the application' of the Convention.[117] The Tribunal determined that this issue of immunity was 'an incidental question that necessarily presents itself in the application of the Convention in respect of the dispute before it'.[118]

The Tribunal was motivated by a need to resolve the dispute 'satisfactorily' and 'conclusively'.[119] There was little elaboration on the rationale for this view, however. From India's perspective, this position would mean that there should have been no decision rendered on its authority to prosecute the Italian Marines as that jurisdiction could not be determined without considering immunity. As immunity was not a question of interpretation or application of UNCLOS, India's exercise of criminal jurisdiction over the Italian Marines could not be challenged before an UNCLOS tribunal.[120] Instead, as Churchill has observed, the question could have been left for the Indian courts in this situation.[121] By contrast to the need espoused by the majority of the Tribunal, Judge Robinson in dissent emphasised the importance of consent to jurisdiction and not proceeding beyond the bounds of State party consent.[122] Moreover, he emphasised the 'package deal' nature of the Convention and that 'conferring jurisdiction on a court or tribunal over a question that does not fall within the provisions of the Convention may disturb the balance in the compromise solutions that were reached in the negotiations that led to its adoption'.[123]

Judge Robinson emphasised that the questions of jurisdiction and immunity were intertwined throughout the pleadings of the parties and characterised the dispute as one concerning both immunity and the exercise of jurisdiction rather than 'primarily' concerning immunity.[124] Both, in his view, were 'core elements' of the dispute.[125] Judge Rao similarly found the Italy's claim to jurisdiction was a core aspect of its case, rather than being incidental.[126] Judge Rao disputed that there was an 'inseparable or integral link between the issue of immunity and the issue of exclusive jurisdiction' to warrant reliance on incidental jurisdiction in line with the *Certain German Interests* case.[127] Judge Robinson characterised Italy's arguments as acknowledging these elements as 'central and inseparable',[128] and noted that immunity was 'definitionally incapable of being independent'. In his view, given

[114] ibid para 767.
[115] ibid paras 798–99.
[116] ibid para 809.
[117] ibid para 808.
[118] ibid para 811.
[119] ibid para 811. Devaney and Tams have observed that the majority was possibly motivated by a principle of effectiveness, even though it was not explicitly articulated as such. James G Devaney, and Christian J Tams, 'In re Arbitration between the Italian Republic and the Republic of India concerning the "Enrica Lexie" Incident' (2021) 115(3) AJIL 513, 518–19.
[120] *Enrica Lexie*, Award (n 105) para 753.
[121] Robin Churchill, 'Dispute Settlement in the Law of the Sea: Survey for 2020' (2021) 36 IJMCL 1, 19.
[122] *Enrica Lexie*, Award (n 105) (Dissenting Opinion of Judge Robinson) para 30. See also para 37 ('the Majority has not been deferential to and protective of the limits of India's consent' to jurisdiction).
[123] ibid para 43.
[124] ibid para 8.
[125] ibid para 10.
[126] *Enrica Lexie*, Award (n 105) (Concurring and Dissenting Opinion of Judge Rao) para 39.
[127] ibid para 36.
[128] *Enrica Lexie*, Award (n 105) (Dissenting Opinion of Judge Robinson) para 19.

the centrality of the issue of immunity to the dispute, it was necessary to find a firmer basis for jurisdiction under UNCLOS rather than relying solely on incidental jurisdiction.[129] Whereas the *Chagos MPA* Tribunal had considered incidental jurisdiction emerges for necessary and ancillary questions, the *Enrica Lexie* Tribunal instead focused only on what was necessary.[130] Simply claiming there is a need to resolve a dispute 'satisfactorily' and 'conclusively' does not justify an exercise of jurisdiction beyond the terms of Article 288. Devaney and Tams have astutely observed that the 'Tribunal's approach to its own jurisdiction tells us something about how it sees its role not only as a legal means for settling disputes between two states but also as actor in the international legal order'.[131]

Determining what constitutes a 'dispute concerning the interpretation or application' of UNCLOS has thus evolved into a more complicated question than may have initially been envisaged from what is a relatively standard type of compromissory treaty clause. Boyle's early recognition of the potential for 'salami-slicing' litigation tactics has arguably been realised in complex disputes that in part concern the law of the sea.[132] It is perhaps this approach to the disputes and possibilities for judicial resolution that has led to some focus on the 'characterisation' of the dispute. Harris has argued that characterising UNCLOS disputes is misplaced and the focus must be on whether the dispute concerns the interpretation or application of the Convention or not.[133] Clearly, questions of State official immunity and territorial sovereignty do not, but then account of incidental jurisdiction is still needed.[134] The *Chagos MPA* and *Coastal State Rights in the Black Sea* decisions indicate a focus on matters that are preliminary and minor relative to the UNCLOS dispute that must be resolved; *Enrica Lexie* would allow for a matter that is very closely intertwined with an UNCLOS dispute to be determined when necessary for the satisfactory conclusion of the case. Diverse claims beyond UNCLOS, and beyond the law of the sea, may ultimately be determined by a Part XV tribunal on the reasoning of the majority in the *Enrica Lexie*. The latter approach risks being too expansive and could reach beyond the expectations of stakeholders, especially as any goal of effectiveness must remain tempered by the limits of State consent.[135]

III. Article 297 Limitations

Article 297 of UNCLOS, headed 'Limitations on Applicability of Section 2', was not subjected to judicial scrutiny in the early case law under UNCLOS, but has received greater consideration in more recent cases, such as the *Chagos MPA* arbitration and the *South China Sea* arbitration. Not all aspects of Article 297 have been raised in arguments before

[129] Judge Robinson remarked, 'A core element of the dispute cannot at the same time be an incidental question in relation to that dispute': ibid para 39.

[130] Devaney and Tams (n 119) 518.

[131] ibid 519.

[132] Boyle (n 2) 41–42.

[133] Callista Harris, 'Claims with an Ulterior Purpose: Characterising Disputes Concerning the "Interpretation or Application" of a Treaty' (2020) 18(3) LPICT 279, 286–90.

[134] Tzeng has usefully captured different categories of 'supplemental jurisdiction' that exists beyond the grant of jurisdiction in art 288(1). See Peter Tzeng, 'Supplemental Jurisdiction under UNCLOS' (2016) 38(2) Hous J Intl L 499.

[135] The balance is of course difficult. The ICJ has observed these tensions in noting that it 'must not exceed the jurisdiction conferred upon it by the Parties, but it must also exercise that jurisdiction to its full extent': *Continental Shelf (Libya/Malta)* (Judgment) [1985] ICJ Rep 13, para 19.

Part XV tribunals, but attention has been given to the aspects dealing with the environment and fisheries.[136] The relevant parts of Article 297 provide:

> 1. Disputes concerning the interpretation or application of this Convention with regard to the exercise by a coastal State of its sovereign rights or jurisdiction provided for in this Convention shall be subject to the procedures provided for in section 2 in the following cases:
>   (a) when it is alleged that a coastal State has acted in contravention of the provisions of this Convention in regard to the freedoms and rights of navigation, overflight or the laying of submarine cables and pipelines, or in regard to other internationally lawful uses of the sea specified in article 58;
>   (b) when it is alleged that a State in exercising the aforementioned freedoms, rights or uses has acted in contravention of this Convention or of laws or regulations adopted by the coastal State in conformity with this Convention and other rules of international law not incompatible with this Convention; or
>   (c) when it is alleged that a coastal State has acted in contravention of specified international rules and standards for the protection and preservation of the marine environment which are applicable to the coastal State and which have been established by this Convention or through a competent international organization or diplomatic conference in accordance with this Convention. . . .
>
> 3(a) Disputes concerning the interpretation or application of the provisions of this Convention with regard to fisheries shall be settled in accordance with section 2, except that the coastal State shall not be obliged to accept the submission to such settlement of any dispute relating to its sovereign rights with respect to the living resources in the exclusive economic zone or their exercise, including its discretionary powers for determining the allowable catch, its harvesting capacity, the allocation of surpluses to other States and the terms and conditions established in its conservation and management laws and regulations.

An initial question emerged as to whether Article 297 defined the totality of disputes that could be subjected to compulsory arbitration or adjudication or whether all disputes fall within UNCLOS unless there is an exception or limitation stipulated in either Articles 297 or 298.[137] The *Chagos MPA* Tribunal confirmed the latter viewpoint, based on the drafting history of Article 297.[138] This history demonstrates that an initial proposal to exclude all disputes involving the coastal State's exercise of sovereign rights and jurisdiction was not finally adopted but instead Article 297 reaffirmed jurisdiction in certain of these cases, excluded jurisdiction in those explicitly listed, and further allowed for jurisdiction over 'certain disputes involving the contravention of legal instruments beyond the four corners of

[136] Article 297(1) was considered in conjunction with art 297(3) in *Chagos Marine Protected Area* and was only briefly addressed in other cases. See Serdy (n 65) paras 14–16.

[137] See eg *Southern Bluefin Tuna (New Zealand v Japan; Australia v Japan)* (Jurisdiction and Admissibility) (2000) 23 RIAA 1, para 61. See further Stefan Talmon, 'The Chagos Marine Protected Area Arbitration: Expansion of the Jurisdiction of UNCLOS Part XV Courts and Tribunals' (2016) 65 ICLQ 927 (Talmon, 'Expansion of Jurisdiction'); Stephen Allen, 'Article 297 of the United Nations Convention on the Law of the Sea and the Scope of Mandatory Jurisdiction' (2017) 48 ODIL 313.

[138] See also *South China Sea*, Award (n 18) para 359.

the Convention itself and ensures that such disputes will not be dismissed as being insufficiently related to the interpretation and application of the Convention'.[139] Article 297 is thus to be understood as reaffirming the grant of jurisdiction as broadly stated in Article 288(1) and then carving out particular exceptions as articulated therein.[140]

The *Chagos MPA* Tribunal therefore confirmed that, if a dispute falls within Article 288(1), a claimant does not also need to establish that the dispute also falls within Article 297(1).[141] Instead, the Tribunal noted that Article 297(1) expands the jurisdiction over disputes that might not fall within Article 288(1), because:

(a) Article 297(1)(a) establishes jurisdiction 'in regard to other internationally lawful uses of the sea specified in article 58' and Article 58 provides that 'other pertinent rules of international law' apply to the conduct of third States in the exclusive economic zone.
(b) Article 297(1)(b) establishes jurisdiction over the exercise of freedoms, rights, and uses of the sea 'in contravention of... the laws and regulations adopted by the coastal State in conformity with this Convention and other rules of international law not incompatible with this Convention'.
(c) Article 297(1)(c) establishes jurisdiction over acts 'in contravention of specified international rules and standards for the protection and preservation of the marine environment', including those established 'through a competent international organization or diplomatic conference'.[142]

Even where a dispute might be excluded by virtue of Article 297 (or Article 298), States still have the option of agreeing to the dispute being submitted to arbitration or adjudication under Article 299. The applicability of the exception may be waived explicitly or implicitly,[143] and has occurred in relation to the *Virginia G*,[144] which addressed questions relating to fishing in the EEZ.

A. Fishing

Article 297(3) provides for compulsory procedures entailing binding decisions to be available for disputes relating to fishing 'except that the coastal State shall not be obliged to accept the submission to such settlement of any dispute relating to its sovereign rights with respect to the living resources in the exclusive economic zone or their exercise'. This provision *prima facie* denies the availability of adjudication or arbitration to challenge any actions

[139] *Chagos MPA* (n 17) para 316, although Kunoy (n 88) has doubted whether art 297(1) could expand jurisdiction beyond art 288(1): see 31.

[140] This was the position adopted by the *Guyana v Suriname* Tribunal, which held: 'Thus, any dispute concerning the interpretation or application of the Convention which is not excluded by the operation of Part XV, Section 3 (Articles 297 and 298) falls under the compulsory procedures in Section 2': *Guyana v Suriname* (Award of the Arbitral Tribunal of 17 September 2007) PCA Case No 2004-04, para 414.

[141] *Chagos MPA* (n 17) para 317.

[142] ibid para 316.

[143] Rüdiger Wolfrum, 'Conciliation under the UN Convention on the Law of the Sea' in Christian Tomuschat, Riccardo Pisillo Mazzeschi, and Daniel Thürer (eds), *Conciliation in International Law: The OSCE Court of Conciliation and Arbitration* (Brill 2016) 171, 187.

[144] *M/V Virginia G (Panama/Guinea-Bissau)* (Judgment) ITLOS Reports 2014, 4 (*Virginia G*).

of the coastal State in relation to fishing in its EEZ. *A contrario*, fishing disputes arising from other maritime areas are within compulsory jurisdiction, consistent with Article 286 of UNCLOS. In *Guyana v Suriname*, the Tribunal dismissed a challenge from Suriname that Guyana's claims relating to non-living resources were also excluded from compulsory jurisdiction under Article 297(3).[145]

In the *Chagos MPA* arbitration, the United Kingdom asserted that the MPA around the Chagos Archipelago was a measure concerning 'sovereign rights with respect to living resources'. The United Kingdom emphasised that the MPA 'is properly characterized as a fisheries measure',[146] and as such was to be excluded from jurisdiction under Article 297(3)(a). Mauritius considered that even if the MPA was so understood, the limitation from Article 297(3) would not apply because that provision insulated the coastal State's actions from compulsory dispute settlement procedures but would not exclude the consideration of the rights of other States in relation to fishing in the EEZ.[147]

The Tribunal did not accept the United Kingdom's characterisation of the MPA as 'solely a measure relating to fisheries'.[148] There was considerable evidence before the Tribunal, including many government pronouncements, which demonstrated the purposes of the MPA went well beyond fisheries management.[149] Nonetheless, the Tribunal still had to consider whether a dispute about fishing rights, which were protected under what was known as the Lancaster House Undertakings, was justiciable in light of the exclusion in Article 297(3)(a). In this regard, the Tribunal rejected the submission by Mauritius that it was possible to consider a dispute relating to the rights of other States within the EEZ as distinct from the rights of the coastal State in the EEZ so that the former would fall within jurisdiction whereas a dispute on the latter would be excluded. The Tribunal remarked:

> In nearly any imaginable situation, a dispute will exist precisely because the coastal State's conception of its sovereign rights conflicts with the other party's understanding of its own rights. In short, the two are intertwined, and a dispute regarding Mauritius' claimed fishing rights in the exclusive economic zone cannot be separated from the exercise of the United Kingdom's sovereign rights with respect to living resources.[150]

The approach of the *Chagos MPA* Tribunal would therefore maintain the strong position that any dispute relating to fishing activities occurring in the EEZ are excluded from compulsory arbitration or adjudication under UNCLOS.

However, doubt was cast on the inter-connected nature of sovereign rights relating to fishing in the EEZ in the *South China Sea* Award. The Philippines challenged China's fishing activities in an area determined in that Award to be part of the Philippines' EEZ. Seemingly, a challenge to China's assertion of fishing rights against the fishing rights claimed by the Philippines would constitute a dispute relating to fishing in the EEZ. Yet, the Philippines

[145] *Guyana v Suriname* (n 140) paras 411–12.
[146] *Chagos MPA* (n 17) para 245.
[147] ibid para 250.
[148] ibid para 286.
[149] ibid paras 286–90.
[150] ibid para 297. Russia supported this position in its pleadings in *Coastal State Rights in the Black Sea* (n 19) and further sought to extend the application of the exception to fishing claims concerning the territorial sea: see paras 394, 397. However, the Tribunal did not resolve these points because it would have implications for the territorial sovereignty case: see para 402.

argued that Article 297(3) did not apply because that provision only excluded disputes relating to the coastal State's actions. As China was not considered the coastal State, there was no examination of the coastal State's exercise of sovereign rights over fish required.[151] It could well be expected that if a third State has acted inconsistently with the fisheries requirements of a coastal State then the dispute may well concern the coastal State's decision-making over fisheries in the EEZ.

As with *Chagos MPA*, an argument could certainly be raised that these issues are once again intertwined and thus fall within the exclusion of Article 297(3). Yet a difference appears to exist between the two cases, albeit quite a subtle one. In *Chagos MPA*, Mauritius was complaining about the lack of due regard shown by the coastal State for other users. In *South China Sea*, the Tribunal noted that the *Chagos MPA* arbitration therefore concerned a 'reversed situation [to the one before the Tribunal] of the regard owed by the coastal State to the rights and duties of other States within its exclusive economic zone'.[152] The Tribunal considered that Article 297(3)(a) limited access to compulsory dispute settlement 'where a claim is brought against a State's exercise of its sovereign rights in respect of living resources in its own exclusive economic zone. These provisions do not apply where a State is alleged to have violated the Convention in respect of the exclusive economic zone of another State'.[153] As a consequence of these decisions, coastal State rights over fisheries are not only firmly insulated from compulsory dispute settlement under Article 297(3), but coastal States are further protected—if not empowered—by allowing the coastal State recourse to arbitration and adjudication if necessary to challenge any unlawful fishing activity by a third State in its EEZ. In other words, coastal State authority over fishing in its EEZ is thus virtually unreviewable,[154] but can be prevailed upon by the coastal State if it wishes to challenge the fishing activities of other States within its EEZ. At the same time, the exception in Article 297(3), which seemed to exclude any and all disputes concerning fishing in the EEZ from arbitration or adjudication, has been narrowed in the *South China Sea* arbitration.

It can finally be noted that the *Chagos MPA* Tribunal would further have excluded from compulsory dispute settlement any disputes relating to straddling stocks or highly migratory species where the dispute concerns measures pertaining to those fish within the EEZ of a State.[155] Judge Paik, however, in the *SRFC Advisory Opinion* commented:

> [A]ny dispute arising from the alleged failure to comply with this obligation under article 63, paragraph 1, of the Convention, unlike those disputes arising from the exercise of sovereign rights of the coastal State with respect to the living resources in its EEZ, can be submitted to the compulsory procedure under Part XV, section 2, of the Convention.[156]

Kunoy has also argued that Article 297(3) should be read strictly so that only those EEZ fisheries disputes explicitly listed in Article 297(3) are excluded from compulsory procedures

[151] *South China Sea*, Award (n 18) para 682.

[152] ibid para 742, citing *Chagos MPA* (n 17).

[153] *South China Sea*, Award (n 18) para 695.

[154] Article 297 does allow for the possibility of compulsory conciliation but the factual predicate to allow for this process would be difficult to achieve. See Natalie Klein, *Dispute Settlement in the UN Convention on the Law of the Sea* (CUP 2005) 185–88 (*Dispute Settlement*).

[155] *Chagos MPA* (n 17) para 300.

[156] *Request for Advisory Opinion Submitted by the Sub-Regional Fisheries Commission* (Advisory Opinion) ITLOS Reports 2015, 4 (Separate Opinion of Judge Paik) para 37.

entailing binding decisions, hence leaving open the possibility of more EEZ-related fisheries disputes remaining within the jurisdiction provided under Section 2 of Part XV.[157] This interpretation may allow disputes arising under Article 63 to be considered as subject to compulsory procedures entailing binding decisions. The inclusion of disputes relating to straddling stocks within Section 2 of Part XV could not be definitively stated at the time of UNCLOS negotiations and commentary has subsequently varied on the question.[158] Judicial consideration of this issue to date has not resolved the matter and will necessitate close consideration of the different legal regimes that may have bearing on any dispute in the future to ensure good ocean governance, especially of vulnerable fish stocks.

B. Marine Environment

Another provision in Article 297 that has been assessed in UNCLOS dispute settlement proceedings is paragraph (1)(c), which addresses disputes relating to the protection and preservation of the marine environment. This provision affirms the authority of courts or tribunals to examine such disputes but prompts questions as to what disputes concerning the marine environment may be outside the scope of compulsory dispute settlement under UNCLOS.

In *Chagos MPA*, the United Kingdom argued for a restrictive reading of Article 297(1)(c) in the event the Tribunal did not accept its argument that the MPA in question constituted a fisheries measure excluded from compulsory jurisdiction under Article 297(3). Mauritius took the position that the MPA was an environmental measure, and as such it was undoubtedly within the jurisdiction of the Tribunal in accordance with Article 297(1)(c). The United Kingdom contended that this provision had to be understood in the context of navigational rights and should be viewed as a protection against coastal States misusing their powers to regulate marine pollution.[159]

The Tribunal assessed whether environmental disputes within compulsory procedures entailing binding decisions were limited to those addressing international rules and standards on marine pollution. The Tribunal considered that references to rules and standards were not only to those established by UNCLOS but could also include the obligation to consult with or give due regard to the rights of other States.[160] In this regard, the narrow position of the United Kingdom was rejected. This interpretation was appropriate because of the important role that procedural obligations have in international environmental law along with substantive standards.[161] Similarly, in the *South China Sea* arbitration, the Tribunal had no difficulty in considering that it had jurisdiction to resolve disputes concerning provisions relating to the protection and preservation of the marine environment.[162]

In rejecting a narrow interpretation of Article 297(1)(c), as well as accepting jurisdiction over disputes relating to Article 194, the *Chagos MPA* Tribunal and the *South China Sea*

[157] Kunoy (n 88) 33–34.
[158] See Klein, *Dispute Settlement* (n 154) 199–204.
[159] *Chagos MPA* (n 17) paras 235, 239.
[160] ibid para 322.
[161] ibid.
[162] The only issue concerned the potential relevance of the military activities exception: *South China Sea*, Award (n 18) para 938. This argument is discussed further below in relation to that exception.

Tribunal have affirmed the importance of UNCLOS dispute settlement in resolving a wide variety of marine environmental law disputes. It could be argued that this embrace of a judicial role in marine environmental protection is reinforced by the decision to adjudicate claims that coastal States might pursue against other States violating their fisheries rights in the EEZ. Holding flag States to account under Part XV of UNCLOS for failures to ensure that their vessels fish lawfully in the EEZ of other States may enhance efforts to conserve and manage fisheries. Yet given the parlous condition of many coastal fisheries, which could reflect failures by the coastal State to conserve and manage marine living resources consistently with UNCLOS, the inability to challenge coastal State decisions in relation to fisheries does not support strong protection of different marine ecosystems and undermines this aspect of ocean governance.

IV. Article 298 Optional Exceptions

In accordance with Article 298, a State party to UNCLOS may declare when it ratifies or accedes to the Convention, or at any time thereafter, that it does not accept compulsory procedures under Section 2 of Part XV in relation to specified disputes.[163] Zou and Ye have noted that Article 298 'serves as a "safety valve" by allowing state parties to exclude certain disputes related to sensitive issues of sovereignty from the application of Section 2 of Part XV in order to accommodate near-global acceptance of the Convention'.[164] The exclusion applies on a reciprocal basis between States.[165] States may, and have in practice, withdrawn their declarations excluding disputes for the purposes of commencing proceedings against another State party.[166]

Article 298(1) allows for declarations in relation to the following categories of disputes:

(a)(i) disputes concerning the interpretation or application of articles 15, 74 and 83 relating to sea boundary delimitations, or those involving historic bays or titles

(b) disputes concerning military activities, including military activities by government vessels and aircraft engaged in non-commercial service, and disputes concerning law enforcement activities in regard to the exercise of sovereign rights or jurisdiction excluded from the jurisdiction of a court or tribunal under article 297, paragraph 2 or 3;

(c) disputes in respect of which the Security Council of the United Nations is exercising the functions assigned to it by the Charter of the United Nations, unless the Security

[163] If a State party specifies a procedure for a dispute otherwise excluded under art 298(1)(a), another State party may submit the dispute to that specified procedure: UNCLOS (n 1) art 298(4).

[164] Keyuan Zou and Qiang Ye, 'Interpretation and Application of Article 298 of the Law of the Sea Convention in Recent Annex VII Arbitrations: An Appraisal' (2017) 48 ODIL 331, 331–32.

[165] UNCLOS (n 1) art 298(3), which reads: 'A State Party which has made a declaration under paragraph 1 shall not be entitled to submit any dispute falling within the excepted category of disputes to any procedure in this Convention as against another State Party, without the consent of that party.'

[166] As Argentina did in *ARA Libertad (Argentina v Ghana)* (Provisional Measures, Order of 15 December 2012) ITLOS Reports 2012, 332, para 34. Article 298(2) of UNCLOS (n 1) provides in this regard: 'A State Party which has made a declaration under paragraph 1 may at any time withdraw it, or agree to submit a dispute excluded by such declaration to any procedure specified in this Convention.'

Council decides to remove the matter from its agenda or calls upon the parties to settle it by the means provided for in this Convention.

To date, no State has raised Article 298(1)(c) as a barrier to jurisdiction, although States have included it when making declarations under this provision.[167] This section thus focuses on the other categories of disputes that have thus far been subject to judicial interpretation: maritime boundary delimitations; historic bays or titles; military activities; and law enforcement activities in regard to fishing or marine scientific research in the EEZ.

A. Maritime Boundary Delimitations

Under Article 2981(1)(a) of UNCLOS, States may opt to exclude delimitation disputes concerning the interpretation or application of the UNCLOS provisions relating to the delimitation of the territorial sea, the EEZ, and the continental shelf under Articles 15, 74, and 83, respectively. These provisions are concerned with the delimitation of overlapping maritime entitlements between States with opposite or adjacent coasts. Consequently, disputes about how a State has drawn its baselines, and thereby claimed rights over a sea area that would otherwise be considered the high seas, do not fall within this possible exclusion. Yet the scope of what counts as delimitation under Articles 15, 74, and 83 has prompted consideration of the parameters of the exclusion under Article 298(1)(a) and is addressed in the first sub-section immediately below. Further, even when a State does exclude disputes concerning Articles 15, 74, and 83 from compulsory procedures entailing binding decisions, States may still compel resort to conciliation, provided a range of conditions are met. The use of compulsory conciliation for sea boundary disputes is discussed in the second sub-section below.

1. Maritime Boundary Delimitations Excluded from Arbitration or Adjudication

In the *South China Sea* arbitration, China argued that the dispute essentially concerned maritime boundary delimitation and was excluded from compulsory arbitration by virtue of its declaration under Article 298 of UNCLOS. China maintained that determining whether a maritime feature was a rock or island to ascertain to what maritime zones that feature is entitled was an essential part of a sea boundary delimitation. China argued in its Position Paper that the Philippines could not divide issues into discrete parts given the integral process involved in maritime boundary delimitations.[168] To do so, in China's view, would potentially denude Article 298 exceptions of any value in UNCLOS dispute settlement.[169]

In response, the Philippines submitted that a question of maritime delimitation could only arise once it was determined that there were overlapping maritime entitlements, but such determination was not integral to the process.[170] The Philippines relied on the position

[167] See eg the declarations of Algeria, Chile, China, Ecuador, Egypt, Nicaragua, Portugal, Togo, Tunisia and the United Kingdom, available at: https://treaties.un.org/pages/ViewDetailsIII.aspx?src=TREATY&mtdsg_no=XXI-6&chapter=21&Temp=mtdsg3&clang=_en. For some discussion on this exception see Klein, *Dispute Settlement* (n 154) 284–85, 366.

[168] China's Position Paper (n 46) paras 67–68.

[169] ibid para 74.

[170] *South China Sea*, Jurisdiction and Admissibility (n 47) para 146.

that the entitlement could be determined and the result of such a determination may not lead to overlapping maritime zones (if, for example, the feature was a rock or a low-tide elevation) so no sea boundary delimitation would be necessitated. From the Philippines perspective, these steps should be viewed as discrete and distinct.

The Philippines presented a strict interpretation of Article 298 to limit the scope of the exception. As such, the Philippines considered that Article 298(1)(a) was only relevant if the Tribunal was called on to interpret or apply one of the provisions expressly mentioned in that clause—namely, Articles 15, 74, and 83 on the delimitation of the territorial sea, the EEZ, and the continental shelf, respectively.[171] In the opinion of the Philippines, to look beyond the specific provisions listed would lead to an overly expansive exclusion of jurisdiction at the behest of one of the parties to the dispute.

The key point of distinction between the Philippines' and China's positions thus centred on what was integral to maritime boundary delimitation and what was not. The Tribunal noted its agreement with China 'that maritime boundary delimitation is an integral and systemic process'.[172] Nonetheless, the Tribunal was not willing to accept that a determination of maritime entitlements of features situated between States, and hence potentially creating States with opposite or adjacent coasts, would form part of that integral process. The Tribunal stated:

> In particular, the Tribunal considers that a dispute concerning the existence of an entitlement to maritime zones is distinct from a dispute concerning the delimitation of those zones in an area where the entitlements of parties overlap. While fixing the extent of parties' entitlements and the area in which they overlap will commonly be one of the first matters to be addressed in the delimitation of a maritime boundary, it is nevertheless a distinct issue. A maritime boundary may be delimited only between States with opposite or adjacent coasts and overlapping entitlements.[173]

A better view is that something that will 'commonly be one of the first matters to be addressed in the delimitation of a maritime boundary' should be excluded from jurisdiction under Article 298. That should be the case because such matters are part of the delimitation of the territorial sea, EEZ or continental shelf, which fell outside the *South China Sea* Tribunal's jurisdiction. The Tribunal provided no reason for separating out the process as it did. Indeed, it runs counter to practice that is typically followed in maritime boundary cases whereby entitlements are determined as a preliminary step in establishing a maritime boundary. For example, in *Bay of Bengal Delimitation*, ITLOS stated: 'Delimitation presupposes an area of overlapping entitlements. Therefore, the first step in any delimitation is to determine whether there are entitlements and whether they overlap.'[174]

The interconnectedness of the delimitation process was evident in the Tribunal's initial decision on jurisdiction in *South China Sea*. The Tribunal considered that the resolution of certain Philippines submissions could be prevented at the merits stage if the Tribunal

[171] ibid para 374.
[172] ibid para 155.
[173] ibid para 156.
[174] *Delimitation of the Maritime Boundary in the Bay of Bengal (Bangladesh/Myanmar)* (Judgment) ITLOS Reports 2012, 4, para 397. The Tribunal went on to state: 'Thus the question the Tribunal should first address in the present case is whether the Parties have overlapping entitlements': see para 399.

determined that China had an overlapping entitlement in the area in question; it would only be in the absence of China's overlapping entitlement that the claims could otherwise be resolved.[175] This recognition highlighted that the Tribunal was indeed presupposing an entitlement—i.e. conducting the first part of a maritime boundary delimitation, and arguably the Tribunal should have been prevented from undertaking this task by virtue of Article 298(1)(a).[176] The decision begs the question as to what other parts of the maritime delimitation process will be segregated in the same manner. Could we arrive at the point that the 'delimitation' is considered to be the actual drawing of the line and a court or tribunal may otherwise undertake all steps leading up to that point, including the articulation of the principles to be utilised in the delimitation as occurred in the *North Sea Continental Shelf Cases*?[177] It seems unlikely that States opting to exclude maritime boundary disputes from compulsory jurisdiction would countenance this level of engagement by judicial decision-makers.

Subsequent to the *South China Sea* arbitration, the Tribunal in *Coastal State Rights in the Black Sea* was presented with a question where the delimitation of a maritime area was not explicitly at issue between the parties but rather the question was whether the Tribunal 'would implicitly have to delimit maritime areas over which the Parties' entitlements overlap; and whether in such event the optional exception from arbitral jurisdiction is triggered'.[178] However, as the Tribunal could not rule explicitly or implicitly on sovereignty over Crimea, there was no scope to determine if the parties had entitlements to the maritime areas around Crimea or if they overlapped.[179]

2. Maritime Boundary Delimitations and Compulsory Conciliation

As noted above, even if a State has excluded a maritime boundary dispute under the terms of Article 298(1)(a), it must still face the prospect of another State party instituting compulsory conciliation under Annex V of UNCLOS, provided various conditions are met. In the *Timor Sea Conciliation*,[180] Timor-Leste pursued this course of action against Australia in relation to their undefined maritime boundary that had been subject to a joint exploration and exploitation regime. This joint regime was elaborated on in three separate treaties.[181]

Article 298(1)(a) of UNCLOS anticipates that parties that have excluded maritime boundary disputes from compulsory procedures entailing binding decisions are to resort to conciliation instead. Conciliation is compulsory in this situation inasmuch as a party

[175] *South China Sea*, Jurisdiction and Admissibility (n 47) para 157.

[176] See Stefan Talmon, 'The South China Sea Arbitration: Is There a Case to Answer?' in Stefan Talmon and Bing Bing Jia (eds), *The South China Sea Arbitration: A Chinese Perspective* (Hart Publishing 2014) 56.

[177] *North Sea Continental Shelf* (n 14).

[178] *Coastal State Rights in the Black Sea* (n 19) para 377.

[179] ibid para 382.

[180] *Conciliation between The Democratic Republic of Timor-Leste and the Commonwealth of Australia* (Report and Recommendations of the Compulsory Conciliation Commission, 9 May 2018) PCA Case No 2016-10.

[181] Following Timor-Leste's independence in 2002, it entered into a series of bilateral agreements with Australia to allow for joint exploitation. See Timor Sea Treaty between the Government of East Timor and the Government of Australia (signed 20 May 2002, entered into force 2 April 2003) 2258 UNTS 3 (Timor Sea Treaty); Agreement between the Government of Australia and the Government of the Democratic Republic of Timor-Leste relating to the Unitisation of the Sunrise and Troubadour Fields (adopted 6 March 2003, entered into force 23 February 2007) [2007] ATS 11; Treaty between Australia and the Democratic Republic of Timor-Leste on Certain Maritime Arrangements in the Timor Sea (adopted 12 January 2006, entered into force 23 February 2007) 2483 UNTS 359 (CMATS Treaty). The CMATS Treaty left the maritime boundary undefined and established a moratorium in relation to the fixing of a permanent maritime boundary as between the two countries for a period of fifty years, or five years after exploitation of the Greater Sunrise gas field ceases, whichever occurs earlier: art 4.

to UNCLOS may institute conciliation proceedings against another party that has issued a declaration under Article 298(1)(a) without any further act of consent.

Nonetheless, for the purposes of compulsory conciliation under Article 298(1)(a), there are a number of preconditions that must be satisfied. If the parties disagree as to the competence of the conciliation commission, particularly because one party alleges the preconditions are not met, the commission is to resolve whether it has jurisdiction to proceed.[182] The conditions include that the dispute has arisen subsequent to the entry into force of UNCLOS; no agreement is reached in negotiations within a reasonable period of time; and the dispute does not involve the concurrent consideration of unsettled territorial disputes.[183] Further, compulsory conciliation is not available for 'any sea boundary dispute finally settled by an arrangement between the parties, or to any such dispute which is to be settled in accordance with a bilateral or multilateral agreement binding upon those parties'.[184]

Several of these preconditions were tested by Australia in challenging the competence of the Commission in the *Timor Sea Conciliation*. Australia submitted that the dispute had in fact arisen prior to the entry into force of UNCLOS for the parties. Australia argued that as Timor-Leste did not become a party to UNCLOS until 2013, UNCLOS only entered into force as between Australia and Timor-Leste at that time. By then, the dispute concerning the maritime boundary in the Timor Sea had already crystallised between the parties. The Commission considered that the relevant date was the entry into force of UNCLOS more generally, which was 1994, as the 'ordinary meaning of the unqualified phrase'.[185] Any presumption in favour of the non-retroactivity of treaties that would normally have operated was seemingly overridden in light of the perceived plain meaning of the phrase.[186]

There are two important consequences following from the Commission's decision. First, setting the date at 1994 will mean any new State, such as Timor-Leste, or perhaps Palestine, coming into existence subsequent to that date and only acceding to UNCLOS after 1994 will also be more likely to have disputes that emerge subsequent to 1994. There is thus a greater potential for 'newer' maritime boundary disputes to be addressed through the compulsory conciliation process involving these new States. Secondly, where States did not formally declare their EEZ until after UNCLOS entered into force, as the EEZ was formally a creation of UNCLOS, it is more likely that a maritime boundary dispute relating to overlapping EEZs could be subjected to compulsory conciliation as compared to continental shelf disputes. States' rights to continental shelves were already recognised prior to the UNCLOS negotiations and it is therefore more likely that disputes as to overlapping entitlements to continental shelves would have emerged at an earlier date. It may still be the case, however, that disputes relating to overlapping continental shelves only emerged with the change in definition to the breadth of the continental shelf under UNCLOS. Arguably, on this approach overlapping entitlements to outer continental shelves could fall within compulsory conciliation without a bar caused by the entry into force dates.

[182] UNCLOS (n 1) Annex V, art 13.

[183] ibid art 298(1)(a)(i).

[184] ibid art 298(1)(a)(iii).

[185] *Conciliation between The Democratic Republic of Timor-Leste and the Commonwealth of Australia* (Decision on Australia's Objections to Competence of 19 September 2016) PCA Case No 2016-10, para 74 (*Timor Sea Conciliation*, Decision on Competence).

[186] ibid para 76.

In relation to other barriers to compulsory conciliation, Australia could not rely on the precondition to compulsory conciliation that the dispute concerned a 'sea boundary dispute finally settled by an arrangement', as the Timor Sea Treaty explicitly referenced the arrangement as falling within Article 83(3) of UNCLOS, as a 'provisional arrangement[] of a practical nature pending agreement on the final delimitation'.[187] It must, however, be generally expected that States that have concluded agreements incorporating provisional arrangements pending the delimitation of their maritime boundaries could not rely on this provision to preclude resort to compulsory conciliation. The provision would rather be directed at preventing States from re-opening final maritime boundary agreements or arrangements that were already in place. This policy would be consistent with the temporal limitation concerning the entry into force of UNCLOS, which is also underlined by a desire not to jeopardise pre-existing maritime boundary agreements.[188] A preference for stability and continuity in maritime boundaries is discernible from this provision and from the requirements limiting third-party engagement enshrined therein.

Australia did dispute whether another precondition to conciliation was met, arguing that the parties had not negotiated for a reasonable period of time prior to the institution of the conciliation, and the requirement could not in any event be fulfilled because of the stipulations of Article 4 of the Treaty on Certain Maritime Arrangements in the Timor Sea (CMATS Treaty).[189] The Commission noted that there was no express requirement for negotiations but rather that no agreement was reached within a reasonable period of time in the event that there were negotiations.[190] As a question of fact, the parties undertook negotiations between 2003 and 2006, prior to the adoption of the CMATS Treaty.[191] Those discussions may have produced the CMATS Treaty, but they did not produce an agreement on the actual sea boundary delimitation. Moreover, Timor-Leste had attempted to raise the question of the boundary with Australia subsequent to the adoption of the CMATS Treaty, which the Commission considered to be permissible in light of various provisions within that Treaty.[192] Consequently, no agreement was reached in negotiations within a reasonable period of time as to the interpretation or application of Articles 74 and 83 of UNCLOS, which concern delimitation of overlapping EEZs and continental shelves.[193]

Arguably, the CMATS Treaty also constituted a binding bilateral agreement that settled the dispute in accordance with the terms of that agreement. The CMATS Treaty thus fell within the terms of Article 298(1)(a)(iii) as well, even if Timor-Leste was no longer happy with the terms of the particular binding bilateral agreement. On the information available, Australia does not seem to have pursued this argument and the Commission therefore did not address the question. Nonetheless, if 'the dispute' was to be understood as only the maritime boundary delimitation rather than the management and exploitation of the maritime resources then the CMATS Treaty would not have met this requirement because it did not definitively set out the maritime boundary. The Commission would have been unlikely

[187] Timor Sea Treaty (n 181) art 2.

[188] A policy enshrined in the Vienna Convention on the Law of Treaties (adopted 23 May 1969, entered into force 27 January 1980) 1155 UNTS 331, art 62(2)(a) (VCLT).

[189] CMATS Treaty (n 181). See *Timor Sea Conciliation*, Decision on Competence (n 185) para 77.

[190] ibid para 78.

[191] ibid para 79.

[192] ibid para 81.

[193] ibid para 82.

to countenance the view that an agreement to delimit the boundary at a later point in time 'settled' the dispute.[194]

A consequence of the Commission's decision that it had jurisdiction was that the engagement of the parties in the conciliation process under UNCLOS seemingly placed them in violation of commitments under the CMATS Treaty.[195] Timor-Leste argued that Article 4(4) of the CMATS Treaty was not applicable because UNCLOS conciliation could not be viewed as a 'dispute settlement mechanism' as it cannot settle the dispute.[196] If conciliation cannot settle a dispute then what is its point? In any event, the Commission was of the view that this international law violation had to be addressed elsewhere,[197] as it did not fall to the Commission to consider or decide.[198] Australia's objections to competence based on a 'clean hands' argument were thereby rejected.[199] Instead, Timor-Leste opted to withdraw from the CMATS Treaty and the parties reached agreement on the resulting arrangements as a consequence of the termination of that treaty.[200]

In addition, it was notable that the Commission resolved a question on the scope of its competence in light of submissions by Timor-Leste that sought the Commission's consideration not only of the maritime boundary but also of transitional arrangements.[201] The Commission endorsed Timor-Leste's position on the basis that Articles 74 and 83 both address provisional arrangements of a practical nature and so its work would not have to be restricted to the delimitation itself.[202]

The Decision on Competence by the Commission was consistent with the ongoing trend in case law under UNCLOS to adopt an expansive approach to jurisdiction and admissibility.[203] In each instance, the Commission opted for an interpretation that would permit, rather than limit, the exercise of its competence. The *Timor Sea Conciliation* has thus demonstrated that even when States exclude maritime boundary delimitation disputes from arbitration or adjudication, conciliation may be contemplated as an accessible alternative. While there remain important jurisdictional barriers to compulsory conciliation under UNCLOS for maritime boundary delimitation disputes,[204] most notably where there is contested territorial disputes also at issue, parties in dispute would also need to consider diverse factors, such as the history of cooperation, third party interests, economic, political and military interests at play, that would also influence the likely success of this process in resolving these disputes.[205]

[194] Consistent with its approach to art 281, which is discussed in ch 3(II)(B)(1).

[195] Timor-Leste disputed such an assertion by Australia: *Timor Sea Conciliation*, Decision on Competence (n 185) para 87.

[196] ibid para 23.

[197] ibid para 92.

[198] ibid para 91.

[199] See ibid paras 90–92. See also discussion in Peter Tzeng, 'The Peaceful Non-Settlement of Disputes: Article 4 of *CMATS* in *Timor-Leste v Australia*' (2017) 18 Melb J Intl L 349, 367–68.

[200] See Permanent Court of Arbitration, 'Joint Statement by the Governments of Timor-Leste and Australia and the Conciliation Commission constituted pursuant to Annex V of the United Nations Convention on the Law of the Sea' (24 January 2017) https://pcacases.com/web/sendAttach/2346.

[201] *Timor Sea Conciliation*, Decision on Competence (n 185) para 93.

[202] ibid para 97.

[203] See generally Klein, 'The Vicissitudes' (n 54); Talmon, 'Expansion of Jurisdiction' (n 137).

[204] See Natalie Klein, '*Timor Sea Conciliation*: A Harbinger for Dispute Settlement under UNCLOS?' in Hélène Ruiz Fabri and others (eds), *Dispute Resolution in the Law of International Watercourses and the Law of the Sea: A Bridge Over Troubled Waters* (Brill Nijhoff 2020) 116–22.

[205] ibid. See also Ulf Linderfalk, 'The Jan Mayen Case (Iceland/Norway): An Example of Successful Conciliation' in Christian Tomuschat, Riccardo Pisillo Mazzeschi, and Daniel Thürer (eds), *Conciliation in International Law: The OSCE Court of Conciliation and Arbitration* (Brill 2017) 203–11.

B. Historic Bays and Titles

Article 298(1)(a) also potentially excludes disputes relating to historic bays and title from the scope of compulsory dispute settlement under UNCLOS. This provision was at issue in the *South China Sea* arbitration because one of the possible justifications for China's nine-dash line encompassing large parts of this semi-enclosed sea could be based on historic rights.[206] The Philippines sought to separate out claims relating to historic rights to those specifically referenced in Article 298(1)(a), namely those 'involving historic bays or titles'. A decision on the Philippines claim challenging China's asserted historic rights could only be made at the merits stage, as the Tribunal reasoned it needed to determine the nature and validity of China's historic rights before being able to conclude if such a decision would fall within Article 298.[207]

At the merits stage, the Philippines addressed the distinction between the 'historic rights' claimed by China, and the concept of 'historic bays or titles' as noted in Article 298 of UNCLOS. Based on the evidence before the Tribunal, the Philippines drew three conclusions that supported the proposition that China's claim of historic rights was distinct from historic bays or titles. The first was that China's statements and actions demonstrated that its 'historic rights' claim was not a claim to 'historic bays or historic title'; the second was that China itself did not characterise its claim as one of 'historic bays or historic title'; and the third was that China chose not to invoke the Article 298 exclusion of disputes concerning 'historic bays or historic title' in its Position Paper, despite invoking the exception in respect to maritime delimitation.[208] Further, the Philippines argued the importance of the distinction between the terms 'historic rights' and 'historic title' in Chinese,[209] and submitted that 'historical title' could only apply to waters directly appurtenant to the coast that lie within the limits of the territorial sea, and not beyond.[210] Although there were difficulties in determining the nature of China's claim as it did not participate in the arbitration or make submissions on the issue, the Philippines relied on the above points to demonstrate that China's claim of historic rights was to be considered distinct from 'historic bays or titles'.

In its Award, the *South China Sea* Tribunal looked to the evolution of references to historic bays, titles, and rights in the international law of the sea.[211] The various terms were differentiated as follows:

> The term 'historic rights' is general in nature and can describe any rights that a State may possess that would not normally arise under the general rules of international law, absent particular historical circumstances. Historic rights may include sovereignty, but may equally include more limited rights, such as fishing rights or rights of access, that fall well short of a claim of sovereignty. 'Historic title', in contrast, is used specifically to refer to historic sovereignty to land or maritime areas. 'Historic waters' is simply a term for historic title over maritime areas, typically exercised either as a claim to internal waters or as

[206] *South China Sea*, Award (n 18) para 186.
[207] *South China Sea*, Jurisdiction and Admissibility (n 47) para 398.
[208] *South China Sea Arbitration (Philippines v China)* (Transcript of Proceedings, Hearing on Merits and Remaining Issues of Jurisdiction and Admissibility, 24 November 2015) PCA Case No 2013-19, 44.
[209] ibid 34.
[210] ibid 47.
[211] *South China Sea*, Award (n 18) para 217.

> a claim to the territorial sea, although 'general international law ... does not provide for a single "régime" for "historic waters" or "historic bays", but only for a particular régime for each of the concrete, recognised cases of "historic waters" or "historic bays"'. Finally, a 'historic bay' is simply a bay in which a State claims historic waters.[212]

On this basis, it appeared that the exception in Article 298(1)(a) would only cover those disputes that involve historic sovereignty rather than broader, and lesser, claims of historic rights or historic waters.[213] The elucidation of the substantive body of law should therefore clarify the scope of the exception in Article 298(1)(a), if the reasoning from the *South China Sea* arbitration is followed in subsequent cases. A further consequence of this decision was the affirmation of a narrow restriction on accessing compulsory arbitration or adjudication under UNCLOS.

One of the issues that emerged in the *South China Sea* arbitration that reappeared in *Coastal State Rights in the Black Sea* concerned the timing for determining if there was a dispute involving historic bays or titles. As mentioned above, the *South China Sea* Tribunal had considered the questions relating to historic rights were not exclusively preliminary and were resolved once full pleadings on the nature of the rights had occurred. Similarly, in *Coastal State Rights in the Black Sea*, the Tribunal determined that the dispute between Russia and Ukraine over the status of the Sea of Azov and the Kerch Strait was 'interwoven with the merits' and could not be resolved at the jurisdictional phase.[214] In that case, the questions for resolution concerned 'whether historic title to the waters in question existed, whether such title continued after 1991, and, if so, what the contents of the regime applicable to such waters has been'.[215] A difficulty with this approach is that a tribunal will need to make a number of important legal findings on the existence of historic title, historic bays or historic rights for the purpose of determining whether the tribunal has jurisdiction. The very act of determining that a maritime area is an historic bay and hence outside jurisdiction may at the same time settle an outstanding question that exists between the parties.

In light of the decisions on this issue to date,[216] drawing distinctions between the different types of historic rights or title to determine if a dispute is within a tribunal's jurisdiction under UNCLOS or not may not be helpful. Arguably, once a dispute 'involves' historic title, it falls within Article 298. As such, even a dispute as to whether a claim is based on historic rights or historic title still 'involves' historic title and should be excluded from jurisdiction. This latter view aligns with the common-sense approach articulated in the *Chagos MPA* arbitration in recognising that States did not necessarily want key sovereignty-related issues subjected to UNCLOS arbitration or adjudication.[217]

[212] ibid para 225.
[213] 'The Tribunal is of the view that this usage was understood by the drafters of the Convention and that the reference to 'historic titles' in art 298(1)(a)(i) of the Convention is accordingly a reference to claims of sovereignty over maritime areas derived from historical circumstances:' ibid para 227.
[214] *Coastal State Rights in the Black Sea* (n 19) para 389.
[215] ibid para 388.
[216] Noting that the *Coastal State Rights in the Black Sea* (n 19) case had not been resolved on the merits at time of writing.
[217] *Chagos MPA* (n 17) para 217.

C. Military Activities

Article 298 does not specify what 'military activities' might be excluded from the scope of compulsory procedures entailing binding decisions. The negotiating history of this exception indicates that States did not necessarily want their military conduct placed under scrutiny before an international tribunal, but also recognised that such review may be needed because of the sovereign immunity that would otherwise protect the actions of naval vessels from interference.[218] An optional exception to compulsory dispute settlement thus met these concerns. There is considerable potential for judicial discretion in determining what may or may not constitute 'military activities' for the purpose of this exception.

The first opportunity to review the scope of the military activities exception arose in the *South China Sea* arbitration in the context of its assessment of the legality of China's land reclamation activities, which the Philippines claimed were in violation of various provisions relating to the protection and preservation of the marine environment. The Philippines argued that the identity of the actor was not dispositive but regard must be had to the nature and purpose of the activity in question.[219] Moreover, while it could usually be assumed that non-military actors or vessels were not engaged in military activities, evidence may be presented to the contrary that would prompt a designation of the conduct as such.[220] Given the political controversy concerning China's activities and concerns as to whether the land reclamation activity was for military purposes, the Tribunal considered briefly if the military activities exception would preclude examination of this conduct. In this regard, the Tribunal indicated that where a State disavows that its activities are military in nature then this characterisation is of distinct relevance. Consequently, the exception could not apply in these circumstances.[221]

Whereas disavowing the military nature of certain conduct had implications in assessing the applicability of this exception, a State's failure to make a claim objecting to jurisdiction under the military activities exception did not prevent the exception from applying. This latter perspective was articulated in the *South China Sea* in response to the Philippines' claims that China had unlawfully aggravated the dispute in its actions subsequent to the commencement of the arbitration.

Contrary to the view of the Philippines that the military activities exception did not apply because it had never been invoked by China, the Tribunal considered that such an explicit claim was not necessary.[222] ITLOS progressed this view in *Detention of Three Ukrainian Naval Vessels* when it noted that the characterisation of the activities by one of the parties was not determinative.[223] Instead of relying on the parties' perspectives, the *South China Sea* Tribunal emphasised 'the relevant question to be whether the dispute itself concerns military activities, rather than whether a party has employed its military in some manner in

[218] Myron H Nordquist (ed), *United Nations Convention on the Law of the Sea 1982: A Commentary* (Martinus Nijhoff 1985–2012) vol 5, 135 (*Virginia Commentary*); Klein, *Dispute Settlement* (n 154) 290–91.

[219] See *South China Sea*, Jurisdiction and Admissibility (n 47) para 377.

[220] ibid.

[221] *South China Sea*, Award (n 18) paras 893, 934 ff. See further paras 1012, 1028 in relation to Mischief Reef.

[222] ibid para 1156.

[223] *Detention of Three Ukrainian Naval Vessels (Ukraine v Russia)* (Provisional Measures Order of 25 May 2019) ITLOS Case No 26, para 65 (*Detention of Three Ukrainian Naval Vessels*, Provisional Measures). See further Yoshifumi Tanaka, 'Release of a Detained Warship and Its Crew through Provisional Measures: A Comparative Analysis of the ARA Libertad and Ukraine v Russia Cases' (2020) 96 ILS 223, 232–34 (Tanaka, 'Release of a Detained Warship').

relation to the dispute'.[224] An objective evaluation is required, 'taking into account the relevant circumstances in each case'.[225]

One of the incidents considered by the *South China Sea* Tribunal concerned a stand-off between the Philippines' armed forces and ships from China's Navy and Coast Guard where the Chinese vessels sought to prevent the resupply and rotation of Philippine troops at Second Thomas Shoal on two occasions.[226] The facts before the Tribunal relating to the incidents at Second Thomas Shoal were deemed to be a 'quintessentially military situation', entailing 'the military forces of one side and a combination of military and paramilitary forces on the other, arrayed in opposition to one another'.[227] The situation thus fell 'well within' Article 298(1)(b) and the Tribunal did not have jurisdiction to consider the Philippines' claims based on these incidents.[228]

The *Coastal State Rights in the Black Sea* case considered the decisions reached in the *South China Sea* arbitration. As many of Ukraine's claims under the Convention were connected to the question of disputed sovereignty over Crimea, Russia sought to rely on the military activities exception 'because Ukraine has made express and specific allegations of acts of military aggression and unlawful use of force'.[229] Ukraine disputed that the existence of an unlawful use of force necessarily meant that any conduct pursuant to that use of force 'would be immunised' from compulsory proceedings under UNCLOS.[230] Arguably, a question should arise as to the applicability of UNCLOS generally during any time of armed conflict and whether the actions that might be complained of under UNCLOS are part of a military campaign in an armed conflict and hence constitute 'military activities'.[231] In *Detention of Three Ukrainian Vessels*, Judge Lijnzaad raised the question of whether a situation of armed conflict existed between Russia and Ukraine in light of the *notes verbale* that were exchanged between the parties.[232] While she agreed with the majority on the existence of prima facie jurisdiction for the purposes of prescribing provisional measures, Judge Lijnzaad considered this question could be addressed further by the Annex VII Tribunal.[233] Even if UNCLOS remained the applicable law, actions taken pursuant to military strategies in an armed conflict would presumably count as a 'quintessentially military situation' and should fall outside the jurisdiction of a tribunal constituted under UNCLOS where a State party has made a declaration under Article 298(1)(b). This question did not need to be resolved in *Coastal State Rights in the Black Sea* as the Tribunal was not concerned with the 'background' of a 'broader alleged armed conflict' but examined specific acts that were subject to complaint.[234]

[224] *South China Sea*, Award (n 18) para 1158.
[225] *Detention of Three Ukrainian Naval Vessels*, Provisional Measures (n 223) para 66.
[226] *South China Sea*, Award (n 18) para 1161.
[227] ibid.
[228] ibid.
[229] *Coastal State Rights in the Black Sea* (n 19) para 303.
[230] ibid para 317.
[231] Klein, *Dispute Settlement* (n 154) 282–84.
[232] See *Detention of Three Ukrainian Naval Vessels*, Provisional Measures (n 223) (Declaration of Judge Lijnzaad) para 5. For further discussion on this point see Ion Gâlea, 'The Interpretation of "Military Activities" as an Exception to Jurisdiction: The ITLOS Order of 25 May 2019 in the Case Concerning the Detention of Three Ukrainian Naval Vessels' (2019) 21 Romanian J Intl L [31], Section 3.1.
[233] *Detention of Three Ukrainian Naval Vessels*, Provisional Measures (n 223) (Declaration of Judge Lijnzaad) paras 5, 8.
[234] *Coastal State Rights in the Black Sea* (n 19) para 331.

In *Coastal State Rights in the Black Sea*, the Tribunal engaged more closely with the meaning of 'military activities' and was particularly concerned with the deployment of military forces in differing contexts. Russia argued that the Ukrainian claims could not be separated into 'civilian' components beyond the allegations surrounding the use of force;[235] instead, military activities should not be interpreted restrictively.[236] Ukraine instead emphasised that 'the military activities exception should only apply where the specific conduct complained of is military in nature'.[237] Ukraine further argued that 'had the States Parties to the Convention intended that the military activities exception extend to any dispute having a causal link to a military activities, they would have drafted [Article 298(1)(b)] so that it covers all disputes "arising out of" or "in connection with" military activities'.[238] The Tribunal agreed that 'concerning' limited the disputes that would be excluded under Article 298(1)(b). For the Tribunal, 'a mere "causal" or historical link between certain alleged military activities and the activities in dispute' would not be enough.[239]

Equally, the 'mere involvement or presence of military vessels is in and by itself' insufficient to bar the exercise of jurisdiction.[240] This holding reinforces the position taken in the *South China Sea* arbitration that more has to be considered than 'whether a party has employed its military in some manner in relation to the dispute'.[241] In *Coastal State Rights in the Black Sea*, the 'mere involvement' of military vessels and personnel in relation to undertaking archaeological expeditions and the construction of the Kerch Strait bridge, which impeded navigation, were agreed to be outside the military activities exception.[242]

The spectrum thus lies between 'mere involvement' of military vessels and personnel to 'quintessentially military situation[s]'; the difficult question is drawing the line between what is or is not justiciable in UNCLOS dispute settlement. It is important to acknowledge that military forces are deployed in diverse settings by countries, subject to the internal organisation of their defence, police and other security services. In *Detention of Three Ukrainian Vessels*, ITLOS noted that 'the traditional distinction between naval vessels and law enforcement vessels in terms of their roles has become considerably blurred'.[243] Further, there may be settings where military forces are used for law enforcement purposes, which might involve the use of physical force, but the use of force in this context would not warrant the characterisation of the activities as 'military' activities.

The specific activities that were identified in *Coastal State Rights in the Black Sea* that could not 'be objectively classified' as military activities were:

(a) the detention and release of the captain of a civilian vessel;
(b) standing guard and supervising works on oil platforms; and
(c) harassing vessels through 'dangerously close approaches, failures to establish radio communication, and general violations of the rules of safe navigation and seamanship'.[244]

[235] ibid para 305.
[236] ibid para 306.
[237] ibid para 316.
[238] ibid para 317.
[239] ibid para 330.
[240] ibid para 334.
[241] *South China Sea*, Award (n 18) para 1158.
[242] *Coastal State Rights in the Black Sea* (n 19) paras 339, 340.
[243] *Detention of Three Ukrainian Naval Vessels*, Provisional Measures (n 223) para 64.
[244] *Coastal State Rights in the Black Sea* (n 19) para 338.

This harassment was not considered a 'military activity' even when it was Russian military vessels and aircraft impeding the Ukrainian navy.[245] To exclude the latter from the scope of military activities creates an especially fine—and perhaps unrealistic—distinction between what might be considered 'non-military' harassment and 'military forces arrayed against one another'.[246]

While the jurisdiction decision in *Coastal State Rights in the Black Sea* was pending, Ukraine instituted further proceedings against Russia to address a specific incident occurring in late 2018 that resulted in Russia arresting and detaining three Ukrainian naval vessels (two warships and an auxiliary vessel) and the twenty-four crew onboard. Ukraine sought provisional measures pending the constitution of the Annex VII tribunal in accordance with Article 290(5). At this stage of the proceedings, Russia raised the military activities exception to deny that ITLOS had even prima facie jurisdiction and refused to appear.[247]

According to Ukraine, the three naval vessels departed from a port in the Black Sea and sought to transit the Kerch Strait to reach a port in the Sea of Azov. The Russian Coast Guard advised that the Strait was closed, sought to block the Ukrainian vessels, and subsequently pursued and detained the vessels and crew onboard.[248] Russia arrested the vessels and crew for criminal violations relating to an 'aggravated illegal crossing of the State border'.[249] Ukraine thus argued that the military activities exception was inapplicable because the incident concerned law enforcement.[250]

In examining the application of the military activities exception in *Detention of Three Ukrainian Naval Vessels*, ITLOS noted three particular circumstances surrounding the incident. First, the Tribunal commented that the passage of naval vessels through a strait was not per se a military activity because passage is undertaken by all vessels.[251] This observation might suggest that if the activities in question can be conducted by both military and non-military vessels then the activity is less likely to be considered 'military'. Other activities that might fit into this category could include search and rescue, routine surveying (e.g. bathymetry) for the purposes of navigation or safety manoeuvres. In his Dissenting Opinion, Judge Kolodkin instead took the view that 'the navigational activities at sea of a State's warships are inherently, or at least on their face, military'.[252] As such, he suggested that the starting presumption was that all activities undertaken by warships are military (and hence outside jurisdiction in accordance with Article 298(1)(b)) and this position only changed where 'specific circumstances in a particular situation may warrant a different conclusion'.[253] No examples of those specific circumstances were provided.

Secondly, ITLOS took into account the fact that the incident involved a denial of passage and the attempt to undertake passage irrespective.[254] As such, the dispute was focused on

[245] ibid.
[246] *South China Sea*, Award (n 18) para 1161.
[247] *Detention of Three Ukrainian Naval Vessels*, Provisional Measures (n 223) para 8.
[248] ibid para 31.
[249] ibid para 32.
[250] ibid para 50.
[251] ibid para 68.
[252] ibid (Dissenting Opinion of Judge Kolodkin) para 9.
[253] ibid.
[254] *Detention of Three Ukrainian Naval Vessels*, Provisional Measures (n 223) para 71. Judge Gao divided these two stages whereby the first related to a question of passage, but the second stage was more properly characterised as a military stand-off: see Separate Opinion of Judge Gao, para 23.

differing interpretations of the applicable passage regime and 'such a dispute is not military in nature'.[255] In this respect, Judge Jesus considered that the focus should be on the Ukrainian ships and measuring the nature of their passage against the requirements for innocent passage.[256] He concluded that there was insufficient information to determine if the nature of their passage was military in nature in view of the types of conduct that would be considered as 'non-innocent' under Article 19 of the Convention.

Thirdly, ITLOS took into account the amount of force used and how its escalation was commensurate with the force escalation deployed in law enforcement operations.[257] Judge Gao, however, raised the critical point that law enforcement against a commercial vessel is very different to force undertaken by State authorities against another State's warships.[258] The Ukrainian vessels were all subject to sovereign immunity and law enforcement could not be anticipated against such vessels.[259]

ITLOS additionally relied on the subsequent proceedings and charges against the vessels and crew as further aligning the situation with law enforcement operations, instead of a military situation.[260] Implicit in this last point is that there was seemingly no suggestion from the Tribunal that the vessels were being seized as enemy belligerents or that the crew were being held as prisoners of war, which may have been the case if there was a situation of armed conflict. These arguments were, however, used by Ukraine in fora other than the Tribunal.[261] Even absent an armed conflict, a more limited military engagement would entail different rules of engagement. Judge Kolodkin, in his Dissenting Opinion, highlighted the content of a 'Checklist for Readiness to Sail', which was prepared by the Ukrainian navy, and demonstrated to him the military nature of the operation to pass through the Kerch Strait.[262]

Distinguishing between military activities and law enforcement was thus a difficult factor in the *Detention of Three Ukrainian Naval Vessels* provisional measures order.[263] The benchmark for doing so rested on a 'primarily' 'objective evaluation'.[264] The scheme of UNCLOS on the exercise of coastal State powers in the territorial sea may have provided some indication as to the characterisation of the activities. The exercise of law enforcement powers may be most readily anticipated when a coastal State seeks to suppress criminal activities within its territorial sea,[265] rather than in either the 'necessary steps' a coastal State may

[255] *Detention of Three Ukrainian Naval Vessels*, Provisional Measures (n 223) para 72.

[256] ibid (Separate Opinion of Judge Jesus) paras 15–16.

[257] *Detention of Three Ukrainian Naval Vessels*, Provisional Measures (n 223) para 74. See also Declaration of Judge Kittichaisaree, para 5 (referring to *M/V Saiga (No 2) (Saint Vincent and the Grenadines v Guinea)* (Judgment) ITLOS Reports 1999, 10 (*Saiga No 2*, Judgment) and the description of the permissible use of force in the context of law enforcement operations).

[258] *Detention of Three Ukrainian Naval Vessels*, Provisional Measures (n 223) (Separate Opinion of Judge Gao) para 34.

[259] ibid para 2.

[260] *Detention of Three Ukrainian Naval Vessels*, Provisional Measures (n 223) para 76.

[261] These assertions are summarised in James Kraska, 'Did ITLOS Just Kill the Military Activities Exemption in Article 298?' *EJIL: Talk!* (27 May 2019) https://www.ejiltalk.org/did-itlos-just-kill-the-military-activities-exemption-in-article-298/.

[262] See *Detention of Three Ukrainian Naval Vessels*, Provisional Measures (n 223) (Dissenting Opinion of Judge Kolodkin) paras 12–17.

[263] For criticism see Yurika Ishii, 'The Distinction between Military and Law Enforcement Activities: Comments on Case Concerning the Detention of Three Ukrainian Naval Vessels (Ukraine v Russian Federation), Provisional Measures Order' *EJIL: Talk!* (31 May 2019) https://www.ejiltalk.org/the-distinction-between-military-and-law-enforcement-activities-comments-on-case-concerning-the-detention-of-three-ukrainian-naval-vessels-ukraine-v-russian-federation-provisional-measures-order/.

[264] *Detention of Three Ukrainian Naval Vessels*, Provisional Measures (n 223) para 66.

[265] As anticipated under art 27 of UNCLOS (n 1).

deploy to prevent passage that is not innocent[266] or the request to warships to leave the territorial sea immediately.[267] The latter are not equivalent to law enforcement, even though the gradual escalation in the coastal State's reactions in each instance (whether for suppression of criminal activity or in response to unlawful passage) are comparable. In *Detention of Three Ukrainian Naval Vessels*, Russia arrested the Ukrainian vessels under Article 91 of its Criminal Procedure Code.[268] This aspect should have influenced the Tribunal's evaluation, but should not be considered decisive given that the actions leading up to the arrest more properly reflected military activities that are necessarily involved in both the assertion of denied navigational rights and in responses to alleged unlawful passage in the territorial sea.

Judge Gao was concerned about the wider ramifications of setting a low threshold for the application of the military activities exception, commenting: 'A high threshold for the military activities exception may serve as an incentive for States to escalate rather than de-escalate a conflict by deploying a great numbers [sic] of naval vessels and increasing the level of forces in order to qualify for the military activities exception to compulsory dispute settlement jurisdiction.'[269] He continued, '[t]he recent judicial developments in this respect may therefore cause general concern that the UNCLOS dispute settlement organs might intrude upon military activities excluded from their jurisdiction'.[270] The Annex VII Tribunal will need to examine this jurisdictional limitation more closely as ITLOS only had to establish a prima facie basis of jurisdiction.[271] Any determination will ultimately be very fact specific but must account for the primary intention that States opting for this exception did not want the core activities of their military forces subjected to mandatory third party review and their acceptance of the UNCLOS dispute settlement regime is conditioned on this exception being properly recognised.[272]

D. Specified Law Enforcement Activities

Under Article 298(1)(b), States further have the option of excluding disputes involving certain law enforcement activities from arbitration or adjudication. The law enforcement activities that may be excluded are those 'disputes concerning law enforcement activities in regard to the exercise of sovereign rights or jurisdiction excluded from the jurisdiction of a court or tribunal under article 297, paragraph 2 or 3'. Article 297(2) addresses marine scientific research and Article 297(3) concerns fisheries.

The scope of this exception was considered in *Arctic Sunrise*, as the Netherlands challenged the legality of Russia's actions in arresting Greenpeace protestors who had staged a protest against an offshore oil platform in the Russian EEZ. Rather than adopt a broad reading of the exception so as to apply to any law enforcement activities undertaken by

[266] UNCLOS (n 1) art 25(1).
[267] ibid art 30.
[268] *Detention of Three Ukrainian Naval Vessels*, Provisional Measures (n 223) para 32.
[269] ibid (Separate Opinion of Judge Gao) para 45.
[270] ibid para 47.
[271] Tanaka has suggested that the Annex VII Tribunal should consider the 'preponderance' of the evidence in assessing activities that are a mix of law enforcement and military: Tanaka, 'Release of a Detained Warship' (n 223) 238.
[272] Kraska has cautioned against 'eviscerating' the military activities exception, particularly as it may reduce the willingness of States to either become party to UNCLOS or participate in its dispute settlement proceedings. See Kraska (n 261).

a coastal State,[273] the Annex VII Tribunal confirmed that the exception in Article 298(1)(b) only applied to law enforcement actions for fishing or marine scientific research in the EEZ.[274] Law enforcement in relation to artificial installations or in connection with the exploration and exploitation of continental shelf resources could thus be resolved under Section 2 of Part XV. The *Arctic Sunrise* Tribunal therefore affirmed the narrow scope of this exception.

Russia also sought to extend the application of Article 298(1)(b)'s law enforcement exception to cover events in the territorial sea or on the continental shelf in *Coastal State Rights in the Black Sea*.[275] Although Ukraine countered this position, it was not ultimately resolved by the Tribunal.[276] It seems unlikely that the exception would be extended beyond the ordinary meaning of the text, especially in light of the interpretation in *Arctic Sunrise*.

The *South China Sea* Tribunal also examined the applicability of this exception under Article 298 in assessing the Philippines' claims that China had violated UNCLOS through its enforcement of its fisheries regulations in a disputed maritime area. In the course of its Final Award, the Tribunal determined that the maritime area in question would be part of the Philippines' EEZ and thus assessed China's fishing regulation and enforcement in this context. While on its face, it would appear that China's actions constituted law enforcement actions over fisheries in the EEZ and would thus be excluded under Article 298(1)(b), the Tribunal accepted that this exception would not apply in relation to law enforcement activities undertaken by third States in a coastal State's EEZ; the exception only applied to exclude disputes concerning the coastal State's law enforcement activities in its own EEZ from compulsory arbitration or adjudication. In doing so, the Tribunal determined it had jurisdiction to decide that China was in violation of UNCLOS. This decision further narrowed the instances where the law enforcement exception may be considered applicable, and thereby expanded the scope of compulsory jurisdiction.

* * *

In any interpretation of Article 298 exceptions, it is critical to note that these exceptions were devised in the knowledge that parties to the Convention would not otherwise be allowed to enter reservations. It could thus be seen that allowing for these exceptions to compulsory jurisdiction was a considerable deviation from what was otherwise intended to be a comprehensive approach to dispute settlement. In this setting, the position may well be taken that exceptions should be read narrowly so as not to disrupt a 'universalist' model.[277] Equally, however, the fact that exceptions were allowed demonstrates that some issues were of such importance to States that they wished to maintain their control over how disputes

[273] Which was the language used in Russia's declaration pertaining to art 298: 'law-enforcement activities in regard to the exercise of sovereign rights or jurisdiction'. See *Arctic Sunrise (Netherlands v Russia)* (Award on Jurisdiction of 26 November 2014) PCA Case No 2014-02, para 9 (*Arctic Sunrise*, Jurisdiction).

[274] ibid paras 69, 76.

[275] *Coastal State Rights in the Black Sea* (n 19) para 345.

[276] As questions relating to sovereignty over Crimea were outside jurisdiction and the law enforcement activities were within an area of potentially overlapping entitlements, the Tribunal considered the conditions for the applicability of this provision were not met. The Tribunal commented, 'both the sovereign character of the rights allegedly exercised by the declaring State and the entitlement of the declaring State to the area in question as that State's [EEZ] must be objectively established for the optional exception to apply': ibid paras 356, 358.

[277] As described by Tanaka. See Tanaka, *Toward an International Legal Order* (n 102) 110–11. But see also ch 1(III).

relating to those matters would be resolved.[278] Further, where a State party to UNCLOS makes a declaration consistent with Article 298, it has made a very clear gesture as to its position on the role of compulsory jurisdiction for disputes relating to Article 298 exceptions.[279] Decisions that run counter to this deliberate effort to protect sovereign prerogatives must account for the complex interests and principles involved. As Sheehan has noted, it is important to recall that the dispute settlement provisions in UNCLOS were a 'package deal' in their own right.[280] Giving appropriate weight to State decision-making in this context will enhance the overall dispute resolution regime and ensure its proper use for the resolution of other law of the sea disputes into the future.

V. Applicable Law and Subject Matter Jurisdiction

Distinguishing between applicable law and subject matter jurisdiction has caused difficulties in the jurisprudence of UNCLOS dispute settlement.[281] Article 293 of UNCLOS, entitled 'Applicable Law', provides in its paragraph 1 that: 'A court or tribunal having jurisdiction under this section shall apply this Convention and other rules of international law not incompatible with this Convention.'[282] The question that has arisen in a number of disputes is the extent to which Article 293(1), with its reference to 'other rules of international law', might be relied upon to expand the subject matter jurisdiction of an UNCLOS tribunal beyond disputes 'concerning the interpretation or application' of UNCLOS. Part XV tribunals have been divided on the effect of Article 293(1), and, as a consequence, have reached quite different conclusions on the scope of their jurisdiction to address such claims.

The *Virginia Commentary* to UNCLOS is silent as to the precise effect of Article 293(1). It notes that early versions of Article 293 included as an element that the dispute settlement processes 'should ensure that the rule of law is observed in the interpretation and application of the Convention', suggesting a very limited role for 'other rules of international law' pursuant to the applicable law provision.[283] Commentators on UNCLOS have argued that Article 293(1) should not be used as a means to expand a Part XV tribunal's jurisdiction. Oxman has emphasised that:

> [C]are should be taken to avoid conflating the question of applicable law with the question of jurisdiction. Under Section 2 of Part XV of the LOSC, jurisdiction is limited to disputes concerning the interpretation and application of the Convention. Other rules of

[278] Allen, for example, has noted that 'the traditional, or background, assumption of the need for state consent to be specifically established in relation to a particular dispute (or in a given situation) still informs the extent to which advance consent can be invoked to justify expansive readings of the interpretation and application of the compulsory procedures contained in part XV'. Allen (n 137) 327.

[279] Although Churchill has noted that the 'small number of declarations under Article 298 suggests that the assumptions on which those exceptions are based may be questionable'. Robin Churchill, 'The General Dispute Settlement System of the UN Convention on the Law of the Sea: Overview, Context, and Use' (2017) 48 ODIL 216, 219.

[280] Anne Sheehan, 'Dispute Settlement under UNCLOS: The Exclusion of Maritime Delimitation Disputes' (2005) 24 UQLJ 165, 166.

[281] The analysis that follows draws on Kate Parlett, 'Beyond the Four Corners of the Convention: Expanding the Scope of Jurisdiction of Law of the Sea Tribunals' (2017) 48 ODIL 284.

[282] UNCLOS (n 1) art 293(1).

[283] *Virginia Commentary* (n 218) vol 5, 72, para 293.1.

> international law may be applied as such in that context, only if they relate to matters not regulated by the Convention, and only if they are not incompatible with the Convention.[284]

Similarly, Sir Michael Wood has argued that:

> The reference to law other than the Convention in Article 293, paragraph 1, cannot be used to extend the jurisdiction conferred on the court or tribunal by the Convention ... Except where extended by agreement between the parties to the proceedings (as provided for in Article 288, paragraph 2, of the Convention, and Articles 21 and 22 of the Statute), a court or tribunal's jurisdiction under Part XV, section 2, is limited to disputes 'concerning the interpretation or application of the Convention' (Article 286). It does not have jurisdiction over other disputes. In particular, it does not have jurisdiction in respect of disputes arising under general international law.[285]

As a textual matter, Article 293 refers to tribunals 'having jurisdiction' are to apply rules under UNCLOS and other rules of international law thus suggesting that jurisdiction must be established in the first instance before any consideration of what law to apply arises.[286]

Nonetheless, the case law under UNCLOS has reflected an evolving and, at times, contrasting approach to the use of Article 293. This section first considers this inter-relationship of Article 293 and subject matter jurisdiction in general before considering how other rules of international law might be incorporated either through *renvoi* or through 'interaction with UNCLOS'.

A. Distinguishing or Conflating Applicable Law with Subject Matter Jurisdiction?

In *Saiga (No 2)*,[287] in its decision on the merits, ITLOS addressed the effect of Article 293, albeit briefly. Saint Vincent and the Grenadines had claimed that Guinea had used excessive and unreasonable force in stopping and arresting the Saiga. In assessing that claim, ITLOS stated:

> In considering the force used by Guinea in the arrest of the *Saiga*, the Tribunal must take into account the circumstances of the areas in the context of the applicable rules of international law. Although the Convention does not contain express provisions on the use of force in the arrest of ships, international law, which is applicable by virtue of article 293 of the Convention, requires that the use of force must be avoided as far as possible and, where force is unavoidable, it must not go beyond what is reasonable and necessary in the

284 Bernard H Oxman, 'Courts and Tribunals: The ICJ, ITLOS, and Arbitral Tribunals' in Donald Rothwell and others (eds), *The Oxford Handbook of the Law of the Sea* (OUP 2015) 414 (reference omitted).

285 Michael Wood, 'The International Tribunal for the Law of the Sea and General International Law' (2007) 22 IJMCL 351, 357.

286 Peter Tzeng, 'Jurisdiction and Applicable Law under UNCLOS' (2016) 126 Yale LJ 242 ('Jurisdiction and Applicable Law') 247.

287 *Saiga (No 2)*, Judgment (n 257).

> circumstances. Considerations of humanity must apply in the law of the sea, as they do in other areas of international law.[288]

On that basis of its jurisdiction to examine rules beyond the scope of the Convention, ITLOS proceeded to conclude that Guinea had used excessive force, violating the rights of Saint Vincent and the Grenadines under international law.[289] In the *dispositif* on this point, ITLOS did not refer explicitly to a provision of UNCLOS, but held that Guinea had 'used excessive force contrary to international law and thereby violated the rights of Saint Vincent and the Grenadines'.[290] Although it is not entirely clear, it is arguable that ITLOS made a finding of breach of rules of international law outside of UNCLOS, and did so on the basis that Article 293(1) of UNCLOS entitled it to decide a claim relating to the use of force under rules of international law extraneous to UNCLOS;[291] certainly that conclusion is supported by the *dispositif*, which found a violation of international law by the use of excessive force, a matter not regulated by any provision of UNCLOS.

Subsequently, in a 2003 Order, the *MOX Plant*[292] Annex VII Tribunal briefly discussed the relationship between Articles 288(1) and 293. It noted that Ireland had made claims arising under treaties beyond UNCLOS (such as the OSPAR Convention)[293] and on other instruments, such as a Ministerial Statement adopted at a meeting of the OSPAR Commission. Although it did not decide on the scope of its jurisdiction, the Tribunal stated:

> The Tribunal agrees with the United Kingdom that there is a cardinal distinction between the scope of its jurisdiction under article 288, paragraph 1, of the Convention, on the one hand, and the law to be applied by the Tribunal under article 293 of the Convention, on the other hand. It also agrees that, to the extent that any aspects of Ireland's claims arise directly under legal instruments other than the Convention, such claims may be inadmissible. However, the Tribunal does not agree that Ireland has failed to start and plead a case arising substantially under the Convention.[294]

On the basis of that statement, it appears that the *MOX Plant* Tribunal would not have considered that it had jurisdiction to determine a claim based on any legal instrument beyond UNCLOS (unlike ITLOS in *Saiga (No 2)*).

Yet the question addressed in *Saiga (No 2)* was revisited in *Guyana v Suriname* in which an Annex VII tribunal addressing a maritime boundary dispute was called upon to decide on one of Guyana's submissions seeking damages for Suriname's allegedly unlawful actions in an incident in an area of sea that was disputed.[295] Guyana argued that Suriname was responsible for violating obligations under UNCLOS, 'the Charter of the United Nations, and

[288] ibid para 155.

[289] ibid para 159.

[290] ibid para 183(9).

[291] cf Wood (n 285) 364, who suggests that the approach of the tribunal here was to 'consider a primary rule of general international law that arises incidentally in the course of deciding an issue within its jurisdiction'.

[292] *MOX Plant (Ireland v United Kingdom)* (Order No 3 on Suspension of Proceedings on Jurisdiction and Merits, and Request for Further Provisional Measures, Order of 24 June 2003) PCA Case No 2002-01 (*MOX Plant*, Order No 3).

[293] Convention for the Protection of the Marine Environment of the North-East Atlantic (opened for signature 22 September 1992, entered into force 25 March 1998) 2354 UNTS 67.

[294] *MOX Plant*, Order No 3 (n 292) para 19.

[295] *Guyana v Suriname* (n 140) para 401 (Guyana's Third Submission).

general international law to settle disputes by peaceful means'.[296] Suriname argued that the Tribunal had no jurisdiction over disputes relating to breaches of the UN Charter or customary international law, and to the extent that its claims were based on those violations, Guyana's claims must be dismissed.[297]

The Tribunal referred to Article 293(1),[298] and to the preamble of UNCLOS, which 'preserved the applicability of general international law, when, in its ultimate paragraph, it affirmed "that matters not regulated by this Convention continued to be governed by the rules and principles of general international law"'.[299] It also referred to the interpretation of Article 293 by ITLOS in *Saiga (No 2)*, and concluded that that interpretation 'is a reasonable interpretation of Article 293', and on that basis concluded that Suriname's jurisdictional objection must be dismissed.[300] On the merits, it found that Suriname had breached UNCLOS, the UN Charter, and general international law by its conduct that amounted to a threat of force.[301] Thus, like ITLOS in *MV Saiga (No 2)*, the *Guyana v Suriname* Tribunal appears to have relied on Article 293 to assert its jurisdiction over a claim based on the UN Charter and general international law.

As noted in Section 1(a) above, in the *Chagos MPA* arbitration, the Tribunal held that the first and second submissions of Mauritius fell outside the scope of Article 288(1) and therefore were beyond jurisdiction. Having reached that conclusion, the Tribunal did not find it necessary to address the question of the potential for Article 293(1) to expand the scope of a Part XV tribunal's jurisdiction. However, it may be helpful to record the parties' submissions on the effect of Article 293(1).

Mauritius' primary position was that the dispute fell within Article 288(1), and it also considered that Article 293(1) allowed an UNCLOS tribunal to 'decide matters of general international law that are not part of the law of the sea'.[302] Mauritius did not go so far as to argue that Article 293(1) expanded an UNCLOS tribunal's subject matter jurisdiction beyond disputes falling within Article 288, but instead said that the Tribunal should apply other rules of international law in deciding a dispute relating to interpretation and application of UNCLOS.[303]

The United Kingdom contended that Article 293 could not be used 'to support an expanded vision of the jurisdiction of a court or tribunal acting under section 2 of Part XV'.[304] The United Kingdom argued that:

[296] ibid.
[297] ibid para 402.
[298] ibid para 403.
[299] ibid para 404. See also paras 439–40, where the Tribunal considers when a threat of force is unlawful under general international law (and UNCLOS, although it does not identify a specific provision of UNCLOS).
[300] ibid para 406.
[301] ibid para 488(2).
[302] *Chagos MPA* (n 17) para 182, quoting *Chagos MPA*, Final Transcript (n 38) 435:1–15; and citing Boyle (n 2). Mauritius relied on several decisions in which ITLOS and Annex VII tribunals had applied other rules of international law: the application of the provisions of the UN Charter on the use of force in *Guyana v Suriname* (n 140); the determination of the permissibility of the use of force under general international law in *Saiga No 2*, Judgment (n 257); and considerations of human rights law in *Arctic Sunrise (Netherlands v Russia)* (Award on the Merits of 14 August 2015) PCA Case No 2014-02 (*Arctic Sunrise*, Merits) (discussed further below): *Chagos MPA* (n 17) para 183.
[303] *Chagos MPA* (n 17) para 182.
[304] ibid para 184, citing *Chagos MPA*, Final Transcript (n 38) 659:14–15.

> The purpose of the reference to 'other rules of international law not incompatible with this Convention' is to dispel any doubt that, in interpreting and applying the provisions of the Convention, a Part XV court [or] tribunal may have recourse to such secondary rules as the law of treaties, State responsibility, diplomatic protection et cetera, and may apply other rules of international law when directed to do so expressly by a provision of the Convention.[305]

In the United Kingdom's view, Article 293 would not empower a Part XV tribunal to decide disputes arising in fields of international law outside the provisions of the Convention.[306] However, it is apparent that it took a narrower view than Mauritius, since it considered that Article 293 authorised recourse only to secondary rules, unless a provision of the Convention contained a specific *renvoi*.

The relationship between Articles 288(1) and 293(1) was then the subject of further consideration in *Arctic Sunrise*. In its request for provisional measures, the Netherlands asserted that, in arresting and detaining crew members and initiating judicial proceedings against them, Russia had breached obligations owed to the Netherlands including under the International Covenant on Civil and Political Rights (ICCPR) and customary international law.[307] The case was then heard by an Annex VII tribunal. Although it did not address that submission in its decision on jurisdiction,[308] it returned to consider it in addressing jurisdiction and admissibility issues in its award on the merits.[309]

In comparison to earlier tribunals, the *Arctic Sunrise* Tribunal was more guarded in its reliance on Article 293. It first noted: 'Article 293(1) does not extend the jurisdiction of a tribunal. Rather, it ensures that, in exercising its jurisdiction under the Convention, a tribunal can give full effect to the provisions of the Convention. For this purpose, some provisions of the Convention directly incorporate other rules of international law.'[310] The Tribunal also referred to Article 311(2), which provides '[t]his Convention shall not alter the rights and obligations of States Parties which arise from other agreements compatible with this Convention and which do not affect the enjoyment by other States Parties of their rights or the performance of their obligations under this Convention.'[311]

The Tribunal noted further that, in order to interpret and apply provisions of UNCLOS, it might need to resort to foundational or secondary rules of general international law, such as the law of treaties or of State responsibility.[312] It noted further that it could be necessary to rely on other primary rules of international law, outside the Convention, to interpret and apply some broadly worded or general provisions of the Convention, and it considered that this had been the approach of ITLOS in *Saiga (No 2)*, in taking into account general international law rules on the use of force in considering the use of force for the arrest of a vessel.[313] (Although arguably ITLOS went further in finding that Guinea had violated rules

[305] *Chagos MPA* (n 17) para 185, quoting *Chagos MPA*, Final Transcript (n 38) 656:8–12.
[306] *Chagos MPA* (n 17) para 186.
[307] *Arctic Sunrise (Netherlands v Russia)* (Provisional Measures, Order of 22 November 2013) ITLOS Reports 2013, 230, para 33(1)(c), citing International Covenant on Civil and Political Rights (adopted 16 December 1966, entered into force 23 March 1976) 999 UNTS 171.
[308] *Arctic Sunrise*, Jurisdiction (n 273).
[309] *Arctic Sunrise*, Merits (n 302) paras 142 ff.
[310] ibid para 188 (references omitted).
[311] ibid para 189, citing UNCLOS (n 1) art 311(2).
[312] *Arctic Sunrise*, Merits (n 302) para 190.
[313] ibid para 191.

governing threats of force under general international law.) However, the *Arctic Sunrise* Tribunal drew a sharp distinction between the use of extraneous sources as a source of jurisdiction, stating:

> Article 293 is not, however, a means to obtain a determination that some treaty other than the Convention has been violated, unless that treaty is otherwise a source of jurisdiction [referring in a footnote to Article 288(2) of the Convention], or unless the treaty otherwise directly applies pursuant to the Convention.[314]

Noting that at times, the Netherlands appeared to invite the Tribunal to determine that there had been a breach of provision of the ICCPR, the Tribunal considered that such a request would be beyond the scope of its jurisdiction:

> The Tribunal considers that, if necessary, it may have regard to general international law in relation to human rights in order to determine whether law enforcement action such as the boarding, seizure, and detention of the *Artic Sunrise* and the arrest and detention of those on board was reasonable and proportionate. This would be to interpret the relevant Convention provisions by reference to relevant context. This is not, however, the same as, nor does it require, a determination of whether there has been a breach of Articles 9 and 12(2) of the ICCPR as such. That treaty has its own enforcement regime and it is not for this Tribunal to act as a substitute for that regime.
>
> In determining the claims by the Netherlands in relation to the interpretation and application of the Convention, the Tribunal may, therefore, pursuant to Article 293, have regard to the extent necessary to rules of customary international law, including international human rights standards, not incompatible with the Convention, in order to assist in the interpretation and application of the Convention's provisions that authorise the arrest or detention of a vessel and persons. This Tribunal does not consider that it has jurisdiction to apply directly provisions such as Articles 9 and 12(2) of the ICCPR or to determine breaches of such provisions.[315]

Although it referred to *Saiga (No 2)* in relying on Article 293, the *Arctic Sunrise* Tribunal appears to have taken an approach more consistent with *MOX Plant* and *Chagos MPA* (and inconsistent with *Guyana v Suriname*), in finding that it could not 'apply directly' rules beyond UNCLOS or 'determine breaches' thereof.

The approach of the *Arctic Sunrise* Tribunal was endorsed by the Annex VII Tribunal in the *Duzgit Integrity* arbitration.[316] There, Malta sought to rely on 'fundamental human rights' as falling within the scope of 'other rules of international law' in Article 293(1), and claimed that São Tomé had not respected its human rights obligations in its dealings with Malta's flagged vessels.[317] Referring to the decision in *Arctic Sunrise*, the Tribunal noted that Article 288(1), together with Article 293(1), meant 'that the Tribunal does not have jurisdiction to determine breaches of obligations not having their source in the Convention

[314] ibid para 192 (references omitted).
[315] ibid paras 197–98.
[316] *Duzgit Integrity* (n 5).
[317] ibid para 203.

(including human rights obligations) as such', but the Tribunal may have regard to other rules of international law in order to assist in the interpretation and application of provisions of UNCLOS concerning the arrest or detention of a vessel or persons.[318] The Tribunal identified the specific role for Article 293(1) as 'ensur[ing] that a tribunal can give full effect to the provisions of the Convention'.[319] Consequently, relying on Article 293(1), the Tribunal concluded that it could have regard to the principles of necessity and proportionality when assessing the exercise of enforcement powers by a coastal State under the Convention, but a claim that fundamental human rights obligations were violated by São Tomé would be beyond its jurisdiction.[320]

In *South China Sea*, the Philippines argued that China had, by its conduct, breached its obligations to protect and preserve the marine environment. In making those submissions, the Philippines had referred to provisions of the Convention on Biological Diversity (CBD).[321] In its award on jurisdiction and admissibility, the Tribunal considered whether the Philippines' submissions on environmental issues were disputes within Article 288(1), or whether they were disputes concerning the interpretation or application of the CBD.[322] The Tribunal was satisfied that the incidents alleged by the Philippines could involve violations of provisions of UNCLOS, specifically Article 194, read together with Article 192.[323] It stated:

> The Tribunal also accepts the Philippines' assertion that, while it considers China's actions and failures to be inconsistent with the provisions of the CBD, the Philippines has not presented a claim arising under the CBD as such. The Tribunal is satisfied that Article 293(1) of the Convention, together with Article 31(3) of the Vienna Convention on the Law of Treaties, enables it in principle to consider the relevant provisions of the CBD for the purposes of interpreting the content and standard of Articles 192 and 194 of the Convention.[324]

While this statement well reflects the use of Article 293, the *South China Sea* Tribunal did not adhere to this approach on all issues.

For example, the Philippines alleged that China had, since the commencement of the arbitration, aggravated and extended the dispute by its conduct in relation to inter alia, the Philippines' rights of navigation, by dredging and construction activities at various reefs.[325] In support of its claim for aggravation and extension of the dispute, the Philippines referenced Article 279 of UNCLOS, which requires parties to 'settle any dispute between them ... by peaceful means', and on Article 300,[326] contending that aggravation and extension of the dispute are inconsistent with those two provisions.[327] It also relied on the 'universally accepted' principles that parties in a case must refrain from aggravating the dispute.[328]

[318] ibid para 207, relying on *Arctic Sunrise*, Merits (n 302) para 198.
[319] *Duzgit Integrity* (n 5) para 208.
[320] ibid paras 209–10.
[321] Convention on Biological Diversity (adopted 5 June 1992, entered into force 29 December 1993) 1760 UNTS 79.
[322] *South China Sea*, Jurisdiction and Admissibility (n 47) para 174.
[323] ibid para 175.
[324] ibid para 176, citing VCLT (n 188).
[325] *South China Sea*, Award (n 18) para 1110.
[326] ibid para 1135.
[327] ibid.
[328] ibid paras 1136–37.

Referring to decisions of the ICJ, the Tribunal's view was that there was 'a duty on parties engaged in a dispute settlement procedure to refrain from aggravating or extending the dispute or disputes during the pendency of the settlement process'.[329] It considered that such a duty was inherent in the requirement of good faith in international legal relations between States.[330] It noted that 'these same principles find expression in Article 279' of UNCLOS, and in Article 300. The Tribunal also observed that aggravation and extension of a dispute were incompatible with the recognition and performance in good faith of the obligations of States parties to comply with an award (under Article 296 and Article 11 of Annex VII).[331]

Although it found the relevant obligation to arise under UNCLOS, the Tribunal found that it would also apply pursuant to Article 293(1). It stated:

> In the Tribunal's view, there is no need to reach beyond the text of the Convention to identify the source of the law applicable to the conduct of parties in the course of dispute settlement proceedings under Part XV. To the extent that it were necessary to do so, however, the Tribunal considers, for the reasons set out above, that the duty to 'abstain from any measure capable of exercising a prejudicial effect in regard to the execution of the decision to be given and, in general, not allow any step of any kind to be taken which might aggravate or extend the dispute' constitutes a principle of international law that is applicable to States engaged in dispute settlement as such. Pursuant to Article 293 of the Convention, this principle constitutes one of the 'other rules of international law not incompatible with this Convention' to which the Tribunal may have recourse.[332]

This holding reflects once more a broader understanding of Article 293 and its relationship to the subject matter jurisdiction of a tribunal constituted under UNCLOS.

A further dimension to the relationship of the applicable law and subject matter jurisdiction in UNCLOS dispute settlement proceedings was added at the merits stage of the *Norstar* case.[333] The Tribunal confirmed that Article 293 could not be used to extend the jurisdiction of the Tribunal.[334] However, unlike the other cases considered to date, the Tribunal in this instance considered if other provisions of UNCLOS could still be addressed following its earlier decision on jurisdiction that had limited the case to claims under Articles 87 and 300.[335] The Tribunal determined that it could refer to other UNCLOS provisions to inform its interpretation of Article 87, including Articles 92 and 94, as part of the applicable law and in doing so, there would not be further decisions on whether those other provisions were also violated.[336] While Panama had argued that Italy had violated human rights, the Tribunal did not decide on these claims, as to whether they were within the Tribunal's jurisdiction or as a substantive matter, on the basis that Panama had not included such claims in its final submissions.[337]

329 ibid para 1169; see also paras 1167–68.
330 ibid para 1171.
331 ibid para 1172.
332 ibid para 1173 (references omitted).
333 *M/V Norstar (Panama v Italy)* (Judgment of 10 April 2019) ITLOS Case No 25 (*Norstar*, Merits).
334 ibid para 136.
335 ibid para 137.
336 ibid para 138.
337 ibid para 146.

Ultimately, it is clear that Article 293(1) provides an explicit basis upon which a Part XV tribunal may have regard to other rules of international law, whether found in another convention, treaty, agreement, or customary international law, to assist in the interpretation and application of provisions of UNCLOS—that is, to determine whether a State has breached the Convention's provisions. Of course, the use of customary international law to ascertain the meaning of a particular provision of a treaty is not without precedent in international law more generally.[338]

More controversial is the extent to which a Part XV tribunal can rely on Article 293(1) to exercise jurisdiction over a claim based on other rules of international law. There is a clear and convincing line of authority suggesting that Article 293(1) is not a means to obtain a determination that some treaty or obligation other than UNCLOS has been violated (unless that other treaty or obligation is either an independent source of jurisdiction for the Part XV tribunal (under Article 288(2)), or it otherwise directly applies pursuant to another provision of UNCLOS (a possibility which is discussed further in the following section).

There are, however, some decisions suggesting otherwise. ITLOS addressed claims on the lawful use or threat of force in *Saiga (No 2)*[339] and in *Virginia G.*[340] The *Guyana v Suriname* Tribunal found that Article 293(1) provided a basis for it to decide that Suriname had breached the UN Charter and general international law by the unlawful threat of force. These decisions appear not to have been followed or relied upon, and more recent authorities such as *Arctic Sunrise* and *Duzgit Integrity* have denied that Part XV tribunals can exercise claims based on obligations that find a source outside of UNCLOS in analogous circumstances.

The award in *South China Sea* also suggested that there was scope for a more expansive role for Article 293(1), using it to import principles of international law governing the conduct of parties in the course of dispute settlement proceedings. The Tribunal expressly relied on a principle of international law, applicable to States engaged in dispute settlement, not to aggravate or extend the dispute. That principle formed the basis of the Tribunal's decision that China had breached 'general international law'. Thus, like the *Guyana v Suriname* Tribunal, the *South China Sea* Tribunal determined that China had breached general international law, and not only the provisions of UNCLOS. At best, these decisions going beyond the provisions of UNCLOS could be justified as an exercise of incidental jurisdiction,[341] but that option was not expressly relied upon in these judgments.

These authorities suggest that the precise scope and effect of Article 293(1), and its potential to expand the jurisdiction of a Part XV tribunal beyond the four corners of the Convention, are still open to debate, even if a number of authorities have emphasised that Article 293(1) cannot and should not have any such expansive effect. Tzeng has observed that those tribunals expanding jurisdiction to address claims relating to the use of force may have good policy reasons for promoting the public order of the oceans;[342] although it

[338] See eg *AMOCO International Finance Corporation v Iran* (1987) 15 Iran-USCTR 189, para 112.

[339] *Saiga No 2*, Judgment (n 257) para 155.

[340] *Virginia G* (n 144) paras 359, 362. See further ch 7(IV)(B).

[341] See Loris Marotti, 'Between Consent and Effectiveness: Incidental Determinations and the Expansion of the Jurisdiction of UNCLOS Tribunals' in Angela Del Vecchio and Roberto Virzo (eds), *Interpretations of the United Nations Convention on the Law of the Sea by International Courts and Tribunals* (Springer 2019) 388.

[342] Tzeng, 'Jurisdiction and Applicable Law' (n 286) 256–57. Tzeng also considers legal, political and individual reasons among the specific judges as to why the line of cases following *MV Saiga (No 2)* have not been rejected: see 256–57.

is notable that similar good public policy to address human rights claims has not yet prevailed in other cases.[343] Moreover, it is at least highly questionable whether public policy grounds suffice to expand the scope of a tribunal operating under a compulsory system of dispute settlement, and ultimately may undermine other fundamental principles of international law, including the principles of States sovereignty, consent to jurisdiction, and the rule of law.

B. *Renvoi* and Reference Provisions within UNCLOS

Apart from the general provision on applicable law in Article 293(1), there are a number of specific provisions in UNCLOS that refer to the potential application of other rules of international law. There are more than forty provisions of UNCLOS that make express reference to international law, or to rights, obligations or rules of international law.[344] Such references may have the effect of incorporating those other rules of international law into UNCLOS, such that a dispute concerning the interpretation or application of the Convention entails the interpretation or application of those other rules. As explained by Sir Michael Wood:

> [A] provision of the Convention may itself contain a direct reference to general international law, or to general international law concepts. Such references—depending on their precise terms and context—may have the effect of incorporating the relevant rules of international law into the Convention.[345]

The effect of any particular reference provision can only be assessed by its precise terms. The extent to which such a provision incorporates international law may well be controversial, and this question has arisen in other contexts, notably in the *Oil Platforms* case, where a majority of the ICJ concluded that a provision of the Treaty of Amity between the United States and Iran[346] incorporated international law governing the use of force, including self-defence.[347]

There have been some instances where a State has relied on a reference provision to incorporate specific rules or regulations outside of UNCLOS. In recent cases, these have ranged from the very specific to the extremely broad. These recent invocations of reference provisions are examined immediately below.

In the *Chagos MPA* arbitration, Mauritius argued that the United Kingdom's establishment of a MPA around the Archipelago infringed its rights under Article 2(3) in relation to the territorial sea, and Article 56(2) in relation to the EEZ. With regard to the territorial sea, it can be recalled that Article 2(3) provides that '[t]he sovereignty over the territorial sea is exercised subject to this Convention and to other rules of international law'. Mauritius

[343] See eg *Arctic Sunrise*, Merits (n 302) paras 197–98.

[344] Wood (n 285) 358. Forteau has estimated 100 such provisions in UNCLOS. See Mathias Forteau, 'Regulating the Competition between International Courts and Tribunals: The Role of Ratione Materiae Jurisdiction under Part XV of UNCLOS' (2016) 15 LPICT 190, 195.

[345] Wood (n 285) 358.

[346] Treaty of Amity, Economic Relations and Consular Rights (Iran/United States) (signed 15August 1955, entered into force 16 June 1957) 284 UNTS 93.

[347] *Oil Platforms (Iran v United States)* (Merits) [2003] ICJ Rep 161, paras 40–41; cf (Separate Opinion of Judge Higgins) para 46.

argued that this provision imposed an obligation to comply with other rules of international law in the exercise of sovereignty in the territorial sea, whereas the United Kingdom considered Article 2(3) to be merely descriptive.[348] Referring to other authentic language versions, from which a sense of legal obligation is more readily apparent, and to the placement of Article 2(3) in UNCLOS, its object and purpose, and the negotiating history, the Tribunal concluded that it imposed an obligation on States to exercise their sovereignty subject to 'other rules of international law'.[349]

Concerning the interpretation of the phrase 'other rules of international law', the Tribunal placed significant weight on the International Law Commission (ILC)'s commentary on Article 1(2) of its Draft Articles concerning the Law of the Sea, which relevantly provides:

> (3) Clearly, sovereignty over the territorial sea cannot be exercised otherwise than in conformity with the provisions of international law.
> (4) Some of the limitations imposed by international law on the exercise of sovereignty in the territorial sea are set forth in the present articles which cannot, however, be regarded as exhaustive. Incidents in the territorial sea raising legal questions are also governed by the general rules of international law, and these cannot be specially codified in the present draft for the purposes of their application to the territorial sea. That is why 'other rules of international law' are mentioned in addition to the provisions contained in the present articles.
> (5) It may happen that, by reason of some special relationship, geographical or other, between two States, rights in the territorial sea of one of them are granted to the other in excess of the rights recognized in the present draft. It is not the Commission's intention to limit in any way any more extensive right of passage or other right enjoyed by States by custom or treaty.[350]

The Tribunal noted that the ILC understood Article 1(2) of its Draft Articles to require States to exercise their sovereignty in the territorial sea subject to the general rules of international law, and it also recognised that States may possess particular rights by bilateral agreement or local custom, but noted merely that the Articles were not intended to interfere with such rights.[351] On that basis, the Tribunal concluded that Article 2(3) of UNCLOS imposes an obligation to exercise its sovereignty subject to the general rules of international law:

> There is no indication that through [Article 1(2) of the Draft Articles] the Commission intended to create an obligation of compliance with any bilateral commitment a State might undertake in the territorial sea, nor is there any basis to assume that the intent of the provision changed between the Commission's formulation of the Draft Articles and the adoption of the Convention in 1982. The Tribunal therefore concludes that the obligation in Article 2(3) [of UNCLOS] is limited to exercising sovereignty subject to the general rules of international law.[352]

348 *Chagos MPA* (n 17) para 499.
349 ibid paras 500–14.
350 International Law Commission, 'Report of the International Law Commission on the Work of its 8th Session' (23 April–4 July 1956) [1956] 2 UNYBILC 253, 265 (also available as UN Doc A/CN.4/104) (ILC, LOS Draft Articles), quoted in *Chagos MPA* (n 17) para 515.
351 *Chagos MPA* (n 17) para 516.
352 ibid.

It followed that Article 2(3) did not extend to the Lancaster House Undertakings, since those Undertakings do not form part of the general rules of international law. However, the Tribunal found further that pursuant to the general rules of international law, the United Kingdom was required to act in good faith in its relations with Mauritius, including with respect to undertakings.[353] Therefore, although it had found that Article 2(3) did not effect a *renvoi* to the Lancaster House Undertakings, by finding that the general rule of good faith in international relations was covered by the *renvoi* in Article 2(3), the result was arguably the same as if it found that Article 2(3) did cover bilateral undertakings. For all practical purposes, the Tribunal's approach had the result that it was therefore considering whether the United Kingdom had complied with the Lancaster House Undertakings, which extended its jurisdiction considerably.

The *Chagos MPA* Tribunal's heavy reliance on the ILC's commentary on its Draft Articles effectively led to it to limit the phrase 'other rules of international law' to general rules of international law and not to obligations arising from bilateral agreements or unilateral undertakings. Yet the latter obligations also affect sovereignty under the Convention. The Tribunal's conclusion may thus strike as counter-intuitive when it is considered that States consent to limitations on their sovereignty in a variety of ways, either through the ongoing development of customary international law, or in the context of specific bilateral agreements with other States. Why should some of these limitations be recognised as falling within Article 2(3) but not others? Giraudeau has commented that the Tribunal's approach to Article 2(3) (and Article 56(2)) 'shows that this decision is not only about applying the technical law of the sea, but also about rending justice in a very wider context of postcolonialism policy'.[354] Barnes has suggested the difference may be explained because 'bilateral limitations entered into on a voluntary basis are at the discretion of the coastal State, whereas general rules of international law, such as abuse of right or good faith, cannot impose mandatory restrictions on the exercise of sovereignty in territorial sea'.[355]

Further, it could be argued that the Tribunal's reliance on the *travaux* for Article 2(3) is not strictly consistent with the Vienna Convention on the Law of Treaties (VCLT),[356] since the ordinary meaning of the term 'rules of international law' is not limited to 'general' rules, but to any rule arising in a multilateral or bilateral context. Nevertheless, the Tribunal's conclusion that the 'general rules of international law' including an obligation of good faith in performance of undertakings, including bilateral undertakings, effectively incorporates a broad range of obligations under the umbrella of Article 2(3), doing away with the limitation that would otherwise have existed as a result of the interpretation of 'rules of international law' as general rules of international law. Applying the *Chagos MPA* Tribunal's approach, the jurisdiction of UNCLOS tribunals has potentially a very broad reach, to cover good faith compliance with all bilateral (and multilateral) obligations with respect to the territorial sea, unless those obligations are otherwise excluded from the Part XV tribunal's jurisdiction.

353 ibid para 517.

354 Géraldine Giraudeau, 'A Slight Revenge and a Growing Hope for Mauritius and the Chagossians: The UNCLOS Arbitral Tribunals' Award of 18 March 2015 on Chagos Marine Protected Area (Mauritius v. United Kingdom) (2015) 12 Revista de Direito Internacional 705, 724.

355 Richard Barnes, 'Article 2' in *Proelss Commentary* (n 65) 27, para 23.

356 VCLT (n 188).

In applying Article 2(3) in *Chagos MPA*, the Tribunal reviewed the context by which the MPA was established and concluded that the United Kingdom did not adequately consult with Mauritius, nor did it balance its own rights and interests with Mauritius' rights arising from the Lancaster House Undertakings.[357] It concluded that the United Kingdom had breached Article 2(3) and therefore the proclamation of the MPA was incompatible with UNCLOS.[358]

On this point, Judges Kateka and Wolfrum dissented; they would have found that Article 2(3) directly incorporated bilateral obligations and not only rules of general international law. Referring to the ILC Commentary quoted above, they stated:

> The first sentence in paragraph 5 of the commentary to article 1(2) of the ILC Draft makes it quite plain that the draft encompasses obligations that may arise from a 'special relationship, geographical or other', where one State recognises or grants the other State rights in the territorial sea. This has the consequence that the reference to 'other rules of international law' not only refers to general international law but has a broader scope ... Taking the ILC Commentary into account means, in our view, that the reference to 'other rules of international law' encompasses obligations arising from commitments by the coastal State bilaterally or even unilaterally, as well as commitments based upon customary international law or the binding decisions of an international organization. For these reasons the undertakings of the United Kingdom in the Lancaster House Understanding have to be read directly into Article 2(3) of the Convention.[359]

The dissenting judges would have thus read 'other rules of international law' to encompass *all* rules of international law. This approach has the potential to greatly expand the scope of jurisdiction available for dispute settlement under UNCLOS.

In relation to the EEZ, the *Chagos MPA* Tribunal noted that Article 56(2) imposed an obligation on the United Kingdom to have 'due regard' to the rights of Mauritius.[360] Article 56(2) provides: 'In exercising its rights and performing its duties under this Convention in the exclusive economic zone, the coastal State shall have due regard to the rights and duties of other States and shall act in a manner compatible with the provisions of this Convention.'[361] The Tribunal considered that this requirement was equivalent to the obligation arising under Article 2(3), set out above.[362] For the same reasons that it considered that the MPA was incompatible with Article 2(3) of UNCLOS, the Tribunal concluded that it was also in breach of Article 56(2).[363]

Interestingly, an earlier draft (the draft of the Group of 77) of Article 56(2) indicated that States 'shall have due regard to the rights of other States in the Exclusive Economic Zone as specified in this Convention'.[364] The *Virginia Commentary* appears to assume that the reference to 'rights' in Article 56(2) indicates only rights under UNCLOS itself, and does not anticipate coverage of broader rights under other agreements or arising by way of unilateral

[357] *Chagos MPA* (n 17) paras 534–35.
[358] ibid para 536.
[359] ibid (Dissenting and Concurring Opinion of Judges Kateka and Wolfrum) para 84.
[360] *Chagos MPA* (n 17) para 519.
[361] UNCLOS (n 1) art 56(2).
[362] *Chagos MPA* (n 17) para 520.
[363] ibid para 536.
[364] *Virginia Commentary* (n 218) vol 2, 533 (excerpting the Group of 77 draft art 56(4)).

acts.[365] Yet the Tribunal's approach to Article 56(2) was effectively the same as its approach to Article 2(3), and it equally has the potential to expand jurisdiction of UNCLOS tribunals considerably, to cover all rights relating to the EEZ, unless otherwise excluded from jurisdiction under another provision of Part XV.

The scope of the reference to 'other rules of international law' in Article 2(3) was subsequently at issue in the *South China Sea* arbitration. In that case, the Philippines argued that China violated its obligations under Article 2(3) of UNCLOS, by preventing Filipino fishers from fishing in the waters of Scarborough Shoal,[366] in exercise of their traditional fishing rights in the territorial sea.[367] The Philippines also argued that China's conduct was in breach of its obligations under Article 2(3) (and Article 279) of UNCLOS to settle disputes through peaceful means.[368]

The Tribunal expressed agreement with the finding in *Chagos MPA* that Article 2(3) 'contains an obligation on States to exercise their sovereignty subject to 'other rules of international law''.[369] The Tribunal further stated that traditional fishing rights constituted a vested right and that 'the rules of international law on the treatment of the vested rights of foreign nationals' fell squarely within the 'other rules of international law' applicable in the territorial sea.[370] It did not comment as to whether these rules constituted rules of 'general international law', nor did it consider whether there was a subsidiary rule of general international law requiring States to comply with such rule in good faith. Moreover, the Tribunal appeared to accept that an obligation to settle disputes by peaceful means was encompassed within the *renvoi* in Article 2(3), but dismissed the Philippines' claim of a breach, noting that both parties found fault with each other in their handling of the issue and both alleged breaches of the UN Charter.[371]

The *South China Sea* Tribunal's approach to Article 2(3) can be seen as more expansive than that of the *Chagos MPA* Tribunal. As noted above, Barnes suggested that the two approaches can be reconciled on the basis that 'rules of general international law' cover all rules that are not 'bilateral limitations entered into on a voluntary basis'.[372] However, this distinction is difficult to sustain: many rules of customary international law that are long-established are not necessarily contracted into, but would not fall within the category of 'general rules of international law' as it is commonly understood. Thus, the two approaches are more difficult to reconcile than by simply excluding bilateral agreements.

Other reference provisions of UNCLOS were also addressed in the *South China Sea* arbitration. The Philippines requested a declaration that China had breached its obligations under the Convention by operating its enforcement vessels in a dangerous manner causing serious risk of collision to Philippine vessels navigating in the vicinity of Scarborough Shoal.[373] The Philippines relied on obligations relating to safe navigation under Articles 94

365 See ibid 543–44, para 56.11(f): 'Provisions protecting the rights and freedoms of other States in various maritime zones appear throughout the Convention, for example in article 24, paragraph 1(territorial sea); article 43, paragraph 2, and article 44 (straits used for international navigation); article 51 (archipelagic waters); article 58 (exclusive economic zone); article 78, paragraph 2 (continental shelf); and article 87, paragraph 2 (high seas).'

366 *South China Sea*, Award (n 18) paras 771–72.

367 ibid paras 774–79. See further ch 8(II).

368 ibid para 780.

369 ibid para 808.

370 ibid (reference omitted). See further ch 8(II).

371 ibid para 813.

372 Barnes (n 355) 27, para 23.

373 *South China Sea*, Award (n 18) para 1044.

(high seas) and 21 (territorial sea) of UNCLOS, and related provisions in the Convention on the International Regulations for Preventing of Collisions at Sea 1972 (COLREGS).[374] The COLREGS have 156 State parties.[375] Both China and the Philippines are parties to the COLREGS, but the Philippines only became a party in 2013.[376]

In referring to the COLREGS, the Philippines relied in particular on Article 94(5),[377] which provides that, in taking measures under paragraph 3 of that Article that are necessary to ensure safety at sea, including measures concerning the prevention of collisions, 'each State is required to conform to generally accepted international regulations ... and to take any steps which may be necessary to secure their observance'.[378] It also relied on Article 21(4), which provides that foreign ships exercising the right of innocent passage through the territorial sea shall comply with 'all generally accepted international regulations relating to the prevention of collisions at sea'.[379] Although this provision technically applied only to foreign ships in innocent passage through a coastal State's territorial sea, the Philippines argued that if a coastal State fails to ensure that its ships respect the COLREGS in the territorial sea and therefore endangers the navigation of foreign ships in the territorial sea, this omission violates coastal States' duties under Article 24 to refrain from hampering innocent passage and to publicise dangers to navigation.[380]

The Tribunal accepted that the COLREGS were incorporated into UNCLOS by Article 94.[381] In particular, it noted that Article 94(1) requires flag States to effectively exercise jurisdiction and control over ships flying their flag, and Article 94(3) clarifies the scope of the flag States' duties, as including taking measures concerning the prevention of collisions. The precise scope of those duties is clarified by Article 94(5), which refers to 'generally accepted international regulations'.[382] It followed that 'a violation of the COLREGS, as "generally accepted international regulations" concerning measures necessary to ensure maritime safety, constitutes a violation of the Convention itself'.[383] The Tribunal then proceeded to interpret and apply the COLREGS to decide on the Philippines' submissions concerning the manoeuvres of China's enforcement vessels near Scarborough Shoal.[384] It concluded that China had violated Rules 2, 6, 7, 8, 15, and 16 of the COLREGS and therefore, as a consequence, was in breach of Article 94 of UNCLOS.[385]

[374] ibid para 1059, relying on Convention on the International Regulations for Preventing Collisions at Sea (adopted 20 October 1972, entered into force 15 July 1977) 1050 UNTS 1976.

[375] *South China Sea*, Award (n 18) para 1081.

[376] ibid paras 1081–82.

[377] ibid para 1061.

[378] UNCLOS (n 1) art 94(5).

[379] *South China Sea*, Award (n 18) para 1062.

[380] ibid para 1064. A further difficulty with this argument was that the Tribunal was not able to identify the relevant 'coastal State' as it was not resolving issues of territorial sovereignty. Without this information, the Tribunal had to rely more on art 94, even though that provision is strictly not applicable within the territorial sea in accordance with art 86 of UNCLOS (n 1).

[381] *South China Sea*, Award (n 18) para 1083.

[382] ibid para 1082.

[383] ibid para 1083. This approach is consistent with the *Virginia Commentary* (n 218) which suggested that the formulation in art 94(5) would cover 'regulations which are a product of international co-operation, without necessarily having been confirmed by formal treaties', and would not cover regulations 'accepted by only a few States ... unless they are well-established as being of regional application': vol 3, 148, para 94.8(i). The *Virginia Commentary* approach relied on the ILC's commentary on draft Article 34 in 1956, explaining similar language ('to observe internationally accepted standards'); ILC, 'LOS Draft Articles' (n 349) 281.

[384] *South China Sea*, Award (n 18) para 1090.

[385] ibid para 1109.

The parties in *Enrica Lexie* similarly asserted violations of the COLREGS as part of their cases,[386] but the Tribunal did not reach any decision on this specific point. Nonetheless, the way in which the Tribunal in *South China Sea* considered pertinent provisions of the COLREGS as incorporated via Article 94(5)'s reference to 'generally accepted international regulations' can be considered as falling within this largely uncontroversial category of incorporated obligations.

The scope of Articles 2(3) and 56(2) was questioned again in the *Enrica Lexie* case. Italy argued that the immunity of its marines could be considered within the jurisdiction of the Tribunal based on the varied references to international law in Articles 2(3), 56(2), 58(2),[387] as well as Article 297(1)(a).[388] The majority did not have cause to examine the scope of the possible *renvoi* in these provisions on the basis that the arrest happened in the internal waters of India and enforcement occurred on its land territory, and the Articles concerned were hence inapplicable to the case.[389] However, the majority's summary approach to the *renvoi* provisions was criticised by Judge Robinson in his dissenting opinion, who suggested that the Tribunal 'did not conduct any enquiry, and therefore did not make any finding, as to whether customary international law was imported into the Convention on the basis of the Articles relied on by Italy'.[390] Judge Robinson in his dissent relied on the ICJ's preliminary objections judgment in *Immunities and Criminal Proceedings*,[391] and stated that the Articles concerned do not constitute a *renvoi* to customary international law.[392] He did not express a view as to whether 'general rules of international law' would be caught by the *renvoi*, nor did he address the findings of the *Chagos MPA* or *South China Sea* Tribunals, so it is not clear whether he would have accepted their approaches to Article 2(3). Further, Judge Robinson suggested that the *renvoi* provisions could not in any event be used as a basis for ascertaining whether the Tribunal had jurisdiction over the two marines,[393] again without addressing the findings of the two earlier tribunals that arguably had the effect of expanding those tribunals' jurisdiction to cover claims under 'general' or 'other' rules of international law. In Judge Robinson's view, the provisions would, at most, influence the applicable law in their interpretation rather than expanding the Tribunal's jurisdiction.[394] This approach would reflect a less expansive approach to subject matter jurisdiction for Part XV tribunals.

The scope of the reference to 'other rules of international law' in Article 2(3) is unclear in light of the cases discussed above. Those decisions indicate that Article 2(3) does not cover bilateral agreements, and therefore it is unlikely that this provision could be used to expand compulsory jurisdiction to a wide variety of other international treaties. However, the extent to which it covers only 'general rules' or also extends to any other rules (including potentially all rules of customary international law) is uncertain, and future tribunals may take a different approach to its interpretation. Furthermore, even if Article 2(3) (and Article 56(2)) covers only 'general rules', as the *Chagos MPA* Tribunal found, these provisions have

[386] *Enrica Lexie*, Award (n 105) paras 565–75.
[387] ibid paras 734, 762–78.
[388] ibid paras 779, 791–94.
[389] ibid paras 798, 801–802.
[390] *Enrica Lexie*, Award (n 105) (Dissenting Opinion of Judge Robinson) para 31.
[391] *Immunities and Criminal Proceedings (Equatorial Guinea v France)* (Preliminary Objections) [2018] ICJ Rep 292, paras 78, 90, 93–102.
[392] *Enrica Lexie*, Award (n 105) (Dissenting Opinion of Judge Robinson) para 31.
[393] ibid.
[394] ibid.

significant potential to cover a wide range of bilateral and multilateral obligations concerning the territorial sea and the EEZ, since these could be caught by the 'general rule' of good faith performance under general international law.[395] This potential is likely to be the subject of argument on more expansive claims in new Part XV proceedings. By contrast, the reliance on the COLREGs as part of 'generally accepted international regulations' in articulating flag State duties under Article 94(5) reflects an appropriate incorporation of external obligations into UNCLOS. While claimant States may seek to take advantage of the compulsory dispute settlement procedures in UNCLOS to resolve disputes that may not be closely related to the exercise of rights and obligations under provisions of UNCLOS as such, it will be incumbent on future tribunals to consider how 'deferential' or 'protective' they should be of a State's consent to jurisdiction.[396]

C. Law that Interacts with or Informs UNCLOS

In the *South China Sea* arbitration, the Tribunal discussed the relationship between UNCLOS and other possible sources of rights under international law in the context of the Philippines' arguments challenging the validity of the nine-dash line. The Tribunal noted its understanding that China claimed historic rights to the living and non-living resources in the waters of the South China Sea within the nine-dash line.[397] By its Submissions Nos 1 and 2, the Philippines requested the Tribunal to declare that China's entitlements in the South China Sea were limited to those provided for in UNCLOS and that any claim to historic rights or other sovereign rights or jurisdiction within the area of the nine-dash line in excess of that provided for by the Convention was prohibited.[398]

On that basis, the *South China Sea* Tribunal first considered whether UNCLOS allowed for the preservation of rights to living and non-living resources that are at variance with the provisions of the Convention and which may have been established prior to the Convention's entry into force by agreement or unilateral act.[399] The Tribunal considered that the relationship between UNCLOS and other international agreements and/or other norms of international law, such as historic rights, was governed by Article 311 of UNCLOS.[400] It also noted that the relationship between UNCLOS and other rules of international law was 'also made clear in Article 293(1) of the Convention', which applied to dispute resolution, including these proceedings.[401] Those provisions mirrored general rules of international law, including as reflected in Articles 30(2) and 30(3) of the VCLT.[402] On the basis of these rules, the Tribunal set out four propositions:

[395] That this approach could lead to a very broad range of rights and obligations being adjudicated by Part XV tribunals is borne out by the dissenting opinion in *Chagos MPA* (n 17): the minority would have addressed the question whether the excision of the Chagos archipelago was contrary to the legal principles of decolonization (referred to in 'Declaration on the Granting of Independence to Colonial Countries and Peoples', UN GA Res 1514(XV) (14 December 1960) UN Doc A/RES/1514(XV)) and to the principle of self-determination. See *Chagos MPA* (n 17) (Dissenting and Concurring Opinion of Judges Kateka and Wolfrum) para 70.

[396] A point highlighted by Judge Robinson in his dissent in *Enrica Lexie*, Award (n 105) (Dissenting Opinion of Judge Robinson) para 37.

[397] *South China Sea*, Award (n 18) para 232.

[398] ibid para 233.

[399] ibid para 234(a).

[400] ibid para 235.

[401] ibid para 236.

[402] ibid para 237, citing VLCT (n 188).

(a) Where the Convention expressly permits or preserves other international agreements, Article 311(5) provides that such agreements shall remain unaffected. The Tribunal considers that this provision applies equally where historic rights ... are expressly permitted or preserved, such as in Articles 10 and 15, which expressly refer to historic bays and titles.
(b) Where the Convention did not expressly permit or preserve a prior agreement, rule of customary international law, or historic right, such prior norms will not be incompatible with the Convention where their operation does not conflict with any provision of the Convention, or to the extent that interpretation indicates that the Convention intended the prior agreements, rules, or rights to continue in operation.
(c) Where rights and obligations arising independently of the Convention are not incompatible with its provisions, Article 311(2) provides that their operation will remain unaltered.
(d) Where independent rights and obligations have arisen prior to the entry into force of the Convention and are incompatible with its provisions, the principles set out in Article 30(3) of the Vienna Convention and Article 293 of the Convention provide that the Convention will prevail over the earlier, incompatible rights or obligations.[403]

The Tribunal noted that no provision of UNCLOS expressly provided for or permitted the continued existence of historic rights to the living or non-living resources of the EEZ.[404]

The Philippines argued that a dispute concerning historic rights lay outside of UNCLOS, but that the connection to UNCLOS still meant the dispute was one that concerned its interpretation or application. Agreeing with this argument, the Tribunal noted: 'A dispute concerning the interaction of the Convention with another instrument or body of law, including the question of whether rights arising under another body of law were or were not preserved by the Convention, is unequivocally a dispute concerning the interpretation and application of the Convention.'[405] This statement could be read very broadly to allow the resolution of disputes concerning legal rights that touch on UNCLOS to be settled within the UNCLOS dispute settlement regime. Yet it would seemingly be more reasonable to understand the statement as focused on resolving what is or is not covered by the Convention rather than also resolving any matter regulated by a body of law that interacts with UNCLOS. Future decisions will need to have close regard to what properly falls within its incidental jurisdiction in resolving a dispute.[406]

* * *

The starting point for discussions on applicable law should be, consistent with the terms of Article 293, establishing that jurisdiction exists in accordance with Articles 286 and 288. Once that is established, a Part XV tribunal can then consider other provisions of the Convention and other rules of international law as necessary to interpret and apply

[403] *South China Sea*, Award (n 18) para 238.
[404] ibid para 239.
[405] *South China Sea*, Jurisdiction and Admissibility (n 47) para 168.
[406] See section II(B) above.

the provisions of UNCLOS that are in dispute between the parties based on the facts and claims presented. Despite suggestions in cases like *Saiga (No 2)*, tribunals constituted under UNCLOS may not expand their jurisdiction of resolving disputes relating to the interpretation or application of UNCLOS to claims covering other bodies of law. Other areas of international law may be relevant as applicable law where there is a *renvoi* or, possibly, an 'interaction' with UNCLOS or as an aid to interpretation consistent with the rules set out under the VCLT. Maintaining a clear understanding of the purpose of the applicable law provision will ensure the resolution of disputes under UNCLOS is consistent with the rule of law as well as the peaceful settlement of disputes.

VI. Concluding Remarks

Harrison has rightly observed that as decisions on subject matter jurisdiction concern not only the States party to UNCLOS but also the 'overall legitimacy' of the UNCLOS dispute settlement regime, UNCLOS tribunals 'must also take into account the broader systemic concerns to inform their decision'.[407] Decisions on subject matter jurisdiction have been controversial by their nature because they determine whether a specific dispute may be resolved by a tribunal rather than through other peaceful means. It is undeniable that compulsory third-party dispute settlement is of fundamental importance in the operation of UNCLOS and in oceans governance more generally. However, at the same time, other peaceful means of dispute settlement have an important role to play. While perhaps unsatisfactory, the nature of the international legal system is such that compulsory third-party dispute resolution is dependent on State consent. For that form of dispute resolution to serve its purpose, the parameters of that consent and the role of judicial decision-makers must be carefully considered.

This chapter has indicated that judicial engagement in dispute settlement under UNCLOS has been greater than may have otherwise been expected because of the interpretation of subject matter jurisdiction. So much has been manifest in the decisions emanating from the *South China Sea* arbitration in particular. The relatively low number of cases under UNCLOS, coupled with the varied factual scenarios and differently styled claims, has further meant that we cannot consider the scope of some exceptions to compulsory jurisdiction definitively resolved. The military activities exception and the scale of examination to determine if the historic title or bays exception applies are notable instances that currently indicate a generous grant of subject matter jurisdiction but may be refined in future decisions. This chapter has also discussed cases where a State party's claim for expansive jurisdiction in relation to territorial sovereignty disputes or through the applicable law provision in Article 293 have not succeeded. These decisions have underlined that UNCLOS dispute settlement procedures should not be used as vehicles to resolve international law disputes that have their own mechanisms of dispute settlement or rely on means other than compulsory third-party settlement.

[407] James Harrison, 'Defining Disputes and Characterizing Claims: Subject-Matter Jurisdiction in Law of the Sea Convention Litigation' (2017) 48 ODIL 269, 283.

Decisions on subject matter jurisdiction may be cast within the frames of 'substantive' or 'procedural' models, which were discussed in Chapter 1.[408] The substantive model is a 'regime-building' perspective that promotes the use of UNCLOS compulsory dispute settlement. The expansive views on jurisdiction may be explained in this way because they are seemingly predicated on a fundamental belief that it is best for international disputes to be resolved in international tribunals to promote the rule of law and the public order of the oceans. In this setting, judicial engagement is to be welcomed wherever possible. The 'procedural' model accounts for a 'Westphalian' perspective that recognises the ongoing importance of State consent. Resisting the increase in subject matter jurisdiction under UNCLOS shows deference to the importance of State engagement in compulsory third-party dispute settlement mechanisms and recognises that the goal of settling disputes by peaceful means may be achieved through diverse avenues, which may not include judicial involvement. The extreme version of either model can be readily denounced for their respective shortcomings so the more difficult task is arriving at a balance between these approaches in future decisions.

408 See ch 1(III), referring to the descriptions of Oxman. Bernard H Oxman, 'Complementary Agreements and Compulsory Jurisdiction' (2001) 95 AJIL 277, 279.

5
Maritime Space

I. Introduction

Given the constitutive status of the UN Convention on the Law of the Sea (UNCLOS or Convention),[1] its terms providing for the source of State authority in varied ocean areas are of critical importance. While the oceans cover over 70 per cent of the Earth's surface, it is a State's sovereignty over land that provides the starting point for determining its rights over maritime areas.[2] UNCLOS accords juridical status to a variety of landforms and features in that the land provides the basis for States to claim different maritime entitlements. These landforms and features include reefs, rocks, low-tide elevations, bays, mouths of rivers, and islands. UNCLOS further sets out a variety of maritime zones that most typically are measured from the coast of a State. These maritime areas include internal waters, the territorial sea, contiguous zone, exclusive economic zone (EEZ), continental shelf, and the high seas. Article 1 of UNCLOS defines the Area as 'the seabed and ocean floor and subsoil thereof, beyond the limits of national jurisdiction'. The designation of these different maritime spaces then has implications for the rights and duties of States, as well as other actors.

Deciding on the status of a particular landform or feature, and determining the extent of any maritime zone are predominantly the tasks of individual coastal States. Where maritime entitlements overlap, a maritime boundary is necessary and disputes relating to maritime boundary delimitation are addressed in the following chapter. This chapter is concerned with the contests that have emerged in State decision-making as to the status of specific land features, given the consequences for maritime rights and duties, and the disputes as to the distribution of rights and duties between State actors in different maritime zones. While coastal States may have a primary role in determining the extent of their maritime zones, as the International Court of Justice (ICJ) has recognised, this task has an international aspect.[3] Judges may therefore have an important role to play in resolving competing views as to the proper allocation of maritime space and what rights and duties flow from the existence of that maritime space. The potential for international courts or tribunals to 'quiet' title to maritime space may be critical for both the peaceful resolution of disputes as well as the ongoing governance of the ocean area in question.[4]

[1] United Nations Convention on the Law of the Sea (adopted 10 December 1982, entered into force 16 November 1994) 1833 UNTS 397 (UNCLOS).

[2] As recognised in the principle of 'the land dominates the sea': see *North Sea Continental Shelf (Federal Republic of Germany/Denmark; Federal Republic of Germany/Netherlands)* (Judgment) [1969] ICJ Rep 3, para 96 (*North Sea*, Judgment), and further discussion in ch 6.

[3] *Anglo-Norwegian Fisheries (United Kingdom v Norway)* (Judgment) [1951] ICJ Rep 116, 132 ('The delimitation of sea areas always has an international aspect; it cannot be dependent merely upon the will of the coastal State as expressed in its municipal law').

[4] For discussion on the role of international courts and tribunals in deciding title to maritime areas as opposed to territorial disputes see Lea Brilmayer and Natalie Klein, 'Land and Sea: Two Sovereignty Regimes in Search of a Common Denominator' (2001) 33 NYU J Intl L & Pol 703.

This chapter assesses the court decisions that have analysed these different dimensions of maritime space that are part of UNCLOS. The focus is on the division of exclusive coastal State rights and inclusive interests of other States. The judicial assessments of rights and duties on the high seas and in the Area are addressed in subsequent chapters dealing with different maritime activities. Section II analyses the cases that have determined the legal status of different land features: low-tide elevations, rocks, and islands. Section III examines baselines, which are the critical starting point for measuring a coastal State's maritime zones. What might count for the purposes of serving as a base point or a baseline will have implications for the extent of authority a coastal State may be able to lawfully assert over the adjacent maritime space. Section IV turns to the core attributes of the maritime zones in UNCLOS that have been subjected to judicial scrutiny to date. The allocation of rights and duties to different States within each of the maritime zones has occasionally proved controversial and it is essential to have a clear understanding of how those rights and duties may need to be balanced. The discussion in this chapter provides a foundation for the further examination of rights and duties relating to navigation, fisheries, as well as protection, and preservation of the marine environment that follows in later chapters.

II. Low-tide Elevations, Rocks, and Islands

The presence of islands and low-tide elevations along the coast of a State can have an impact on the outer limits of that State's maritime zones. In addition, a State may be able to claim entitlement to further maritime zones around islands that are distant to it on the basis of the State's sovereignty over that remote island. The opportunity to claim exclusive rights to more ocean resources based on sovereignty over islands has been a key element to some ongoing territorial disputes.[5] Even where sovereignty may not be contested, disputes may still emerge as to whether the land feature in question is an island or a rock in light of the implications for the maritime entitlements that flow from that status.[6] As discussed in Chapter 4, territorial sovereignty disputes do not fall within the scope of jurisdiction under Article 288(1) of UNCLOS.[7] However, a dispute concerning the classification of a feature as a low-tide elevation, rock, or island does concern the interpretation or application of UNCLOS .

The regime of islands is dealt within in a single article in UNCLOS, Article 121, as follows:

1. An island is a naturally formed area of land, surrounded by water, which is above water at high tide.

[5] Among the most well-known disputes are those concerning Senkaku/Diaoyu, Dokdo/Takeshima, Hans Island, and Abu Musa, as well as the island grounds in the South China Sea. See further Sean D Murphy, 'International Law Relating to Islands' (2017) 836 Hague Recueil des Cours 5, 25–40.

[6] One example being Japan's claim to Okinotorishima: see eg Yoshifumi Tanaka, *The International Law of the Sea* (3rd edn, CUP 2019) 77; Eiichi Usuki, 'China's Three Distinctive Assertions under the "Nine-dash-line" Claims and the Annex VII Arbitral Tribunal's Interpretation of Article 121 Regarding an Island and Rocks under the 1982 UN Convention on the Law of the Sea' (2014) 21 Asian Yrbk Intl L 141.

[7] Unless possibly falling within the category of an incidental or ancillary matter, as described in the *Chagos Marine Protected Area Arbitration (Mauritius v United Kingdom)* (Award of 18 March 2015) PCA Case No 2011-03 (*Chagos MPA*). See ch 4(II).

2. Except as provided for in paragraph 3, the territorial sea, the contiguous zone, the exclusive economic zone and the continental shelf of an island are determined in accordance with the provisions of this Convention applicable to other land territory.
3. Rocks which cannot sustain human habitation or economic life of their own shall have no exclusive economic zone or continental shelf.[8]

Low-tide elevations are defined in Article 13 of UNCLOS, which provides:

1. A low-tide elevation is a naturally formed area of land which is surrounded by and above water at low tide but submerged at high tide. Where a low-tide elevation is situated wholly or partly at a distance not exceeding the breadth of the territorial sea from the mainland or an island, the low-water line on that elevation may be used as the baseline for measuring the breadth of the territorial sea.
2. Where a low-tide elevation is wholly situated at a distance exceeding the breadth of the territorial sea from the mainland or an island, it has no territorial sea of its own.[9]

These provisions were the subject of only limited judicial consideration before the 2016 award in *South China Sea*.[10] There, the Tribunal embarked on a comprehensive interpretation and application of these provisions, and its Award has been subjected to considerable scrutiny as a result.[11]

Prior to *South China Sea*, the ICJ considered aspects of Articles 121 and 13 in two cases: *Qatar v Bahrain*,[12] and *Territorial and Maritime Dispute*.[13] In *Qatar v Bahrain*, the ICJ stated that Article 121(2) 'reflects customary international law', and that 'islands, regardless of their size, in this respect enjoy the same status and therefore generate the same maritime rights, as other land territory'.[14] In *Territorial and Maritime Dispute*, the Court confirmed, as was agreed between the parties to that case, that Article 121 as a whole was declaratory of customary international law,[15] and explicitly expressed the view that the legal regime of islands set out in Article 121 'forms an indivisible regime, all of which ... has the status of customary international law'.[16]

In both those cases, the Court had to consider the legal status of features claimed by one State to qualify as an island. In *Qatar v Bahrain*, there was a dispute between the parties as to the legal status of a small landform, Qit'at Jaradah, which was within the twelve-mile limit of both States. Bahrain claimed sovereignty over it, whereas Qatar argued it was a low tide elevation that could not be appropriated, and fell within Qatar's territorial sea.[17] Bahrain argued it was permanently above water, and thus an island.[18] The Court considered the

[8] UNCLOS (n 1) art 121.
[9] ibid art 13.
[10] *South China Sea Arbitration (Philippines v China)* (Award of 12 July 2016) PCA Case No 2013-19 (*South China Sea*, Award).
[11] See discussion in ch 5(II) below.
[12] *Maritime Delimitation and Territorial Questions between Qatar and Bahrain (Qatar v Bahrain)* (Merits) [2001] ICJ Rep 40 (*Qatar v Bahrain*, Merits).
[13] *Territorial and Maritime Dispute (Nicaragua v Colombia)* (Judgment) [2012] ICJ Rep 624 (*Territorial and Maritime Dispute*, Judgment).
[14] *Qatar v Bahrain*, Merits (n 12) para 185.
[15] *Territorial and Maritime Dispute*, Judgment (n 13) para 138.
[16] ibid para 139.
[17] *Qatar v Bahrain*, Merits (n 12) paras 191–97.
[18] ibid paras 193–94.

evidence, including the fact that Qatar's experts did not themselves maintain that it was scientifically proven that Qit'at Jaradah was a low-tide elevation, and the majority concluded that it was an island to be taken into consideration as such for the drawing of the maritime boundary.[19] In dissent, Judges Bedjaoui, Ranjeva, and Koroma considered that the fact that land rises above the high water line was insufficient to establish island status, as it was also necessary to show that the feature was 'terra firma'—ie whether the land, a product of nature, was the consequence of geological action or of sedimentation.[20] As Qit'at Jaradah was formed by accretion, in the view of the dissenting judges, its geomorphological characteristics were such that it was not an island in accordance with Article 121.[21]

The Court also clarified that the legal status of a feature as an island or a low-tide elevation impacts not only the question of whether it generates any maritime entitlement, but also the question of whether it is 'territory' subject to State sovereignty. It noted that '[i]t has never been disputed that islands constitute terra firma, and are subject to the rules and principles of territorial acquisition',[22] whereas '[t]he few existing rules do not justify a general assumption that low-tide elevations are territory in the same sense as islands'.[23] The Court thus concluded that it was not established that 'low-tide elevations can, from the viewpoint of the acquisition of sovereignty, be fully assimilated with islands or other land territory'.[24]

In *Territorial and Maritime Dispute*, the ICJ was confronted with the question of whether maritime features in dispute were capable of appropriation.[25] These maritime features were in the Caribbean Sea, with Nicaragua to the east and Colombia to the south.[26] Nicaragua had claimed sovereignty over some of the features, but at the jurisdictional stage, the Court held that it had no jurisdiction over that claim, because the question of sovereignty had been determined by a 1928 treaty by which Nicaragua recognised Colombian sovereignty over the islands.[27] Some were islands and others were cays, atolls, or banks.[28] In that context, the Court confirmed that 'islands, however small, are capable of appropriation',[29] whereas 'low-tide elevations cannot be appropriated', although low-tide elevations within the territorial sea fall within the coastal State's sovereignty as part of the territorial sea, and may be taken into account for the purposes of measuring the breadth of the territorial sea (consistently with Article 13(1) of UNCLOS).[30] The parties were agreed that several of the features were islands, but were in disagreement as to whether any of the features on Quitasueño (a large bank/shoal approximately 57 km long and 20 km wide[31]) qualified as islands.[32] The issue for the Court was whether any naturally formed areas of land that were above water at high tide existed at Quitasueño.[33] The Court referred principally to the contemporary expert

[19] ibid para 195.
[20] *Qatar v Bahrain*, Merits (n 12) (Dissenting Opinion of Judges Bedjaoui, Ranjeva, and Koroma) para 198. See also *Qatar v Bahrain*, Merits (n 12) (Declaration of Judge Vereschchetin) para 13.
[21] *Qatar v Bahrain*, Merits (n 12) (Dissenting Opinion of Judges Bedjaoui, Ranjeva, and Koroma) para 199.
[22] *Qatar v Bahrain*, Merits (n 12) para 206.
[23] ibid.
[24] ibid.
[25] *Territorial and Maritime Dispute*, Judgment (n 13) para 25.
[26] ibid paras 18–19.
[27] ibid para 23.
[28] ibid para 24.
[29] ibid para 26.
[30] ibid. See also para 182.
[31] ibid para 24(e).
[32] ibid para 27.
[33] ibid para 35.

evidence,[34] including the evidence of Colombia's expert identifying thirty-four individual features within Quitasueño, and twenty low-tide elevations (referred to as QS1 to QS54).[35] The Court focused on the largest of the features, QS32. The Court noted that, whichever tidal method was used, QS 32 (at Quitasueño) was above water at high tide.[36] Nicaragua argued that it could nevertheless not be regarded as an island because it was composed of coral debris.[37] The Court disagreed. It noted that the photographic evidence confirmed that QS 32 was composed of solid material, attached to the substrate, and not of loose debris; the fact that it was composed of coral was irrelevant to its legal status.[38] Nor did it matter that QS 32 was very small 'since international law does not prescribe any minimum size which a feature must possess in order to be considered an island'.[39] The Court therefore concluded that QS 32 was capable of appropriation,[40] while all the other features at Quitasueño did not qualify as islands.[41]

The Court's conclusion in *Territorial and Maritime Dispute*, that Article 121(3) reflected customary international law, was considered controversial. In 1992, the UN Secretary-General reported that States had generally not applied Article 121(3) of UNCLOS in practice, stating:

> Article 121(3), regarding rocks, has not had a great impact upon the practice of States. Existing claims to 200-mile zones made before the adoption of the Convention have, in the main, not been withdrawn. New claims since 1982 to 200-mile zones measures from small features, which may be described as rocks, have generated protests in some cases. As a result, the practice of States displays unevenness.[42]

Commentators generally agree that it is difficult to find support in State practice for a customary rule reflecting Article 121(3). For example, Tanaka has argued that if Article 121(3) reflects customary international law, 'State practice is highly diverse in the interpretation and application of this provision',[43] and his views have been echoed by other commentators.[44]

The Tribunal in *South China Sea* was the first UNCLOS tribunal to have the opportunity to undertake a comprehensive interpretation of Article 121, together with Article 13. As discussed in Chapter 4, although sovereignty over different land features in the South China Sea is disputed between the Philippines and China, the Philippines submitted that its case was focused on the maritime entitlements of those land features through interpretations of

[34] ibid para 36.
[35] ibid para 29.
[36] ibid para 37.
[37] ibid.
[38] ibid.
[39] ibid.
[40] ibid.
[41] ibid.
[42] 'Law of the Sea: Report of the Secretary-General: Progress Made in the Implementation of the Comprehensive Regime Embodied in the United Nations Convention on the Law of the Sea' (5 November 1992) UN Doc A/47/512, para 46.
[43] Tanaka (n 6) 84.
[44] See eg Stefan Talmon, 'Article 121' in Alexander Proelss (ed), *United Nations Convention on the Law of the Sea: A Commentary* (CH Beck, Hart, and Nomos 2017) 861, para 6.

Articles 121 and 13 without seeking to resolve which State would be entitled to any territorial sea, EEZ, and/or continental shelf generated from the land.[45]

In respect of the definition of low-tide elevations in Article 13(1), the Tribunal noted that it 'operates in parallel with that of an island in Article 121(1)'.[46] From both definitions, it followed that 'the status of a feature is to be evaluated on the basis of its natural condition',[47] and any human modification cannot change the seabed into a low-tide elevation, or a low-tide elevation into an island, regardless of the scale of the island or installation built atop it.[48] Consideration of the relevance of human modification was necessary because of the extensive land-reclamation activities that China had undertaken, including during the pendency of the proceedings.[49]

As to the status and entitlements of low-tide elevations, the Tribunal noted that Article 13(2) of UNCLOS provides that, unless within an exception, a low-tide elevation generates no territorial sea of its own.[50] Although Article 13(2) does not expressly state that a low-tide elevation does not generate an EEZ or continental shelf, the Tribunal considered that this outcome was necessarily implied in the Convention, given that the breadth of the EEZ (Article 57) and the continental shelf (Article 76) are measured from the baseline of the territorial sea, and given that Article 121(3) provides that even certain high-tide features that are deemed to be rocks do not generate an EEZ or continental shelf.[51] The Tribunal further stated that, notwithstanding the use of the term 'land' in the physical description of a low-tide elevation, such features do not form part of the land territory of the coastal State in a legal sense, and accordingly, they cannot be appropriated, citing with approval the ICJ's treatment of this issue in *Territorial and Maritime Dispute*.[52] The consistency of these views may hold positive implications for the future resolution of disputes between other States where further contests as to low-tide elevations may arise. Whether a feature is a low tide-elevation or not may remain disputed as a factual matter.

Finally, in respect of the meaning of 'high tide', the Tribunal noted that it was not a technical term and was potentially subject to a number of different interpretations and, in particular, that different datums may be used for measuring high water.[53] The Tribunal considered that there was nothing in the Convention, and no rule of customary international law, that mandates that the status of features as low-tide elevations and/or islands be determined against any particular high-water datum.[54] Thus, 'States are free under the Convention to claim a high-tide feature or island on the basis of any high-water datum that reasonably corresponds to the ordinary meaning of the term "high tide" in Articles 13 and 121'.[55] Where the features in questions are claimed by multiple States,[56] and/or their status is disputed on the basis of the use of different high-water datums,[57] it would be for a tribunal

[45] See ch 4(II).
[46] *South China Sea*, Award (n 10) para 304.
[47] ibid para 305.
[48] ibid.
[49] These activities were subject to separate claims by the Philippines for violating UNCLOS obligations relating to the protection and preservation of the marine environment. See ch 9(II)(A).
[50] *South China Sea*, Award (n 10) para 308.
[51] ibid.
[52] ibid para 309.
[53] ibid para 310.
[54] ibid para 311.
[55] ibid.
[56] ibid para 312.
[57] ibid para 313.

to consider the issue further, particularly if a feature is near enough to high water that its status would differ as a result of the datum used.[58] In light of this analysis, the Tribunal examined the evidence with respect to the particular features in dispute, addressing them in turn, and determining whether they were high-tide features or low-tide elevations.[59]

For those features identified as high-tide features (ie not low-tide elevations), the Tribunal proceeded to consider whether they qualified as rocks or islands under Article 121. The Tribunal noted that Article 121 had not previously been the subject of significant consideration by any courts or tribunals and that divergent interpretations were given by commentators.[60] It noted at the outset that Article 121 was to be interpreted in accordance with the principles on interpretation set out in Articles 31 and 32 of the Vienna Convention on the Law of Treaties (VCLT).[61] The Tribunal thereby focused on Article 121(3) and on the particular textual elements thereof 'that merit consideration'.[62]

First, the term 'rocks', and in particular, whether Article 121(3) applies only to features that are composed of solid rock or are otherwise rock-like in nature.[63] The Tribunal noted that the dictionary meaning of 'rock' does not confine the term so strictly, and that the ICJ in *Territorial and Maritime Dispute* considered a protrusion of coral to be a 'rock'.[64] It further noted that introducing a geological qualification in Article 121(3) would mean that any high-tide features formed by sand, mud, gravel, or coral would not be rocks, but would necessarily be islands within Article 121 that generated extended maritime entitlements.[65] The Tribunal therefore concluded that 'rocks' for the purposes of Article 121(3) need not necessarily be composed of rock in the geological sense,[66] and further noted that the name given to a feature (eg rock or island) would have no bearing on whether it qualified as a 'rock' for the purposes of Article 121(3).[67]

Second, the term 'cannot', which indicates a concept of capacity, ie does the feature in its natural form have the capability of sustaining human habitation or an economic life?[68] The Tribunal took the view that what is relevant here is whether the feature is apt, able to, or lends itself to human habitation or economic life, not whether it actually does (or has) sustain(ed) human habitation or an economic life.[69] It also noted that historical evidence of habitation or economic life in the past may be relevant to establishing the relevant capacity.[70]

Third, the term 'sustain': the Tribunal took account of the ordinary meaning of 'sustain', including in the context of land/a place, a person, and an activity.[71] It considered that it had three components: the first is the concept of the support and provision of essentials; the second is that support and provision must be over a period of time and not one-off or short-lived; and the third is a qualitative concept, entailing at least a minimal 'proper standard'.[72]

[58] ibid.
[59] ibid paras 333–84.
[60] ibid para 474.
[61] ibid paras 476–77.
[62] ibid para 478.
[63] ibid para 479.
[64] ibid para 480.
[65] ibid para 481.
[66] ibid para 482.
[67] ibid.
[68] ibid para 483.
[69] ibid.
[70] ibid para 484.
[71] ibid paras 485–86.
[72] ibid para 487.

Thus, habitation and economic life must be able to extend over a certain duration and occur to an adequate standard.[73]

Fourth, for the term 'human habitation', the Tribunal considered that this included a qualitative element that was reflected in the notions of settlement and residence that are inherent in that term.[74] It implied a non-transient presence of persons who have chosen to stay and reside on the feature in a settled manner.[75] At a minimum, it required that a feature be able to support, maintain, and provide food, drink, and shelter to some humans to enable them to reside there permanently or habitually over an extended period of time.[76] While there was no precise minimum number of persons, ordinarily a feature that provided the basic necessities for a sole individual would not meet the criteria of human habitation, since humans need company and community.[77]

Fifth, the term 'or': whether it meant that the specified capacities were *both* required for a feature to be entitled to an EEZ and continental shelf, or whether *one* sufficed.[78] The Philippines argued that it was a 'double negative' so that a feature must be able both to sustain human habitation and economic life to be entitled to an EEZ and continental shelf.[79] The Tribunal disagreed, finding that if a feature is capable of sustaining *either* human habitation *or* an economic life of its own, it will qualify as a fully entitled island.[80] It noted that in practical terms, the two concepts are nevertheless linked, because economic activity is carried out by humans and humans will rarely inhabit areas where no economic activity or livelihood is possible.[81] The Tribunal's conclusion has been criticised on the basis that it effectively changed the 'or' in Article 121(3) to an 'and'.[82]

Sixth, in addressing the phrase 'economic life of their own', the Tribunal emphasised that 'economic life' implied the development and regulation of material resources, and some level of local human activity to exploit, develop, and distribute those resources.[83] 'Of their own' made clear that a feature (or group of related features) must have the ability to support an independent economic life, and the resources must be local, not imported.[84] The Tribunal considered that economic activity derived from an EEZ or continental shelf would not of itself meet this criterion, as it would be circular and absurd if the mere presence of economic activity in the EEZ or continental shelf were sufficient to endow a feature with an entitlement to those zones.[85] However, economic activity in the territorial sea could form part of the economic life of a feature, because any high-tide feature will generate a territorial sea.[86]

[73] ibid paras 487, 504(c).
[74] ibid para 489.
[75] ibid.
[76] ibid para 490.
[77] ibid para 491.
[78] ibid para 493.
[79] ibid.
[80] ibid paras 494–96.
[81] ibid para 497.
[82] See eg Erik Franckx, 'The Arbitral Tribunal's Interpretation of Paragraph 3 in Article 121: A first but Important Step Forward' in S Jayakumar and others (eds), *The South China Sea Arbitration: The Legal Dimension* (Edward Elgar Publishing 2018) 174.
[83] *South China Sea*, Award (n 10) para 499.
[84] ibid para 500.
[85] ibid paras 501–502.
[86] ibid para 503.

The Tribunal then turned to consider the context of Article 121(3) and the object and purpose of the Convention, focusing first on the context of the system of classifying features that includes fully entitled islands, rocks, low-tide elevations, and submerged features. Thus, Article 121(3) had to be interpreted in conjunction with the other paragraphs of Article 121 and with Article 13 concerning low-tide elevations.[87] Taking account of the context and purpose of those provisions, the Tribunal emphasised that the status of a feature must be assessed on the basis of its natural condition,[88] and that the capacity of a feature must be assessed without artificial additions or human modifications.[89] The Tribunal also noted that, as Article 121(3) concerned the circumstances in which a feature would be denied entitlements to an EEZ or a continental shelf, it had to be interpreted in the context of those maritime areas and the purpose behind the introduction of the EEZ.[90] It noted that the purpose of the EEZ was to extend the jurisdiction of States over the waters adjacent to their coasts and to preserve the resources of those waters for the benefit of the coastal State's population.[91] Article 121(1) serves '[a]s a counterpoint to the expanded jurisdiction of the EEZ'—to 'prevent such expansion from going too far'.[92] Thus, the meaning given to the terms in Article 121(3) 'should serve to reinforce, rather than counter, the purposes that the [EEZ] and Article 121(3) were respectively intended to serve'.[93] In the Tribunal's view, that was best accomplished by recognising the connection between 'human habitation' and the population of the coastal State, for the benefit of whom the resources of the EEZ were to be preserved.[94] Thus, the Tribunal considered that the human habitation with which the drafters of Article 121(3) were concerned was the habitation by a portion of the population for whose benefit the EEZ was being introduced. This perspective suggests that habitation for the purposes of Article 121(3) is habitation by a settled group or community for whom the feature is a home.[95]

The Tribunal then considered the negotiating history of Article 121(3),[96] although noting that it was 'an imperfect guide', because the key compromise was reached through informal consultations for which no records were kept.[97] Nevertheless, it noted the following general conclusions from the negotiating history:

- Article 121(3) is a provision of limitation; the conditions therein were introduced with the object and purpose of preventing encroachment on the international seabed reserved for the common heritage of humankind and avoiding the inequitable distribution of maritime spaces under national jurisdiction.[98]
- The definitions in Article 121(3) were discussed in the context of other aspects of the Convention, including the introduction and purpose of the EEZ; the questions of islands under foreign control or colonial dependence; the introduction of the international

[87] ibid para 507.
[88] ibid para 508.
[89] ibid paras 509–510.
[90] ibid paras 507, 512.
[91] ibid para 513. See also paras 514–15.
[92] ibid para 516.
[93] ibid.
[94] ibid para 517.
[95] ibid para 520.
[96] ibid paras 522–33.
[97] ibid para 534.
[98] ibid para 535.

seabed area; the protection of the interests of archipelagic States; the role of islands in maritime delimitation; and concerns about the potential for artificial installations to generate maritime zones.[99]

- There are diverse high-tide features, and the negotiating history demonstrated the difficulty of setting bright-line rules for all cases, and especially for defining or categorising features by reference to size.[100]

Taking account of the text, context, object, and purposes, as well as negotiating history, the Tribunal set out the following conclusions with respect to the interpretation of Article 121(3):[101]

(1) The term 'rock' did not limit Article 121(3) to features composed of solid rock: the geological and geomorphological characteristics of a feature were not relevant to its classification under Article 121(3).[102]
(2) The status of a feature was determined on the basis of its natural capacity, without external additions or modifications.[103]
(3) The critical factor for 'human habitation' was the non-transient character of the inhabitation—it required inhabitation of the feature by a stable community of people for whom the feature constituted a home and on which they could remain.[104]
(4) The term 'economic life of their own' was linked to and would in most instances go hand in hand with the requirement of human habitation.[105] The economic life must be oriented around the feature itself and not focused solely on the waters or seabed, and extractive economic activity to harvest the natural resources for the benefit of a population elsewhere could not reasonably be considered to constitute the economic life of a feature as its own.[106]
(5) The ability to sustain either human habitation or an economic life of its own sufficed to entitle a high-tide feature to an EEZ and continental shelf.[107]
(6) Article 121(3) is concerned with the *capacity* of a feature, rather than whether it is presently, or has been, inhabited or home to economic life.[108]
(7) The capacity of a feature to sustain human habitation or an economic life of its own had to be assessed on a case-by-case basis, rather than by application of a specific or abstract test.[109]
(8) The capacity of a feature should be assessed with due regard for the potential for a group of small features collectively to sustain human habitation or economic life.[110]
(9) Evidence of the objective, physical conditions on a particular feature could only take the Tribunal so far in its task; it was difficult to determine from the physical

[99] ibid para 536.
[100] ibid paras 537–38.
[101] ibid para 539.
[102] ibid para 540.
[103] ibid para 541.
[104] ibid para 542.
[105] ibid para 543.
[106] ibid.
[107] ibid para 544.
[108] ibid para 545.
[109] ibid para 546.
[110] ibid para 547.

> characteristics alone whether the feature had the capacity to sustain settled habitation by a human community.[111] The most reliable evidence of the capacity of a feature would usually be the historical use to which it had been put,[112] but it was also important to consider whether there was evidence that any historical habitation was only possible though outside support.[113] The same mode of analysis would apply to the criterion of economic life of its own.[114]

Finally, the Tribunal noted that Article 31(3) of the VCLT provides that any subsequent practice in the application of a treaty that establishes the agreement of the parties regarding its interpretation is to be taken into account together with the context.[115] Noting that the ICJ has applied a high threshold for accepting an agreement on interpretation,[116] the Tribunal concluded that there was no evidence for an agreement based on State practice on the interpretation of Article 121(3) that differed from the Tribunal's interpretation of that provision.[117] The Tribunal, however, did not engage in any assessment of the diversity of State practice in relation to the points it addressed in classifying rocks and islands.

The *South China Sea* Tribunal's detailed analysis of Article 121 has been a signature judicial contribution to the interpretation of UNCLOS since the Convention's entry into force. The stakeholders in this process included not only the Philippines and China as parties to the dispute (even in China's absence from the proceedings), but all State parties to UNCLOS as well as non-State parties interested in better understanding what the ICJ has described as customary international law.[118] The factors discussed by the Tribunal in interpreting Article 121 were of high relevance for a number of other States that claim extended maritime zones from what may be considered as 'rocks' pursuant to the Tribunal's assessment.[119]

For the immediate case at hand, the interpretation was important because when applied to the features in question, the Tribunal determined that none of them qualified as 'fully-entitled islands',[120] which meant that there were no areas of overlapping maritime entitlements between the Philippines and China. This holding not only had significance for the Tribunal's jurisdiction,[121] but also had the potential, if accepted by the parties, to reduce competition between States in this semi-enclosed sea. Such an outcome would have been an extraordinary contribution to the good order of the oceans and contributed positively to efforts at cooperation, as required under Article 123 of UNCLOS. However, China's rejection of the award and actions subsequent to the arbitration have to date diminished the practical significance of the determination.

[111] ibid para 548.
[112] ibid para 549.
[113] ibid para 550.
[114] ibid para 551.
[115] ibid para 552.
[116] ibid.
[117] ibid para 553.
[118] See further Natalie Klein, 'Stakeholders in Dispute Settlement under the UN Convention on the Law of the Sea' in Marta Chantal Ribeiro, Fernando Loureiro Bastos, and Tore Henrikson (eds), *Global Challenges and the Law of the Sea* (Springer 2020) 250–56.
[119] See discussion in: Natalie Klein, 'Rocks and Islands after the South China Sea Arbitration' (2016) 34 Aust YBIL 21.
[120] The assessment of Itu Aba as a 'rock' has generated criticism in this regard. See Myron H Nordquist, 'UNCLOS Article 121 and Itu Aba in the South China Sea Final Award: A Correct Interpretation?' in S Jayakumar and others (eds), *The South China Sea Arbitration: The Legal Dimension* (Edward Elgar Publishing 2018).
[121] See ch 4(IV)(A)(1).

Further, the Tribunal's reasoning and conclusions with respect to Article 121 have been the subject of significant criticism by commentators and appear not to have been adopted by States in their ongoing characterisation of various offshore features as islands. Much of the criticism in the literature has focused on the Tribunal's disregard of State practice claiming offshore features as islands that would not qualify under the Tribunal's interpretation of Article 121(3).[122] The Tribunal's treatment of this State practice was summary and did not explain the grounds on which the Tribunal concluded that there was 'no evidence for an agreement based upon State practice'. It has been suggested that 'if the relevant maritime claims and state practice had been thoroughly examined, the tribunal might have come to a different conclusion on the interpretation and application of Article 121 and in particular 121(3)'.[123] It has also been suggested that the Tribunal disregarded the case law of the ICJ, recognising maritime entitlements of features where there is no evidence of the capacity of the feature to sustain human habitation or economic life of its own, without outside support.[124] Commentators have also pointed out that no State appears to have altered its practice in light of the Tribunal's interpretation; a fact that may eventually lead a subsequent tribunal to reconsider and depart from aspects of the Tribunal's approach.[125]

Given that this case was the first comprehensive interpretation of Article 121 by a tribunal, it is perhaps unsurprising that it has been subjected to significant critique. There is clearly scope for the same questions to come before another tribunal in due course and it remains to be seen whether the *South China Sea* Tribunal's interpretation is adopted, or disregarded, in future cases.

III. Baselines

As noted at the outset, a primary function of the law of the sea is to determine the spatial extent of, and scope of rights to, coastal State sovereignty and jurisdiction over maritime areas. The seaward limits of each of the relevant maritime zones are measured from the coastal State's baselines, and it follows that the way in which baselines are drawn may have a significant influence on the spatial extent of the coastal State's rights. UNCLOS provides for four types of baselines: normal baselines (Article 5), straight baselines (Article 7), closing lines across river mouths and bays (Articles 9 and 10), and archipelagic baselines (Article 47). In addition, Article 11 provides that 'permanent harbour works' may be regarded as forming part of the coast for the purposes of delimiting the territorial sea. As such, in

[122] See eg Klein (n 119); A Oude Elferink, 'The South China Sea Arbitration's Interpretation of Article 121(3) of the LOSC: A Disquieting First' *NCLOS Blog* (7 September 2016) https://site.uit.no/nclos/2016/09/07/the-south-china-sea-arbitrations-interpretation-of-article-1213-of-the-losc-a-disquieting-first/; Stefan Talmon, 'The South China Sea Arbitration and the Finality of "Final" Awards' (2019) 8 JIDS 338; Yann-huei Song, 'The July 2016 Arbitral Award, Interpretation of Article 121(3) of the UNCLOS, and Selecting Examples of Inconsistent State Practice' (2019) 49 ODIL 247; Sondra Faccio, 'Human Habitation or Economic Life of their Own: The Definition of Features Between History, Technology and the Law' (2021) 42 Liverpool LR 15; Gilbert Guillaume, 'Rocks in the Law of the Sea: Some Comments on the South China Sea Arbitration Award' *EJIL: Talk!* (25 February 2021) https://www.ejiltalk.org/ricks-in-the-law-of-the-sea-some-comments-on-the-south-china-sea-arbitration-award/; Irini Papanicolopulu, 'The Land Dominates the Sea (Dominates the Land Dominates the Sea)' (2018) 47 Questions of Intl L 39.

[123] Song (n 122) 250.

[124] Guillaume (n 122).

[125] W Gullett, 'The South China Sea Arbitration's Contribution to the Concept of Juridical Islands' (2018) 47 Questions of Intl L 5, 38.

certain circumstances, base points may be placed on them, and therefore have an impact on the outer limit as well as delimitation of the territorial sea with neighbouring States. Article 16 requires coastal States to give due publicity to baselines under Articles 7, 9, and 10. The interpretation of these provisions is primarily undertaken by the relevant coastal States in preparing charts and/or promulgating national laws for the regulation of ocean areas. The discussion immediately below considers the occasions where courts or tribunals have been called on to examine these UNCLOS provisions and clarified their potential application in the practice of States.

A. Normal Baselines

The normal baseline is the low-water line drawn along the coast. Article 5 of UNCLOS provides: 'Except where otherwise provided in this Convention, the normal baseline for measuring the breadth of the territorial sea is the low-water line along the coast as marked on large-scale charts officially recognized by the coastal State.'[126] The default rule under Article 5 reflects the approach taken by the ICJ in *Anglo-Norwegian Fisheries*,[127] which noted that the low-water mark (as opposed to the high-water mark, or the mean between them) had generally been adopted in the practice of States for the purpose of measuring the breadth of the territorial sea.[128]

In *Guyana v Suriname*,[129] a dispute arose as to the accuracy of the depiction of one of Suriname's claimed base points located on a shoal. The chart depicting the low-water line was produced after the arbitration had commenced and that chart showed a line several kilometres seaward of an earlier chart.[130] After hearing evidence, the Tribunal declared that it was 'not convinced' that the base point was inaccurate and therefore accepted Suriname's base point on the shoal.[131] This holding indicates that where a claimed base point or baseline impacts on a maritime boundary delimitation, the Tribunal will consider the validity of the claimed base point or baseline. However, for any errors to be corrected, they need to be significant. As Trümpler has pointed out, the decision in *Guyana v Suriname* affirmed that errors must be clear and convincingly shown, and that those errors have considerable influence on the coastline in order for a tribunal to correct them.[132]

More recently, in *Maritime Delimitation in the Indian Ocean*, the Court refused to accept the base points proposed by the parties on offshore features, and used only base points on the mainland coasts of the two States.[133] While noting that it would have regard to the proposals of the parties as to base points, the Court emphasised that it could review the appropriateness of the use of a particular base point, even if agreed by the parties.[134] The use

126 UNCLOS (n 1) art 5.

127 *Anglo-Norwegian Fisheries* (n 3).

128 ibid 128.

129 *Guyana v Suriname* (Award of the Arbitral Tribunal of 17 September 2007) PCA Case No 2004-04 (*Guyana v Suriname*).

130 ibid para 395.

131 ibid para 396.

132 Kai Trümpler, 'Article 5' in Alexander Proelss (ed), *United Nations Convention on the Law of the Sea: A Commentary* (CH Beck, Hart, and Nomos 2017) 54, para 26.

133 *Maritime Delimitation in the Indian Ocean (Somalia v Kenya)* (Judgment of 12 October 2021) General List No 161 (*Maritime Delimitation in the Indian Ocean*, Judgment) paras 111–14.

134 ibid para 111.

of base points on the mainland coastlines resulted in the Court ignoring several offshore features, and in particular those off the Somali coast, which had an impact on the near-shore course of the equidistance line. The Court's approach to base points had the effect of pushing the equidistance line so that more of the disputed area was allocated to Kenya, even beyond the equidistance line it had drawn in the territorial sea. As discussed in more detail in Chapter 6, this aspect of the Court's decision was heavily criticised by Judge Yusuf in his separate opinion. It appears to mark a significant shift away from the approach of the Tribunal in *Guyana v Suriname*, which set a high bar to depart from base points claimed by a party.

B. Straight Baselines

Straight baselines have been one of the most controversial aspects of claims to maritime space because States may utilise them in circumstances that augment the ocean area considered as internal waters (those waters located between the straight baseline and the actual coast) and thereby extend the reach of other maritime zones where the breadth is measured from that baseline.[135] The ICJ had early influence in this regard in acknowledging State practice and articulating a method for drawing straight baselines in *Anglo-Norwegian Fisheries*.[136] The criteria derived from that method were included in the Convention on the Territorial Sea and Contiguous Zone (Territorial Sea Convention).[137] During UNCLOS negotiations, it was agreed that only small variations should be made to the provision in the Territorial Sea Convention to account for the status of atolls, islands with fringing reefs, and unstable coastlines.[138] Article 7 of UNCLOS addresses straight baselines as follows:

1. In localities where the coastline is deeply indented and cut into, or if there is a fringe of islands along the coast in its immediate vicinity, the method of straight baselines joining appropriate points may be employed in drawing the baseline from which the breadth of the territorial sea is measured.
2. Where because of the presence of a delta and other natural conditions the coastline is highly unstable, the appropriate points may be selected along the furthest seaward extent of the low-water line and, notwithstanding subsequent regression of the low-water line, the straight baselines shall remain effective until changed by the coastal State in accordance with this Convention.
3. The drawing of straight baselines must not depart to any appreciable extent from the general direction of the coast, and the sea areas lying within the lines must be sufficiently closely linked to the land domain to be subject to the regime of internal waters.
4. Straight baselines shall not be drawn to and from low-tide elevations, unless lighthouses or similar installations which are permanently above sea level have been built on them

[135] See International Law Association, 'Baselines under the International Law of the Sea' (Final Report, 2018) https://www.ila-hq.org/images/ILA/DraftReports/DraftReport_Baselines.pdf.

[136] *Anglo-Norwegian Fisheries* (n 3) 128.

[137] Convention on the Territorial Sea and Contiguous Zone (opened for signature 29 April 1958, entered into force 10 September 1964) 516 UNTS 205, art 4.

[138] UN Office for Ocean Affairs and the Law of the Sea, *Baselines: An Examination of the Relevant Provisions of the United Nations Convention on the Law of the Sea* (UN 1989) viii–ix https://www.un.org/depts/los/doalos_publications/publicationstexts/The%20Law%20of%20the%20Sea_Baselines.pdf.

or except in instances where the drawing of baselines to and from such elevations has received general international recognition.

5. Where the method of straight baselines is applicable under paragraph 1, account may be taken, in determining particular baselines, of economic interests peculiar to the region concerned, the reality and the importance of which are clearly evidenced by long usage.
6. The system of straight baselines may not be applied by a State in such a manner as to cut off the territorial sea of another State from the high seas or an exclusive economic zone.[139]

There have been few cases in which a tribunal has directly addressed claims to straight baselines. In maritime delimitation cases, there is a trend for the parties to ignore their straight baselines and to identify base points on the low water line for the purposes of delimitation.[140] To date, no tribunal constituted under UNCLOS has had cause to resolve a dispute concerning the interpretation or application of Article 7.

In *Qatar v Bahrain*, the ICJ affirmed that the straight baselines method is exceptional. Bahrain argued that, as a multiple-island State characterised by a cluster of islands off the coasts of its main islands, it was entitled to draw a line connecting the outermost islands and low-tide elevations, and the external fringe should serve as a baseline for its territorial sea.[141] However, the Court noted that:

> [T]he method of straight baselines, which is an exception to the normal rules for the determination of baselines, may only be applied if a number of conditions are met. This method must be applied restrictively. Such conditions are primarily that either the coastline is deeply indented and cut into, or that there is a fringe of islands along the coast in its immediate vicinity.[142]

The Court held that Bahrain did not meet either of these conditions. As to the first, Bahrain did not claim that its main islands formed a deeply indented coasts.[143] As to the second, the Court noted that the islands concerned were relatively small in number and 'it would be going too far ... to qualify them as a fringe of islands along the coast'.[144] In the view of the Court, there could only be a 'cluster of islands' or an 'island system' if Bahrain included its main islands, and in such a situation, the method of straight baselines would apply only if the State had declared itself to be an archipelagic State, which Bahrain had not.[145] Archipelagic baselines are discussed further below, together with the potential application of straight baselines under Article 7 to offshore archipelagos.

In *Eritrea/Yemen*, the Tribunal declined to use base points on Eritrea's claimed straight baseline relying on Negileh Rock, a reef that was not above water at any stage of the tide.[146]

[139] UNCLOS (n 1) art 7.

[140] See eg *Bay of Bengal Maritime Boundary Arbitration (Bangladesh v India)* (Award of 7 July 2014) PCA Case No 2010-16 (*Bay of Bengal Arbitration*) para 249; Alexander Proelss, 'Article 7' in Alexander Proelss (ed), *United Nations Convention on the Law of the Sea: A Commentary* (CH Beck, Hart, and Nomos 2017) 84, para 50.

[141] *Qatar v Bahrain*, Merits (n 12) para 211.

[142] ibid para 212.

[143] ibid.

[144] ibid para 214.

[145] ibid para 214.

[146] *Eritrea/Yemen—Sovereignty and Maritime Delimitation in the Red Sea* (Award of the Arbitral Tribunal in the Second Stage of the Proceedings—Maritime Delimitation of 17 December 1999) PCA Case No 1996-04 (*Eritrea/Yemen*, Second Stage).

Referring to Article 6 of UNCLOS, which provides that for islands with fringing reefs, the baseline is the seaward low-water line of the reef, and Article 7(4), the Tribunal determined that these provisions precluded the use of 'a reef that is not proud of the water at low-tide as a baseline of the territorial sea'.[147] These interpretations of Article 7 may be brought to bear in future cases submitted under UNCLOS. Future tribunals may do well to note that the tendency in the existing cases has been to restrict generous interpretations of Article 7 that would otherwise allow the coastal State to claim exclusive rights over larger stretches of ocean space.

C. Bays and River Mouths

UNCLOS permits the use of straight baselines across mouths of rivers under Article 9, and across bays meeting certain criteria under Article 10. Pursuant to Article 10(1), UNCLOS only relates to single-State bays, and pursuant to Article 10(6), it does not apply 'to so-called "historic" bays'. It can be recalled that historic bays may fall outside the scope of compulsory procedures under Section 2 of Part XV of UNCLOS if a State has issued a declaration to this effect under Article 298(1)(a).[148]

Article 9 has not been considered in any cases.[149] Article 10 has only been addressed indirectly. In *Land, Island and Maritime Dispute*, the Court suggested that Article 10 'must be found to express general customary international law',[150] without going into any detail on that assessment. In that case, the bay in question, the Gulf of Fonseca, did not fall within the scope of Article 10, as it is a pluri-State bay (bordered by El Salvador, Honduras, and Nicaragua). However, the Court agreed with the parties that it is an 'historic bay',[151] and stated that '[t]here can be no serious doubt that the closing line of an historic bay is the baseline of the territorial sea'.[152]

In *Maritime Delimitation in the Caribbean Sea and the Pacific Ocean*, the Court accepted the parties' agreement as to the starting point of the maritime boundary in the Pacific Ocean at the midpoint of the closing line of Salinas Bay, a shared bay, without referring to Article 10 or to the characterisation of Salinas Bay.[153] It remains to be seen how Article 10 may prove contentious and how future tribunals will interpret it.

[147] ibid paras 143–45.

[148] See ch 4(IV)(B).

[149] In *Maritime Delimitation in the Black Sea (Romania v Ukraine)* (Judgment) [2009] ICJ Rep 61 (*Maritime Delimitation in the Black Sea*) it appears that the parties had agreed to part of the boundary extending from a point on a river boundary continuing along the middle of the channel of the river for a short distance and then in a straight line to a point defined with coordinates where there was a beacon, but there was no finally agreed closing line across the river and no discussion of Article 9: see paras 51–58.

[150] *Case Concerning the Land, Island and Maritime Frontier Dispute (El Salvador/Honduras: Nicaragua Intervening)* (Judgment) [1992] ICJ Rep 351, para 383.

[151] ibid.

[152] ibid para 417.

[153] *Maritime Delimitation in the Caribbean Sea and the Pacific Ocean (Costa Rica v Nicaragua)* and *Land Boundary in the Northern Part of Isla Portillos (Costa Rica v Nicaragua)* (Judgment) [2019] ICJ Rep 139, para 169.

D. Archipelagic Baselines

Article 47 of UNCLOS permits an archipelagic State to draw straight baselines under certain conditions. Article 46(1) defines 'archipelagic State' to mean 'a State constituted wholly or by one or more archipelagos and may include other islands'. The recognition of 'archipelagic States' was one of the innovations of UNCLOS and Part IV of the Convention details *inter alia* the legal status of archipelagic waters and the interaction of this new concept with existing agreements.[154] The determination of archipelagic baselines is important for demarcating the waters that fall within the sovereignty of the archipelagic State and that are subject to the regimes of either innocent or archipelagic sea lanes passage.[155] The archipelagic baselines also represent the starting point for measuring maritime zones extending from the archipelagic State.[156] Archipelagic baselines have been addressed in three cases.

As noted above, in *Qatar v Bahrain*, the Court rejected Bahrain's argument that it could connect its outermost islands and low-tide elevations in a straight baseline system, on the grounds that it had not included its main islands, and it had not declared itself to be an archipelagic State.[157] In *Barbados v Trinidad and Tobago*, in describing the maritime boundary, the Tribunal referred to the turning point or turning points 'of the archipelagic baselines of Trinidad and Tobago',[158] without discussing the criteria for use of baselines under Article 47. In *South China Sea*, the Tribunal discussed whether China could claim that the Spratly Islands should be enclosed within a system of archipelagic or straight baselines. It noted that China is constituted principally by territory on the mainland of Asia and cannot meet the definition of an archipelagic State in Article 46 of UNCLOS.[159] It noted further that although the Philippines is an archipelagic State (being constituted wholly by an archipelago), and had employed archipelagic baselines for its territorial sea,[160] it could not declare archipelagic baselines surrounding the Spratly Islands, as Article 47(1) limits their use to circumstances where 'within such baselines are included the main islands and an area in which the ratio of the area of the water to the area of the land, including atolls, is between 1 to 1 and 9 to 1'. The Tribunal noted that 'under any conceivable system of baselines' the ratio of water to land would greatly exceed 9 to 1.[161]

The Tribunal went on to consider whether straight baselines might be drawn under Article 7, noting the practice of some States to use straight baselines with respect to offshore archipelagos. The Tribunal expressed the firm view that Article 7 could not be used to justify straight baselines around an offshore archipelago, stating:

> In the Tribunal's view, any application of straight baselines to the Spratly Islands in this fashion would be contrary to the Convention. Article 7 provides for the application of straight baselines only '[i]n localities where the coastline is deeply indented and cut into, or if there is a fringe of islands along the coast in its immediate vicinity'. These conditions

[154] UNCLOS (n 1) arts 49, 51.
[155] ibid arts 52, 53.
[156] ibid art 48.
[157] *Qatar v Bahrain*, Merits (n 12) para 214.
[158] *Barbados v Trinidad and Tobago* (Award of the Arbitral Tribunal of 11 April 2006) PCA Case No 2004-02, para 381 (*Barbados v Trinidad and Tobago*).
[159] *South China Sea*, Award (n 10) para 573.
[160] ibid.
[161] ibid para 574.

> do not include the situation of an offshore archipelago. Although the Convention does not expressly preclude the use of straight baselines in other circumstances, the Tribunal considers that the grant of permission in Article 7 concerning straight baselines generally, together with the conditional permission in Articles 46 and 47 for certain States to draw archipelagic baselines, excludes the possibility of employing straight baselines in other circumstances, in particular with respect to offshore archipelagos not meeting the criteria for archipelagic baselines. Any other interpretation would effectively render the conditions in Articles 7 and 47 meaningless.[162]

Referring to the practice of some States to the contrary, the Tribunal considered that there was 'no evidence that any deviations from this rule have amounted to the formation of a new rule of customary international law that would permit a departure from the express provisions of the Convention'.[163] Commentators such as Symmons have taken issue with the Tribunal's approach, suggesting that it 'seems to fly in the face of present State practice'.[164] In this particular case, the Tribunal may have been influenced by the rather extreme claim in respect of the Spratly Islands (taking account of the ratio of water to land, as noted above). In future disputes, tribunals may be more amenable to interpreting the conditions in Article 47 in light of State practice, as they have done in respect of other issues.

E. Harbour Works

Article 11 of UNCLOS, entitled 'Ports', provides:

> For the purpose of delimiting the territorial sea, the outermost permanent harbour works which form an integral part of the harbour system are regarded as forming part of the coast. Off-shore installations and artificial islands shall not be considered as permanent harbour works.[165]

The first sentence of Article 11 is identical to Article 8 of the Territorial Sea Convention. In the 1981 *Dubai/Sharjah Arbitration*, both parties relied on that provision to contend that their respective harbour works should be used to construct the boundary line.[166] Both sets of work were substantial: those of Sharjah were approximately two miles in length and projected about half a mile seaward; and the works of Dubai were approximately two miles in length and projected one and a half miles seaward. The Court of Arbitration held that both sets of works were to be treated as part of the coast for the purpose of identifying the baselines from which their boundary was to be constructed and considered that giving full effect to both sets of works did not produce an inequitable result.[167]

[162] ibid para 575.

[163] ibid para 576.

[164] Clive R Symmons, 'Article 47' in Alexander Proelss (ed), *United Nations Convention on the Law of the Sea: A Commentary* (CH Beck, Hart, and Nomos 2017) 357, para 9, fn 42. Reaching a contrary conclusion, see Catherine Redgwell and Antonios Tzanakopoulos, 'Custom and Treaty Entanglements Revisited: The Concept of an Offshore or Outlying Archipelago in the Law of the Sea', 15 March 2022, <http://dx.doi.org/10.2139/ssrn.4059266>.

[165] UNCLOS (n 1) art 11.

[166] *Dubai-Sharjah Border Arbitration* (Judgment of the Court of Arbitration of 19 October 1981) (1981) 91 ILR 543.

[167] ibid 662.

Article 11 was directly considered by the ICJ in *Maritime Delimitation in the Black Sea*.[168] Romania argued that the Sulina dyke, a 7.5 km-long dyke out to sea on the southern headland of the Musura Bay, was to be treated as a 'permanent harbour work' under Article 11 of UNCLOS. Romania had notified its baselines to the UN under Article 16 of UNCLOS relying on the seaward end of the dyke, and Ukraine had not objected. Further, Ukraine had accepted the use of the seaward end of the dyke for the purposes of determining the provisional equidistance line.[169] Nevertheless, the Court considered whether the dyke qualified under Article 11—specifically, whether base points on it should be used for the purposes of the delimitation.

It was accepted by the parties that the dyke was 'permanent': the Court had to determine whether it was 'harbour works' that formed 'an integral part of the harbour system'.[170] The Court noted that the term 'works' 'denotes a combination of apparatus, structures and facilities installed for a specific purpose'.[171] Noting that these terms were not defined in UNCLOS (or in the Territorial Sea Convention), the Court stated that 'harbour works' 'which form an integral part of the harbour system' are 'generally installations which allow ships to be harboured, maintained or repaired and which permit or facilitate the embarkation and disembarkation of passengers and the loading or unloading of goods'.[172] The Court noted that the functions of a dyke are different from those of a port; the Sulina Dyke 'may be of use in protecting shipping destined for the mouth of the Danube and for the ports situated there'.[173]

As to the length of qualifying harbour works, the Court noted that in its preparatory work for the Territorial Sea Convention, the International Law Commission (ILC) had queried whether structures of excessive length could qualify under Article 8 of the Territorial Sea Convention, without defining precisely the limit beyond which a dyke, jetty, or works could no longer form 'an integral part of the harbour system'.[174] However, the Court declined to decide the matter on the basis of length, concluding that 'irrespective of its length, no convincing evidence has been presented that this dyke serves any direct purpose in port activities'.[175] The Court thus declined to use the seaward end of the Sulina dyke as a base point for the purposes of the construction of a provisional equidistance line for the delimitation,[176] although it used the landward end of the dyke as a base point, since it was a fixed point on the Romanian mainland.[177]

As noted by Symmons, the modern trend of construction of extensive seaward structures is likely to create difficulties in future cases, and the Court's cautious approach in *Maritime Delimitation in the Black Sea* to the problem of excessive length is likely to be picked up by tribunals in the future.[178]

[168] *Maritime Delimitation in the Black Sea* (n 149).
[169] ibid para 125.
[170] In accordance with UNCLOS (n 1) art 11.
[171] *Maritime Delimitation in the Black Sea* (n 149) para 133.
[172] ibid.
[173] ibid para 134. For a different view on the purpose of the dyke see discussion in Chris Carleton, 'Problems Relating to Non-Natural and Man-Made Basepoints under UNCLOS' in Clive R Symmons (ed), *Selected Contemporary Issues in the Law of the Sea* (Martinus Nijhoff 2011) 31–65 (see especially 63). Carleton argues that the dyke performed the function of facilitation of safe navigation of vessels to and from a river port and is therefore part of the port's structure.
[174] *Maritime Delimitation in the Black Sea* (n 149) para 134.
[175] ibid para 138.
[176] ibid.
[177] ibid paras 139–40.
[178] Clive R Symmons 'Article 11' in Alexander Proelss (ed), *United Nations Convention on the Law of the Sea: A Commentary* (CH Beck, Hart, and Nomos 2017) 124, para 14.

F. Publicity and Notification of Baselines

Article 16 of UNCLOS requires coastal States to show the baselines for measuring the breadth of the territorial sea in accordance with Articles 7, 9, or 10 on charts, or on a list of geographical coordinates of points, and to give due publicity to such charts or lists, and to deposit copies with the Secretary-General of the UN. However, notification of baselines or base points under Article 16 is a distinct question from the validity of those baselines or base points, and in particular, notification does not mean that those baselines or base points will automatically have effect in a maritime delimitation.

In *Maritime Delimitation on the Black Sea*, Romania had notified a base point on the dyke, as discussed above, under Article 16 of UNCLOS. The Court distinguished between the determination of base points for the purpose of measuring the breadth of a maritime zone (here, the EEZ and continental shelf), in respect of which 'the coastal State, in conformity with the relevant provisions of UNCLOS ... may determine the relevant basepoints',[179] and the use of base points in maritime delimitation between two States, where 'the Court should not base itself solely on the choice of base points made by one of those Parties'.[180] The fact that the Court ultimately used the landward end of the dyke as a base point for the provisional equidistance line, rather than the base point claimed by Romania and notified to the UN, suggests that mere notification of a base point by the coastal State under Article 16 will not necessarily bind other States, even if those other States did not object to the claim.[181] This finding may be significant for the small island developing States that are endeavouring to set permanent limits for their maritime zones in the face of rising sea-levels.[182]

The question of non-compliance with Article 16 has not been addressed by an UNCLOS tribunal. In *Maritime Delimitation on the Black Sea*, the ICJ affirmed that 'normal baselines, defined as the low-water line along the coast, do not have to be notified to the [UN], as straight baselines have to be'.[183] However, given that the Court found that it could deviate from the base points selected by the parties for their territorial seas,[184] it ultimately felt it unnecessary to deal with the issue of non-compliance with Article 16 directly,[185] an approach that has been criticised by some commentators.[186] Symmons and Reed have argued that the Court's approach suggests that, where a State has failed to comply with the publicity requirements of Article 16, it would appear that third States may be entitled, even in the absence of protest, to ignore claimed baselines until there is compliance with procedural

179 *Maritime Delimitation in the Black Sea* (n 149) para 137.

180 ibid.

181 See Clive R Symmons and Michael W Reed 'Baseline Publicity and Charting Requirements: An Overlooked Issue in the UN Convention on the Law of the Sea' (2010) 41 ODIL 77, 97.

182 See further David Freestone, Davor Vidas, and Alejandra Torrse Camprubi, 'Sea Level Rise and Impacts on Maritime Zone and Limits: The Work of the ILA Committee on International Law and Sea Level Rise' (2017) 5 Korean J Intl L 5; Clive H Schofield, 'Climate Change and Changing Coasts: Geophysical and Jurisdictional Implications of Sea Level Rise for Pacific Island States' (2017) 5 Korean J Intl L 36.

183 *Maritime Delimitation in the Black Sea* (n 149) para 137.

184 ibid paras 135–37.

185 Similarly, in *Bay of Bengal Delimitation*, Myanmar argued that neither State had publicized or submitted charts or coordinates relating to the 'Agreed Minutes', but as the Court found the 'Minutes' not to be binding, it stated that it was unnecessary 'to address the relevance, if any ... of the failure to deposit' such information in accordance with Article 16(2): *Delimitation of the Maritime Boundary in the Bay of Bengal (Bangladesh/Myanmar)* (Judgment) ITLOS Reports 2012, 4, paras 86 and 99 (*Bay of Bengal Delimitation*).

186 See Clive R Symmons, 'Article 16' in Alexander Proelss (ed), *United Nations Convention on the Law of the Sea: A Commentary* (CH Beck, Hart, and Nomos 2017) 174, para 21. See also Symmons and Reed (n 181) 96.

requirements.[187] While this is a tenable consequence that follows from the Court's approach in *Maritime Delimitation on the Black Sea*, it is perhaps equally arguable that the procedural requirements matter less than the question of substantive compliance—ie whether the base point itself is valid and meets the substantive requirements of UNCLOS.

* * *

The use of particular baselines, and the placement of base points on them, has the potential to impact significantly on the seaward limits of a coastal State's maritime spaces, as well as the delimitation of maritime boundaries with its neighbours. A State's unilateral claims to baselines or base points thus has the potential to impact on other States, as well as other stakeholders. Tribunals have had several opportunities to address specific aspects of baselines and corresponding base points and have generally assessed those claims against the criteria set out in UNCLOS; in some cases rejecting unilateral claims and interpreting the provisions of UNCLOS in a way that prevents coastal States from claiming exclusive rights over large portions of maritime space. Tribunals have also been generally reluctant to accept arguments based on State practice where they consider it deviates from the text of the applicable provisions.

IV. Nature and Extent of Maritime Zones

UNCLOS has a detailed set of provisions governing the spatial extent and scope of rights of the coastal State—and other States—in respect of the various maritime zones. Articles 2–32 govern the rights and obligations of States within the territorial sea, which is limited to a breadth of 12 NM. Articles 55–75 govern the rights and obligations of State within the EEZ, up to a breadth of 200 NM. Articles 76–85 address the rights and obligations of States in respect of the continental shelf, which is limited to 200 NM unless the coastal State can establish an entitlement to an extended continental shelf. As the Tribunal observed in *South China Sea*, '[t]he Convention thus provides—and defines limits within—a comprehensive system of maritime zones that is capable of encompassing any area of sea or seabed'.[188] This section examines the judicial assessment of the UNCLOS provisions dealing with the different maritime zones, their designation, and the distribution of rights and duties between States in those maritime zones. The latter aspect is detailed further in later chapters whereas this chapter considers the initial allocation of authority between States with a focus on Articles 2, 56, and 58.

A. Internal Waters

Pursuant to Article 2 of UNCLOS, the coastal State has full sovereignty over its internal waters. The ICJ affirmed this view in *Certain Activities Carried Out by Nicaragua in the Border Area/Construction of a Road*, noting that '[t]he basic legal concept of State sovereignty in

[187] ibid 97–98.
[188] *South China Sea*, Award (n 10) para 231.

customary international law ... extends to the internal waters and territorial sea of every State and to the air space above its territory'.[189] Article 8 of UNCLOS defines the internal waters of the coastal State as follows:

> 1. Except as provided in Part IV, waters on the landward side of the baseline of the territorial sea form part of the internal waters of the State.
> 2. Where the establishment of a straight baseline in accordance with the method set forth in article 7 has the effect of enclosing as internal waters areas which had not previously been considered as such, a right of innocent passage as provided in this Convention shall exist in those waters.[190]

The extent of internal waters, and the application of UNCLOS to them, has not yet been the subject of consideration by any tribunal. In *Coastal State Rights in the Black Sea*, which has not been decided on the merits at the time of writing, there is an extant dispute between the parties as to whether the Sea of Azov and the Kerch Strait are Russia's internal waters.[191] Russia initially objected to jurisdiction on the basis that UNCLOS does not regulate a regime of internal waters, such that a dispute relating to events that occurred in internal waters cannot concern the interpretation or application of UNCLOS.[192] The Tribunal joined that jurisdictional objection to the merits, given its inter-relationship with the merits of the dispute, since the question of whether the Sea of Azov and the Kerch Strait are internal waters requires consideration of how the parties treated them after Ukraine's independence.[193] Moreover, the question of whether the application of UNCLOS to the Sea of Azov and the Kerch Strait was excluded from jurisdiction under Article 298(1)(a) on the basis of historic title also required consideration of matters interwoven with the merits.[194] The Tribunal noted, however, that it was unconvinced by the 'rather sweeping premise' that UNCLOS does not regulate a regime of internal waters,[195] noting that Article 8(2) provides for a right of innocent passage in certain circumstances;[196] that the *SRFC Advisory Opinion* affirmed that the obligation to protect and preserve the marine environment applies to 'all maritime areas';[197] and that the Tribunal in *ARA Libertad* held that some provisions of Part III of the Convention may apply to all maritime areas.[198] It stated that it was not inclined to accept the proposition that a dispute is beyond the scope of UNCLOS because the underlying events occurred in internal waters; rather:

[189] *Certain Activities Carried Out by Nicaragua in the Border Area (Costa Rica v Nicaragua), Construction of a Road in Costa Rica along the San Juan River (Nicaragua v Costa Rica)* (Judgment) [2015] ICJ Rep 665, para 212.

[190] UNCLOS (n 1) art 8.

[191] *Dispute Concerning Coastal State Rights in the Black Sea, Sea of Azov, and Kerch Strait (Ukraine v Russia)* (Preliminary Objections Award of 21 February 2020) PCA Case No 2017-06, para 290 (*Coastal State Rights in the Black Sea*).

[192] ibid para 294.

[193] ibid paras 290–91.

[194] ibid paras 292–93. See further ch 4(IV)(B).

[195] ibid para 294.

[196] ibid.

[197] ibid para 295, citing *Request for Advisory Opinion Submitted by the Sub-Regional Fisheries Commission* (Advisory Opinion) ITLOS Reports 2015, 4 (*SRFC Advisory Opinion*).

[198] *Coastal State Rights in the Black Sea* (n 191) para 295, citing *ARA Libertad (Argentina v Ghana)* (Provisional Measures, Order of 15 December 2012) ITLOS Reports 2012, 332.

> the relevant question for the Arbitral Tribunal appears to be whether a particular issue raised by the Parties' dispute is regulated by the Convention or whether the particular conduct complained of implicates, or raises questions of the interpretation or application of the Convention.[199]

The hearing on the merits in *Coastal State Rights in the Black Sea* was held in October 2021; a decision is currently awaited and will likely address the qualification of waters as internal under Article 8, as well as the extent to which provisions of UNCLOS apply to such waters.[200]

B. Territorial Sea

In *Anglo-Norwegian Fisheries*, the ICJ described the character of the territorial sea 'as appurtenant to land territory'.[201] The territorial sea as a maritime space is principally addressed in three provisions of UNCLOS: Article 2 addresses its legal status; Article 3 addresses its breadth; and Article 4 addresses its outer limit. While disputes may still emerge as to the delimitation of overlapping territorial sea between opposite or adjacent States,[202] the question of the breadth of the territorial sea was resolved with the adoption of UNCLOS.[203] To date, it is the scope of coastal State sovereignty within the territorial sea and the concomitant impact of other States' rights within the territorial sea that has prompted judicial consideration. Concerning the legal status of the territorial sea, Article 2(1) confirms that '[t]he sovereignty of a coastal State extends ... to an adjacent belt of sea, described as the territorial sea'. However, Article 2(3) confirms that the sovereignty of the coastal State in the territorial sea is not unfettered: it 'is exercised subject to this Convention and to other rules of international law'. That provision has been the subject of judicial consideration with firm views expressed as to its meaning and effect.

The scope of the *renvoi* in Article 2(3) has been considered by multiple tribunals and the implications for the scope of jurisdiction available to Part XV tribunals has been discussed in Chapter 4 above.[204] In relation to the substantive obligations emerging in relation to Article 2(3), Mauritius argued in the *Chagos Marine Protected Area* arbitration (*Chagos MPA*)[205] that the United Kingdom's declaration of a marine protected area (MPA) around

[199] ibid para 296.

[200] On the issues to be addressed see Valentin J Schatz and Dmytro Koval, 'Ukraine v Russia: Passage through Kerch Strait and the Sea of Azov—Part I: The Legal Status of Kerch Strait and the Sea of Azov' *Völkerrechtsblog* (10 January 2018) https://voelkerrechtsblog.org/ukraine-v-russia-passage-through-kerch-strait-and-the-sea-of-azov/; Nilüfer Oral, 'Ukraine v. The Russian Federation: Navigating Conflict over Sovereignty under UNCLOS' (2021) 97 ILS 478; and Valentin J. Schatz and Dmyto Koval, 'Russia's Annexation of Crimea and the Passage of Ships Through Kerch Strait: A Law of the Sea Perspective' (2019) 50 ODIL 278.

[201] *Anglo-Norwegian Fisheries* (n 3) 128.

[202] See ch 6(II).

[203] The controversy concerning the breadth of the territorial sea had been critical at the First and Second Law of the Sea Conferences and was relevant to the *Anglo-Norwegian Fisheries* (n 3) and *Fisheries Jurisdiction (United Kingdom v Iceland)* (Jurisdiction) [1973] ICJ Rep 3: see discussion in Kai Trümpler 'Article 3' in Alexander Proelss (ed), *United Nations Convention on the Law of the Sea: A Commentary* (CH Beck, Hart, and Nomos 2017) 34, paras 3–8.

[204] See ch 4(V)(B).

[205] *Chagos Marine Protected Area Arbitration (Mauritius v United Kingdom)* (Award of 18 March 2015) PCA Case No 2011-03 (*Chagos MPA*).

the Chagos Archipelago was incompatible with substantive and procedural obligations under UNCLOS, including international law obligations incorporated into UNCLOS via the *renvoi* in Article 2(3).

As explored in more detail in Chapter 4, the majority in *Chagos MPA* held that 'Article 2(3) contains an obligation on States to exercise their sovereignty subject to "other rules of international law" '.[206] As to the scope of 'other rules of international law', the Tribunal placed significant weight on the ILC's commentary on Article 1(2) of its Draft Articles concerning the Law of the Sea,[207] and concluded that Article 2(3) of UNCLOS required States to exercise their sovereignty in the territorial sea subject to the general rules of international law, and found no indication that the Commission intended to create an obligation of compliance with any bilateral commitment a State may undertake in the territorial sea.[208] The Tribunal thus concluded that the obligation in Article 2(3) 'is limited to exercising sovereignty subject to the general rules of international law'.[209]

In the specific case at hand, Mauritius had argued that Article 2(3) required the United Kingdom to comply with the so-called Lancaster House Undertakings, which recorded conditions on the agreement to detach the Chagos Islands, including that 'if the need for the [US defence] facilities on the islands disappeared the islands should be returned to Mauritius' and that the United Kingdom would ensure that fishing rights would remain available to Mauritius.[210] The Tribunal found that Article 2(3) did not extend to the Lancaster House Undertakings, since they were not general rules of international law, but that pursuant to the general rules of international law, the United Kingdom was required to act in good faith in its relations with Mauritius, including with respect to Undertakings.[211] In applying Article 2(3), the Tribunal reviewed the context by which the MPA was established, and concluded that the United Kingdom did not adequately consult with Mauritius, nor did it balance its own rights and interests with Mauritius' rights arising from the Lancaster House Undertakings.[212] It concluded that the United Kingdom had breached Articles 2(3) and therefore the proclamation of the MPA was incompatible with UNCLOS.[213] On the scope of the obligations encompassed by Article 2(3), Judges Kateka and Wolfrum dissented; they would have found that Article 2(3) directly incorporated bilateral obligations and not only rules of general international law.[214]

The scope of the reference to 'other rules of international law' in Article 2(3) was also at issue in the *South China Sea* arbitration. The Philippines argued that China violated its obligations under Article 2(3) of UNCLOS, by preventing Filipino fishers from fishing in the waters of Scarborough Shoal,[215] in exercise of their traditional fishing rights in the territorial sea.[216] The Philippines also argued that China's conduct was in breach of its

[206] ibid para 514.
[207] International Law Commission, Articles concerning the Law of the Sea with Commentaries [1956] II UNYBILC 265, 265, quoted in ibid para 515 (Articles on LOS).
[208] *Chagos MPA* (n 205) para 516.
[209] ibid.
[210] ibid para 77.
[211] ibid para 517.
[212] ibid paras 534–35.
[213] ibid para 536.
[214] *Chagos MPA* (n 205) (Dissenting and Concurring Opinion of Judges Kateka and Wolfrum) para 84. See further ch 4(V)(B).
[215] *South China Sea*, Award (n 10) paras 771–72.
[216] ibid paras 774–79. See further ch 8(II).

obligations under Article 2(3) (and Article 279) of UNCLOS to settle disputes through peaceful means.[217]

As to the scope of 'other rules of international law', the Tribunal considered that traditional fishing rights constituted a vested right and that 'the rules of international law on the treatment of the vested rights of foreign nationals' fell squarely within the 'other rules of international law' applicable in the territorial sea.[218] It did not comment as to whether these rules constituted rules of 'general international law', nor did it consider whether there was a subsidiary rule of general international law requiring States to comply with such rule in good faith. As explained further in Chapter 4,[219] in this sense, the *South China Sea* Tribunal's approach to Article 2(3) can be seen as more expansive than that of the *Chagos MPA* Tribunal.

In applying that conclusion to the facts, the *South China Sea* Tribunal found that Chinese government vessels had acted to prevent entirely fishing by Filipino fishers at Scarborough Shoal for significant periods of time,[220] and concluded that the complete prevention of such fishing was not compatible with the respect due under international law to the traditional fishing rights of Filipino fishers.[221] Moreover, as noted in Chapter 4, the Tribunal appeared to accept that an obligation to settle disputes by peaceful means was encompassed within the *renvoi* in Article 2(3), but dismissed the Philippines' claim of a breach, noting that both parties found fault with each other in their handling of the issue and both alleged breaches of the UN Charter.[222]

Finally, in *Enrica Lexie*, Italy had argued that the Tribunal had jurisdiction to determine the claim of its marines to immunity from criminal jurisdiction, including on the basis of Article 2(3) of UNCLOS (as well as Articles 56(2) and 58(2)).[223] The Tribunal dismissed these arguments summarily, noting that Articles 2(3), 56(2), and 58(2) apply only to the exercise of rights and duties in the territorial sea and the EEZ, respectively, and that India enforced its jurisdiction over the marines only in its internal waters and on land, when the marines were arrested and detained.[224] It ultimately held that it had jurisdiction to address the question of immunity of the marines as it was an issue 'that necessarily arises as an incidental question in the application of the Convention'.[225] As discussed in Chapter 4, the majority's summary approach to the *renvoi* provisions was criticised by Judge Robinson in his dissenting opinion.[226] He suggested that those provisions 'do not constitute a *renvoi* to customary international law',[227] and could not in any event be used as a basis for ascertaining whether the Tribunal had jurisdiction to assess the immunity claims of the marines.[228]

As noted in Chapter 4, the scope of the reference to 'other rules of international law' in Article 2(3) is unclear in the light of these decisions. The extent to which it covers only

217 *South China Sea*, Award (n 10) para 780.
218 ibid (citation omitted).
219 See ch 4(V)(B).
220 *South China Sea*, Award (n 10) para 810.
221 ibid para 812.
222 ibid para 813.
223 *Enrica Lexie (Italy v India)* (Award of 21 May 2020) PCA Case No 2015-28, paras 796–97 (*Enrica Lexie*, Award).
224 ibid para 798.
225 ibid para 809. See further ch 4(II).
226 *Enrica Lexie*, Award (n 223) (Dissenting Opinion of Judge Robinson) para 31. See also ch 4(V)(B).
227 ibid para 31.
228 ibid.

'general rules' or also extends to any other rules (including potentially all rules of customary international law) is uncertain, and future tribunals may take a different approach to its interpretation in assessing the scope of their jurisdiction. Irrespective of the jurisdictional question for tribunals constituted under UNCLOS, it should be generally understood that coastal States exercise their sovereignty over the territorial sea subject to other applicable rules of international law, irrespective of whether they apply by virtue of UNCLOS or in addition or complementary to the UNCLOS regime.

C. Contiguous Zone

Article 33 of UNCLOS addresses the contiguous zone, as follows:

> 1. In a zone contiguous to its territorial sea, described as the contiguous zone, the coastal State may exercise the control necessary to:
>   (a) prevent infringement of its customs, fiscal, immigration or sanitary laws and regulations within its territory or territorial sea;
>   (b) punish infringement of the above laws and regulations committed within its territory or territorial sea.
> 2. The contiguous zone may not extend beyond 24 nautical miles from the baselines from which the breadth of the territorial sea is measured.[229]

The scope of a coastal State's rights to prevent infringement or punish infringements of its laws and regulations in the contiguous zone has been raised in two cases. In *Saiga (No 2)*,[230] Guinea claimed in the proceedings that the Saiga supplied gas oil in its contiguous zone, but, as noted in the Separate Opinion of Judge Vukas, eventually it based its claim only on alleged rights to enforce customs legislation in its EEZ.[231] In his Separate Opinion, Judge Laing noted that there was 'uncertainty attending Guinea's apparent invocation of the Convention's provisions on the contiguous zone in support of its actions',[232] but nevertheless he considered it necessary to discuss various issues concerning the scope and effect of Article 33, given the underlying facts and issues.[233] Judge Laing addressed three matters:

(a) He considered whether the word 'control' in Article 33(1) encompasses authority to exercise prescriptive and enforcement jurisdiction. Taking account of the context of Article 33(1), including related provisions of UNCLOS, the drafting history, and State practice, he concluded that 'control' conferred broad authority, including 'taking such actions ... as inspections, verifications, instructions and warnings, all

[229] UNCLOS (n 1) art 33.

[230] *M/V Saiga (No 2) (Saint Vincent and the Grenadines v Guinea)* (Judgment) ITLOS Reports 1999, 10 (*Saiga (No 2)*, Judgment).

[231] *Saiga (No 2)*, Judgment (n 230) (Separate Opinion of Judge Vukas) para 3. See also *Saiga (No 2)*, Judgment (n 230) (Separate Opinion of Judge Laing) para 2.

[232] *Saiga (No 2)*, Judgment (n 230) (Separate Opinion of Judge Laing) para 2.

[233] ibid para 8.

with the purpose of subserving laws and restraining their possible violation in territorial areas'.[234]

(b) Judge Laing also affirmed that although 'control' could be taken pursuant to prescription, Article 33 makes clear that coastal States are not authorised to prescribe customs and other types of laws and regulations for conduct occurring inside the contiguous zone: it is only for 'control' in relation to prescription of conduct in the territorial sea that is authorised.[235]

(c) Finally, he considered whether Article 33 authorised Guinea to punish infringements of its laws committed in the contiguous zone and outside of the territorial sea. He answered in the negative, given that the ordinary meaning of Article 33 linked the power of the coastal State in the contiguous zone to conduct that had a relevant connection with the territorial sea.[236]

The question of the scope of a coastal State's authority in the contiguous zone is currently pending before the ICJ in *Alleged Violations of Sovereign Rights and Maritime Spaces in the Caribbean Sea (Nicaragua v Colombia)*. At the time of writing, the hearing has been concluded but the Court's judgment is pending.[237] Colombia has argued that its declaration of a contiguous zone around the Colombian islands comprising the San Andrés Archipelago (which covers areas within Nicaragua's EEZ) is consistent with customary international law,[238] and that its rights over the contiguous zone are not extinguished by Nicaragua's EEZ rights.[239] Nicaragua has argued that Colombia's declaration of a contiguous zone is inconsistent with customary international law, and that its rights in Nicaragua's EEZ, as a third State, are limited to those set out in Article 58 of UNCLOS.[240]

Colombia, which is not a party to UNCLOS, further contended that Article 33 of UNCLOS does not reflect customary international law, and the interests for the protection of which the coastal State may exercise control in the contiguous zone have evolved with the threats posed to coastal States, including in respect of security and protection of the environment.[241] As to the interpretation of Article 33, Colombia argued that it extended to the right to prevent actions taken by ships within the contiguous zone that may infringe Colombia's vital interests, including ships suspected of intending to infringe Colombia's customs, fiscal, immigration or sanitary laws and regulations.[242] Nicaragua's position was that Article 33(1) reflects customary international law,[243] and that Colombia's claimed rights in the contiguous zone are inconsistent with international law.[244]

234 ibid paras 9–13.

235 ibid para 14.

236 ibid para 15.

237 For the most recent phase of proceedings at the time of writing see *Alleged Violations of Sovereign Rights and Maritime Spaces in the Caribbean Sea (Nicaragua v Colombia)* (Preliminary Objections) [2016] ICJ Rep 3.

238 'Rejoinder of the Republic of Colombia', *Alleged Violations of Sovereign Rights and Maritime Spaces in the Caribbean Sea (Nicaragua v Colombia)* (General List No 155, 15 November 2018) paras 1.22–1.26, 4.47–4.105 (Columbia's Rejoinder). Colombia's declared contiguous zone extends beyond 24 NM from its baselines. Nicaragua has argued that its declaration is inconsistent with customary international law: see 'Reply of the Republic of Nicaragua', *Alleged Violations of Sovereign Rights and Maritime Spaces in the Caribbean Sea (Nicaragua v Colombia)* (General List No 155, 15 May 2018) paras 3.1–3.20 (Nicaragua's Reply).

239 Colombia's Rejoinder (n 238) paras 4.17–4.46.

240 Nicaragua's Reply (n 238) paras 3.1–3.25.

241 Colombia's Rejoinder (n 238) paras 4.52–4.105.

242 ibid para 4.74.

243 Nicaragua's Reply (n 238) paras 3.28–3.40.

244 ibid paras 3.41–3.52.

Thus, the Court is likely to have to address directly the customary law status of Article 33(1) of UNCLOS, and the question of the scope of a coastal State's authority therein, including the question of whether it encompasses enforcement powers. Given the increasing discussion of maritime security goals of coastal States, including in respect of irregular migration and the smuggling of illicit goods, it is likely that authority within the contiguous zone will continue to be exercised increasingly by coastal States. As a result, the precise scope of authority that may be exercised in this maritime zone may come under greater scrutiny in the future in efforts to enhance the public order of the oceans.

D. EEZ

The EEZ is an area beyond and adjacent to the territorial sea, extending not more than 200 NM from the baseline of the territorial sea. Its origins have been traced to the practice of Latin American States in the late 1940s, in claiming full sovereignty up to 200 NM from their coasts. Claims for a 200 NM zone were later made by a majority of coastal developing States, but it also became clear that other States were unwilling to accept such an extensive territorial sea. The concept of the EEZ was formally proposed by Kenya to the UN Seabed Committee in 1972, by which the natural resources of the zone would be placed under the jurisdiction of the coastal State, while freedom of navigation was to be guaranteed. The following year, Colombia, Mexico, and Venezuela submitted a similar proposal to the UN Seabed Committee, for the 'patrimonial sea'.[245] During UNCLOS negotiations, the two concepts were merged and the right of coastal States to claim an EEZ was incorporated in Article 55 of UNCLOS, as follows:

> The exclusive economic zone is an area beyond and adjacent to the territorial sea, subject to the specific legal regime established in this Part, under which the rights and jurisdiction of the coastal State and the rights and freedoms of other States are governed by the relevant provisions of this Convention.[246]

Article 57 of UNCLOS provides that the EEZ 'shall not extend beyond 200 nautical miles from the baselines from which the breadth of the territorial sea is measured'.

The vast majority of coastal States have claimed an EEZ. In its 1985 judgment in *Libya/Malta*, the ICJ stated that it 'is incontestable that . . . the institution of the exclusive economic zone, with its rule on entitlement by reason of distance, is shown by the practice of States to have become a part of customary law'.[247]

There are three aspects of the EEZ that have been the subject of consideration by tribunals and are discussed below. First, the co-existence of the EEZ and continental shelf, including where rights to them are held by different States in the same area; secondly, the scope and extent of the sovereign rights and jurisdiction of coastal States over the EEZ; and thirdly, the rights and freedoms of other States in the EEZ, most notably in the context of

[245] See the draft articles on the territorial sea submitted by Colombia, Mexico, and Venezuela (originally issued as UN Doc A/AC.138/SC.II/L.21), reproduced in 'Report of the Committee on the Peaceful Uses of the Sea-Bed and the Ocean Floor Beyond the Limits of National Jurisdiction' vol 3 (1973) UN Doc A/9021, 19.

[246] UNCLOS (n 1) art 55.

[247] *Continental Shelf (Libya/Malta)* (Judgment) [1985] ICJ Rep 13, 33, para 34 (*Libya/Malta*).

reconciling or balancing those against the sovereign rights and jurisdiction of the coastal State. Tribunals have thus had the opportunity to address the question of the balance of the rights between coastal and other States, performing the dual function of resolving a dispute between two States, whilst also contributing to the elaboration of provisions that confer rights on third States. This setting is a clear example of tribunals having to account for (and serving) both the interests of the parties and the international community more broadly, and thereby fulfilling the objectives of the peaceful settlement of disputes, the rule of law, and public order of the oceans.

1. Co-existence of the EEZ and Continental Shelf

The Tribunal in *Barbados v Trinidad and Tobago* made clear that coastal States remain entitled to a continental shelf within their EEZ. It noted:

> In spite of some early doubt about the continuing existence of the concept of the continental shelf within an area appertaining to the coastal state by virtue of its entitlement to an EEZ, it became clear that the latter did not absorb the former and that both coexisted with significant elements in common arising from the fact that within 200 nm from a State's baselines distance is the basis for the entitlement to each of them.[248]

As noted in Chapter 6, the co-existence of a continental shelf and EEZ may mean, in practice, that there is a so-called 'grey area', where one State is entitled to EEZ, and another State is entitled to continental shelf.[249] In *Bay of Bengal Delimitation*, the Tribunal confirmed that:

> [I]n the area beyond Bangladesh's exclusive economic zone that is within the limits of Myanmar's exclusive economic zone, the maritime boundary delimits the Parties' rights with respect to the seabed and subsoil of the continental shelf but does not otherwise limit Myanmar's rights with respect to the exclusive economic zone, notably those with respect to the superjacent waters.[250]

A similar situation resulted from the delimitation in the *Bay of Bengal Arbitration*.[251] In both cases, the Tribunals emphasised the need for cooperation to ensure that each of the States concerned was able to exercise its rights and perform its duties within the 'grey area'. In the *Bay of Bengal Arbitration*, the Tribunal stated:

> The establishment of a maritime area in which the States concerned have shared rights is not unknown under the Convention. The Convention is replete with provisions that recognize to a greater or lesser degree the rights of one State within the maritime zones of another. Within the provisions of the Convention relating to the exclusive economic zone and continental shelf, articles 56, 58, 78, and 79 all call for States to exercise their rights and perform their duties with due regard to the rights and duties of other States. It is for the Parties to determine the measures they consider appropriate in this respect, including

[248] *Barbados v Trinidad and Tobago* (n 158) para 226, citing *Libya/Malta* (n 247) 13. See also *Barbados v Trinidad and Tobago* (n 158) paras 234, 296.
[249] See ch 6(V).
[250] *Bay of Bengal Delimitation* (n 185) para 474.
[251] *Bay of Bengal Arbitration* (n 140) paras 498–508.

> through the conclusion of further agreements or the creation of a cooperative arrangement. The Tribunal is confident that the Parties will act, both jointly and individually, to ensure that each is able to exercise its rights and perform its duties within this area.[252]

The difficulties that may arise from a tribunal's delimitation that creates a 'grey area' are discussed in more detail in Chapter 6: as explained there, the 'grey area' may be an unfortunate but necessary consequence of the need to reach an equitable solution, which is paramount under the provisions of UNCLOS on delimitation. If requested by parties to a dispute, there would be scope for a tribunal to pronounce upon the rights and duties of States in such a 'grey area', including the rights and duties of third States. So far, no such request has been made.

2. Sovereign Rights and Jurisdiction of Coastal States over the EEZ

The sovereign rights of the coastal State over the EEZ are essentially limited to economic exploration and exploitation, which is made clear in the key provision governing coastal State jurisdiction over the EEZ. Article 56(1) provides:

> 1. In the exclusive economic zone, the coastal State has:
>   (a) sovereign rights for the purpose of exploring and exploiting, conserving and managing the natural resources, whether living or non-living, of the waters superjacent to the seabed and of the seabed and its subsoil, and with regard to other activities for the economic exploitation and exploration of the zone, such as the production of energy from the water, currents and winds;
>   (b) jurisdiction as provided for in the relevant provisions of this Convention with regard to:
>   (i) the establishment and use of artificial islands, installations and structures;
>   (ii) marine scientific research;
>   (iii) the protection and preservation of the marine environment;
>   (c) other rights and duties provided for in this Convention.[253]

Article 73(1) of UNCLOS confirms that a coastal State exercises both legislative and enforcement jurisdiction in the EEZ over living marine resources. It states:

> The coastal State may, in the exercise of its sovereign rights to explore, exploit, conserve and manage the living resources in the exclusive economic zone, take such measures, including boarding, inspection, arrest and judicial proceedings, as may be necessary to ensure compliance with the laws and regulations adopted by it in conformity with this Convention.[254]

Aspects of coastal States' rights and jurisdiction in the EEZ are elaborated in other provisions of UNCLOS. With respect to coastal State jurisdiction over artificial islands, Article 60 provides (in relevant part):

[252] ibid paras 507–508. See also *Bay of Bengal Delimitation* (n 185) paras 471–72.
[253] UNCLOS (n 1) art 56(1).
[254] ibid art 73(1).

1. In the exclusive economic zone, the coastal State shall have the exclusive right to construct and to authorize and regulate the construction, operation and use of:
   (a) artificial islands;
   (b) installations and structures for the purposes provided for in article 56 and other economic purposes;
   (c) installations and structures which may interfere with the exercise of the rights of the coastal State in the zone.
2. The coastal State shall have exclusive jurisdiction over such artificial islands, installations and structures, including jurisdiction with regard to customs, fiscal, health, safety and immigration laws and regulations.[255]

Article 61 of UNCLOS addresses the coastal State obligations in relation to conservation and management of the living resources in the EEZ. Article 62 further provides that coastal States shall promote optimum utilisation of the living resources of the EEZ, and sets out an indicative list of conservation measures and other terms and conditions that a coastal State may impose on fishing in the EEZ.

In *Virginia G*, the Tribunal addressed the scope of a coastal State's 'sovereign rights' under Article 56(1) of UNCLOS, in the context of the question of whether Guinea-Bissau was entitled to regulate bunkering of fishing vessels in its EEZ.[256] The Tribunal confirmed that the coastal State's sovereign rights 'encompasses all rights *necessary for and connected with* the exploration, exploitation, conservation, and management of the natural resources, including the right to take the necessary enforcement measures.'[257] A narrow interpretation limited to the explicit terms listed in Article 56(1) was thus avoided. The Tribunal noted that the rights of coastal States 'go beyond conservation in its strict sense', as confirmed by the fact that Article 61 of UNCLOS addresses the issue of conservation, whereas Article 62 addresses both conservation and management.[258] Referring to Articles 56(1) and 62(4), the Tribunal confirmed that the coastal State is entitled to adopt laws and regulations establishing the terms and conditions for access by foreign fishing vessels to its EEZ,[259] and that the list of matters in Articles 62(4), which the laws and regulations may relate to, is a non-exhaustive list.[260] The Tribunal further noted that for all activities that may be regulated by a coastal State 'there must be a direct connection to fishing', and such connection exists for bunkering of foreign fishing vessels in the EEZ 'since this enables them to continue their activities without interruption at sea'.[261] In reaching its conclusion, the Tribunal was guided by the definitions of 'fishing' and 'fishing-related' activities in several other agreements, including the Agreement on Port State Measures to Prevent, Deter and Eliminate Illegal, Unreported and Unregulated Fishing;[262] the Convention on the Determination of the Minimum Conditions for Access and Exploitation of Marine Resources within the

[255] ibid art 60.
[256] *Virginia G (Panama/Guinea-Bissau)* (Judgment) ITLOS Reports 2014, 4 (*Virginia G*).
[257] ibid para 211 (emphasis added).
[258] ibid para 212.
[259] ibid para 213.
[260] ibid.
[261] ibid para 215.
[262] Agreement on Port State Measures to Prevent, Deter and Eliminate Illegal, Unreported and Unregulated Fishing (adopted 22 November 2009, entered into force 5 June 2016) [2016] ATS 21

Maritime Areas under Jurisdiction of the Member States of the Sub-Regional Fisheries Commission,[263] and several other conventions relating to conservation of fish stocks and fishery resources.[264] It also noted that its conclusion was consistent with State practice that had developed after the adoption of UNCLOS,[265] including the national legislation of coastal States that provided for regulation of bunkering of foreign fishing vessels and with which there was general compliance.[266]

As discussed further in Chapter 8, the Tribunal went on to consider the scope of the competence of coastal States to regulate bunkering of fishing vessels in the EEZ, taking account of the freedom of navigation and other internationally lawful uses of the sea under Article 58 of UNCLOS.[267] It considered that Article 58 does not prevent coastal States from regulating bunkering of foreign fishing vessels in the EEZ under Article 56.[268] It emphasised that the coastal State does not have such competence with regard to other bunkering activities, unless otherwise determined under other provisions of the Convention.[269]

ITLOS reiterated its conclusion in *Virginia G* with respect to activities that may be regulated by the coastal State in its EEZ in *SRFC Advisory Opinion*,[270] emphasising in particular that for all activities regulated under Article 62(4) of UNCLOS, there must be a direct connection to fishing.[271] Further, taking account of the special rights and responsibilities of the coastal State with respect to conservation and management of natural resources in the EEZ, the Tribunal concluded that 'the primary responsibility for taking the necessary measures to prevent, deter and eliminate IUU fishing rests with the coastal State'.[272]

Concerning coastal State jurisdiction in the EEZ, in *Saiga (No 2)*, the Tribunal considered whether Article 60(2) might be invoked to justify Guinea's application of its customs laws in its EEZ to a foreign vessel engaged in bunkering of fishing vessels. Noting that Article 60(2) addressed only a coastal State's jurisdiction with respect to customs laws and regulations over artificial islands, installations, and structures in the EEZ, the Tribunal held that UNCLOS does not empower a coastal State to apply its customs laws in respect of any other parts of the EEZ.[273] It ultimately concluded that, by applying its customs laws to areas including parts of its EEZ, Guinea acted in a manner contrary to UNCLOS.[274]

In *South China Sea*, the Tribunal confirmed that the coastal State has exclusive decision-making and regulatory power over the construction and operation of artificial islands, and of installations and structures covered by Article 60(1), in its EEZ.[275] As the Tribunal found that Mischief Reef was within the EEZ of the Philippines,[276] it followed that any

[263] Convention on the Determination of the Minimum Conditions for Access and Exploitation of Marine Resources within the Maritime Areas under Jurisdiction of the Member States of the Sub-Regional Fisheries Commission (adopted 8 June 2012, entered into force 16 September 2012).
[264] *Virginia G* (n 256) paras 216, 219.
[265] ibid para 217.
[266] ibid para 218.
[267] ibid para 220.
[268] ibid para 222.
[269] ibid para 223.
[270] *SRFC Advisory Opinion* (n 197) paras 98–100.
[271] ibid para 100.
[272] ibid para 106. See also paras 101–105.
[273] *Saiga (No 2)*, Judgment (n 230) para 127.
[274] ibid para 136. For further discussion see David Anderson, 'Coastal State Jurisdiction and High Seas Freedoms in the EEZ in the Light of the Saiga Case' in Clive R Symmons (ed), *Selected Contemporary Issues in the Law of the Sea* (2011) 105–15.
[275] *South China Sea*, Award (n 10) para 1035. See also paras 1031–33.
[276] ibid para 1031.

construction or authorisation of such structures by China was in violation of its obligations under UNCLOS.[277]

These cases on the scope of coastal State authority within the EEZ reflect an important balance that must be struck in judicial decision-making. On the one hand, where the coastal State has exclusive jurisdiction or sovereign rights, there is an opportunity to allow that authority to be exercised consistent with the overarching grant of power in Article 56(1). This perspective is manifest in the *Virginia G* decision in recognising rights 'necessary for and connected with' those listed in Article 56(1) and in the recognition of the Philippines' authority under Article 60(1) in *South China Sea*. On the other hand, tribunals were not willing to condone the application of laws that were not 'necessary for and connected with' coastal State rights but appeared to extend coastal State authority from the contiguous zone. The application of Guinea's customs laws thus could not stand in *Saiga (No 2)*, although in light of *Virginia G*, it would seem that Guinea may be able to achieve a similar end if the relevant laws are cast in a frame of fisheries regulations and enforcement rather than as a customs matter. Chapter 8 further explores how judges are striking this balance between the rights of coastal States and other States in the EEZ in the context of fisheries.

3. Rights and Freedoms of Other States in the EEZ

Article 56(2) imposes an obligation on the coastal State to have due regard to the rights and duties of other States. It provides:

> In exercising its rights and performing its duties under this Convention in the exclusive economic zone, the coastal State shall have due regard to the rights and duties of other States and shall act in a manner compatible with the provisions of this Convention.[278]

The rights and duties of other States in the EEZ are set out in Article 58. They are limited to freedoms of navigation and overflight, the laying of submarine cables and pipelines, and other internationally lawful uses of the sea related to those freedoms. Article 58 provides:

> 1. In the exclusive economic zone, all States, whether coastal or land-locked, enjoy, subject to the relevant provisions of this Convention, the freedoms referred to in article 87 of navigation and overflight and of the laying of submarine cables and pipelines, and other internationally lawful uses of the sea related to these freedoms, such as those associated with the operation of ships, aircraft and submarine cables and pipelines, and compatible with the other provisions of this Convention.
> 2. Articles 88 to 115 and other pertinent rules of international law apply to the exclusive economic zone in so far as they are not incompatible with this Part.
> 3. In exercising their rights and performing their duties under this Convention in the exclusive economic zone, States shall have due regard to the rights and duties of the coastal State and shall comply with the laws and regulations adopted by the coastal State in accordance with the provisions of this Convention and other rules of international law in so far as they are not incompatible with this Part.[279]

[277] ibid paras 1036–38.
[278] UNCLOS (n 1) art 56(2).
[279] ibid art 58.

Additionally, in respect of fishing, Article 62(3) provides that, in giving access to other States to its EEZ, the coastal State shall take into account, inter alia, 'the need to minimise economic dislocation in States whose nationals have habitually fished in the zone or which have made substantial efforts in research and identification of stocks'. Under Article 62(2), such access applies only where the coastal State does not have the capacity to harvest the entire allowable catch, and under Article 62(4), any fishing by nationals of other States is subject to the laws and regulations of the coastal State. The scope of the rights and freedoms of other States in the EEZ under Articles 56(2), 58, and/or 62 have been directly considered by four tribunals.

In *Chagos MPA*, the Tribunal considered the meaning of Article 56(2), confirming that it imposed an obligation on the coastal State. The dispute between the United Kingdom and Mauritius concerned what was meant by 'due regard', and the extent to which it implied an obligation to consult, or an obligation of non-impairment.[280] The Tribunal held that Article 56(2) did not lay down a specific rule of universal application; instead, the scope of the obligation of 'due regard' depended on the nature of the rights of the non-coastal State, the nature and importance of the activities contemplated by the coastal State, and the availability of alternative approaches. It stated:

> In the Tribunal's view, the ordinary meaning of 'due regard' calls for the United Kingdom to have such regard for the rights of Mauritius as is called for by the circumstances and by the nature of those rights. The Tribunal declines to find in this formulation any universal rule of conduct. The Convention does not impose a uniform obligation to avoid any impairment of Mauritius' rights; nor does it uniformly permit the United Kingdom to proceed as it wishes, merely noting such rights. Rather, the extent of the regard required by the Convention will depend upon the nature of the rights held by Mauritius, their importance, the extent of the anticipated impairment, the nature and importance of the activities contemplated by the United Kingdom, and the availability of alternative approaches. In the majority of cases, this assessment will necessarily involve at least some consultation with the rights-holding State.[281]

Mauritius argued that the United Kingdom's unilateral establishment of the MPA around the Chagos Archipelago breached its obligation of due regard under Article 56(2). The Tribunal addressed this argument together with the claim for breach of Article 2(3) in respect of the territorial sea, discussed above. It considered that the obligations under Article 2(3) to exercise good faith with respect to Mauritius' rights in the territorial sea, and under Article 56(2) to have 'due regard' to Mauritius' rights in the EEZ, were 'for all intents and purposes, equivalent'.[282]

The Tribunal considered that the obligation to have 'due regard' to Mauritius' rights and interests arising out of the Lancaster House Undertakings 'entails, at least, both consultation and a balancing exercise with its own rights and interests'.[283] It did not accept that the United Kingdom had fulfilled the basic purpose of consulting, given the lack of information

280 *Chagos MPA* (n 205) para 518.
281 ibid para 519.
282 ibid para 520.
283 ibid para 534.

actually provided to Mauritius and the absence of a reasoned exchange between the two States.[284] It also held that the United Kingdom failed properly to balance its own rights and interests with Mauritius' rights.[285] It therefore concluded that the United Kingdom had breached Article 56(2) (as well as Article 2(3)) and that the declaration of the MPA was incompatible with UNCLOS.[286]

In *Arctic Sunrise*, the Netherlands argued that Russia's conduct in boarding, seizing, and detaining the vessel and crew engaged in protest at and around the Prirazlomnaya, a Russian offshore oil production platform in its EEZ, was in breach of inter alia, the obligation of due regard under Article 56(2).[287] The Tribunal emphasised the obligation of due regard,[288] and proceeded to consider the law enforcement measures and other bases of authority that may have been available to Russia under UNCLOS.[289] So far as concerns the balance between coastal State rights and the rights of other States, the Tribunal noted that 'the protection of a coastal State's sovereign rights is a legitimate aim that allows it to take appropriate measures for that purpose. Such measures must fulfil the tests of reasonableness, necessity, and proportionality'.[290] However, it also noted that 'the coastal State should tolerate some level of nuisance through civilian protest', and '[d]ue regard must be given to the rights of other States, including the right to allow vessels flying their flag to protest'.[291] The Tribunal concluded that the conduct of the Arctic Sunrise did not interfere with Russia's rights as a coastal State,[292] and ultimately found that Russia had breached its obligation under Article 56(2).[293]

In *SRFC Advisory Opinion*, the Tribunal noted the specific obligations of flag States in the EEZ of the coastal State under Article 58(3), and the stipulation in Article 62(4) that nationals of other States fishing in the EEZ shall comply with conservation measures and other terms and conditions established in the laws and regulations of the coastal State.[294] As discussed further in Chapter 8, the Tribunal considered that Article 62(4) imposes an obligation on States to ensure that their nationals engaged in fishing in the EEZ of other States comply with the conservation measures and other applicable terms and conditions.[295] It followed in the Tribunal's view that flag States 'are obliged to take the necessary measures to ensure that their nationals and vessels flying their flag are not engaged in IUU fishing activities'.[296]

In *South China Sea*, the Tribunal considered whether China could rely on 'historic rights' in the EEZ of the Philippines.[297] Referring to Articles 56, 58, and 62 of UNCLOS, the Tribunal noted that the Convention is clear in according sovereign rights to living and non-living resources in the EEZ to the coastal State.[298] This interpretation was, in the

[284] ibid.
[285] ibid para 535.
[286] ibid para 536.
[287] *Arctic Sunrise (Netherlands v Russia)* (Award on the Merits of 14 August 2015) PCA Case No 2014-02, para 140 (*Arctic Sunrise*, Merits).
[288] ibid para 230.
[289] ibid paras 234–35.
[290] ibid para 326.
[291] ibid para 328.
[292] ibid para 330.
[293] ibid para 333.
[294] *SRFC Advisory Opinion* (n 191) paras 121–22.
[295] ibid para 123.
[296] ibid para 124.
[297] Historic fishing rights in the EEZ are addressed in ch 8(II).
[298] *South China Sea*, Award (n 10) para 243. See also paras 240–42.

Tribunal's view, generally incompatible with another State having historic rights to the same resources, and it was also incompatible with the express inclusion of an article setting out the rights of other States (Article 58) and with attention given to the rights of other States in the allocation of any excess catch in the EEZ (Article 62).[299] The Tribunal further noted that the system of maritime zones created by UNCLOS was intended to be comprehensive and to cover any area of sea or seabed.[300] Thus, so far as China claimed that its historic rights to living and non-living resources in the EEZ were protected by UNCLOS, the Tribunal rejected that claim. It stated:

> The Convention does not include any express provisions preserving or protecting historic rights that are at variance with the Convention. On the contrary, the Convention supersedes earlier rights and agreements to the extent of any incompatibility. The Convention is comprehensive in setting out the nature of the exclusive economic zone and continental shelf and the rights of other States within those zones. China's claim to historic rights is not compatible with these provisions.[301]

The Tribunal concluded that the text and the context of UNCLOS were clear in superseding any historic rights that a State may have in another State's EEZ (and continental shelf), and there was thus no need to have recourse to supplementary means of interpretation under Article 32 of the VCLT.[302] Nevertheless, the Tribunal did recount the negotiation of the EEZ provisions of UNCLOS,[303] noting that in the debates China was resolutely opposed to any suggestion that coastal States could be obliged to share the resources of the EEZ with other States that had historically fished in those waters.[304] China's position was 'largely representative of the position that prevailed in the final text of the Convention'.[305] The Tribunal also placed emphasis on the prohibition on reservations in Article 309 of UNCLOS as confirming the intention of the contracting States to find a consensus text,[306] which would have been entirely inconsistent with allowing the Convention to 'be subordinate to broad claims of historic rights'.[307] The Tribunal thus concluded that China's claim to historic rights to the living and non-living resources within the so-called 'nine dash line' (which incorporated parts of the Philippines' EEZ) was incompatible with UNCLOS,[308] and any such historic rights were superseded by the limits of the maritime zones provided for by UNCLOS.[309]

The Tribunal then addressed several specific claims of breach to the Philippines' sovereign rights in its EEZ, which are addressed further in Chapter 8. It confirmed that Article 56 allocated to the coastal State specific sovereign rights, and that the rights of other States under Article 58 were limited and did not include 'restricting a coastal State from exploiting the living resources of its own [EEZ]'.[310] In respect of fishing by Chinese vessels in

299 ibid para 243.
300 ibid para 245.
301 ibid para 246.
302 ibid para 247.
303 ibid paras 248–54.
304 ibid para 251.
305 ibid para 252.
306 ibid paras 253–54.
307 ibid para 254.
308 ibid para 261.
309 ibid para 262.
310 ibid para 700.

the Philippines' EEZ, the Tribunal noted that, under Articles 61 and 62 of UNCLOS, the Philippines controlled the process of granting and regulating access to the fisheries of its EEZ, subject to the provisions of the Convention.[311] Article 62(4) imposes an obligation on nationals of other States to comply with the laws and regulations of the coastal State, setting out an illustrative list of the areas that may be regulated.[312] Thus, Article 62(4) expressly required Chinese vessels to comply with the licensing and other access procedures of the Philippines within any area forming part of its EEZ.[313] The Tribunal noted that this obligation was directly imposed on private parties engaged in fishing in the Philippines' EEZ,[314] and that UNCLOS also imposes obligations on States parties, under Article 58(3) of UNCLOS, to have 'due regard to the rights and duties' of the coastal State in the EEZ.[315] Referring to *Chagos MPA*[316] and to the *SRFC Advisory Opinion*,[317] the Tribunal concluded that 'anything less than due diligence by a State in preventing its nationals from unlawfully fishing in the [EEZ] of another would fall short of the regard due pursuant to Article 58(3) of the Convention'.[318]

The Tribunal's treatment of historic rights in this context has been both applauded and criticised by commentators. Joseph Klein argued that the Tribunal had no general authority to 'retrospectively extinguish historical rights' that existed before UNCLOS, on the basis that there is nothing in the text of UNCLOS that would 'reverse the presumption of non-retroactivity [of treaties]'.[319] Pemmaraju similarly suggested that the Tribunal appeared 'to give the provisions of UNCLOS hierarchically a status higher than the general or customary law', and proposed that disputes over historic rights remain governed by general international law.[320] On the other hand, Symmons welcomed the Tribunal's treatment of historic rights in this context, agreeing with the Tribunal that Article 62(3) had an exclusionary effect on any pre-existing claimed historic rights, and noting that 'this provision is the death knell of any continuing exercise of any meaningful claimed historic rights in a post-UNCLOS setting in an EEZ by a third State'.[321] He placed particular emphasis on the Tribunal's reasoning relying on the fact that UNCLOS provides a comprehensive system of maritime zones, confirming that the clear aim was to eliminate all historically claimed rights in what is now another State's EEZ.[322] Similarly, Lee and Bautista have suggested that this part of the Tribunal's award is a significant contribution to the development of the law in this area, particularly in clearly stating that 'historic rights claims that are incompatible or inconsistent with the rights provided for under UNCLOS are basically nullified once a state

[311] ibid paras 736–38.
[312] ibid para 739.
[313] ibid para 740.
[314] ibid.
[315] ibid paras 741–42.
[316] ibid para 742.
[317] ibid para 743.
[318] ibid para 744.
[319] See Joseph Klein, 'South China Sea: UN Law of the Sea Arbitral Tribunal Sinks the Rule of Law' *Foreign Policy Journal* (20 August 2016) https://www.foreignpolicyjournal.com/2016/08/20/south-china-sea-un-law-of-the-sea-arbitration-tribunal-sinks-the-rule-of-law/.
[320] Sreeniva Rao Pemmaraju, 'The South China Sea Arbitration (the Philippines v. China Case): Assessment of the Award on Jurisdiction and Admissibility' (2016) 15(2) Chinese JIL 265, 293.
[321] Clive R Symmons, 'Historic Rights in the Light of the Award in the South China Sea Arbitration: What Remains of the Doctrine Now?' in S Jayakumar and others (eds), *The South China Sea Arbitration: The Legal Dimension* (Edward Elgar Publishing 2018) 101, 122. See also ibid 118–21.
[322] ibid 122.

has acceded to or ratified the Convention'.[323] It follows that historic rights will not deprive another State of what has been lawfully allocated to it by the Convention.[324] They have suggested that the careful treatment of this issue by the Tribunal means that its conclusion is likely to carry substantial precedential weight in future cases.[325]

In *Enrica Lexie*, India argued that Italy had breached its rights under Articles 56 and 58 of UNCLOS by interfering with the ability of its fishing vessel, the St Antony, to fish within India's EEZ.[326] Italy argued that the marines on board the *M/V Enrica Lexie* had not acted to impede India's rights in its EEZ, but rather on the basis of the apprehension of a threat of the risk of collision and of pirate boarding.[327] The Tribunal accepted on the basis of the evidence that the marines and the *M/V Enrica Lexie* crew believed that the vessel was under a pirate attack and took actions to protect the vessel against that perceived attack.[328] So far as concerned Article 56, the Tribunal considered that the actions of the marines were not directed at undermining or interfering with India's sovereign rights, and that it was a single and isolated incident that did not rise to the level of interference with India's sovereign rights in the EEZ.[329] In their Joint Dissenting Opinion, Dr Rao and Judge Robinson would have determined that a 'singular and isolated incident' can still be a violation of Article 56 rather than requiring a pattern of behaviour or a 'numerical threshold'.[330] These judges instead considered that necessarily the killing of two Indian fishers while they were exploiting the natural resources of the EEZ was a clear interference with India's sovereign right to exploit those resources.[331]

In respect of Article 58, India argued that the term 'due regard' implied that 'if another State's activity clashes with the coastal State's competence in respect of economic utilization of the zone, the determination must be in favour of the coastal State'.[332] Italy argued that the content of the 'due regard' obligation depended on the circumstances, and contended that in the context of the apprehension of the risk by the marines, there was no breach by Italy of its obligation to have due regard to India's rights.[333] The Tribunal noted that 'due regard' is not defined in UNCLOS, but its ordinary meaning is 'with the proper care or concern for', and as a matter of ordinary meaning, it did not contemplate priority for one activity over another.[334] It noted that the absence of hierarchy was reflected in the complementarity of Articles 56(2) and 58(3):[335] these provisions reflect a need to ensure balance between concurrent rights belonging to coastal and other States.[336] Referring to the definition of 'due regard' in Article 56(2) of *Chagos MPA*,[337] the Tribunal considered that the same notion also applied to Article 58(3),[338] such that the extent of 'due regard' required was

[323] Seokwoo Lee and Lowell Bautista, 'Historic Rights' in Øystein Jensen (ed), *The Development of the Law of the Sea Convention: The Role of International Courts and Tribunals* (Edward Elgar Publishing 2020) 260.
[324] ibid.
[325] ibid 261.
[326] *South China Sea*, Award (n 10) paras 947–48.
[327] ibid para 494.
[328] *Enrica Lexie*, Award (n 223) paras 947–52.
[329] *South China Sea*, Award (n 10) para 953.
[330] *Enrica Lexie*, Award (n 223) (Joint Dissenting Opinion of Dr Rao and Judge Robinson) para 11.
[331] ibid.
[332] *Enrica Lexie*, Award (n 223) para 971.
[333] ibid para 972.
[334] ibid para 973.
[335] ibid para 974.
[336] ibid para 975.
[337] ibid para 976.
[338] ibid para 977.

dependent, inter alia, on the nature of the rights enjoyed by a State.[339] Noting that Article 58(2) of UNCLOS extends the application of Articles 88–115 to the EEZ, including the specific rights and duties of States as regards suppression of piracy,[340] the Tribunal noted that if protection from and repression of piracy was both a right and a duty of Italy and India, including within India's EEZ, the conduct of the marines in responding to a perceived piracy threat could not have unreasonably interfered with, and failed to show 'due regard' to, India's rights as a coastal State.[341] Thus, the Tribunal concluded that the actions of the marines did not result in a breach of Italy's obligation of 'due regard' for the sovereign rights of India and did not breach Article 58(3) of UNCLOS.[342]

It has been noted that these tribunals, when interpreting Articles 56(2) and 58(3), have generally not adopted a strict application of the ordinary rules for treaty interpretation codified in the VCLT. Churchill has described the Tribunal's interpretive approach to the meaning of 'due regard' under Article 56(2) in *Chagos Marine Protected Area* as 'remarkable' in light of the 'open-textured nature of Article 56(2)'.[343] He noted that, after setting out 'what it calls 'the ordinary meaning' of the provision', the Tribunal 'cites no authority for its view and makes no reference, explicit or otherwise, to received canons of interpretation'.[344] Churchill commented further that, while the *South China Sea* Tribunal adopted a more rigorous application of Articles 31 and 32 of the VCLT in relation to China's claim to historic rights, it was content merely to follow the interpretation of 'due regard' set out in *Chagos MPA* when interpreting Article 58(3).[345] However, not all commentators have been critical of the approach of tribunals to this question. Chircop has approved of what he describes as the 'mixed teleological and functionalist' approach to the interpretation of Article 58(3) alongside Article 62(4), which was adopted by ITLOS in the *SRFC Advisory Opinion*.[346] He argued that the absence of any reference to the *travaux préparatoires* reflects a forward-looking methodology, and that the interpretations reached by ITLOS 'make sense in the result achieved, even where the text of those provisions falls short'.[347]

More generally, Proelss has argued that the case-by-case analysis put forward by the *Chagos MPA* Tribunal does not give sufficient guidance to States as to how they may lawfully conduct the balancing exercise required of them under Articles 56(2) and 58(3), particularly for coastal States carrying out marine spatial planning. Accordingly, in the interests of legal certainty and in order properly to take into account the *sui generis* legal status of the EEZ, he has argued in favour of a rebuttable presumption in favour of the coastal State in the event of a conflict concerning coastal and flag States' respective due regard obligations.[348]

339 ibid para 978.
340 ibid para 979.
341 ibid para 980.
342 ibid para 981.
343 Robin Churchill, 'Revealing a Mosaic: International Jurisprudence Concerning the Non-fisheries Elements of the Exclusive Economic Zone Regime' in Øystein Jensen (ed), *The Development of the Law of the Sea Convention: The Role of International Courts and Tribunals* (Edward Elgar Publishing 2020) 69.
344 ibid.
345 ibid 70–71.
346 Aldo Chircop, 'Obligations of Flag States in the Exclusive Economic Zone' in Øystein Jensen (ed), *The Development of the Law of the Sea Convention: The Role of International Courts and Tribunals* (Edward Elgar Publishing 2020) 160.
347 ibid 161.
348 Alexander Proelss, 'Article 56' in Alexander Proelss (ed), *United Nations Convention on the Law of the Sea: A Commentary* (CH Beck, Hart, and Nomos 2017) 432–34, paras 26–31. See also Alexander Proelss, 'The Law on the Exclusive Economic Zone in Perspective: Legal Status and Resolution of User Conflicts Revisited' (2012) 26(1) Ocean YB 87.

Gaunce, on the other hand, and after conducting a thorough application of Articles 31 and 32 of the VCLT (including a detailed review of the *travaux préparatoires*), has concluded that the approach of the Tribunals in *Chagos MPA*, *Arctic Sunrise*, and *South China Sea* correctly reflects a relationship of legal equality amongst coastal and flag States in the EEZ, similar to that in the high seas.[349]

Given the balancing exercise involved, and taking account of the fact that the obligation of 'due regard' necessitates a relative assessment, it is difficult to see how tribunals could approach the question of balance other than on a case-by-case basis. The tribunals that have so far grappled with these issues have, on the whole, engaged in a reasoned approach to the balancing of rights of coastal States and other States, and have generally been reluctant to accord broad rights to coastal States at the cost of the interests of other States, and the international community as a whole.

E. Continental Shelf

The continental shelf is defined in Article 76(1), which sets out two alternative criteria for the outer limit of the continental shelf: a distance of 200 NM (distance criterion) or the limit of the outer edge of the continental margin (geological criterion). It provides:

> 1. The continental shelf of a coastal State comprises the seabed and subsoil of the submarine areas that extend beyond its territorial sea throughout the natural prolongation of its land territory to the outer edge of the continental margin, or to a distance of 200 nautical miles from the baselines from which the breadth of the territorial sea is measured where the outer edge of the continental margin does not extend up to that distance.[350]

The continental margin is defined in Article 76(3) as follows:

> 3. The continental margin comprises the submerged prolongation of the land mass of the coastal State, and consists of the seabed and subsoil of the shelf, the slope and the rise. It does not include the deep ocean floor with its oceanic ridges or the subsoil thereof.[351]

So far as concerns the continental shelf beyond 200 NM, Article 76(4) sets out two criteria for fixing the seaward limit: the first is the sedimentary thickness test; the second is the fixed distance test, a line delineated by reference to fixed points not more than 60 NM from the foot of the continental slope. Given the technical and scientific issues involved in establishing the outer limits of the continental shelf, UNCLOS established and allocated competence on these matters to the Commission on the Limits of the Continental Shelf (CLCS). Under Article 76(8) and Annex II of UNCLOS, the coastal State is required to submit information on continental shelf limits to the CLCS, and the CLCS makes recommendations to the

[349] Julia Gaunce, 'On the Interpretation of the General Duty of "Due Regard"' (2018) 32(1) Ocean YB 27. See also Rolf Einar Fife, 'Obligations of "Due Regard" in the Exclusive Economic Zone: Their Context, Purpose and State Practice' (2019) 34 IJMCL 43.

[350] UNCLOS (n 1) art 76(1).

[351] ibid art 76(3).

coastal State on those limits. The limits of the shelf established by the coastal State on the basis of the CLCS' recommendations are said to be 'final and binding'.[352]

The rights of the coastal State over the continental shelf are set out in Article 77, as follows:

1. The coastal State exercises over the continental shelf sovereign rights for the purpose of exploring it and exploiting its natural resources.
2. The rights referred to in paragraph 1 are exclusive in the sense that if the coastal State does not explore the continental shelf or exploit its natural resources, no one may undertake these activities without the express consent of the coastal State.
3. The rights of the coastal State over the continental shelf do not depend on occupation, effective or notional, or on any express proclamation.
4. The natural resources referred to in this Part consist of the mineral and other non-living resources of the seabed and subsoil together with living organisms belonging to sedentary species, that is to say, organisms which, at the harvestable stage, either are immobile on or under the seabed or are unable to move except in constant physical contact with the seabed or the subsoil.[353]

In addition to the rights set out in Article 77, the coastal State has jurisdiction over the shelf with regard to artificial islands,[354] marine scientific research,[355] dumping,[356] and drilling.[357]

Article 78(1) clarifies that the rights of the coastal State over the continental shelf 'do not affect the legal status of the superjacent waters or the airspace above those waters'. It follows that where a coastal State has not claimed an EEZ to 200 NM, and/or in the continental shelf beyond 200 NM, the waters above the shelf are high seas.[358] Further, Article 78(2) provides that: 'The exercise of the rights of the coastal State over the continental shelf must not infringe or result in any unjustifiable interference with navigation and other rights and freedoms of other States as provided for in this Convention.'[359]Given that the CLCS has competence to make recommendations as to the seaward limit of the extended continental shelf, it is unsurprising that the issue has not come before any tribunal. However, as noted in Chapter 6, more recently, tribunals have been willing to delimit the extended continental shelf even in the absence of any established outer limits,[360] and in that context have addressed aspects of Article 76. In *South China Sea*, the Tribunal also briefly addressed the rights of the coastal State under Article 77.

1. Article 76

The Tribunal in *Bay of Bengal Delimitation* affirmed that under Article 76(8) the limits of the continental shelf beyond 200 NM can only be established by the coastal State, and opposability of those limits with regard to other States is dependent on satisfaction of the

[352] ibid art 76(8).
[353] ibid art 77.
[354] See ibid arts 80, 60.
[355] See ibid arts 56(1)(b)(ii), 246.
[356] See ibid art 210(5).
[357] See ibid art 81.
[358] On the rights of the coastal State to the continental shelf and the rights of freedoms of other States in the high seas above them see Joanna Mossop, *The Continental Shelf Beyond 200 Nautical Miles: Rights and Responsibilities* (OUP 2016) 173–202.
[359] UNCLOS (n 1) art 78(2).
[360] See ch 6(IV).

requirements set out in Article 76, most notably a recommendation from the CLCS.[361] However, the Tribunal clarified that entitlement to a continental shelf does not depend on procedural requirements, referring to Article 77(3), which specifies that the rights of the coastal State do not depend on occupation or on any proclamation.[362] Thus, it concluded that the existence of an entitlement to an outer continental shelf does not depend on the establishment of outer limits of that shelf,[363] and the fact that the outer limits had not been determined did not imply that the Tribunal must refrain from determining the existence of entitlement to the shelf and delimiting it.[364] As to the division of competence between the CLCS and UNCLOS tribunals, in particular in interpreting Article 76, the Tribunal said:

> The Tribunal's consideration of whether it is appropriate to interpret article 76 of the Convention requires careful examination of the nature of the questions posed in this case and the functions of the Commission established by that article. It takes note in this regard that, as this article contains elements of law and science, its proper interpretation and application requires both legal and scientific expertise. While the Commission is a scientific and technical body with recommendatory functions entrusted by the Convention to consider scientific and technical issues arising in the implementation of article 76 on the basis of submissions by coastal States, the Tribunal can interpret and apply the provisions of the Convention, including article 76. This may include dealing with uncontested scientific materials or require recourse to experts.[365]

As is detailed in Chapter 6, the question of the competence of a tribunal to delimit the continental shelf absent a recommendation from the CLCS has been treated differently by different tribunals. Initially, the ICJ suggested that it would not delimit the extended continental shelf without a recommendation of the CLCS,[366] and it declined to delimit the extended continental shelf before the coastal State had made a full submission to the CLCS,[367] but after the Tribunal's decision in *Bay of Bengal Delimitation*, the Tribunal in *Bay of Bengal Arbitration* held it could proceed to a delimitation,[368] and the ICJ has more recently indicated that it could proceed to a delimitation absent a CLCS recommendation.[369] Other tribunals have proceeded to delimit the outer continental shelf where one State has received a CLCS recommendation,[370] and the ICJ most recently proceeded to a delimitation where both States had made submissions to the CLCS and neither disputed the other's claim to an extended shelf.[371] These cases are discussed in Chapter 6 below.

[361] *Bay of Bengal Delimitation* (n 185) para 407.
[362] ibid para 408.
[363] ibid para 409.
[364] ibid para 410.
[365] ibid para 411.
[366] *Territorial and Maritime Dispute between Nicaragua and Honduras in the Caribbean Sea (Nicaragua v Honduras)* (Preliminary Objections) [2007] ICJ Rep 659, para 318.
[367] *Territorial and Maritime Dispute*, Judgment (n 13) para 127.
[368] *Bay of Bengal Arbitration* (n 140) paras 82–83.
[369] *Delimitation of the Continental Shelf between Nicaragua and Colombia beyond 200 Nautical Miles from the Nicaraguan Coast (Nicaragua v Colombia)* (Preliminary Objections) [2016] ICJ Rep 100, paras 105–15.
[370] *Delimitation of the Maritime Boundary between Ghana and Côte d'Ivoire in the Atlantic Ocean (Ghana/Côte d'Ivoire)* (Judgment of 23 September 2017) ITLOS Case No 23, paras 493–95.
[371] *Maritime Delimitation in the Indian Ocean*, Judgment (n 133) para 194.

As to the substantive provisions of Article 76, in *Bay of Bengal Delimitation*, the Bangladesh and Myanmar disagreed as to the meaning of 'natural prolongation' in Article 76(1), resulting in judicial interpretation of this term. Bangladesh argued that it required geological as well as geomorphological continuity between the territory of the coastal State and the seabed beyond 200 NM.[372] It pointed out that the Indian plate slides under the adjacent Burma plate close to and along the coast of Myanmar, resulting in the Sunda Subduction Zone, making a collision between the two separate tectonic plates. Bangladesh argued that this subduction resulted in a fundamental geological discontinuity in the Bay of Bengal,[373] and, as a consequence, Myanmar's coastal territory had no 'natural prolongation' beyond 200 NM.[374] Myanmar argued that 'natural prolongation' was not an independent criterion or test for entitlement to the continental shelf beyond 200 NM, and that the controlling concept was 'outer edge of the continental margin' defined by the two formulae in Article 76(4).[375] Thus, according to Myanmar, the tectonics underlying the continents were not relevant to the extent of entitlement to the continental shelf under Article 76.[376]

Noting that the parties did not differ on the 'scientific aspects' of Article 76, but instead had a dispute as to the meaning of 'natural prolongation' in Article 76(1) and the relationship between that and Article 76(4) on the outer limit of the continental margin,[377] the Tribunal considered that the parties' entitlement to a continental shelf beyond 200 NM 'raises issues that are predominantly legal in nature' that could and should be determined by the Tribunal.[378] The Tribunal then proceeded to address the meaning of 'natural prolongation' in Article 76(1),[379] considering that the notion of 'the outer edge of the continental margin' is an 'essential element in determining the extent of the continental shelf',[380] and that the two notions are 'closely interrelated' and refer to the same area.[381] Noting that one of the principal objects and purposes of Article 76 is to define the outer limits of the continental shelf, the Tribunal noted that it was difficult to accept that 'natural prolongation' constituted a separate and independent criterion that a coastal State must satisfy to establish an entitlement to continental shelf beyond 200 NM.[382] It also noted that the CLCS in its Scientific and Technical Guidance on the Limits of the Continental Shelf had adopted a 'test of appurtenance' on the basis of Article 76(4).[383] Taking account of these factors, the Tribunal concluded that:

> [T]he reference to natural prolongation in article 76, paragraph 1, of the Convention, should be understood in light of the subsequent provisions of the article defining the continental shelf and the continental margin. Entitlement to a continental shelf beyond 200 nm should thus be determined by reference to the outer edge of the continental margin, to be

[372] *Bay of Bengal Delimitation* (n 185) para 426.
[373] ibid para 424.
[374] ibid para 425.
[375] ibid para 427.
[376] ibid.
[377] ibid para 412.
[378] ibid para 413.
[379] ibid paras 424–25, 428–38.
[380] ibid para 429.
[381] ibid para 434. See also paras 430–33.
[382] ibid para 435.
[383] ibid para 436.

> ascertained in accordance with article 76, paragraph 4. To interpret otherwise is warranted neither by the text of article 76 nor by its object and purpose.[384]

It therefore rejected Bangladesh's argument that, by reason of the geological discontinuity dividing the Burma plate from the India plate, Myanmar was not entitled to a continental shelf beyond 200 NM.[385]

This aspect of the Tribunal's approach has been criticised, including on the basis that, as a technical matter, the foot of the slope will be at the limit of the natural prolongation and not at the same point as the outer limit of the continental margin.[386] It has also been suggested that the Tribunal's approach is confusing: as it appears to elevate the formula in Article 76(4) (which prescribes specific methods to locate the precise position of the outer limit of the continental shelf) over that in Article 76(1) (which provides the legal basis for entitlement to an extended continental shelf).[387] Schofield, Telesetsky, and Lee suggested that, although the Tribunal offered a means by which natural prolongation can be interpreted with enhanced objectivity and precision, there may be cases where geophysical factors can and should continue to play a role in the delimitation of the outer continental shelf. Where there is no clear geological or geomorphological distinction between the entitlements of the parties then the Tribunal's approach is likely to work; where there is a geomorphic or geological feature in the area to be delimited (such as a trough or a plate boundary), then that feature is likely to be relevant to the delimitation.[388]

In the *Timor Sea Conciliation* proceedings, Australia relied on the concept of natural prolongation and geological and geomorphological factors in contending that the delimitation of the continental shelf boundary with Timor-Leste should not necessarily coincide with the delimitation of the EEZ.[389] Timor-Leste argued that the concept of natural prolongation and the geology and geomorphology were not relevant to the delimitation of the continental shelf between the two States at a distance of less than 400 NM.[390] Although the Commission did not address these arguments in any detail, its Report noted that it had invited the parties to consider a single maritime boundary.[391]

2. Rights of the Coastal State under Article 77

As noted in Chapter 7,[392] the *Arctic Sunrise* Tribunal commented on the scope of a coastal State's rights of enforcement under Article 77,[393] although it did not have to decide the point since there was no evidential basis to conclude that Russia's actions were taken to enforce laws and regulations relating to non-living resources. It considered that Article 77

[384] ibid para 437.
[385] ibid para 438.
[386] Lindsay Parson, 'Article 76' in Alexander Proelss (ed), *United Nations Convention on the Law of the Sea: A Commentary* (CH Beck, Hart, and Nomos 2017) 587, para 26.
[387] Yao Huang and Xuexia Liao, 'Natural Prolongation and Delimitation of the Continental Shelf Beyond 200 nm: Implications of the Bangladesh/Myanmar Case' (2014) 4(2) Asian JIL 281, 292–93.
[388] Clive Schofield, Anastasia Telesetsky, and Seokwoo Lee, 'A Tribunal Navigating Complex Waters: Implications of the *Bay of Bengal Case*' (2013) 44 ODIL 363, 374–75.
[389] *Conciliation between The Democratic Republic of Timor-Leste and the Commonwealth of Australia* (Report and Recommendations of the Compulsory Conciliation Commission, 9 May 2018) PCA Case No 2016-10, para 234.
[390] ibid para 232.
[391] ibid para 239.
[392] See ch V(IV)(A).
[393] *Arctic Sunrise*, Merits (n 287) paras 281–82.

encompassed a right to exercise enforcement powers in relation to the prevention and punishment of violations of laws and regulations with respect to the exploration and exploitation of the resources of the continental shelf.[394] So far as concerns the scope of permissible enforcement action, the Tribunal in *Guyana v Suriname* confirmed that the use of force in law enforcement activities may amount to a use or threat of use of force in contravention of the UN Charter.[395]

The *South China Sea* Tribunal addressed the rights of the coastal State under Article 77 of UNCLOS in the context of the Philippines' claim that China had prevented a seismic survey vessel from conducting surveys for an oil and gas production company in an area of its continental shelf. The Tribunal noted that Article 77 of UNCLOS provides that a coastal State exercises sovereign rights for the purposes of exploring and exploiting natural resources of the shelf, and as a consequence, only the Philippines, or another State acting with its permission, could exploit the resources of the seabed.[396] The Tribunal concluded that, with respect to the survey operations, China had breached Article 77 of UNCLOS.[397]

So far, tribunals have had few opportunities to engage substantively with Article 77 of UNCLOS. The cases that have addressed it have not considered the question of balancing coastal States' rights against those of third States and/or the international community, but have rather been focused on defining the extent of coastal States' rights. The question of the existence, scope, and extent of coastal States' enforcement powers under Article 77 is an area where there is the potential for future disputes. The *Arctic Sunrise* Tribunal suggested enforcement powers are quite broad, in the absence of any express language in Article 77 itself. It remains to be seen whether other tribunals reach the same conclusion.

V. Concluding Remarks

The entitlements of a coastal State to maritime spaces, and their rights and duties in those maritime spaces, have clear implications for other States, the international community, and a variety of other actors. The interpretation of rules on maritime space entitlements, as well as on the characterisation of certain features that may also have maritime space entitlements, is therefore critical to the fundamental objective of public order of the oceans. Given that the provisions of UNCLOS addressing the source and extent of State authority in the oceans apply to coastal States across the board, interpretation of those provisions by tribunals is also essential to the rule of law, and the peaceful settlement of disputes: including but potentially extending beyond the scope of the particular bilateral dispute.

Tribunals have had significant opportunities to address the interpretation of provisions of UNCLOS governing entitlement to maritime spaces and the question of the scope of rights and duties in them, as well as the balancing of coastal State rights and rights of third States. The treatment of these issues has necessarily been rather piecemeal, since all depends on the particular claims and disputes that are submitted to each tribunal. As regards entitlements to maritime spaces, on the whole, tribunals have generally assessed coastal States'

394 ibid para 283, referring to ILC, 'Articles on LOS' (n 207) 297.

395 *Guyana v Suriname* (n 129) para 445. See also paras 439–44. This decision is discussed in more detail in ch 7(IV)(B).

396 *South China Sea*, Award (n 10) para 698.

397 ibid paras 707–708, 716.

unilateral claims against the criteria set out in UNCLOS; in some cases rejecting them and interpreting the provisions of UNCLOS in a way that prevents coastal States from claiming exclusive rights over large portions of maritime space. Tribunals have also been generally reluctant to accept arguments based on State practice where they consider it deviates from the text of the applicable provisions. As regards the scope and extent of coastal States' rights, and the balancing of those rights against the rights and interests of other States, tribunals have, on the whole, engaged in a reasoned approach to the balancing of rights of coastal States and other States, and have generally been reluctant to accord broad rights to a coastal State at the cost of the interests of other States, and the international community as a whole. It is highly likely that the balancing of coastal and third States' rights, including in the EEZ and continental shelf, will continue to be a source of contention and disputes, and thus tribunals are likely to have further opportunities to clarify the way in which this balance is to be struck in future cases.

6

Maritime Boundary Delimitation

I. Introduction

There have been ample opportunities for tribunals to consider maritime boundary disputes, and hence to interpret and apply the United Nations Convention on the Law of the Sea (UNCLOS or Convention) provisions on delimitation.[1] Notably, the provisions on delimitation of the exclusive economic zone (EEZ) and the continental shelf are cast in very broad terms: they require delimitation on the basis of agreement and to achieve an 'equitable solution'.[2] From those very general requirements, the Court and international tribunals have developed a very specific approach to delimitation and hence have exerted considerable influence, both in interpreting provisions of UNCLOS and on the parallel emergence of customary international law on maritime delimitation. The case law is also notable for its consistency, with deviations from the developed standard methodology being reasoned on the basis of case-specific circumstances. In this way, it can be considered to contribute to and fulfil the fundamental objectives of international dispute settlement in the context of UNCLOS—the peaceful settlement of disputes, the rule of law, and public order of the oceans. All of those objectives are reinforced by clarity and certainty as to the definition of maritime zones, so that there is then clarity and certainty as to the relevant entitlements of coastal States and other States in those zones. In addition to this significant influence on the elaboration of an approach to the delimitation of the EEZ and the continental shelf, the Court and international tribunals have rendered numerous decisions on Article 15 of UNCLOS on delimitation of the territorial sea, which provides for an equidistance line absent 'special circumstances' or 'historic title'.

Commentators have remarked on the very significant influence of judicial decision-makers on the development of rules on maritime delimitation. Even before the methodology for delimitation of the EEZ/continental shelf had been fully articulated, in 1989 Weil remarked that:

> [T]he legal conquest of maritime delimitation is not the work of either treaty or custom but of the courts which, far from being a subsidiary source of international law, here play the role of a primary and direct source of law, even if they have chosen modesty to ascribe the credit to customary law.[3]

[1] This jurisprudence has been analysed in book-length studies: Alex G Oude Elferink, Tore Henriksen, and Signe Veierud Busch (eds), *Maritime Delimitation: The Case Law—Is It Consistent and Predictable?* (CUP 2018); Massimo Lando, *Maritime Delimitation as Judicial Process* (CUP 2019) (Lando, *Maritime Delimitation*); Stephen Fietta and Robin Cleverly, *A Practitioner's Guide to Maritime Boundary Delimitation* (OUP 2016).

[2] United Nations Convention on the Law of the Sea (adopted 10 December 1982, entered into force 16 November 1994) 1833 UNTS 397, arts 74(1) and 83(1) (UNCLOS).

[3] Prosper Weil, *The Law of Maritime Delimitation: Reflections* (CUP 1989) 8.

Indeed, tribunals have even articulated that their own approach to delimitation has become a source of law to be read into UNCLOS, giving further content to the open-textured delimitation provisions. In this way, tribunals have made a significant contribution to the peaceful settlement of disputes with regards to an issue of high importance in inter-State relations given the economic, strategic, and other interests at stake. Moreover, as previously noted, the increasing consistency in the cases supports the public order of the oceans in providing future guidance to other stakeholders. This chapter commences with a brief introduction to general principles of delimitation and commonly used delimitation methods, which will assist with the analysis of the cases given in the rest of the chapter (section II). Section III addresses delimitation of the territorial sea, and section IV addresses delimitation of the EEZ and the continental shelf, including the continental shelf beyond 200 NM. The obligations pending delimitation are discussed in section V, before some concluding remarks in section VI.

II. A Brief Introduction to Commonly Used Delimitation Methods

Before surveying the development of case law, it is useful to recall a fundamental principle that underlies maritime limitation: the principle that the 'land dominates the sea'. This principle was first set out by the ICJ in the *North Sea* cases, and it has been confirmed repeatedly by the Court and international tribunals. In *North Sea*, the Court stated:

> [T]he land dominates the sea; it is consequently necessary to examine closely the geographical circumstances of the coastlines of the countries whose continental shelves are to be delimited ... [S]ince the land is the legal source of the power which a State may exercise over territorial extensions to seaward, it must first be clearly established what features do in fact constitute such extensions.[4]

Consistently with this principle, the outer limits of a coastal State's maritime zones are defined by reference to distances from the baselines from which the breadth of the territorial sea is measured.[5]

Much of the early case law explained in this chapter has focused on the various methods of delimitation, with the 'equidistance' method coming to occupy a particularly prominent position. An equidistance line, which is also referred to as a 'median' line, is one drawn so that it is the same distance from the nearest base points on both States' coasts. This method is specified in Article 15 of UNCLOS. A crucial first step is therefore the identification of relevant base points, which may be located on the low-water line of the mainland coast, or islands, low-tide elevations, and harbour works, depending on the circumstances.[6] The resulting provisional equidistance line will consist of a series of straight lines which, depending on the coastline, will be likely to have a series of turning points. It can be thus defined by coordinates setting out a series of points and connected by lines. A provisional

[4] *North Sea Continental Shelf (Federal Republic of Germany/Denmark; Federal Republic of Germany/Netherlands)* (Judgment) [1969] ICJ Rep 3, para 96 (*North Sea*, Judgment).
[5] See UNCLOS (n 2) arts 3 (territorial sea), 57 (EEZ), and 76 (continental shelf).
[6] See further ch 5(III).

equidistance line is now usually constructed using technical expertise of hydrographers, and can be precisely defined. It may consist of thousands of specified points, and is commonly reduced to a simplified line that has fewer turning points and results in a more practical line.

A common alternative to an equidistance line for adjacent Stares is the 'bisector' method.[7] This method involves the construction of a straight line representing the general direction of each State's coast, and drawing a line that bisects the angle between those two straight lines. It can be appropriate, for example, where there are no reliable or stable base points, so that an equidistance line is not feasible. A further alternative is a perpendicular boundary, ie a boundary following a line perpendicular to the general direction of the coast. This method may be appropriate in circumstances where two adjacent States share a coastal front that faces the same general direction.

In practice, States have reached agreements on maritime boundaries that do not necessarily bear a direct relationship to the coastline or the coastal fronts. These agreements may take the form of boundaries following parallels of latitudes, meridians of longitude, or lines following a particular azimuth (ie following a constant angle). Judicial decisions have largely favoured the use of an equidistance line, with some adjustments, and/or employed a bisector method to reach an 'equitable solution', as perceived by the judges.

III. Delimitation of the Territorial Sea

A. Article 15 of UNCLOS

Delimitation of the territorial sea is addressed in Article 15 of UNCLOS, which provides for delimitation by an equidistance line, unless there is historic title or other 'special circumstances'. Article 15 provides:

> Where the coasts of two States are opposite or adjacent to each other, neither of the two States is entitled, failing agreement between them to the contrary, to extend its territorial sea beyond the median line every point of which is equidistant from the nearest points on the baselines from which the breadth of the territorial seas of each of the two States is measured. The above provision does not apply, however, where it is necessary by reason of historic title or other special circumstances to delimit the territorial seas of the two States in a way which is at variance therewith.

Article 15 of UNCLOS is materially identical to Article 12 of the 1958 Geneva Convention on the Territorial Sea and Contiguous Zone (Territorial Sea Convention),[8] which substantially

[7] See eg *Delimitation of the Maritime Boundary in the Gulf of Maine Area (Canada v United States)* (Merits) [1984] ICJ Rep 246 (*Gulf of Maine*), where a bisector was used in the first segment of the boundary: see paras 212–13.

[8] Convention on the Territorial Sea and Contiguous Zone (opened for signature 29 April 1958, entered into force 10 September 1964) 516 UNTS 205, art 12 (Territorial Sea Convention). As observed in *Maritime Delimitation and Territorial Questions (Qatar v Bahrain)* (Merits) [2001] ICJ Rep 40, para 176 (*Qatar v Bahrain*, Merits): 'Article 15 of the 1982 Convention is virtually identical to Article 12, paragraph 1 of the 1958 Convention on the Territorial Sea and the Contiguous Zone.'

reflected the International Law Commission's (ILC) approach in its final report on the law of the sea prepared in 1956.[9] The same rule was set out in Article 6 of the 1958 Convention on the Continental Shelf (Continental Shelf Convention), which provided for delimitation of the continental shelf between adjacent States, in the absence of agreement, by an equidistance line, 'unless another boundary line is justified by special circumstances'.[10]

The ICJ has affirmed that Article 15 of UNCLOS represents customary international law. In *Qatar v Bahrain* the Court noted that '[t]he Parties agree that the provisions of the Article 15 of [UNCLOS] ... are part of customary law'[11] and, referring to the fact that Article 15 is 'virtually identical' to Article 12 of the Territorial Sea Convention, said that it 'is to be regarded as having a customary character'.[12]

Article 15 'places primacy on the [equidistance] line as the delimitation line between the territorial seas of opposite or adjacent States',[13] as the tribunal in *Guyana v Suriname* observed. Thus, a territorial sea delimitation would normally commence with the construction of a provisional equidistance line. It also mandates departure from an equidistance line only where it is 'necessary by reasons of historic title or other special circumstances'.[14] This decision requires assessment 'on a case by case basis'.[15]

B. Early Decisions

As noted above, Article 15 of UNCLOS is materially identical to Article 12 of the Territorial Sea Convention. There were no cases in which a delimitation of the territorial sea was carried out on the basis of the Territorial Sea Convention as the applicable law. However, it is notable that in the *Beagle Channel* arbitration award,[16] issued in 1977 by a court of arbitration constituted under a 1971 arbitration agreement between Argentina and Chile, the Court delimited the territorial sea using an adjusted equidistance line. Under Article I of the arbitration agreement, the applicable law was 'the principles of international law'.[17] The Court emphasised the principle of appurtenance (closely related to the principle that the land dominates the sea), noting that 'an attribution of territory must *ipso facto* carry with it the waters appurtenant to the territory attributed; and therefore, on the Channel, those extended up to some sort of median line'.[18] It said that, in drawing its boundary line:

[9] International Law Commission, 'Articles concerning the Law of the Sea with Commentaries' [1956] II UNYBILC 265, 271 (art 12), 272 (art 14).

[10] Convention on the Continental Shelf (opened for signature 29 April 1958, entered into force 10 June 1964) 499 UNTS 311, art 6(1) (Continental Shelf Convention).

[11] *Qatar v Bahrain*, Merits (n 8) para 175.

[12] ibid para 176. See also *Territorial and Maritime Dispute between Nicaragua and Honduras in the Caribbean Sea (Nicaragua v Honduras)* (Preliminary Objections) [2007] ICJ Rep 659 (*Nicaragua v Honduras*) ('It is recalled that Article 15 of UNCLOS, which was adopted without any discussion as to the method of delimitation of the territorial sea, is virtually identical (save for minor editorial changes) to the text of Article 12, paragraph 1, of the 1958 Convention on the Territorial Sea and the Contiguous Zone').

[13] *Guyana v Suriname* (Award of the Arbitral Tribunal of 17 September 2007) PCA Case No 2004-04, para 296 (*Guyana v Suriname*).

[14] UNCLOS (n 2) art 15.

[15] *Guyana v Suriname* (n 13) para 303.

[16] *Beagle Channel Arbitration (Argentina/Chile)* (Report and Decision of the Court of Arbitration dated 18 February 1977) 21 RIAA 53 (*Beagle Channel*).

[17] Agreement for Arbitration (Compromiso) of a Controversy between the Argentine Republic and the Republic of Chile concerning the Region of the Beagle Channel (1971) 10 ILM 1182, art 1.

[18] *Beagle Channel* (n 16)para 107.

> the Court has been guided by the considerations indicated in Annex IV hereto (which shows how the line has been traced)—in particular by mixed factors of appurtenance, coastal configuration, equidistance, and also of convenience, navigability, and the desirability of enabling each Party so far as possible to navigate in its own waters. None of this has resulted in much deviation from the strict median line except, for obvious reasons, near Gable Island where the habitually used navigable track has been followed.[19]

Although no reference was made to the equidistance/special circumstances rule, nor to the Territorial Sea Convention,[20] it is notable that the Court took an approach that gave primacy to equidistance, and then adjusted it on the grounds of, inter alia, navigational interests.[21]

The Court of Arbitration in the *Dubai-Sharjah Border Arbitration*,[22] in its award issued in 1981, referred to the equidistance/special circumstances rule in its delimitation of both the territorial sea and the continental shelf. This case involved the delimitation of maritime boundaries between internal units of a federal State (the emirates of Dubai and Sharjah of the United Arab Emirates (UAE)), and so neither of the 1958 Geneva Conventions were directly applicable. However, the Court considered that the applicable law was UAE federal law, and in the event that it did not exist or was incomplete, 'recourse must be made to international law'.[23] It concluded that it should determine the maritime boundaries 'by reference to the governing rules and principles of customary international law', and noted that it took into account developments within the Third Conference on the Law of the Sea and to State practice in the region,[24] as well as the 1958 Geneva Conventions.[25] The Court said:

> It has sought to ensure that the boundary line conforms to equitable principles and produces a result that allows, in equity, a proportionate influence on the existence of 'special circumstances' or 'special and unusual features' which call for special treatment.[26]

So far as concerns the territorial sea, the Court agreed with Dubai that it should treat the permanent harbour works of both parties as part of the coast for the purposes of drawing baselines from which the equidistance line was to be constructed. It noted that this decision resulted in a 'slight' deflection but did not give rise to any inequitable result, and therefore the Court delimited the territorial seas using an unadjusted equidistance line.[27]

[19] ibid para 110.

[20] Argentina had signed but not ratified the Territorial Sea Convention (n 8), while Chile never signed it.

[21] See Fietta and Cleverly (n 1) 184–85. Argentina subsequently rejected the award, and Chile rejected Argentina's declaration of nullity: see Exchange of Diplomatic Notes concerning the Beagle Channel Arbitration (1978) 17 ILM 738. The two States then recommenced negotiations, resulting in a treaty concluded in 1984 which referred to the 'existing boundary in the Beagle Channel', implicitly accepting the territorial sea delimitation made in the 1977 award, and using its end point as the starting point for delimiting the EEZ and continental shelf boundary: see Treaty of Peace and Friendship (Chile–Argentina) (29 November 1984) 1390 UNTS 89.

[22] *Dubai-Sharjah Border Arbitration* (Judgment of the Court of Arbitration of 19 October 1981) (1981) 91 ILR 543.

[23] ibid 586. See also 590 ('The Court has, in the light of the above considerations, come to the conclusion that the applicable law in the present case is international law adapted to the special conditions of the region in question').

[24] ibid 654. The two parties also agreed that the 'Court had full competence to determine the territorial sea boundary and the continental shelf boundary by reference to customary international law since neither Party was bound by the 1958 Geneva Conventions on the Territorial Sea and Contiguous Zone or the Continental Shelf': see 658.

[25] ibid 663 (referring to art 12 of the Territorial Sea Convention (n 8)). See also 669–70 (referring to art 6 of the Continental Shelf Convention (n 10)).

[26] ibid 654.

[27] ibid 663. See also 662.

As noted above, the equidistance/special circumstances rule was also set out in Article 6 of the Continental Shelf Convention. That rule was addressed by several tribunals in early decisions on continental shelf delimitations, and those cases shed some light on the meaning of 'special circumstances'. For example, in *Dubai-Sharjah Border Arbitration*, the Court of Arbitration adjusted the equidistance line to account for the distorting effect that Abu Musa, a substantial island approximately 35 NM offshore, and accorded it no effect in the delimitation.[28] In *United Kingdom/France Continental Shelf Case* (*UK/France*), decided by an ad hoc court of arbitration in 1977, the Court of Arbitration ultimately did not apply Article 6, but it noted that if the equidistance/special circumstances rule had applied, then 'the presence of the Channel Islands close to the French coast must be considered, prima facie, as constituting a 'special circumstance' justifying a delimitation other than the median line'.[29] As for the navigational, defence, and security interests, the Court noted that these 'cannot be regarded by the Court as exercising a decisive influence on the delimitation'.[30] Finally, although it rejected a submission from France that the situation of the coasts was in itself a 'special circumstance', it considered that the Scilly Islands had a considerable and material influence on the line, and as a special circumstance, would have given them half-effect.[31] As noted by Fietta and Cleverly, the decision in *Delimitation of the Continental Shelf* (*UK/France*) emphasised the role of geography in determining the existence of 'special circumstances': the circumstances that led to variation in the equidistance line were all of a geographical character, and arguments based upon geology, navigation, security, and defence were all rejected.[32] In addition, this decision was the first modern example of 'special circumstances' being taken into account by giving half effect to a group of islands.[33]

C. The *Travaux* of the Third Conference: 1973–82

During UNCLOS negotiations, proposals on delimitation of the territorial sea generally reflected two approaches: either to use equidistance or to emphasise equitable principles, reflecting the decision of the ICJ in *North Sea*.[34] The same debate took place with respect to the question of the delimitation of the EEZ and the continental shelf; in respect of the latter, the equidistance/special circumstances rule in the Continental Shelf Convention was not ultimately carried over into UNCLOS.[35]

[28] ibid 673–77.

[29] *Delimitation of the Continental Shelf (United Kingdom/France)* (Decision of 30 June 1977) 18 RIAA 3, para 196 (*UK/France*).

[30] ibid para 188.

[31] ibid paras 244–51.

[32] Fietta and Cleverly (n 1) 207.

[33] See ibid 208.

[34] See Myron H Nordquist (ed), *United Nations Convention on the Law of the Sea 1982: A Commentary*, vol 2 (Martinus Nijhoff 1985) 135 (*Virginia Commentary*). Some proposals to replace the equidistance/special circumstances rule with a reference to equitable solutions also referred to 'special' or 'relevant' circumstances: see eg 'Proposal of Turkey', reproduced in *Virginia Commentary* (n 34) vol 2, 136; 'Turkey: Draft Article on the Delimitation of the Territorial Sea; Various Aspects Involved' (15 July 1974) UN Doc A/CONF.62/C.2/L.9 (Revised Proposal of Turkey); 'Netherlands: Draft Article on Delimitation between States with Opposite or Adjacent Coasts' (19 July 1974) UN Doc A/CONF.62/C.2/L.14 (Proposal of Netherlands); 'Romania: Draft Articles on Delimitation of Marine and Ocean Space between Adjacent and Opposite Neighbouring States and Various Aspects Involved' (23 July 1974) UN Doc A/CONF.62/C.2/L.18 (Proposal of Romania).

[35] See section IV(A) below.

Most of the proposals favouring equidistance were largely based on Article 12 of the Territorial Sea Convention,[36] although some proposed deleting the references to 'historic rights or other special circumstances';[37] while others proposed retaining them.[38] The draft proposed in the Informal Single Negotiating Text in 1975, the Revised Single Negotiating Text in 1976 and the Informal Composite Negotiating Text in 1977 reflected in substance the rule set out in Article 12 of the Territorial Sea Convention.[39] In the introduction to the 1977 text, the President of Conference noted that the absence of any substantive change was that 'it had not been possible to devise a formula which would narrow the differences between the opposing points of view'.[40] In 1978, the delimitation of maritime boundaries was identified as a 'hard-core issue',[41] which was referred to Negotiating Group 7. Within that Group, the discussion focused on delimitation of the EEZ and the continental shelf and dispute settlement, rather than on delimitation of the territorial sea.[42] Thus, Article 15 of UNCLOS as adopted remained as proposed in 1975, and reflected in substance the rule set out in Article 12 of the Territorial Sea Convention.

D. Delimitation of the Territorial Sea: Decisions under UNCLOS

Article 15 of UNCLOS provides for a method of delimitation in the absence of agreement, but it does not permit review of agreed territorial sea boundaries. Likewise, as the tribunal in *Guinea Bissau/Senegal* confirmed, no customary law rule or general principle of law allows States, or their successors, to review or verify the equitable character of a valid treaty concerning maritime delimitation.[43] That conclusion is consistent with the fundamental principle of stability of boundaries, which applies to land boundaries as well as maritime boundaries,[44] as well as with the broader principle of respect for the rule of law.

[36] *Virginia Commentary* (n 34) vol 2, 136.

[37] See eg the proposal of Cyprus, reproduced in *Virginia Commentary* (n 34) vol 2, 136 ; the proposal of Uruguay (originally issued as UN Doc A/AC.138/SC.II/L.25), reproduced in 'Report of the Committee on the Peaceful Uses of the Sea-Bed and the Ocean Floor Beyond the Limits of National Jurisdiction', vol 3 (1973) UN Doc A/9021, 23, 25 (1973 SBC Report, vol 3); 'Greece: Draft Articles' (25 July 1974) UN Doc A/CONF.62/C.2/L.22 (Proposal of Greece).

[38] See eg proposals of Uganda and Zambia (originally issued as UN Doc A/AC/138/SC.II/L.31), reproduced in 1973 SBC Report, vol 3 (n 37), 89–90, art 3 [2]; 'United Kingdom: Draft Articles on the Territorial Sea and Straits' (3 July 1974) UN Doc A/CONF.62/C.2/L.3 (Proposal of the United Kingdom); 'Bulgaria, German Democratic Republic, Poland, Union of Soviet Social Republics: Draft Articles on the Territorial Sea' (29 July 1974) UN Doc A/CONF.62/C.2/L.26 (Proposal of Four East European Socialist States).

[39] See *Virginia Commentary* (n 34) vol 2, 138 (referring to 'Informal Single Negotiating Text, Part II', UN Doc A/CONF.62/WP.8/Part II)) 139 (reproducing 'Revised Single Negotiating Text, Part II', UN Doc A/CONF.62/WP.8/Rev.1/Part II); 139 (referring to 'Informal Composite Negotiating Text' (15 July 1977) UN Doc A/CONF.62/WP.10).

[40] ibid vol 2, 139 [15.7], citing HS Amerasinghe, 'Memorandum by the President of the Conference on Document A/CONF.62/WP.10' (22 July 1977) UN Doc A/CONF.62/WP.10/Add.1.

[41] *Virginia Commentary* (n 34) vol 2, 139, citing 'Organization of Work' (18 April 1978) UN Doc A/CONF.62/62, p 8, para 5, item (7).

[42] *Virginia Commentary* (n 34) vol 2, 140.

[43] *Delimitation of Maritime Boundary (Guinea-Bissau/Senegal)*, 31 July 1989, 83 ILR 1, para 79 (*Guinea-Bissau/Senegal*).

[44] See Vienna Convention on the Law of Treaties (adopted 23 May 1969, entered into force 27 January 1980) 1155 UNTS 331, art 62(2)(a) (VCLT); *Grisbådarna (Norway v Sweden)* (Award of 23 October 1909) 11 RIAA 161; *Aegean Sea Continental Shelf (Greece v Turkey)* (Judgment) [1978] ICJ Rep 3, para 8 (*Aegean Sea Continental Shelf*); *Territorial Dispute (Libya/Chad)* (Judgment) [1994] ICJ Rep 6, 72–73; *Territorial and Maritime Dispute (Nicaragua v Colombia)* (Preliminary Objections) [2007] ICJ Rep 832 *(Territorial and Maritime Dispute,* Preliminary Objections) para 89.

As noted above, Article 15 of UNCLOS requires delimitation by an equidistance line, unless 'it is necessary by reason of historic title or other special circumstances to delimit the territorial seas' by another method. Consistently with the text of Article 15, the Tribunal in *Guyana v Suriname* confirmed that Article 15 'places primacy on the median line as the delimitation line between the territorial seas of opposite or adjacent States'.[45]

In practice, when delimiting the territorial sea, courts and tribunals have rarely departed from an equidistance line. When they have done so, they have either used another method or adjusted a provisional equidistance line. As the ICJ observed in *Nicaragua v Honduras*, nothing in the wording of Article 15 suggests that "special circumstances' may only be used as a corrective element to a line already drawn',[46] and the same interpretive logic would apply to the exception for historic title.

In several cases rendered under UNCLOS, tribunals have delimited territorial sea boundaries with equidistance lines, finding no circumstances calling for an adjustment. In *Bangladesh/Myanmar (Bay of Bengal Delimitation)*, the International Tribunal for the Law of the Sea (ITLOS) found that there was no existing agreement between the parties on their territorial sea boundary.[47] It dismissed Myanmar's argument that the island of St Martin's was a special circumstance necessitating adjustment of the provisional equidistance line to give that island less than full effect, noting that it was a significant maritime feature by virtue of its size, population, and the extent of economic and other activities.[48] As noted by Fietta and Cleverly, this decision confirmed the tendency in modern territorial sea delimitations to give full effect to any significant island features.[49] ITLOS thus delimited the territorial sea with an equidistance line.[50] Similarly, as noted below, in *Costa Rica v Nicaragua* (*Maritime Delimitation in the Caribbean Sea and the Pacific Ocean*), the ICJ delimited the territorial sea in the Pacific Ocean by an unadjusted equidistance line. Likewise, in *Somalia v Kenya* (*Maritime Delimitation in the Indian Ocean*), the ICJ delimited the territorial sea with an equidistance line that was not adjusted to take account of any special circumstances, but was drawn using base points different to those proposed and/or agreed by the parties, in effect resulting in an adjustment to the equidistance line.[51] This aspect of the Court's approach was heavily criticised by two judges in separate and individual opinions.[52]

There have been no cases where the territorial sea delimitation was adjusted on the basis of historic title. In *Croatia/Slovenia Arbitration*, Slovenia argued for an adjustment to the equidistance line on the basis of historic title, claiming that, as former parts of the Socialist Federal Republic of Yugoslavia (SFRY), Slovenia and Slovenian entities were entitled to exercise the same territorial sea and other maritime rights that the SFRY possessed. It said that this exercise was long-standing, and well known to the other republics of the SFRY. It argued further that a 'historic title' does not need to be exclusive to be relevant under

[45] *Guyana v Suriname* (n 13) para 296.
[46] *Nicaragua v Honduras* (n 12) para 280.
[47] *Delimitation of the Maritime Boundary in the Bay of Bengal (Bangladesh/Myanmar)* (Judgment) ITLOS Reports 2012, 4, paras 88–89, 112–18 (*Bay of Bengal Delimitation*).
[48] ibid paras 151–52.
[49] Fietta and Cleverly (n 1) 506.
[50] *Bay of Bengal Delimitation* (n 47) para 164.
[51] *Maritime Delimitation in the Indian Ocean (Somalia v Kenya)* (Judgment of 12 October 2021) General List No 161, paras 111–14 (*Maritime Delimitation in the Indian Ocean*, Judgment).
[52] See nn 106–14 below and accompanying text.

Article 15.[53] Croatia argued that Slovenia did not produce sufficient evidence of its alleged historic title, and disputed whether it could have established such title prior to its independence.[54] The Tribunal did not accept Slovenia's claim to historic title. It noted that any entitlements that Slovenia had were entitlements under SFRY law to share and participate in the uses of the maritime zones of the SFRY and were not entitlements of Slovenia in its own right to its own maritime zones under international law.[55]

In contrast, in several cases, tribunals have found that special circumstances required either an adjustment to the equidistance line or the use of a different method of delimitation. In a majority of cases, adjustment or a different method was used on the basis of geographical circumstances, such as the configuration of the coast or the presence of islands.

In *Qatar v Bahrain*, while not applying UNCLOS, the ICJ found that Article 15 reflected customary law.[56] In delimiting the territorial sea, the Court found that the presence of the small islands[57] of Fasht al Azm, and of Qit'at Jaradah,[58] were both special circumstances warranting adjustment of the provisional equidistance line.[59] The Court also simplified the delimitation line in the area of the Hawar Islands, in accordance with common practice.[60]

In *Guyana v Suriname*, the Tribunal, having found that there was an agreement between the predecessors of the parties to delimit their territorial sea out to three NM by the use of an azimuth,[61] held that these 'historical arrangements of an unusual nature', justified by navigational and security interests, constituted a special circumstance.[62] It therefore delimited the remainder of the territorial sea using a line drawn diagonally by the shortest distance from the terminus of the agreed three NM line, to meet the line adopted by the Tribunal to delimit the continental shelf and EEZ.[63] This decision was a relatively rare example of the use of non-geographical special circumstances, as noted by Fietta and Cleverly.[64]

In *Nicaragua v Honduras*, the ICJ identified 'geomorphological problems' in that both the configuration and the unstable nature of the coastal area made it impossible to identify base points from which to construct a provisional equidistance line. It found that these difficulties were a 'special circumstance' within the meaning of Article 15 of UNCLOS, and justified the use of a different method for delimitation of the territorial sea.[65] The factors that the Court identified included the sharply convex coastline in the vicinity of the land boundary at Cape Gracias a Dios, as a result of which two base points on either side of the River Coco would have had a substantial and disproportionate effect on the equidistance line; and the movement of sediment in the area around the mouth of the River Coco, which resulted in

[53] *Arbitration between the Republic of Croatia and the Republic of Slovenia* (Final Award of 29 June 2017) PCA Case No 2012-04, para 955 (*Croatia/Slovenia Arbitration*, Final Award).

[54] ibid paras 960–61.

[55] ibid para 1006.

[56] *Qatar v Bahrain*, Merits (n 8) para 176.

[57] The Court left open whether Fasht al Azm was an island or a low-tide elevation: either way it constituted a special circumstance: ibid para 218.

[58] As noted in ch 5(II) above, the Court decided that Qit'at Jaradah was an island, not a low-tide elevation: ibid para 195.

[59] ibid paras 217–23.

[60] ibid paras 222–23.

[61] *Guyana v Suriname* (n 13) para 307.

[62] ibid para 323.

[63] ibid paras 323–25.

[64] Fietta and Cleverly (n 1) 449.

[65] *Nicaragua v Honduras* (n 12) paras 277–82 (*Nicaragua v Honduras*). Judge *ad hoc* Torres Bernárdez dissented on this point, contending that the majority disregarded the general rule of equidistance set out in art 15: see para 161 (Dissenting Opinion of Judge ad hoc Torres Bernárdez).

significant shifts in the location of islands immediately off the mainland coast, and which meant that there would probably be significant shifts in the base points over time. Taking into account the geographical configuration of the coast, and the geomorphological features of the area where the endpoint of the land boundary is located,[66] the Court delimited the territorial sea using a bisector line.[67] Noting the parties' mutual preference to a starting point three miles seaward of the mouth of the River Coco, with their intention to negotiate a solution for the first three miles, the Court set the starting point at a point three miles out to sea along the azimuth of the Court's bisector line.[68]

The majority's approach to delimitation of the territorial sea was criticised by Judge Ranjeva in his separate opinion, who emphasised that Article 15 provided for departure from an equidistance line only where 'necessary', and contended that 'the notion of necessity involves an absence of solution such that no alternative can be envisaged'.[69] He considered that instability of the coastline did not constitute an impossibility, noting that Article 7(2) of UNCLOS provided that, where the coastline is highly unstable, appropriate points may be selected on the furthest seaward extent of the low-water line for the purposes of drawing straight baselines.[70] Judge Ranjeva further noted that in practice, an equidistance line could have been constructed from points equidistant from the two States' coastal fronts.[71] In his view, the majority's approach assigned a 'rule-making function to the special circumstances' and failed to recognise the prominence assigned to equidistance by the drafters of UNCLOS.[72]

In *Bangladesh v India* (*Bay of Bengal Arbitration*), the Tribunal dismissed Bangladesh's argument that coastal instability was a special circumstance warranting application of a bisector rather than an equidistance line, and it also rejected the contention that concavity or the geographical peculiarities of the area in question justified departure from an equidistance line.[73] In contrast, the Tribunal adjusted the provisional equidistance line in the continental shelf and EEZ in order to avoid an unreasonable cut-off effect for Bangladesh. The Tribunal then noted that the land boundary terminus identified by it was not a point equidistant from the base points selected by the tribunal for the delimitation of the territorial sea. Thus, the Tribunal considered that the need to connect the land boundary terminus to the median line constructed by the Tribunal for delimitation of the territorial sea constituted a 'special circumstance' justifying departure from an equidistance line, drawing a parallel with the approach of the Tribunal in *Guyana v Suriname*.[74] Thus, the Tribunal decided that the boundary should follow a 12 NM geodetic line from the land boundary terminus to meet the median line that delimited the EEZ/continental shelf.[75] The geodetic delimitation line followed a line slightly to the east of the provisional equidistance line for about half of its length, as shown on Map 3 in the Award.[76] Lando has criticised the Tribunal

[66] ibid para 292.
[67] ibid paras 294–98.
[68] ibid paras 307, 311.
[69] ibid (Separate Opinion of Judge Ranjeva) paras 4–7.
[70] ibid para 7.
[71] ibid paras 7–10.
[72] ibid para 8.
[73] *Bay of Bengal Maritime Boundary Arbitration (Bangladesh v India)* (Award of 7 July 2014) PCA Case No 2010-16, paras 248 and 272 (*Bay of Bengal Arbitration*).
[74] ibid paras 273–75, citing *Guyana v Suriname* (n 13).
[75] ibid para 276.
[76] ibid 77 (Map 3).

on the basis that it considered special circumstances twice, an approach he describes as an 'erratic *modus operandi*',[77] but it appears that the special circumstance requiring adjustment only became apparent once the Tribunal had identified the relevant base points, and had identified the delimitation line for the EEZ/continental shelf, thus necessitating further consideration of the territorial sea boundary.

In *Croatia/Slovenia Arbitration*, the Tribunal emphasised the convergence of the principles applicable to delimitation of the territorial sea and to the EEZ/continental shelf.[78] In this respect, the Tribunal noted that in delimiting the territorial sea, it was necessary to accommodate two fundamental principles. First, the principle of natural prolongation of the continental shelf, which could not be secured in respect of the continental shelf unless it was also applied to the territorial sea.[79] Secondly, the principle that an unjustifiable difference of treatment arising from incidental special features should be abated, so that where particular local geographic features of configurations have a greatly exaggerated effect, the delimitation should seek to mitigate that effect.[80]

The Tribunal's statements in relation to convergence of the delimitation methods have been criticised by commentators, and the reference to the law applicable to the delimitation of the EEZ and the continental shelf has rightly been described as confusing.[81] As discussed further below, an argument made to the same effect was rejected by the ICJ in *Maritime Delimitation in the Caribbean Sea and the Pacific Ocean*.[82]

Notwithstanding its reference to convergence, the Tribunal ultimately applied a two-stage methodology to delimit the territorial sea, consistently with other cases under Article 15. Slovenia argued that special circumstances, including its position at the head of the Adriatic Sea and on the concave coast of the Gulf of Trieste, and the confinement of its territorial sea by the territorial sea of its neighbours, necessitated adjustment of the provisional equidistance line.[83] The Tribunal rejected arguments that the disparity in coastal fronts and historic title were special circumstances, but it considered that certain features of the coastal configuration 'produce an exaggeratedly adverse effect if the strict equidistance line is used, and do constitute a special circumstance'.[84] The Tribunal noted in particular that the coastline of Croatia turns sharply southwards around Cape Savudrija, which resulted in an exaggeration of the 'boxed-in' nature of Slovenia's maritime zone.[85] The Tribunal thus delimited

[77] Massimo Lando, 'Judicial Uncertainties on Territorial Sea Delimitations under Article 15 UNCLOS' (2017) 66(3) ICLQ 589, fn 56.

[78] *Croatia/Slovenia Arbitration*, Final Award (n 53) para 1000.

[79] ibid para 1008.

[80] ibid para 1009.

[81] See eg Massimo Lando, 'The Croatia/Slovenia Arbitral Award of 29 June 2017: Is There a Common Method for Delimiting All Maritime Zones Under International Law?' (2017) 100(4) Rivista di dirritto internazionale 1184, 1187; Alex G Oude Elferink, 'Slovenia/Croatia Arbitration—Is the Territorial Sea Delimitation Inconsistent with the Case Law on Maritime Delimitation?' *NCLOS Blog* (16 August 2017) https://site.uit.no/nclos/2017/08/16/sloveniacroatia-arbitration-is-the-territorial-sea-delimitation-inconsistent-with-the-case-law-on-maritime-delimitation/. See also Andrea Insolia, 'The Law of Maritime Delimitation in the Croatia/Slovenia Final Award' in Angela Del Vecchio and Roberto Virzo (eds), *Interpretations of the United Nations Convention on the Law of the Sea by International Courts and Tribunals* (Springer 2019) 249–55 (concluding that the Tribunal reached a balanced result, although reservations can be made about the methods employed to reach it).

[82] *Maritime Delimitation in the Caribbean Sea and the Pacific Ocean (Costa Rica v Nicaragua)* and *Land Boundary in the Northern Part of Isla Portillos (Costa Rica v Nicaragua)* (Judgment) [2019] ICJ Rep 139 (*Maritime Delimitation in the Caribbean Sea and Pacific Ocean*).

[83] *Croatia/Slovenia Arbitration*, Final Award (n 53) para 1005.

[84] ibid para 1011.

[85] ibid paras 1011–12.

the maritime boundary not with an equidistance line, but with an azimuth in a direction approximately parallel to a segment of the maritime boundary between Slovenia and Italy.[86] It subsequently delimited an area to the southwest of the territorial sea boundary to provide Slovenia with a 'junction to the high seas', as had been agreed between the parties.[87]

In *Ghana/Côte d'Ivoire*, the Special Chamber of ITLOS noted that delimitation of the territorial sea is governed by Article 15, which sets out different rules to those governing delimitation of the EEZ and the continental shelf.[88] However, noting that neither party raised sovereignty-related considerations in respect of delimitation of the territorial sea, it considered it appropriate to use the same methodology in respect of delimitation of the entire single maritime boundary.[89] In this respect, the Special Chamber's approach was a departure from the accepted approach in different cases: it appears to have concluded that the parties' request for a single maritime boundary was an implicit acceptance that the same delimitation methodology should apply to all three zones (territorial sea, EEZ, and continental shelf).[90] However, in the event, the approach made no difference, since the Special Chamber rejected all arguments for an adjustment to the provisional equidistance line and other approaches. It rejected Côte d'Ivoire's argument for the application of an angle bisector, in favour of equidistance/relevant circumstances;[91] and it rejected all of the arguments put forward for an adjustment, and delimited the territorial sea, EEZ, and continental shelf within 200 NM using an equidistance line.[92]

In *Maritime Delimitation in the Caribbean Sea and the Pacific Ocean*, the ICJ delimited the maritime boundaries on both sides of the isthmus. Citing to *Croatia/Slovenia Arbitration*, Nicaragua argued that the approach to delimitation of the territorial sea under Article 15 and to the EEZ/continental shelf under Articles 74 and 83 'are convergent' and 'all relevant provisions of UNCLOS must be read together and in context'.[93] The Court did not address this argument explicitly but it notably applied a two-stage equidistance/special circumstances approach for the territorial sea and a separate methodology for the EEZ/continental shelf.[94] In his separate opinion, Judge Robinson squarely rejected the contention that there was convergence in methodology for the three maritime zones, referring to the *travaux* of the Convention, and emphasising the difference in the legal regime for the territorial sea, on the one hand, and the EEZ and the continental shelf, on the other.[95]

On the Caribbean Sea, the Court rejected Nicaragua's contention that the combined effect of the concavity of Nicaragua's coast west of the land boundary and the convexity of Costa Rica's coast east of that point was a special circumstance justifying an adjustment of the equidistance line under Article 15.[96] However, the Court found that the high instability and narrowness of the sandspit in Costa Rica near the land boundary terminus was a special circumstance affecting maritime delimitation in the territorial sea. This instability did not

[86] ibid para 1014.
[87] ibid paras 1062–83.
[88] *Delimitation of the Maritime Boundary between Ghana and Côte d'Ivoire in the Atlantic Ocean (Ghana/Côte d'Ivoire)* (Judgment of 23 September 2017) ITLOS Case No 23, paras 261–62 (*Ghana/Côte d'Ivoire*, Judgment).
[89] ibid paras 262–63.
[90] ibid para 262.
[91] ibid para 324.
[92] ibid paras 480–81.
[93] *Maritime Delimitation in the Caribbean Sea and the Pacific Ocean* (n 81) para 92.
[94] ibid para 98.
[95] ibid (Separate Opinion of Judge Robinson) paras 3–10 and 21.
[96] ibid para 103.

allow one to select a basepoint on that part of Costa Rica's territory, or to connect a point on the sandspit to a fixed point at sea for the first part of the delimitation line. Thus, the Court concluded that it was more appropriate that the fixed point at sea on the median line be connected by a mobile line to the point on solid land on Costa Rica's coast closest to the mouth of the river. The Court also found that another special circumstance was the fact that there was instability of the sandbar separating a small Nicaraguan lagoon on Costa Rica's territory (Harbor Head Lagoon) from the Caribbean Sea. The delimitation of the territorial sea did not take into account any entitlement that might otherwise have resulted from this small Nicaraguan enclave.[97]

On the Pacific side, Nicaragua argued for an adjustment to the provisional equidistance line on the basis of an alleged cut-off due to the prominence of the Santa Elena peninsula close to shore.[98] The Court rejected this argument. The Court noted that 'islets, rocks and minor coastal projections' can have a disproportionate effect on the median line, calling for an adjustment of the provisional median line. However, it considered that the Santa Elena Peninsula 'cannot be considered to be a minor coastal projection that has a disproportionate effect on the delimitation line. The coast of the Santa Elena Peninsula accounts for a large portion of Costa Rica's coast in the area in which the Court is requested to delimit the territorial sea'. It further noted that if it adjusted the line as Nicaragua requested, the resulting boundary would significantly cut off Costa Rica's coastal projections within the territorial sea.[99] Consequently, the Court delimited the territorial sea using an equidistance line.[100]

In *Maritime Delimitation in the Indian Ocean*, the Court rejected Kenya's argument that there was an agreed maritime boundary following a parallel of latitude. The Court therefore proceeded to delimit the maritime boundary. Somalia argued that the territorial sea boundary should be delimited by an equidistance line,[101] while Kenya argued that the boundary should follow the parallel of latitude (on the basis of the parties' agreement, although the Court had rejected that argument).[102] The Court agreed with Somalia that the territorial sea should be delimited by an equidistance line. Although it did not adjust the equidistance line, it selected base points for the equidistance line that differed from those used by the parties on offshore features, and used only base points on the mainland coasts of the two States.[103] Noting that it would have regard to the proposals of the parties as to base points, the Court emphasised that it need not select a particular base point, even if agreed by the parties, if it does not consider it to be appropriate.[104] The Court recalled that it had in the past (for example in *Qatar v Bahrain*) not selected a base point on small maritime features, and that 'there may be situations in which "the equitableness of an equidistance line depends on whether the precaution is taking of eliminating the disproportionate effect of certain 'islets, rocks and minor coastal projections'"'.[105] The use of base points on the mainland coasts resulted in the Court ignoring several offshore features, and in particular those off the Somali coast, which had an impact on the near-shore course of the equidistance line.

97 ibid paras 104–105.
98 ibid para 117.
99 ibid para 174.
100 ibid para 175.
101 *Maritime Delimitation in the Indian Ocean*, Judgment (n 51) paras 101–104.
102 ibid paras 105–106.
103 ibid paras 111–14.
104 ibid para 111.
105 ibid.

The Court's approach therefore had the effect of pushing the equidistance line so that more of the disputed area was allocated to Kenya, even beyond the equidistance line it had drawn in the territorial sea.

The Court concluded its discussion of base points by noting that the course of the line it had drawn 'corresponds closely to the course of a line "at right angles to the general trend of the coastline"', which was a phrase used in the '1927/1933 treaty arrangement'.[106] That 'arrangement' consisted of an agreement signed by Great Britain and Italy (at the time the colonial authorities in Kenya and Somalia, respectively) and a 1933 Exchange of Notes that redefined the land boundary in its southernmost section.[107] Kenya had argued that the 1927/1933 treaty arrangement provided for the establishment of a boundary in the territorial sea, emphasising that Appendix I of the 1927 Agreement stated that the line proceeds from the last point on the land boundary 'in a south-easterly direction, to the limit of territorial waters in a straight line at right angles to the general trend of the coast-line at Dar Es Salam, leaving the islets of Diua Damasciaca in Italian territory'. According to Kenya, the resulting line, which it describes as running perpendicular to the general direction of the coast, 'must be extended further into the territorial sea (which extended up to 3 nautical miles at the time)'.[108] However, Kenya did not ask the Court to delimit any segment of the maritime boundary on the basis of the 1927/1933 treaty arrangement;[109] it argued that there was an agreement for the maritime boundary to proceed along the parallel of latitude.[110]

The Court's approach to base points was heavily criticised by Judge Yusuf in his separate opinion. He noted that the Court and other tribunals have plotted provisional equidistance lines by reference to base points on the low-water line, but the judgment deviated from this practice 'without providing adequate reasons for this seemingly random selection of basepoints'.[111] He also noted that it was well established that the court or tribunal will respect the parties' agreement on the placement of base points, unless particular reasons warrant a different conclusion. Since the parties had here both proposed base points 'which reflect the geographical reality in the vicinity of the land boundary terminus',[112] and their proposed base points were 'largely concordant',[113] the Court should not have disregarded them.[114] He further noted that the Court's approach resulted in it disregarding a material feature in Somalia's coastline, which marked a 'significant shift' in the direction of its coast,[115] and that it also acted inconsistently by placing base points on an island off Kenya's main coast, without giving reasons for the difference in approach.[116] Judge Yusuf was also highly critical of the Court's reference to the 1927/1933 treaty arrangement, which he said 'can only create misunderstandings'.[117] He concluded that:

106 ibid para 118.
107 ibid para 32.
108 ibid para 105.
109 ibid para 106.
110 ibid.
111 ibid (Separate Opinion of Judge Yusuf) paras 8–10.
112 ibid (Separate Opinion of Judge Yusuf) para 11.
113 ibid (Separate Opinion of Judge Yusuf) para 13.
114 ibid (Separate Opinion of Judge Yusuf) para 14.
115 ibid (Separate Opinion of Judge Yusuf) para 16.
116 ibid (Separate Opinion of Judge Yusuf) para 17.
117 ibid (Separate Opinion of Judge Yusuf) para 21.

> The Judgment's approach in the selection of base points has resulted in a contrived median line, the construction of which appears to have been aimed at producing a line which comes as close as possible to a bisector line, although there is nothing that justifies the use of a bisector for the delimitation of the territorial sea between Somalia and Kenya. Paragraph 118 in the Judgment reinforces this impression. Indeed, this paragraph suggests that the approach adopted by the Court for the construction of the median line may have been dictated by the search for a median line that 'corresponds closely to the course of a line 'at right angles to the general trend of the coastline', assuming that the 1927/1933 treaty arrangement, in using this phrase, had as an objective to draw a line that continues into the territorial sea, a question that the Court need not decide.

The Court's references to the 1927/1933 treaty arrangement were also addressed in the individual opinion of Judge Robinson, who noted that the Court had not explained 'how [it] is in a position to take cognizance of this treaty'.[118] Referring to principles of State succession and self-determination, Judge Robinson concluded that 'those treaties are inapplicable in the determination of the maritime dispute between Somalia and Kenya'.[119]

The approaches of tribunals to territorial sea delimitations can be said to promote certainty (and therefore reinforce the rule of law), by a generally strict application of the equidistance/relevant circumstances rule unless there are clear reasons for departure from it. Certainty also has the potential to make a broader contribution to both the rule of law and public order of the oceans, as States that have yet to delimit their territorial sea boundaries have a relatively predictable basis on which to assert claims on specific grounds, thus potentially avoiding conflict and disputes (and possibly also opening the way to territorial sea delimitation agreements being reached without the need for recourse to third-party dispute settlement procedures).

In terms of other potential stakeholder interests, there has been little scope for tribunals to take account of interests of third States, given that territorial sea delimitations address near-shore areas where such interests do not come into play. The extent to which the interests of other stakeholders, for example, individuals undertaking fishery or navigation activities, have been taken into account has generally been limited, because the adjustment of provisional equidistance lines on account of non-geographic factors has been relatively rare—but the cases demonstrate that there is scope for such interests to be taken into account in appropriate circumstances. The way in which tribunals have generally given full effect to islands and other coastal features (such as peninsulas) in territorial sea delimitations might also be considered to take account of the interests of the inhabitants of those features, who may benefit from the full extension of a territorial sea, and whose livelihoods might be adversely impacted if the full extent of a territorial sea is not attributed to the relevant features.

118 ibid (Individual Opinion, Partly Concurring and Partly Dissenting of Judge Robinson) para 36. See also para 37.

119 ibid (Individual Opinion, Partly Concurring and Partly Dissenting of Judge Robinson) paras 37–45.

IV. Delimitation of the Exclusive Economic Zone and Continental Shelf

A. Articles 74(1) and 83(1) of UNCLOS

Articles 74(1) and 83(1) of UNCLOS set out identical rules for delimitation of the EEZ and the continental shelf, as follows:

> The delimitation of the [exclusive economic zone/continental shelf] between States with opposite or adjacent coasts shall be effected by agreement on the basis of international law, as referred to in Article 38 of the Statute of the International Court of Justice, in order to achieve an equitable solution.[120]

This formulation was a notable departure from Article 6 of the Continental Shelf Convention, which provided for delimitation under the equidistance/special circumstances rule. That rule was retained for the territorial sea, as discussed above, but it was not retained for the continental shelf; nor was it adopted for the EEZ. This approach was no doubt influenced by the 1969 judgments of the ICJ in the *North Sea* cases, in which the Court rejected the argument that there was a customary international law of delimitation by reference to the equidistance/special circumstances rule. The Court observed that '[i]t has never been doubted that the equidistance method is a very convenient one, the use of which is indicated in a considerable number of cases',[121] and that 'it would probably be true to say that no other method of delimitation has the same combination of practical convenience and certainty of application'.[122] Yet, the Court considered that these factors did 'not suffice of themselves to convert what is a method into a rule of law'.[123] It did not accept that Article 6 of the Continental Shelf Convention reflected or crystallised a rule of customary international law,[124] and it concluded that no such rule had emerged following the adoption of that Convention.[125] Instead, the Court found that there were 'certain basic legal notions' that applied, notably 'that delimitation must be the object of agreement between the States concerned, and that such agreement must be arrived at in accordance with equitable principles'.[126]

An arguably different approach was taken by the ad hoc court of arbitration in *UK/France* in 1977, which considered that the equidistance/special circumstances rule in Article 6 was a particular expression of the customary international law rule that, failing agreement, the continental shelf boundary was to be delimited in accordance with equitable principles.[127] Whilst emphasising that what is equitable in the circumstances will be influenced by the relevant geography, the Court of Arbitration suggested that the equidistance method was an appropriate starting point for delimitation:

[120] UNCLOS (n 2) arts 74(1) (for EEZ), 83 (for continental shelf).
[121] *North Sea*, Judgment (n 4) para 22.
[122] ibid para 23.
[123] ibid para 23.
[124] ibid para 62.
[125] ibid para 81.
[126] ibid para 84.
[127] *UK/France* (n 29) paras 70, 75.

> The Court notes that in a large proportion of the delimitations known to it, where a particular geographical feature has influenced the course of a continental shelf boundary, the method of delimitation has been some modification or variant of the equidistance principle rather than its total rejection ... Consequently, it seems to the Court to be in accord not only with the legal rules governing the continental shelf but also with State practice to seek the solution in a method modifying or varying the equidistance method rather than to have recourse to a wholly different criterion of delimitation.[128]

Consistently with that finding, the Court carried out a delimitation on the basis of an equidistance line, adjusted to the extent necessary to achieve an equitable solution.

In light of these differing approaches, it is perhaps unsurprising that discussion on delimitation of the EEZ and the continental shelf during UNCLOS negotiations was dominated by the debate between equidistance and equitable principles. Agreement was only reached at a very late stage, when President Koh proposed a draft article representing a compromise position, which was, with a few modifications, approved on 24 September 1982, less than three months before UNCLOS was adopted. That compromise was to omit any reference to a method of delimitation, and merely to indicate that delimitation should 'achieve an equitable solution'.[129] As noted by Evans:

> The equidistance versus equitable principles debate became something of a 'cause célèbre' during the Third United Nations Conference on the Law of the Sea (UNCLOS III) and produced a near 'cliff hanger' of an outcome which proved satisfactory to everyone only because of its dearth of substance.[130]

The formulation in Articles 74 and 83 has therefore provided considerable scope for courts and tribunals interpreting those provisions to contribute to understandings of what constitutes an 'equitable solution'. The flexibility accorded to States, as well as to international tribunals with responsibility for maritime boundary delimitations, has not, however, been fully realised given the emergence of a 'standard' approach, as discussed below.

B. Pre UNCLOS Decisions: Equitable Solution but No Prioritised Method

In February 1982 (before UNCLOS was adopted but after Articles 74 and 83 had been agreed by the Conference), the ICJ rendered judgment in *Continental Shelf* (*Tunisia/Libya*),[131] delimiting the continental shelf. Referring to the ICJ judgment in *North Sea*, as well as the 1977 award in *UK/France*, and the history of Article 83 of UNCLOS, the Court considered 'that equidistance may be applied if it leads to an equitable solution: if not, other methods should be employed'.[132] However, it also noted that equidistance is not 'a

[128] ibid para 249.

[129] UNCLOS (n 2) arts 74(1) and 83(1). See also *Bay of Bengal Arbitration* (n 73) para 339.

[130] Malcolm D Evans, 'Maritime Boundary Delimitation: Where Do We Go From Here?' in David Freestone, Richard Barnes, and David Ong (eds), *The Law of the Sea: Progress and Prospects* (OUP 2006) 138.

[131] *Continental Shelf (Tunisia/Libya)* (Judgment) [1982] ICJ Rep 18 (*Tunisia/Libya*).

[132] ibid para 109.

mandatory legal principle, or a method having some privileged status in relation to other methods'.[133] The Court instead focused on the need to achieve an equitable solution. As such, a method could not be chosen in the abstract, but depended on the relevant circumstances in a particular situation.[134]

A similar approach was taken by the Chamber of the ICJ in *Gulf of Maine* in 1984 in delimiting a single maritime boundary. The Chamber noted that Articles 74(1) and 83(1) of UNCLOS were 'limited to expressing the need for settlement of the problem by agreement and recalling the obligation to achieve an equitable solution'.[135] It rejected the suggestion that customary international law endorsed the equidistance method of delimitation, referring to the judgment in *North Sea*, noting that it was merely 'a practical method that can be applied for the purposes of delimitation'.[136] The Chamber considered that there was a 'fundamental norm' applicable to all maritime delimitations, comprised of two points: first, that delimitation 'must be sought and effected by means of an agreement' and where such agreement cannot be achieved 'delimitation should be effected by recourse to a third party possessing the necessary competence'. Secondly, that:

> delimitation is to be effected by the application of equitable criteria and by the use of practical methods capable of ensuring, with regard to the geographic configuration of the area and other relevant circumstances, an equitable result.[137]

Likewise, the Tribunal in *Delimitation of the Maritime Boundary* (*Guinea/Guinea-Bissau*) considered that the essential objective was to find an 'equitable solution', also referring to Articles 74(1) and 83(1) of UNCLOS.[138] The Tribunal noted that the equidistance method was 'just one among many', and that there was 'no obligation to use it or give it priority, even though it is recognised as having a certain intrinsic value because of its scientific character and the relative ease with which it can be applied'.[139] As to relevant factors and methods, the Tribunal suggested that these were 'not restricted in number', and were 'not restricted to physical facts whether geographical, geological or geomorphological'.[140]

In *Continental Shelf* (*Libya/Malta*), the ICJ noted that '[j]udicial decisions are at one ... in holding that the delimitation of a continental shelf boundary must be effected by the application of equitable principles in all the relevant circumstances in order to achieve an equitable result'.[141] Referring to *North Sea*, and to the UNCLOS negotiations, the Court rejected the suggestion that it was required to use the equidistance method, 'even as a preliminary and provisional step towards the drawing of a delimitation line', and noted that '[t]he application of equitable principles in the particular relevant circumstances may still require the adoption of another method, or combination of methods, of delimitation, even from the outset'.[142] However, the Court held that, in the circumstances, commencing with

[133] ibid para 110.
[134] ibid para 70.
[135] *Gulf of Maine* (n 7) para 295.
[136] ibid para 106.
[137] ibid para 112.
[138] *Delimitation of the Maritime Boundary (Guinea/Guinea-Bissau)* (Award of 18 February 1985) 25(2) (1986) ILM 251, para 88 (*Guinea/Guinea-Bissau*).
[139] ibid para 102.
[140] ibid para 98.
[141] *Continental Shelf (Libya/Malta)* (Judgment) [1985] ICJ Rep 13, para 45 (*Libya/Malta*).
[142] ibid para 43.

a provisional median line 'is the most judicious manner of proceeding with a view to the eventual achievement of an equitable result'.[143] The Court noted that the median line was 'only provisional',[144] and it required adjustment on the basis of the difference in length of the parties' relevant coasts[145] and the southward location of the Maltese islands.[146] The Court therefore adjusted the equidistance line, and confirmed that there was 'no evident disproportion' in the areas of shelf attributed to each State on the basis of the adjusted equidistance line.[147]

Similarly, the Tribunal's 1992 decision in *Delimitation of Maritime Areas* (*St Pierre and Miquelon*) noted the parties' agreement on the 'fundamental norm to be applied, which requires the delimitation to be effected in accordance with equitable principles, or equitable criteria, taking account of all the relevant circumstances in order to achieve an equitable result'.[148] It further noted that 'the underlying premise of this fundamental norm is the emphasis on equity and the rejection of any obligator method'.[149] The Tribunal did not accept either method of delimitation proposed by the parties (equidistance was espoused by France, and Canada proposed that the two islands be effectively enclaved), and instead adopted a modified enclave solution in the western sector together with a method of frontal projection in the southern sector.[150] The Tribunal also concluded with an assessment of proportionality, finding that there was 'certainly no disproportion' arising from the final line.[151]

C. The Emergence of the Two-stage Approach: 1993–2007

The 1993 judgment of the ICJ in *Maritime Delimitation between Greenland and Jan Mayen* has been described as a 'turning point'.[152] The Court was asked to delimit the continental shelf and the fishery zone between Denmark's Greenland and the Norwegian island of Jan Mayen. Both parties had ratified the Continental Shelf Convention, such that the equidistance/special circumstances method in Article 6 applied to the continental shelf delimitation. The Court observed that it was the first occasion on which it applied the Continental Shelf Convention.[153] So far as concerns the continental shelf delimitation, the Court considered that if even customary law applied, 'it is in accord with precedents to begin with the median line as a provisional line and then to ask whether 'special circumstances' require any adjustment or shifting of that line'.[154] For the fishery zone, the Court considered it was also appropriate to begin the delimitation with a provisional median line, with adjustments to be

143 ibid para 62.
144 ibid para 63.
145 ibid para 68.
146 ibid para 69.
147 ibid para 75.
148 *Delimitation of Maritime Areas (St Pierre and Miquelon) (Canada/France)* (Decision of 10 June 1992) 31 (1992) ILM 1145, para 38 (*St Pierre and Miquelon*).
149 ibid para 38.
150 ibid paras 67–70.
151 ibid para 93.
152 Yoshifumi Tanaka, *The International Law of the Sea* (3rd edn, CUP 2019) 244; Lando, *Maritime Delimitation* (n 1) 20.
153 *Maritime Delimitation in the Area between Greenland and Jan Mayen (Denmark v Norway)* (Judgment) [1993] ICJ Rep 38, para 45 (*Maritime Delimitation between Greenland and Jan Mayen*).
154 ibid para 51.

made on the basis of 'relevant circumstances'.[155] It noted, however, that 'there is inevitably a tendency towards assimilation between the special circumstances of Article 6 of the 1958 Convention and the relevant circumstances under customary law, and this if only because they are both intended to enable the achievement of an equitable result'.[156] Thus, the ICJ considered that:

> It cannot be surprising if an equidistance-special circumstances rule produced much the same result as an equitable principles-relevant circumstances rule in the case of opposite coasts, whether in the case of a delimitation of continental shelf, of fishery zone, or of an all-purpose single boundary.[157]

Thus, for both the continental shelf and the fishery zone, the Court commenced with a provisional equidistance line, and it considered that the median should be adjusted as a consequence of the disparity of the lengths of the two States' relevant coasts,[158] and in the southern part of the boundary, to permit equitable access to capelin fishery resources.[159] It rejected both Denmark's argument that major differences between Greenland and Jan Mayen as regards population and socio-economic factors,[160] and Norway's argument that security considerations necessitated further adjustments to the line.[161] In this sense, the Court's approach is consistent with other judgments that have focused on geographic rather than non-geographic circumstances. On the one hand, it might be questioned whether this approach has the potential to minimise other stakeholder interests, for example individual interests in security and socio-economic prosperity. On the other hand, the emphasis on geographic factors might be perceived to promote predictability, stability, and ultimately the rule of law and public order of the oceans. As will be seen in the discussion of more recent case law below, tribunals have in some cases taken non-geographic factors into account, including security and interests in navigation and fisheries, and it may be that in those cases it was considered on the facts to be more equitable to do so than in those cases where such factors were not taken into account.

The arbitral tribunal in *Eritrea/Yemen* was the first to apply UNCLOS as a formal source of law. Although Eritrea was not yet a party to UNCLOS, the Arbitration Agreement required the Tribunal to take account of UNCLOS and 'any other pertinent factor'.[162] As to the latter, the Tribunal noted it was

> a broad concept, and doubtless includes various factors that are generally recognised as being relevant to the process of delimitation such as proportionality, non-encroachment, the presence of islands, and any other factors that might affect the equities of the particular situation.[163]

155 ibid para 54.
156 ibid para 56.
157 ibid.
158 ibid paras 68–69.
159 ibid para 76.
160 ibid paras 79–80.
161 ibid paras 81.
162 *Sovereignty and Maritime Delimitation in the Red Sea (Eritrea/Yemen)* (Award of the Arbitral Tribunal in the Second Stage of 17 December 1999: Maritime Delimitation) PCA Case No 1996-04, para 6 (citing art 2 of the Arbitration Agreement) (*Eritrea/Yemen*, Second Stage).
163 ibid para 130.

Both parties proposed a boundary using the equidistance method, although their proposed delimitations varied broadly. The Tribunal noted:

> It is a generally accepted view, as is evidenced in both the writings of commentators and in the jurisprudence, that between coasts that are opposite to each other the median or equidistance line normally provides an equitable boundary in accordance with the requirements of the Convention, and in particular those of its Articles 74 and 83 which respectively provide for the equitable delimitation of the EEZ and of the continental shelf between States with opposite or adjacent coasts. Indeed both Parties to the present case have claimed a boundary constructed on the equidistance method, although based on different points of departure and resulting in very different lines.[164]

The Tribunal commenced the delimitation with a provisional equidistance line, noting that there were various factors that required careful consideration. It then adjusted the equidistance line: in the northernmost stretch on account of various islands; in the middle stretch to respect the territorial sea of certain islands; and in the southern sector, using an unadjusted equidistance line. The Tribunal rejected arguments that fishing or fisheries were factors relevant to the delimitation,[165] and declined to make any adjustment on account of them or of any traditional fishing regimes. However, the Tribunal recognised the existence of a traditional fishing regime in the region, requiring the parties to perpetuate that regime so as to ensure free access and enjoyment for the fishers of both Eritrea and Yemen. The Tribunal elaborated on the character and practical implications of that regime, and specified that it was to be perpetuated notwithstanding the award on maritime delimitation.

The Tribunal then noted that proportionality 'is not an independent mode or principle of delimitation, but rather a test of the equitableness of a delimitation arrived at by some other means'.[166] After comparing the lengths of the two States' relevant coasts and the division of the relevant area, the Tribunal concluded that the line of delimitation it decided upon resulted in no disproportion.[167]

Notably, although the Tribunal rejected Eritrea's argument that the offshore petroleum contracts of the parties supported a 'historic median line' boundary, the Tribunal also concluded that the parties were under an obligation to consult each other with regard to the exploitation of petroleum resources in the area. It stated:

> [H]aving regard to the maritime boundary established by this Award, the Parties are bound to inform one another and to consult one another on any oil and gas and other mineral resources that may be discovered that straddle the single maritime boundary between them or that lie in its immediate vicinity. Moreover, the historical connections between the peoples concerned, and the friendly relations of the Parties that have been restored since the Tribunal's rendering of its Award on Sovereignty, together with the body of State practice in the exploitation of resources that straddle maritime boundaries, import that Eritrea and

[164] ibid para 131.
[165] ibid para 74.
[166] ibid para 165.
[167] ibid para 168.

> Yemen should give every consideration to the shared or joint or unitised exploitation of any such resources.[168]

This aspect of the Tribunal's decision indicates that it was clearly aware of the broader interests of diverse stakeholders, although ultimately its decision was guided by the geography, reflecting the fundamental principle that the land dominates the sea.

After these two decisions, there followed two ICJ judgments and two arbitral awards that took the same approach: effectively drawing a provisional equidistance line and considering whether adjustment was needed on the basis of relevant circumstances. Thus, in 2001, in *Qatar v Bahrain*, the ICJ delimited the EEZ and the continental shelf on the basis of customary international law,[169] and referring to *Jan Mayen*, determined that it would provisionally draw an equidistance line and then consider whether there were circumstances that would require an adjustment of that line.[170] Notably, in respect of the EEZ and the continental shelf the two States were in a relationship of adjacency.

In 2002, the ICJ in *Land and Maritime Boundary* (*Cameroon v Nigeria*) took the same approach in applying Articles 74 and 83 of UNCLOS, which were in force between the parties.[171] Referring to its earlier decisions in *Qatar v Bahrain*, *Gulf of Maine*, and *Libya/Malta*, the Court noted that it had made clear

> what the applicable criteria, principles and rules of delimitation are when a line covering several zones of coincident jurisdictions is to be determined. They are expressed in the so-called equitable principles/relevant circumstances method. This method, which is very similar to the equidistance/special circumstances method applicable in delimitation of the territorial sea, involves first drawing an equidistance line, then considering whether there are factors calling for the adjustment or shifting of that line in order to achieve an 'equitable result'.[172]

The Court rejected arguments that the concavity of the coastline, the presence of an island under the sovereignty of a third State, disparity between the coastal lengths, and the parties' practice with respect to oil concessions were circumstances requiring adjustment of the equidistance line, but the Court did take into account the interests of a third State, Equatorial Guinea, in the delimitation line it ultimately drew.

In 2006, the arbitral tribunal in *Barbados v Trinidad and Tobago* noted that Articles 74(1) and 83(1) of UNCLOS set out an 'apparently simple and imprecise formula', allowing for 'a broad consideration of the legal rules'.[173] Referring to the judgments of the ICJ in *Qatar v Bahrain* and *Cameroon v Nigeria*, the Tribunal noted that:

168 ibid para 86.

169 Bahrain had ratified UNCLOS but Qatar was only a signatory; and neither State was party to the 1958 Geneva Conventions: *Qatar v Bahrain*, Merits (n 8) para 167.

170 ibid para 230, citing *Maritime Delimitation between Greenland and Jan Mayen* (n 153).

171 *Land and Maritime Boundary (Cameroon v Nigeria)* (Judgment) [2002] ICJ Rep 303, paras 285–86 (*Cameroon v Nigeria*).

172 ibid para 288, citing *Qatar v Bahrain*, Merits (n 8); *Gulf of Maine* (n 135); *Libya/Malta* (n 141).

173 *Barbados v Trinidad and Tobago* (Award of the Arbitral Tribunal of 11 April 2006) PCA Case No 2004-02, para 222 (*Barbados v Trinidad and Tobago*).

> The determination of the line of delimitation thus normally follows a two-step approach. First, a provisional line of equidistance is posited as a hypothesis and a practical starting point. While a convenient starting point, equidistance alone will in many circumstances not ensure an equitable result in the light of the peculiarities of each specific case. The second step accordingly requires the examination of this provisional line in the light of relevant circumstances, which are case specific, so as to determine whether it is necessary to adjust the provisional equidistance line in order to achieve an equitable result. This approach is usually referred to as the 'equidistance/relevant circumstances' principle. Certainty is thus combined with the need for an equitable result.[174]

The following year, the arbitral Tribunal in *Guyana v Suriname* took the same approach, citing the decision in *Barbados v Trinidad and Tobago*, and stating:

> Articles 74 and 83 of the Convention require that the Tribunal achieve an 'equitable' solution. The case law of the International Court of Justice and arbitral jurisprudence as well as State practice are at one in holding that the delimitation process should, in appropriate cases, begin by positing a provisional equidistance line which may be adjusted in the light of relevant circumstances in order to achieve an equitable solution. The Tribunal will follow this method in the present case.'[175]

The only departure from the two-stage equidistance/relevant circumstances approach in this period was the ICJ's judgment in *Nicaragua v Honduras*. Having found that there was no agreed maritime boundary, the Court proceeded to the delimitation. It noted that the equidistance method is 'widely used in the practice of maritime delimitation ... because of its scientific character and the relative ease with which it can be applied'.[176] However, it stated that 'the equidistance method does not automatically have priority over other methods of delimitation and, in particular circumstances, there may be factors which make the application of the equidistance method inappropriate'.[177] As noted above in relation to the territorial sea delimitation, the Court identified factors that rendered, in its view, the construction of base points for an equidistance line impossible. These factors were all geographical: the sharply convex coastline in the vicinity of the land boundary; the 'very active morpho-dynamism' in the coastline around Cape Gracias a Dios, which could 'render any equidistance line so constructed today arbitrary and unreasonable in the near future'.[178] Taking into account the geographical configuration of the coast, and the geomorphological features of the area where the endpoint of the land boundary is located,[179] the Court concluded that equidistance would not be appropriate. As noted above, it adopted the bisector method, noting that the method of delimitation should 'be faithful to the actual geographical situation' and that '[t]he bisector method ... seeks to approximate the relevant coastal relationships ... on the basis of the macro-geography of a coastline as represented by a line drawn between two points on the coast'.[180]

[174] ibid para 242 (citations omitted), citing *Qatar v Bahrain*, Merits (n 8); *Cameroon v Nigeria* (n 171).
[175] *Guyana v Suriname* (n 13) para 342, citing *Barbados v Trinidad and Tobago* (n 173).
[176] *Nicaragua v Honduras* (n 65) para 272.
[177] ibid.
[178] ibid para 277.
[179] ibid para 292.
[180] ibid para 289.

In respect of the islands located north and south of the 15th parallel, the Court confirmed that Honduras was entitled to a 12 NM territorial sea, subject to any overlap with the territorial sea of nearby Nicaraguan islands. It delimited the territorial seas of the islands using equidistance lines, finding that there were no special circumstances in the area warranting adjustment of the equidistance line.[181] The single maritime boundary therefore followed a bisector until it intersected with the islands' equidistance lines, following those until reconnecting with the bisector.[182]

As noted by Fietta and Cleverly, this judgment is particularly notable for having rejected the equidistance/relevant circumstances approach after a series of cases, spanning more than a decade, in which the court and tribunals embraced the drawing of a provisional equidistance line as the first step in the delimitation of the EEZ/continental shelf. Nevertheless, in the very particular and highly unusual geography, the Court adopted the bisector method, while noting the 'primacy' of equidistance in delimitation of the territorial sea and the 'clear role' accorded to equidistance in practice delimiting the EEZ and the continental shelf.[183] This approach suggests that flexibility remains important to achieve an overall equitable solution and that, although predictability is an important objective, it will not trump the particular factual circumstances of any particular situation. The fact that the Court highlighted the very unusual geographic situation may reflect its concern to emphasise the importance of predictability and certainty, both for the resolution of disputes and also for avoiding them, through the reaching of bilateral delimitation agreements.

D. The Three-stage Methodology: Judicial Development of the 'Standard' Approach

The two-stage equidistance/relevant circumstances approach was displaced by the ICJ in 2009 in *Maritime Delimitation in the Black Sea*, in favour of a three-stage methodology, which has since become the established approach. In that case, the Court concluded that there was an agreed boundary between the USSR and Romania following a 12 NM arc around Serpents' Island, but that there was no agreement in force delimiting the EEZ and the continental shelf.[184] It therefore considered the appropriate methodology under Articles 74 and 83, noting that it would proceed in three defined stages.[185]

First, 'the Court establishes a provisional delimitation line … us[ing] methods that are geometrically objective and appropriate for the geography of the area'.[186] As regards adjacent States, an equidistance line will be drawn 'unless there are compelling reasons that make this unfeasible in the particular case', and for opposite coasts, 'the provisional delimitation line will consist of a median line between the two coasts'.[187] To construct a provisional equidistance line, the Court noted that it is also necessary to identify the 'relevant area' and the 'relevant coasts'. In *Maritime Delimitation in the Black Sea*, the Court noted that 'the

181 ibid para 304.
182 ibid para 305.
183 Fietta and Cleverly (n 1) 467.
184 *Maritime Delimitation in the Black Sea (Romania v Ukraine)* (Judgment) [2009] ICJ Rep 61, paras 26–30 (*Maritime Delimitation in the Black Sea*).
185 ibid paras 115–22.
186 ibid para 116.
187 ibid.

coast, in order to be considered as relevant for the purpose of the delimitation, must generate projections which overlap with projections from the coast of the other party'.[188] Next, one identifies appropriate base points on the parties' relevant coasts,[189] and from those base points the provisional equidistance line is constructed. This process is objective in the sense that it produces a line based on the geography of the parties. However, it also involves a degree of subjectivity because the selection of relevant coasts and base points will necessarily influence the line. This subjectivity gives potential scope to facilitate an equitable solution in the particular circumstances, but also may be grounds for criticism, as has been seen in some of the cases discussed below.

Secondly, having established a provisional equidistance line, the Court considered whether there were any relevant circumstances necessitating an adjustment of that line in order 'to achieve an equitable result'.[190]

Thirdly and finally, the Court stated it would:

> [v]erify that the line ... does not, as it stands, lead to an inequitable result by reason of any marked disproportion between the ratio of the respective coastal lengths and the ratio between the relevant maritime area of each State by reference to the delimitation line. A final check for an equitable outcome entails a confirmation that no great disproportionality of maritime areas is evident by comparison to the ratio of coastal lengths.[191]

In its application to the particular case, there are three particular issues of note. First, in respect of its identification of the relevant coasts, the Court recalled the principle that the land dominates the sea, and identified as relevant 'those coasts the projections of which overlap, because the task of delimitation consists in resolving the overlapping claims by drawing a line of separation of the maritime areas concerned'.[192] The Court considered that the coast of Ukraine's Karkinits'ka Gulf was not relevant, because '[t]he coast of this gulf face each other and their submarine extension cannot overlap with the extensions of Romania's coast'. The Court used a closing line on the Gulf to calculate the relevant area but did not include this closing line in its calculation of the relevant coast.[193] This approach was in contradiction with the ICJ Chamber's treatment of the Bay of Fundy in *Gulf of Maine*,[194] and has been criticised, including on the basis that at least the back of the coast of the Gulf does project into the area of overlapping claims.[195]

The second point of issue concerned relevant circumstances. The Court examined several factors that the parties relied upon as relevant circumstances. Ukraine relied on the relative disparity in coastal lengths as a relevant circumstance, at a ratio of 2.8:1 in Ukraine's favour. The Court noted that '[w]here disparities in the lengths of coasts are particularly marked', the Court could choose to treat that as a relevant circumstance necessitating adjustment to the provisional equidistance line, but it did not find such marked disparity in the present case.[196] Romania relied on other delimitation agreements in the enclosed Black

188 ibid para 99.
189 ibid paras 116–17.
190 ibid paras 120, 155.
191 ibid para 122.
192 ibid paras 77, 99.
193 ibid para 100.
194 *Gulf of Maine* (n 7) para 31.
195 Fietta and Cleverly (n 1) 490. See also discussion in Lando, *Maritime Delimitation* (n 1) 60–65.
196 *Maritime Delimitation in the Black Sea* (n 184) paras 164, 168.

Sea as a relevant circumstance, but the Court considered that neither the existing agreements in the Black Sea nor its enclosed character necessitated adjustment to the provisional equidistance line.[197] Romania also argued that Serpents' Island was a relevant circumstance necessitating adjustment to the equidistance line. The Court noted that the Island could not generate any entitlement projecting beyond those generated by the Ukrainian mainland coast, and it followed from this that the Island did not call for adjustment to the equidistance line.[198] Ukraine argued that activities in the relevant area, including hydrocarbon licensing and fisheries regulation, constituted a relevant circumstance. Referring to *Barbados v Trinidad and Tobago*, the Court noted that resource-related circumstances had not generally been considered relevant circumstances, and dismissed Ukraine's arguments in this regard.[199] Both States relied on cut-off as a relevant circumstance, but the Court considered that its line allowed the adjacent coasts of each State 'to produce their effects, in terms of maritime entitlements, in a reasonable and mutually balanced way', and therefore there was no need for an adjustment.[200] Similarly, as to the parties' reliance on security interests, the Court considered that the provisional equidistance line fully respected the legitimate security interests of both States.[201] Thus, the Court concluded that there were no relevant circumstances necessitating adjustment of the provisional equidistance line.

At the final stage of the delimitation, the Court noted that the coastal length ratio was 2.8:1 in favour of Ukraine, and the division of the relevant area, using the Court's equidistance line, yielded a ratio of 2.1:1 in favour of Ukraine It did not consider that this led to any significant disproportionality necessitating adjustment.[202]

The Court's judgment in *Maritime Delimitation in the Black Sea* was unanimous and there were no opinions appended to it. Its statement of the three-stage approach to delimitation and the EEZ was hugely influential, and has been considered, at least as a starting point, in all subsequent delimitation cases. Its unanimity may have contributed to its influence. It may also be considered to have been a timely opportunity for the Court to make a clear statement as to the standard approach that should be taken, and its influence might also be attributed to the recognition of subsequent tribunals as to the value of predictability and certainty in attracting cases. Notably, there has since been a steady stream of delimitation disputes referred to binding dispute settlement under UNCLOS or other agreements.

Thus, in *Bay of Bengal Delimitation*, ITLOS endorsed the three-stage approach, stating that:

> In the *Black Sea* case, the ICJ built on the evolution of the jurisprudence on maritime delimitation. In that case, the ICJ gave a description of the three-stage methodology which it applied … The Tribunal notes that jurisprudence has developed in favour of the equidistance/relevant circumstances method. This is the method adopted by international courts and tribunals in the majority of the delimitation cases that have come before them.[203]

[197] ibid paras 174, 177–78.
[198] ibid paras 187–88.
[199] ibid paras 197–98, citing *Barbados v Trinidad and Tobago* (n 173).
[200] ibid para 201.
[201] ibid para 204.
[202] ibid paras 210–16.
[203] *Bay of Bengal Delimitation* (n 47) paras 233, 238.

In his separate declaration, addressing the delimitation methodology, Judge Wolfrum expressed the view that judges exercise a law-making function, such that their case law constitutes a source of international law to be read into UNCLOS. He stated:

> Case law of international courts and tribunals is more than a means to identify the customary or treaty law relevant for the delimitation of continental shelves and exclusive economic zones, as stated by the Tribunal. In my view international courts and tribunals in respect of maritime delimitation exercise a 'law-making function', a function which is anticipated and legitimized by articles 74 and 83 of the Convention. In this context it is appropriate to mention that article 287 of the Convention entrusts three institutions[204] with the task and responsibility of interpreting the Convention and, within its framework, to progressively develop it. This requires them to harmonize their jurisprudence with the view to avoiding any fragmentation, in particular in respect of delimitation of maritime areas.[205]

He continued, in respect of delimitation methodology for the EEZ/continental shelf:

> The ensuing international case law constitutes an acquis judiciaire, a source of international law to be read into articles 74 and 83 of the Convention. It is the feature of this law not to be static but to be open to progressive development by the international courts and tribunals concerned. It is the responsibility of these international courts and tribunals not only to decide delimitation cases while remaining within the framework of such acquis judiciaire but also to provide for the progressive development of the latter. They are called upon in further developing this acquis judiciaire to take into account new scientific findings.[206]

Through this declaration, Judge Wolfrum expressly set out his views as to the significance of the tribunal's function in law development. Although he did so with specific reference to Articles 74 and 83, it appears that the same principle would apply to other aspects of the Convention that a tribunal is called upon to interpret. He also appears to have taken cognisance of the importance of stability and predictability (by reference to the *acquis judiciaire*), while also suggesting that an important aspect of the tribunal's function is to take account of new and progressive developments.

In the application of the methodology to this case, a particular issue of dispute between the parties concerned the treatment of the Bangladeshi St Martin's Island, which lies about six NM off the coast of Bangladesh close to the land boundary with Myanmar. As noted above, in the territorial sea delimitation, the Tribunal gave St Martin's full effect and held that it was not a special circumstance necessitating adjustment to the provisional equidistance line. However, in respect of the EEZ/continental shelf the Tribunal gave special consideration to St Martin's Island in two ways. First, it accepted Myanmar's contention that using the island as a base point would result in a line that blocked the seaward projection of Myanmar's coast, which would result in an 'unwarranted distortion of the delimitation line,

[204] Judge Wolfrum appears not to have counted Annex VIII arbitration, which is a fourth institution with competence under art 287 of UNCLOS.

[205] *Bay of Bengal Delimitation* (n 47) paras 136–37 (Declaration of Judge Wolfrum).

[206] ibid 138.

and amount to a "judicial refashioning of geography" '.[207] The Tribunal therefore excluded any base points on St Martin's Island for construction of the provisional equidistance line. Secondly, it accepted Myanmar's argument that St Martin's Island was a relevant circumstance warranting adjustment of the equidistance line in the EEZ/continental shelf, noting that '[t]he distorting effect of an island on an equidistance line may increase substantially as the line moves beyond 12 nm from the coast'.[208] The Tribunal therefore gave the island no effect at all in the delimitation of the EEZ/continental shelf.[209]

Bangladesh argued for two other relevant circumstances. First, it considered that the concavity of its coastline and the resulting cut-off effect necessitated an adjustment to the provisional equidistance line. The Tribunal agreed with Bangladesh, noting that Bangladesh was the middle country in a three-State situation with India and Myanmar, and the resulting line produced a cut-off effect on its coast requiring an adjustment to the provisional equidistance line.[210] The Tribunal therefore adjusted the equidistance line, deflecting it from the point where it began to cut off the seaward projection of Bangladesh's coast.[211] Secondly, Bangladesh argued that the Bengal depositional system gave a physical, geological, and geomorphological connection between Bangladesh's landmass and the Bay of Bengal sea floor, and was a special circumstance necessitating that no boundary within 200 NM should cut off its rights in the area beyond 200 NM.[212] The Tribunal rejected Bangladesh's argument, noting that:

> The location and direction of the single maritime boundary applicable both to the seabed and subsoil and to the superjacent waters within the 200 nm limit are to be determined on the basis of geography of the coasts of the Parties in relation to each other and not on the geology or geomorphology of the seabed of the delimitation area.[213]

Finally, the Tribunal carried out the disproportionality test, noting that ratios in favour of Myanmar of 1:1.42 for relevant coast and 1:1.54 for relevant area did not show any significant disproportion necessitating adjustment of the equidistance line.[214]

In 2012, in *Territorial and Maritime Dispute (Nicaragua v Colombia)*,[215] Colombia argued for the application of the three-stage equidistance methodology, whereas Nicaragua argued that the Colombian islands to the east of its mainland coasts should be enclaved in an area forming part of Nicaragua's EEZ and continental shelf. The Court stated that it:

> [h]as made clear on a number of occasions that the methodology which it will normally employ when called upon to effect a delimitation between overlapping continental shelf and exclusive economic zone entitlements involves proceeding in three stages.[216]

[207] ibid 265.
[208] ibid para 318.
[209] ibid paras 318–19.
[210] ibid paras 290–97.
[211] ibid paras 329–36.
[212] ibid para 320.
[213] ibid para 322.
[214] ibid paras 498–99.
[215] *Territorial and Maritime Dispute (Nicaragua v Colombia)* (Judgment) [2012] ICJ Rep 624 (*Territorial and Maritime Dispute*, Judgment).
[216] ibid para 190.

The Court rejected Nicaragua's argument that the geographical situation made the construction of a provisional equidistance line unfeasible. Rather, the unusual geography could be taken into account in the second stage of the delimitation process.[217]

The parties raised a significant number of factors as relevant circumstances. The Court did not accept that the previous conduct of the parties, access to natural resources, security issues, or bilateral delimitation agreements with third States were relevant circumstances.[218] However, it accepted two factors as relevant circumstances. First, the substantial difference in length of relevant coasts, at 1:8.2 in favour of Nicaragua.[219] Notably, the Court calculated Colombia's relevant coasts using a radial projection of its islands, ie including those parts of the coasts that faced away from Nicaragua's mainland coast. That approach was arguably in contrast to its approach to Ukraine's Karkinits'ka Gulf in *Maritime Delimitation in the Black Sea*,[220] but might be explained on the basis that Nicaragua's 200 NM maritime claim extended also to the east of the Colombian islands (ie it surrounded the islands).

The second relevant circumstance that was accepted by the Court was the overall geographical context, whereby Nicaragua was cut-off by a few small Colombian islands. The Court noted that, at the same time, Colombia should not be cut off from the entitlements generated by its islands in the area to the east.[221] Ultimately, it did enclave Quitasueño and Serrana, in light of their size and remote location, and taking account of the disproportionate effect they would otherwise have on the boundary.[222] However, it declined to enclave the small Colombian islands, a number of which had significant human populations, noting that it would have 'unfortunate consequences for the orderly management of maritime resources, policing and the public order of the oceans in general, all of which would be better served by a simpler and more coherent division of the relevant area'.[223] The two features that were enclaved, Quitasueño and Serrana, had no population.[224] Thus, here, the Court took account of the interests of broader and diverse group of stakeholders: those individuals inhabiting the relevant islands, as well as the international community's interest in public order of the oceans more generally.

In the part of the Caribbean between Nicaragua's mainland coasts and Colombia's islands, the Court adjusted the equidistance line using a 3:1 weighting ratio between the Nicaraguan and Colombian base points, which resulted in a line that did not cut across the 12 NM territorial seas generated by Colombia's islands. To the north and south of that line, the Court continued the delimitation lines along parallels of latitude out to Nicaragua's 200 NM limit.[225] The resulting delimitation line divided the relevant area in a ratio of 1:3.44 in Nicaragua's favour, with a relevant coast length ratio of 1:8.2 also in Nicaragua's favour. Noting that the disproportionality test was carried out to ensure that there is not 'a significant disproportionality so gross as to 'taint' the result and render it inequitable',[226] the Court

[217] ibid paras 195–98.
[218] ibid paras 217–28.
[219] ibid para 211.
[220] See n 193 above and accompanying text.
[221] *Territorial and Maritime Dispute*, Judgment (n 215) paras 215–30.
[222] ibid para 238.
[223] ibid para 230.
[224] Fietta and Cleverly (n 1) 529.
[225] *Territorial and Maritime Dispute*, Judgment (n 215) para 236.
[226] ibid para 242.

concluded that there was no disproportionality requiring adjustment to the delimitation line.[227]

The delimitation line as adjusted by the Court has a rather unorthodox appearance, which results in part from the very unusual geographic situation, namely, the presence of Colombian islands opposite the coast of Nicaragua, a significant distance from the Colombian mainland. However, as has been observed, the Court affirmed in this case that the three-step methodology is not to be applied mechanically, and even if one commences with a provisional equidistance line, that does not preclude substantial adjustments to that line.[228] As in other cases, the Court emphasised geographic factors justifying adjustments, and non-geographic factors, including those which were argued to have an impact on public order, were dismissed.

In *Maritime Dispute* (*Peru v Chile*), the ICJ found that the two States had tacitly agreed a maritime boundary along a parallel of latitude out to 80 NM, which coincided with the fishing practices of the two States.[229] Beyond that point, the Court delimited the maritime boundary. In doing so, it followed the three-stage delimitation methodology set out in the earlier cases. However, there were two aspects of the case that were novel.

First, the Court constructed an equidistance line ignoring any Peruvian coast that fell within a radius of 80 NM of the land boundary terminus, and only used coast beyond that point for base points.[230] This decision resulted in an equidistance line shifted to the north, in Chile's favour. From the point where that displaced equidistance line reached Chile's outer limit of 200 NM, the Court decided that the boundary would continue directly southwards to meet Peru's outer limit at 200 NM.[231] This determination had the effect of generating a small area of Peruvian EEZ to the south of the boundary with Chile, in effect wrapping around the Chilean EEZ. Having drawn that provisional modified equidistance line, the Court considered that there were no relevant circumstances necessitating adjustment of it.[232]

Secondly, in carrying out the disproportionality exercise, the Court noted that the agreed boundary out to 80 NM rendered the calculation of the relevant coast length and relevant area 'difficult, if not impossible', so it did not carry out a calculation of relevant ratios, but undertook a 'broad assessment of disproportionality', and concluded that 'no significant disproportion is evident, such as would call into question the equitable nature of the provisional equidistance line'.[233] The Court effectively abandoned its usual approach of comparing ratios of relevant coasts and relevant area by the use of an objective mathematical formula. The resulting 'broad assessment' introduced significant subjectivity into the disproportionality test, and there was a marked absence of any detailed consideration of the factors leading it to conclude that there was 'no significant disproportion'.[234] While

[227] ibid paras 244, 247.

[228] See eg Lawrence H Martin and Yuri B Parkhomenko, 'The Territorial and Maritime Dispute (Nicaragua v. Colombia) and Its Implications for Future Maritime Delimitations in the Caribbean Sea and Elsewhere' in Edgardo Sobrenes Obregon and Benjamin Samson (eds), *Nicaragua Before the International Court of Justice: Impacts on International Law* (Springer 2018) 138.

[229] *Maritime Dispute (Peru v Chile)* (Judgment) [2014] ICJ Rep 3, paras 149, 151 (*Peru v Chile*).

[230] ibid paras 183–86.

[231] ibid para 190.

[232] ibid para 191.

[233] ibid paras 192–94.

[234] This has been criticised by commentators. See eg Lando, *Maritime Delimitation* (n 1) 281, 287; Fietta and Cleverly (n 1) 547–48.

departing from its usual approach to elements of the delimitation methodology due to the particular circumstances of the case, the Court nevertheless affirmed the principal aspects of the methodology, in particular the three-stage approach.

In *Bay of Bengal Arbitration*, the Annex VII Tribunal focused on the delimitation methodology as developed in the existing case law, noting that UNCLOS Articles 74 and 83, unlike Article 15, did not specify a method of delimitation, and that the reference in Article 15 to a median line could not be read into Articles 74 and 83.[235] Drawing upon the language of Judge Wolfrum's separate opinion in *Bay of Bengal Delimitation* (a member of the Annex VII Tribunal in this case), the Tribunal emphasised the special role of the jurisprudence and therefore of UNCLOS tribunals in developing the law and the content of Articles 74 and 83:

> Since articles 74 and 83 of the Convention do not provide for a particular method of delimitation, the appropriate delimitation method—if the States concerned cannot agree—is left to be determined through the mechanisms for the peaceful settlement of disputes. In addressing this question, international courts and tribunals are guided by a paramount objective, namely, that the method chosen be designed so as to lead to an equitable result and that, at the end of the process, an equitable result be achieved. In this connection, the Tribunal recalls the principles stated by the International Tribunal for the Law of the Sea in its judgment in [*Bay of Bengal Delimitation*]. This Tribunal wishes to add that transparency and the predictability of the delimitation process as a whole are additional objectives to be achieved in the process. The ensuing—and still developing—international case law constitutes, in the view of the Tribunal, an *acquis judiciaire*, a source of international law under article 38(1)(d) of the Statute of the International Court of Justice, and should be read into articles 74 and 83 of the Convention.[236]

The Tribunal considered the three-stage equidistance methodology and the angle-bisector approach and noted that both of them are based on 'geometric techniques'.[237] However, it noted that the equidistance method 'clearly separates the steps to be taken and is thus more transparent'.[238] The Tribunal also noted that the identification of relevant coasts as straight lines under the bisector method required subjective considerations, and that the equidistance method allowed for adjustment 'to reflect the particularities of the case', while allowing for a 'high degree of transparency'.[239] It concluded that the three-stage equidistance method 'is preferable unless, as the [ICJ] stated in *Nicaragua v Honduras*, there are "factors which make the application of the equidistance method inappropriate" '.[240] In the present case, it considered that the coastal configuration of the Bay of Bengal did not render the identification of base points impractical or unreliable, and it therefore applied the equidistance methodology, drawing a provisional equidistance line.[241] This emphasis on transparency can be considered as promoting the rule of law.

[235] *Bay of Bengal Arbitration* (n 73) para 338.
[236] ibid para 339, citing *Bay of Bengal Delimitation* (n 48) para 235.
[237] ibid para 343.
[238] ibid.
[239] ibid para 344.
[240] ibid para 345, citing *Nicaragua v Honduras* (n 65) para 272.
[241] ibid paras 345–46.

Bangladesh argued for two relevant circumstances. First, it argued that the coastline was highly unstable, resulting in changes that would accelerate with sea-level rise. The Tribunal accepted that the coastline was unstable, but it did not consider this concern to be a relevant circumstance, taking account only of present conditions. It noted that 'future changes of the coast, including those resulting from climate change, cannot be taken into account in adjusting a provisional equidistance line'.[242] This view may accord with stability and predictability but does not engage in any meaningful way with many of the challenges that emerge in the future for States from sea-level rise, especially in delimiting overlapping maritime entitlements.[243]

Bangladesh also argued that its situation at the back of a three-State coastal concavity meant that the provisional equidistance line cut it off from the maritime areas in front of its coasts. It argued that this situation should be remedied either by the use of an angle bisector line, or a substantial adjustment to the provisional equidistance line. In this context, Bangladesh also argued that its inhabitants depended heavily on fish from the Bay of Bengal, which would exacerbate the effect of any equidistance line delimitation. As noted above, the Tribunal did not accept that there was any cut-off effect necessitating adjustment of the equidistance line in the territorial sea. However, the Tribunal accepted that the provisional equidistance line produced a cut-off effect for Bangladesh's west and south facing coasts in the EEZ and the continental shelf, and observed that this effect became more severe as the line moved further from the coast. It noted that, in order to warrant adjustment of the line, a cut-off effect must prevent a State from extending its maritime boundary as far seaward as international law permits and prevent an equitable solution. The Tribunal considered that the cut-off for Bangladesh was a relevant circumstance necessitating adjustment to the provisional equidistance line.[244] It ultimately adjusted the provisional line by following an azimuth from a specified point, Prov-3, until it met the maritime boundary between Bangladesh and Myanmar.[245] In respect of fishing, the Tribunal concluded that Bangladesh had not produced sufficient evidence to demonstrate its dependence on fishing as a relevant circumstance.[246]

For the final stage of the delimitation, the Tribunal noted that the ratio between the lengths of relevant coasts was 1:1.92 in favour of India, and that its delimitation line divided the relevant area in a ratio of 1:2.81 in favour of India. It considered that this did not produce any significant disproportion necessitating adjustment of the delimitation line.[247]

In *Croatia/Slovenia Arbitration*, the Tribunal was not called upon to delimit the EEZ/continental shelf, but in accordance with the parties' agreement reflected in their *compromis*, it was required to determine the location of Slovenia's 'junction to the high sea'.[248] The

[242] ibid para 399.

[243] For discussion on these issues see eg David D Caron, 'Climate Change, Sea Level Rise and the Coming Uncertainty in Oceanic Boundaries: A Proposal to Avoid Conflict' in Seoung-Yong Hong and Jon M Van Dyke (eds), *Maritime Boundary Disputes, Settlement Processes, and the Law of the Sea* (Brill 2009) 1–17; International Law Commission, 'Sea-Level Rise in Relation to International Law: First Issues Paper by Bogdan Aurescu and Nilüfer Oral, Co-Chairs of the Study Group on Sea-Level Rise in Relation to International Law' (28 February 2020) UN Doc No A/CN.4/740.

[244] *Bay of Bengal Arbitration* (n 73) paras 402–21.

[245] ibid paras 478–80.

[246] ibid para 424.

[247] ibid paras 495–96.

[248] The parties' arbitration agreement did not explicitly refer to UNCLOS but required the Tribunal to apply 'the rules and principles of international law', and both States are party to UNCLOS. See *Croatia/Slovenia Arbitration*, Final Award (n 53) para 1.

Tribunal understood this task to mean determining any area of seas lying beyond the territorial sea, thus including any EEZ.[249] The Tribunal decided in accordance with the parties' agreement and taking account of the particular geographical circumstances, not by reference to Articles 74 and 83. It accorded Slovenia a 'junction area' 2.5 NM wide, from its territorial sea to the outer limit of Croatia's territorial sea.[250]

As noted above in relation to Article 15 of UNCLOS, in *Ghana/Côte d'Ivoire*, the Special Chamber of ITLOS emphasised that delimitation of the territorial sea is governed by Article 15, which sets out different rules to those governing delimitation of the EEZ and the continental shelf.[251] However, noting that neither party raised sovereignty-related considerations in respect of delimitation of the territorial sea, it considered it appropriate to use the same methodology in respect of delimitation of the entire single maritime boundary.[252] The Chamber also noted that the two parties agreed in principle on the three-stage approach as it had been developed in international jurisprudence.[253]

Côte d'Ivoire argued for the application of an angle bisector, on the basis of three geographical circumstances (location and number of the base points, base points on what it termed 'Jomoro Peninsula' at the south-west of Ghana, and instability of the coastline), and one non-geographical factor: the interests of third States, given that this maritime boundary was the first being delimited in the region. The Chamber rejected all of these arguments. It noted that it was possible to identify base points and the fact that they were few in number did not justify departure from the equidistance method.[254] As for Jomoro, the Chamber noted it was part of Ghana's territory and was not a peninsula: it was not to be assimilated to an island or a protruding peninsula and would be given full effect in the delimitation.[255] Nor was the Chamber convinced that the coast was unstable such that it was difficult to identify appropriate base points.[256] So far as concerns the interests of third States, the Chamber noted that:

> [s]uch consideration is alien to the application of articles 74 and 83 of the Convention. It is the mandate of the Special Chamber to decide on the maritime delimitation between Ghana and Côte d'Ivoire. Such delimitation has to be equitable in result for the two Parties concerned. Note also has to be taken that interests of neighbouring States or of the region would have to be voiced by the other States.[257]

It further noted that its judgment had binding effect only vis-à-vis the parties to the case, and not with respect to any third States.[258] The Chamber concluded that there was no reason to depart from the standard equidistance/relevant circumstances methodology.[259] It therefore constructed a provisional equidistance line delimiting territorial sea, the EEZ, and the continental shelf within 200 NM.

[249] ibid paras 1066–70.
[250] See ibid 347 (Map VII).
[251] *Ghana/Côte d'Ivoire*, Judgment (n 88) paras 261–62.
[252] ibid paras 262–63.
[253] ibid para 360.
[254] ibid para 302.
[255] ibid paras 309–10.
[256] ibid para 318.
[257] ibid para 283.
[258] ibid para 323.
[259] ibid para 324.

Both States argued for adjustment of the provisional equidistance line on the basis of relevant circumstances. Ghana relied on the parties' practice with respect to limits of their oil and gas concessions and argued that the line should be adjusted to conform to the 'de facto boundary', established on the basis of a tacit agreement, estoppel, and by the parties' conduct.[260] Côte d'Ivoire invoked the concavity of its coast and the convexity of Ghana's coast, and argued that the equidistance line caused it to be cut-off. It also emphasised the impact of Jomoro on the Ghanaian coast. Côte d'Ivoire also referred to the presence of hydrocarbons in the disputed area and to the east of it, arguing that it was entitled to a 'fair share' of these resources.[261]

The Chamber referred to the need to achieve an equitable solution, and emphasised that 'delimitation must not completely refashion geography or compensate for the inequalities of nature'.[262] In respect of the alleged cut-off, the Chamber referred to the requirements as set out in *Bay of Bengal Arbitration*: that a cut-off effect must prevent a State from extending its maritime boundary as far seaward as international law permits, and prevent an equitable solution.[263] The Chamber noted that Côte d'Ivoire's convexity was not as pronounced as Bangladesh's in the Bay of Bengal, and noted that any cut-off only impacted the projection of part of Côte d'Ivoire's coast at some 163 NM distant from its shores. It also noted that adjusting the provisional equidistance line in favour of Côte d'Ivoire would have cut off the seaward projection of Ghana's coast. In the circumstances, it rejected Côte d'Ivoire's invocation of cut-off as a relevant circumstance.[264] As it did in relation to the delimitation methodology, the Chamber also rejected Côte d'Ivoire's argument that Jomoro was a relevant circumstance, noting that this territory could not be isolated from the land territory of Ghana as a whole.[265]

So far as concerns hydrocarbons, the Chamber noted that there was not sufficient evidence to suggest that most of the deposits fell on the Ghanaian side of the equidistance line, but it considered that this factor would anyway not be decisive, because 'the process of delimiting maritime zones is not meant to refashion nature'.[266] Non-geographical considerations would only be taken into account in 'extreme' cases, and in the present case the Chamber concluded that the location of maritime mineral resources could not be considered a relevant factor.[267]

With respect to Ghana's reliance on the conduct of the parties concerning their oil concessions, the Chamber rejected that this activity reached the level of a tacit agreement. It distinguished the situation in *Continental Shelf (Tunisia/Libya)*, where the ICJ took account of the parties' conduct in issuing petroleum concessions. It noted that in that case, both the subject matter of and approach to delimitation were different than in the present case, and that the practice in *Tunisia/Libya* was supported by the parties' observing a de facto maritime limit.[268] It further noted that, subsequently, international courts and tribunals had all been reluctant to consider oil concessions and oil activities as relevant circumstances. It

[260] ibid para 404.
[261] ibid paras 406, 437–42.
[262] ibid para 409.
[263] ibid para 422, citing *Bay of Bengal Arbitration* (n 73).
[264] ibid paras 424–26.
[265] ibid paras 434–36.
[266] ibid para 451.
[267] ibid paras 452–55.
[268] *Ghana/Côte d'Ivoire*, Judgment (n 88) paras 470–75, citing *Tunisia/Libya* (n 131).

noted that the practice of the parties in the present case was not free of controversy, such that it could not be said to reflect a de facto maritime limit. In any event, the Chamber considered that any de facto line or modus vivendi relating to oil practice 'cannot *per se* be a relevant circumstance in the delimitation of an all-purpose maritime boundary with respect to superjacent water as well as the seabed and subsoil'.[269] Thus, the Chamber rejected Ghana's contention that the conduct of the parties constituted a relevant circumstance.[270] It concluded that there were no relevant circumstances necessitating adjustment of the provisional equidistance line.[271]

In carrying out the disproportionality test, the Chamber noted that the ratio of the lengths of the relevant coasts as 1:2.53 in favour of Côte d'Ivoire, while the delimitation line allocated the relevant area in a ratio of 1:2.02 in favour of Côte d'Ivoire. It concluded that this did not lead to any significant disproportion.[272]

In *Maritime Delimitation in the Caribbean Sea and the Pacific Ocean*, the ICJ applied its 'established methodology' to delimit the EEZ and the continental shelf.[273] It described its approach as follows:

> The Court will delimit the exclusive economic zone and the continental shelf pursuant to its established methodology in three stages. First, it will provisionally draw an equidistance line using the most appropriate base points on the relevant coasts of the Parties. Second, it will consider whether there exist relevant circumstances which are capable of justifying an adjustment of the equidistance line provisionally drawn. Third, it will assess the overall equitableness of the boundary resulting from the first two stages by checking whether there exists a marked disproportionality between the length of the Parties' relevant coasts and the maritime areas found to appertain to them ... The Court notes that the methodology in three stages set out in its Judgment in [*Maritime Delimitation in the Black Sea*] has also been adopted by other international tribunals requested to delimit maritime boundaries.[274]

For the delimitation in the Caribbean Sea, both States argued for relevant circumstances necessitating an adjustment to the provisional equidistance line. Nicaragua argued that it would suffer a cut-off effect due to the configuration of Costa Rica's 'convex and north-facing' coast immediately adjacent to Nicaragua's concave coastline.[275] Costa Rica argued that, on the basis of its concavity, and taking account of a notional delimitation by equidistance with Panama, it suffered a cut-off effect of its seaward projections.[276] Costa Rica also argued that Nicaragua's Corn Islands should be given no effect, taking into account in particular their location at about 26 NM distance from Nicaragua's mainland coast.[277]

The Court accepted Costa Rica's argument that the Corn Islands had an impact on the provisional equidistance line that was out of proportion with their limited size, and taking

[269] ibid paras 476–78.
[270] ibid para 479.
[271] ibid paras 480–81.
[272] ibid paras 537–38.
[273] *Maritime Delimitation in the Caribbean Sea and the Pacific Ocean* (n 82) paras 135, 176.
[274] ibid para 135 (citations omitted).
[275] ibid para 148.
[276] ibid para 150.
[277] ibid para 151.

account their significant distance from the mainland coast, and it gave them only half effect.[278] However, the Court rejected both States' arguments relating to alleged cut-off, considering that any cut-off for either State was not significant.[279]

Taking account of the complexity of the resulting adjusted equidistance line, the Court considered it more appropriate to adopt a simplified line, taking account of the most significant turning points.[280] The resulting line divided the relevant area in a ratio of 1:2.4 in favour of Nicaragua, which did not show any marked disproportion when compared to the ratio of the lengths of relevant coasts, which was 1:2.04 in favour of Nicaragua.[281]

On the Pacific side, Costa Rica did not argue for any adjustments to the provisional equidistance line.[282] Nicaragua argued that it suffered an unjustified cut-off of its seaward projections, if base points were placed on Costa Rica's Santa Elena Peninsula and on its Nicoya Peninsula, and it argued for half effect for both these features.[283] The Court accepted that base points on Santa Elena had a disproportionate effect on the provisional equidistance line, controlling the course of it from the 12 NM limit of the territorial sea to a point approximately 120 NM from the coasts of the parties, and that it resulted in a significant and inequitable cut-off of Nicaragua's maritime projections. The Court therefore gave Santa Elena half-effect.[284] However, the Court gave full effect to the Nicoya Peninsula, noting that its coast accounts for a sizeable portion of Costa Rica's coast and therefore it could not be said to depart from the general direction of its coastline. Further, the Court noted that it could not disregard the geographical realities of the case before it.[285] The resulting delimitation line, adjusted to give half effect to Santa Elena, divided the relevant area in a ratio of 1:1.30 in Costa Rica's favour, while the relevant coastal lengths had a ratio of 1:1.42 in favour of Costa Rica. In the view of the Court, this outcome did not result in gross disproportionality necessitating further adjustment of the delimitation line.[286]

In *Maritime Delimitation in the Indian Ocean*, the Court endorsed[287] and applied the three-stage methodology, although it emphasised that it is 'not mandatory',[288] and will not be used if there are factors that make its application inappropriate.[289]

So far as concerned the adjustment of the provisional equidistance line, Somalia argued that there were no reasons for adjustment,[290] whereas Kenya invoked five relevant circumstances.[291] Two of the alleged relevant circumstances were invoked to support Kenya's argument for a maritime boundary along the parallel of latitude. First, Kenya referred to the regional practice of using parallels of latitude to define the maritime boundaries of States on the Eastern African coast.[292] The Court gave this argument short shrift, noting that it had already concluded that no maritime boundary between Somalia and Kenya following the

278 ibid paras 153–54.
279 ibid paras 155–56.
280 ibid para 158.
281 ibid para 165.
282 ibid para 190.
283 ibid para 191.
284 ibid paras 193–94.
285 ibid para 195–98.
286 ibid paras 202–204.
287 *Maritime Delimitation in the Indian Ocean*, Judgment (n 52) paras 119–25.
288 ibid para 128.
289 ibid para 129.
290 ibid para 148.
291 ibid para 149.
292 ibid para 150.

parallel of latitude was established in the past. It further noted that the adjustment sought by Kenya 'would represent a radical adjustment while clearly not achieving an equitable solution'.[293]

Secondly, Kenya sought to rely on the parties' conduct in relation to oil concessions, naval patrols, fishing, and other activities. It argued that these reflected the existence of a de facto maritime boundary along the parallel of latitude.[294] The Court dismissed this argument, emphasising that conduct such as that related to oil concessions, naval patrols, and fishing activities may only be taken into account if they reflect an express or tacit agreement, and the Court had already concluded that no maritime boundary along the parallel of latitude had been agreed between Somalia and Kenya.[295] It therefore rejected Kenya's argument that this practice constituted a relevant circumstance necessitating adjustment of the provisional equidistance line.

The third and fourth relevant circumstances put forward by Kenya concerned non-geographic factors. One was vital security interests of the parties and the international community, including in relation to terrorism and piracy.[296] The Court acknowledged the serious threats to security in the region, but it considered that the current security situation in Somalia was not of a permanent nature and therefore did not justify the adjustment of the provisional equidistance line.[297]

Another non-geographic factor invoked by Kenya was the fishers who were said to be dependent on fisheries in coastal areas near the Kenya-Somalia boundary.[298] The Court noted that such a factor can be taken into account in exceptional circumstances, but on the basis of the evidence before it, the Court was not convinced that the provisional equidistance line would entail catastrophic consequences for the livelihood and economic well-being of the population of Kenya. The Court therefore dismissed Kenya's argument that this concern constituted a circumstance necessitating adjustment of the provisional equidistance line.[299]

The final factor invoked by Kenya was a significant, pronounced, and unreasonable cut-off effect of Kenya's coastal projection.[300] While the Court noted that concavity in the coastline of Kenya and Somalia 'is not conspicuous',[301] it considered that it should examine the issue of concavity in the context of a broader geographical configuration.[302] In the broader context, it considered that Kenya faces a cut-off of its maritime entitlements as the middle State between Somalia and Tanzania[303] and, although the cut-off effect was less pronounced than in some other cases, it was nonetheless serious enough to warrant some adjustment to the provisional equidistance line, to address the 'substantial narrowing of Kenya's potential entitlements'.[304]

[293] ibid para 156.
[294] ibid para 152.
[295] ibid para 160.
[296] ibid para 151.
[297] ibid para 158. Although she agreed with the Court's conclusion on these factors, in her Declaration Judge Xue emphasised that there was no definitive list of relevant circumstances and suggested that if such circumstances were limited to geographical circumstances, 'equitable principles would vanish from the process of delimitation': see Declaration of Judge Xue, paras 13–16.
[298] ibid para 153.
[299] ibid para 159.
[300] ibid para 140.
[301] ibid para 164.
[302] ibid paras 165–68.
[303] ibid paras 168–69.
[304] ibid paras 170–71.

The Court's conclusion with respect to concavity was criticised by several judges. In his separate opinion, Judge Abraham pointed out that the Court's macro-geographic approach was a significant departure from its established approach, which emphasised the presence of concavity in the sector to be delimited.[305] Judge Yusuf also criticised the Court's approach to concavity, noting that the judgment 'breaks with [the] tradition' of no judicial refashioning of geography but searching for a concavity beyond the coasts of the parties.[306] By taking into account the Tanzanian coastline to determine that Kenya suffered from cut-off caused by concavity, the Court incorrectly took account of coasts other than those of the parties: he described it in very strong terms as an 'arbitrary refashioning of geography to achieved preconceived results'.[307] Judge Robinson also criticised the Court's approach to the macro-geography, describing it as 'problematic'[308] and emphasising that any concavity must fall within the area to be delimited to qualify as a relevant factor necessitating adjustment of the provisional equidistance line.[309] He further queried whether the curvature in the Somali, Kenyan, and Tanzanian coasts had the degree of concavity sufficient to result in a cut-off effect, requiring adjustment of the line.[310]

In respect of the concavity, noting that any adjustment to a provisional equidistance line must be assessed on a case-by-case basis to achieve an equitable solution,[311] the Court decided to adjust the provisional equidistance line from the outer limit of the territorial sea, to the north so that it followed a geodetic line with an initial azimuth of 114°.[312] This decision had the effect of according some 10,000–11,000 km^2 of EEZ/continental shelf to Kenya.

The Court then considered whether the delimitation line led to any significant disproportionality,[313] noting that the ratio of the relevant coasts is 1:1.43 in favour of Somalia, and the delimitation line resulted in a ratio of the relevant area of 1:1.30 in favour of Kenya. The Court considered that this result did not produce any significant or marked disproportionality.[314]

* * *

In the emerging case law, particularly since *Maritime Delimitation in the Black Sea* in 2009, tribunals have developed and increasingly applied the three-stage methodology to delimitation of the EEZ and the continental shelf under Articles 74 and 83.[315] Over time, the three-stage methodology has been effectively read into the open-textured Articles 74 and

305 ibid (Separate Opinion of Judge Abraham) paras 10–15.
306 ibid (Separate opinion of Judge Yusuf) para 23. See also paras 24–25.
307 ibid (Separate Opinion of Judge Yusuf) paras 28–29.
308 ibid (Individual Opinion, Partly Concurring and Partly Dissenting of Judge Robinson) para 30.
309 ibid (Individual Opinion, Partly Concurring and Partly Dissenting of Judge Robinson) paras 31–33.
310 ibid (Individual Opinion, Partly Concurring and Partly Dissenting of Judge Robinson) para 29.
311 ibid para 173.
312 ibid para 174.
313 ibid para 175.
314 ibid paras 176–77. Judge Xue, in her declaration, took issue with the Court's approach to proportionality, referring to the way in which the relevant area had been calculated (by the use of radial rather than frontal projections). She queried whether the disproportionality test was an effective check on the equitableness of a delimitation line: see Declaration of Judge Xue, paras 7–11, 17–20.
315 In this respect, the ICJ's decision in *Maritime Delimitation in the Black Sea* (n 184) has been described as a 'grand arrêt': Alina Miron, 'The acquis judiciaire, a Tool for Harmonization in a Decentralized System of Litigation? A Case-study in the Law of the Sea' in Chiara Giorgetti and Mark Pollack (eds), *Beyond Fragmentation: Cross-Fertilization, Cooperation and Competition among International Courts and Tribunals* (CUP 2022).

83 by tribunals, and any departure therefrom is generally carefully reasoned and justified. Thus, in the absence of a specified method in the provisions of UNCLOS:

> International courts and tribunals have developed a body of case law on maritime delimitation which has reduced the elements of subjectivity and uncertainty in the determination of maritime boundaries and in the choice of methods employed to that end.[316]

Given the emphasis placed on equidistance in the three-stage methodology, one might question whether tribunals have effectively overridden the compromise reached during UNCLOS negotiations for the EEZ and the continental shelf, which was to prefer delimitation on the basis of an equitable solution over the equidistance method. On the other hand, there is an obvious interest in a method that provides States with greater certainty and confidence in judicial outcomes, and it is arguable that the three-stage methodology has done just that. In general, academic commentators have welcomed the certainty that has followed over the last decade,[317] while some have remained critical of the primacy it has given to equidistance.[318]

Whether or not one agrees with the methodology that has been adopted, it is apparent that international tribunals have made a decisive contribution to articulating the methodology and have sought to promote predictability in its application. Moreover, the consistency of application across the different fora is remarkable, if not unprecedented. In this context, Lando has argued that:

> International tribunals could be considered to be makers of the delimitation process. The legal basis of their law-making function stems both from the impossibility for customary rules of international law to develop in maritime delimitation, and from the inability of states to agree on clear treaty rules governing delimitation. Confronted with this normative void, international tribunals seem to have had little choice but to exercise a creative function, which, owing to their jurisprudence over half a century, has crystallised in the three-stage delimitation process. This creative function is connected with the character of international judicial decisions as formal sources of international law. While international tribunals may exercise a law-making function, states can either sanction the law developed through judicial elaboration, or oppose that development.[319]

Lando suggests that States have sanctioned the three-stage methodology as developed by international tribunals, and in this regard he points to the fact that a 'noticeably strong majority' of maritime delimitation agreements delimit boundaries based on equidistance,[320]

[316] *Bay of Bengal Delimitation* (n 47) para 226.

[317] See eg Fietta and Cleverly (n 1) 584; Donald R Rothwell and Tim Stephens, *The International Law of the Sea* (2nd edn, Bloomsbury 2019) 427–31; Robin R Churchill, 'Dispute Settlement under the UN Convention on the Law of the Sea: Survey for 2009' (2010) 25 IJMCL 457, 477–78; Yoshifumi Tanaka, *The International Law of the Sea* (3rd edn, CUP 2019) 246.

[318] See eg Malcolm D Evans, 'Maritime Boundary Delimitation' in Donald R Rothwell and others (eds), *The Oxford Handbook of the Law of the Sea* (OUP 2015) 260; Malcolm D Evans, 'Maritime Boundary Delimitation: Whatever Next?' in Jill Barrett and Richard Barnes (eds), *Law of the Sea: UNCLOS as a Living Treaty* (BIICL 2016) 41–42.

[319] Lando, *Maritime Delimitation* (n 1) 290–91.

[320] ibid 309 and app 2.

and he identifies twenty-four such agreements since 2009 (when the ICJ decided *Maritime Delimitation in the Black Sea*),[321] whereas he has identified only seven such agreements since that date where it was clear that the parties departed from equidistance.[322] He also notes that after *Maritime Delimitation in the Black Sea*, ultimately all States party to maritime delimitation disputes have accepted the three-stage methodology as the established method, even though some of them called for it to be disapplied on the basis of particular circumstances.[323] By this conduct, Lando argues, States have effectively sanctioned the law-making function of tribunals mandated to delimit maritime boundaries.

The consistency in approach of tribunals can be seen to promote the broader goals of predictability, stability, and consistency, as well as the rule of law and certainty in the public order of the oceans. It might also be perceived as contributing to the broader settlement of disputes: by the provision of a stable and certain framework for the delimitation of maritime boundaries, there could be increased scope for delimitation agreements, and as noted above, there has been a trend since 2009 towards the use of equidistance in maritime boundary agreements between States.

In terms of the interests of stakeholders other than States, tribunals have underscored the fundamental principle that the land dominates the sea by retaining a focus on geographic factors in adjusting the provisional equidistance line to achieve an equitable solution. Non-geographic factors, such as fisheries, navigation, security interests, and interests in oil exploration and exploitation, have generally not been taken into account in the cases, although there are some exceptions. Taking account of non-geographic factors might be considered as a way in which tribunals could engage with the interests of more diverse stakeholders, such as those individuals engaged in fisheries, navigation, and exploration and exploitation activities. However, the extent to which a tribunal can feasibly do so will always depend on the facts and the evidence before it: the cases where such factors were dismissed might readily be explained on the basis of the evidence, rather than on the grounds that a tribunal was not prepared to take account of other interests. The Court's recent affirmation in *Maritime Delimitation in the Indian Ocean* that non-geographic factors may be relevant confirms that there continues to be scope for States to establish, by reference to evidence, that the interests of diverse stakeholder should be taken into account, and there may well be further opportunities for tribunals to do so in the future.

V. Delimitation of the Continental Shelf beyond 200 NM

There are two key issues that had been addressed in the jurisprudence on delimitation of the extended continental shelf: the question of jurisdiction or admissibility of requests to delimit beyond 200 NM; and the question of the delimitation itself, including the appropriate methodology. Each of these questions is addressed in turn below.

[321] ibid app 2, 346–48.
[322] ibid app 2, 353–54.
[323] ibid 315–17.

A. Jurisdiction and Admissibility of Requests to Delimit an Extended Continental Shelf

As noted in Chapter 5, every coastal State has an *ipso facto* entitlement to a continental shelf extending to 200 NM from its baselines, and may have entitlements to areas of the shelf further seaward, to the outer edge of the continental margin, if it extends beyond 200 NM.[324] Beyond 200 NM, a State's entitlement is based on geological and geomorphological factors. These conditions are set out in Article 76 of UNCLOS on the definition of the continental shelf.

Under Article 76(8) of UNCLOS, the Commission on the Limits of the Continental Shelf (CLCS) has exclusive competence to determine the outer limits of the continental shelf. Article 76(8) provides:

> Information on the limits of the continental shelf beyond 200 nautical miles from the baselines from which the breadth of the territorial sea is measured shall be submitted by the coastal State to the Commission on the Limits of the Continental Shelf set up under Annex II on the basis of equitable geographical representation. The Commission shall make recommendations to coastal States on matters related to the establishment of the outer limits of their continental shelf. The limits of the shelf established by a coastal State on the basis of these recommendations shall be final and binding.

Annex II of UNCLOS establishes the CLCS.[325] Article 9 of Annex II provides that '[t]he actions of the Commission shall not prejudice matters relating to the delimitation of boundaries between States with opposite or adjacent coasts'.[326] The Commission has adopted Rules of Procedure, and paragraph 5(a) of the Annex to those Rules provides that:

> In cases where a land or maritime dispute exists, the Commission shall not consider and qualify a submission made by any of the States concerned in the dispute. However, the Commission may consider one or more submissions in the area under dispute with prior consent given by all States that are parties to such a dispute.[327]

In practice, therefore, there may be a stalemate in circumstances where there is a pending delimitation dispute, as that dispute could prevent the CLCS from delineating any entitlement of a State to a shelf beyond 200 NM and the outer limit of such shelf.

In several cases, tribunals have declined to delimit the outer continental shelf, pending identification of the outer limits of any entitlements. However, in more recent cases, that approach has been partially reversed, as is explained in more detail below.

In *St Pierre and Miquelon*, France requested that the tribunal extend the delimitation line for the continental shelf beyond 200 NM, to the outer edge of the continental margin. The CLCS had not yet been established. The Tribunal noted that this request gave rise to an issue

[324] See ch 5(IV)(D).

[325] UNCLOS (n 1) Annex II, art 1.

[326] See also ibid art 76(10): 'The provisions of this article are without prejudice to the question of delimitation of the continental shelf between States with opposite or adjacent coasts.'

[327] Commission on the Limits of the Continental Shelf, Rules of Procedure of the Commission, UN Doc No CLCS/40/Rev.1 (adopted 17 April 2008).

as to competence, since '[a]ny decision ... recognizing or rejecting any rights of the Parties over the continental shelf beyond 200 nautical miles, would constitute a pronouncement involving a delimitation, not 'between the Parties' but between each one of them and the international community'.[328] On the basis that it was not competent to carry out a delimitation affecting the rights of a party not before it, and referring to the exclusive competence of the CLCS under Article 76(8) and Annex II of UNCLOS, the Tribunal held that it was not competent to delimit the boundary beyond 200 NM.[329]

The Annex VII tribunal in *Barbados v Trinidad and Tobago* also declined to delimit the outer continental shelf, claimed by Trinidad and Tobago. While it held it had jurisdiction to delimit a maritime boundary extending beyond 200 NM, it held that 'the single maritime boundary which [it] has determined is such that as between Barbados and Trinidad and Tobago, there is no single maritime boundary beyond 200 nm'.[330]

Although neither State sought delimitation of the extended continental shelf in *Nicaragua v Honduras*, the ICJ addressed that issue briefly in connection with the endpoint of the delimitation line. Taking account of the possible interests of third States, the Court declined to specify a precise end point, but it stated that:

> in no case may the line be interpreted as extending more than 200 nautical miles from the baselines from which the breadth of the territorial sea is measured; any claim of continental shelf rights beyond 200 miles must be in accordance with Article 76 of UNCLOS and reviewed by the Commission on the Limits of the Continental Shelf established thereunder.[331]

This statement suggested strongly that the ICJ would not proceed to delimit any outer continental shelf absent a recommendation from the CLCS under Article 76(8) of UNCLOS.

The first tribunal that took a different approach and proceeded to delimit the outer continental shelf was ITLOS in *Bay of Bengal Delimitation*. Both Bangladesh and Myanmar had made submissions to the CLCS claiming outer shelf areas. Myanmar did not dispute that the Tribunal had jurisdiction to delimit the outer continental shelf but argued it should not exercise such jurisdiction because it 'might prejudice the rights of third parties and also those relating to the international seabed area'. It also argued that a 'necessary precondition' of delimitation was that the CLCS had already made recommendations as to the outer limits.[332] ITLOS agreed with the parties that it had jurisdiction to delimit the continental shelf in its entirety.[333] So far as concerns the CLCS' determination, the Tribunal considered that 'the absence of established outer limits of a maritime zone does not preclude delimitation of that zone', noting that lack of agreement on baselines has not been considered an impediment to delimitation of zones within 200 NM.[334] Noting the CLCS' Annex to its Rules of Procedure, and that the CLCS had deferred consideration of both States' submissions, it identified the stalemate in the following terms:

328 *St Pierre and Miquelon* (n 148) para 78.
329 ibid paras 79–82.
330 *Barbados v Trinidad and Tobago* (n 173) para 368.
331 *Nicaragua v Honduras* (n 65) para 318.
332 *Bay of Bengal Delimitation* (n 47) paras 344–45.
333 ibid paras 360–63.
334 ibid para 370.

> A decision by the Tribunal not to exercise its jurisdiction over the dispute relating to the continental shelf beyond 200 nm would not only fail to resolve a long-standing dispute, but also would not be conducive to the efficient operation of the Convention.
>
> In the view of the Tribunal, it would be contrary to the object and purpose of the Convention not to resolve the existing impasse. Inaction in the present case, by the Commission and the Tribunal, two organs created by the Convention to ensure the effective implementation of its provisions, would leave the Parties in a position where they may be unable to benefit fully from their rights over the continental shelf.[335]

Thus, ITLOS concluded that it had an obligation to delimit the continental shelf beyond 200 NM, such delimitation being without prejudice to the establishment of the outer limits in accordance with Article 76(8) of UNCLOS.[336] Further, the fact that the outer limits of the shelf had not been established did not imply, in the view of ITLOS, that it should refrain from determining the existence of any entitlement to extended shelf and delimiting it between the parties concerned.[337] The apparent need to resolve the dispute before it seemingly motivated the Tribunal's decision in this regard.

This approach was a departure from previous cases. Yet, it is also clear from the judgment that ITLOS was heavily influenced by the fact that there was undisputed evidence that the Bay of Bengal was covered with a thick layer of sedimentary rock. As such, the coastal States would be entitled to an extended shelf, even if the outer limits of those shelves had not yet been delineated.

Both States accepted that there was extended continental shelf, but each of them argued that it alone was entitled to the entire area.[338] Bangladesh argued that its land territory had a natural prolongation into the Bay of Bengal, while there was a discontinuity between the Myanmar landmass and the seabed beyond 200 NM. The argument turned on the meaning of 'natural prolongation' in Article 76(1). Bangladesh argued that the term has a physical meaning and must be established on the basis of a geological connection with the claiming State. Myanmar argued it was a legal term with no scientific connotation, and that the controlling concept under Article 76(1) is the 'outer edge of the continental margin', defined by the two formulae set out in Article 76(4). ITLOS considered that the reference to natural prolongation in Article 76(1) had to be understood in light of the subsequent provisions of Article 76 defining the continental shelf and the continental margin. Rejecting Bangladesh's argument, it held that entitlement to an outer shelf should be determined by reference to the outer edge of the shelf, determined in accordance with Article 76(4).[339]

ITLOS noted that both States had claimed extended continental shelf in their submissions to the CLCS, and stated that it 'would have been hesitant to proceed with the delimitation of the area beyond 200 nm had it concluded that there was significant uncertainty as to the existence of a continental margin in the area of question'.[340] However, as noted above, the Tribunal observed that it was undisputed that the sea floor of the Bay of Bengal is covered by a thick layer of sediment some 14 to 22 km deep, and that both States claimed entitlement

335 ibid paras 391–92.
336 ibid para 394.
337 ibid para 410.
338 ibid para 414.
339 ibid paras 428–38.
340 ibid para 443.

based on the thickness of sedimentary rocks under the formula set out in Article 76(4)(a)(i). Thus, ITLOS concluded that both Bangladesh and Myanmar had entitlements to a continental shelf extending beyond 200 NM, and that their entitlements overlapped in the area in dispute in this case.[341] The unique situation of the Bay of Bengal, which was critical to the approach of ITLOS in this case, was picked up by other tribunals in subsequent decisions.

When the question of jurisdiction to delimit the extended continental shelf came before the ICJ again in *Territorial and Maritime Dispute* in 2012, the Court held that it was not in a position to delimit the boundary. Nicaragua requested that the Court delimit a continental shelf boundary delimiting the two State's overlapping entitlements, on the basis of its assertion that its continental margin extended beyond 200 NM from its coast and into areas within 200 NM of Colombia's coasts.[342] It had submitted preliminary information to the CLCS, but had not made a full submission; nor had the CLCS made any recommendations as to the outer limits.[343]

The ICJ distinguished *Bay of Bengal Delimitation* on the basis of the 'unique situation' of the Bay of Bengal, referring to the established evidence as to the thick layer of sedimentary rock covering the Bay. It also noted that both States party to that dispute were parties to UNCLOS and had made full submissions to the CLCS.[344] In contrast, Colombia was not party to UNCLOS, and Nicaragua had submitted only preliminary information to the CLCS. Referring to its judgment in *Nicaragua v Honduras*, to the effect that any claim to continental shelf beyond 200 NM must be in accordance with Article 76 of UNCLOS and reviewed by the CLCS, the Court noted that:

> UNCLOS, according to its Preamble, is intended to establish 'a legal order for the seas and oceans which will facilitate international communication, and will promote the peaceful uses of the seas and oceans, the equitable and efficient utilization of their resources'. The Preamble also stresses that 'the problems of ocean space are closely interrelated and need to be considered as a whole'. Given the object and purpose of UNCLOS, as stipulated in its Preamble, the fact that Colombia is not a party thereto does not relieve Nicaragua of its obligations under Article 76 of that Convention.[345]

The Court further noted that Nicaragua had not established that it had a continental margin extending far enough to overlap with Colombia's 200 NM continental shelf, measured from its mainland coast, and so it concluded that it was not in a position to delimit the boundary as requested by Nicaragua.[346] Thus, the Court declined to take the same approach as ITLOS and proceed to delimit the extended continental shelf, noting that Nicaragua had not made a full submission to the CLCS. By referring to its earlier decision in *Nicaragua v Honduras*, the Court also arguably implied that any such submission would need to be reviewed by the CLCS in advance of delimitation by a court of tribunal.

The Annex VII tribunal in *Bay of Bengal Arbitration* was also requested to delimit the outer continental shelf. Both States had made submissions to the CLCS; the consideration

341 ibid paras 444–49.
342 *Territorial and Maritime Dispute*, Judgment (n 215) paras 108–112.
343 ibid para 127.
344 ibid para 125.
345 ibid para 126, citing *Nicaragua v Honduras* (n 65).
346 ibid para 129.

of both had been deferred.[347] Both parties agreed that the Tribunal had jurisdiction to delimit the continental shelf beyond 200 NM. The Tribunal took note of the decisions in *Barbados v Trinidad and Tobago*, *Bay of Bengal Delimitation*, and *Territorial and Maritime Dispute*. It noted that the outer limits of the continental shelf had not been determined but, recalling the reasoning in *Bay of Bengal Delimitation*, saw no grounds for refraining to exercise its jurisdiction to decide on the delimitation before the outer limits were established. It emphasised that Article 76 embodies the concept of a single continental shelf, and noted that both parties agreed that they had entitlements to continental shelf beyond 200 NM in the Bay of Bengal.[348] It further noted that the consideration of the submissions to CLCS had been deferred, and was of the view that in the circumstances

> the consequence of these decisions by the CLCS is such that, if the Tribunal were to decline to delimit the continental shelf beyond 200 nm, the outer limits of the continental shelf of each of the Parties would remain unresolved, unless the Parties were able to reach an agreement. In light of the many previous rounds of unsuccessful negotiations between them, the Tribunal does not see that such an agreement is likely. Accordingly, far from enabling action by the CLCS, inaction by this Tribunal would in practice leave the Parties in a position in which they would likely be unable to benefit fully from their rights over the continental shelf. The Tribunal does not consider that such an outcome would be consistent with the object and purpose of the Convention.[349]

The need to settle the dispute was again apparent. The Tribunal therefore concluded that it had jurisdiction to delimit the continental shelf between the parties beyond 200 NM.[350] Like in *Bay of Bengal Delimitation*, the Tribunal was in a position to proceed with some certainty as to the existence of the parties' entitlement to an extended shelf, even if the outer limits had not yet been delineated.

In 2013, Nicaragua commenced a new proceeding against Colombia at the ICJ (*Delimitation of the Continental Shelf*),[351] relating to delimitation of the continental shelf beyond 200 NM. It had, by this time, made a full submission to the CLCS, but no recommendation had been made by the CLCS. Following the ICJ's judgment in *Territorial and Maritime Dispute* in 2012, Colombia had withdrawn from the Pact of Bogotá, which was the basis of jurisdiction invoked in that case, and in this further proceeding. Nicaragua also commenced a separate case against Colombia relating to alleged violations of its maritime zones, on account of Colombia's alleged failure to comply with the 2012 judgment.

In *Delimitation of the Continental Shelf*, Colombia raised five preliminary objections against Nicaragua's case, on the grounds of both jurisdiction and admissibility.[352] The first and second concerned jurisdiction *ratione temporis* under the Pact of Bogotá. The third objection was that Nicaragua's claim was barred by *res judicata*, it having been decided in 2012. The fourth was on the basis that Nicaragua's new case was an attempt to appeal and revise

[347] *Bay of Bengal Arbitration* (n 73) para 81.
[348] ibid paras 77–78.
[349] ibid para 82.
[350] ibid para 83.
[351] *Delimitation of the Continental Shelf between Nicaragua and Colombia beyond 200 Nautical Miles from the Nicaraguan Coast (Nicaragua v Colombia)* (Preliminary Objections) [2016] ICJ Rep 100 (*Delimitation of the Continental Shelf*).
[352] ibid para 15.

the 2012 judgment. Finally, it argued that the claim was inadmissible, including because the CLCS had not made recommendations to Nicaragua with respect to the outer limits of its continental shelf.

The Court rejected all of Colombia's objections to jurisdiction. In respect of the delimitation of the outer continental shelf, it clarified that in its 2012 decision in *Territorial and Maritime Dispute*, it had concluded that Nicaragua had not established that it had a continental margin that extended far enough to overlap with Colombia's 200 NM entitlement to the continental shelf, measured from Colombia's mainland coast, because Nicaragua had not yet submitted full information to the CLCS.[353] So far as concerns Colombia's argument that Nicaragua's request for delimitation of the extended shelf was inadmissible because the CLCS had not made any recommendation on Nicaragua's submission, the Court noted that the procedure before the CLCS concerns the delineation of the outer limits of the continental shelf, which is distinct from its delimitation. It considered that a delimitation can be undertaken independently of a recommendation from the CLCS. Accordingly, the Court rejected Colombia's objection to admissibility of Nicaragua's request to delimit the outer continental shelf.[354]

This determination was perceived as a departure from the approach of the Court in earlier cases, in particular from its dicta in *Nicaragua v Honduras* that any claim to an extended shelf must be 'reviewed' by the CLCS, and its reference to that dicta in its 2012 judgment between the same parties. Five of the Court's judges dissented from the Court's decision in *Delimitation of the Continental Shelf* on this point, considering that 'information submitted to the CLCS pursuant to Article 76(8) of UNCLOS will not necessarily be regarded as sufficient to establish the existence of an extended continental shelf'.[355] They emphasised that the function of the CLCS was to examine the submission and to make recommendations as to whether the description of its delineation meets the criteria laid down in Article 76;[356] thus the dissenting judges concluded that it was 'surprising that the majority should maintain that the submission of information ... was considered a prerequisite by the Court in its 2012 Judgment' while at the same time concluding that recommendations are not a prerequisite before a State can ask the Court to settle a dispute over delimitation.[357]

Nonetheless, with this decision, the ICJ has brought itself more closely into alignment with the ITLOS judgment in *Bay of Bengal Delimitation* and the Annex VII award in *Bay of Bengal Arbitration*, in finding that a recommendation by the CLCS as to the outer limit of the continental shelf was not a prerequisite to delimitation of that shelf. Yet its decision was criticised by five of its own judges. It was also criticised by some commentators: for example, Lando has emphasised that the Court left open the question of the proof required for Nicaragua to establish an entitlement beyond 200 NM, and considered that 'in most cases it would seem more appropriate' for tribunals to delimit boundaries only after the CLCS's recommendation.[358] The question of the level of certainty required came back before the Court

353 ibid paras 82–84.

354 ibid paras 105–115.

355 ibid (Joint Dissenting Opinion of Vice-President Yusuf, Judges Cançado Trinidade, Xue, Gaja, Bhandari, Robinson, and Judge ad hoc Brower) para 55.

356 ibid (Joint Dissenting Opinion of Vice-President Yusuf, Judges Cançado Trinidade, Xue, Gaja, Bhandari, Robinson, and Judge ad hoc Brower) para 56.

357 ibid (Joint Dissenting Opinion of Vice-President Yusuf, Judges Cançado Trinidade, Xue, Gaja, Bhandari, Robinson, and Judge ad hoc Brower) para 58.

358 Massimo Lando, 'Delimiting the Continental Shelf Beyond 200 Nautical Miles at the International Court of Justice: The Nicaragua v Colombia Cases' (2017) 16 Chinese JIL 137, 173. cf Bjarni Már Magnússon, 'Is there a

recently, in *Maritime Delimitation in the Indian Ocean*, discussed further below: as will be seen, there continues to be a lack of unanimity of views on the point at the ICJ.

In *Ghana/Côte d'Ivoire*, the parties were agreed that the Chamber had jurisdiction to delimit the extended continental shelf.[359] Nevertheless, the Chamber considered it had to decide on its jurisdiction *proprio motu*.[360] Noting that Ghana had made a submission to the CLCS and had received a recommendation, while Côte d'Ivoire had made a submission but was yet to receive a recommendation, it emphasised that it had 'no doubt' that a continental shelf existed beyond 200 NM for Côte d'Ivoire, because its geological situation was identical to that of Ghana, for which the CLCS had made an affirmative recommendation.[361] Referring to the Tribunal's decision in *Bay of Bengal Delimitation* on the different functions of the CLCS and a tribunal tasked with settling disputes as to maritime boundaries, the Chamber concluded that it had jurisdiction to decide on the delimitation of the continental shelf beyond 200 NM and that their submissions were admissible.[362]

In *Maritime Delimitation in the Indian Ocean*, the Court confirmed the approach taken in its 2016 judgment in *Delimitation of the Continental Shelf*. Both Somalia and Kenya asked the Court to delimit the continental shelf beyond 200 NM. They had both made submissions to the CLCS,[363] but the CLCS had yet to consider their submissions and to make any recommendations.[364] In its judgment on preliminary objections, the Court was reserved about the possibility of delimiting the outer continental shelf in advance of a recommendation from the CLCS, stating that:

> [a] lack of certainty regarding the outer limits of the continental shelf, and thus the precise location of the endpoint of a given boundary in the area beyond 200 nautical miles, does not, however, necessarily prevent either the States concerned or the Court from undertaking the delimitation of the boundary in appropriate circumstances before the CLCS has made its recommendations.[365]

The Court did not elaborate on what 'appropriate circumstances' would be, but one can infer from this statement that unilateral submissions to the CLCS would likely be insufficient.[366]

In its judgment on the merits, in considering whether to proceed with delimitation of the extended shelf, the Court first noted that the entitlement of a State to the continental

Temporal Relationship between the Delineation and the Delimitation of the Continental Shelf beyond 200 nm?' (2013) 28 IJMCL 465 (suggesting that only in cases of significant uncertainty as to the existence of an extended shelf will the tribunal decline to exercise jurisdiction).

359 *Ghana/Côte d'Ivoire*, Judgment (n 88) paras 483–88.
360 ibid para 489.
361 ibid para 491.
362 ibid paras 493–95, citing *Bay of Bengal Delimitation* (n 47).
363 Both States had filed an objection to consideration by the CLCS of the other's submission but these were subsequently withdrawn: *Maritime Delimitation in the Indian Ocean*, Judgment (n 51) para 188.
364 ibid.
365 *Maritime Delimitation in the Indian Ocean (Somalia v Kenya)* (Preliminary Objections) [2017] ICJ Rep 3, para 94.
366 See discussion in Lando, *Maritime Delimitation* (n 1) 97–98; Giovanny Vega-Barbosa, 'The Admissibility of Outer Continental Shelf Delimitation Claims Before the ICJ Absent a Recommendation by the CLCS' (2018) 49 ODIL 103, 112; Bjørn Kunoy, 'The Admissibility of a Plea to an International Adjudicative Forum to Delimit the Outer Continental Shelf Prior to the Adoption of Final Recommendations by the Commission on the Limits of the Continental Shelf' (2010) 25 IJMCL 237; Magnússon (n 358).

shelf beyond 200 NM depends on geological and geomorphological criteria, subject to the constraints in Article 76(5) of UNCLOS, and that '[a]n essential step in any delimitation is to determine whether there are entitlements, and whether they overlap'.[367] The Court acknowledged that the situation was different to that in *Bay of Bengal Delimitation*, because the unique situation in the Bay of Bengal and the negotiation record of UNCLOS were sufficient to enable the Tribunal to proceed with the delimitation of the shelf beyond 200 NM.[368] However, the Court noted that both States had claimed a continental shelf beyond 200 NM; their claims overlapped; and neither State questioned the existence of the other's entitlement to a shelf beyond 200 NM; and both parties had requested the Court to delimit the maritime boundary up to the outer limit of the continental shelf. The Court therefore stated that it would 'proceed to do so'.[369]

Two judges disagreed with the Court's decision to delimit the continental shelf beyond 200 NM on the basis that the Court had insufficient evidence to do so. President Donoghue noted that the Court 'is not well positioned to identify, even approximately, any area of overlapping entitlement and thus to arrive at an equitable delimitation of any area of overlap'.[370] She noted that the case was 'entirely different' from *Bay of Bengal Delimitation*, where there was uncontested scientific evidence that practically the entire Bay of Bengal was covered with a thick layer of sedimentary rocks,[371] and from *Ghana/Côte d'Ivoire*, where there had been an affirmative CLCS recommendation in relation to Ghana.[372] In contrast here, the Court had 'no comparable evidence regarding the existence, extent, shape or continuity of any outer continental shelf appertaining to either Party',[373] and the parties' submissions to the CLCS are 'unilateral assertions'; it could not be assumed that the CLCS would adopt any State's submissions.[374] Judge Robinson also disagreed with the Court's approach, noting that in order to delimit the outer shelf 'the Court must have before it reliable evidence that there is in existence, in the area beyond 200 nautical miles, a "submerged prolongation of the land mass of the coastal State"'.[375] He noted that the Court's judgment 'reflects an awareness of the requirement that the Court must have at hand reliable information confirming the existence of a continental margin in the area beyond 200 nautical miles' if it was to delimit that area,[376] but the Court ignored this requirement.[377] The judgment was thus 'bereft of even a scintilla of reliable evidence that the geological and geomorphological criteria ... have been met'.[378] He stated further that the requests of the parties, and the congruence of their views as to their entitlement to a shelf beyond 200 NM, did not constitute a sufficient basis for delimitation of that area.[379]

The Court appears now to have expressed a firm willingness to proceed to delimit the continental shelf beyond 200 NM absent a high degree of certainty as to the existence of

[367] *Maritime Delimitation in the Indian Ocean*, Judgment (n 51) para 193.
[368] ibid para 193.
[369] ibid para 194.
[370] ibid (Separate Opinion of Judge Donoghue) para 4.
[371] ibid (Separate Opinion of Judge Donoghue) para 6, citing *Bay of Bengal Delimitation* (n 47).
[372] ibid (Separate Opinion of Judge Donoghue) para 7, citing *Ghana/Côte d'Ivoire*, Judgment (n 88).
[373] ibid (Separate Opinion of Judge Donoghue) para 8.
[374] ibid.
[375] ibid (Individual Opinion, Partly Concurring and Partly Dissenting of Judge Robinson) para 6.
[376] ibid (Individual Opinion, Partly Concurring and Partly Dissenting of Judge Robinson) para 9.
[377] ibid.
[378] ibid (Individual Opinion, Partly Concurring and Partly Dissenting of Judge Robinson) para 13.
[379] ibid (Individual Opinion, Partly Concurring and Partly Dissenting of Judge Robinson) para 16.

entitlements in that zone, which represents a move from the position it initially expressed and that was reflected in the tribunals' approaches in *Bay of Bengal Delimitation* and *Bay of Bengal Arbitration*. There are dissenting views, and it may be that the Court backtracks or provides further elaboration of the pre-conditions for such delimitation in future cases. It also remains to be seen whether other tribunals take the same approach as the Court, as they have tended generally to follow suit in maritime boundary delimitation cases.

B. Delimitation of the Extended Continental Shelf

Those tribunals that have proceeded to delimit the extended continental shelf have generally emphasised that no different methodology should apply to delimitation of the shelf within and beyond 200 NM. This point was first made by the Tribunal in *Bay of Bengal Delimitation*. It therefore applied the equidistance/relevant circumstances approach. Bangladesh argued that the geology and geomorphology, notably the connection of the shelf to its landmass, was a relevant circumstance necessitating adjustment of the equidistance line in its favour. It also argued that the continuing cut-off effect, which caused ITLOS to adjust the equidistance line within 200 NM, continued to apply.[380] The Tribunal rejected Bangladesh's argument on the basis of 'the most natural prolongation', but it considered that the concavity of the Bangladesh coast was a relevant circumstance that had continuing effect beyond 200 NM. It therefore delimited the outer shelf using an adjusted equidistance line, continuing the line delimiting the EEZ and the continental shelf within 200 NM in the same direction 'until it reaches the area where the rights of third States may be affected'.[381]

ITLOS noted that the adjusted equidistance line delimitation resulted in a 'grey area': an area on the Bangladeshi side of the line, beyond 200 NM from its coasts but within 200 NM of Myanmar's coast. This area was essentially Myanmar's EEZ, but Bangladeshi continental shelf. The Tribunal reconciled this result with the comment that '[i]t is not unusual in such cases for States to enter into agreements or cooperative arrangements to deal with problems resulting from the delimitation'.[382]

In *Bay of Bengal Arbitration*, the Tribunal applied the same methodology to delimitation of the outer continental shelf as it had for the EEZ/continental shelf within 200 NM. Bangladesh abandoned its unsuccessful argument in *Bay of Bengal Delimitation* that the shelf was 'the most natural prolongation' of its coast, but it argued for a substantial adjustment on the basis of cut-off caused by its concave coast. The Tribunal considered that the provisional equidistance line did cause Bangladesh to suffer a cut-off as a result of its concavity and, in particular, the provisional line did not give sufficient weight to the south-facing coast of Bangladesh. As noted above, the Tribunal ultimately adjusted the provisional line by following an azimuth from a specified point, Prov-3, until it met the maritime boundary between Bangladesh and Myanmar.[383]

The Tribunal's delimitation, as in *Bay of Bengal Delimitation*, created a 'grey area' of Indian EEZ in an area of Bangladeshi continental shelf. That grey area also overlapped

380 *Bay of Bengal Delimitation* (n 47) paras 457–58.
381 ibid paras 460–62.
382 ibid paras 471–72.
383 ibid paras 478–80.

to some extent with Myanmar's grey area, resulting in a smaller zone where both India's and Myanmar's EEZ would overlap. Like the Tribunal in *Bay of Bengal Delimitation*, the Tribunal here emphasised that it was for the parties to determine the measures they consider appropriate, recalling that under UNCLOS States should exercise their rights in the EEZ and the continental shelf with due regard for the rights of other States.[384]

The Tribunal's creation of the grey area was the subject of a strong dissent by Dr PS Rao, who argued that:

> The creation of a grey area is entirely contrary to law and the policies underlying the decision taking in UNCLOS to create the EEZ as one single, common maritime zone within 200 nm which effectively incorporates the regime of the continental shelf within it.[385]

He contended that as entitlement to the continental shelf beyond 200 NM is based on the establishment of its outer limits under Article 76 of UNCLOS, entitlement to it is not as absolute as the entitlement to the EEZ, from which it followed that entitlement to an EEZ takes priority over the outer continental shelf.[386]

A 'grey area' will result in any extended continental shelf delimitation between adjacent States that departs from a strict equidistance line.[387] Departing from the equidistance line may be required to reach an equitable solution to the delimitation,[388] and in that sense it is consistent with fundamental principles of international law, including respect for the rule of law. However, in a very practical sense it creates difficulties, as pointed out in the opinion of Dr PS Rao, and has the potential to create further disputes, which is arguably inconsistent with a primary judicial function: namely, the resolution of disputes.[389] The fact that coordination or cooperation would be required was implicitly acknowledged by both tribunals in *Bay of Bengal Delimitation* and *Bay of Bengal Arbitration*, in stating that it was for the parties to determine measures appropriate to meet their obligations under UNCLOS. A judgment that requires the parties to cooperate to implement it is not unique in international dispute settlement: while of course a dispute may develop in the future, it is difficult to see how these tribunals could have avoided that possibility. It is not clear that they would have had jurisdiction to determine the rights and obligations of each State in the grey area, and the only way in which it could have been avoided in practice would have been if they had reverted to a strict equidistance line through the 200 NM limit, which would—on the reasoning of each tribunal—have been inconsistent with the outcome dictated by international law. In light of these considerations, the grey area might be characterised as an unfortunate but necessary consequence of the need to reach an equitable solution, which is paramount under the applicable provisions of UNCLOS.[390] It appears to be going too far to suggest that this constituted an abdication of the judicial function. Rather, it is a necessary consequence of

[384] ibid paras 506–508.

[385] ibid (Concurring and Dissenting Opinion of Dr PS Rao) para 24.

[386] ibid (Concurring and Dissenting Opinion of Dr PS Rao) para 40.

[387] Fietta and Cleverly (n 1) 112–13; Alex G Oude Elferink, 'Does Undisputed Title to a Maritime Zone Always Exclude its Delimitation: The Grey Area Issue' (1998) 13(2) IJMCL 143.

[388] See Bjarni Már Magnússon, 'The Grey Areas in the Bay of Bengal' (2016) 56(1) Indian J Intl L 41, 57–58.

[389] See also the discussion in Lando, *Maritime Delimitation* (n 1) 140–43.

[390] Jensen noted that the creation of grey areas was 'a highly welcome result' in light of the UNCLOS provisions. øystein Jensen, 'The Delimitation of the Continental Shelf beyond 200 nm: Substantive Issues' in Alex G Oude Elferink, Tore Henriksen, and Signe Veierud Busch (eds), *Maritime Boundary Delimitation: The Case Law—Is It Consistent and Predictable?* (CUP 2018) 372.

the fact that international tribunals have limited jurisdiction, which is itself consistent with the fundamental principle of State sovereignty.

In *Ghana/Côte d'Ivoire*, the Chamber also emphasised that there is only one single continental shelf, and therefore it would be inappropriate to make a distinction between the continental shelf within and beyond 200 NM as far as the delimitation methodology is concerned.[391] It extended the delimitation line it had identified for the EEZ and the continental shelf within 200 NM in the same direction, until it reached the outer limit of the continental shelf.[392]

In *Maritime Delimitation in the Indian Ocean*, the Court took the same approach. It considered that it was appropriate to extend the geodetic line used for the delimitation of the EEZ and the continental shelf within 200 NM to delimit the shelf beyond 200 NM.[393] It therefore concluded that the maritime boundary beyond 200 NM continued along the same geodetic line until it reached the outer limit of the parties' continental shelves on the basis of the recommendations of the CLCS, or until it reached the area where the rights of third States may be affected.[394] The Court represented the delimitation line with an arrow extending beyond 200 NM.[395] The Court noted that, depending on the extent of Kenya's entitlement to a continental shelf beyond 200 NM, the delimitation line might give rise to an area of 'limited size' beyond 200 NM of the coast of Kenya and within 200 NM of the coast of Somalia, but on the Kenyan side of the delimitation line. However, it considered that the existence of this 'grey area' was only a possibility, so it was not necessary for the Court to pronounce itself on the legal regime that would be appliable in that area.[396]

On the method of delimitation, three judges criticised the Court's approach. President Donoghue noted in her separate opinion that beyond 200 NM, the area of overlapping entitlement is determined not by the configuration of the coasts of the two States, but rather by application of the geological and geomorphological criteria set out in Article 76 of UNCLOS.[397] She noted that, although it was simple and inviting to continue the delimitation line past the 200 NM limit, 'it cannot be presumed that a line that achieves an equitable delimitation of the 200-nautical-mile zones will also result in an equitable delimitation of overlapping areas of two States' outer continental shelves'.[398]

Judge Yusuf also criticised the Court's approach, on two grounds: first, he disagreed with the use of the geodetic line that he considered had been unjustifiably adjusted within 200 NM.[399] Secondly, he noted that the Court's reference to the potential for a 'grey area' 'may create a new and unnecessary controversy between these two neighbouring States in the future'.[400] In his individual opinion, Judge Robinson questioned whether the Court's approach to delimitation of the outer shelf was appropriate, noting that the judgment was silent on the question whether the methodology used produced an equitable solution. Judge Robinson

391 *Ghana/Côte d'Ivoire*, Judgment (n 88) para 526.
392 ibid para 527.
393 *Maritime Delimitation in the Indian Ocean*, Judgment (n 51) para 195.
394 ibid para 199.
395 ibid 70 (Sketch Map 12).
396 ibid para 197.
397 ibid (Separate Opinion of Judge Donoghue) para 11.
398 ibid (Separate Opinion of Judge Donoghue) para 13.
399 ibid (Separate Opinion of Judge Yusuf) para 50. See also para 51.
400 ibid (Separate Opinion of Judge Yusuf) para 52.

viewed this matter as a 'significant omission' that 'raises serious questions as to whether the delimitation carried out has been effected in accordance with the Convention'.[401]

The cases are therefore generally consistent as to the appropriate methodology for delimiting the extended continental shelf: the same methodology as for the 200 NM continental shelf (and EEZ) should apply. However, in light of the approach of tribunals to the question of competence to delimit in advance of recommendations from the CLCS as to the delineation of the outer limits of the shelves, the question that arises is whether an equitable solution can be achieved. That point is made strongly in President Donoghue's recent separate opinion and carries some force.

VI. Provisional Arrangements and Obligation Not to Jeopardise a Final Agreement

In respect of the EEZ and the continental shelf, Articles 74(3) and 83(3) of UNCLOS provide that:

> Pending agreement as provided for in paragraph 1, the States concerned, in a spirit of understanding and cooperation, shall make every effort to enter into provisional arrangements of a practical nature and, during this transitional period, not to jeopardize or hamper the reaching of the final agreement. Such arrangements shall be without prejudice to the final delimitation.[402]

In *Guyana v Suriname*, the Annex VII Tribunal articulated two obligations arising from these provisions: first, to make every effort to enter into provisional arrangements of a practical nature; and secondly, to make every effort not to jeopardise or hamper the reaching of a final agreement.[403]

The *Guyana v Suriname* Tribunal considered that the first obligation with respect to provisional arrangements imposed on the parties a duty to negotiate in good faith, while acknowledging that the language 'every effort' left some room for interpretation.[404] The second obligation, it said, did not preclude all activities in a disputed maritime area, only those that would prejudice a final agreement. The Tribunal thus drew a distinction between unilateral acts that would cause a permanent physical change to the marine environment and those that would not. It considered that:

> [A]cts that do cause physical change would have to be undertaken pursuant to an agreement between the parties to be permissible, as they may hamper or jeopardise the reaching of a final agreement on delimitation. A distinction is therefore to be made between activities of the kind that lead to a permanent physical change, such as exploitation of oil and gas reserves, and those that do not, such as seismic exploration.[405]

401 ibid (Individual Opinion, Partly Concurring and Partly Dissenting of Judge Robinson) para 21.
402 UNCLOS (n 1) arts 74(3) (EEZ), 83(3) (continental shelf).
403 *Guyana v Suriname* (n 13) para 459.
404 ibid para 461.
405 ibid para 467.

This holding aligned with the earlier position of the ICJ in the *Aegean Sea* case.[406]

In the context of the dispute, the *Guyana v Suriname* Tribunal found that both States violated their obligation to make every effort to make a provisional arrangement, particularly around the time that Guyana's concession holder carried out drilling operations in the disputed area. After that period, the Tribunal considered that both States had respected their obligation with respect to provisional arrangements.[407] It also found that both States had violated their duty not to jeopardise or hamper reaching a final agreement: Guyana by unilaterally authorising exploratory drilling, and Suriname by responding to that action with a threat of force.[408] The Tribunal issued only declaratory relief for these breaches of the Convention.[409] The holding is an important reminder that State parties may be held accountable for their actions under Articles 74(3) and 83(3) pending the resolution of their maritime boundary dispute.

In *Ghana/Côte d'Ivoire*, the Special Chamber considered a claim by Côte d'Ivoire for breach of Article 83 of the Convention. In 2015, at the request of Côte d'Ivoire, the Chamber issued a provisional measures order, requiring Ghana to take all necessary steps to ensure that no new drilling either by Ghana or under its control took place in areas of maritime space that were disputed.[410] It declined to order Ghana to suspend all exploration or exploitation activities in the disputed area, on the basis that such an order 'would entail the risk of considerable financial loss to Ghana and its concessionaires and could also pose a serious danger to the marine environment'.[411] It is notable that the Chamber did not refer to Articles 74(3) and 83(3) in its order, although the parties did so in their pleadings. One possible explanation might be that it considered the obligations of Articles 74(3) and 83(3) were not relevant in a provisional measures context, where a dispute had been taken to third party settlement.[412]

During the merits phase, Côte d'Ivoire argued that Ghana's conduct in the disputed area violated international law, Article 83 of UNCLOS, and the 2015 Order.[413] In respect of Article 83, Côte d'Ivoire argued that Ghana's unilateral activities in the disputed area, its inflexibility in negotiations, together with the closing off of avenues for settling the dispute all violated the obligation to negotiate in good faith (an obligation arising under Article 83(1)).[414] While the Chamber emphasised that the obligation to negotiate 'occupies a prominent place in the Convention, as well as in general international law', it is an obligation of conduct and not one of result. It noted that negotiations took place between the parties over six years, with ten meetings between 2008 and 2014, all dealing with maritime delimitation. Taking account of that evidence, the Chamber concluded that Côte d'Ivoire had not established that Ghana did not negotiate in good faith and dismissed its claim for breach of Article 83(1) of UNCLOS.[415]

[406] *Aegean Sea Continental Shelf* (n 44) para 30. For further discussion see Natalie Klein, 'Provisional Measures and Provisional Arrangements in Maritime Boundary Disputes' (2006) 21 IJMCL 423, 429–32.

[407] *Guyana v Suriname* (n 13) paras 471–78.

[408] ibid paras 479–84.

[409] ibid paras 485-86.

[410] *Delimitation of the Maritime Boundary between Ghana and Côte d'Ivoire in the Atlantic Ocean (Ghana/Côte d'Ivoire)* (Provisional Measures Order of 25 April 2015) ITLOS Reports 2015, 146, paras 166–67.

[411] ibid para 99.

[412] See discussion in BIICL, 'Report on the Obligations of States under Articles 74(3) and 83(3) of UNCLOS in Respect of Undelimited Maritime Areas' (BIICL 2016) 25–27.

[413] *Ghana/Côte d'Ivoire*, Judgment (n 88) paras 541–44.

[414] ibid paras 598–601.

[415] ibid paras 604–605.

Côte d'Ivoire further argued that the activities undertaken by Ghana violated the obligation under Article 83(3) not to jeopardise or hamper the conclusion of an agreement.[416] Ghana argued that Article 83(3) does not require States to refrain from any particular type of activity; rather it only requires them not to jeopardise or hamper the reaching of a final agreement. Thus, any activity in a disputed area must be judged on the basis of its likely effect on the process of reaching a final agreement, and not on the basis of its physical effects.[417] The Chamber considered that the obligation not to jeopardise or hamper the reaching of a final agreement must be interpreted taking account of the general obligations under Article 83(3) to act 'in a spirit of understanding and cooperation'.[418] In the particular circumstances, the Chamber noted that Ghana had suspended its activities implementing its obligations under the 2015 provisional measures order. It also noted that Ghana had undertaken hydrocarbon activities only in areas that ultimately were held to fall on the Ghanaian side of the delimited boundary. Since those actions did not take place in Côte d'Ivoire's maritime space, the Chamber concluded that it was 'impossible to state that Ghana has undertaken activities which have jeopardised or hampered the conclusion of an agreement as envisaged by [Article 83(3)]'.[419] Accordingly, the Chamber found that Ghana did not violate Article 83(1) or 83(3).[420]

This aspect of the Chamber's decision appears to be somewhat circular: it essentially reasoned that because the activities took place in an area that the Chamber ultimately awarded to Ghana, they were not in breach of the obligation not to jeopardise or hamper an agreement. Arguably, the obligation not to jeopardise or hamper should apply to activities in any area where a neighbouring State has a good faith claim. It seems logical that if one State is undertaking activities in an area that is claimed in good faith by a neighbouring State, there is at least some potential to jeopardise or hamper negotiations to reach a final agreement. However, in circumstances where the Chamber had declined to grant provisional measures ordering the cessation of all petroleum activities, it is perhaps not surprising that it ultimately found that Ghana's continuation of its activities did not fall foul of Article 83. The Chamber's decision also suggests that the obligation not to jeopardise or hamper the reaching of a final agreement would only be breached in circumstances where unilateral acts have caused physical changes and were carried out in areas later found to fall within the other State's maritime areas. In this regard, the decision departs from *Guyana v Suriname*, where the Tribunal premised a breach of the obligation on activities in any part of the disputed area that had a permanent detrimental effect.[421]

In *Maritime Delimitation in the Indian Ocean*, Somalia argued that Kenya, by its unilateral actions in the area, violated Somalia's sovereignty over the territorial sea and its sovereign rights and jurisdiction in the EEZ and the continental shelf.[422] It claimed that these unilateral actions violated Kenya's obligations under Article 74(3) and 83(3), jeopardising and hampering the possibility of reaching a final agreement between the two States.[423]

[416] ibid paras 606–15.
[417] ibid paras 617–18.
[418] ibid para 630.
[419] ibid paras 632–33.
[420] ibid para 634.
[421] See further Natalie Klein, 'Provisional Measures and Provisional Arrangements' in Alex G Oude Elferink, Tore Henriksen, and Signe Veierud Busch, *Maritime Boundary Delimitation: The Case Law—Is It Consistent and Predictable?* (CUP 2018) 117, 120–28.
[422] *Maritime Delimitation in the Indian Ocean*, Judgment (n 51) para 199.
[423] ibid para 200.

Referring to the judgment in *Ghana/Côte d'Ivoire*, the Court noted that where maritime claims overlap, activities undertaken by one State in the area cannot be considered to be a violation of the sovereign rights of the other, if they were carried out before the judgment was delivered, and if the area concerned was the subject of claims made in good faith by both States.[424] As to the claim for breach of Articles 74(3) and 83(3), the Court noted that the maritime delimitation dispute between the parties had been established since 2009, and so it only examined activities conducted by Kenya after that date.[425] The Court noted that certain activities, such as the award of oil concession blocks to private operators and the performance of surveys, were not of a kind as to lead to permanent physical change in the marine environment; nor was it established that they had the effect of jeopardising or hampering the reaching of a final agreement on delimitation of the maritime boundary.[426] Somalia had also complained of certain drilling activities, which the Court acknowledged could alter the status quo and jeopardise or hamper the reaching of a final agreement.[427] However, some of the drilling was authorised but never took place;[428] others took place south of and at a great distance from the equidistance line claimed by Somalia as the maritime boundary.[429] For others, the Court considered that there was insufficient evidence that it took place after 2009.[430] The Court therefore concluded that Kenya had not violated its international obligations through its maritime activities in the disputed area.[431]

This aspect of the Court's decision appears to be consistent with the approach of the Chamber in *Ghana/Côte d'Ivoire*. Underlying both decisions appears to be a general reluctance to find that conduct undertaken before the boundary is delimited was in breach of obligations under UNCLOS, even if it appears to have had significant potential to hamper the reaching of any agreement.

VII. Concluding Remarks

The UNCLOS provisions for delimitation, most notably Articles 74 and 83 concerning the EEZ and the continental shelf, reflect an inherent desire for flexibility in maritime delimitation, with an equitable solution as the goal. As noted at the outset, tribunals have developed a very specific approach to delimitation and hence have exerted considerable influence on the elaboration of provisions of UNCLOS. The consistency of the case law is notable.

The discussion in this chapter has, however, indicated instances where questions have emerged as to the subjectivity of a determination. Choices are necessarily made when, for example, base points are selected and tribunals deviate from the parties' submissions in this regard. Differing views will inevitably emerge as between the parties, and external stakeholders, as to what should count as 'relevant circumstances' in varied factual settings. It has also been apparent that questions of evidence or proof may be decisive, especially in relation to the outer continental shelf but also in demonstrating claims to tacit agreements or the

424 ibid para 203.
425 ibid para 206.
426 ibid para 207.
427 ibid para 208.
428 ibid.
429 ibid para 209.
430 ibid.
431 ibid para 212. See also para 211.

strength of specific concerns in the area to be delimited. Given that not all coastlines are the same, divergences will emerge. Yet the judicial effort to establish a common approach and the strong mutual regard for decisions among the different tribunals is remarkable.

In this way, tribunals have in this field successfully performed the function of dispute settlement, alongside the function of law development. It is a clear example where interests of stakeholders beyond the parties to the dispute are served. The potential to account for both the interests of the parties and the international community more broadly in this context was emphasised by Evans as early as 1989:

> When a dispute comes before a Court, however, there are countervailing pressures. Not only should the result be acceptable to the parties but the international community should also be satisfied, in order to engender respect for, and encourage recourse to, the process of adjudication. Such acceptability requires demonstration, a task which the flexibility of the process has made relatively difficult. In any case, equity is often in the eye of the beholder. What a Court can and must do, however, is to ensure that its result derives from the process indicated by the norms of international law; these norms being drawn from, and functioning in the light of, the circumstances relevant in the context of the particular case, thus ensuring a relatively uniform approach and providing an important basis for future negotiations.[432]

It is clear that the development of a coherent body of law on delimitation, one that provides both certainty and predictability, is of broader interest to the international community. The way in which tribunals have prioritised a common method and developed a consistent body of case law on maritime delimitation serves this interest. In this way, the objectives of both the peaceful settlement of disputes and the rule of law are met. Further, because the international community at large has an interest in knowing which areas of maritime space are attributable to coastal States, and the extent of their rights and jurisdictions in those spaces, the broader objective of public order of the oceans is also served.

[432] Malcolm D Evans, *Relevant Circumstances and Maritime Delimitation* (OUP 1989) 240.

7
Navigation

I. Introduction

A foundational principle of the law of the sea is freedom of the seas. That principle has been critical to the recognition of navigational rights and freedoms in the law of the sea. In the modern law of the sea, reflected in the 1958 Geneva Conventions,[1] the UN Convention on the Law of the Sea (UNCLOS),[2] and through State practice, increasing importance has been given to the balancing of navigational rights and freedoms with the rights and interests of coastal States. Over time, coastal State interests have expanded. While initially they were focused on security issues and sovereignty over waters immediately adjacent to the coasts, they now cover matters such as protection and preservation of the marine environment, the conservation and management of marine living resources, and a broad range of interests in relation to the exclusive economic zone (EEZ) and continental shelf. In addressing claims in relation to navigation, UNCLOS tribunals have had multiple opportunities to address the balance to be struck between freedom of navigation and coastal State interests, particularly in relation to the scope and extent of permitted law enforcement measures.[3] As well as contributing to the settlement of disputes between the States party to proceedings, UNCLOS tribunals have been able to contribute to the broader goals of the rule of law and public order of the oceans. These objectives are reinforced by clarity around the balance between coastal States' rights and interests, and the interests of all States with flagged vessels exercising freedom of navigation, as well as the interests of private entities who own and operate such vessels. While the contribution of UNCLOS tribunals to the interpretation and application of the provisions of UNCLOS governing navigation has necessarily been piecemeal, there have been several opportunities for tribunals to clarify important aspects of navigation, and thereby contribute to the broader objectives of the rule of law and public order of the oceans.

This chapter focuses on those aspects of navigation that have been addressed by UNCLOS tribunals. Section II deals with status of vessels, addressing both the requirements of nationality in Article 91 and immunities of warships and ships owned or operated by a State and used only on government non-commercial service, pursuant to Articles 32, 95, and 96. Section III examines cases addressing different aspects of freedom of navigation under

[1] Convention on the Territorial Sea and Contiguous Zone (opened for signature 29 April 1958, entered into force 10 September 1964) 516 UNTS 205; Convention on the Continental Shelf (opened for signature 29 April 1958, entered into force 10 June 1964) 499 UNTS 311; Convention on the High Seas (adopted 29 April 1958, entered into force 30 September 1962) 450 UNTS 1; Convention on Fishing and Conservation of the Living Resources of the High Seas (adopted 29 April 1958, entered into force 26 September 1968) 599 UNTS 285.

[2] United Nations Convention on the Law of the Sea (adopted 10 December 1982, entered into force 16 November 1994) 1833 UNTS 397 (UNCLOS).

[3] On the balance to be struck see generally Philipp Wendel, *State Responsibility for Interferences with the Freedom of Navigation in Public International Law* (Springer 2007).

UNCLOS: including innocent passage in the territorial sea and archipelagic waters, and freedom of navigation in the EEZ and on the high seas. In respect of the latter, tribunals have addressed issues relating to the spatial extent of freedom of navigation; activities covered by freedom of navigation; what constitutes interference with freedom of navigation; duties of the flag State relating to safety of navigation; and the question of jurisdiction over incidents of navigation on the high seas. Section IV addresses law enforcement by coastal States: examining cases where tribunals have addressed the areas where coastal States have enforcement jurisdiction; limits on the use of force, including the crucial distinction between law enforcement measures and international rules regulating the use of force under the UN Charter; and the scope and exercise of the right of hot pursuit. Concluding remarks are made in section V.

II. Status of Vessels

Flag State jurisdiction, which is established on the basis of the nationality of the ship, is exclusive on the high seas, and hence essential to maintenance of order on the high seas. The flag State is responsible for various matters in respect of its flag vessels,[4] and it is also entitled to exercise diplomatic protection over the ship itself as well as its crew and cargo.[5] Flagged vessels have a general immunity from acts of interference by foreign government vessels on the high seas.

A. Nationality

Article 91 of UNCLOS sets out the general rule that each State is entitled to set the conditions for the grant of its nationality to ships. Article 91(1) provides that there must exist a 'genuine link' between the State and the ship, and Article 91(2) provides for the State to issue documents to its ships to which it has granted the right to fly its flag. Pursuant to Article 94(1), the flag State must 'effectively exercise its jurisdiction and control in administrative, technical and social matters over ships flying its flag'.

UNCLOS sets out some rules regulating the status of ships. Article 92 of UNCLOS provides that ships may sail under the flag of one State only, and shall be subject to its 'exclusive jurisdiction' on the high seas. A ship may not change its flag during a voyage or while in a port of call, except in case of a real transfer of ownership or change of registry. If a ship sails under the flag of two or more States, it may not claim any of the nationalities with respect to any other State, and may be assimilated to a Stateless vessel.

The idea of a genuine link for nationality can be traced to the International Court of Justice (ICJ) in the *Nottebohm* case, stating that 'nationality is a legal bond having as its basis a social fact of attachment, a genuine connection of existence, interests and sentiments, together with the existence of reciprocal rights and duties'.[6] In *Barcelona Traction*, Judge

[4] UNCLOS (n 2) art 94.

[5] See International Law Commission, 'Draft Articles on Diplomatic Protection with Commentaries' (2006) 2(2) UNYBILC 26, 52 (art 18) ('Diplomatic Protection'). See also *M/V Saiga (No 2) (Saint Vincent and the Grenadines v Guinea)* (Judgment) ITLOS Reports 1999, 10, paras 105–107 (*Saiga (No 2)*, Judgment).

[6] *Nottebohm (Liechtenstein v Guatemala)* (Second Phase) [1955] ICJ Rep 4, 23.

Jessup suggested that if a flag State did not assure that its ship 'meet such tests as management, ownership, jurisdiction and control, other States are not bound to recognize the asserted nationality of the ship'.[7]

The requirement of a 'genuine link' was set out in Article 5(1) of the 1958 Geneva High Seas Convention, although it did not specify any consequences of the absence of such a link nor elaborate on its meaning.[8] This approach was in contrast to the proposal of the International Law Commission (ILC) in its 1956 Draft Articles on the Law of the Sea, which provided that 'for purposes of recognition of the national character of the ships by other States, there must exist a genuine link between the State and the ship'.[9] The High Seas Convention approach represented a shift away from ownership requirements and from a right of non-recognition by other States. The language of Article 5(1) of the High Seas Convention was replicated in Article 94(1) of UNCLOS, while the basic requirement of a genuine link was set out in Article 91(1).

In *Saiga (No 2)*,[10] the M/V Saiga was provisionally registered in Saint Vincent and the Grenadines on 12 March 1997, endorsed as valid until 12 September 1997, but a permanent certificate of registration was not issued until 28 November 1997. Guinea objected to the claim brought against it on the basis that the M/V Saiga lacked nationality of the claimant State, as the provisional registration certificate had expired at the time of its arrest in October 1997. The Tribunal noted that Article 91 codifies a well-established rule of general international law, and that '[d]etermination of the criteria and establishment of the procedures for granting and withdrawing nationality to ships are matters within the exclusive jurisdiction of the flag State'.[11] However, noting that disputes concerning nationality may be submitted to the dispute-settlement procedures under Part XV of UNCLOS, the Tribunal stated that 'nationality is a question of fact to be determined, like other facts in dispute before it, on the basis of evidence adduced by the parties'.[12] On the basis of the evidence, the Tribunal concluded that the M/V Saiga retained Vincentian nationality at the time of its arrest.[13] It noted that it was not established that Vincentian nationality of the vessel was extinguished after the provisional certificate expired, and that the consistent conduct of Saint Vincent and the Grenadines supported the conclusion that the M/V Saiga retained Vincentian nationality at all times material to the dispute.[14] It also noted that Guinea had failed to question the assertion of Vincentian nationality when it had reasonable opportunity to do so, and that 'in the particular circumstances of this case, it would not be consistent with justice if the Tribunal were to decline to deal with the merits of the dispute'.[15]

Guinea also argued that there was no 'genuine link' between the M/V Saiga and Saint Vincent and the Grenadines. The Tribunal noted that the first question to be addressed was whether the absence of a genuine link between the State and the ship entitles another State

[7] *Barcelona Traction, Light and Power Company, Limited (Belgium v Spain)* (Second Phase) [1970] ICJ Rep 3, 161, para 46 (Separate Opinion of Judge Jessup).

[8] UNCLOS (n 2) art 5(1) reads in relevant part: 'There must exist a genuine link between the State and the ship; in particular, the State must effectively exercise its jurisdiction and control in administrative, technical and social matters over ships flying its flag.'

[9] International Law Commission, Articles concerning the Law of the Sea with Commentaries [1956] 2 UNYBILC 265, 278 (art 29(1)).

[10] *Saiga (No 2)*, Judgment (n 5).

[11] ibid paras 63–65.

[12] ibid para 66.

[13] ibid paras 72–74.

[14] ibid para 73.

[15] ibid.

to refuse to recognise the nationality of the ship. Referring to the antecedents of Articles 91 and 94 in Article 5(1) of the High Seas Convention, and to the contrasting 1956 Draft Articles proposed by the ILC, the Tribunal concluded that the absence of a genuine link did not entitle Guinea to disregard the M/V Saiga's nationality, stating that:

> [T]he purpose of the provisions of the Convention on the need for a genuine link between a ship and its flag State is to secure more effective implementation of the duties of the flag State, and not to establish criteria by reference to which the validity of the registration of ships in a flag State may be challenged by other States.[16]

It followed that there was no legal basis on which Guinea could refuse to recognise the right of the M/V Saiga to fly the flag of Saint Vincent and the Grenadines on the basis of a requirement of genuine link.[17] In any event, the Tribunal found that the evidence of the absence of a genuine link adduced by Guinea was not sufficient to establish a lack of genuine link between the M/V Saiga and its flag State at the relevant time.[18]

In commenting on *Saiga (No 2)*, O'Keefe suggests that the Tribunal's conclusion of law was not without problems, noting that 'the overarching doctrine of good faith continues to condition a State's competence to grant its nationality'.[19] From this position, he suggests that the condition of good faith might have been enforced in this case. However, as O'Keefe notes, the Tribunal was not satisfied that the evidence supported the denial of a genuine link, and Guinea did not frame its case on the basis of good faith. Thus, if the Tribunal had taken this point, it would have been highly controversial.[20]

Guinea made a further objection to admissibility on the basis that the claims related to violation of persons (i.e. the owner and the crew) who were not nationals of Saint Vincent and the Grenadines. Referring to the duties of flag States set out in Articles 94 and 217 of UNCLOS, the Tribunal noted that these could be discharged only through the exercise of appropriate jurisdiction and control over the master, members of the crew, the owners or operators, and other people involved in the activities of the ship.[21] The Tribunal concluded that:

> [T]he Convention considers a ship as a unit ... Thus the ship, everything on it, and every person involved or interested in its operations are treated as an entity linked to the flag State. The nationalities of these persons are not relevant.[22]

The International Tribunal for the Law of the Sea (ITLOS) returned to consider the question of nationality in the *Grand Prince* case.[23] Belize sought prompt release of the Grand Prince, which bore a provisional patent of navigation dated 16 October 2000 expiring 29 December 2000. In a *note verbale* dated 4 January 2001, Belize informed France that the vessel would

[16] ibid para 83. See also paras 79–82.
[17] ibid para 86.
[18] ibid para 87.
[19] Roger O'Keefe, 'ITLOS Flags Its Intent' (2000) 59(3) CLJ 428, 431.
[20] ibid. More generally see Vincent P Cogliati-Bantz, 'Disentangling the "Genuine Link": Enquiries in Sea, Air and Space Law' (2010) 79 Nord J Intl L 383.
[21] *Saiga (No 2)*, Judgment (n 5) para 105.
[22] ibid para 106. This was subsequently accepted by the ILC in its Articles on Diplomatic Protection: see ILC, 'Diplomatic Protection' (n 5) 52 (art 18).
[23] *Grand Prince (Belize v France)* (Prompt Release, Judgment) ITLOS Reports 2001, 17 (*Grand Prince*).

be de-registered the same day due to repeated fishing violations. Two further communications from the Belize maritime registry dated 26 and 30 March 2001 indicated that Belize was in the process of cancelling registration and wished to invoke nationality in order to facilitate proceedings at ITLOS. Thus, the Tribunal was faced with inconsistent evidence. It affirmed that its task was to determine the nationality of the vessel on the basis of evidence adduced by the parties.[24] It noted that under the Belizean Registration of Merchant Ships Act 1989, 'the right of a fishing vessel to fly the Belizean flag flows from the act of registration'.[25] The only document issued under the Registration of Merchant Ships Act 1989 was the provisional patent of navigation, which expressly stated that its date of expiration was 29 December 2000. The Tribunal did not consider that the statements in the March 2001 letter were substantiated, and also noted that they were contradicted by the January 2001 *note verbale*, which indicated that the Grand Prince had been de-registered.[26] The Tribunal concluded that the documentary evidence submitted by Belize failed to establish that it was the flag State of the Grand Prince when the application was made, and dismissed the claim for lack of jurisdiction.[27] It did not examine any genuine link between the vessel and Belize.

Nine judges dissented in *Grand Prince*, contending that Belize had discharged its burden to show that the vessel had Belizean nationality, and suggesting that the Tribunal might have exercised its evidence-gathering powers under Article 77 of its Rules.[28] They also questioned the majority's assumption that an applicant in a proceeding under Article 292 must be the flag State at the time of application, as opposed to at the time of detention, and at the time that an allegation is made of non-compliance with UNCLOS.[29] Oxman and Bantz highlight that the case concerned the reflagging of a fishing vessel, a problem that has attracted international concern,[30] and they suggested that there were important reasons why the majority chose not to request more information, in particular that if the Tribunal had proceeded with the case, it would have had to consider complex issues concerning the confiscation order imposed by France.[31] Oxman and Bantz conclude that dealing with the case on the basis that the applicant 'failed to get its formal documentation in order may have seemed not only the easiest, but the most prudent, approach'.[32]

In its judgment in *Virginia G*,[33] ITLOS affirmed its approaches to nationality issues as set out in *Saiga (No 2)*. The M/V Virginia G, an oil tanker with a Panamanian flag, was arrested by Guinea-Bissau. The Tribunal noted that the requirement of a 'genuine link' set out in Article 91(1) was not a pre-requisite for a grant of nationality. It noted, however, that once a ship is registered, the flag State is required, under Article 94(1) of UNCLOS, 'to exercise effective jurisdiction and control over that ship in order to ensure that it operates in accordance with generally accepted international regulations. This is the meaning of "genuine link"'.[34] On the basis of the evidence, ITLOS saw no reason to question that

[24] ibid para 81.
[25] ibid para 83.
[26] ibid para 87.
[27] ibid paras 84–93.
[28] ibid (Dissenting Opinion of Judges Caminos, Marotta Rangel, Yankow, Yamamoto, Aki, Vukas, Marsit, Eiriksson, and Jesus) paras 3, 13–14.
[29] ibid para 15.
[30] Bernard H Oxman and Vincent P Bantz, 'The "Grand Prince" (Belize v. France) Judgment (2002) 96(1) AJIL 219, 222.
[31] ibid 222–23.
[32] ibid 225.
[33] *M/V Virginia G (Panama/Guinea-Bissau)* (Judgment) ITLOS Reports 2014, 4 (*Virginia G*).
[34] ibid paras 110–13.

Panama exercised effective jurisdiction and control over the M/V Virginia G at the time of the incident. It noted that Panamanian legislation set out conditions for the grant of nationality, including by carrying out certain activities and submitting substantial information and documentation; that Panama also delegated the conduct of an annual safety inspection and the issuance of a technical certificate to a recognised organisation in accordance with the relevant International Maritime Organization (IMO) conventions, and that the M/V Virginia G met the standard set out in the International Convention for the Prevention of Pollution from Ships (also known as MARPOL 73/78).[35] Taking that into account, the Tribunal concluded that there was a genuine link between the vessel and Panama at the time of the relevant incident.[36]

Guinea-Bissau also objected to Panama's standing on the basis that the owner and crew members were nationals of third States. As in *Saiga (No 2)*, ITLOS gave this argument short shrift, dismissing the objection and affirming that the M/V Virginia G was to be considered as a unit, so that its crew, cargo on board, owner, and every person involved or interested in its operations are to be treated as an entity linked to the flag State.[37] Panama explicitly relied on Article 18 of the ILC's Articles on Diplomatic Protection as conferring on it a right to exercise diplomatic protection.[38]

The impact of confiscation of a vessel on nationality was squarely at issue in the *Tomimaru* case. There, the Tomimaru, a Japanese fishing vessel was arrested in Russia's EEZ, and following a Russian court order was subject to a confiscation order. On Japan's application for prompt release, ITLOS considered whether confiscation had an impact on the nationality of a vessel. It noted that confiscation had an impact on ownership of a vessel, but it could not be assumed that a change in ownership automatically leads to a change in nationality or loss of its flag.[39] Russia had not claimed to have initiated any procedures leading to a change or loss in the Japanese flag of the Tomimaru.[40] As discussed in Chapter 3,[41] the confiscation on the facts of this case led to a determination that an application for prompt release under Article 292 was without object. This conclusion was warranted given the interplay between prompt release proceedings under UNCLOS with domestic law enforcement proceedings.[42] The impact of national confiscation measures on a ship's nationality has not yet fallen squarely within UNCLOS jurisprudence but may be tested in the future on the merits and not only as a question of standing, as in *Tomimaru*.

Nationality was most recently considered by an Annex VII Tribunal in *Enrica Lexie*.[43] The Indian fishing boat, the St Antony, which was involved in the incident with the Italian oil tanker Enrica Lexie, was not flying a flag at the relevant time. The Tribunal therefore had to determine whether the vessel had Indian nationality, as argued by India. The Tribunal affirmed that, under Article 91 of UNCLOS, it was for each State to fix conditions for the grant

[35] International Convention for the Prevention of Pollution from Ships (adopted 2 November 1973, entered into force 2 October 1983) 1340 UNTS 62; Protocol of 1978 Relating to the International Convention for the Prevention of Pollution from Ships (adopted 17 February 1978, entered into force 2 October 1983) 1340 UNTS 61.

[36] *Virginia G* (n 33) paras 114–17.

[37] ibid paras 125–29.

[38] ibid para 121.

[39] *Tomimaru (Japan v Russian Federation)* (Prompt Release, Judgment) ITLOS Reports 2005–2007, 74, paras 69–70.

[40] ibid paras 69–70.

[41] See ch 3(III)(A).

[42] As manifest in art 292(3) of UNCLOS (n 2).

[43] *Enrica Lexie (Italy v India)* (Award of 21 May 2020) PCA Case No 2015-28 (*Enrica Lexie*, Award).

of its nationality to ships.[44] The nationality of a ship is a question of fact to be determined on the basis of the evidence adduced by the parties. Here, the Tribunal examined the provisions of Indian law, which provided that an Indian vessel included vessels wholly owned by a citizen of India, and which is registered under the Indian Merchant Shipping Act 1958, or under any other central, provincial, or State Act. Noting that the St Antony was a fishing vessel owned by an Indian national and registered under the Tamil Nadu Marine Fishing Regulation Act 1983, and the Marine Products Export Development Authority Act 1972, the Tribunal concluded that the *St Antony* was an Indian vessel.[45]

The Tribunal also addressed the relevance of the absence of a flag on the St Antony, and concluded that the presence of a flag is not determinative of nationality, but it is merely visual evidence or a symbol of nationality.[46] The fact that small vessels were exempted from the requirement to maintain a register under Article 94(2) did not deprive them of the fundamental rights to freedom of navigation under Article 87.[47] The Tribunal also held that any failure by the flag State to fulfil its duties under Article 94 had no impact on the right to freedom of navigation under Articles 87 and 90.[48]

* * *

The approach of tribunals to nationality issues have focused—properly in our view—on whether the applicant State is able to assert its rights or its vessel's rights in relation to a specific claim or incident. They also seem to generally align with the commercial realities of ship operations: this reflection is particularly evident in the approach of the *Enrica Lexie* Tribunal to small vessels and their nationality and concomitant rights. While there are undoubtedly highly challenging dimensions to flag State control over ships and whether that authority is properly exercised in all instances (given the recognised issues associated with flags of convenience), this issue is a broader systemic problem in ocean governance and an UNCLOS tribunal has a limited role to play in this regard.

B. Immunity

UNCLOS confers complete immunity (save for the jurisdiction of the flag State) on two categories of vessels on the high seas: warships under Article 95, and ships owned or operated by a State and used only on government non-commercial service under Article 96. These two provisions fall within the scope of those referred to in Article 58(2), concerning the rights and duties of other States in the EEZ: it provides that: 'Articles 88 to 115 and other pertinent rules of international law apply to the exclusive economic zone in so far as they are not incompatible with this Part.' Immunities of these vessels are also referred to in Article 32 of UNCLOS, as follows: 'With such exceptions as are contained in subsection A and in

44 ibid para 1022.
45 ibid paras 1022–25.
46 ibid paras 1028–29.
47 ibid paras 1032–34.
48 ibid para 1035.

articles 30 and 31, nothing in this Convention affects the immunities of warships and other government ships operated for non-commercial purposes.'[49]

The scope and extent of the immunity of warships or other non-commercial government vessels have not been directly considered by any UNCLOS tribunal to date. However, Article 32 has been invoked before two tribunals in provisional measures requests, and their decisions suggest a broad application of immunity to qualifying vessels and potentially also to their crews (even though crews are not specifically mentioned in the UNCLOS provisions).

In *ARA Libertad*,[50] Argentina argued that Ghana's detention of an Argentine warship (in its internal waters) violated Article 32 and that it also violated the rights of innocent passage and freedom of navigation. Ghana argued that Article 32 applied only to territorial seas, and not to internal waters. In its order on provisional measures, ITLOS noted that Article 32 did not specify the geographical scope of its application, but that it also is situated with Part II of the Convention (entitled 'Territorial Sea and Contiguous Zone'), and some provisions in this Part may apply to all maritime areas, such as the definition of warships in Article 29.[51] It concluded that a difference of opinion existed between the parties with respect to the applicability of Article 32, and that difference appeared to be a dispute concerning the interpretation and application of UNCLOS, which provided a basis on which prima facie jurisdiction of the Annex VII Tribunal might be founded.[52] It did not decide whether Article 32 applied to actions in internal waters, although it noted that 'in accordance with general international law, a warship enjoys immunity, including in internal waters, and that this is not disputed by Ghana'.[53] However, in a strongly worded dissent, Judges Wolfrum and Cot considered that any immunity in internal waters would have to be established on the basis of customary international law. They considered that the Tribunal ought to have found that it did not have prima facie jurisdiction on the basis of a dispute as to the interpretation and application of Article 32.[54]

The Tribunal's treatment of Article 32 was recently referred to by the Annex VII Tribunal in *Coastal State Rights in the Black Sea*:[55] noting that ITLOS had observed that some of the provisions in Part II of UNCLOS 'may be applicable to all maritime areas', alongside the ITLOS decision in *SRFC Advisory Opinion* that the obligation to protect and preserve

[49] Subsection A of Section 3 of Part II sets out the rule applicable to all ships, and notably defines innocent passage (arts 18 and 19) and permits the coastal State to impose laws and regulations relating to innocent passage, for example in respect of safety of navigation (see arts 21 and 22). Article 30 permits a coastal State to require a warship to leave the territorial sea immediately if it does not comply with the laws and regulations of the coastal State concerning passage through the territorial sea and disregards any request for compliance with such laws and regulations. Article 31 provides that a flag State bears responsibility for any loss or damage to the coastal State resulting from the non-compliance of a warship or other government ship operated for non-commercial purposes with the laws and regulations of the coastal State concerning passage through the territorial sea, or with the provisions of UNCLOS or other rules of international law.

[50] *ARA Libertad (Argentina v Ghana)* (Provisional Measures, Order of 15 December 2012) ITLOS Reports 2012, 332 (*ARA Libertad*).

[51] ibid paras 63–64. Some provisions in Part II apply only to internal waters; the Tribunal did not address any implication of those provisions for the scope of application of art 32.

[52] ibid paras 65–67. The implications of the jurisdictional analysis are discussed in Nuwan Peiris, 'ARA Libertad from ITLOS: How Provisional a Provisional Measure Should Be' (2012) 25 Hague YB Intl L 159. See also Vincent P Cogliati-Bantz, 'Immune or Not; Warships in Foreign Internal Waters and the UN Convention on the Law of the Sea' (2013) 4 Durham L Rev 1.

[53] *ARA Libertad* (n 50) para 95.

[54] *ARA Libertad* (n 50) (Separate Opinion of Judges Wolfrum and Cot) paras 38–51.

[55] *Dispute Concerning Coastal State Rights in the Black Sea, Sea of Azov, and Kerch Strait (Ukraine v Russia)* (Preliminary Objections Award of 21 February 2020) PCA Case No 2017-06 (*Coastal State Rights in the Black Sea*).

the marine environment applies to 'all maritime areas',[56] the Annex VII Tribunal rejected Russia's argument that a dispute falls entirely outside the scope of UNCLOS because the underlying events occurred in internal waters. The Tribunal has joined Russia's preliminary objection to the ongoing proceedings on the merits.[57]

Scholars had anticipated that the scope and extent of Article 32 would be finally resolved on the merits of *ARA Libertad*, but the case did not proceed to a final award. Nevertheless, the approach was received by some as an 'encouraging precedent for stability of expectations and the rule of law at sea and in port', given the importance that States place on sovereign immunity for warships.[58] It seems unlikely that future tribunals will depart from it, especially in light of the endorsement in *Coastal State Rights in the Black Sea*.

The approach of ITLOS in *ARA Libertad* has been criticised on the basis that the Tribunal effectively recognised an absolute immunity of the warship under Article 32, and did not go on to consider whether Argentina's immunity had been waived in the particular context of the case. The ARA Libertad was arrested in Ghana to enforce a judgment against Argentina obtained in United States' courts, in respect of which the underlying documents provided for an irrevocable waiver, although it was arguable whether it covered immunity from execution, as the Ghanaian courts had found. Argentina argued that military property is absolutely excluded from any kind of execution measure by a foreign State, and could only be waived explicitly. Ghana did not address the immunity on the basis of waiver, having argued that immunity under Article 32 did not apply to vessels in port. In the circumstances, the Tribunal was able to avoid addressing this question at all, leading some to conclude that it recognised an absolute immunity under Article 32,[59] and to contend that the Tribunal had overlooked the waiver of immunity.[60] This issue would probably have been explored had the case proceeded to the merits.

In *Detention of Three Ukrainian Naval Vessels*, Ukraine brought proceedings following the detention of three of its naval warships and their servicemen by Russia in the Black Sea, near the Kerch Strait and sought provisional measures from ITLOS.[61] At the provisional measures stage, Ukraine argued that the detention of the vessels was in breach of Russia's obligations under Articles 32, 58, 95, and 96 of UNCLOS. Ukraine argued that Articles 95 and 96 conferred complete immunity on its three vessels from the jurisdiction of any State other than the flag State. Two of the detained vessels, the Berdyansk and the Nikopol, were warships and the third, the Yani Kapu, was a naval auxiliary vessel. Ukraine also argued that Article 58 extended the application of immunity under Articles 95 and 96 to the EEZ, and that Article 32 and customary international law guaranteed the same immunity in the territorial sea. It also argued that the immunity protected not only warships and naval auxiliary vessels, but also their crews.[62] On the basis of Russia's conduct in arresting and detaining

[56] *Request for Advisory Opinion Submitted by the Sub-Regional Fisheries Commission* (Advisory Opinion) ITLOS Reports 2015, 4.

[57] *Coastal State Rights in the Black Sea* (n 55) paras 295–96. The decision on the merits was pending at time of writing.

[58] See eg James Kraska, 'The "ARA Libertad"' (2013) 107(2) AJIL 404, 410. See also Massimo Lando, 'State Jurisdiction and Immunity of Warships in the ARA Libertad Case' (2015) 58 Japanese YB Intl L 336.

[59] See eg Moudachirou Djibril, 'Does a Sovereign State Immunity Say More than We Think: ITLOS's Decisions in ARA Libertad Case' (2015) 37 J L Poly & Globalization 6, 10–12; Kraska (n 58) 408–409.

[60] See eg, Editorial, 'Lawless at Sea' *Wall St Journal* (New York, 24 December 2012) A12.

[61] *Detention of Three Ukrainian Naval Vessels (Ukraine v Russian Federation)* (Provisional Measures Order of 25 May 2019) ITLOS Case No 26, paras 22–23 (*Detention of Three Ukrainian Naval Vessels*, Provisional Measures).

[62] ibid para 93.

the Ukrainian vessels, and commencing criminal proceedings against the Ukrainian servicemen, the Tribunal considered that a dispute concerning the interpretation or application of UNCLOS prima facie existed when the proceedings were commenced.[63] After examining the circumstances in which the arrest and detention of the vessels took place, the Tribunal considered that the dispute was not—on a prima facie basis—one concerning 'military activities' that would fall within the exclusion in Article 298(1)(b) of UNCLOS.[64] It also considered that the rights claimed by Ukraine under Articles 95, 96, 58, and 32 in respect of both its vessels and servicemen were plausible, although in respect of the crew, it immediately noted that 'the nature and scope of their immunity may require further scrutiny';[65] this determination might be taken as an indication from the Tribunal that the claim of the crew to immunity at least needed further explanation, albeit it did not consider it necessary at the provisional measures stage. Concerning the vessels, the Tribunal distinguished between the Berdyansk and the Nikopol, which it noted were warships within the meaning of Article 29, and the Yani Kapu, which it treated as a ship owned or operated by a State and used only on government non-commercial service, within the meaning in Article 96 of UNCLOS.[66] The Tribunal thus resolved the question of whether vessels ancillary to warships qualify under Article 96 of UNCLOS.[67] The Tribunal proceeded to order the release of the Ukrainian vessels and the detained Ukrainian servicemen.[68] Although Russia initially did not comply with the Tribunal's provisional measures order,[69] later in 2019 the Ukrainian servicemen were released, reportedly as part of an exchange of prisoners, and the vessels were also returned to Ukraine.[70]

Immunities of persons on board vessels were directly at issue in the recent *Enrica Lexie* award.[71] The M/V Enrica Lexie was a commercial oil tanker carrying a Vessel Protection Detachment comprising Italian marines operating under Italian law. The issue before the Annex VII Tribunal was whether the Indian courts could exercise criminal jurisdiction over the two Italian marines who fired shots at the Indian fishing vessel, the St Antony. The Tribunal considered that the two States had concurrent jurisdiction over the incident.[72] However, Italy claimed that the two marines were immune from criminal jurisdiction, and that the dispute as to their immunity fell within the jurisdiction of the Annex VII Tribunal. The Tribunal therefore had to consider whether it could decide Italy's claim to immunity—whether that fell within its jurisdiction under UNCLOS.

Italy argued that certain articles of UNCLOS constituted a basis for the Tribunal's jurisdiction over the claim of immunity. Italy relied on Articles 2(3), 56(2), and 58(2) of UNCLOS, which refer to 'other rules of international law', 'the rights and duties of other

63 ibid paras 44–45.

64 ibid paras 67–77. See discussion in ch 4(IV)(C).

65 *Detention of Three Ukrainian Naval Vessels*, Provisional Measures (n 61) paras 97–98.

66 ibid para 97.

67 See Yoshifumi Tanaka, 'Release of a Detained Warship and Its Crew through Provisional Measures: A Comparative Analysis of the ARA Libertad and Ukraine v Russia Cases' (2020) 96 ILS 223, 255.

68 *Detention of Three Ukrainian Naval Vessels*, Provisional Measures (n 61) paras 124(1)–(2).

69 'Report of Ukraine', *Detention of Three Ukrainian Naval Vessels (Ukraine v Russia)* (PCA Case No 2019-28, 25 June 2019).

70 See Ministry of Foreign Affairs of Ukraine, 'Ukraine Pleads Today Before the Arbitration Tribunal in the Hague in the Case of Russia's Seizure of Three Ukrainian Naval Vessels and Their Crew' (12 October 2021) https://mfa.gov.ua/en/news/ukraine-pleads-today-arbitration-tribunal-hague-case-russias-seizure-three-ukrainian-naval-vessels-and-their-crew.

71 See also the discussion of the Tribunal's approach to jurisdiction over this issue in ch 4(II)(B).

72 *Enrica Lexie*, Award (n 43) para 839.

States', and 'other pertinent rules of international law'. The Tribunal considered that these provisions were irrelevant because they applied to the territorial sea and the EEZ, and India had enforced its jurisdiction over the marines only in its internal waters and on land.[73] Italy also relied on Articles 95 and 96 of UNCLOS but, as the Tribunal noted, these provisions do not address immunity of persons, but only of vessels.[74] Italy also relied on Article 297(1)(a) and (b), which explicitly extends compulsory jurisdiction to, respectively, disputes about 'other internationally lawful uses of the sea specified in Article 58' and to 'other rules of international law not incompatible with this Convention'. However, the Tribunal also dismissed this argument, considering that the claim to immunity did not fall within Article 297(1)(a) nor Article 297(1)(b), given that the dispute did not concern the exercise of freedoms, rights, and uses of the sea 'in contravention of ... the laws and regulations adopted by the coastal State in conformity with this Convention and other rules of international law not incompatible with this Convention'.[75] Thus, the Tribunal considered that none of the articles of UNCLOS invoked by Italy constituted a basis for jurisdiction over Italy's claim to immunity for the marines.[76]

The Tribunal then considered whether the issue of the Tribunal's entitlement to exercise jurisdiction over the incident could be satisfactorily answered without addressing the question of the immunity of the marines. Even though UNCLOS did not provide a basis for entertaining an independent immunity claim under general international law, as discussed further in Chapter 4, the Tribunal considered whether the question of immunity necessarily arose as an incidental question in the application of UNCLOS.[77] Given that immunity from jurisdiction operates as an exception to an otherwise existing right to exercise jurisdiction, the Tribunal concluded that it could not provide a complete answer to the question of which Party could exercise jurisdiction without incidentally examining whether the marines enjoyed immunity. It therefore found that the issue of immunity was an incidental question that fell within the Tribunal's jurisdiction.[78]

Two judges dissented from the Tribunal's conclusion. Judge Robinson contended that the immunity of the marines was not an incidental question, but 'a core element of the dispute; ... the real issue on the dispute between the Parties'.[79] Dr Pemmaraju Sreenivasa Rao considered that there were 'two distinct and separate disputes', and that 'the claim concerning immunity is not and cannot be treated as an incidental issue to the other dispute over which the Arbitral Tribunal found jurisdiction'.[80] As noted in Chapter 4, the Tribunal's approach to incidental jurisdiction has been considered significant by commentators, and suggests that the Tribunal considered it had a role beyond dispute settlement, serving as an 'actor in the international legal order'.[81]

The Tribunal then proceeded to consider whether the marines had immunity from jurisdiction under customary international law. The answer turned on whether, first, the

[73] ibid para 798.
[74] ibid para 799.
[75] ibid para 802
[76] ibid paras 802–803.
[77] See discussion in ch 4(II)(B).
[78] *Enrica Lexie*, Award (n 43) paras 805–811.
[79] ibid (Dissenting Opinion of Judge Robinson) para 81(ii).
[80] ibid (Concurring and Dissenting Opinion of Dr Rao) paras VII(i)–(ii).
[81] James G Devaney and Christian J Tams, 'In re Arbitration between the Italian Republic and the Republic of India concerning the "Enrica Lexie" Incident' (2021) 115(3) AJIL 513, 519. See further discussion in ch 4(II)(B) above.

marines were 'State officials'; secondly, whether they were undertaking 'official acts' or 'acts performed in an official capacity'; and thirdly, whether any exceptions applied to preclude them from enjoying such immunity. Noting that the marines were members of the Italian Navy, and officers and agents of the judicial police entrusted with guaranteeing the maritime defence of the State, the Tribunal considered that they were 'State officials of the Italian Republic'.[82] As to their functions, the Tribunal noted that the marines were deployed on the M/V Enrica Lexie as members of Italy's armed forces, pursuant to a mandate under Italian law.[83] In the specific incident, the marines appeared to have followed the applicable rules of engagement. Thus, the Tribunal considered that the evidence demonstrated that during the incident, the marines were under an apprehension of a piracy threat and engaged in conduct that was in the exercise of their official functions.[84] Finally, the Tribunal considered that even if there was a 'territorial tort' exception to immunity under customary international law, it would not apply in this case, since the marines were on board the M/V Enrica Lexie, and not on Indian territory, at the time of the incident.[85] The Tribunal thus concluded that the marines enjoyed immunity in relation to the acts occurring during the incident, and India was precluded from exercising jurisdiction over them.[86]

Two judges also dissented on the majority's findings with respect to immunity. Judge Robinson emphasised the commercial nature of the transaction that led to the marines being placed on the M/V Enrica Lexie, and considered that it followed that the marines did not have immunity.[87] Dr Rao noted that the application of immunity to foreign State officials in cases involving commercial and non-government service is highly contested,[88] and the marines here were deployed on a commercial cargo vessel as part of a commercial transaction between the Italian government and the Italian ship owners.[89] He determined that the conclusion reached by the majority, that the marines were entitled to immunity from jurisdiction, was not supported by State practice, and was without foundation in treaty or customary international law.[90]

Ultimately, the Tribunal's conclusion on immunity turned on its assessment of the customary international law position, since UNCLOS does not provide for or express a position on the immunity of foreign State officials (or individuals engaged by the government to carry out security services) on commercial vessels.

* * *

The scope and extent of immunities of State officials at sea has potentially far-reaching consequences, particularly as concerns about maritime security become more prevalent. Clarity as to the circumstances in which vessels and those onboard have immunity from jurisdiction will necessarily contribute to the overarching objectives of the rule of law and public order of the oceans. Moreover, as with all circumstances in which immunity

[82] *Enrica Lexie*, Award (n 43) paras 848–55.
[83] ibid paras 850–55.
[84] ibid pars 856–62.
[85] ibid paras 863–72.
[86] ibid paras 873–74.
[87] *Enrica Lexie*, Award (n 43) (Dissenting Opinion of Judge Robinson) para 63.
[88] ibid (Concurring and Dissenting Opinion of Dr Rao) para 70.
[89] ibid para 78.
[90] ibid para 80.

is invoked, there is not necessarily an absence of jurisdiction or impunity: it is merely a question of which State or tribunal may exercise jurisdiction. Further, even if State officials onboard vessels are immune from proceedings against them, there remains the possibility that an international tribunal has jurisdiction in inter-State proceedings with respect to the violations of UNCLOS, such as violations of the freedom of navigation. UNCLOS tribunals have so far made important clarifications to the immunities of vessels under Article 32 of UNCLOS, and the Tribunal in *Detention of Three Ukrainian Vessels* is anticipated to return to this question in its decision on the merits.

III. Navigation under UNCLOS

UNCLOS tribunals have so far addressed two aspects of navigation: innocent passage in archipelagic waters; and freedom of navigation on the high seas and in the EEZ. As can be seen from the discussion that follows, tribunals have had opportunities to clarify provisions that are critical to the exercise of navigational rights under UNCLOS, and to address the way in which those rights should be balanced against other States' rights and duties, particularly in the EEZ.

A. Innocent Passage in the Territorial Sea and Archipelagic Waters

In the territorial sea, ships of all States enjoy the right of innocent passage. The right of innocent passage is well established in customary international law,[91] and is reflected in Article 17 of UNCLOS. Passage is defined in Article 18(1) to include 'lateral passage: i.e. traversing the territorial sea without entering internal waters or calling at a port outside internal waters; passage to or from internal waters or to a call at a port facility outside internal waters'. Article 18(2) adds a further condition for innocent passage: it must be 'continuous and expeditious'. Stopping and anchoring are only permitted as incidental to ordinary navigation or as necessary by *force majeure* or distress. 'Innocent passage' is defined in Article 19, principally by reference to the activities undertaken while in passage.

Under Article 52(1) of UNCLOS, the right of innocent passage applies to archipelagic waters other than in those sea lanes subject to the right of archipelagic sea lane passage.[92] In *Duzgit Integrity*,[93] the Tribunal considered whether ship-to-ship operations could fall within the scope of innocent passage in archipelagic waters, and determined that they did not. In that case, the Maltese-flagged vessel had attempted to initiate a transfer of cargo from ship-to-ship in the archipelagic waters of São Tomé and Príncipe. Subsequently, the

[91] *Military and Paramilitary Activities in and against Nicaragua (Nicaragua v United States)* (Merits) [1986] ICJ Rep 14, para 214.

[92] As to the purpose of passage, the ICJ's judgment in *Corfu Channel* suggests that what is relevant is what the vessels actually do in passage, rather than their intent. In respect of the passage of British warships on 22 October 1946, the 'mission' of the UK was to ascertain Albania's attitude to passage, but the Court concluded that the passage engaged in was in exercise of the right of innocent passage: *Corfu Channel (United Kingdom v Albania)* [1949] ICJ Rep 4, 30–32 (*Corfu Channel*).

[93] *Duzgit Integrity Arbitration (Malta v São Tomé and Príncipe)* (Award of 5 September 2016) PCA Case No 2014-07.

vessel and its master were detained, and the local court ordered confiscation of the vessel and cargo and imposed fines.[94] There was a dispute as to whether the operations were authorised and the Tribunal ultimately found that they were not. Malta also argued that the operations were covered by the right of innocent passage. The Tribunal noted that 'passage' requires continuous and expeditious navigation, and that stopping and anchoring are only covered by 'passage' if these acts are incidental to ordinary navigation. The Tribunal therefore dismissed Malta's claim that São Tomé breached Article 25(1) of UNCLOS in respect of actions taken against the Duzgit Integrity during ship-to-ship operations.[95]

Although there have been controversies arising from State practice on matters such as prior authorisation or notification for the passage of warships or the lawful steps States may take in response to non-innocent passage, these questions have not yet been the subject of scrutiny before any tribunal constituted under UNCLOS.[96]

B. Freedom of Navigation

Article 87 of UNCLOS on freedom of the high seas addresses freedom of navigation in paragraph (1)(a). It states:

> 1. The high seas are open to all States, whether coastal or land-locked. Freedom of the high seas is exercised under the conditions laid down by this Convention and by other rules of international law. It comprises, inter alia, both for coastal and land-locked States:
>   (a) freedom of navigation.[97]

Pursuant to Article 87(2), freedoms of the high seas 'shall be exercised by all States with due regard for the interests of other States in their exercise of the freedom of the high seas', as well as with due regard for the rights with respect to activities in the Area. Article 90 further sets out the 'right of navigation' in the following terms: 'Every State, whether coastal or land-locked, has the right to sail ships flying its flag on the high seas.'

Article 58(1) of UNCLOS provides that all States enjoy the freedom of navigation referred to in Article 87 in the EEZ, subject to relevant provisions of the Convention. In exercising their rights in the EEZ, Article 58(3) requires States to have due regard to the rights and duties of coastal States (some of which are set out in Article 56(1)) and to comply with laws and regulations adopted by the coastal State in accordance with UNCLOS, and other rules of international law.

In the discussion below, the analysis first addresses the cases concerned with the scope of application of freedom of navigation on the high seas and in the EEZ, before addressing questions of what activities fall with the scope of the freedom of navigation—in particular, whether bunkering activities form part of the freedom of navigation, and whether acts of

[94] ibid paras 48–120.

[95] ibid para 310.

[96] In the *Corfu Channel* case, the ICJ decided as a matter of customary international law that warships were not required to give notice or obtain prior authorisation to transit through an international strait: *Corfu Channel* (n 92) 29–30.

[97] UNCLOS (n 2) art 87(1).

protest fall within freedom of navigation. Tribunals have further addressed the question of what constitutes interference with freedom of navigation. Finally, a tribunal has recently addressed the meaning of an 'incident of navigation' under Article 97 of UNCLOS, which provides for the exclusive jurisdiction of the flag State for penal and disciplinary matters relating to such incidents. The cases addressing these questions are discussed in the subsections below.

1. The Spatial Extent of Freedom of Navigation: Application to Vessels in Port

In two cases, flag States have argued that the freedom of navigation on the high seas was impaired by restrictions imposed on a vessel in port.[98] These arguments would have potentially augmented the opportunities for third-party review of port State action through UNCLOS dispute settlement. However, in both cases, the claims were dismissed, the tribunals holding that restrictions imposed on a vessel in port did not breach freedom of navigation on the high seas.

In the *Louisa* case, Saint Vincent and the Grenadines claimed that the detention of the vessel in a Spanish port prevented it from reaching the high seas and exercising its freedom of navigation under Article 87. The Tribunal held that freedom of navigation under Article 87 was not violated by the detention in a port: 'Article 87 cannot be interpreted in such a way as to grant the M/V "Louisa" a right to leave the port and gain access to the high seas notwithstanding its detention in the context of legal proceedings against it.'[99] In his Declaration, Judge Paik addressed this argument in some detail, concluding that:

> To extend the freedom of the high seas to include a right of the State to have access to the high seas to enjoy that freedom is warranted neither by the text of the relevant provisions or the context of the Convention, nor by established State practice on this matter.[100]

In his dissenting opinion in *Louisa*, Judge Lucky agreed with the majority as to the inapplicability of Article 87(1), noting that 'even if given the widest and most generous interpretation, [A]rticle 87 cannot be deemed to include the territorial sea or internal waters',[101] but also noting that the right to freedom of navigation may be infringed by conduct preventing a vessel from leaving port to sail to the high seas 'where a vessel is detained without just cause'.[102]

In a similar manner, Panama argued in the *Norstar* case that freedom of navigation under Article 87 includes a right to 'sail towards the high seas', and that the M/V Norstar enjoyed that freedom even in a port of a coastal State.[103] The Tribunal dismissed that claim, noting that interpreting freedom of navigation as encompassing a right to leave port and gain access to the high seas would be inconsistent with the legal regime of internal waters.[104] In his

[98] *M/V Louisa (Saint Vincent and the Grenadines v Spain)* (Judgment) ITLOS Reports 2013, 4 (*Louisa*, Judgment); *M/V Norstar (Panama v Italy)* (Judgment of 10 April 2019) ITLOS Case No 25 (*Norstar*, Judgment). In *ARA Libertad* (n 50) Argentina argued that the detention of the vessel by Ghana prevented it from exercising freedom of navigation on the high seas: at para 43). This argument was not specifically addressed by the Tribunal.

[99] *Louisa*, Judgment (n 98) para 109.

[100] ibid (Declaration of Judge Paik) para 29.

[101] ibid (Dissenting Opinion of Judge Lucky) para 36.

[102] ibid para 35.

[103] *Norstar*, Judgment (n 98) paras 190–91.

[104] ibid paras 220–21.

Separate Opinion, Judge Lucky expressed the view that Spain on behalf of Italy exercised its rights under UNCLOS in a manner amounting to an abuse of rights under Article 300, by denying the M/V Norstar its right to access the high seas.[105] He emphasised that the M/V Norstar was prevented from having access to the high seas because of its arrest and detention, and it was on this basis that he concluded that there had been a breach of Article 300 of UNCLOS.[106]

The majorities in these tribunals have showed restraint about the extent of their jurisdiction, effectively excluding potential claims for breach of the right of freedom of navigation on the high seas arising from issues relating to port access and the exercise of port State jurisdiction. In both cases, Judge Lucky took the view that an unlawful exercise of port jurisdiction might also breach a right of access to the high seas to exercise freedom of navigation, effectively finding a compound breach of UNCLOS (i.e. an unlawful exercise of port jurisdiction, as well as unlawful prevention of access to the high seas), albeit via Article 300. Nevertheless, this position was not adopted by the majority.

2. Activities Covered by Freedom of Navigation: Bunkering and Protest

Another issue that has been addressed by multiple tribunals is the extent to which bunkering activities fall within the scope of freedom of navigation. This question is also addressed in Chapter 8 in relation to fisheries disputes.[107]

In *Saiga (No 2)*, the M/V Saiga entered Guinea's EEZ and supplied fuel to three fishing vessels. It was arrested by Guinean customs patrol boats outside Guinea's EEZ, purportedly in exercise of the right of hot pursuit. Saint Vincent and the Grenadines (the flag State of the M/V Saiga) claimed that Guinea's arrest violated the right of freedom of navigation under Article 58, amongst other Convention rights. The Tribunal considered that Guinea's application of its custom laws to bunkering activities in its EEZ was in breach of UNCLOS, and it followed that Guinea's arrest and detention of the M/V Saiga, prosecution and conviction of its master, and confiscation of cargo and seizure of the ship were contrary to UNCLOS.[108] The parties disagreed as to whether bunkering in the EEZ was an exercise of the freedom of navigation under Articles 56 and 58 of UNCLOS.[109] However, the Tribunal declined to decide the point, having already held that the actions taken by Guinea were inconsistent with UNCLOS.[110]

In his Separate Opinion, Judge Zhao expressed the firm view that 'bunkering of fishing vessels in the [EEZ] is not navigation under the Convention' and therefore 'bunkering must not be regarded as falling within the high seas freedom of navigation or related to it'.[111] Judge Anderson considered that bunkering 'could well amount to an 'internationally lawful use of the sea' related to the freedom of navigation', and considered that the Tribunal was right not to decide the question in the context of the particular case.[112] Judge Laing also concluded that Guinea violated the freedom of navigation of Saint Vincent and the Grenadines, but considered that further evidence and argument would be required in order to determine

[105] *Norstar*, Judgment (n 98) (Separate Opinion of Judge Lucky) paras 6, 137–140, 163.
[106] ibid para 6.
[107] See ch 8(IV)(A).
[108] *Saiga (No 2)*, Judgment (n 5) paras 126–36.
[109] ibid paras 126–36.
[110] ibid paras 137–38.
[111] *Saiga (No 2)*, Judgment (n 5) (Separate Opinion of Judge Zhao) para 3.
[112] ibid (Separate Opinion of Judge Anderson) 137–38.

whether the M/V Saiga was involved in activities encroaching on the coastal State's jurisdiction in the EEZ.[113]

The competence of the coastal State to regulate bunkering vessels in the EEZ arose again in *Virginia G*. There, the Panamanian-flagged bunkering vessel had been arrested by Guinea-Bissau in its EEZ for unauthorised selling of fuel to ships fishing within that EEZ. Panama claimed that Guinea-Bissau had violated, inter alia, the right of free navigation, on the grounds that the bunkering service provided by the M/V Virginia G fell within the freedom of navigation and other internationally lawful uses of the sea in Article 58(1). The Tribunal considered that Article 58 had to be read together with Article 56, and that the former did not prevent coastal States from regulating bunkering of foreign vessels fishing in the EEZ, in accordance with their sovereign rights to explore, exploit, conserve and manage natural resources.[114] However, the Tribunal considered that '[t]he coastal State ... does not have such competence with regard to other bunkering activities, unless otherwise determined in accordance with the Convention'.[115] In this way, the Tribunal struck a balance between the freedom of navigation under Article 58(1) and coastal State jurisdiction in Article 56(1), and aligned itself with the practice of parties to UNCLOS in such a way as to increase the likelihood that the Tribunal's approach would be welcomed by governments and promote stability.[116] Guinea-Bissau had also argued that its regulation was justified on the basis of the purpose of protecting the marine environment: in this regard, the Tribunal noted that the relevant regulations on bunkering were incorporated in Guinea-Bissau's legislation on fishing rather than in legislation concerning protection of the marine environment,[117] leaving open the question of whether regulations adopted on the basis of protection of the environment could fall with the scope of permissible regulations of the coastal State.

In *Norstar*, the Tribunal also addressed the question whether bunkering on the high seas fell within the freedom of navigation. The Tribunal noted that the parties did not dispute the lawfulness of bunkering on the high seas. It also recalled its findings in *Virginia G*, that bunkering of foreign vessels in the EEZ may be regulated by the coastal State, but that the coastal State does not have such competence with regard to other bunkering activities. The Tribunal concluded that bunkering on the high seas is part of the freedom of navigation under Article 87 of UNCLOS.[118] Obviously the competing interests of coastal States were not at issue in this instance and greater attention is required on the allocation of rights and duties for activities occurring within the EEZ, as compared to the high seas.

Most recently, at the provisional measures stage of *San Padre Pio*,[119] ITLOS addressed Switzerland's claim that its oil tanker, engaged in ship-to-ship (STS) bunkering of oil within Nigeria's EEZ, was exercising freedom of navigation. The oil was intended to supply an oil installation. The vessel was arrested on the basis that it did not have the appropriate documents relating to an import levy. Before the Tribunal, Nigeria argued it had rights to

[113] ibid (Separate Opinion of Judge Laing) para 53.

[114] *Virginia G* (n 33) para 222. See further ch 8(IV)(A).

[115] ibid para 223.

[116] See Bernard H Oxman and Vincent P Cogliati-Bantz, 'The M/V Virginia G' (2014) 108 AJIL 769, 773–74. For a different view, suggesting that the tribunal unduly restricted freedom of navigation in favour of an expansive approach to coastal State jurisdiction see Clayton Vignocchi, 'ITLOST? The International Tribunal for the Law of the Sea Sounds the Charge to Expand Coastal State Jurisdiction' (2015) 39 Tul Mar LJ 791.

[117] *Virginia G* (n 33) para 224.

[118] *Norstar*, Judgment (n 98) para 219.

[119] *M/T San Padre Pio (Switzerland v Nigeria)* (Provisional Measures, Order of 6 July 2019) ITLOS Case No 27 (*San Padre Pio*, Provisional Measures).

exercise enforcement jurisdiction under Articles 56(1)(a) (conservation and management of natural resources and other activities for economic exploitation), 208, and 214 (both of which concern enforcement relating to pollution of the marine environment). The Tribunal concluded that the rights claimed by Switzerland, including under Article 58, were plausible.[120] In this respect, the Tribunal appears to have taken the same approach as the Tribunal in *Virginia G*, such that coastal States may regulate bunkering to the extent that it relates to some other right recognised under UNCLOS.

On the merits, the Tribunal may have needed to address more closely the question of whether the M/T San Padre Pio was engaged in STS transfers rather than bunkering,[121] and what legal difference emerges in distinguishing between these activities. Testa suggested that STS transfers do not facilitate navigation and as such, it may not be appropriate to classify them as part of the freedom of navigation under Article 58.[122] The allocation of rights and duties in relation to bunkering and STS operations has relevance not only in relation to navigation, but also for the protection and preservation of the marine environment and in the suppression of maritime crime.[123]

The scope of freedom of navigation in the EEZ was also discussed in *Arctic Sunrise*.[124] The Dutch ship, Arctic Sunrise, had been chartered by Greenpeace and was used in protest activities against the Prirazlomnaya, a Russian offshore oil production platform in its EEZ. The Arctic Sunrise was given a warning by the Russian authorities, referring to Articles 60, 149, and 259 of UNCLOS concerning safety of navigation around artificial islands and structures and the impermissibility of causing damage to the Prirazlomnaya.[125] Individuals from the Arctic Sunrise subsequently attempted to scale the platform but were unsuccessful.[126] The vessel was then seized and detained by Russia.

The Netherlands argued that Russia had breached, inter alia, its freedom of navigation in the EEZ under Article 58(1) of UNCLOS. The Tribunal considered that protest fell within freedom of navigation under UNCLOS. It stated:

> Protest at sea is an internationally lawful use of the sea related to the freedom of navigation. The right to protest at sea is necessarily exercised in conjunction with the freedom of navigation. The right to protest derives from the freedom of expression and the freedom of assembly, both of which are recognised in several international human rights instruments to which the Netherlands and Russia are parties, including the ICCPR. The right to protest at sea has been recognised by resolutions of international organisations.

[120] ibid paras 106–108.

[121] At the provisional measures stage, Judge ad hoc Murphy observed that it was 'difficult to assess whether the situation is best approached as simply a STS transfer, which normally is understood as a transfer of cargo between two seagoing vessels, or is best approached as offshore bunkering, which normally is understood as the replenishment by one vessel of a second vessel's fuel bunkers with fuel intended for the operation of the second vessel's engines': *San Padre Pio*, Provisional Measures (n 118) (Separate Opinion of Judge ad hoc Murphy) para 13. As this case was settled prior to the merits, this issue remains unresolved from a judicial perspective.

[122] David Testa, 'Comments on Coastal and Flag State Jurisdiction in the M/T "San Padre Pio" Dispute' *EJIL: Talk!* (3 September 2019) https://www.ejiltalk.org/comments-on-coastal-and-flag-state-jurisdiction-in-the-m-t-san-padre-pio-dispute/.

[123] On the latter point see Yurika Ishii, 'Informal Lawmaking and International Cooperation on Illegal Bunkering at Sea' in Natalie Klein (ed), *Unconventional Lawmaking in the Law of the Sea* (OUP 2022).

[124] *Arctic Sunrise (Netherlands v Russia)* (Award on the Merits of 14 August 2015) PCA Case No 2014-02 (*Arctic Sunrise*, Merits).

[125] ibid para 82.

[126] ibid paras 88–92.

The right to protest is not without its limitations, and when the protest occurs at sea its limitations are defined, *inter alia*, by the law of the sea. Article 88 of UNCLOS provides that '[t]he high seas shall be reserved for peaceful purposes' and Article 58(2) makes that applicable to the EEZ. Article 58(3) of UNCLOS requires that in exercising their rights and performing their duties in the EEZ, states shall have 'due regard to the rights and duties of the coastal State and shall comply with the laws and regulations adopted by the coastal State in accordance with this Convention and other rules of international law in so far as they are not incompatible with [Part V of the Convention]'.[127]

The Tribunal then proceeded to consider whether there was any legal basis for the enforcement actions taken by Russia against the Arctic Sunrise. In this context, it considered whether Russia's actions could be justified on the basis of the right of visit on suspicion of piracy;[128] violation of coastal State laws applicable to artificial islands, installations, and structures and their safety zones, under exercise of a right of hot pursuit;[129] commission of terrorist offences;[130] enforcement of laws regarding non-living resources;[131] enforcement jurisdiction relating to protection of the marine environment;[132] dangerous manoeuvring;[133] prevention of adverse ecological or environmental consequences;[134] prevention of terrorism;[135] and sovereign rights for the exploration and exploitation of non-living resources in the EEZ.[136] It concluded that none of these provided justification for the boarding, seizure, and detention of the Arctic Sunrise, and thus found that Russia had breached its obligations under UNCLOS, including under Article 58(1).[137] The Tribunal's treatment of permissible enforcement measures is discussed in section 4 below.

3. Interference with Freedom of Navigation

The question of what constitutes an interference with freedom of navigation has also been considered by several tribunals. The balance between the freedom of navigation and other rights and duties under UNCLOS is of critical importance to the broader principle of public order of the oceans, and is also an issue that frequently arises in State practice. Thus, tribunals are well-placed to provide guidance to States on the correct balance to be struck, as their findings are likely to be relevant to a broad range of coastal and other States.

This issue was considered in some detail by the Tribunal in *Norstar*. There, the Panamanian flagged M/V Norstar had bunkered private leisure boats on the high seas off the coast of Italy. After investigating, Italy declared that the M/V Norstar had been involved in selling fuel purchased in Italy without paying the appropriate tax duties. The Italian authorities issued a decree of seizure, which was implemented by Spanish authorities when the Norstar was moored in Spanish waters. Panama argued that Italy had breached its freedom of navigation on the high seas under Article 87 of UNCLOS.

127 ibid paras 227–28 (citations omitted).
128 ibid paras 236–41.
129 ibid paras 242–75.
130 ibid para 278.
131 ibid paras 281–85.
132 ibid paras 286–97.
133 ibid paras 298–305.
134 ibid paras 307–13.
135 ibid paras 314–23.
136 ibid paras 324–32.
137 ibid para 333.

So far as concerns acts that constitute a breach of the freedom of navigation under Article 87, the Tribunal noted that any acts of physical or material interference with navigation of foreign ships on the high seas would violate the freedom of navigation.[138] Italy accepted that acts falling short of enforcement action on the high seas could be relevant to a breach of Article 87, but argued that such acts had to produce a 'chilling effect', and none was produced in the present case because the Decree of Seizure issued by the Italian authorities was not known or knowable. The Tribunal did not accept that a 'chilling effect' was required: it considered that any act that subjects activities of a foreign ship on the high seas to the jurisdiction of a State other than the flag State would constitute a breach of the freedom of navigation, save in exceptional cases provided for in UNCLOS or under international treaties.[139]

The Tribunal then proceeded to find that the principle of exclusive flag State jurisdiction in Article 92 'prohibits not only the exercise of enforcement jurisdiction on the high seas by States other than the flag State but also the extension of their prescriptive jurisdiction to lawful activities conducted by foreign ships on the high seas'.[140] Thus, Italy's application of its criminal and customs laws to bunkering activities of foreign ships on the high seas could constitute a breach of freedom of navigation under Article 87 of UNCLOS.[141]

Italy further argued that Article 87 was not applicable because the Decree of Seizure was enforced in internal waters. The Tribunal dismissed this argument, noting that although the locus of enforcement was relevant, it was not the 'sole criterion'.[142] The Tribunal concluded that by extending its criminal and customs laws to the high seas, by issuing the Decree of Seizure, and by requesting the Spanish authorities to execute it, Italy breached the freedom of navigation under Article 87 of UNCLOS.[143]

In respect of the majority judgment on Article 87, seven judges dissented, expressing the view that Article 87 did not apply; and if it had applied, it would not have been violated. They noted that:

> [N]othing in the text of the Convention, in its travaux préparatoires, in other international treaties, in customary international law, or in the practice of States suggests that article 87 and its corollary article 92 altogether excludes the right of non-flag States to exercise their prescriptive criminal jurisdiction with respect to activities on the high seas.[144]

The dissenting minority considered that Article 87(1) prohibits only prescriptive jurisdiction of a State to the 'lawful activities' of foreign vessels on the high seas: the non-flag State is not excluded from extending, in conformity with international law, its prescriptive jurisdiction to the unlawful activities of foreign vessels or persons on the high seas.[145] The minority considered that the majority had mischaracterised Italy's exercise of jurisdiction; that it was not exercising jurisdiction with respect to the M/V Norstar's activities in bunkering vessels

[138] *Norstar*, Judgment (n 98) para 222.
[139] ibid paras 223–24
[140] ibid para 225.
[141] ibid paras 222–25.
[142] ibid para 226.
[143] ibid.
[144] *Norstar*, Judgment (n 98) (Dissenting Opinion of Judges Cot, Pawlak, Yanai, Hoffmann, Kolodkin, Lijnzaad, and Judge ad hoc Treves) para 19, citing Douglas Guilfoyle, 'Article 92' in Alexander Proelss (ed), *United Nations Convention on the Law of the Sea: A Commentary* (CH Beck, Hart, and Nomos 2017) 700–701.
[145] *Norstar*, Judgment (n 98) (Dissenting Opinion of Judges Cot, Pawlak, Yanai, Hoffmann, Kolodkin, Lijnzaad and Judge ad hoc Treves) para 20.

on the high seas, but that it was investigating the use of the vessels as a means to transport and supply fuel for the purposes of which it was alleged that appropriate taxes had not been paid in Italy's territory and which was subsequently smuggled into its territory.[146] Yet even if the exercise of jurisdiction involved the extension of prescriptive criminal jurisdiction to bunkering activities on the high seas, that would not have violated Article 87(1), because an integral part of the alleged criminal activity was commenced and completed in its territory, and had effects in its territory.[147] The minority was firmly of the view that a State may exercise its prescriptive criminal jurisdiction with respect to conduct on the high seas where such conduct is integral to an alleged crime committed in the State's territory, and that is not prohibited by Article 87.[148]

The majority's approach to Article 87(1), and in particular its finding that the exclusivity of flag State jurisdiction under Article 92 covers prescriptive and not only enforcement jurisdiction, was at odds with most academic opinion and has been criticised, principally on the basis that the tribunal failed to provide reasons (while noting that the minority could be subjected to the same critique), and because it is at odds with State practice.[149] This result may be an example of a compromise or common sense outcome taking account of the particular facts of this case, but the approach of the Tribunal to Article 92 is potentially of broad application in practice, and the criticism to the effect that the Tribunal failed to take account of significant State practice to the contrary appears to be well-placed.

The Tribunal in *Enrica Lexie* also considered the question of what acts can constitute a breach of freedom of navigation under Article 87(1) of UNCLOS. Italy argued that India violated its right to freedom of navigation by directing, interdicting, and escorting the Italian-flagged M/V Enrica Lexie beyond India's territorial waters.[150] Referring to *Norstar*, the Tribunal noted that any act of interference with navigation of foreign ships or any exercise of jurisdiction over such ships on the high seas constitutes a breach of freedom of navigation, unless justified by UNCLOS or other international treaties.[151] That interference, the Tribunal confirmed, could take physical or non-physical forms.[152] With regards to the *Croatia/Slovenia Arbitration*,[153] the Tribunal noted that interference of a physical nature could include boarding, arrest, detention, or diversion of a vessel.[154] Yet it further confirmed that even acts that do not involve physical interference or enforcement on the high seas may constitute a breach of the freedom of navigation. It stated that:

[146] ibid paras 22–30.
[147] ibid paras 31–35.
[148] ibid para 36.
[149] See Arron N Honniball, 'Freedom of Navigation Following the M/V "Norstar" Case' *The NCLOS Blog* (4 June 2019) https://site.uit.no/nclos/2019/06/04/freedom-of-navigation-following-the-m-v-norstar-case/; Richard Collins, 'Delineating the Exclusivity of Flag State Jurisdiction on the High Seas: ITLOS Issues Its Ruling in the M/V "Norstar" Case' *EJIL: Talk!* (4 June 2019) https://www.ejiltalk.org/delineating-the-exclusivity-of-flag-state-jurisdiction-on-the-high-seas-itlos-issues-its-ruling-in-the-m-v-norstar-case/; Cameron Miles, 'The M/V "Norstar" Case' (Panama v Italy)' 119 (2020) AJIL 116. For earlier scholarly work on this point see Arron N Honniball, 'The Exclusive Jurisdiction of Flag States: A Limitation on Pro-active Port States?' (2016) 31 IJMCL 499; Douglas Guilfoyle, 'The High Seas' in Donald R Rothwell and others (eds), *The Oxford Handbook of the Law of the Sea* (OUP 2015) 209–10. cf RR Churchill and AV Lowe, *The Law of the Sea* (3rd edn, Juris Publishing 1999) 208–209.
[150] *Enrica Lexie*, Award (n 43) para 435.
[151] ibid para 468.
[152] ibid para 469
[153] *Arbitration between the Republic of Croatia and the Republic of Slovenia* (Final Award of 29 June 2017) PCA Case No 2012-04 (*Croatia/Slovenia Arbitration*, Final Award).
[154] *Enrica Lexie*, Award (n 43) para 470. In *Croatia/Slovenia Arbitration*, Final Award (n 153) the Tribunal was addressing freedom of communication rather than navigation: see para 1129 and dispositif, para IV(B)(f).

> [A] breach of freedom of navigation may result from acts including physical or material interference with navigation of a foreign vessel, the threat or use of force against a foreign vessel, or non-physical forms of interference whose effect is that of instilling fear in, or causing hindrance to, the exercise of the freedom of navigation.
>
> Additionally, as stated in M/V 'Norstar', the exercise of jurisdiction over a foreign ship on the high seas, unless justified by the Convention or other international treaties, is generally agreed to constitute a breach of freedom of navigation.[155]

The Tribunal then examined Italy's claim by reference to the principle of exclusive flag State jurisdiction, pursuant to Article 92, which applies to the EEZ under Article 58(2). Interestingly, the Tribunal adopted an expansive approach to exclusive flag State jurisdiction under Article 92, following *Norstar*, to the effect that it covers prescriptive, as well as enforcement, jurisdiction.[156]

Ultimately, the Tribunal found that Italy had not discharged its burden to show that the Indian authorities had exercised jurisdiction over the Enrica Lexie in the EEZ.[157] It followed that no issue arose as to violation of Italy's freedom of navigation in the EEZ. Like the decision in *Norstar*, the Tribunal's finding in *Enrica Lexie* that the principle of exclusive flag State jurisdiction covers both prescriptive and enforcement jurisdiction is open to criticism on the basis of a paucity of reasoning. The majority did not take the opportunity to address the numerous dissenting opinions in *Enrica Lexie* at the provisional measures stage before ITLOS, which had suggested that UNCLOS is silent as to extraterritorial prescriptive jurisdiction at sea.[158] While the issue may have arisen again when ITLOS considered the merits in *San Padre Pio (No 2)*, and the possibility of a clarifying judgment was anticipated by commentators,[159] that case was settled prior to the merits phase.

India brought a counterclaim against Italy in *Enrica Lexie*, alleging that Italy had breached India's freedom and right of navigation in its EEZ, under Articles 87(1) and 90, by the actions of the marines against the vessel St Antony. As noted above, the Tribunal affirmed that small vessels exempted from the requirement to maintain a register under Article 94(2) were still entitled to the fundamental rights to freedom of navigation under Article 87.[160] The Tribunal also held that any failure by the flag State to fulfil its duties under Article 94 had no impact on the right to freedom of navigation under Articles 87 and 90.[161] The Tribunal noted that the act of shooting at the St Antony caused it to change direction and ultimately to head back to shore: thus, it was prevented from navigating its intended course. It concluded that this physical interference with the navigation was a breach of Articles 87(1)(a) and 90 of UNCLOS.[162]

155 *Enrica Lexie*, Award (n 43) paras 472–73.

156 ibid paras 524–27.

157 ibid paras 535–36.

158 *Enrica Lexie (Italy v India)* (Provisional Measures, Order of 24 August 2015) ITLOS Reports 2015, 182 (Dissenting Opinion of Judge Lucky) paras 36 and 60, (Dissenting Opinion of Vice President Bougetaia) para 15, (Dissenting Opinion of Judge Ndiaye) para 23. See further Arron N Honniball, 'The "Enrica Lexie" Incident Award and Exclusive Flag State Jurisdiction' *CIL Blog* (10 August 2020) https://cil.nus.edu.sg/the-enrica-lexie-incident-award-and-exclusive-flag-state-jurisdiction-by-arron-n-honniball/ (Honniball, 'The *Enrica Lexie* Incident').

159 See Honniball, 'The *Enrica Lexie* Incident' (n 158).

160 *Enrica Lexie*, Award (n 43) paras 1032–34.

161 ibid para 1035.

162 ibid paras 1036–43.

4. Article 94 and Safety of Navigation

As noted above, pursuant to Article 94(1) of UNCLOS, the flag State must 'effectively exercise its jurisdiction and control in administrative, technical and social matters over ships flying its flag'. In *South China Sea*,[163] the Philippines argued that China had operated its law enforcement vessels in a dangerous manner, causing a serious risk of collision. It argued that China had breached its obligations relating to safe navigation under Articles 94 and 21 of UNCLOS and related provisions in the 1972 Convention on the International Regulations for Preventing of Collision at Sea (COLREGS).[164]

The Tribunal noted that Article 94(1) of UNCLOS requires flag States effectively to exercise their jurisdiction and control in administrative, technical, and social matters over their flagged vessels. Article 94(3) clarifies that the scope of flag States' duties includes measures 'as are necessary to ensure safety at sea', including inter alia, the prevention of collisions. Article 94(5) further provides that in taking the measures called for in Article 94(3) 'each State is required to conform to generally accepted international regulations, procedures and practices and to take any steps which may be necessary to secure their observance.'[165]

The Tribunal further considered that Article 94 incorporates the COLREGS, so that any violation of the COLREGS is a violation of UNCLOS.[166] Noting that the tribunal-appointed expert concluded that China had breached its obligations under Rules 2, 6, 8, 15, and 16 of the COLREGS,[167] the Tribunal considered the evidence relating to the specific incidents and concluded that the activities of Chinese vessels constituted violations of the COLREGS, and a breach of Article 94 of UNCLOS.[168]

The Tribunal's determination will be relevant to the conduct of law enforcement activities,[169] but will probably also have ramifications for navigation in general, as it makes clear that the flag State's responsibilities include compliance with generally accepted regulations in respect of safety of navigation, including relevant provisions of the COLREGS.[170]

5. Penal Jurisdiction Relating to Incidents of Navigation on the High Seas

A further provision that reinforces the limited jurisdiction of coastal States in respect of navigation is Article 97. It addresses penal jurisdiction in matters of collision or any other incident of navigation on the high seas. It states:

[163] *South China Sea Arbitration (Philippines v China)* (Award of 12 July 2016) PCA Case No 2013-19 (*South China Sea*, Award).

[164] Convention on the International Regulations for Preventing Collisions at Sea (adopted 20 October 1972, entered into force 15 July 1977) 1050 UNTS 1976 (COLREGS).

[165] *South China Sea*, Award (n 163) para 1082.

[166] ibid para 1083. See further ch 4(V)(B).

[167] *South China Sea*, Award (n 163) para 1085.

[168] ibid paras 1092, 1105, 1109.

[169] See Clive Schofield, 'A Landmark Decision in the South China Sea: The Scope and Implications of the Arbitral Tribunal's Award' 38 (2016) Contemporary Southeast Asia 339. In its Critical Study of the Award, the Chinese Society of International Law argued that the COLREGS would in any event only apply to the normal navigation of ships, and not to law enforcement activities of the coastal State aiming to prevent the non-innocent passage of foreign vessels: see Chinese Society of International Law, 'The South China Sea Arbitration Awards: A Critical Study' (2018) 17 Chinese JIL 207, 599–602, paras 840–47.

[170] There are other international treaties addressing aspects of navigational safety that might too be included within the general obligation under art 4 of UNCLOS, including the IMO's International Convention for the Safety of Life at Sea (adopted 1 November 1974, entered into force 25 May 1980) 1184 UNTS 278; and the International Convention on Standards of Training, Certification and Watchkeeping for Seafarers (adopted 7 July 1978, entered into force 28 April 1984) 1361 UNTS 2.

1. In the event of a collision or any other incident of navigation concerning a ship on the high seas, involving the penal or disciplinary responsibility of the master or of any other person in the service of the ship, no penal or disciplinary proceedings may be instituted against such person except before the judicial or administrative authorities either of the flag State or of the State of which such person is a national.
2. In disciplinary matters, the State which has issued a master's certificate or a certificate of competence or licence shall alone be competent, after due legal process, to pronounce the withdrawal of such certificates, even if the holder is not a national of the State which issued them.
3. No arrest or detention of the ship, even as a measure of investigation, shall be ordered by any authorities other than those of the flag State.[171]

Article 97 falls within the provisions referred to in Article 58(2) as applying also to the EEZ.

In *Arctic Sunrise*, Russia accused the Arctic Sunrise of dangerous manoeuvring, and asserted that the captain of the vessel did not react to lawful requests to stop, nor to signals under the International Code of Signals.[172] It alleged that the vessel carried out dangerous manoeuvres in violation of the COLREGS.[173] The Tribunal considered whether this allegation could form the basis of a lawful justification for the measures taken against the Arctic Sunrise. The Netherlands argued that the regulations to which Russia referred did not permit States to board a foreign ship, nor to take other enforcement measures, and this position was corroborated by Article 97(3) of UNCLOS.

The Tribunal noted that the international rules and standards referred to by Russia did not provide any legal basis for boarding, seizure, or detention of a foreign ship for dangerous manoeuvring.[174] It noted also that under Article 97, only the flag State may institute penal or administrative proceeding against a person, or arrest or detain a vessel, for any incident of navigation.[175] The Tribunal concluded that even if the Arctic Sunrise had engaged in dangerous manoeuvring, this action would not have provided Russia with a legal basis to board, seize, and detain the vessel.[176]

Article 97(3) arose again in *Enrica Lexie*. There, Italy argued that India breached Italy's exclusive flag State jurisdiction under Article 97(3) by ordering the detention of the Enrica Lexie. Italy argued that Article 97(3) prohibits arrest and detention of a foreign vessel in the territorial sea in respect of incidents of navigation occurring on the high seas or in the EEZ.[177] India argued that Article 97 was inapplicable because the incident involving the Enrica Lexie was not a collision or an incident of navigation. It also argued that Article 97 did not apply to an arrest in port.[178]

The Tribunal dealt at some length with the meaning of 'incident of navigation', applying a Vienna Convention on the Law of Treaties[179] analysis. Referring to the dictionary meaning

171 UNCLOS (n 2) art 97.

172 *Arctic Sunrise*, Merits (n 124) paras 94, 256, 298, referring to the International Code of Signals for Visual, Sound, and Radio Communications (1969).

173 ibid para 299, referring to the COLREGS (n 164).

174 *Arctic Sunrise*, Merits (n 124) para 301.

175 ibid para 304.

176 ibid paras 298–305.

177 *Enrica Lexie*, Award (n 43) para 624.

178 ibid paras 631–32.

179 Vienna Convention on the Law of Treaties (adopted 23 May 1969, entered into force 27 January 1980) 1155 UNTS 331.

of the terms 'incident' and 'navigation', the Tribunal noted that an 'incident of navigation' should involve 'a distinct or noteworthy event that occurs in relation to the movement and directing or manoeuvring of a ship'.[180] The Tribunal also noted that the term 'incident of navigation' appears in Articles 221(2) and 94(7) of UNCLOS. Article 221(2) suggests that 'incident of navigation' must be taken to refer to an occurrence on board a vessel or external to it resulting in material damage or imminent threat of material damage to a vessel or cargo. This interpretation was corroborated by Article 94(7), which refers to 'incidents of navigation' 'causing loss of life or serious injury to nationals of another State or serious damage to ships or installations of another State or to the marine environment'.[181] The Tribunal also referred to the object and purpose of Article 97, which could be traced to the *SS Lotus* case,[182] which referred to 'the object of protecting ships and their crews from the risk of penal proceedings before foreign courts in the event of collision on the high seas, since such proceedings may constitute an intolerable interference with international navigation'.[183] The Tribunal held that the *travaux préparatoires* of the Convention suggested that:

> [A]n exception to the otherwise prevailing rules on allocating jurisdiction was created specifically for a situation where the master or any other person in the service of a ship are at risk of facing penal proceedings before foreign courts in respect of navigational conduct on the high seas; such risk would typically arise only where some form of damage or harm has occurred as a result of navigation.[184]

The Tribunal also noted that during the discussion in the ILC of the precursor to Article 97, all examples of 'incidents of navigation' concerned the manoeuvring of the ship and damage caused by the operation of the vessel.[185] On the basis of its analysis, the Tribunal concluded that an 'incident of navigation' within the meaning of Article 97(1) is an event:

(a) that occurs in relation to the movement and manoeuvring of a ship; and
(b) which allegedly causes some form of serious damage or harm, including to the ships involved, their cargo, or the individuals on board.[186]

In its assessment of Italy's claim, the Tribunal noted that no collision occurred between the Enrica Lexie and the St Antony and, although there was a risk of collision, no damage resulted from the manoeuvring or movement of a ship.[187] The Tribunal also rejected the argument that the entire incident related to navigation because the origin of it was the course steered by each of the two approaching vessels, finding that the link between any navigational aspect and the damage and harm caused was too tenuous to sustain the claim that the firing of shots by the marines related to navigation.[188] The Tribunal thus found that no 'incident of navigation' had occurred that would trigger the application of Article 97(1).[189]

180 *Enrica Lexie*, Award (n 43) para 639.
181 ibid paras 640–43.
182 *SS 'Lotus' (France v Turkey)* (Judgment of 7 September 1927) [1927] PCIJ Rep Series A No 10, para 14.
183 *Enrica Lexie*, Award (n 43) paras 644–45.
184 ibid para 646.
185 ibid para 649.
186 ibid para 650.
187 ibid para 652.
188 ibid para 653.
189 ibid para 656.

The Tribunal declined to address the question as to whether Article 97 applies to arrest and detention of vessels in the territorial sea in respect of incidents of navigation occurring on the high seas, since it had found that Article 97(1) was not applicable.[190]

* * *

UNCLOS tribunals have had several opportunities to provide some useful interpretations of provisions that are critical to the exercise of navigational rights under UNCLOS, notably Articles 92, 94, and 97, as well as the general scope of freedom of navigation under Articles 87 and 58(1). The balance of navigational rights with other States' rights and duties, especially in the EEZ, has been a work in progress as tribunals respond to different factual scenarios. While the conclusions reached in each instance may properly be limited to the specific facts of the case, there are some broad statements of principle that will undoubtedly be influential in future State decision-making on the interpretation and application of UNCLOS. Most notable in this regard are the statements relating to the exclusivity of prescriptive and enforcement jurisdiction for flag States on the high seas, what actions may amount to a violation of the freedom of navigation beyond the territorial sea, and the relevance of other international agreements in defining the standards of conduct for which a flag State will be held responsible.

IV. Law Enforcement

Freedom of navigation in the EEZ may be limited to the extent that the coastal State exercises its rights under UNCLOS. Several tribunals have addressed the question of whether an interference with navigation could be justified on the basis of lawful enforcement measures under UNCLOS. This question is addressed immediately below, and also in relation to fisheries and the marine environment in Chapters 8 and 9, respectively. The question as to whether enforcement measures involved excessive force has also been considered, as has the question whether enforcement measures could be justified on the basis of the exercise of the right of hot pursuit under UNCLOS. The latter two questions are also addressed in this section.

A. Coastal States' Rights of Enforcement

UNCLOS balances the freedom of navigation with a substantial number of functional jurisdictional competences that States may exercise against foreign vessels under certain conditions. Some of these have been addressed by UNCLOS tribunals. In particular, tribunals have addressed the question of the lawfulness of enforcement measures taken by coastal States in interference with freedom of navigation in several cases. Article 73(1) provides an express basis for enforcement measures relating to the coastal State's rights to living

[190] ibid paras 658–59. The Tribunal could equally have dismissed the claim under art 97(3) on the basis that it did not apply to the territorial sea, but given the approach taken by this Tribunal, the question remains undecided and will be a matter to be addressed by future tribunals.

resources in the EEZ and is discussed in relation to fisheries in Chapter 8. The *Arctic Sunrise* Tribunal considered the question of the extent of a coastal State's rights of enforcement beyond those set out in Article 73(1). It addressed rights of enforcement with respect to rights to non-living resources in the EEZ; with respect to rights to protection of the marine environment; and whether enforcement action could be taken on the basis of dangerous manoeuvring in the course of navigation.

As an initial matter, it should be noted that Article 73 applies only to enforcement for the purpose of conservation and management of living resources in the EEZ. In *Louisa*, Saint Vincent and the Grenadines argued that Spain should have notified it of the detention of its vessel in accordance with Article 73. The Tribunal dismissed this argument, noting that the M/V Louisa was not detained for violation of the laws and regulations of Spain concerning living resources in the EEZ, but instead in the context of criminal proceedings relating to alleged violations of laws for the protection of underwater cultural heritage and the possession and handling of weapons of war. Consequently, the requirement promptly to notify under Article 73(4) did not apply to the Louisa.[191]

The question of the extent of a coastal State's rights of enforcement beyond those set out in Article 73(1) was considered by the Tribunal in *Arctic Sunrise*. The Tribunal first considered rights of enforcement with respect to rights to non-living resources in the EEZ. The Tribunal noted that Russia's actions did not concern living resources, so that Article 73(1) could not form the basis of the measures taken by Russia.[192] The Tribunal also noted that proposals were made at the Third United Nations Conference on the Law of the Sea to extend enforcement powers with respect to living resources to non-living resources, but these proposals were not accepted.[193] However, the Tribunal suggested that enforcement powers existed in relation to laws and regulations concerning non-living resources, on the basis of Article 77 of UNCLOS, which was based on the 1958 Geneva Convention on the Continental Shelf,[194] for which draft articles of the ILC had been prepared. The commentary to the ILC draft states that the words setting out the rights of the coastal State in relation to the continental shelf:

> [L]eave no doubt that the rights conferred upon the coastal state cover all rights necessary for and connected with the exploration and exploitation of the resources of the continental shelf. Such rights include jurisdiction in connexion with the prevention and punishment of violations of the law.[195]

The Tribunal considered that it was not necessary 'to reach a view on the extent of the coastal State's right to enforce its laws in relation to non-living resources in the EEZ', and found that there was no basis on the evidence to conclude that Russia's actions were taken in respect of violations of Russian laws in relation to exploration and exploitation activities on non-living resources in the EEZ, but it expressed the view that 'it is clear' that a right to enforce laws in relation to non-living resources in the EEZ' exists.[196]

[191] *Louisa*, Judgment (n 98) paras 101–105.
[192] *Arctic Sunrise*, Merits (n 124) para 282.
[193] ibid para 281.
[194] Convention on the Continental Shelf (n 1).
[195] *Arctic Sunrise*, Merits (n 124) para 283, referring to ILC, Articles concerning the Law of the Sea with Commentaries (n 9) 297.
[196] *Arctic Sunrise*, Merits (n 124) para 284.

As Mossop has noted, this conclusion appears at first glance inconsistent with the general structure of UNCLOS, which granted exclusive jurisdiction to the flag State on the high seas and in the EEZ, subject to specific express exceptions. However, she also notes that Article 111(2) provides for a right of hot pursuit regarding violations 'on the continental shelf, including safety zones around continental shelf violations'.[197] This provision implies an enforcement right over the continental shelf that covers and extends beyond safety zones.[198]

The *Arctic Sunrise* Tribunal also considered whether Russia's measures could be justified on the basis of interference with its sovereign rights for the exploration and exploitation of the non-living resources in the EEZ. The Tribunal considered that, in the context of the types of protest actions that could be considered to interfere with the exercise of those sovereign rights, and held that it would be reasonable for a coastal State to act to prevent:

(a) violations of its laws adopted in conformity with the Convention;
(b) dangerous situations that can result in injuries to persons and damage to equipment and installations;
(c) negative environmental consequences; and
(d) delay or interruption in essential operations.[199]

The Tribunal noted that at the time it was boarded and seized, the Arctic Sunrise was no longer engaged in any actions that could have potentially interfered with Russia's exercise of its rights as a coastal State, but was exercising the freedom of navigation. Pursuant to Article 78, the exercise of a coastal State's rights over the continental shelf 'must not infringe or result in any unjustifiable interference with navigation and other rights and freedoms of other States as provided in this Convention'. The Tribunal considered that, if the boarding and seizure of the Arctic Sunrise were done in the exercise of Russia's rights over the continental shelf, they would not have been consistent with UNCLOS, because they would have infringed and unjustifiably interfered with the navigation and other rights and freedoms of the Netherlands, as flag State of the Arctic Sunrise.[200]

The Tribunal thus appears to have taken the view that the arrest must coincide with the breach or breaches, and that any delay in enforcement measures could result in the measures being unjustifiable. As Mossop has noted, this approach imposes a significant limitation on the ability of coastal States to enforce measures against vessels that have violated the coastal State's laws and regulations on the continental shelf.[201] It also calls into doubt whether a coastal State is entitled to take measures to prevent breaches of its legitimate laws and regulations unless the vessel is engaged in breaches already or they are imminent.[202] The Tribunal appears to have missed an opportunity to provide guidance as to the balance to be struck under Article 78 between enforcement measures and freedom of navigation, and in particular the meaning of 'unjustifiable interference'.

[197] Joanna Mossop, 'Protests against Oil Exploration at Sea: Lessons from the *Arctic Sunrise* Arbitration' (2016) 31 IJMCL 60, 71.

[198] ibid 71; see also 79–80. The Tribunal's conclusion also raises the spectre of whether there are implicit enforcement powers in other instances where the Convention recognises prescriptive jurisdiction of the coastal state, such as in relation to international straits subject to the transit passage regime.

[199] *Arctic Sunrise*, Merits (n 124) para 327.

[200] ibid paras 328–32.

[201] Mossop (n 197) 73.

[202] ibid 73. See also 86.

Also in relation to the law enforcement rights of a coastal State to non-living resources in its EEZ, the Tribunal noted that a reasonable belief that a vessel may be involved in a terrorist attack on an installation or structure of the coastal State could justify some form of preventative action against a vessel. However, the Tribunal considered that on the facts there was no reasonable basis for Russia to suspect that the Arctic Sunrise was engaged or was likely to engage in terrorist acts, noting that the Russian authorities were familiar with the Arctic Sunrise, its objectives, and the manner in which it staged protest actions.[203] It also considered that Russia's conduct, and in particular its delay in boarding and arresting the vessel, were inconsistent with any reasonable suspicion of terrorism.[204] It therefore concluded that Russia's right to take measures to protect its rights in the EEZ against terrorism did not provide a legal basis for the measures taken against the Arctic Sunrise.[205]

B. Limits to the Use of Force

The scope of permissible enforcement action will be guided by: (a) the applicable domestic laws and regulations, which will usually indicate the degree of force permissible in taking enforcement measures; and (b) the international law conditions under which force may be used and the limits on the degree of force that may be used.[206] It follows that officers engaged in law enforcement action at sea 'must take into account more questions than is ordinarily required of authorities ashore because [they are] operating in a domain regulated fundamentally by international law'.[207] Maritime law enforcement has become the main context in which force is used at sea.[208] That some force may be used in this context is confirmed by the Convention for the Suppression of Unlawful Acts against the Safety of Maritime Navigation, as amended by its Protocol of 2005, in situations where the persons concerned have unlawfully and intentionally committed an offence within the meaning of that Convention.[209]

UNCLOS is mostly silent on issues associated with the use of force. Article 301 provides that in exercising rights and performing duties under UNCLOS, 'States Parties shall refrain from any threat or use of force against the territorial integrity or political independence of any State, or in any other manner inconsistent with the principles of international law embodied in the Charter of the United Nations'. Together with Article 293(1), which requires an UNCLOS tribunal to apply 'other rules of international law not incompatible with this Convention', Article 301 effectively reaffirms the prohibition on the use of force

[203] *Arctic Sunrise*, Merits (n 124) para 314.
[204] ibid para 319.
[205] ibid paras 314–23.
[206] DP O'Connell, *The International Law of the Sea*, vol 2 (IA Shearer ed, 1st edn, Clarendon Press 1988) 1062.
[207] ibid 1062–63.
[208] See Jinxing Ma and Shiyan Sun, 'Restrictions on the Use of Force at Sea: An Environmental Protection Perspective' (2016) 98 Intl Rev Red Cross 515, 521.
[209] Convention for the Suppression of Unlawful Acts Against the Safety of Maritime Navigation (adopted 10 March 1988, entered into force 1 March 1992) 1678 UNTS 221; Protocol of 2005 to the Protocol for the Suppression of Unlawful Acts against the Safety of Fixed Platforms Located on the Continental Shelf (adopted 14 October 2005, entered into force 28 July 2010) IMO Doc LEG/CONF.15/22.

under Article 2(4) of the UN Charter, as well as Article 51 of the Charter, dealing with self-defence.[210]

The use of police force in maritime law enforcement is to be distinguished from the use of force in international relations. However, forcible measures taken against foreign vessels can constitute a use of force against the flag State in the sense of Article 2(4), and in practice the distinction may be difficult to apply.[211] In *Oil Platforms*, the ICJ confirmed that forcible measures against foreign vessels (in that case, not in the exercise of enforcement powers, but mine and missile attacks) could fall within the scope of the international prohibition on the use of force.[212] The Tribunal in *Guyana v Suriname* confirmed that the use of force in law enforcement activities may amount to a use or threat of use of force in contravention of the UN Charter: while accepting that under international law force may be used in law enforcement activities provided that it is unavoidable, reasonable, and necessary, it found that the action taken by Suriname was more akin to a threat of military action than a mere law enforcement activity.[213] It ultimately concluded, albeit somewhat controversially,[214] that Suriname had threatened force in breach of UNCLOS, the UN Charter, and general international law.[215]

More recently, in *Enrica Lexie*, India argued that Italy infringed its right under Article 88 of UNCLOS, relating to the use of seas for peaceful purposes, by the use of force by the Italian marines. India argued that Article 88 should be read together with Article 301 of UNCLOS, which prohibits the threat or use of force or any other action inconsistent with the UN Charter.[216] Italy argued that Article 88 of UNCLOS was not engaged because it did not have a purpose that was not peaceful.[217] It identified 'an important distinction' between States' purposes under Article 88 and the attribution to Italy of 'a particular purpose based on the conduct of the Marines in a particular incident in which they responded to a perceived threat to … security and safe navigation'.[218] The Tribunal observed that the use of force is not completely prohibited provided it is consistent with Article 2(4) of the UN Charter, as reflected in Article 301 of UNCLOS.[219] Rather, States can take 'the necessary measures, including enforcement measures' consistent with UNCLOS and the UN Charter, to protect their vessels against piracy.[220] Taking account of the purpose for which the marines had been deployed on the M/V Enrica Lexie (to protect it against potential pirate attacks), and its conclusion that the marines acted under the apprehension that the

[210] See eg Natalie Klein, *Maritime Security and the Law of the Sea* (Oxford University Press 2011) 261. As discussed in ch 4(IV)(A), Article 293 does not extend the subject matter jurisdiction of any UNCLOS court or tribunal.

[211] See Patricia Jimenez Kwast, 'Maritime Law Enforcement and the Use of Force: Reflections on the Categorisation of Forcible Action at Sea in the Light of the Guyana/Suriname Award' (2008) 13 JC&SL 49. See especially 53–63.

[212] *Oil Platforms (Iran v United States)* (Merits) [2003] ICJ Rep 161, paras 50–61, 78.

[213] *Guyana v Suriname* (Award of the Arbitral Tribunal of 17 September 2007) PCA Case No 2004-04, para 445 (*Guyana v Suriname*). See also paras 439–44.

[214] See discussion in ch 4(IV)(A).

[215] *Guyana v Suriname* (n 213) para 488(2). For a useful commentary on the decision see David H Anderson, 'Some Aspects of the Use of Force in Maritime Law Enforcement' in Nerina Boschiero and others (eds), *International Courts and the Development of International Law* (Springer 2013).

[216] *Enrica Lexie*, Award (n 43) paras 1065–66.

[217] ibid para 1067.

[218] ibid para 1058.

[219] ibid para 1073.

[220] ibid para 1074.

vessel was under a pirate attack,[221] the Tribunal concluded that Italy did not breach Article 88 of UNCLOS.

In the context of navigational rights and freedoms, claims that a coastal State's use of force against a vessel has been excessive have been considered in *Saiga (No 2)*, and *Virginia G*. In both cases, the issue was analysed through the prism of the standard for lawful force in the context of law enforcement measures, rather than under the international law rules governing the use of force, reflected in Article 2(4) of the UN Charter. The tribunals affirmed that the relevant test was one of reasonableness and necessity, with force to be avoided as far as possible.[222]

In *Saiga (No 2)*, Saint Vincent and the Grenadines alleged that Guinea had used excessive force in arresting the M/V Saiga, in particular by firing at the ship from a fast-moving patrol boat without issuing any signals or warnings in advance, and upon boarding, continuing to discharge firearms. In respect of the applicable law, the Tribunal stated:

> Although the Convention does not contain express provisions on the use of force in the arrest of ships, international law, which is applicable by virtue of article 293 of the Convention, requires that the use of force must be avoided as far as possible and, where force is unavoidable, it must not go beyond what is reasonable and necessary in the circumstances. Considerations of humanity must apply in the law of the sea, as they do in other areas of international law.[223]

The Tribunal noted that the usual practice used to stop a ship at sea is first to give an auditory or visual signal to stop, using internationally recognised signals. Where that does not succeed, other actions may be taken, including firing of shots across the bows. Only after those actions fail, the pursuing vessel may use force, as a last resort.[224] However, even then, appropriate warning must be issued and all efforts should be made to ensure that life is not endangered.[225] In articulating these requirements, the Tribunal reaffirmed the customary law standards as set out by the Anglo-American Arbitral Tribunal in *SS I'm Alone* arbitration (stating that the US was entitled to 'use necessary and reasonable force for the purpose of effecting the objects of boarding, searching, seizing and bringing into port the suspected vessel')[226] and the Danish–British Commission of Inquiry in relation to *The Red Crusader* arbitration (finding that the Danish patrol vessel had 'exceeded legitimate use of armed force' because it acted 'without proved necessity').[227]

The Tribunal assessed the question whether excessive force had been used in breach of Guinea's obligations under international law and UNCLOS by reference to the specific circumstances. In respect of the use of force to arrest, it noted that the M/V Saiga was almost fully laden and low in the water, and its maximum speed was ten knots.[228] It was initially alleged that the M/V Saiga had attempted to sink the patrol boat but during that hearing the

221 ibid para 1076.
222 For a useful elaboration of the applicable test see Matteo Tondini, 'The Use of Force in the Course of Maritime Law Enforcement Operations' (2017) 4(2) J Use of Force & Intl L 253, 260–66.
223 *Saiga (No 2)*, Judgment (n 5) para 155.
224 ibid para 156.
225 ibid.
226 *SS I'm Alone (Canada/United States)* (1935) 7 ILR 203, 205.
227 *Red Crusader (Denmark/United Kingdom)* (1962) 35 ILR 485, 499.
228 *Saiga (No 2)*, Judgment (n 5) para 157.

allegation was modified to suggest that there was danger to the sinking of the patrol boat from the wake of the M/V Saiga.[229] The Tribunal noted that, 'whatever the circumstances, there is no excuse for the fact that the officers fired at the ship itself with live ammunition from a fast-moving patrol boat without issuing any of the signals and warnings required by international law and practice'.[230]

The Tribunal also considered that the Guinean officers used excessive force on board the M/V Saiga:

> Having boarded the ship without resistance, and although there is no evidence of the use or threat of force from the crew, they fired indiscriminately while on the deck and used gunfire to stop the engine of the ship. In using firearms in this way, the Guinean officers appeared to have attached little or no importance to the safety of the ship and the persons on board. In the process, considerable damage was done to the ship and to vital equipment in the engine and radio rooms. And, more seriously, the indiscriminate use of gunfire caused severe injuries to two of the persons on board.[231]

The Tribunal thus concluded that Guinea had violated the rights of Saint Vincent and the Grenadines, by using excessive force and endangering human life before and after boarding the M/V Saiga.[232] It is notable that the question of the applicability of the international law rules on use of force generally was not raised in *Saiga (No 2)*, with the focus remaining on the customary international law standards governing the resort to force in the context of law enforcement activities.

The same approach was taken in *Virginia G*. There, the Tribunal considered whether Guinea-Bissau had used excessive force in the arrest of the vessel. The Tribunal noted that the patrol vessels were clearly marked and the inspectors who boarded the vessel were dressed in a way that identified them.[233] The Tribunal considered that '[d]uring boarding, the use of force did not go beyond what was reasonable and necessary in the circumstances and after the initial stage of detention the captain was no longer prevented from communicating with the owner of the vessel'.[234] On the basis of the information provided by the parties, the Tribunal considered that excessive force was not used against the vessel or its crew.[235]

UNCLOS tribunals addressing questions concerning the limits of the use of permissible force have focused on the specific circumstances of the facts of each case, and in that context have emphasised the use of reasonable and necessary force in the particular circumstances. They have also affirmed that considerations of humanity apply in the law of the sea, as they do in other areas. It is likely that claims in relation to excessive use of force will continue to come before UNCLOS tribunals, particularly as States engage more actively in issues of maritime security.

[229] ibid.
[230] ibid.
[231] ibid para 158.
[232] ibid para 159.
[233] *Virginia G* (n 33) para 361.
[234] ibid.
[235] ibid para 362.

C. Hot Pursuit

The right of hot pursuit is set out in Article 111 of UNCLOS, as follows:

1. The hot pursuit of a foreign ship may be undertaken when the competent authorities of the coastal State have good reason to believe that the ship has violated the laws and regulations of that State. Such pursuit must be commenced when the foreign ship or one of its boats is within the internal waters, the archipelagic waters, the territorial sea or the contiguous zone of the pursuing State, and may only be continued outside the territorial sea or the contiguous zone if the pursuit has not been interrupted. It is not necessary that, at the time when the foreign ship within the territorial sea or the contiguous zone receives the order to stop, the ship giving the order should likewise be within the territorial sea or the contiguous zone. If the foreign ship is within a contiguous zone, as defined in article 33, the pursuit may only be undertaken if there has been a violation of the rights for the protection of which the zone was established.
2. The right of hot pursuit shall apply *mutatis mutandis* to violations in the exclusive economic zone or on the continental shelf, including safety zones around continental shelf installations, of the laws and regulations of the coastal State applicable in accordance with this Convention to the exclusive economic zone or the continental shelf, including such safety zones.
3. The right of hot pursuit ceases as soon as the ship pursued enters the territorial sea of its own State or of a third State.
4. Hot pursuit is not deemed to have begun unless the pursuing ship has satisfied itself by such practicable means as may be available that the ship pursued or one of its boats or other craft working as a team and using the ship pursued as a mother ship is within the limits of the territorial sea, or, as the case may be, within the contiguous zone or the exclusive economic zone or above the continental shelf. The pursuit may only be commenced after a visual or auditory signal to stop has been given at a distance which enables it to be seen or heard by the foreign ship.
5. The right of hot pursuit may be exercised only by warships or military aircraft, or other ships or aircraft clearly marked and identifiable as being on government service and authorized to that effect.
6. Where hot pursuit is effected by an aircraft:
   (a) the provisions of paragraphs 1 to 4 shall apply *mutatis mutandis*;
   (b) the aircraft giving the order to stop must itself actively pursue the ship until a ship or another aircraft of the coastal State, summoned by the aircraft, arrives to take over the pursuit, unless the aircraft is itself able to arrest the ship. It does not suffice to justify an arrest outside the territorial sea that the ship was merely sighted by the aircraft as an offender or suspected offender, if it was not both ordered to stop and pursued by the aircraft itself or other aircraft or ships which continue the pursuit without interruption.
7. The release of a ship arrested within the jurisdiction of a State and escorted to a port of that State for the purposes of an inquiry before the competent authorities may not be claimed solely on the ground that the ship, in the course of its voyage, was escorted

across a portion of the exclusive economic zone or the high seas, if the circumstances rendered this necessary.

8. Where a ship has been stopped or arrested outside the territorial sea in circumstances which do not justify the exercise of the right of hot pursuit, it shall be compensated for any loss or damage that may have been thereby sustained.[236]

In the prompt release stage of *Saiga*, Guinea argued that it arrested the vessel in accordance with the right of hot pursuit.[237] The argument was dismissed by the Tribunal as unarguable (not being of a sufficiently plausible character).[238] In particular, the Tribunal highlighted that the pursuit was commenced one day after the alleged violation, at a time when the M/V Saiga 'was certainly not within the contiguous zone of Guinea'.[239]

In *Saiga (No 2)*, Guinea pursued its argument based on the right of hot pursuit. The Tribunal confirmed that the conditions under Article 111 are cumulative: 'each of them has to be satisfied for the pursuit to be legitimate under the Convention'.[240] Guinea presented different accounts of the pursuit: the Tribunal noting that in some of its assertions, the pursuit commenced on 27 October 1997 sooner or after the authorities had information that the M/V Saiga had committed or was about to commit violations of its laws, and that the pursuit was continued throughout the period until the vessel was arrested in the morning of 28 October 1997. In other of its assertions, Guinea argued that the pursuit commenced in the early morning of 28 October 1997, when the M/V Saiga was still in its EEZ.

In respect of the pursuit alleged to have commenced on 27 October 1997, the Tribunal noted that:

(a) the authorities could have had no more than a suspicion that a tanker had violated Guinea's laws in its EEZ;
(b) no visual or auditory signals could have been given to the *Saiga*; and
(c) the alleged pursuit was interrupted, since the small patrol boat sent onto search for the *Saiga* was recalled.[241]

In respect of the pursuit alleged to have commenced on 28 October 1997, the Tribunal noted that there was conflicting evidence as to whether any signals were given, and that any signals given could not be said to have been given at the time of commencement of the pursuit.[242] The Tribunal further noted that no laws or regulations of Guinea applicable in accordance with UNCLOS were violated and therefore there was no legal basis for the exercise of the right of hot pursuit. The Tribunal thus concluded that Guinea's arrest of the M/V Saiga could not be justified on the basis of the right of hot pursuit.[243]

236 Hot pursuit came up in the *Volga* case, as Russia argued that Australia had done the arrest following an unlawful hot pursuit and it did seem that Australia might have been outside its EEZ when pursuit started. However, as it was prompt release case, the Tribunal did not examine it further. See *Volga (Russia v Australia)* (Prompt Release, Judgment) ITLOS Reports 2002, 10.

237 *M/V Saiga (Saint Vincent and the Grenadines v Guinea)* (Prompt Release, Judgment) ITLOS Reports 1997, 16, para 60.

238 ibid para 61.

239 ibid.

240 *Saiga (No 2)*, Judgment (n 5) para 146.

241 ibid para 147.

242 ibid para 148.

243 ibid paras 149–150.

At the merits stage of the *Arctic Sunrise*, the Tribunal considered whether Russia's enforcement action against the vessel in the EEZ could be justified on the basis of the right of hot pursuit. It noted that the Russian authorities had charged the crew with the offence of hooliganism, and that the Russian coastguard vessel had invoked an alleged violation of a prohibition to enter a safety zone around the Prirazlomnaya as a ground for ordering the Arctic Sunrise to stop. It further observed that the alleged commission of these offences did not provide a basis under international law for boarding a foreign vessel in the EEZ without the consent of the flag State. The boarding, seizure, and detention of the vessel on suspicion of those offences would only have a lawful basis if the requirements of hot pursuit were satisfied.[244]

Referring to *Saiga (No 2)*, the *Arctic Sunrise* Tribunal affirmed that the conditions set out in Article 111 are cumulative.[245] The first requirement is that the competent authorities of the coastal State must have good reason to believe that the vessel has violated the laws or regulations of that State. Noting that Russia had unequivocally stated that a 500-metre zone prohibited to navigation existed around the Prirazlomnaya, the Tribunal proceeded on the assumption that a safety zone had been validly established around the platform and that navigation was prohibited in that zone. In such a case, the Tribunal noted, the Russian authorities would have had good reason to believe that there had been a violation of that prohibition on navigation, and that would have constituted sufficient reason to commence pursuit under Article 111.[246]

The second and third conditions are the signal after which and the location from where pursuit may be commenced. The Tribunal addressed these requirements together. So far as concerns the signal, the Tribunal accepted that the Arctic Sunrise had been given an order to stop by very high frequency (VHF) radio. Noting that municipal courts have recognised that radio messages may constitute valid signals under UNCLOS, and that at the time when the radio messages were transmitted the Arctic Sunrise and the pursuing vessel were within approximately three nautical miles of each other, the Tribunal accepted that the radio messages were a valid 'auditory signal' under Article 111(4).[247] This understanding of the requirement under Article 111(4) reflected an understanding that the use of new technology may be validly contemplated in interpreting UNCLOS provisions. In this way, the Tribunal interpreted UNCLOS (and in particular the criteria set out in Article 111) in line with modern technology.[248]

So far as concerns the location, the Tribunal considered that the pursuit of the Arctic Sunrise had to commence while at least one of its rigid-hull inflatable boats (RHIBs) was within the 500-metre safety zone around the Prirazlomnaya.[249] The Tribunal determined that the 'relevant area' was the safety zone: that is a special zone within the continental shelf or EEZ,[250] where the coastal State has additional rights that it does not otherwise have in the continental shelf or EEZ.[251] While noting that Article 111(1) requires that the foreign ship

[244] *Arctic Sunrise*, Merits (n 124) paras 242–45.
[245] ibid para 246.
[246] ibid paras 247–250.
[247] ibid para 259.
[248] See Klein (n 210) 109, where the author contends that the criteria in Article 111 should take into account the evolving technology that may improve the efficiency of law enforcement operations.
[249] *Arctic Sunrise*, Merits (n 124) para 253.
[250] ibid para 253.
[251] See Alex G Oude Elferink, 'The Russian Federation and the Arctic Sunrise Case: Hot Pursuit and Other Issues under the LOSC' (2016) 92 ILS 381, 393.

'must be' in the relevant area at the commencement of the pursuit, it also took account of the test in Article 111(4), which it described as 'less stringent[]', and provides that pursuit is not deemed to have commenced unless 'the pursuing ship has satisfied itself by such practicable means as may be available' that the pursued ship is in the relevant area. In light of this, the Tribunal considered that:

> [T]he location of the foreign ship at the time of the first stop order should not be evaluated with the full benefit of hindsight, but rather looked at from the perspective of the pursuing ship. The Tribunal is also conscious that, in the present case, the relevant maritime area within which the foreign ship or its boats must have been located for the commencement of the pursuit—the 500-metre safety zone—is small enough that leaving it may have been a matter of only a few minutes. It may therefore be that, given the closeness in time of the first stop order and the departure of the Arctic Sunrise RHIBs from the relevant zone, and the fact that the Ladoga ostensibly began radioing the stop order as soon as it realised that the Arctic Sunrise RHIBs were returning to their ship, the Ladoga should be seen as having 'satisfied itself by such practicable means as [were] available' that the Arctic Sunrise RHIBs were in the correct zone.[252]

Ultimately, the Tribunal did not decide whether the pursuit was lawfully commenced, given its finding (discussed below) that the requirement of continuity was not met.

The correctness of the Tribunal's approach to the location requirement has been questioned. Oude Elferink has argued that the Tribunal's approach 'seems to introduce an undesirable measure of subjectivity', while the test in Article 111(1) that the foreign ship or its vessels 'must be' in the maritime zone concerned is objective.[253] He also rightly questioned 'whether practical considerations in relation to one specific zone should play a role in interpreting the provisions on hot pursuit that are generally applicable to all coastal State maritime zones'.[254] Finally, in terms of practical considerations, Oude Elferink noted that the actions involving the Arctic Sunrise played out over a considerable period of time, and a determination that hot pursuit should be commenced could have been made in that time frame, before the departure from the safety zone.[255]

The Tribunal then turned to the fourth condition: continuity of pursuit. The Tribunal noted that the pursuing vessel had initially engaged in conduct consistent with the notion of pursuit, but after some three hours, and for a further thirty-three hours, the vessel shadowed the Arctic Sunrise, positioning itself between that vessel and the Prirazlomnaya. The Tribunal considered that this conduct was 'not consistent with continuous pursuit, the final objective of which would have been to board, as soon as possible, the pursued ship'. It also noted that the Arctic Sunrise did not behave consistently with a pursued ship, as it remained in the area and did not attempt to flee.[256] The Tribunal concluded that the pursuit was interrupted, and therefore one of the necessary conditions in Article 111 was not met: therefore, the right of hot pursuit could not serve as the legal basis for the boarding, seizure, and detention of the Arctic Sunrise.[257]

252 *Arctic Sunrise*, Merits (n 124) para 267.
253 Oude Elferink (n 251) 394.
254 ibid.
255 ibid.
256 *Arctic Sunrise*, Merits (n 124) paras 270–71.
257 ibid para 275.

The Tribunal's approach to the continuity requirement has also been criticised. There is no requirement in UNCLOS that the final objective of a hot pursuit should be to board the pursued ship as soon as possible. As Oude Elferink points out, the Tribunal itself acknowledged that a pursuing vessel may need to await reinforcements.[258] He suggested that in judging the question whether a hot pursuit is interrupted, the intent of the coastal State authorities should be decisive.[259] Oude Elferink noted that, in *Arctic Sunrise*, the Tribunal did not have the benefit of Russia's participation in the proceedings, although the position paper of the Russian Ministry of Foreign Affairs denied that Russia was exercising the right of hot pursuit in boarding and arresting the vessel.[260] Russia instead argued that it could arrest the Arctic Sunrise anywhere in its EEZ, on the basis that the vessel was not exercising any right to freedom of navigation, and also on the basis that a coastal State can take enforcement action to protect its right safely to exploit resources of its continental shelf and its EEZ.[261]

The Tribunal did not consider the application of the condition in Article 111(5) that the right of hot pursuit may only be exercised 'by warships or military aircraft, or other ships or aircraft clearly marked and identifiable as being on government service and authorized to that effect'. In an earlier part of its award, the Tribunal noted that the vessel was boarded by helicopter, from which men descended onto the Arctic Sunrise. The helicopter was unmarked save for a red star on its bottom side. The men descending from it did not, in the recollection of the crew of the Arctic Sunrise, identify themselves. The Tribunal stated that it was:

> [s]atisfied, in context, that the vessel was boarded by Russian officials. This conclusion is apparent from their subsequent action, which included allowing the Russian Coast Guard vessel Ladoga to tow the Arctic Sunrise ... as well as from contemporaneous Russian statements.[262]

Although the Tribunal did not make a finding on this point in addressing the question whether the actions were justified on the basis of the exercise of the right of hot pursuit, it appears it considered that the condition in Article 111(4) could be met by reference to subsequent conduct.[263] The approach of the Tribunal to this question has also been met with criticism, as effectively overlooking the express conditions of clear marking and identification.[264]

UNCLOS tribunals have had several opportunities to interpret and apply the specific elements of Article 111, and thus to clarify the conditions governing the exercise of the right of hot pursuit. In particular, the *Arctic Sunrise* Tribunal clarified that radio messages are a valid 'auditory signal' under Article 111(4), and also interpreted the location requirement, emphasising that the perspective of principal importance is that of the pursuing ship, as

[258] Oude Elferink (n 251) 396.
[259] ibid.
[260] ibid 396–98, 406.
[261] Ministry of Foreign Affairs of the Russian Federation 'On Certain Legal Issues Highlighted by the Action of the *Arctic Sunrise* Against *Prirazlomnaya* Platform' (5 August 2015) https://www.mid.ru/en/web/guest/foreign_policy/news/-/asset_publisher/cKNonkJE02Bw/content/id/1639745.
[262] *Arctic Sunrise*, Merit (n 124) paras 100–101.
[263] Oude Elferink (n 251) 394–95.
[264] ibid 394–95, 405–406. The Tribunal's approach also raises interesting questions concerning the use of autonomous vehicles for law enforcement. The Tribunal's views appear to cut against the suggestion that drones should be properly marked.

well as the continuity requirement, finding that the objective must be to board the pursued ship as soon as possible. Some elements of flexibility and subjectivity that were accommodated by the *Arctic Sunrise* Tribunal will potentially be helpful to law enforcement officials in their daily conduct of operations at sea: for example, assessing the location requirement on the basis of the information available to the pursuing ship at the time, rather than with the benefit of hindsight, is likely to accord some leeway to coastal States in avoiding lost opportunities of enforcement where they act in good faith in applying the conditions in Article 111.

V. Concluding Remarks

The provisions of UNCLOS relating to freedom of the high seas reflect the increasing importance of balancing navigational rights and freedoms with the rights and interests of coastal States, which have themselves been expanded over time to cover a broad range of issues including protection of the marine environment, and the conservation and management of marine living resources. UNCLOS tribunals have had several opportunities to address the right balance to be struck between coastal State interests and the rights of other stakeholders, including other States as well as private entities engaged in navigation on the high seas and in other maritime zones. While these decisions are marked by their focus on the particular facts and circumstances of each case, they have also provided some guiding principles that have the potential to contribute to the broader objectives of the rule of law and public order of the oceans.

Aspects of navigation that have been addressed by UNCLOS tribunals include the status of vessels, in particular the requirements of nationality and immunities of ships and their crew. In addressing nationality issues, the decisions of tribunals can be seen to be generally aligned with the commercial realities of ship operations. UNCLOS tribunals have also clarified the immunities of vessels under Article 32 of UNCLOS and confirmed the immunities that apply under Articles 95 and 96 of UNCLOS. So far as concerns the exercise of navigational rights, tribunals have interpreted critical provisions, including Articles 93, 94, and 97, and have made broad statements of principle in addressing claims with respect to the balance of navigational rights with other States' rights and duties, which will probably be influential in future State practice. Tribunals have also provided useful guidance on the scope of lawful enforcement measures under UNCLOS, including assessing whether excessive force has been used, or whether actions are justifiable as an exercise of the right of hot pursuit. While the contributions of UNCLOS tribunals to aspects of navigation have undoubtedly been piecemeal, as it is dependent on the particular disputes referred to it, tribunals have on the whole been able to make a significant contribution to clarifying the scope of the right of navigation while taking account of other rights and interests.

8
Fisheries

I. Introduction

Fisheries disputes have long presented challenges to inter-State relationships and have led to violent altercations as well as litigation before international courts.[1] Notably, in the 1950s, Iceland's efforts to enforce an exclusive fisheries zone beyond its territorial sea and in its adjacent waters led to confrontations between British fishing trawlers and Icelandic gunboats, prompting the intervention of the British Royal Navy.[2] This clash ultimately resulted in the *Fisheries Jurisdiction* (*Icelandic Fisheries*) case at the International Court of Justice (ICJ) between the United Kingdom and Iceland.[3] While some of these disputes were resolved with the recognition of the exclusive economic zone (EEZ),[4] the 'turbot war' between Canadian authorities and Spanish fishing vessels[5] prompted not only the conclusion of the Fish Stocks Agreement,[6] but also another case being referred to the ICJ.[7] Judicial engagement with fisheries issues has been largely driven by responses to claims concerning authority over maritime space,[8] as well as concerns about conservation and management.[9]

One of the greatest conservation issues in relation to the world's fisheries at present has been the increased incidence of illegal, unreported, and unregulated (IUU) fishing. The UN

[1] One early twentieth century case was *North Atlantic Coast Fisheries (United Kingdom v United States of America)* (Award of 7 September 1910) 11 UNRIAA 167, where the Tribunal recognised the obligations of the coastal State to protect and preserve its fisheries. See James Harrison and Elisa Morgera, 'Article 61' in Alexander Proelss (ed), *United Nations Convention on the Law of the Sea: A Commentary* (CH Beck, Hart, and Nomos 2017) (*Proelss Commentary*) 480, para 5.

[2] Richard Nelsson, 'Iceland v Britain: The Cod Wars Begin—Archive, September 1958' *The Guardian* (7 September 2018) https://www.theguardian.com/business/from-the-archive-blog/2018/sep/07/first-cod-war-iceland-britain-fish-1958.

[3] With a finding that recognised Iceland's preferential fishing rights. See *Fisheries Jurisdiction (United Kingdom v Iceland)* (Jurisdiction) [1973] ICJ Rep 3 (*Icelandic Fisheries*).

[4] For example, the 'cod war' occurred around the same time as the 'tuna war', which involved South American naval forces seizing US fishing vessels that did not have a license to fish within 200 miles of their coasts. James Kraska, *Maritime Power and the Law of the Sea: Expeditionary Operations in World Politics* (OUP 2011) 98.

[5] *Fisheries Jurisdiction (Spain v Canada)* (Jurisdiction) [1998] ICJ Rep 432 (*Spain v Canada*). See eg Allen L Springer, 'The Canadian Turbot War With Spain: Unilateral State Action in Defense of Environmental Interests' (1997) 6 J Env & Dev 26.

[6] See Michael Byers, 'Policing the High Seas: The Proliferation Security Initiative' (2004) 98 AJIL 526, 537–38.

[7] This case failed for lack of jurisdiction: *Spain v Canada* (n 5) paras 84, 87.

[8] Falling in this category are *Anglo-Norwegian Fisheries (United Kingdom v Norway)* (Judgment) [1951] ICJ Rep 116; *Icelandic Fisheries* (n 3); *Spain v Canada* (n 5); *South China Sea Arbitration (Philippines v China)* (Award of 12 July 2016) PCA Case No 2013-19 (*South China Sea*, Award); and *Chagos Marine Protected Area Arbitration (Mauritius v United Kingdom)* (Award of 18 March 2015) PCA Case No 2011-03 (*Chagos MPA*), in addition to fisheries claims raised in the context of maritime boundary delimitations.

[9] Cases in this category include *Southern Bluefin Tuna (New Zealand v Japan; Australia v Japan)* (Jurisdiction and Admissibility) (2000) 23 RIAA 1 (*Southern Bluefin Tuna*, Jurisdiction and Admissibility); *South China Sea*, Award (n 8); *M/V Virginia G (Panama/Guinea-Bissau)* (Judgment) ITLOS Reports 2014, 4 (*Virginia G*); and the art 292 prompt release cases. *Volga (Russia v Australia)* (Prompt Release, Judgment) ITLOS Reports 2002, 10 (*Volga*); *Camouco (Panama v France)* (Prompt Release, Judgment) ITLOS Reports 2000, 10 (*Camouco*); and *Monte Confurco (Seychelles v France)* (Prompt Release, Judgment) ITLOS Reports 2000, 86 (*Monte Confurco*) arguably fall into both categories.

General Assembly has characterised IUU fishing as: '[O]ne of the greatest threats to fish stocks and marine ecosystems and [it] continues to have serious and major implications for the conservation and management of ocean resources, as well as the food security and the economies of many States, particularly developing States.'[10] There are consequently diverse stakeholders in fisheries disputes, including the coastal and flag States as well as the fishing companies owning and operating the fishing vessels, communities and individuals dependent on the fishing industry for their livelihoods, and civil society groups concerned with conservation.

For fisheries disputes, any tribunal constituted under the United Nations Convention on the Law of the Sea (UNCLOS or Convention)[11] is especially confronted with a core tension from the time UNCLOS was drafted concerning increased coastal State rights over living marine resources and ongoing interests of flag States with vessels seeking to fish with as few restrictions as possible throughout the oceans. With the recognition of the coastal State's sovereign rights over the EEZ, including for the conservation and management of living marine resources, the Convention also builds in protection of these coastal State rights as well as safeguards for flag States. The protection of coastal States' interests in the EEZ is demonstrated in the broad insulation of coastal State decision-making from third party review.[12] Flag State interests are shielded to some extent through restrictions on law enforcement and the mechanism for the prompt release of vessels upon payment of a reasonable bond.[13] Balancing these competing perspectives has inevitably coloured judicial decision-making in fisheries disputes under UNCLOS.

This chapter assesses the judicial decisions under UNCLOS that concern fisheries. First, the discussion reflects on challenges to traditional fishing rights, which also encapsulates historic rights claims to fisheries, across different maritime zones. Second, fishing in the territorial sea, predominantly an issue in the *Chagos Marine Protected Area* (*Chagos MPA*) arbitration,[14] is examined. Third, despite the limitations on subject matter jurisdiction over fisheries disputes in the EEZ,[15] tribunals have illuminated the meaning of some UNCLOS provisions pertaining to fishing rights and duties. The International Tribunal for the Law of the Sea (ITLOS) especially had opportunity to do so in the *Sub-Regional Fisheries Commission Advisory Opinion* (*SRFC Advisory Opinion*).[16] The aspect of fisheries management that has witnessed the most judicial assessment has been law enforcement, and particularly the prompt release of fishing vessels. The final two sections of the chapter consider the few cases generated to date that concern straddling stocks and highly migratory species, and high seas fisheries. As will be evident from this examination of the jurisprudence, the question of how to balance the interests of diverse stakeholders has been a core concern in

[10] 'Sustainable Fisheries, including through the 1995 Agreement for the Implementation of the Provisions of the United Nations Convention on the Law of the Sea of 10 December 1982 relating to the Conservation and Management of Straddling Fish Stocks and Highly Migratory Fish Stocks, and Related Instruments', UNGA Res 69/109 (9 December 2014) UN Doc A/RES/69/109, para 56.

[11] United Nations Convention on the Law of the Sea (adopted 10 December 1982, entered into force 16 November 1994) 1833 UNTS 397 (UNCLOS).

[12] See Natalie Klein, *Dispute Settlement in the UN Convention on the Law of the Sea* (CUP 2005) 176–88 (Klein, *Dispute Settlement*). See further ch 4(III)(A).

[13] See UNCLOS (n 11) arts 73 and 292.

[14] *Chagos MPA* (n 8).

[15] As discussed in ch 4(III)(A).

[16] *Request for Advisory Opinion Submitted by the Sub-Regional Fisheries Commission* (Advisory Opinion) ITLOS Reports 2015, 4 (*SRFC Advisory Opinion*).

judicial considerations of fisheries rights and responsibilities. In addition, the judges involved in making these decisions have further needed to interpret obligations to align with current practices and concerns associated with the conservation and management of living marine resources.

II. Traditional Fishing

Consideration of traditional fishing rights in international litigation may be traced back to the *Bering Fur Seal Arbitration*.[17] In that case, the Tribunal recognised the need to conserve and manage marine mammals on the high seas and further accounted for the long-standing aboriginal practices in setting out regulations for pelagic sealing.[18] Other cases that have focused on traditional fishing rights include the *Eritrea/Yemen* arbitration,[19] the *South China Sea* arbitration,[20] and maritime boundary delimitation cases where historic fishing claims have been argued to be a relevant circumstance necessitating adjustment of the boundary.[21]

The terms 'traditional' and 'artisanal' fishing have been used interchangeably,[22] with the main emphasis on distinguishing this type of fishing from large-scale commercial or industrial fishing.[23] The ICJ recognised the importance of traditional fishing rights at the time of the UNCLOS negotiations in upholding Iceland's preferential fishing rights beyond its territorial sea in the *Icelandic Fisheries* case.[24]

Traditional fishing rights are only explicitly referenced in UNCLOS in Article 51(1), which requires archipelagic States to recognise traditional fishing rights 'of the immediately adjacent neighbouring States in certain areas falling within archipelagic waters'.[25] There is also recognition of foreign nationals who have habitually fished in an EEZ in determining access to a coastal State's EEZ pursuant to Article 62(3). The extent such rights are recognised is dependent on coastal State consent and discretion. Although no further protection of traditional fishing rights is included within UNCLOS, the *Eritrea/Yemen* arbitral tribunal determined the traditional fishing rights in that case were enforceable wherever they exist and were not qualified by the existence of UNCLOS maritime zones.[26]

[17] *Rights of Jurisdiction of United States in the Bering's Sea and the Preservation of Fur Seals (United Kingdom v United States)* (Award) (1893) 28 RIAA 263, 271. See Ryan North, 'Traditional Fishing Rights in International Law: The South China Sea Arbitration' (2017) 36 University of Tasmania Law Review 101, 102.

[18] See Alexander Proelss, 'Marine Mammals' in Anne Peters (ed), *Max Planck Encyclopedia of Public International Law* (OUP July 2007) paras 5–8.

[19] *Sovereignty and Maritime Delimitation in the Red Sea (Eritrea/Yemen)* (Award of the Arbitral Tribunal in the First Stage of 3 October 1996: Territorial Sovereignty and Scope of the Dispute) PCA Case No 1996-04 (*Eritrea/Yemen*, First Stage); *Sovereignty and Maritime Delimitation in the Red Sea (Eritrea/Yemen)* (Award of the Arbitral Tribunal in the Second Stage of 17 December 1999: Maritime Delimitation) PCA Case No 1996-04 (*Eritrea/Yemen*, Second Stage).

[20] *South China Sea*, Award (n 8).

[21] This case law is also considered in ch 6(IV).

[22] The Food and Agriculture Organization of the United Nations (FAO) defines artisanal fishing as 'traditional fisheries involving fishing households (as opposed to commercial companies) using relatively small amount of capital and energy, relatively small fishing vessels (if any), making short fishing trips, close to shore, mainly for local consumption'. FAO, 'FAO Term Portal' (2021) http://www.fao.org/faoterm/en/.

[23] See *Eritrea/Yemen*, Second Stage (n 19) para 106. See also *South China Sea*, Award (n 8) para 809.

[24] *Icelandic Fisheries* (n 3) 28.

[25] UNCLOS (n 11) art 51(1).

[26] *Eritrea/Yemen*, Second Stage (n 19) para 109; North (n 17) 103.

Traditional fishing rights may be grounded within historic rights and such rights were considered in this context in the *South China Sea* arbitration. The Philippines alleged that China had interfered with the exercise of traditional fishing rights in waters within 12 NM of Scarborough Shoal.[27] The *South China Sea* Tribunal contemplated what might be meant by the terms 'traditional' or 'artisanal' fishing, noting that there was no settled definition in international law.[28] Yet the Tribunal still considered that '[i]ts distinguishing characteristic will always be that, in contrast with industrial fishing, artisanal fishing will be simple and carried out on a small scale, using fishing methods that largely approximate those that have historically been used in the region'.[29] In this respect, the Tribunal does not initially appear to allow for some improvement in fishing and navigation techniques to the extent contemplated in the *Eritrea/Yemen* arbitration.[30] The *South China Sea* Tribunal also observed that it did not have to engage with how traditional fishing practices may change over time based on technological advances.[31] For artisanal fishing to be 'traditional', there had to be a 'longstanding practice of the community', exercised 'continuously through the ages'.[32]

To support the existence of traditional fishing rights in the face of coastal State claims to exclusivity in its maritime zones, the Philippines relied on Article 2(3) of UNCLOS, which, the Philippines argued, 'impose[s] substantive obligations informed by general rules of international law, including the preservation of pre-existing rights'.[33] The Tribunal agreed that traditional fishing rights within the territorial sea were not altered with the adoption of UNCLOS, and the vested rights of foreign nationals could be preserved under Article 2(3).[34] As is addressed in detail in Chapter 4,[35] the Tribunal's conclusion appears to stand in contrast to the *Chagos MPA*, which considered that 'other rules' in Article 2(3) encompassed only 'general rules' of international law. The *Chagos MPA* Tribunal's findings are also discussed further below.

The *South China Sea* Tribunal acknowledged that the coastal State had authority to regulate traditional fishing, particularly for conservation and for protection of the marine environment.[36] Such reasonable regulation may extend to moderating the scale and technological development that would be permissible within the scope of 'traditional' fishing.[37] The difficulty in the *South China Sea* arbitration was the lack of information as to which State was the relevant coastal State for the purposes of decision-making on this regulation in the territorial sea around Scarborough Shoal. The Tribunal nonetheless considered that China's decisions in completely excluding the Filipino fishing vessels from these waters while allowing

[27] *South China Sea*, Award (n 8) para 758. These traditional fishing rights existed even in the absence of any definitive finding as to the relevant sovereign over Scarborough Shoal: see paras 759, 793.

[28] ibid para 797 (referring to a study within the World Trade Organization on the different usages and meanings accorded to the term).

[29] ibid.

[30] *Eritrea/Yemen*, Second Stage (n 8) para 106, referenced in *South China Sea*, Award (n 8) para 796.

[31] *South China Sea*, Award (n 8) para 806.

[32] ibid para 798, citing *Eritrea/Yemen*, Second Stage (n 8) para 104.

[33] *South China Sea*, Award (n 8) para 774.

[34] ibid para 808. Although it is unclear who are the 'foreign' nationals without knowing which State has sovereignty over Scarborough Shoal. The Tribunal further observed the protection of traditional fishing rights in relation to archipelagic waters under art 51(1) of UNCLOS: see para 804. This provision would seem inapposite given that the Tribunal rejected the notion of offshore archipelagos applying on the facts, as China had maintained: see para 573.

[35] See ch 4(V)(B).

[36] *South China Sea*, Award (n 8) para 809. See also Richard Barnes, 'Article 2' in *Proelss Commentary* (n 1) 27, para 22.

[37] *South China Sea*, Award (n 8) para 809.

Chinese fishing vessels to continue fishing was discriminatory.[38] This determination begs the question of whether such decision would have still been impermissibly discriminatory if it was clear that China was the coastal State with sovereignty over the waters and its decision was informed by a need to reduce the extent of fishing in its territorial sea for conservation and management purposes. The Tribunal's decision suggests that Article 2(3) would arguably still require the coastal State to allow traditional fishing by foreign nationals even if at the expense of its own nationals or food security.

Nonetheless, China's actions were not considered to be 'compatible with the respect due under international law to the traditional fishing rights of Filipino fishermen'.[39] As this respect is required irrespective of which State has sovereignty over Scarborough Shoal, it could be concluded that respect for traditional fishing rights within a territorial sea applies *erga omnes*. This interpretation aligns with the wording of Article 2(3), which refers to 'sovereignty over the territorial sea' in contrast to the 'sovereignty of a coastal State' used in Article 2(1).

More controversial has been the status of traditional fishing rights in another State's EEZ, with some commentators considering that such rights ceased to exist beyond what was indicated in UNCLOS.[40] Nonetheless, States have recognised such rights in their practice.[41] In the *South China Sea* arbitration, the Tribunal decided that traditional fishing rights were extinguished with the establishment of the EEZ in maritime areas beyond 12 NM from a State's coast apart from the consideration to be afforded to 'habitual' fishing in coastal State decision-making over allocation of any fishing rights in Article 62(3).[42] The Tribunal's reasoning on the incompatibility of historic rights with sovereign rights in the EEZ is discussed further in Chapter 5.[43] The decision relied on an assessment of UNCLOS negotiations,[44] and the Tribunal further considered its position as consistent with the *Gulf of Maine*.[45] The latter holding was distinguished from the finding in *Eritrea/Yemen* as to the existence of traditional fishing rights throughout the maritime zones of those States on the basis that the Tribunal in *Eritrea/Yemen* was not required to apply only UNCLOS in reaching its conclusions.[46] The Tribunal also distinguished the *Chagos MPA* arbitration and *Icelandic*

[38] ibid para 812.

[39] ibid.

[40] Leonardo Bernard, 'The Effect of Historic Fishing Rights In Maritime Boundaries Delimitation' in Harry N Scheiber and Moon Sang Kwon (eds), *Securing the Ocean for the Next Generation* (Law of the Sea Institute, UC Berkeley–Korea Institute of Ocean Science and Technology Conference, Seoul, May 2012) 2; Harrison and Morgera (n 1) 493, para 12.

[41] Examples of State practice recognising the existence of traditional fishing rights are reviewed in Polite Dyspriani, *Traditional Fishing Rights: Analysis of State Practice* (Division for Ocean Affairs and the Law of the Sea, Office of Legal Affairs, UN 2011).

[42] *South China Sea*, Award (n 8) para 804. North has argued that it is questionable that traditional fishing rights of foreign nationals should be viewed as permissible in areas of sovereignty close to land compared to an area of sovereign rights further from shore: see North (n 17) 106. Although it is understandable to make this distinction from a policy perspective, it would seem that the permissible legal derogations in relation to each maritime zone are distinct and that with respect to fishing, there is more allowance for an exception to sovereignty by virtue of art 2(3) than there is in relation to sovereign rights over living marine resources.

[43] See ch 5(IV)(D)(3).

[44] *South China Sea*, Award (n 8) paras 248–52. See also Bernard (n 40) 7–8.

[45] *Delimitation of the Maritime Boundary in the Gulf of Maine Area (Canada v United States)* (Merits) [1984] ICJ Rep 246, para 235; *South China Sea*, Award (n 8) paras 256–57.

[46] *South China Sea*, Award (n 8) para 803. Notably, the *Eritrea/Yemen* Tribunal applied an Islamic law concept as the basis for the existence and recognition of the traditional fishing rights in the relevant waters: *Eritrea/Yemen*, First Stage (n 19) paras 129–130. In addition, the *Eritrea/Yemen* Tribunal was expressly allowed to look to historic title as a source of law.

Fisheries cases.[47] The *South China Sea* decision had the effect of curtailing Chinese claims to fishing rights throughout the area enclosed within its nine-dash-line, even when pre-existing fishing rights in EEZ areas had been acknowledged in the context of bilateral fisheries agreements in the region prior to the arbitration.[48] The Tribunal acknowledged that such recognition was permissible in the context of bilateral or regional agreements or in coastal State legislation,[49] presumably as an exercise of the coastal State's sovereign rights.

Historic fishing rights have also been discussed in the context of maritime boundary delimitation cases,[50] and particularly in relation to whether those rights are to be recognised for the purpose of adjusting the maritime boundary in one State's favour or creating a right of access to maritime spaces allocated to one State through a delimitation. These claims are more commonly asserted in relation to specific areas or specific fish or marine resources.[51] For example, Barbados submitted in its dispute with Trinidad and Tobago (*Barbados v Trinidad and Tobago*) that Barbadian fisherfolk had been fishing off Tobago for flying fish for centuries and as such an adjustment in the equidistance line was required.[52] The Tribunal did not accept that Barbados had established its claims in this regard,[53] and stated:

> Determining an international maritime boundary between two States on the basis of traditional fishing on the high seas by nationals of one of those States is altogether exceptional. Support for such a principle in customary and conventional international law is largely lacking.[54]

Unlike the *South China Sea* Tribunal, it is nonetheless notable that the Tribunal in *Barbados v Trinidad and Tobago* did not deny the possible existence of traditional fishing rights in the EEZ in the absence of a formal agreement.[55]

The exceptional nature of traditional fishing rights places a high burden on any State wishing to have such a claim accepted. Judges have evinced greater sympathy for such claims when these practices occur in the territorial sea. This increased sympathy may be explicable on the basis that the coastal State has long recognised sovereignty, and potentially greater physical control over the territorial sea, so exceptions are more easily discernible and manageable. Within the EEZ, the (relatively) more recent assertion of coastal State rights may have been more vulnerable to opposing claims from distant-water fishing States. Establishing the legal pre-eminence of the coastal State and its interests in response to these

[47] *Spain v Canada* was distinguished because it predated UNCLOS whereas the *Chagos MPA* arbitration (n 8) was viewed as a modification of the rights of the UK and Mauritius pursuant to art 311 of UNCLOS (n 1). *South China Sea*, Award (n 8) paras 258–260.

[48] See Huan-Sheng Tseng and Ching-Hsiewn Ou, 'The Evolution and Trend of the Traditional Fishing Rights' (2010) 53 Ocean & Coastal Manag 270, 276 (discussing a bilateral agreement between China and Viet Nam in which the transitional arrangements in effect were viewed as reflecting the historic fishing practices).

[49] *South China Sea*, Award (n 8) para 804(b). See also Yen Hoang Tran, 'The South China Sea Arbitral Award: Legal Implications for Fisheries Management and Cooperation in the South China Sea' (2017) 6 CILJ 87, 89.

[50] See further ch 6(III)(B). See also Bernard (n 40) 12–18.

[51] Bernard (n 40) 5.

[52] *Barbados v Trinidad and Tobago* (Award of the Arbitral Tribunal of 11 April 2006) PCA Case No 2004-02, paras 247–51.

[53] ibid para 265.

[54] ibid para 269.

[55] North (n 17) 104.

claims was hence essential. Supporting the central role of the coastal State in its decision-making over the management of the EEZ further aligns with this perspective.

III. Fishing in the Territorial Sea

As the coastal State has sovereignty over the territorial sea, it has exclusive rights to control and manage fishing activities within this zone. Any fishing activities by a foreign ship would constitute a violation of the right of innocent passage,[56] and be subject to the coastal State's enforcement jurisdiction by dint of its sovereignty. These aspects of UNCLOS have not yet been subject to judicial scrutiny.[57] However, the coastal State's sovereignty is to be 'exercised subject to [UNCLOS] and to other rules of international law'.[58] This latter reference may provide a basis for a State to argue that it has entitlements to fish within the territorial sea of another State (beyond any claim to traditional fishing).

This scenario arose in the *Chagos MPA* arbitration between Mauritius and the United Kingdom because of what the Tribunal termed as the 'Lancaster House Undertakings', which were given in September 1965.[59] The Lancaster House Undertakings, which recorded conditions on the agreement to detach the Chagos Islands, including that 'if the need for the [US defence] facilities on the islands disappeared the islands should be returned to Mauritius' and that the United Kingdom would ensure that fishing rights would remain available to Mauritius.[60]

In assessing the actions of the United Kingdom in declaring a Marine Protected Area (MPA) over the EEZ of the Chagos Archipelago, Mauritius argued that it was essential to consider the nature of the Lancaster House Undertakings, and whether they constituted legal obligations or mere political commitments. Mauritius considered that the undertakings given by the United Kingdom were intended to be legally binding and, moreover, that the United Kingdom was now estopped from claiming otherwise.[61] Moreover, Mauritius submitted that the undertaking in relation to fishing rights was to be broadly construed.[62] The United Kingdom, by contrast, characterised the Lancaster House Undertakings as important political commitments.[63] Even if a binding unilateral undertaking could be said to exist, the United Kingdom argued it was nonetheless entitled to revoke these commitments.

The Lancaster House Undertakings were viewed by the Tribunal as 'part of the *quid pro quo* through which Mauritian agreement to the detachment of the Chagos Archipelago from Mauritius was procured'.[64] These undertakings became binding as a matter of international law upon Mauritius' independence and were reaffirmed between the parties subsequent to

[56] UNCLOS (n 11) art 19(2)(i).

[57] Fishing in the territorial sea of Scarborough Shoal was addressed in the *South China Sea* arbitration in the context of historic fishing rights, which are addressed in the preceding section.

[58] UNCLOS (n 11) art 2(3).

[59] *Chagos MPA* (n 8) para 77.

[60] ibid para 77. See also the Secretary of State, Lord Taylor, Sir Hilton Poynton, Sir John Rennie, Mr PR Noakes, Mr J Stacpoole, Sir S Ramgoolam, Mr S Bissoondoyal, Mr JM Paturau, Mr AR Mohamed, 'Record of a Meeting held in Lancaster House at 2:30pm on Thursday 23rd September: Mauritius Defence Matters' (Final Record of the Lancaster House Meeting, London, 23 September 1965) (Lancaster House Undertakings) para 22(vi).

[61] *Chagos MPA* (n 8) para 397.

[62] ibid para 408.

[63] ibid para 399.

[64] ibid para 421. See further para 422.

independence.[65] After a close examination of the requirements of estoppel, the Tribunal further determined that the United Kingdom was estopped from denying the binding effect of the commitments relating to the return of the Archipelago, the preservation of benefits of mineral resources and fishing rights being available as far as practicable.[66] In relation to the fishing rights, the express words of the undertaking reflected that the United Kingdom had to 'ensure' that fishing rights 'would remain available' to Mauritius, but subject to 'the overarching defence needs of the United States and the United Kingdom's discretion in the routine management of the fishery'.[67]

Having determined the nature of the obligations the United Kingdom owed to Mauritius, the Tribunal was able to assess whether the declaration of the MPA infringed the rights of Mauritius as recognised within UNCLOS. As addressed in detail in Chapter 4 in relation to Article 2(3),[68] considerable attention was accorded to what was encompassed within the reference to sovereignty being subject 'to other rules of international law'. Did the Lancaster House Undertakings fall within these rules and limit the United Kingdom's action? The Tribunal closely examined the original formulation of Article 2(3) from its counterpart in the 1958 Territorial Sea Convention and discussions within the International Law Commission and at conference negotiations. The indication drawn by the majority of the Tribunal from these materials was that the interpretation of 'other rules of international law' was intended to reference general international law rather than specific bilateral commitments between States.[69] General international law required the United Kingdom to act in good faith in its relations with Mauritius with regard to the exercise of sovereignty over the territorial sea.[70] The failure by the United Kingdom to balance Mauritius's fishing rights as set out in the Lancaster House Undertakings with its interests showed a lack of good faith and constituted a violation of Article 2(3). Whether the violation of a fishing agreement that applies within the territorial sea would similarly be viewed as a lack of good faith and amount to a violation of Article 2(3) remains to be determined in the future.[71]

IV. Fishing in the Exclusive Economic Zone

The international legal recognition of the EEZ in Part V of UNCLOS was a significant achievement for coastal States, especially developing States seeking to assert more strongly their rights over natural resources. Article 56 sets out the sovereign rights of the coastal State in managing and conserving its living marine resources within its EEZ. Articles 61 to 68 detail the parameters of coastal State management of its fisheries, although—as will be discussed in this section—the precise scope of the rights and duties for State parties has needed elucidation. As highlighted at the outset of this chapter, IUU fishing has proven

65 ibid para 434.

66 ibid para 448.

67 ibid para 455.

68 See ch 4(V)(B); see also ch 5(IV)(B).

69 ibid para 516. Judges Kateka and Wolfrum dissented on this limitation to art 2(3) on their review of the International Law Commission's commentaries. See Chagos *MPA* (n 8) (Dissenting and Concurring Opinion of Judges Kateka and Wolfrum) para 94.

70 See further ch 4(V)(B).

71 The existence of a separate fishing agreement may indicate that it has its own dispute settlement provision and Section 1 of Part XV of UNCLOS (n 11) may be relevant in determining jurisdiction. See further ch 3(II)(B).

especially challenging for fisheries conservation and management.[72] The balance of rights, duties, and interests has been problematic not only in the conservation and management of living marine resources but also in law enforcement efforts in responding to diverse facets of IUU fishing. This section examines different aspects of fishing in the EEZ that have been discussed in UNCLOS dispute settlement proceedings: sovereign rights,[73] conservation and utilisation, due diligence, law enforcement, and prompt release.

While the EEZ regime in Part V of UNCLOS is quite detailed (compared to the high sea fisheries regime), judges have needed to consider closely the meaning and scope of diverse provisions. This exercise needs to account for the dynamics of a vast global fishing industry, which varies in scale and importance across different countries. Not only has the nature of the fishing industry changed since UNCLOS negotiations, but fishing techniques have also shifted and need to be taken into account in interpreting and applying UNCLOS in the present day. While it is apparent that there are diverse stakeholders in the fisheries industry, for governance purposes, the role of regional and other fisheries organisations may necessitate particular consideration. Given the vast competition for fish resources, both within the EEZ and on the high seas, judicial decisions that support sustainable conservation and management measures would seemingly be those that contribute most to the public order of the oceans and the peaceful resolution of disputes.

A. Sovereign Rights over Fishing in the EEZ

With the creation of the EEZ in UNCLOS, coastal States gained sovereign rights to conserve and manage the marine living resources located within this maritime zone under Article 56.[74] This general grant of authority provides a broad basis for coastal States to challenge the actions of other States and their vessels. In the *South China Sea* arbitration, the Philippines claimed that China had interfered with these sovereign rights through enacting and enforcing fisheries laws in an area that the Philippines claimed to be its EEZ, including through the prevention of fishing by Philippine fishing vessels around Mischief Reef and Second Thomas Shoal.[75] China did so on the basis that it considered that it was the relevant coastal State with sovereign rights in the maritime areas in question.[76] However, the Tribunal concluded that China did not have any historic rights or sovereign rights generated from any land features in the relevant areas,[77] and so it followed that the relevant areas were within the Philippines' EEZ. For China to restrict the Philippines from exploiting the living resources of the Philippines' own EEZ was, in the Tribunal's view, incompatible with 'the central objective motivating' the introduction of the EEZ and clearly fell outside the rights of other States as set out in Article 58 of UNCLOS.[78]

[72] ITLOS noted the wide use of the definition of IUU fishing from the International Plan of Action on IUU Fishing and the Food and Agriculture Organizations' Code of Conduct for Responsible Fisheries in binding international agreements as well as in the practice of regional organisations and in national legislation: *SRFC Advisory Opinion* (n 16) para 92. The Tribunal did not go so far as to suggest the definition reflected customary international law, however.

[73] This issue is also considered in more detail in ch 5(IV)(C).

[74] See ch 5(IV)(C).

[75] *South China Sea*, Award (n 8) para 686.

[76] ibid para 689.

[77] ibid para 694.

[78] ibid para 700.

The *South China Sea* Tribunal found as a factual matter that China had violated the Philippines' sovereign rights over the living resources in its EEZ in respect of a fishing moratorium promulgated in 2012 that threatened punitive measures and 'may have [had] a deterring effect on Filipino fishermen and their activities'.[79] The mere assertion of jurisdiction in this context was sufficient for a finding of violation of Article 56.[80] The Philippines failed to establish any further violation of Article 56, as it did not include evidence of actual interference with its fishing vessels in the waters around Mischief Reef or Second Thomas Shoal.[81] Moreover, another regulation that was said to apply within 12 NM of the Chinese island of Hainan could not be considered as breaching the Philippines' rights in the EEZ, because it was clearly applicable within China's territorial sea.[82]

Beyond interference with its own fishing vessels, the Philippines also argued that China had violated its rights in failing to prevent Chinese nationals and fishing vessels from exploiting marine living resources in the Philippines' EEZ.[83] The Philippines submitted that under Article 56, China had an 'obligation to take the measures necessary to prevent' Chinese nationals from exploiting resources in the Philippines' EEZ.[84] Further, the Philippines argued that the 'obligation to ensure', as set out in the *SRFC Advisory Opinion*, required China to 'deploy adequate means, to exercise best possible efforts, to do the utmost' to ensure compliance with the Philippines' laws and regulations and prevent unauthorised fishing activity by its nationals.[85] As discussed further below, the *South China Sea* Tribunal rightly did not read an 'obligation to ensure' into Article 56. Instead, the Tribunal assessed China's conduct against Article 58(3), which mandates that States show due regard for the rights and duties of the coastal State.[86]

The due regard requirement set out in Article 58(3) does not create a 'universal rule of conduct' but requires a contextual assessment.[87] To this end, the *Chagos MPA* Tribunal considered that:

> [T]he extent of the regard required by the Convention will depend upon the nature of the rights held by [one State], their importance, the extent of the anticipated impairment, the nature and importance of the activities contemplated by the [other State], and the availability of alternative approaches.[88]

The Tribunal further anticipated that this assessment would entail consultation among the States concerned.[89] Goodman considers that the appraisal required under Article

[79] ibid para 712.
[80] ibid.
[81] ibid para 714.
[82] ibid para 713.
[83] ibid para 717.
[84] ibid para 725.
[85] ibid paras 726–27.
[86] ibid para 744. See further nn 125–28 and accompanying text. The due diligence requirements for fisheries conservation and management are set out further below in this section.
[87] As discussed in ch 5(IV)(C).
[88] *Chagos MPA* (n 8) para 519.
[89] ibid. Scovazzi has observed that there is thus substantive and procedural elements involved in assessing due regard in light of the *Chagos Marine Protected Area* decision. Tullio Scovazzi, '"Due Regard" Obligations, with Particular Emphasis on Fisheries in the Exclusive Economic Zone' (2019) 34 IJMCL 56, 63.

58(3) is relevant to the regulation of living marine resources, given that coastal State rights over fisheries are part of the jurisdiction exercised more generally by coastal States in the EEZ.[90]

The range of fishing activities that may be subject to the sovereign rights of the coastal State was considered in *Virginia G*.[91] In that case, the question arose as to whether bunkering (the supply of fuel to fishing vessels)[92] constituted an exercise of the freedom of navigation under Article 58, as alleged by Panama,[93] or whether, as argued by Guinea-Bissau, it could be regulated by the coastal State as part of its sovereign rights over the exploitation, conservation, and management of the resources of the EEZ,[94] or for the purposes of protecting the marine environment.[95] Guinea-Bissau considered that an 'evolutionary interpretation' of the Convention was required.[96] Although bunkering is not explicitly addressed in UNCLOS, ITLOS considered that Article 56, when read together with Articles 61 to 68 on living resources,[97] provided an answer as to whether coastal States have competence to regulate the bunkering of foreign fishing vessels in the EEZs.[98] The Tribunal's views were thus limited to one sort of bunkering rather than considering bunkering of all vessels located in a foreign EEZ.[99]

To this end, the Tribunal observed that the reference to 'conserving and managing' in Article 56, when taken with Articles 61 and 62, 'go beyond conservation in the strict sense'.[100] The Tribunal took the position, as discussed further below, that the coastal State's sovereign rights extend to fishing-related activities, which included the bunkering of fishing vessels. The Tribunal did not, however, consider that bunkering of other vessels necessarily fell within the sovereign rights of the coastal State, 'unless otherwise determined in accordance with the Convention'.[101] The inclusion of bunkering of foreign fishing vessels within the coastal State's sovereign rights reflects a decision that further enhances coastal State rights in relation to fishing in its EEZ and will shore up coastal State regulatory and enforcement powers in the future.

[90] Camille Goodman, 'Rights, Obligations, Prohibitions: A Practical Guide to Understanding Judicial Decisions on Coastal State Jurisdiction over Living Resources in the Exclusive Economic Zone' (2018) 33 IJMCL 558, 564.

[91] *Virginia G* (n 9).

[92] Bunkering was described in the *Virginia G* as 'the term used in the shipping industry to describe the selling of fuel from specialised vessels, such as oil tankers, which supply fuel (such as light fuel, gas oil and marine diesel) to other vessels whilst at sea': ibid para 162.

[93] ibid paras 165–70.

[94] ibid para 188.

[95] ibid para 196.

[96] ibid para 187.

[97] Judge Nelson noted in a separate declaration that the Tribunal failed to refer to art 59 in dealing with a matter that was not explicitly referenced in UNCLOS (n 1). *Virginia G* (n 9) (Declaration of Judge Nelson) para 10. See also *Virginia G* (n 9) (Declaration of Judge ad hoc Treves) para 8.

[98] *Virginia G* (n 9) para 209.

[99] 'The coastal State, however, does not have such competence with regard to other bunkering activities, unless otherwise determined in accordance with the Convention': ibid para 223. The Tribunal leaves open the possibility that bunkering might be regulated by the coastal State as a means to protect its marine environment, which had been argued by Guinea-Bissau: see para 224.

[100] ibid para 212.

[101] ibid para 223.

B. Conservation and Utilisation of Living Resources in the EEZ

Consistent with all the rights granted to the coastal State within the EEZ, the coastal State must exercise its rights and perform its duties in relation to living marine resources with due regard to the rights and duties of other States.[102] Articles 61 and 62 are the key provisions of UNCLOS articulating coastal State rights and duties, as well as the concomitant rights and duties of other States, in respect of fisheries in the EEZ. They read as follows:

ARTICLE 61

CONSERVATION OF THE LIVING RESOURCES

1. The coastal State shall determine the allowable catch of the living resources in its exclusive economic zone.
2. The coastal State, taking into account the best scientific evidence available to it, shall ensure through proper conservation and management measures that the maintenance of the living resources in the exclusive economic zone is not endangered by over-exploitation. As appropriate, the coastal State and competent international organizations, whether subregional, regional or global, shall cooperate to this end.
3. Such measures shall also be designed to maintain or restore populations of harvested species at levels which can produce the maximum sustainable yield, as qualified by relevant environmental and economic factors, including the economic needs of coastal fishing communities and the special requirements of developing States, and taking into account fishing patterns, the interdependence of stocks and any generally recommended international minimum standards, whether subregional, regional or global.
4. In taking such measures the coastal State shall take into consideration the effects on species associated with or dependent upon harvested species with a view to maintaining or restoring populations of such associated or dependent species above levels at which their reproduction may become seriously threatened.
5. Available scientific information, catch and fishing effort statistics, and other data relevant to the conservation of fish stocks shall be contributed and exchanged on a regular basis through competent international organizations, whether subregional, regional or global, where appropriate and with participation by all States concerned, including States whose nationals are allowed to fish in the exclusive economic zone.[103]

ARTICLE 62

UTILIZATION OF THE LIVING RESOURCES

1. The coastal State shall promote the objective of optimum utilization of the living resources in the exclusive economic zone without prejudice to article 61.
2. The coastal State shall determine its capacity to harvest the living resources of the exclusive economic zone. Where the coastal State does not have the capacity to harvest the entire allowable catch, it shall, through agreements or other arrangements and pursuant to the terms, conditions, laws and regulations referred to in paragraph 4, give

[102] UNCLOS (n 11) art 56(2).
[103] ibid art 61.

other States access to the surplus of the allowable catch, having particular regard to the provisions of articles 69 and 70, especially in relation to the developing States mentioned therein.

3. In giving access to other States to its exclusive economic zone under this article, the coastal State shall take into account all relevant factors, including, inter alia, the significance of the living resources of the area to the economy of the coastal State concerned and its other national interests, the provisions of articles 69 and 70, the requirements of developing States in the subregion or region in harvesting part of the surplus and the need to minimize economic dislocation in States whose nationals have habitually fished in the zone or which have made substantial efforts in research and identification of stocks.
4. Nationals of other States fishing in the exclusive economic zone shall comply with the conservation measures and with the other terms and conditions established in the laws and regulations of the coastal State. These laws and regulations shall be consistent with this Convention and may relate, inter alia, to the following:
   (a) licensing of fishermen, fishing vessels and equipment, including payment of fees and other forms of remuneration, which, in the case of developing coastal States, may consist of adequate compensation in the field of financing, equipment and technology relating to the fishing industry;
   (b) determining the species which may be caught, and fixing quotas of catch, whether in relation to particular stocks or groups of stocks or catch per vessel over a period of time or to the catch by nationals of any State during a specified period;
   (c) regulating seasons and areas of fishing, the types, sizes and amount of gear, and the types, sizes and number of fishing vessels that may be used;
   (d) fixing the age and size of fish and other species that may be caught;
   (e) specifying information required of fishing vessels, including catch and effort statistics and vessel position reports;
   (f) requiring, under the authorization and control of the coastal State, the conduct of specified fisheries research programmes and regulating the conduct of such research, including the sampling of catches, disposition of samples and reporting of associated scientific data;
   (g) the placing of observers or trainees on board such vessels by the coastal State;
   (h) the landing of all or any part of the catch by such vessels in the ports of the coastal State;
   (i) terms and conditions relating to joint ventures or other cooperative arrangements;
   (j) requirements for the training of personnel and the transfer of fisheries technology, including enhancement of the coastal State's capability of undertaking fisheries research;
   (k) enforcement procedures.
5. Coastal States shall give due notice of conservation and management laws and regulations.[104]

(From United Nations Convention on the Law of the Sea, by United Nations Division for Ocean Affairs and the Law of the Sea, © 1982), United Nations. Reprinted with the permission of the United Nations.)

[104] ibid art 62.

These two provisions were assessed in a 1986 arbitration between Canada and France, *Filleting within the Gulf of St Lawrence*,[105] which primarily concerned the interpretation of a bilateral agreement between these States and whether French fishing vessels were allowed to undertake processing of fish catch in Canada's Gulf of St Lawrence, which is in the vicinity of the French islands of St Pierre and Miquelon. In that case, the Tribunal had regard to Article 61(3) in its effort to determine the extent of Canadian regulatory authority and how that authority was to be exercised in the context of the 1972 bilateral agreement.[106] A majority concluded that Canada was not permitted to regulate processing, but only harvesting and allocation of fish.

Burke has criticised the Tribunal's reading of Article 61(3) as too narrow in its approach to fishery management, including for limiting the language of Article 61(3) that refers to 'the economic needs of coastal fishing communities' as meaning 'the resource needs of such communities and not the whole of the other economic needs and interests'.[107] Burke considers that the fisheries management approach in the Convention is more holistic, consistent with the drafters' intentions, for considering more than the maximum sustainable yield, and also taking into account environmental, economic, and social factors.[108] The dissenting opinion of Professor Pharand supported this broader reading of Article 61, especially when considered in light of the range of management measures set out in Article 62.[109] Further, Burke has observed that the scope of coastal State authority was necessarily broad when considered in light of the sovereign rights enshrined in Article 56.[110] The broader reading of these UNCLOS provisions has been preferred in more recent jurisprudence, particularly in relation to the scope of coastal State authority as discussed below on bunkering.

Notably, ITLOS interpreted Articles 61 and 62 in the *SRFC Advisory Opinion*. This Advisory Opinion was requested via the Convention on the Determination of the Minimal Conditions for Access and Exploitation of Marine Resources within the Maritime Areas under Jurisdiction of the Member States of the Sub-Regional Fisheries Commission (MCA Convention),[111] which was also interpreted by the Tribunal. ITLOS was requested to consider questions that concerned, put simply, flag State obligations over vessels conducting IUU fishing in the EEZ of SRFC members; the responsibility of flag States and/or international organisations for those actions; and the rights and responsibilities of coastal States in relation to straddling stocks and highly migratory species.[112]

In relation to the question as to the obligations of flag States in relation to IUU fishing in the EEZ of third States,[113] the opinion was to be limited to non-member States of the SRFC

[105] *Dispute Concerning Filleting within the Gulf of St Lawrence between Canada and France*, (Decision of 17 July 1986) (1990) 82 ILR 591 (*Filleting Award*).

[106] ibid para 52.

[107] ibid. See William T Burke, 'Coastal State Fishery Regulation Under International Law: A Comment on the La Bretagne Award of July 17, 1986' (1988) 25 San Diego L Rev 495, 520.

[108] Burke (n 107) 519–21.

[109] *Filleting Award* (n 105) (Dissenting Opinion of Professor Pharand) para 17.

[110] Burke (n 107) 522–23.

[111] Convention on the Determination of the Minimal Conditions for Access and Exploitation of Marine Resources within the Maritime Areas under Jurisdiction of the Member States of the Sub-Regional Fisheries Commission (adopted 8 June 2012, entered into force 16 September 2012).

[112] *SRFC Advisory Opinion*, para 2 (setting out the questions in full).

[113] ibid para 85.

that had vessels fishing within the EEZs of the SRFC members.[114] Although such an observation ensures the opinion aligned with the scope of jurisdiction of ITLOS, it can readily be anticipated that the views expressed will be examined for general and broader application in addressing the duties and performance of flag States with respect to IUU fishing.[115] For example, the Tribunal recognised that flag State responsibilities in relation to IUU fishing are not specifically addressed in the Convention and it thus considered any determination was to be drawn from the general and specific obligations applying to flag States in UNCLOS both in relation to conservation and management of living marine resources generally and in the EEZ specifically.[116]

The *SRFC Advisory Opinion* largely confirms the legal schemata relating to the conservation and management of living resources set out in the Convention, particularly in Articles 55, 56, 61, and 62, as well as Article 73 addressing enforcement, without further elaboration on the precise content of those provisions.[117] From this schemata, the Tribunal affirms that a 'primary responsibility' is accorded to the coastal State for taking the necessary measures to prevent, deter and eliminate IUU fishing.[118] This primary responsibility accorded to the coastal State does not remove responsibility from other States, however.[119] Through its consideration of the law of State responsibility and international environmental law, the *SRFC Advisory Opinion* is credited with bringing a more integrated approach to ocean issues.[120]

As set out in the *SRFC Advisory Opinion*, the particular responsibilities of flag States in relation to IUU fishing in the EEZ are to be drawn from Articles 58(3) and 62(4), general obligations under Articles 91, 92, and 94,[121] as well as two provisions concerning the protection and preservation of the marine environment, Articles 192 and 193.[122] The Tribunal observed that flag State obligations are usually elaborated on in the context of fisheries access agreements as between flag States and coastal States,[123] which was the case in relation to the SRFC members.[124]

In considering the content of Article 62(4), ITLOS broadened out the reference therein to nationals fishing in the EEZ complying with coastal State measures, laws, and regulations to refer to a flag State ensuring that its nationals comply with coastal State measures, laws, and regulations.[125] Judge Paik queried whether this approach was necessary or whether the

[114] ibid para 89. The Tribunal also limited its views to the EEZ and not other maritime zones, such as the high seas.

[115] Harrison takes this view on the bases that interpretations of UNCLOS have relevance for State parties and in light of the wide participation of States in the proceedings. James Harrison, 'Significant International Environmental Law Cases: 2014–15' (2015) 27 JEL 541, 546. See also Michael A Becker, 'Request for an Advisory Opinion Submitted by the Sub-Regional Fisheries Commission (SRFC)' (2015) 109 AJIL 851, 856 ('Significant International Environmental Law Cases').

[116] *SRFC Advisory Opinion* (n 16) para 109.

[117] Despite invitations to go further in written statements. See R Rajesh Babu, 'State Responsibility for Illegal, Unreported and Unrelated Fishing and Sustainable Fisheries in the EEZ: Some Reflections on the ITLOS Advisory Opinion of 2015' (2015) 55 Indian J Intl L 239, 263–64.

[118] *SRFC Advisory Opinion* (n 16) para 106.

[119] ibid para 108.

[120] See Victor Alencar Mayer Feitosa Ventura, 'Tackling Illegal, Unregulated and Unreported Fishing: The ITLOS Advisory Opinion on Flag State Responsibility for IUU Fishing and the Principle of Due Diligence' (2015) 12 Revista de Direito Internacional 50, 63.

[121] Curiously, the Tribunal states that these general obligations apply 'in all maritime areas regulated by the Convention': *SRFC Advisory Opinion* (n 16) para 111. This assertion would seem to run counter to art 86.

[122] See further ch 9(II)(A).

[123] *SRFC Advisory Opinion* (n 16) para 112.

[124] See ibid para 114.

[125] ibid para 123. See also Harrison, 'Significant International Environmental Law Cases' (n 115) 547. A similar approach was taken in Joined Cases C-103/12 and C-165/12 *European Parliament and European Commission*

provision could instead be viewed as reflecting the prescriptive jurisdiction of the coastal State.[126] If that were the case, it would render the reference to the '[n]ationals of other States' otiose, given that the coastal State's fisheries laws and regulations can already apply to all nationals within its EEZ. The ITLOS interpretation is consistent with the fact that State parties are bound by the requirements of UNCLOS, and that private individuals are not necessarily bound.[127] ITLOS affirmed this approach in its assessment of the due regard requirement in Article 58(3).[128] Reading these provisions to establish flag State duties aligns with other instances in UNCLOS where the Convention requires States to take action to regulate the conduct of private individuals: so the obligation falls properly on the State to adopt and enforce the necessary laws to meet its international law duties.[129]

According to ITLOS in the *SRFC Advisory Opinion*, flag States must therefore ensure under Article 62(4) that their nationals comply with a coastal State's conservation measures and other laws and regulations when fishing in that coastal State's EEZ.[130] This obligation 'to ensure' encapsulates a due diligence standard,[131] which is discussed in more detail below. The Tribunal then read this obligation together with the core obligation to protect and preserve the marine environment in Article 192,[132] as well as the requirement in Article 58(3) that States are to show due regard to the rights of the coastal State and comply with the relevant and applicable laws and regulations of that State in the EEZ.[133] When taken together, the Tribunal concluded 'that flag States are obliged to take the necessary measures to ensure that their nationals and vessels flying their flag are not engaged in IUU fishing activities'.[134] The Tribunal's cumulative assessment of the various UNCLOS provisions facilitated a finding of a much deeper commitment than might have otherwise been apparent on a prima facie reading of Article 62(4).

The consequences of this perspective were revealed in the *South China Sea* arbitration. The *South China Sea* Tribunal noted that Article 62(4) imposed an obligation directly on private parties, requiring compliance with the laws and regulations of the coastal State.[135] In linking this direct obligation on private parties to the due regard requirement of Article 58(3), the Tribunal considered that the flag State is to take all necessary measures to ensure

v Council of the European Union [2015] OJ/C26/2, paras 62–65. See also Valentin Schatz, 'Fishing for Interpretation: The ITLOS Advisory Opinion on Flag State Responsibility for Illegal Fishing in the EEZ' (2016) 47 ODIL 327, 330.

[126] *SRFC Advisory Opinion* (n 16) (Separate Opinion of Judge Paik) para 15. See also Schatz (n 125) 330; Jianjun Gao, 'The ITLOS Advisory Opinion for the SRFC' (2015) 14 Chinese JIL 735, 750.

[127] But see *South China Sea*, Award (n 8) para 740 (taking the approach that private actors are directly bound).

[128] *SRFC Advisory Opinion* (n 16) para 129.

[129] Other examples include art 98, which requires States to have masters of their ships render assistance or rescue persons in distress, and arts 114 and 115, which regulate submarine cables and pipelines. A similar approach could potentially be anticipated in relation to the freedom of navigation given that it is a right that belongs to States but is also exercised by private, commercial operators.

[130] *SRFC Advisory Opinion* (n 16) para 123. But see Gao (n 126) 750 (arguing that a responsibility to ensure should not be inferred from UNCLOS provisions in light of other UNCLOS provisions mentioning this responsibility explicitly).

[131] *SRFC Advisory Opinion* (n 16) para 129.

[132] See ibid para 120.

[133] ibid para 124.

[134] ibid.

[135] *South China Sea*, Award (n 8) para 740.

compliance and to prevent IUU fishing by those vessels flying its flag.[136] The Tribunal concluded:

> Given the importance of fisheries to the entire concept of the [EEZ], the degree to which the Convention subordinates fishing within the [EEZ] to the control of the coastal State, and the obligations expressly placed on the nationals of other States by Article 62(4) of the Convention, the Tribunal considers that anything less than due diligence by a State in preventing its nationals from unlawfully fishing in the [EEZ] of another would fall short of the regard due pursuant to Article 58(3) of the Convention.[137]

The *South China Sea* Tribunal acknowledged that the due diligence requirements may be difficult to articulate in terms of the precise scope required and in establishing the relevant factual base because of the covert nature of IUU fishing.[138] However, the close involvement of Chinese government vessels in escorting, protecting, organising, and coordinating Chinese fishing vessels made it clear that China 'unequivocally breached' the due regard requirement under Article 58(3).[139]

The flag State responsibilities for fishing activities in the EEZ are layered into the core duties of flag States set out in Article 94. Article 94 refers to the requirement that every State 'effectively exercise its jurisdiction and control in administrative, technical and social matters over ships flying its flag'.[140] Article 94 has an inclusive list of measures 'to ensure safety at sea'.[141] Certainly one key focus of this provision was the navigational operations of a ship and the flag State responsibilities to ensure conformity with relevant standards as set forth in International Maritime Organization (IMO) treaties dealing with issues of seaworthiness, crew, collisions and other related matters.[142] In the *SRFC Advisory Opinion*, ITLOS, however, considered that the 'administrative' matters over which flag States must exercise effective jurisdiction and control include those for the conservation and management of marine living resources.[143] The reasoning for this approach was that the inclusive language used in Article 92(2), (3), and (5) allowed for a broader reading.

Judge Paik examined this issue in his separate opinion in the *SRFC Advisory Opinion*, arguing that flag State duties were more general and extended beyond issues of safety at sea and that they applied throughout the oceans because of the general nature of the provision.[144] Judge Paik would have applied a 'dynamic interpretation',[145] as he took the position that flag State jurisdiction and control 'have evolved to cope with new issues, reflecting the changing needs of society and the new demands of the time' and that account should be

[136] ibid para 743, relying on *SRFC Advisory Opinion* (n 16) para 129. Schatz (n 125) disputes the validity of this reasoning: see 331.

[137] *South China Sea*, Award (n 8) para 744.

[138] 'Often, unlawful fishing will be carried out covertly, far from any official presence, and it will be far from obvious what the flag State could realistically have done to prevent it': ibid para 754.

[139] ibid para 756.

[140] UNCLOS (n 11) art 94(1).

[141] ibid arts 94(2) and (3).

[142] Drawing on arts 5(1) and 10 of the 1958 High Seas Convention. See Douglas Guilfoyle, 'Article 94' in *Proelss Commentary* (n 1) 707, paras 3, 4.

[143] *SRFC Advisory Opinion* (n 16) para 119.

[144] *SRFC Advisory Opinion* (n 16) (Separate Opinion of Judge Paik) paras 8–10 (grounding this view on the earlier versions of art 94 from the High Seas Convention).

[145] Schatz (n 125) 332.

taken of the 'evolving, open-ended context of the duties of the flag State'.[146] This reasoning is understandable when considered against a background of international effort to devise better legal responses to IUU fishing and the central role of flag States in needing to exercise better control over their vessels.[147]

The Tribunal made several findings under Article 94 as regards flag State obligations in respect of fisheries in the *SRFC Advisory Opinion*. The Tribunal found that Articles 94(1) and (2) established an obligation to exercise effective jurisdiction and control over administrative matters, which would include the proper marking of a vessel.[148] Ensuring the proper marking and flagging of vessels has been an issue in fisheries management and facilitates the identification of vessels when located in waters outside the flag State's jurisdiction.[149] From Article 94(6), which requires a flag State to investigate and possibly remedy matters reflecting a failure to exercise effective jurisdiction and control, the Tribunal considered this responsibility would also arise in relation to coastal State reports of IUU fishing activities.[150] This duty of the flag State is not to prejudice the enforcement rights of the coastal State under Article 73, however.[151] In considering the Tribunal's elaboration of flag State responsibilities in relation to fisheries, Gavouneli has commented that it was 'a valid effort to regulate an area neglected by the letter of the Convention'.[152]

Beyond an allocation of responsibilities for fishing activities to both coastal and flag States, a question further arises as to the scope of those duties. Anticipating what is allowed for 'conservation' and 'management' in the EEZ necessitates an understanding of these terms. In the *Virginia G* case, the Tribunal observed that the contents of Articles 61 and 62 informed the use of both the terms 'conserving' and 'managing' in Article 56.[153] Moreover, the 'management' measures in Article 62(4) was an inclusive listing,[154] and elaboration of the actions allowed may be expected over time as technologies improve and fishing practices change.[155]

When determining what falls within the scope of coastal State authority for conserving and managing the living marine resources of the EEZ, 'it is apparent from the list in article 62, paragraph 4, of the Convention that for all activities that may be regulated by a coastal State there must be a direct connection to fishing'.[156] In requiring a 'direct connection', ITLOS set a contrary standard than the arbitral tribunal in *Filleting in the Gulf of St*

[146] *SRFC Advisory Opinion* (n 16) (Separate Opinion of Judge Paik) para 11.

[147] As reflected in FAO initiatives on flag State responsibility. Discussed in Natalie Klein, 'Strengthening Flag State Performance in Compliance and Enforcement' in Richard Caddell and Erik J Molenaar (eds), *Strengthening International Fisheries Law in an Era of Changing Oceans* (Hart Publishing 2019) 351. Against this interpretation see Schatz (n 125) 333. For discussion on flag State responsibilities under different international agreements see generally Günther Handl, 'Flag State Responsibility for Illegal, Unreported and Unregulated Fishing in Foreign EEZs' (2014) 44 Env Poly & L 158.

[148] *SRFC Advisory Opinion* (n 16) para 137.

[149] The standard for marking fishing vessels is set out in 1989 FAO Standard Specifications for the Marking and Identification of Fishing Vessels. See FAO, 'The Marking and Identification of Fishing Vessels' (2017) 4 http://www.fao.org/3/a-i7783e.pdf. See also FAO, 'Code of Conduct for Responsible Fisheries' (31 October 1995) FAO Res 4/95, art 8.2.3.

[150] *SRFC Advisory Opinion* (n 16) para 139.

[151] ibid.

[152] Maria Gavouneli, 'Request for an Advisory Opinion Submitted by the Sub-Regional Fisheries Commission (SRFC) (ITLOS)' (2015) 54 ILM 890, 891.

[153] Virginia G (n 9) paras 212, 213.

[154] ibid.

[155] The meaning of conservation and management was also discussed in relation to high seas fisheries in *Spain v Canada* (n 5). This case is discussed in section VI below.

[156] *Virginia G* (n 5) para 215.

Lawrence, which simply denied regulation 'of a different nature than those described'.[157] As noted above, the Tribunal in *Filleting in the Gulf of St Lawrence* would have limited coastal State authority under Article 62 purely to harvesting and allocation decisions.[158] Instead, ITLOS considered that a direct connection existed in relation to bunkering of fishing vessels because the activity enabled fishing vessels to stay at sea and continue their operations without interruption.[159] This approach was considered in line with various international agreements that reference 'fishing' and 'fishing-related' activities to include support vessels providing fuel and other provisions at sea,[160] as well as State practice subsequent to the adoption of the Convention.[161]

This decision of ITLOS in *Virginia G* resolved a question that had been left open in *M/V Saiga No 2*.[162] ITLOS has not to date determined whether the coastal State may regulate bunkering of vessels other than fishing vessels, although Judges Kelly and Attard suggested in their joint declaration in *Virginia G* that the coastal State would have such authority because of the environmental implications that arise from the activity.[163] In his declaration, Judge Gao described the clarification in relation to fisheries bunkering 'as breaking new ground in international case law'.[164] Judge Lucky, in his separate opinion, was critical of this act of 'judge-made' law,[165] but did not provide an alternative option to address advances in fishing practices that largely developed subsequent to the adoption of UNCLOS.[166]

Judge Paik's separate opinion was critical of the majority of the Tribunal for not considering in more detail the legal developments since the adoption of the Convention, particularly in light of the increased focus on flag State performance in international fisheries law over the previous two decades.[167] He did not agree with the majority's view that the core obligations were all to be found in UNCLOS. Judge Paik noted in particular that the 'prohibition of vessels of the flag State from fishing in the [EEZ] unless so authorised by the coastal State, proper marking of fishing vessels, and the imposition of adequate sanctions' are not found within UNCLOS provisions.[168] Judge Paik did acknowledge, however, that these requirements are to be found in other instruments adopted after UNCLOS that address flag

[157] *Filleting Award* (n 105) para 52. See further Ted L McDorman, 'French Fishing Rights in Canadian Waters: The 1986 La Bretagne Arbitration' (1989) 4 IJECL 52, 58–59 (criticising the decision as 'at odds with state practice, the intent of the negotiators of the LOS Convention and the interpretation placed on the LOS Convention provisions by knowledgeable commentators'); Burke (n 107) 505 ('The award does not merit emulation either for the process of legal analysis, for its approach to treaty interpretation or for its views about substantive law').

[158] McDorman (n 157) 59.

[159] *Virginia G* (n 5) para 215.

[160] ibid para 216. The Tribunal did not, however, mention whether both parties were also party to these treaties, consistent with an interpretation following art 31(3)(c) of the Vienna Convention on the Law of Treaties (adopted 23 May 1969, entered into force 27 January 1980) 1155 UNTS 331.

[161] *Virginia G* (n 5) para 217. The Tribunal explicitly referenced practice in western African States, as well as 'some other regions of the world' without protest in this regard: see para 218.

[162] *M/V Saiga (No 2) (Saint Vincent and the Grenadines v Guinea)* (Judgment) ITLOS Reports 1999, 10 (*Saiga (No 2)*, Judgment). See Klein, *Dispute Settlement* (n 12) 137–38.

[163] *Virginia G* (n 5) (Joint Declaration of Judges Kelly and Attard). They relied on UNCLOS (n 1) arts 56(1)(b)(iii), 211(5) and 220(3), (5), and (6).

[164] *Virginia G* (n 5) (Declaration of Judge Gao) para 12.

[165] *Virginia G* (n 5) (Separate Opinion of Judge Lucky) para 27.

[166] *Virginia G* (n 5) (Declaration of Judge Gao) para 5. Judge Ndiaye provides information on when various States adopted legislation on bunkering, noting a spread both pre-UNCLOS, prior to its entry into force and subsequent to then. The majority of this legislation was adopted after UNCLOS was concluded. See *Virginia G* (n 5) (Dissenting Opinion of Judge Ndiaye) para 227.

[167] *SRFC Advisory Opinion* (n 16) (Separate Opinion of Judge Paik) para 22.

[168] ibid para 21.

State performance. He considered that these could be counted as part of flag State duties under UNCLOS because of the 'rule of reference' in Article 94(5), which permits inclusion of 'generally accepted international regulations, standards or practice'.[169] Judge Paik would have further added to these measures: establishment and maintenance of a national record of fishing vessels, as well as monitoring, control, and surveillance of the flag State's fishing vessels and their operations.[170]

The obligations imposed on States in relation to IUU fishing extend to a duty to cooperate, which is again not specified in the Convention but is characterised by ITLOS in the *SRFC Advisory Opinion* as a fundamental principle under Part XII of UNCLOS and general international law.[171] There is no further rationale or explanation as to the bases for extending this duty to efforts to combat IUU fishing or to improve flag State performance. While the sentiment is laudable, it remains to be seen in contentious proceedings whether there is a duty to cooperate in relation to fisheries that is distinct to a duty to cooperate in the protection and preservation of the marine environment,[172] or whether the factual predicate for claims of violating Articles 56 or 58(3) would automatically entail a violation of the duty to cooperate as well. While a failure to cooperate would suggest a failure to show due regard, would a failure to show due regard necessarily mean that there has also been a failure to cooperate? If the answer is yes, the obligation to cooperate from general international law may not add anything to the substantive obligations that already exist under UNCLOS.

C. Due Diligence Standard

Due diligence has been described as 'part of the framework for accountability in international law, in which it plays an important role in establishing standards of conduct, while preserving flexibility and autonomy for sovereign States in the implementation of their international obligations'.[173] Due diligence obligations in UNCLOS serve the purpose of ensuring that State parties take the necessary steps to implement their obligations vis-à-vis the actions of private actors who are within the State's jurisdiction. To meet a due diligence standard, a State must prescribe necessary laws and regulations, as well as seek to enforce those requirements.[174] This standard has been assessed in some cases arising under UNCLOS in relation to the conservation and management of living marine resources, as well as in relation to the protection and preservation of the marine environment.[175]

The 'responsibility to ensure' was aligned in the *SRFC Advisory Opinion* with an obligation of conduct and of due diligence, as had been discussed in the *Seabed Advisory Opinion*.[176] In the context of flag States responding to IUU fishing in the EEZ of another

[169] He also considered the rules of reference located within Part XII of the Convention, addressing protection and preservation of the marine environment, further justified this approach: ibid para 24.

[170] ibid para 29.

[171] *SRFC Advisory Opinion* (n 16) para 140.

[172] The parameters of the duty to cooperate for the protection and preservation of the marine environment are discussed in ch 9(III).

[173] Goodman (n 90) 567–68.

[174] For further discussion on due diligence requirements see ch 9(VII).

[175] See further ch 9(VII).

[176] *Responsibilities and Obligations of States with Respect to Activities in the Area* (Advisory Opinion) ITLOS Reports 2011, 10 (*Seabed Advisory Opinion*). See *SRFC Advisory Opinion* (n 16) para 125.

State, the requirement is for them to '"to deploy adequate means, to exercise best possible efforts, to do the utmost" to prevent IUU fishing by ships flying its flag'.[177] Flag States are thus required to take the necessary measures to ensure compliance of their vessels with the coastal State's laws and regulations applying in its EEZ,[178] or otherwise to prohibit their vessels from fishing in the coastal State's EEZ unless authorised to do so.[179] From Articles 192 and 193, the Tribunal considered that there was a further obligation on flag States to ensure that their vessels complied with the protection and preservation measures of the coastal States.[180] In taking these steps, it would not be enough for a flag State to implement laws and regulations but steps would be required to enforce those laws and to impose sanctions to deter offenders and prevent them from benefitting from their IUU fishing activities.[181] Whether there is an isolated act or a repeated pattern of offences does not matter, because the focus must be on whether the flag State has taken all necessary and appropriate measures required to meet its due diligence obligations.[182]

To determine if China had violated its obligations to protect and preserve the marine environment in the conservation and management of living marine resources, the *South China Sea* Tribunal endorsed the due diligence standard that had been applied by the ICJ and ITLOS.[183] In assessing China's responsibility, the *South China Sea* Tribunal determined on the facts that China was aware of the illegal fishing conduct.[184] Moreover, the Tribunal concluded that there was 'no evidence in the record that would indicate that China has taken any steps to enforce those rules and measures against fishermen engaged in poaching of endangered species'.[185] Requiring enforcement of laws to ensure compliance by a State's nationals to meet the due diligence standard was consistent with the approach of the ICJ in the *Pulp Mills* case.[186] Instead, the Tribunal found that China 'must have known of, and deliberately tolerated, and protected the harmful acts' in relation to harvesting of endangered species and to using the propeller chopping method.[187]

French has observed that the *South China Sea* Tribunal reached different conclusions in relation to catching sea turtles and giant clams as opposed to the use of cyanide and explosives for fishing;[188] for the former, the Tribunal noted there was no evidence to show China had sought to enforce its laws, whereas for the latter, there was no evidence that China failed

[177] *SRFC Advisory Opinion* (n 16) para 129, citing *Seabed Advisory Opinion* (n 176).

[178] Consistent with UNCLOS (n 1) art 58(3) and art 62(4). *SRFC Advisory Opinion* (n 16) para 134.

[179] *SRFC Advisory Opinion* (n 16) para 135.

[180] ibid para 136.

[181] ibid para 138.

[182] ibid para 150.

[183] *South China Sea*, Award (n 9) para 944, noting views in the *Pulp Mills on the River Uruguay (Argentina v Uruguay)* (Merits) [2010] ICJ Rep 14 (*Pulp Mills*, Merits) decision and the advisory opinions of ITLOS and the Seabed Disputes Chamber in *SRFC Advisory Opinion* (n 16) and *Seabed Advisory Opinion* (n 176), respectively.

[184] *South China Sea*, Award (n 9) para 962.

[185] ibid para 963. But see Chinese Society of International Law, 'The South China Sea Arbitration Awards: A Critical Study' (2018) 17 Chinese JIL 207, paras 793–802. However, it does not appear that this information about China's efforts was available to the Tribunal at the time of the arbitration.

[186] 'It is an obligation which entails not only the adoption of rules and measures, but also a certain high level of vigilance in their enforcement and the exercise of administrative control applicable to public and private operators, such as monitoring of activities undertaken by such operators, to safeguard the rights of other [parties]': *Pulp Mills*, Merits (n 183) para 197. See also *Seabed Advisory Opinion* (n 176) para 218.

[187] *South China Sea*, Award (n 9) paras 964–66.

[188] Duncan French, 'In the Matter of the South China Sea Arbitration: Republic of Philippines v People's Republic of China, Arbitral Tribunal Constituted under Annex VII to the 1982 United Nations Law of the Sea Convention, Case No. 2013-19, Award of 12 July 2016' (2017) 19 Env L Rev 48, 54.

to enforce its laws.[189] The Tribunal therefore made no finding as to China's international responsibility in relation to its fishers' use of cyanide or dynamite but held that it had violated UNCLOS in relation to the harvesting of clams. The difference appears quite subtle, but perhaps was ultimately fortified by the facts indicating active Chinese support for the harvesting of endangered species.[190]

D. Law Enforcement under Article 73

The coastal State has authority to enforce its laws and regulations relating to the exploitation, conservation, and management of living marine resources in the EEZ by virtue of Article 73 of UNCLOS.[191] This provision has been the subject of judicial proceedings as the basis for claims under Article 292 relating to the prompt release of vessels upon payment of a reasonable bond and as the basis for substantive claims as to the correct interpretation or application of the Convention between State parties.[192]

The *Virginia G* dispute involved allegations of violations of each of the paragraphs of Article 73, which provides in full:

> 1. The coastal State may, in the exercise of its sovereign rights to explore, exploit, conserve and manage the living resources in the exclusive economic zone, take such measures, including boarding, inspection, arrest and judicial proceedings, as may be necessary to ensure compliance with the laws and regulations adopted by it in conformity with this Convention.
> 2. Arrested vessels and their crews shall be promptly released upon the posting of reasonable bond or other security.
> 3. Coastal State penalties for violations of fisheries laws and regulations in the exclusive economic zone may not include imprisonment, in the absence of agreements to the contrary by the States concerned, or any other form of corporal punishment.
> 4. In cases of arrest or detention of foreign vessels the coastal State shall promptly notify the flag State, through appropriate channels, of the action taken and of any penalties subsequently imposed.[193]

In *Virginia G*, Panama instituted proceedings against Guinea-Bissau challenging its arrest and detention of the M/V Virginia G, a bunkering vessel that had been supplying fuel to fishing vessels in the EEZ of Guinea-Bissau. In particular, Panama challenged the confiscation of the Virginia G as a sanction for violating Guinea-Bissau's laws. Noting that a coastal State is permitted under Article 73(1) to take measures 'as may be necessary to ensure compliance with the laws and regulations adopted by it in conformity with this Convention', the

[189] *South China Sea*, Award (n 9) para 975. In the context of this submission, the Tribunal referenced a possible violation of art 194(2) in addition to arts 194(5) and 192, but no further discussion of the interpretation or application of art 194(2) was provided in this context in the *South China Sea* award. See further French (n 188) 54.

[190] *South China Sea*, Award (n 9) para 755.

[191] Law enforcement beyond art 73, especially as assessed in *Arctic Sunrise (Netherlands v Russia)* (Award on the Merits of 14 August 2015) PCA Case No 2014-02 (*Arctic Sunrise*, Merits), is discussed in ch 7(IV)(A).

[192] Questions on the amount of force that is permissible in the context of law enforcement operations have also been raised and are addressed in ch 7(IV)(B).

[193] UNCLOS (n 1) art 73.

Tribunal confirmed that it was competent to establish: (a) whether the relevant legislation is in conformity with the Convention; and (b) whether the measures taken in implementing the legislation are necessary.[194] The Tribunal thus confirmed that Article 73(1) implicitly covers both legislative and enforcement jurisdiction.

In his separate opinion, which concerned the interpretation of Article 73(1), Judge Paik underlined three questions: 'first, whether the laws and regulations of the coastal State are "in conformity with the Convention"; second, whether an enforcement measure taken by the coastal State is to "ensure compliance" with them; and third, whether the enforcement measure is "necessary" for that purpose'.[195] He noted that a negative answer to any of these questions would amount to a violation of Article 73(1).[196] The Tribunal concluded in the *Virginia G* that Guinea-Bissau was in violation of Article 73(1) because the confiscation of the vessel was not accepted as 'necessary' to ensure compliance.

However, in a Joint Dissenting Opinion, judges from developing countries observed how difficult it may be for developing States to detect bunkering violations in their EEZ.[197] They emphasised that a margin of appreciation was necessary in assessing a State's implementation of its international obligations, including in the decisions of the national courts.[198] In this regard, they commented '[i]t is in no way the task of the Tribunal to take the place of the competent national authorities but rather to review the decisions they delivered in the exercise of their power of appreciation'.[199] Their emphasis was on supporting the deterrence effect of Guinea-Bissau's decision.[200] In their dissenting opinions, Judges Ndiaye and Jesus similarly underlined the challenges presented to coastal States in relation to IUU fishing in their respective dissenting opinions.[201] Likewise, in the *Camouco* prompt release case, Judge Wolfrum had advocated for a margin of appreciation in respect of the coastal State's competence to enforce its fisheries law.[202] Judge ad hoc Sérvulo Correia commended this approach in relation to Article 73(1) in his dissenting opinion in the *Virginia G*.[203]

The majority of the Tribunal in *Virginia G* were concerned about whether the confiscation of the vessel was necessary, however. The Tribunal noted that Article 73(1) does not provide explicitly for the confiscation of fishing vessels but that such measures were taken in practice by State parties,[204] and this practice had to be considered in the interpretation of

[194] *Virginia G* (n 9) paras 255–56.

[195] *Virginia G* (n 9) (Separate Opinion of Judge Paik) para 5.

[196] ibid.

[197] *Virginia G* (n 9) (Dissenting Opinion of Vice-President Hoffman and Judges Marotta Rangel, Chandreskhara Rao, Kateka, Gao, and Bouguetaia) para 60. See also *Virginia G* (n 9) (Dissenting Opinion of Judge Ndiaye) para 206 (referring to developing States implementing stricter controls over navigation to regulate access and transit of foreign fishing vessels).

[198] *Virginia G* (n 9) (Dissenting Opinion of Vice-President Hoffman and Judges Marotta Rangel, Chandreskhara Rao, Kateka, Gao, and Bouguetaia) para 51. They considered a measure was unnecessary only if 'there was a manifest error in the exercise of power or the exercise of power is manifestly arbitrary or if the power is exercised on the basis of facts which do not exist and which are patently erroneous': see para 54.

[199] ibid para 53.

[200] ibid para 59.

[201] *Virginia G* (n 9) (Dissenting Opinion of Judge Ndiaye) paras 5–18; *Virginia G* (n 9) (Dissenting Opinion of Judge Jesus) para 21.

[202] See Camouco (n 9) (Dissenting Opinion of Judge Wolfrum) paras 8, 11. Judge Wolfrum was reflecting on art 73(2) in relation to prompt release rather than art 73(1).

[203] *Virginia G* (n 9) (Dissenting Opinion of Judge ad hoc Sérvulo Correia) paras 17, 21.

[204] *Virginia G* (n 9) para 253, citing *Tomimaru (Japan v Russia)* (Prompt Release, Judgment) ITLOS Reports 2005–2007, 74 (*Tomimaru*). Judge Kulyk observed that confiscation was a penalty, rather than 'a measure to ensure compliance: *Virginia G* (n 9) (Declaration of Judge Kulyk) para 9. He therefore seemed to suggest that it was better addressed in relation to art 73(3).

Article 73(1).[205] This decision aligned with the approach of ITLOS in the *Tomimaru* prompt release decision.[206] Any confiscation of a fishing vessel pursuant to Article 73(1) must remain consistent with the balance of interests as between coastal States and flag States in the EEZ.[207] To achieve this balance, considerations as to the legality of the confiscation would include whether it was consistent with international due process, whether it still allowed for the prompt release proceedings under UNCLOS to occur, and whether the shipowner would still have recourse to available domestic judicial remedies.[208] Confiscation may extend to the vessel, the catch as well as equipment.[209] The Tribunal suggested that confiscation without regard to the severity of the violation and without possible judicial recourse may not comply with Article 73(1).[210]

On the facts before it in *Virginia G*, the Tribunal found that the relevant legislation of Guinea-Bissau provided for some discretion as well as possibilities for legal challenge.[211] The Tribunal took the view that the law afforded the relevant authorities 'flexibility in sanctioning of violations of its fishing laws and regulations', so it considered in providing for confiscation, Guinea-Bissau was not per se in violation of Article 73(1).[212] This position suggests that reasoned determinations of penalties by law enforcement authorities and domestic courts in the light of the particular circumstances of the violation are unlikely to be second-guessed by UNCLOS tribunals.[213]

The Tribunal then turned to consider the confiscation of the vessel and its gas oil in the particular circumstances. It noted that the vessel did not have written authorisation for bunkering as required by the legislation of Guinea-Bissau and it had not paid the prescribed fee of €112.00. The Tribunal considered these infractions to be a 'serious violation'. However, it took into account that violations of similar gravity were committed by the four fishing vessels that received the bunkering services: two of them were arrested but received only fines and were not confiscated; the other two were neither arrested nor fined at all. In the circumstances, the Tribunal considered that the failure to obtain the required authorisation was not an intentional violation of the laws and regulations of Guinea-Bissau, and that the confiscation of the vessel and the gas oil on board was not necessary either to sanction the violation committed or to deter future violations. Considering that the principle of reasonableness applied generally to enforcement measures taken under Article 73, the Tribunal determined that the measures taken against the M/V Virginia G were not reasonable in the light of the particular circumstances of the case, and therefore violated Article 73(1).[214]

Judge Jesus, in his dissenting opinion in *Virginia G*, considered that Article 73(1) had to be interpreted in light of the whole provision, and not just focusing on the words of that

[205] *Virginia G* (n 9) para 253.
[206] *Tomimaru* (n 204) para 72.
[207] ibid para 75.
[208] ibid para 76.
[209] Bernard H Oxman, 'The "Tomimaru" (Japan v Russian Federation). Judgment: ITLOS Case No 15' (2008) 102 AJIL 316; Abdul Ghafur Hamid and Khin Maung Sein, 'Prompt Release of Vessel and Crew Under Article 292 of the UNCLOS: Is It An Adequate Safeguard Against the Powers of Coastal States?' (2011) 7 J App Sci Res 2421, 2426.
[210] *Virginia G* (n 9) para 257.
[211] ibid.
[212] ibid.
[213] See Bernard H Oxman and Vincent P Cogliati-Bantz, 'The M/V "Virginia G" (Panama/Guinea-Bissau). Case No 19' (2014) 108 AJIL 769, 775.
[214] *Virginia G* (n 9) paras 258–270.

paragraph. In this respect, he commented that Article 73(1) sets out a general policy of empowerment of the coastal State and Article 73(3) then sets out exceptions as to how the coastal State powers are to be exercised. Judge Jesus considered that the Tribunal introduced a third exception to the general policy by stating that confiscation of the vessel was not a necessary measure.[215] He criticised the Tribunal for creating an exception 'not by decision of the framers of the Convention but rather by the constructive interpretation made in this Judgment'.[216] Yet in taking this position, Judge Jesus appears to elide the point that the Tribunal thought confiscation was not a necessary measure in the circumstances of the case at hand. It did not create a blanket prohibition against confiscation under Article 73, rather just indicated that there are limits to the coastal State's powers of enforcement in making a relative assessment of what is 'necessary'. The tension between coastal State conservation and management efforts with navigational interests was again one that was difficult to balance.

In assessing enforcement action taken by a coastal State pursuant to Article 73, the *Virginia G* Tribunal considered that the actions of the coastal State had to be reasonable.[217] It stated, 'in applying enforcement measures due regard has to be paid to the particular circumstances of the case and the gravity of the violation'.[218] This reasonableness requirement incorporates standards of necessity and proportionality,[219] especially where there is consideration of the use of force during law enforcement actions.[220] In addition, the criteria for enforcement action set out in Article 225 of UNCLOS, which requires a State 'not to endanger the safety of navigation or otherwise create any hazard to a vessel, or bring a vessel to an unsafe port or anchorage, or expose the marine environment to an unreasonable risk', were held to apply to Article 73(1) in *Virginia G*.[221]

In relation to Article 73(2), the Tribunal in *Virginia G* commented that the provision entails three core requirements: 'arrested vessels and their crews be released upon posting of bond or other security, that such release be done promptly and that the bond or other security be reasonable'.[222] It is then up to the coastal State to determine how these requirements are met within the framework of its domestic law.[223] In the *Juno Trader*,[224] the Tribunal remarked that Article 73(2) had to be read in conjunction with Article 73 as a whole, and that 'elementary considerations of humanity and due process of law' were also part of the prompt release obligation.[225] The requirements relating to the setting of a reasonable bond are addressed further below in relation to the prompt release proceedings

[215] *Virginia G* (n 9) (Dissenting Opinion of Judge Jesus) para 18.

[216] ibid.

[217] *Virginia G* (n 9) para 270, referring to prompt release jurisprudence that looks to the reasonableness of the bond set. See *Hoshinmaru (Japan v Russia)* (Prompt Release, Judgment) ITLOS Reports 2005–2007, 18, para 88 (*Hoshinmaru*). This element of reasonableness was said to apply to all aspects of law enforcement under art 73: *Virginia G* (n 9) para 270.

[218] *Virginia G* (n 9) para 270. Judge Jesus, in his dissenting opinion, criticised this standard as 'arbitrary' and 'subjective'. See *Virginia G* (n 9) (Dissenting Opinion of Judge Jesus) para 20.

[219] *Duzgit Integrity Arbitration (Malta v São Tomé and Príncipe)* (Award of 5 September 2016) PCA Case No 2014-07, paras 209, 254; Arctic Sunrise, Merits (n 191) para 222. See further Goodman (n 90) 565.

[220] See *Saiga No 2*, Judgment (n 162) para 155.

[221] *Virginia G* (n 9) para 373.

[222] ibid para 283.

[223] ibid para 284.

[224] *Juno Trader (Saint Vincent and the Grenadines v Guinea-Bissau)* (Prompt Release, Judgment) ITLOS Reports 2004, 17 (*Juno Trader*).

[225] ibid para 77.

that protect flag States in the event a coastal State does not meet its requirements under this provision.

One aspect to be noted in this regard is that non-financial measures may not be imposed upon fishing vessels in the exercise of a coastal State's enforcement jurisdiction over fishing in its EEZ. In the *Volga* prompt release proceedings, Russia contested Australia's imposition of a requirement that the Volga be fitted with a vessel monitoring system upon release so Australia could better monitor its whereabouts.[226] Australia also calculated the bond with a view to ensuring future good behaviour by the *Volga*.

The *Volga* Tribunal examined the language used in Article 73, along with the other provisions of UNCLOS that require the prompt release of vessels upon payment of a reasonable bond.[227] It considered that the emphasis was on financial payment and not on any other conditions.[228] A bond to prevent future conduct could not be included.[229] Judge Anderson and Judge ad hoc Shearer each dissented on this point, with Judge Anderson emphasising the word 'bond' in its own right and focusing on whether it was reasonable or not.[230] Judge ad hoc Shearer was willing to go further in his interpretation of Article 73(2) in light of the vast increase in IUU fishing since the adoption of the Convention. He argued that the words 'bond' and 'financial security':

> [S]hould be given a liberal and purposive interpretation in order to enable the Tribunal to take full account of the measures—including those made possible by modern technology—found necessary by many coastal [S]tates (and mandated by regional and sub-regional fisheries organisations) to deter by way of judicial and administrative orders the plundering of the living resources of the sea.[231]

The tension between the different stakeholders was palpable in this regard with Australia and Judge ad hoc Shearer emphasising the need to use diverse legal tools to respond to IUU fishing. Rothwell and Stephens have highlighted the important role for the Commission on the Conservation of Antarctic Marine Living Resources and its interests, along with those of its members (including Russia), in seeking to conserve and manage the living marine resources of the Southern Ocean.[232] The majority of the Tribunal was not prepared to recalibrate the balance between navigational interests and fishing interests in this way. Instead, it is possible that such conditions may be imposed in the context of authority to fish within a coastal State's EEZ in the first place.[233]

In assessing the requirement in Article 73(3) that coastal States may not impose imprisonment or corporal punishment in response to violations of their fisheries laws, the *Virginia*

226 *Volga* (n 9) para 75.

227 UNCLOS (n 1) arts 220(7) and 226(1)(b).

228 *Volga* (n 9) para 77.

229 ibid para 80. See also Hamid and Sein (n 209) 2429.

230 *Volga* (n 9) (Dissenting Opinion of Judge Anderson) paras 13–14.

231 *Volga* (n 9) (Dissenting Opinion of Judge ad hoc Shearer) para 17.

232 Donald R Rothwell and Tim Stephens, 'Illegal Southern Ocean Fishing and Prompt Release: Balancing Coastal and Flag State Rights and Interests' (2004) 53 ICLQ 171, 184. They do go on to note that the Tribunal's authority under art 292 may be too limited to appreciate these dynamics and that further effort is required within the regional organisation as a result: see 185.

233 *Volga* (n 9) para 76. See also Robin Churchill, 'The Jurisprudence of the International Tribunal for the Law of the Sea Relating to Fisheries: Is There Much in the Net?' (2007) 22 IJMCL 383, 409–410 ('Fisheries Jurisprudence of ITLOS').

G Tribunal was not willing to consider the temporary confiscation of passports and the resulting stay of the crew on the vessel until its release as tantamount to imprisonment.[234] No further restrictions on the type of penalties are otherwise provided in UNCLOS.

In the *Juno Trader* prompt release case, a question arose as to whether the confiscation of a fishing vessel would violate the requirements of Article 73(3). In the context of prompt release proceedings, Guinea Bissau argued that the effect of the confiscation was that St Vincent and the Grenadines was no longer the flag State and hence not in a position to submit an application for prompt release.[235] ITLOS did not agree, however, that in the circumstances of the case that there had been a change in nationality.[236] Judges Mensah and Wolfrum explored this point further in their joint separate opinion, noting that to consider confiscation as a means of depriving a vessel of its nationality, as opposed to changing the ownership of the vessel, would run counter to the intentions of Articles 94 and 292, which set out the rights and duties of flag States.[237]

The requirement to notify the flag State under Article 73(4) was violated by Guinea-Bissau in *Virginia G* because Guinea-Bissau had notified Spain and Cuba, as the States of nationality of the owner and crew,[238] but had not advised Panama as flag State.[239] Although Guinea-Bissau considered Panama to be a flag of convenience with no genuine link to the vessel,[240] the Tribunal determined that Panama did in fact exercise effective jurisdiction and control over the vessel.[241] As a consequence, Guinea-Bissau had to meet its requirement to notify Panama as stipulated in Article 73(4).[242] The negative implication from the judgment is that if a State had failed to satisfy the requirements of Article 94, a coastal State may potentially be relieved of its obligation of notification under Article 73(4). This decision in *Virginia G* reinforced the finding in *M/V Saiga (No 2)* that 'the ship, every thing on it, and every person involved or interested in its operations are treated as an entity linked to the flag state. The nationalities of these persons are not relevant'.[243] In this setting, it would seem that any protections to be afforded to the individuals onboard are to be derived from Article 73(2) and Article 73(3).[244]

In the *Juno Trader* and *Camouco* prompt release decisions, ITLOS also connected Article 73(4) to Article 73(2), in that a failure to notify the flag State may result in the terms of Article 73(2) not being met; a flag State that is not notified is presumably unable to post a reasonable bond or other security. Equally, the failure to notify might implicate the flag State's rights to institute prompt release proceedings under Article 292.[245]

[234] *Virginia G* (n 9) paras 308, 310. The Tribunal noted that the crew members were free to leave the ship: see 308.

[235] *Juno Trader* (n 224) para 58. See discussion in Churchill, 'Fisheries Jurisprudence of ITLOS' (n 233) 407–408. See also ch 3(III)(A).

[236] *Juno Trader* (n 224) para 63.

[237] *Juno Trader* (n 224) (Separate Opinion of Judges Mensah and Wolfrum) para 10. They also raised concerns about international human rights law violation in this context: *Juno Trader* (n 224) (Separate Opinion of Judges Mensah and Wolfrum) paras 3–6. See further *Juno Trader* (n 224) (Separate Opinion of Judge Treves) paras 3-6 (also stressing the importance of due process and fairness).

[238] *Virginia G* (n 9) para 321.

[239] ibid para 328.

[240] ibid para 319.

[241] ibid para 325.

[242] ibid para 326.

[243] *Saiga No 2*, Judgment (n 162) para 106.

[244] Protections would also be derived from the Vienna Convention on Consular Relations. James Harrison, 'Article 73' in *Proelss Commentary* (n 1) 556, para 21.

[245] *Camouco* (n 9) para 59; *Juno Trader* (n 224) para 76.

In *Virginia G*, Panama further alleged that Guinea-Bissau had violated other provisions of UNCLOS relating to the boarding of its bunkering vessel, including Articles 110 and 224.[246] Panama considered that general principles of international law encapsulated in these provisions were equally applicable to law enforcement under Article 73 of UNCLOS.[247] The Tribunal agreed that general international law applied in relation to all law enforcement operations, but did not consider that the fact that these were reflected in Articles 110 and 224 meant that operations under Article 73 also triggered the operation of these provisions as well and would expose a State to further findings of international responsibility.[248]

E. Prompt Release of Vessels under Article 292

Article 292 of UNCLOS sets out a distinct procedure for the prompt release of vessels and crews.[249] It is available where States have exercised their enforcement powers under Article 73 in relation to fisheries regulations in the EEZ, or under Articles 220 or 226 concerning pollution.[250] To date, prompt release proceedings before ITLOS have only concerned challenges to State action under Article 73 and these cases are therefore addressed in relation to the fisheries regime under UNCLOS. Under Article 292, State parties may agree to submit the question of release from detention to any court or tribunal listed under Article 287, but if no such agreement is reached within ten days from the time of detention, ITLOS is the default forum for this procedure.[251] ITLOS has decided every prompt release case thus far.

The central question to be resolved under Article 292 is whether the 'detaining State has not complied with the provisions of this Convention for the prompt release of the vessel or its crew upon the posting of a reasonable bond or other financial security'.[252] For present purposes, it can therefore be noted that Article 292 correlates to the requirement in Article 73(2) that '[a]rrested vessels and their crews shall be promptly released upon the posting of a reasonable bond or other security'. Proceedings under Article 292 may only deal with the question of the prompt release upon posting of a reasonable bond, and are without prejudice to the merits of any case before the domestic forum dealing with the vessel, its owner or crew,[253] and do not address allegations of any other possible violation of UNCLOS.[254]

A central purpose of Article 292 was captured by Judge Chandrasekhara Rao in the following terms: 'Article 292 is designed to free ships and their crews from prolonged detention resulting from the imposition of unreasonable bonds in municipal jurisdictions which inflict deleterious effects on the owner of the vessel and also on international commercial transactions.'[255] This statement recognises the interests of a large number of stakeholders,

[246] Article 110 sets out the right of visit on the high seas and art 224 limits the exercise of enforcement powers to State officials and State vessels or aircraft.

[247] *Virginia G* (n 9) para 340.

[248] ibid para 342.

[249] See discussion in ch 3(IV)(B).

[250] States may not rely upon art 292 for the release of vessels arrested on other bases apart from these three provisions. See Klein, *Dispute Settlement* (n 12) 103–108. Instead, separate proceedings under Section 2 of Part XV of UNCLOS (n 1) must be pursued.

[251] The parties may still agree after ten days on a different forum. See UNCLOS (n 1) art 292(1). However, as noted in ch 3(IV)(B), the timing involved makes this unlikely as a practical matter.

[252] UNCLOS (n 1) art 292(1).

[253] ibid art 292(3).

[254] See *Camouco* (n 9) para 59; *Monte Confurco* (n 9) para 63. See also Klein, *Dispute Settlement* (n 12) 95.

[255] *Juno Trader* (n 224) (Separate Opinion of Judge Chandrasekhara Rao) para 4.

including the owner of the vessel, the owner of the cargo, the master and crew of the vessel, national court judges, and national law enforcement officers, in addition to the flag State. The important commercial interests at stake are underlined by the possibility that prompt release proceedings under Article 292 may be instituted 'on behalf of' the flag State of the vessel.[256]

Yet this protection of the navigational rights of the flag State, its vessels, and other interested stakeholders is to be balanced against the right of the coastal State to enforce its fisheries laws and regulations under Article 73.[257] Article 73 further reflects a balance between the rights of the flag State and those of the coastal State in that Article 73(1) 'includes a broad and non-exhaustive list of measures the coastal State may take to ensure compliance with its laws and regulations',[258] whereas the remaining provisions of Article 73 impose some constraints on coastal State action. Judge Treves described these provisions as having:

> [T]he purpose to ensure that these measures will not have the effect of limiting the freedom of the persons involved (prompt release of the crew, prohibition of imprisonment as a penalty) and of unduly jeopardizing the rights of shipowners and of the flag State (prompt release of the vessel), while ensuring timely protective action by the flag State (obligation to notify in case of arrest and of the imposing of penalties).[259]

These purposes have underscored a range of decisions relating to Article 292 procedures,[260] including most notably the assessment of what constitutes a reasonable bond.

In assessing the reasonableness of the bond, ITLOS will consider this question either where a bond has not been set at all, or where the amount of the bond set is alleged to be unreasonable.[261] There is no specific time limit on when a bond must be set following the detention of a fishing vessel.[262] Requests from the applicant not to have to post a bond at all have been denied as contrary to the nature of prompt release proceedings.[263]

The requirements for setting a reasonable bond have been well-rehearsed within the prompt release proceedings under Article 292 of UNCLOS.[264] They were summarised in the *Hoshinmaru* prompt release decision as follows:

[256] UNCLOS (n 1) art 292(2).

[257] See *Monte Confurco* (n 9) para 72; *Volga* (n 9) para 65.

[258] *Juno Trader* (n 224) (Separate Opinion of Judge Treves) para 2.

[259] ibid.

[260] Including, for example, discussions on the time limits involved for submitting proceedings and the consequences if a State fails to submit a response. See *Juno Trader* (n 224) (Separate Opinion of Judge Chandrasekhara Rao); *Juno Trader* (n 224) (Separate Opinion of Judge Lucky) (discussing the respondent's failure to submit a written response and implications for the timing stipulated under the Rules of the Tribunal). In the *Tomimaru* prompt release decision, the Tribunal noted that allowing time for an application under art 292 prior to the execution of a decision to confiscate a fishing vessel was part of maintaining the balance between arts 73 and 292: *Tomimaru* (n 204) para 75 ('It is the view of the Tribunal that confiscation of a fishing vessel must not be used in such a manner as to upset the balance of the interests of the flag State and of the coastal State established in the Convention').

[261] See *Hoshinmaru* (n 217) para 65, confirming the position from *M/V Saiga (Saint Vincent and the Grenadines v Guinea)* (Prompt Release, Judgment) ITLOS Reports 1997, 16, para 77 (*Saiga*, Prompt Release).

[262] *Hoshinmaru* (n 217) para 80; *Camouco* (n 9) para 54. In *Hoshinmaru*, Judge Türk commented that it would be consistent with the 'fundamental objective and purpose' of the prompt release proceedings for the bond to be set 'at the earliest possible point in time'; further suggesting a one month timeframe from the time of detention. See *Hoshinmaru* (n 217) (Declaration of Judge Türk).

[263] See *Saiga (No 2)*, Prompt Release (n 261) para 81; *Juno Trader* (n 224) para 97.

[264] For discussion see eg Igor V Karaman, *Dispute Resolution in the Law of the Sea* (Martinus Nijhoff 2012) 77–89; LDM Nelson, 'The Jurisprudence of the International Tribunal for the Law of the Sea: Some Observations' in Tafsir Malick Ndiaye and Rüdiger Wolfrum (eds), *Law of the Sea, Environmental Law and Settlement of Disputes:*

> The Tribunal has expressed its views on the reasonableness of the bond in a number of its judgments. In the 'Camouco' Case it stated: 'the Tribunal considers that a number of factors are relevant in an assessment of the reasonableness of bonds or other financial security. They include the gravity of the alleged offences, the penalties imposed or imposable under the laws of the detaining State, the value of the detained vessel and of the cargo seized, the amount of the bond imposed by the detaining State and its form'... In the 'Monte Confurco' Case it added that: 'This is by no means a complete list of factors. Nor does the Tribunal intend to lay down rigid rules as to the exact weight to be attached to each of them' ... In the 'Volga' Case it stated that: 'In assessing the reasonableness of the bond or other security, due account must be taken of the terms of the bond or security set by the detaining State, having regard to all the circumstances of the particular case' ... In the 'Juno Trader' Case the Tribunal further declared that: .The assessment of the relevant factors must be an objective one, taking into account all information provided to the Tribunal by the parties.[265]

That the bond must be reasonable 'indicates that a concern for fairness is one of the purposes of this provision'.[266] Nonetheless, the circumstances of the seizure of the vessel are not a factor to be considered in determining the reasonableness of the bond.[267]

The amount of the bond 'is to be proportionate to the gravity of the offences'.[268] In this context, ITLOS has examined coastal State responses to IUU fishing through law enforcement. In *Hoshinmaru*, the Tribunal compared a lack of accurate reporting with unlicensed fishing or overfishing,[269] with the implication that the latter was more serious than the former. Yet, the Tribunal still acknowledged: 'Monitoring of catches, which requires accurate reporting, is one of the most essential means of managing marine living resources.'[270] The bond set by the Tribunal in this case did not include an amount encompassing the value of the vessel, as Russia had done,[271] which may have reflected the Tribunal's view that confiscation of the Hoshinmaru was unlikely given the offence in question.

In the *Volga* decision, the Tribunal only considered the broader setting of IUU fishing in the Southern Ocean to the extent that it held implications for the gravity of the penalty assessed against an arrested vessel.[272] The problems of IUU fishing in this region that were highlighted in Australia's submissions, including the Volga's involvement in ongoing illegal fishing activities,[273] were at least noted with concern by the Tribunal.[274] The Tribunal's decision was criticised for its failure to account for Australia's efforts within a cooperative regime to improve the conservation status of Patagonian toothfish.[275]

Liber Amicorum *Judge Thomas A Mensah* (Brill 2007) 967, 969–78; Vincent P Bantz, 'Views from Hamburg: The Juno Trader Case or How to Make Sense of the Coastal State's Rights in the Light of Its Duty of Prompt Release' (2005) 24 UQLJ 415, 436–39.

265 *Hoshinmaru* (n 217) para 82 (citations omitted).
266 *Juno Trader* (n 224) para 77.
267 ibid para 95.
268 *Hoshinmaru* (n 217) para 88.
269 ibid para 98.
270 ibid para 99.
271 ibid para 51.
272 Volga (n 9) paras 67–68.
273 'Verbatim Record', *Volga (Russia v Australia)* (Prompt Release) (ITLOS Case No 11, 12 December 2002) ITLOS/PV.02/02, 26 (David Bennett QC). See also Rothwell and Stephens (n 232) 180.
274 *Volga* (n 9) para 68.
275 See Rothwell and Stephens (n 232) 180–81, 184–85; Klein, *Dispute Settlement* (n 12) 111–12.

Subsequent to the *Volga* decision, in *Hoshinmaru* the importance of the cooperative fishing regime established between Russia and Japan was noted by the Tribunal in considering the reasonableness of the bond.[276] Moreover, in this instance, the Tribunal was willing to consider a possible agreement between States with long-standing fishing relationships that reflected expectations on how a reasonable bond would be calculated.[277] Such an approach 'may contribute to mutual confidence, help resolve misunderstandings and prevent disputes'.[278] Nonetheless, any agreement could not be established on the facts of the *Hoshinmaru* case.[279] The Tribunal's efforts in this regard may indicate the possibility of Regional Fisheries Management Organizations (RFMOs) seeking to reach agreement on a reasonable sum for fisheries offences within their jurisdiction, which could then better inform any tribunal's assessment of the bond set by a coastal State. It could not necessarily be viewed as decisive, however, given that the tribunal will still look to other factors.

Due process considerations have come to the fore in assessing the legal effect of coastal State laws requiring the confiscation of fishing vessels in the context of prompt release proceedings under Article 292. The concern that arises in this instance is that if a vessel has been confiscated and now belongs to the detaining State, the flag State may no longer have standing to assert the rights of the vessel in Article 292 proceedings.[280] Confiscation is not an enforcement measure explicitly anticipated in Article 73, but, as discussed above, ITLOS has acknowledged that many States provide for such a penalty in national legislation.[281] While confiscation may be a permissible measure, ITLOS has observed that it may only occur consistent with international due process, which anticipates that there is no 'unjustified haste'.[282] Flag States must be afforded the opportunity to act in a timely manner, either to institute proceedings under Article 292 or to pursue proceedings before the domestic courts of the detaining State.[283] Due process again demands that proper formalities be followed before a flag State could be deprived of its right to take up the claim of one of its vessels.[284]

* * *

In some respects, it is remarkable that so much judicial elucidation has been achieved in relation to fisheries in the EEZ given that disputes emerging in relation to fishing in the EEZ are largely excluded from third party review.[285] Further elaboration of the respective rights

[276] *Hoshinmaru* (n 217) para 98.
[277] ibid para 85.
[278] ibid.
[279] ibid paras 85–87.
[280] As noted above, Guinea-Bissau submitted this argument in the *Juno Trader* (n 224) para 58.
[281] See *Tomimaru* (n 204) para 72. Judge Jesus in his Separate Opinion endorsed this interpretation, referring to 'undisputed State practice'. *Tomimaru* (n 204) (Separate Opinion of Judge Jesus) para 6.
[282] *Tomimaru* (n 204) para 76. Judges Nelson and Jesus queried whether the Tribunal should consider the merits of any confiscation decision, and particularly whether there should be value judgments about the national decision-making on this point. See *Tomimaru* (n 204) (Separate Opinion of Judge Jesus) para 9; *Tomimaru* (n 204) (Declaration of Judge Nelson).
[283] *Tomimaru* (n 204) para 77. See also Bantz (n 264) 427–32.
[284] *Juno Trader* (n 224) (Separate Opinion of Judge Ndiaye) paras 28–29. As noted above, judges have further queried whether the transfer of ownership necessarily also involves a transfer of nationality. Judge Ndiaye in his Separate Opinion in the *Juno Trader* considered that if such a conclusion was allowed, it would contribute to the creation of a 'phantom flag': see para 30.
[285] See ch 4(III)(A). See further Klein, *Dispute Settlement* (n 12) 176–85.

and duties of coastal and flag States will potentially calibrate the range of claims and counter-claims between stakeholders in EEZ fisheries. As mentioned at the outset of this section, given the many loci for international fisheries governance, judges who have perspective on their role vis-à-vis broader ocean governance may contribute better to the overall efforts in conservation and management of coastal fisheries. Although this perspective has been only signalled in prompt release proceedings to date, the *SRFC Advisory Opinion* has contributed further in this regard. In particular, highlighting the roles and responsibilities of flag States advances current understanding of the operation of the legal regime. Translating these expectations more widely into State implementation of the Convention remains a challenge. Tribunals with jurisdiction under UNCLOS to resolve EEZ fisheries disputes will need to ensure a balance between the stakeholders that sustains the world's fisheries into the future.

V. Straddling Stocks and Highly Migratory Species

Obligations under UNCLOS relating to straddling stocks and highly migratory species are primarily set out in Articles 63 and 64,[286] which potentially impinge on the high seas right to fish, as recognised in Article 116 of UNCLOS.[287] The rights and duties associated with straddling stocks and highly migratory species are further elaborated in the Fish Stocks Agreement. While the latter agreement anticipates that UNCLOS dispute settlement procedures apply *mutatis mutandis* to any disputes concerning the interpretation or application of the Fish Stocks Agreement,[288] no such cases have been instituted directly under this Agreement to date.[289]

ITLOS was asked to set out the responsibilities of coastal States in the *SRFC Advisory Opinion* in relation to the 'sustainable management' of 'shared stocks and stocks of common interest' within the region.[290] The Tribunal had to consider the meaning of the particular terms used in the request for advice, as they did not reflect the exact terms used in UNCLOS or the Fish Stocks Agreement. In examining UNCLOS and the MCA Convention, the Tribunal considered that the meaning of 'shared stocks' and 'stocks of common interest' correlated with the description of stocks in Articles 63(1) and (2).[291]

Article 63 provides:

1. Where the same stock or stocks of associated species occur within the exclusive economic zones of two or more coastal States, these States shall seek, either directly or

[286] Annex I of UNCLOS (n 1) lists highly migratory species protected under art 64 of UNCLOS.

[287] Article 116 recognises the right of all States for their nationals to fish on the high seas, subject to the rights and duties 'provided for, *inter alia*, in article 63, paragraph 2, and articles 64 to 67': ibid art 116.

[288] United Nations Agreement for the Implementation of the Provisions of the United Nations Convention on the Law of the Sea of 10 December 1982 relating to the Conservation and Management of Straddling Fish Stocks and Highly Migratory Fish Stocks (adopted 4 August 1995, entered into force 11 December 2001) 2167 UNTS 3, art 30(1) (Fish Stocks Agreement).

[289] There have been challenges under art 28 of the Fish Stocks Agreement, which relates to the prevention of disputes, and are addressed in relation to high seas fisheries below. Curiously, there was no discussion of the Fish Stocks Agreement in the *SRFC Advisory Opinion* (n 16) (except in Judge Ndiaye's separate opinion). It could not do so, according to Judge Paik, because the jurisdictional limit of the *SRFC Advisory Opinion* related to the EEZs of the SRFC member States and the Fish Stocks Agreement is concerned primarily (albeit not exclusively) with areas beyond national jurisdiction.

[290] *SRFC Advisory Opinion* (n 16) para 175.

[291] ibid para 186.

> through appropriate subregional or regional organizations, to agree upon the measures necessary to coordinate and ensure the conservation and development of such stocks without prejudice to the other provisions of this Part.
>
> 2. Where the same stock or stocks of associated species occur both within the exclusive economic zone and in an area beyond and adjacent to the zone, the coastal State and the States fishing for such stocks in the adjacent area shall seek, either directly or through appropriate subregional or regional organizations, to agree upon the measures necessary for the conservation of these stocks in the adjacent area.[292]

In considering the term 'sustainable management' in the *SRFC Advisory Opinion*, there was an opportunity for the Tribunal to address the variety of management techniques, and accompanying descriptions, for fisheries management, such as ecosystem-based management or maximum sustainable yield. Article 63(1) further requires coordination for the purposes of 'conservation and development'.

The Tribunal took the view that the meaning of 'sustainable management' was to be informed by the requirements of Article 61, which provides the basic framework for the conservation and management of marine living resources.[293] In reviewing paragraphs (2) and (4) of Article 61, the Tribunal observed 'the ultimate goal of sustainable management of fish stocks is to conserve and develop them as a viable and sustainable resource'.[294] On this basis, the Tribunal determined that 'sustainable management' could be understood as 'conservation and development' as set out in Article 63(1) and as informed by the requirements of Article 61.[295] More information is provided on 'conservation' than 'development' in Article 61 and so the Tribunal elaborated on what could be comprehended by 'development': namely, the use of the fisheries resources within a 'framework of a sustainable fisheries management regime'.[296] The Tribunal continued:

> This may include the exploitation of non-exploited stocks or an increase in the exploitation of under-exploited stocks through the development of responsible fisheries, as well as more effective fisheries management schemes to ensure the long-term sustainability of exploited stocks. This may also include stock restoration, guided by the requirement under article 61 of the Convention that a given stock is not endangered by over-exploitation, thus preserving it as a long-term viable resource.[297]

Despite ongoing concerns about the consequences for fisheries,[298] the Tribunal endorsed the principle of optimum utilization of fish resources given its repeated use in UNCLOS.[299]

As ITLOS was also asked to address the sustainable management of tuna, a highly migratory species, the Tribunal had regard to the terms of Article 64 of UNCLOS as well. Article 64 reads:

[292] UNCLOS (n 11) art 63.

[293] *SRFC Advisory Opinion* (n 16) para 189.

[294] ibid para 190.

[295] ibid para 191.

[296] ibid para 198.

[297] ibid.

[298] See generally Abdullah Al Arif, 'Exploring the Legal Status and Key Features of Ecosystem-Based Fisheries Management in International Fisheries Law' (2018) 27 RECIEL 320.

[299] In arts 61, 63, and 64. *SRFC Advisory Opinion* (n 16) para 213.

1. The coastal State and other States whose nationals fish in the region for the highly migratory species listed in Annex I shall cooperate directly or through appropriate international organizations with a view to ensuring conservation and promoting the objective of optimum utilization of such species throughout the region, both within and beyond the exclusive economic zone. In regions for which no appropriate international organization exists, the coastal State and other States whose nationals harvest these species in the region shall cooperate to establish such an organization and participate in its work.
2. The provisions of paragraph 1 apply in addition to the other provisions of this Part.[300]

The Tribunal did not elaborate in detail on the obligations imposed on coastal States under Articles 63 and 64 in the *SRFC Advisory Opinion*, but largely reiterated the obligations set out in the text of those provisions of UNCLOS.[301] In relation to highly migratory species, the Tribunal did note that the cooperation anticipated in Article 64 would entail adopting measures consistent and compatible with those adopted by the appropriate regional fisheries organisation.[302] Judge Paik gave more detailed consideration to the content of the obligation to cooperate in his separate opinion. He underlined that Articles 63(1) and 64 entail requirements to seek to agree, rather than requiring agreement, and that these efforts must be bona fide and meaningful.[303] He contemplated that '[t]he obligation to cooperate may include duties to notify, to exchange information, and to consult and negotiate'.[304] Judge Paik suggested that further indication of what is entailed in the obligation to cooperate may be drawn from Article 7(3) and (4) of the Fish Stocks Agreement.[305] These provisions refer to the effort of States to agree on compatible conservation and management measures within a reasonable period of time in line with their duty to cooperate or otherwise refer the matter to dispute settlement.

The Tribunal recognised that the UNCLOS requirements relating to straddling stock and highly migratory species were due diligence obligations and that in consulting with one another in good faith,[306] there should be a substantial effort by the concerned States to adopt the necessary and effective measures for coordination and to ensure the conservation and development of shared stocks.[307] Harrison has noted that a 'similar result arises by virtue of the obligations in Articles 56, 58, 192 and 193 of the Convention, all of which require [implicitly] cooperation on the protection and preservation of the marine environment'.[308] On this basis, it would seem that obligations to cooperate (or coordinate) in relation to straddling stock and highly migratory species would still be within jurisdiction of a court or tribunal constituted under UNCLOS, even if Article 297(3) was relied upon to exclude disputes concerning these fish within the coastal State's EEZ.[309]

300 UNCLOS (n 11) art 64.

301 See eg *SRFC Advisory Opinion* (n 16) paras 207–209. Judge Paik is critical of the Advisory Opinion in this regard. See *SRFC Advisory Opinion* (n 16) (Separate Opinion of Judge Paik) para 34.

302 *SRFC Advisory Opinion* (n 16) para 207(iii).

303 Consistent with the view of the ICJ from *North Sea Continental Shelf Cases (Germany/Denmark; Germany/Netherlands)* (Judgment) [1969] ICJ Rep 3. See *SRFC Advisory Opinion* (n 16) (Separate Opinion of Judge Paik) para 35.

304 *SRFC Advisory Opinion* (n 16) (Separate Opinion of Judge Paik) para 36.

305 ibid.

306 As required by art 300 of UNCLOS (n 11). *SRFC Advisory Opinion* (n 16) para 210.

307 *SRFC Advisory Opinion* (n 16) para 210.

308 Harrison, 'Significant International Environmental Law Cases' (n 115) 548.

309 See discussion in ch 4(III)(A).

Moreover, in the context of discussing the rights of coastal States to conserve and manage the living marine resources that are shared across the EEZ, the Tribunal highlighted that there is an obligation to show due regard to the rights and duties of other users.[310] This requirement is based on Articles 56(2) and 58(3) and also flows from the requirements to protect and preserve the marine environment as set out in Articles 192 and 193.[311] Again, a due regard requirement might also overcome jurisdictional limitations if a claim under either Article 56(2) or Article 58(3) is to be assessed by reference to the standards anticipated under Articles 63 and 64.

Yet beyond the obligations of the coastal States, the Tribunal suggested that there are corresponding rights.[312] What these exact rights are was not explicitly articulated.[313] Presumably, the rights arise in relation to the obligation to cooperate give the mutuality of the nature of the obligation. The implication is that a coastal State has a right that another State cooperate in accordance with Articles 63 and 64 and a right that another State seek to agree pursuant to Article 63. In casting the obligations set out in the Convention as entailing corresponding rights, it remains unclear as to whether, or if at all, a rights framework provides any stronger (or different) legal basis for a coastal State in managing its relationships with other States or with organisations in the conservation and management of straddling stocks and highly migratory species.[314]

As noted in Chapter 4, there remains a jurisdictional question mark over disputes relating to straddling stock and highly migratory species under UNCLOS.[315] If disputes relating to those provisions proceed, many of the judicial considerations pertaining to fisheries in the EEZ will arguably pertain here. Notably, judges need to account for a range of contemporary interests and practices, as well as activity in other fora that might influence the standard of conduct to be expected and accepted, especially in determining the regard shown to other ocean users and the level of cooperation that must be reached.

VI. Fishing on the High Seas

While fishing on the high seas was once considered one of the traditional freedoms of the high seas, it has become increasingly regulated in light of ongoing concerns about the conservation and survival of a number of species. The UNCLOS provisions relating to fishing on the high seas are quite broad, setting general requirements for cooperation (Articles 117 and 118) and for conservation and management of marine living resources on the high seas (Article 119). They are also 'umbrella' in nature in that there is a dependence on other international agreements providing more detailed obligations and hence greater substance to the requirements set out in the Convention.[316] So much is clear in Article 116, which subjects the right of nationals to engage in fishing on the high seas to the treaty obligations of the State.

[310] *SRFC Advisory Opinion* (n 16) para 216.
[311] ibid.
[312] ibid para 205.
[313] Goodman (n 90) 563.
[314] Perhaps the political rhetoric in a dispute is stronger if a State is claiming that its rights are being violated rather than asserting that another actor is not meeting its international obligations.
[315] See ch 4(III)(A).
[316] See Klein, *Dispute Settlement* (n 12) 192–93.

Although not specifically based on the UNCLOS high seas fishing provisions, in *Spain v Canada*, which concerned the latter's attempt to regulate and enforce national fisheries laws beyond its EEZ, the ICJ considered what was meant by a measure for conservation and management. The Court considered that for a measure to be characterised as a conservation and management measure, it was 'sufficient that its purpose is to conserve and manage living marine resources and that, to this end, it satisfies various technical requirements'.[317] Conservation and management of living marine resources entails actions such as establishing catch limitations (quantity of fish and size of fish), fishing periods, specific fishing areas, and prescribing what fishing gear may be used.[318] As such, Article 119 can provide States with a wide scope of action in regulating their vessels and nationals on the high seas.[319] As with the ICJ decision in *Spain v Canada*, an interpretation would need to look to international law and practice in considering what measures would fall within the scope of a State's permissible action.

To date, the UNCLOS high seas fisheries provisions have prompted international litigation in two instances: the *Conservation of Swordfish Stocks* case instituted by special agreement between Chile and the European Union in 2000[320] and the *Southern Bluefin Tuna* case that Australia and New Zealand brought against Japan in 1998.[321] Neither case resulted in a decision on the merits, so the precise content of these obligations has not yet been subject to elaboration or explanation by any tribunal constituted under UNCLOS.[322]

All that can be noted at this point are the arguments that were formulated by each of the States in these cases or the actions taken in the shadow of the proceedings as possible indicators as to how State parties to UNCLOS understood these provisions. The *Conservation of Swordfish Stocks* case concerned a dispute relating to the conservation and sustainable exploitation of swordfish stocks in the south-eastern Pacific Ocean. Chile challenged the actions of the European Union in taking swordfish from high seas areas adjacent to Chile's EEZ, whereas the European Union protested Chile's attempt to apply conservation managements on the high seas.[323] Prior to any written submissions or arguments before the ITLOS Special Chamber constituted to hear the case, the parties entered into an agreement on fisheries cooperation, including freezing the peak total of fishing effort as at 2008, as well as the establishment of a Bilateral Scientific and Technical Committee to assist decision-making on conservation measures.[324] As a consequence of this agreement, there were no submissions reflecting the parties' views on the content of the high seas fisheries provisions under

[317] *Spain v Canada* (n 5) para 70. In this regard, the Court considered that was the sense that 'conservation and management measures' was used in art 62(4) of the Convention.

[318] ibid.

[319] Marcos A Orellana, 'The Law on Highly Migratory Fish Stocks: ITLOS Jurisprudence in Context' (2004) 34 Golden Gate U L Rev 459, 466.

[320] *Conservation and Sustainable Exploitation of Swordfish Stocks (Chile/European Community)* (Order of 16 December 2009) ITLOS Reports 2008–2010, 13 (*Conservation of Swordfish Stocks*).

[321] *Southern Bluefin Tuna*, Jurisdiction and Admissibility (n 9).

[322] A reflection on the substantive obligations may be discerned from the provisional measures order in *Southern Bluefin Tuna*, but there is little concrete that can be drawn from the discussion. See Churchill, 'Fisheries Jurisprudence of ITLOS' (n 233) 412–14; *Southern Bluefin Tuna (New Zealand v Japan; Australia v Japan)* (Provisional Measures, Order of 27 August 1999) ITLOS Reports 1999, 280 (*Southern Bluefin Tuna*, Provisional Measures).

[323] See ITLOS, 'Press Release: Case on Conservation of Swordfish Stocks between Chile and the European Community in the South-Eastern Pacific Ocean before Special Chamber of the Tribunal' (ITLOS/Press 43, 21 December 2000) https://www.itlos.org/fileadmin/itlos/documents/press_releases_english/press_release_43_en.pdf.

[324] As reflected in the ITLOS Order. See *Conservation of Swordfish Stocks* (n 320).

UNCLOS. At most, it could be speculated that the agreement reached reflected the views of the parties as satisfying the requirements under UNCLOS so that there was no more dispute between them.

In *Southern Bluefin Tuna*, Australia and New Zealand challenged Japan's establishment of an experimental fishing programme that necessitated Japan taking more tuna than was allocated to it under the national allocations previously agreed within the Commission for the Conservation of Southern Bluefin Tuna.[325] The Commission was established under the (then) trilateral Convention for the Conservation of Southern Bluefin Tuna (SBT Convention), which has the key objective of ensuring conservation and optimum utilisation of southern bluefin tuna.[326] Australia, New Zealand, and Japan all considered that UNCLOS was an umbrella or framework agreement to the implementation of measures for southern bluefin tuna under the SBT Convention.[327] Australia and New Zealand further argued that while the SBT Convention implemented UNCLOS obligations, the trilateral treaty should not be seen as a means of escaping UNCLOS obligations.[328]

In discussing potential violations of the high seas fisheries provisions, Australia and New Zealand argued as follows:

> Australia and New Zealand contended that Japan's conduct also placed it in violation of Articles 116, 117, 118, and 119, inter alia by failing to adopt necessary conservation measures for its nationals so as to maintain or restore [southern bluefin tuna] stock to levels which can produce the maximum sustainable yield, by ignoring credible scientific evidence presented by Australia and New Zealand and by pursuing a course of unilateral action in its exclusive interest contrary to their rights as coastal States while enjoying the benefits of restraint by Australia and New Zealand, with discriminatory effect upon nationals of the Applicants.[329]

More specifically, Australia and New Zealand argued that Article 116 sets out conditions for the exercise of the right of nationals to fish on the high seas, such as the right being subject to treaty obligations, including those set out in UNCLOS, so that it was clear that the right to fish is qualified in different ways.[330] Another qualification was included in Article 117, which requires States to take, and to cooperate in taking, conservation measures as necessary for the living resources of the high seas.[331] Article 119 was said to prevent a State from engaging in additional, unilateral fishing of a seriously depleted stock where scientific evidence indicated that such unilateral fishing may threaten its recovery.[332] Further, Article 118 sets out a requirement to cooperate with the SBT Commission to the effect that where an impasse is reached, unilateral actions taken have to be assessed against the other requirements in UNCLOS.[333] Australia and New Zealand underlined how Japan considered

[325] *Southern Bluefin Tuna*, Jurisdiction and Admissibility (n 9) paras 24–25.
[326] Convention for the Conservation of Southern Bluefin Tuna (adopted 10 May 1993, entered into force 20 May 1994) 1819 UNTS 359, art 3.
[327] *Southern Bluefin Tuna*, Jurisdiction and Admissibility (n 9) para 29.
[328] ibid para 33.
[329] ibid.
[330] ibid para 41(g).
[331] ibid.
[332] ibid.
[333] ibid.

that it could decide on its own terms how much it was allowed to take and what limits it was willing to accept without further reference to UNCLOS requirements once the trilateral treaty was in place.[334] In this respect, the suggestion from Australia and New Zealand was that the obligations relating to high seas fishing continued to regulate fishing activities beyond national jurisdiction even when States have otherwise agreed on more detailed obligations for their fishing activities in a regional or other agreement. The Tribunal accepted this view, noting that it was common for more than one treaty to bear upon a dispute and that a given act of a State could violate more than one treaty obligation.[335] At the provisional measures stage, ITLOS also indicated that it would be relevant to have regard to a State's conduct within a RFMO to determine if it had complied with its obligations under UNCLOS.[336]

Conduct within a RFMO may further be challenged through the implementation of the Fish Stocks Agreement and its dispute resolution processes. In accordance with Article 28 of the Fish Stocks Agreement, States are to agree on effective decision-making procedures within RFMOs as a means of preventing disputes. Notably, some RFMOs have adopted procedures to challenge the justifiability of a State's objection to be bound by a binding decision of the organisation. Such a procedure is laid out in the Convention on the Conservation and Management of High Seas Fisheries Resources in the South Pacific Ocean (Auckland Convention).[337] It was first utilised in 2013 when Russia challenged the catch decisions of the South Pacific RFMO (SPRFMO) Commission in a Conservation and Management Measure.[338] In those proceedings, Russia had to demonstrate how this Conservation and Management Measure was inconsistent with UNCLOS, the Fish Stocks Agreement or the Auckland Convention.[339] The key issue before the 2013 SPRFMO Review Panel was whether the Conservation and Management Measure unjustifiably discriminated against Russia in form or in fact in the SPRFMO Commission's decision on what data to rely in deciding national allocations.[340] The 2013 SPRFMO Review Panel agreed that this discrimination had occurred.[341]

Russia had also suggested that Articles 87, 116, and 119 of UNCLOS were violated, as well as Article 8 of the Fish Stocks Agreement, which addresses non-discrimination.[342] These submissions were contested by Chile and New Zealand.[343] Ultimately, Russia's arguments

[334] ibid (arguing: 'This is the old anarchy returned in procedural guise').

[335] ibid para 52.

[336] *Southern Bluefin Tuna*, Provisional Measures (n 322) para 50. See further Churchill, 'Fisheries Jurisprudence of ITLOS' (n 233) 413.

[337] Convention on the Conservation and Management of High Seas Fishery Resources in the South Pacific Ocean (adopted 14 November 2009 entered into force 24 August 2012) 2899 UNTS 211, art 17(2).

[338] *Review Panel Established Under the Convention on the Conservation and Management of High Seas Fishery Resources in the South Pacific Ocean* (Findings and Recommendations of the Review Panel of 5 July 2013) PCA Case No 2013-14 (*2013 SPRFMO Review Panel*). For an overview see Robin Churchill, 'Dispute Settlement in the Law of the Sea: Survey for 2013' (2015) 30 IJMCL 1, 48–52 ('Survey for 2013'); Rosemary Rayfuse, 'Settling Disputes in Regional Fisheries Management Organisations: Dealing with Objections' in Hélène Ruiz Fabri and others (eds), *Dispute Resolution in the Law of International Watercourses and the Law of the Sea: A Bridge Over Troubled Waters* (Brill Nijhoff 2021) 240.

[339] See *2013 SPRFMO Review Panel* (n 338) (Procedural Directive No 1) para 1.

[340] For detailed discussion see Andrew Serdy, 'Implementing Article 28 of the UN Fish Stocks Agreement: The First Review of a Conservation Measure in the South Pacific Regional Fisheries Management Organisation' (2016) 47 ODIL 1. See also Harrison, 'Significant International Environmental Law Cases' (n 115) 536–38.

[341] *2013 SPRFMO Review Panel* (n 338) para 92.

[342] ibid para 70.

[343] ibid paras 71–72. See Serdy (n 340) 19.

were not examined in detail by the 2013 SPRFMO Review Panel but a finding was made that the Conservation and Management Measure was consistent with both UNCLOS and the Fish Stocks Agreement.[344] Serdy has instead supported the Russian contention and argued that a finding of discrimination against Russia in relation to the Conservation and Management Measure under the Auckland Convention necessarily violated both Article 8(3) of the Fish Stocks Agreement and Article 119(3) of UNCLOS.[345] These claims were not finally tested in adjudication following the acceptance of the 2013 SPRFMO Review Panel's findings and recommendations.[346] Rayfuse has noted that while the Review Proceedings settled the immediate dispute for Russia efficiently, the broader issues relating to Russia's fishing vessel at issue and the conservation and management of jack mackerel remained pressing and unresolved.[347]

Ecuador also sought to challenge an allocation decision within SPRFMO in early 2018 on the grounds that it was discriminatory and inconsistent with the Auckland Convention, the Fish Stocks Agreement and UNCLOS.[348] However, in that instance, the 2018 SPRFMO Review Panel determined that there was no discrimination, recognising that a wide margin of discretion was necessary in allocation decisions of the Commission.[349] The 2018 SPRFMO Review Panel supported Ecuador's argument that the interests of developing States 'need to be treated with the utmost seriousness'.[350] Moreover, this approach was said to be 'consistent with well-established international principles supporting the sustainable development of developing States, and also with the view that developing States should not be disadvantaged because their economic status has prevented them from developing a high seas fishery'.[351] In relation to UNCLOS, the 2018 SPRFMO Review Panel considered that this regard for developing States' interests was implicit in Articles 61, 62, and 119.[352] In a step beyond the 2013 SPRFMO Review Panel, the 2018 SPRFMO Review Panel explicitly stated that if the Commission acted outside its wide margin of discretion then there would be violations of the Auckland Convention, the Fish Stocks Agreement, and UNCLOS (albeit without specifying which provisions of the latter).[353] At their highest, the 2018 SPRFMO Review Panel findings indicate that a principle of non-discrimination and a requirement to show special regard for the interests of developing States must form part of the broad obligations relating to fishing on the high seas. However, given the formally non-binding nature of these proceedings, the lack of any detailed analysis in relation to UNCLOS provisions,

[344] *2013 SPRFMO Review Panel* (n 338) paras 93 and 100(d). For analysis see Serdy (n 340) 19–20.

[345] Serdy (n 340) 23.

[346] The matter may have progressed to compulsory dispute settlement in accordance with the Auckland Convention, Annex II, para 10(d). As Russia did not object, the Review Panel's recommendation became binding. Churchill has observed that this outcome renders the process more akin to arbitration than conciliation. See Churchill, 'Survey for 2013' (n 338) 52. See also Peter Tzeng, 'Fisheries Review Panels: Lessons from Russia v. Commission and Ecuador v. Commission' (2019) 37 Chinese (Taiwan) YB Intl L & Aff 221, 227–28.

[347] Rayfuse (n 338) 267.

[348] *Review Panel established under the Convention on the Conservation and Management of High Seas Fishery Resources in the South Pacific Ocean* (Findings and Recommendations of the Review Panel of 5 June 2018) PCA Case No 2018-3 (*2018 SPRFMO Review Panel*). For discussion see Harrison, 'Significant International Environmental Law Cases' (n 115) 536–38.

[349] *2018 SPRFMO Review Panel* (n 348) para 92.

[350] ibid para 94.

[351] ibid.

[352] ibid para 91.

[353] ibid para 95. For discussion see Rayfuse (n 338) 267–69.

and the restricted context of RFMO dispute procedures as between the members of the specific organisation, these points may not be applied more broadly.

Judicial resolution of many questions relating to the regulation of high seas fisheries under UNCLOS remains for the future. One judicial engagement in relation to fishing in the high seas may be discerned from a statement of the ICJ in the *Icelandic Fisheries* case. The Court stated that 'the former *laissez faire* treatment of the living resources of the sea in the high seas has been replaced by a recognition of a duty to have due regard to the rights of other States and the needs of conservation for the benefit of all'.[354] What the 'needs of conservation for the benefit of all' might entail includes reference to equitable exploitation,[355] or potentially resolving claims and counter-claims based on considerations of equity.[356] A tribunal constituted under UNCLOS will need to determine if these reflections are pertinent for the future interpretation of the Convention's provisions relating to high seas fisheries.

VII. Concluding Remarks

The extent of judicial interpretation of the UNCLOS provisions relating to fisheries has steadily increased. The challenges faced by judges in this area have been summarised by Judge Lucky in *Virginia G* as follows:

> That this case would result in one or more dissenting or separate opinions should come as no surprise or be the cause of any discomfort. In my view, the ventilation of interpretation of the relevant law and findings of fact will be the subject of the highest international scrutiny and will augur well for the development of the jurisprudence of this specialized court. This is a case where the judge has to make findings of fact having predominantly in focus the determination of the truth.[357]

The importance of facts will of course arise in other issue areas in dispute under the Convention. For fisheries, available scientific information and data are likely to be especially significant. These factual settings may mean that States may not want judges to deal with their cases but prefer to turn to experts, potentially as anticipated under Annex VIII of UNCLOS or in the dispute resolution mechanisms in RFMOs.[358]

While resource scarcity and food security may indicate an increase in fisheries disputes is inevitable, the role of tribunals under UNCLOS may vacillate. Jurisdictional impediments may prevent judicial resolution of many fisheries disputes. Nonetheless, international obligations under UNCLOS relating to EEZ fisheries and straddling stocks have been elucidated through the *SRFC Advisory Opinion*, *South China Sea*, and *Virginia G*. By contrast, where there is scope for judicial resolution in relation to high seas fisheries, this avenue is yet to be fully used by States. States may continue to prefer other processes to compulsory

[354] *Icelandic Fisheries* (n 3) para 72.

[355] In the *dispositif*, the Court refers to negotiations between the parties taking account of 'the obligation to pay due regard to the interests of other States in the conservation and equitable exploitation of these resources': ibid para 79.

[356] *Icelandic Fisheries* (n 3) (Declaration of Judge Nagendra Singh) 40.

[357] *Virginia G* (n 9) (Separate Opinion of Judge Lucky) para 3.

[358] Churchill discusses reasons as to why there may not be too many fisheries cases: Churchill, 'Fisheries Jurisprudence of ITLOS' (n 233) 417–19.

procedures entailing binding decisions under UNCLOS. Given the opportunity, we might well expect a tribunal constituted under UNCLOS to embrace a role in elaborating requirements pertaining to high seas fisheries. Such elaboration should, though, still pay close attention to the other legal regimes that have bearing on this activity and how best to meet the interests of key stakeholders. A close assessment of the interests of coastal States and the rights and responsibilities of flag States, as was undertaken in the *SRFC Advisory Opinion* and the *South China Sea* arbitration, will remain critical in contributing to the future conduct of all stakeholders in the public order of the oceans.

9
Marine Environment

I. Introduction

Part XII of the United Nations Convention on the Law of the Sea (UNCLOS)[1] on the protection and preservation of the marine environment has become one of the more litigated Parts of UNCLOS. The use of adjudication or arbitration to resolve marine environmental disputes may not be an immediately obvious means of resolving environmental disputes in light of the importance accorded to dispute avoidance or prevention in many multilateral environmental treaties adopted in the 1990s and beyond.[2] Moreover, the initial cases instituted under the UNCLOS dispute settlement system that related to the marine environment faltered at different jurisdictional and admissibility hurdles,[3] or were settled before proceeding to the merits.[4] The foreshadowed claims in these cases, as well as the arguments of the parties, provide some indication of the potential for judicial contribution to the protection and preservation of the marine environment under UNCLOS. This potential has been subsequently realised in two advisory opinions under UNCLOS,[5] as well as the *Chagos Marine Protected Area* (*Chagos MPA*)[6] and the *South China Sea* arbitrations.[7] Other decisions, such as the Annex VII arbitration in *Duzgit Integrity*,[8] and the ITLOS decisions in *Virginia G*[9] and the *Louisa*,[10] have also elaborated on more specific elements of

[1] United Nations Convention on the Law of the Sea (adopted 10 December 1982, entered into force 16 November 1994) 1833 UNTS 397 (UNCLOS).

[2] See Tim Stephens, *International Courts and Environmental Protection* (CUP 2009) 10–11.

[3] See eg *MOX Plant (Ireland v United Kingdom)* (Provisional Measures, Order of 3 December 2001) ITLOS Reports 2001, 95 (*MOX Plant*, Provisional Measures); *MOX Plant (Ireland v United Kingdom)* (Order No 6 on Termination of Proceedings, Order of 6 June 2008) PCA Case No 2002-01 (*MOX Plant*, Termination); *Southern Bluefin Tuna (New Zealand v Japan; Australia v Japan)* (Jurisdiction and Admissibility) (2000) 23 RIAA 1 (*Southern Bluefin Tuna*, Jurisdiction and Admissibility).

[4] See eg *Conservation and Sustainable Exploitation of Swordfish Stocks (Chile/European Community)* (Order of 16 December 2009) ITLOS Reports 2008–2010, 13; *Land Reclamation by Singapore in and around the Straits of Johor (Malaysia v Singapore)* (Award on Agreed Terms of 1 September 2005) PCA Case No 2004-05 (*Land Reclamation*, Award). Some commentators have been positive about the modest contribution made to the protection and preservation of the marine environment through even these preliminary judicial encounters. See eg Xiaoyi Jiang and Jianwei Zhang, 'Marine Environment and the International Tribunal for the Law of the Sea: Twenty Years' Practices and Prospects' (2017) 5 China L Sci 84; Alan Boyle, 'The Environmental Jurisprudence of the International Tribunal for the Law of the Sea' (2007) 22 IJCML 369 (Boyle, 'Environmental Jurisprudence').

[5] *Responsibilities and Obligations of States with Respect to Activities in the Area* (Advisory Opinion) ITLOS Reports 2011, 10 (*Seabed Advisory Opinion*); *Request for Advisory Opinion Submitted by the Sub-Regional Fisheries Commission* (Advisory Opinion) ITLOS Reports 2015, 4 (*SRFC Advisory Opinion*).

[6] *Chagos Marine Protected Area Arbitration (Mauritius v United Kingdom)* (Award of 18 March 2015) PCA Case No 2011-03 (*Chagos MPA*).

[7] *South China Sea Arbitration (Philippines v China)* (Award of 12 July 2016) PCA Case No 2013-19 (*South China Sea*, Award).

[8] *Duzgit Integrity Arbitration (Malta v São Tomé and Príncipe)* (Award of 5 September 2016) PCA Case No 2014-07 (*Duzgit Integrity*).

[9] *M/V Virginia G (Panama/Guinea-Bissau)* (Judgment) ITLOS Reports 2014, 4 (*Virginia G*).

[10] *M/V Louisa (Saint Vincent and the Grenadines v Spain)* (Judgment) ITLOS Reports 2013, 4 (*Louisa*, Judgment).

the legal regime protecting the marine environment under UNCLOS. These cases sit within a growing body of environmental jurisprudence from diverse international courts and tribunals,[11] and contribute to the overall development of international environmental law.[12]

The governance of international environmental law has evolved into a dense collection of principles, standards, actors, and institutions.[13] UNCLOS provides an overarching legal structure in relation to the normative framework for the marine environment and anticipates that other international treaties, as well as different international and national actors, will be involved in implementing the requirements set out in UNCLOS. Provisions in Part XII of UNCLOS explicitly refer to these external standards,[14] and judicial engagement with Part XII has further resulted in other environmental principles and understandings being built into the interpretation and application of UNCLOS, as will be discussed in this chapter. This approach is arguably consistent with a method of 'systemic integration' provided for under Article 31(3)(c) of the Vienna Convention on the Law of Treaties (VCLT).[15]

Part XII consists of eleven Sections addressing different dimensions of the protection and preservation of the marine environment. The general provisions in Section 1 set out the core obligations in this regard, as well as the key duties relating to marine pollution. 'Pollution' is one of the few defined terms in UNCLOS, which is in Article 1(1)(4) of UNCLOS, along with a definition of 'dumping'. Section 2 of Part XII contains provisions on global and regional cooperation, including obligations relating to notification, contingency planning, and scientific programmes. Technical assistance to developing countries is addressed in Section 3. Section 4 sets out different procedural obligations relating to monitoring and environmental impact assessments (EIAs). Sections 5 and 6 set out, respectively, requirements for the regulation of different forms of pollution and their enforcement. Section 5 is particularly notable for its reference to external norms for benchmarking national action and for the formulation of the necessary regulations. Given the increased enforcement powers accorded to coastal and port States in relation to the protection and preservation of the marine environment, Section 7 provides various safeguards for foreign vessels and their flag States. Further protections are set out in Section 9 on responsibility and liability, as well as Section 10, which confirms sovereign immunity, and Section 11, which reinforces the ongoing applicability of more specific environmental rules that were adopted prior to

[11] Key decisions of the ICJ include *Pulp Mills on the River Uruguay (Argentina v Uruguay)* (Merits) [2010] ICJ Rep 14 (*Pulp Mills*, Merits); *Gabčíkovo-Nagymaros Project (Hungary/Slovakia)* (Judgment) [1997] ICJ Rep 7;and *Certain Activities Carried Out by Nicaragua in the Border Area (Costa Rica v Nicaragua), Construction of a Road in Costa Rica along the San Juan River (Nicaragua v Costa Rica)* (Judgment) [2015] ICJ Rep 665 (*Construction of a Road*). For general discussion of the contribution of courts and tribunals to international environmental law see Stephens (n 2); Natalie Klein, 'International Environmental Law Disputes before International Courts and Tribunals' in Jacqueline Peel and Lavanya Rajamani (eds), *Oxford Handbook of International Environmental Law* (2nd edn, OUP 2021).

[12] In this regard, Peel, writing in 2001, noted that 'judicial analysis and exposition is crucial in areas such as international environmental law which is still in a formative stage of development': Jacqueline Peel, 'A Paper Umbrella Which Dissolves in the Rain? Implications of the Southern Bluefin Tuna Case for the Compulsory Resolution of Disputes Concerning the Marine Environment under the 1982 LOS Convention' (2001) 6 APJEL 297, 304.

[13] This framework is explained by various theories on environmental governance. For an overview see Erika J Techera and Natalie Klein, *International Law of Sharks: Obstacles, Options and Opportunities* (Martinus Nijhoff 2017) 67–76.

[14] See eg UNCLOS (n 1) arts 197, 207(1) and 208(3).

[15] Vienna Convention on the Law of Treaties (adopted 23 May 1969, entered into force 27 January 1980) 1155 UNTS 331, art 31(3)(b) (VCLT). For discussion see Chie Kojima, 'South China Sea Arbitration and the Protection of the Marine Environment: Evolution of UNCLOS Part XII Through Interpretation and the Duty to Cooperate' (2015) 21 Asian Ybk Intl L 166, 170–71.

UNCLOS. Section 8, uniquely containing Article 234 on ice-covered areas, was a provision for which Canada advocated to ensure proper protection of the Arctic from pollution.[16] From this overview, it is immediately apparent that there are diverse disputes that may arise in relation to the protection and preservation of the marine environment given the balance that must be struck between different States' interests in a variety of scenarios. To date, it is the core obligations as well as the requirements associated with EIAs that have been most frequently subject to international litigation.

Not all aspects of Part XII have been interpreted in international adjudication or arbitration thus far. It is nonetheless important to note the potential for this Part to be used in an increasing number of international disputes resolved under Part XV of UNCLOS for four reasons. First, the broad terms found in Part XII provide scope for many activities that potentially affect the marine environment to be challenged. Secondly, the reliance on external rules and standards in interpreting the provisions in Part XII allows for claims that implicate rights and duties under diverse treaties to be presented under the UNCLOS dispute settlement procedure.[17] Thirdly, the geographic scope of many requirements under Part XII is extensive, addressing conduct in all maritime areas, including the territorial sea, exclusive economic zone (EEZ) and the high seas. Finally, and particularly when coupled with the geographic application of environmental obligations, the generous jurisdictional remit to tribunals constituted under UNCLOS in terms of subject matter jurisdiction means that all environmental disputes will most commonly be subject to compulsory arbitration or adjudication.[18]

In addition, issues of contested sovereignty or particular responsibilities or obligations that might accrue to a State based on the maritime zone in which activities occur are not necessarily relevant in assessing whether a State is in violation of the Convention's requirements for the protection and preservation of the marine environment.[19] More relevant is whether the respondent State had jurisdiction or control over the harmful activities at issue.[20] It therefore does not matter which maritime zone is at issue, or indeed if ownership rights over the maritime zone are disputed, when considering obligations relating to the marine environment as those duties apply throughout the oceans.[21]

To discuss the judicial interpretation of the marine environmental provisions of UNCLOS, this chapter focuses on the limited number of provisions from Part XII that have been interpreted and applied in judgments and advisory opinions. The core obligations of Articles 192 and 194 are the first focus, including their applicability in relation to the conservation and management of marine living resources, as well as activities in the Area. The

[16] See Suzanne Lalonde, 'Evaluating Canada's Position on the Northwest Passage in Light of Two Possible Sources of International Protection' in Clive Schofield, Seokwoo Lee, and Moon-Sang Kwon (eds), *The Limits of Maritime Jurisdiction* (Martinus Nijhoff 2014) 576–82.

[17] Although this potential overlap may present a jurisdictional hurdle under Articles 281 and 282. The *South China Sea* Tribunal addressed this issue in relation to the Convention on Biological Diversity (adopted 5 June 1992, entered into force 29 December 1993) 1760 UNTS 79 (CBD), but did not consider it a basis to deny jurisdiction. See *South China Sea Arbitration (Philippines v China)* (Award on Jurisdiction and Admissibility of 29 October 2015) PCA Case No 2013-19, paras 281–89, 317–21. See also ch 3(II)(A)(1).

[18] For discussion on the jurisdictional scope to examine environmental disputes under UNCLOS see ch 4(III)(B).

[19] *South China Sea*, Award (n 7) para 927.

[20] ibid para 944.

[21] See Myron H Nordquist (ed), *United Nations Convention on the Law of the Sea 1982: A Commentary*, vol 4 (Martinus Nijhoff 1990) 43 (*Virginia Commentary*) (discussing the scope of Article 192).

chapter then discusses the analysis of substantive environmental norms, such as the duty to cooperate, the conduct of EIAs and the precautionary approach. The enforcement of environmental standards and due diligence standards are subsequently addressed. Judicial activity has been largely beneficial for the development of international law relating to the protection and preservation of the marine environment but there remains potential for much more in this space. Nonetheless, questions must be raised as to how much development is to occur within judicial settings and what should more properly be resolved directly among the State parties and other stakeholders, including conservation NGOs, civil society, and maritime industries.

II. Core Obligations

The core obligations consist of the general provisions set out in Section 1 of Part XII. They are intended to set the framework for Part XII and it has been suggested that they do not 'impos[e] specific obligations or confer[] quantifiable rights on States'.[22] Nonetheless, the judicial evolution of various of these provisions within Section 1 has resulted in a situation where the standards enshrined in Articles 192 and 194 provide very concrete bases for asserting claims of breach. The content that has evolved under these general provisions is discussed below in relation to the obligations in Articles 192 and 193; core obligations protecting the environment from marine pollution as set out in Article 194; conservation and management of marine living resources, and environmental protection of the Area.

A. Articles 192 and 193

Articles 192 and 193 of UNCLOS set out the broadest international law principles relating to the protection and preservation of the marine environment. While Article 192 contains the core obligation to protect and preserve the marine environment, Article 193 anticipates more of a balance between States' obligations towards the environment and their right to development through the exploitation of natural resources.[23] To this end, Article 193 provides: 'States have the sovereign right to exploit their natural resources pursuant to their environmental policies and in accordance with their duty to protect and preserve the marine environment'. The cases addressing the core obligations have focused more on elucidating the content of Article 192 rather than clarifying what balance is appropriate under Article 193. As Schatz has observed, the open wording of Article 192 lends itself to a dynamic interpretation.[24]

In the interpretation of Article 192 of the Convention, the *South China Sea* Tribunal noted that the content of this obligation was 'informed by the other provisions of Part XII

[22] ibid 36. But see Detlef Czybulka, 'Article 192' in Alexander Proelss (ed), *United Nations Convention on the Law of the Sea: A Commentary* (CH Beck, Hart, and Nomos 2017) (*Proelss Commentary*) 1284, paras 19–20 (arguing there was an intention for these core obligations to have a legal effect rather than reflect simply a political statement).

[23] Boyle, 'Environmental Jurisprudence' (n 4) 376.

[24] Valentin Schatz, 'Fishing for Interpretation: The ITLOS Advisory Opinion on Flag State Responsibility for Illegal Fishing in the EEZ' (2016) 47 ODIL 327, 333.

and other applicable rules of international law'.[25] The latter dimension was envisaged by Article 237 of UNCLOS, according to the Tribunal.[26] Such an approach is consistent with the view that Article 192 as a general formulation 'would be the binding element or organic link between the general treaty and particular treaties or national measures dealing with individual aspects of marine pollution'.[27] At its base, 'Article 192 thus entails the positive obligation to take active measures to protect and preserve the marine environment, and by logical implication, entails the negative obligation not to degrade the marine environment'.[28]

Article 192 was relevant to the *South China Sea* arbitration in light of China's construction activities on different maritime features in the South China Sea.[29] The Philippines' claims particularly concerned construction activities on Cuarteron Reef, Fiery Cross Reef, Gaven Reef (North), Johnson Reef, Hughes Reef, Subi Reef, and Mischief Reef in the Spratly Islands group. These activities accelerated from the end of 2013 when China 'deployed a large fleet of vessels to the seven reefs, primarily using heavy "cutter-suction dredge" equipment, to create more than 12.8 million square metres [12.8 km^2] of new land in less than three years'.[30] The reef systems were impacted through construction and dredging activities either directly, in terms of destruction of reef habitat through burial, or indirectly, in terms of harm to benthic organisms (including corals and seagrasses), and to organisms in the water column caused by changes to the marine environment.[31]

In assessing whether China had violated UNCLOS requirements for the protection and preservation of the marine environment in its island-building activities, and given China's non-appearance, the *South China Sea* Tribunal had regard to documents that had previously been prepared by a Chinese agency. The Tribunal-appointed expert refuted many of the claims set out in this Chinese report.[32] The Tribunal thus concluded that the weight of evidence demonstrated that 'China's artificial island-building activities on the seven reefs in the Spratly Islands have caused devastating and long-lasting damage to the marine environment'.[33] On that basis, the Tribunal found China to have violated Articles 192, 194(1), and 194(5) of the Convention.[34] With reference to two previous arbitral awards, the *South China Sea* Tribunal considered there was a duty to prevent, or at least mitigate, significant harm to the marine environment during the pursuit of large-scale construction activities.[35] Failure to do so constituted a breach of Article 192.

[25] *South China Sea*, Award (n 7) para 941.

[26] ibid para 942. Article 237 refers to 'special conventions' and 'agreements concluded previously' addressing the protection and preservation of the marine environment. Although there is no explicit reference to customary international law, the Tribunal proceeds on the basis that customary international law also informs the interpretation of Article 192.

[27] *Virginia Commentary* (n 21) vol IV, 37.

[28] *South China Sea*, Award (n 7) para 941. See also ibid 39–40, which notes: 'Article 192 would appear to fall into the latter category [of a general principle of law], explicitly proclaiming in positive terms, as a general principle of law, that all States have the obligation to protect and preserve the marine environment, and implicitly (in negative terms) the obligation not to degrade it deliberately (or perhaps even carelessly).'

[29] China's construction of artificial islands in the South China Sea prompted the Philippines to claim that these activities violated Articles 123, 192, 194, 197, 205 and 206 of UNCLOS (n 1). *South China Sea*, Award (n 7) para 820. Article 123 is not located in Part XII of UNCLOS concerning the protection and preservation of the marine environment, but falls within Part IX, which is concerned with enclosed or semi-enclosed seas.

[30] *South China Sea*, Award (n 7) para 854.

[31] ibid para 857.

[32] ibid para 982.

[33] ibid para 983.

[34] ibid.

[35] ibid para 941, citing *Indus Waters Kishenganga Arbitration (Pakistan v India)* (Partial Award of 18 February 2013) PCA Case No 2011-01 and *Iron Rhone Arbitration (Belgium/Netherlands)* (Award of 25 May 2005) 27 RIAA 35, which did not concern the interpretation of UNCLOS (n 1).

Article 192 thus provides an umbrella for claims of a variety of environmental law violations caused by activities at sea. The *South China Sea* arbitration addressed activities on a large scale that caused 'significant harm'. It remains to be seen if less damaging conduct would also trigger a finding that Article 192 has been violated.[36] It is, however, questionable whether a State would elect to bring a claim based on minor damage, given the political and financial costs involved in international litigation.

B. Protecting the Marine Environment from Pollution

Article 194 of the Convention establishes the core obligations relating to the adoption of measures to prevent, reduce and control pollution of the marine environment from any source. It reads:

1. States shall take, individually or jointly as appropriate, all measures consistent with this Convention that are necessary to prevent, reduce and control pollution of the marine environment from any source, using for this purpose the best practicable means at their disposal and in accordance with their capabilities, and they shall endeavour to harmonize their policies in this connection.
2. States shall take all measures necessary to ensure that activities under their jurisdiction or control are so conducted as not to cause damage by pollution to other States and their environment, and that pollution arising from incidents or activities under their jurisdiction or control does not spread beyond the areas where they exercise sovereign rights in accordance with this Convention.
3. The measures taken pursuant to this Part shall deal with all sources of pollution of the marine environment. These measures shall include, inter alia, those designed to minimize to the fullest possible extent:
   (a) the release of toxic, harmful or noxious substances, especially those which are persistent, from land-based sources, from or through the atmosphere or by dumping;
   (b) pollution from vessels, in particular measures for preventing accidents and dealing with emergencies, ensuring the safety of operations at sea, preventing intentional and unintentional discharges, and regulating the design, construction, equipment, operation and manning of vessels;
   (c) pollution from installations and devices used in exploration or exploitation of the natural resources of the seabed and subsoil, in particular measures for preventing accidents and dealing with emergencies, ensuring the safety of operations at sea, and regulating the design, construction, equipment, operation and manning of such installations or devices;
   (d) pollution from other installations and devices operating in the marine environment, in particular measures for preventing accidents and dealing with

[36] See eg Mossop, who has argued: 'It is possible that a future tribunal, interpreting the obligation in Article 192 of UNCLOS to protect and preserve the marine environment, might consider the application of the precautionary approach a part of the state's obligation to exercise due diligence to implement Article 192': Joanna Mossop, 'Can We Make the Oceans Greener: The Successes and Failures of UNCLOS as an Environmental Treaty' (2018) 49 VUWLR 573, 588–89.

emergencies, ensuring the safety of operations at sea, and regulating the design, construction, equipment, operation and manning of such installations or devices.

4. In taking measures to prevent, reduce or control pollution of the marine environment, States shall refrain from unjustifiable interference with activities carried out by other States in the exercise of their rights and in pursuance of their duties in conformity with this Convention.
5. The measures taken in accordance with this Part shall include those necessary to protect and preserve rare or fragile ecosystems as well as the habitat of depleted, threatened or endangered species and other forms of marine life.

Article 194 was intended to 'link … the two statements of general principle contained in articles 192 and 193 to the formal rules of law appearing in the subsequent articles of Part XII'.[37]

The scope and meaning of Article 194(1) were considered in the *Chagos MPA* arbitration. In its broad setting, this case concerned Mauritius' ongoing challenge to and concerns about the United Kingdom's exercise of sovereignty over the Chagos Archipelago. These concerns encompassed the removal of the Chagossian population from the Archipelago, the use of and access to Diego Garcia, an island within the Archipelago that the United States uses as a defence facility, as well as contested sovereignty over the Archipelago. More particularly in the arbitration, Mauritius challenged the legality of the United Kingdom's declaration of a marine protected area (MPA) over the EEZ of the Archipelago. In relation to potential violations of the provisions of UNCLOS through the declaration of the MPA, the principal basis of Mauritius' complaints was set out as follows:

> The UK did not inform Mauritius of its plans; it provided Mauritius with inaccurate information; and it ignored Mauritius' repeated calls for bilateral consultations, insisting on proceeding instead with a fundamentally flawed Public Consultation all despite a commitment by the UK Prime Minister to his Mauritian counterpart that the MPA would be put on hold.[38]

Mauritius thus alleged that the United Kingdom was in violation of Article 194 of the Convention.

Mauritius argued that Article 194(1) required that 'States must try hard to do or achieve harmonization of policies regarding pollution prevention'.[39] As such, it was necessary for States to share information, exchange ideas, and engage in some consultation.[40] The United Kingdom's interpretation was that Article 194(1), as one of the general provisions in Part XII, was intended as a chapeau to more specific requirements set out in relation to

[37] *Virginia Commentary* (n 21) vol IV, 53. See also Czybulka (n 22) 1297, para 1 ('it is in Art 194 where the rather general principles of Arts 192 and 193 are concretised and transformed into specific obligations of States'). The *Virginia Commentary* further notes that all the negotiations on this provision occurred in informal meetings and there are thus scant records and little guidance for interpretation: see vol IV, 64.

[38] *Chagos MPA* (n 6) para 457, citing *Chagos Marine Protected Area Arbitration (Mauritius v United Kingdom)* (Final Transcript) PCA Case No 2011-03, 336:18 to 337:2.

[39] *Chagos MPA* (n 6) para 483.

[40] ibid.

pollution control measures, as indicated in Article 194(3) and subsequently in Section 5 of Part XII.[41]

In examining the scope of Article 194(1), the Tribunal concluded that the obligation to 'endeavour to harmonise' policies between States was not limited to controlling pollution but, in light of Article 194(5), 'extends to measures focused primarily on conservation and the preservation of ecosystems'.[42] Article 194(5) thus informed the content of the other sub-paragraphs of Article 194,[43] and this decision has the effect of ensuring that the obligations in Part XII of UNCLOS are not confined to questions of pollution in particular but should address marine environmental protection *in toto*.[44] Moreover, the Tribunal considered that the obligation in Article 194(1) is prospective and sets a standard of 'best efforts'.[45] When all these dimensions were considered, the *Chagos MPA* Tribunal concluded that the short life of the MPA had not resulted in any violation on the part of the United Kingdom.[46]

The *South China Sea* Tribunal also considered that China's artificial island-building activities were a violation of Article 194(1) of UNCLOS. The evidence before the Tribunal as to the environmental harm caused by the construction activity was considered compelling and left 'no doubt' that China's activities had caused 'devastating and long-lasting damage to the marine environment'.[47] The Tribunal had not previously discussed any interpretation of Article 194(1) but simply found that China had conducted its dredging 'in such a way as to pollute the marine environment with sediment'.[48] There was no further engagement with the definition of pollution on this point.

Mauritius further argued in *Chagos MPA* that the United Kingdom's declaration of the MPA had violated Article 194(4) of UNCLOS. As set out above, this provision requires States to refrain from unjustifiable interference with activities carried out by other States in taking pollution measures. Mauritius argued that this obligation necessitated an assessment by the United Kingdom of whether the interference was justifiable but no evidence of such an assessment was forthcoming.[49] In the view of Mauritius, the total ban on activities in the MPA was an obvious and unjustifiable interference with its fishing rights within the area.[50] The United Kingdom disputed that there was interference as a matter of fact.[51]

The *Chagos MPA* Tribunal considered that the obligation in Article 194(4) to 'refrain from unjustifiable interference with activities carried out by other states' could be assessed similarly to the due regard requirement in Article 56(2) and the good faith requirement of Article 2(3).[52] The Tribunal noted: 'Like these provisions, Article 194(4) requires a balancing act between competing rights, based upon an evaluation of the extent of the interference, the availability of alternatives, and the importance of the rights and policies at issue.'[53] However,

[41] ibid para 488. This position aligns with the authoritative Virginia commentary to UNCLOS, as noted above. See n 22 and accompanying text.

[42] *Chagos MPA* (n 6) para 538.

[43] ibid.

[44] Prior to this decision, Boyle had commented: 'it is clear from the totality of Articles 192–196 that Part XII was never intended to be simply about pollution, and that it encompasses protection of ecosystems, conservation of depleted or endangered species of marine life, and control of alien species.' Boyle (n 4) 373.

[45] *Chagos MPA* (n 6) para 539.

[46] ibid.

[47] *South China Sea*, Award (n 7) para 983.

[48] ibid.

[49] *Chagos MPA* (n 6) para 485.

[50] ibid para 486.

[51] ibid para 489.

[52] ibid para 540.

[53] ibid.

in relation to Article 194(4), as opposed to Articles 2(3) and 56(2), the Tribunal observed that the interference related to activities carried out on the basis of rights held, rather than interference with the rights themselves.[54] This interpretation limited the Tribunal's consideration to interference with fishing activities, rather than any prospective fishing rights that Mauritius might hold.[55] In applying the facts, the United Kingdom's failure to engage in any consideration of Mauritius's fishing rights in the territorial sea in establishing the MPA led to a violation of Article 194(4), in addition to Articles 2(3) and 56(2) of the Convention.[56] This decision confirms that cumulative violations of the Convention may occur where the same activities can be found to violate different international legal obligations.

In relation to Article 194 of UNCLOS, the *South China Sea* Tribunal focused on paragraph 5 of that provision, which concerns protection and preservation of 'rare or fragile ecosystems as well as the habitat of depleted, threatened or endangered species and other forms of marine life'.[57] As mentioned above, the *Chagos MPA* Tribunal relied on this provision to determine that Part XII was not uniquely concerned with questions of controlling marine pollution, but was to address environmental protection more broadly.[58] The *South China Sea* Tribunal examined this requirement more extensively. In interpreting 'ecosystems', the *South China Sea* Tribunal relied on 'internationally accepted definitions' as reflected in Article 2 of the Convention on Biological Diversity.[59] What might constitute a 'rare or fragile' ecosystem was not parsed in any detail by the Tribunal. Harrison has noted that this element is 'inherently flexible' and 'must be understood by reference to scientific information concerning the state of the marine environment'.[60] Nonetheless, the Tribunal has been commended for adopting an 'ecosystem approach' based on Article 194,[61] rather than limiting its focus to marine pollution.

Further, the *South China Sea* Tribunal found that the identification of 'depleted, threatened or endangered species' in Article 194(5) is to be informed by the Convention on the International Trade in Endangered Species (CITES).[62] The Tribunal considered that CITES 'forms part of the general corpus of international law that informs the content of Article 192 and 194(5) of the Convention'.[63] Yet, while Article 194(5) refers to 'depleted, threatened or endangered species', the *South China Sea* Tribunal reduced the scope of the variety

[54] ibid.
[55] ibid.
[56] ibid.
[57] UNCLOS (n 1) art 194(5). The Philippines had developed an argument based on Articles 194(1), (3), and (5) whereby the broad obligation to protect and preserve the marine environment from pollution meant that dumping of cyanide was prohibited for the harm caused to a fragile ecosystem. See Ilias Plakokefalos, 'Environmental Law Aspects of the Arbitral Tribunal Award in the South China Sea Dispute' (2016) 6 https://papers.ssrn.com/sol3/papers.cfm?abstract_id=2880624.
[58] *Chagos MPA* (n 6) paras 320, 538. The Chinese Society of International Law's response to the *South China Sea* arbitration similarly argued that Article 194(5) must be understood as a provision relating to pollution so that any harmful harvesting activities had to be shown to have caused pollution of the marine environment. See Chinese Society of International Law, 'The South China Sea Arbitration Awards: A Critical Study' (2018) 17 Chinese JIL 207, para 791.
[59] *South China Sea*, Award (n 7) para 945, citing CBD (n 17) art 2.
[60] James Harrison, *Saving the Oceans Through Law: The International Legal Framework for the Protection of the Marine Environment* (OUP 2017) 30.
[61] Plakokefalos (n 57) 12. See also Stephen Fietta, Jiries Saadeh, and Laura Rees-Evans, 'The South China Sea Award: A Milestone for International Environmental Law, the Duty of Due Diligence and the Litigation of Maritime Environmental Disputes' (2017) 29 Geo Intl Envtl L Rev 711, 745 ('a welcome development in the "joining up" of international environmental law standards relating to conservation and the protection of biodiversity').
[62] *South China Sea*, Award (n 7) para 956.
[63] ibid.

of marine species that may otherwise be protected under this provision, as it referred to those species that 'are recognised internationally as being at risk of extinction and requiring international protection'.[64] Does this holding mean that only those marine species listed in Appendix I or II of CITES will now be protected under UNCLOS? Varying levels of restrictions on the international trade in these species apply depending on whether or not a species is listed, and depending on which appendix it is listed. The International Union for Conservation of Nature (IUCN) Red List is an authoritative guide on the status of species, rating them as extinct to critically endangered to vulnerable, through to least concern or data deficient.[65] The IUCN Red List informs decisions taken by the States party to CITES to list any species on the CITES Appendices. The *South China Sea* Tribunal's approach to identifying 'depleted, threatened or endangered species' prompts questions as to the relevant benchmark for the purposes of assessing violations under Article 194(5). For example, what of those marine species that have been identified on the IUCN Red List as near threatened (so 'depleted') or endangered but are not yet subject to international protection under CITES because of political disagreement? Arguably, the UNCLOS protection applies more broadly and not only to those species listed in the CITES Appendices.

The linkage to Appendix I and II of CITES does, however, allow for the possibility that the interpretation of Article 194(5) may shift depending on State decisions to change or update the status of species listed under those Appendices.[66] It allows for quite a dynamic form of treaty interaction as a result.[67] Nonetheless, it would be worth asking whether the linkage should be drawn too closely between CITES and UNCLOS. If the interpretation of Article 194(5) is to rely on CITES listings, it may be argued that consideration must be given as to which States were parties to CITES as well as to UNCLOS, and whether the fact that a State was not bound by a CITES listing would necessarily preclude an interpretation of the species as 'depleted, threatened, or endangered' under UNCLOS. Commentators suggest that what would be more informative in this situation should be the level of international consensus around the status of a species.[68] This approach favours the establishment of a legal standard as to what species are considered as depleted, threatened, or endangered rather than relying solely on scientific evidence as the key, or only, indicator. This approach may be politically justifiable, but the narrowed scope of Article 194(5) would no doubt disappoint conservation advocates.

While the precise contours of what species are protected will typically be determined on a case-by-case basis,[69] the *South China Sea* Tribunal did consider that Articles 192 and 194(5), when read together, required the prevention of indirect harm to such species.[70] The protection afforded is thus appropriately broad in this context. Recognising that habitat destruction may also constitute a violation of Article 194(5) of UNCLOS is consistent with an

[64] ibid.

[65] See International Union for Conservation of Nature (IUCN), *Red List Categories and Criteria* (2nd edn, version 3.1, 2012).

[66] See Kojima (n 15) 173.

[67] ibid 173. See also Harrison (n 60) 30.

[68] See Alan Boyle, 'Further Development of the Law of the Sea Convention: Mechanisms for Change' (2005) 54 ICLQ 563, 569; Kojima (n 15) 174.

[69] See Czybulka (n 22) 1312, para 33.

[70] *South China Sea*, Award (n 7) para 959.

ecosystem approach.[71] However, there is a risk that the ecosystem approach is undermined if the number of species protected under Article 194(5) is narrowly construed.

Even if a narrow reading of Article 194(5) reduces the scope of species protection required of States under that specific provision of UNCLOS, it can nonetheless be borne in mind that in the *SRFC Advisory Opinion*, ITLOS affirmed that 'living resources and marine life are part of the marine environment'.[72] Through this recognition that marine life protection is inherent in the general obligation to protect and preserve the marine environment under Article 192, there is once again potential to broaden out what conduct might be considered unlawful when directed against the preservation or conservation of particular marine species.[73]

In reading Articles 192 and 194(5) together, on the reasoning of the *South China Sea* Tribunal, it appears that a breach of the latter necessarily means that there is also a breach of the former. Presumably, a tribunal constituted under UNCLOS could still find a breach of Article 192 in the absence of a breach of another provision in Part XII of the Convention. Such a finding would be foreseeable where there is a violation of 'other applicable rules of international law'.[74] Yet Article 194 itself has now been used as an expansive basis for asserting environmental claims and has moved well beyond a framework clause that does not specify obligations or 'confer[] quantifiable rights'.[75]

C. Conservation of Marine Living Resources

Within the core obligations, and particularly Article 192, the UNCLOS jurisprudence has endorsed the inclusion of the conservation and management of marine living resources as part of the protection and preservation of the marine environment. When ITLOS declared in its provisional measures order in *Southern Bluefin Tuna* that 'the conservation of the living resources of the sea is an element in the protection and preservation of the marine environment',[76] there was no explicit invocation of any provision of the Convention to justify such a holding. At most, this statement linked the orders ITLOS prescribed to the head of power granted in Article 290(5). That is, the Tribunal had to make this connection between conservation of marine living resources and protection of the marine environment given that provisional measures may be prescribed under Article 290 to prevent serious harm to the marine environment.[77] This limited understanding of the provisional measures order has not been followed subsequently but the statement has instead been used to envelop the conservation and management of living marine resources into the protection and preservation of the marine environment more generally. Fisheries disputes have thus been considered in the context of Part XII of UNCLOS, as well as in relation to UNCLOS provisions addressing fisheries.

[71] Tim Stephens, 'The Collateral Damage from China's "Great Wall of Sand": the Environmental Dimensions of the South China Sea Case' (2016) 34 Aust YBIL 41, 48.
[72] *SRFC Advisory Opinion* (n 5) para 216.
[73] See ch 9(II)(A) above (discussing the scope of Article 192).
[74] *South China Sea*, Award (n 7) para 941.
[75] See n 22.
[76] *Southern Bluefin Tuna (New Zealand v Japan; Australia v Japan)* (Provisional Measures, Order of 27 August 1999) ITLOS Reports 1999, 280 (*Southern Bluefin Tuna*, Provisional Measures) para 70.
[77] ibid para 67.

In the *South China Sea* arbitration, the Philippines alleged that harmful fishing practices violated China's duties to protect and preserve the marine environment under the Convention.[78] The facts before the *South China Sea* Tribunal indicated that Chinese fishers had engaged in the harvesting of corals and giant clams using destructive fishing techniques. Corals and giant clams are endangered species, with their conservation status considered as near-threatened or vulnerable on the IUCN Red List.[79] Tribunal-appointed experts, as well as expert reports presented by the Philippines, indicated that the propellers of small ships had been extensively used to break up coral and release giant clams.[80] The Philippines also presented evidence claiming that Chinese fishers had used dynamite, cyanide, and other chemicals as part of their fishing practices.[81]

In the Philippines' view, China's encouragement of and failure to prevent harvesting of endangered species and fishing techniques violated Articles 192 and 194 of UNCLOS.[82] The Philippines' arguments were cast as 'five obligations ... applicable to States under Part XII of the Convention'.[83] As such, these were not specific references to provisions of the Convention but what the Tribunal should read into Articles 192 and 194, as well as Articles 197 and 123 in relation to the obligations to consult and cooperate.[84] The Philippines sought to amplify the content of Article 192 by reference to Principle 21 from the Stockholm Declaration.[85] As discussed above, the Tribunal determined that China was in violation of Article 194(5).[86] China's conduct also violated Article 192 'read in the context of Article 194(5) and the international law applicable to endangered species'.[87] This finding was based on the determination that China was aware of, tolerated, and failed to prevent harvesting of endangered species on a significant scale and harvesting giant clams in a manner severely destructive of the coral reef ecosystem.[88]

The environmental requirements relating to the conservation and management of marine living resources were also addressed in the *SRFC Advisory Opinion*. This Advisory Opinion was issued by ITLOS further to a request from the Sub-Regional Fisheries Commission (SRFC), which sought guidance on the responsibilities and liability of flag States in relation to illegal, unregulated, and unreported (IUU) fishing, as well as advice on the coastal State's rights and obligations in ensuring the sustainable management of shared stocks.[89] As

[78] Philippines Submission 12(b): see *South China Sea*, Award (n 7) para 816, described as such by the Tribunal: see para 817.

[79] See IUCN, 'Red List of Threatened Species'<https://www.iucnredlist.org/>. There are many different species of coral, which range from critically endangered to least concern. The majority of the species of coral included on the IUCN list are vulnerable or near-threatened. The *South China Sea* award did not address what species of coral were targeted in China's operations. In light of the large areas destroyed through the island-building and illicit fishing activities, it would be reasonable to assume that vulnerable species of coral were affected.

[80] *South China Sea*, Award (n 7) para 848.

[81] ibid paras 827–31, 845. However, this claim was not ultimately upheld by the Tribunal: see para 975. For discussion see Fietta, Saadeh, and Rees-Evans (n 61) 738.

[82] *South China Sea*, Award (n 7) para 894.

[83] ibid para 910.

[84] ibid.

[85] Principle 21 of the Stockholm Declaration provides for an obligation to 'ensure that activities within their jurisdiction or control do not cause damage to the environment of other States or of areas beyond the limits of national jurisdiction': 'Declaration of the United Nations Conference on the Human Environment' (adopted 16 June 1972) UN Doc A/Conf.48/14/Rev.1, Principle 21 (Stockholm Declaration). See also 'Memorial of the Philippines, Vol I', *South China Sea Arbitration (Philippines v China)* (Memorial of the Philippines: Volume 1) PCA Case No 2013-19, para 6.71.

[86] See nn 57–70 above and accompanying text.

[87] *South China Sea*, Award (n 7) para 964.

[88] ibid paras 964–66.

[89] *SRFC Advisory Opinion* (n 5) para 2.

discussed in Chapter 8, although the *SRFC Advisory Opinion* was specifically for the members of the SRFC, it could be anticipated that the interpretations of the Convention provisions in the Advisory Opinion may be applied to other State parties in the future.[90]

In its *SRFC Advisory Opinion*, ITLOS noted that Articles 192 and 193 of UNCLOS concern 'general obligations which are to be met by the flag State in all maritime areas regulated by the Convention', including the coastal State's EEZ.[91] ITLOS considered that a flag State's failure to ensure that its vessels comply with the coastal State's conservation measures would be a violation of Article 192.[92] More particularly, Article 192 supported an interpretation of Article 62(4) that requires flag States to take the necessary measures to ensure their nationals and vessels are not engaged in IUU fishing activities.[93] Articles 192 and 193 were also held to be bases for requiring flag States to take the necessary measures to ensure that their vessels comply with a regional fisheries organisation's protection and preservation measures.[94] It thus seems that Articles 192 and 193 may be used to build out the due regard requirement that is imposed on States by virtue of Article 58(3) of the Convention. Equally, a violation of Article 58(3) caused by fishing activities may also entail violations of Articles 192 and 193.

This due regard requirement is seemingly extended to straddling stocks as well, given that ITLOS outlined the requirement and noted it is part of Articles 192 and 193 and '[a]ccordingly' noted that States are to agree upon measures as required in Article 63(2).[95] The connection is by no means explicit in the *SRFC Advisory Opinion*, but the reiteration of the due regard requirement and its connection to the protection and preservation of the marine environment across all maritime zones may prompt a possible argument in the future that the measures agreed in relation to straddling stocks entail a requirement to have due regard to the rights and duties of all users.[96]

D. Core Obligations in the Protection of the Area

The judicial interpretation of environmental obligations applicable to the Area arose in the context of an advisory opinion requested of the Seabed Disputes Chamber pursuant to Article 191 of the Convention. The Council of the International Seabed Authority (ISA) sought the views of the Chamber in light of Nauru and Tonga's concerns as to their potential responsibilities and obligations as sponsoring States in the exploration and exploitation of the deep seabed.[97] In responding to questions on the substantive obligations adhering to sponsoring States, the Chamber had cause to address environmental protection requirements. This process involved a consideration of UNCLOS provisions relating to the Area specifically, as well as provisions addressing the marine environment more generally. The

[90] See ch 8(IV)(B).
[91] *SRFC Advisory Opinion* (n 5) para 111. See also para 120.
[92] ibid para 120.
[93] ibid para 124. A conclusion that is also drawn from UNCLOS (n 1) Articles 58(3) and 62(4).
[94] *SRFC Advisory Opinion* (n 5) para 136.
[95] ibid para 216.
[96] See also ch 8(V).
[97] For further detail on the background to the *Seabed Advisory Opinion* (n 5) see Yoshifumi Tanaka, 'Obligations and Liability of Sponsoring States Concerning Activities in the Area: Reflections on the ITLOS Advisory Opinion of 1 February 2011' (2013) 60 NILR 205, 206–208.

Chamber further relied on the 1994 Agreement and regulations that have been adopted by the ISA that govern prospecting and exploration for polymetallic sulphides and for polymetallic nodules in the Area.[98] A distinction is drawn in the *Seabed Advisory Opinion* as between direct obligations imposed on sponsoring States and due diligence obligations, requiring the sponsoring States to ensure their conduct, or the conduct of private actors within their jurisdiction or control, is consistent with environmental protection requirements. This section discusses the direct obligations arising under the core obligations of environmental protection.[99]

In assessing the application of environmental norms to 'activities in the Area', the Seabed Disputes Chamber pursued an interpretation of the Convention and the 1994 Agreement to ascertain what 'activities' would engage State obligations. In doing so, the Chamber excluded transporting and processing as 'activities in the Area'.[100] Such an interpretation suggests that States are not obliged under Article 145 to take 'necessary measures' to protect the marine environment from the harmful effects of transportation or any processing that may occur. An indicative list of activities was instead included, and referred to 'drilling, dredging, coring, and excavation; disposal, dumping and discharge into the marine environment of sediment, wastes or other effluents; and construction and operation or maintenance of installations, pipelines and other devices related to such activities'.[101] The Chamber noted that transporting and processing were included in the definitions of 'exploration' and 'exploitation' in the ISA's Nodules and Sulphides Regulations.[102] However, as the Regulations are subordinate to the Convention, the Chamber determined that there must be a consistent interpretation across all references to 'activities in the Area' throughout the Convention provisions.[103] Consequently, transporting and processing remain excluded from the scope of the environmental requirements set out in Article 145.[104] According to the Chamber, it must instead be expected that any environmental harm resulting from transporting or processing associated with activities in the Area would still fall under the broader environmental obligations set out in Article 192.[105] The Chamber did not, however, contemplate the use of Article 194 in a similar regard. Commentators have further suggested that Article 235, which addresses responsibility and liability, could be relied upon for this purpose.[106]

[98] The two sets of regulations are: International Seabed Authority, 'Regulations on Prospecting and Exploration for Polymetallic Sulphides in the Area' (15 November 2010) https://www.isa.org.jm/files/documents/EN/Regs/PolymetallicSulphides.pdf UN Doc ISBA/16/A/12/Rev.1 (Sulphides Regulations); International Seabed Authority, 'Regulations on Prospecting and Exploration for Polymetallic Nodules in the Area' (22 July 2013) https://www.isa.org.jm/files/documents/EN/Regs/PN-en.pdf UN Doc ISBA/19/C/17 (Nodules Regulations).

[99] The due diligence obligations are addressed in ch 8(IV)(D) above.

[100] *Seabed Advisory Opinion* (n 5) para 87.

[101] UNCLOS (n 1) art 145(a). See *Seabed Advisory Opinion* (n 5) para 87.

[102] *Seabed Advisory Opinion* (n 5) para 92.

[103] ibid para 93.

[104] ibid paras 95–96. 'Prospecting' is also excluded: see para 98. For discussion see David Freestone, 'Advisory Opinion of the Seabed Disputes Chamber of the International Tribunal for the Law of the Sea on "Responsibilities and Obligations of States Sponsoring Persons and Entities With Respect to Activities in the Area"' (2011) 15 ASIL Insights www.asil.org/insights/volume/15/issue/7/advisory-opinion-seabed-disputes-chamber-international-tribunal-law-sea-.

[105] *Seabed Advisory Opinion* (n 5), para 97.

[106] Donald K Anton, Robert A Makgill, and Cymie R Payne, 'Seabed Mining: Advisory Opinion on Responsibility and Liability' (2011) 41 Env Poly & L 60, 62. Article 235(1) reads: 'States are responsible for the fulfilment of their international obligations concerning the protection and preservation of the marine environment. They shall be liable in accordance with international law': UNCLOS (n 1) art 235(1).

Further environmental obligations that the Chamber considered as directly applying to States included a guarantee in the event of an emergency order by the ISA for marine environment protection,[107] and allowing recourse for prompt and adequate compensation or other relief in respect of damage caused by pollution of the marine environment, in accordance with Article 235(2) of UNCLOS.[108] The first of these requirements had been embodied in the Nodules and Sulphides Regulations.[109] As such, there was some circularity in the Chamber's reasoning in that the obligations set out in the subordinate instruments also became the obligations enshrined in the ordinate instrument, even though the ordinate instrument did not include that detail. With the Chamber's interpretation, the ordinate instrument does seemingly now include such an obligation directly applying to sponsoring States in the conduct of activities in the Area. The Chamber's reasoning therefore allowed the Regulations to amplify the Convention obligations but, as discussed in relation to transporting and processing, could not contradict the Convention. The Chamber moreover affirmed that the environmental obligations identified in the Advisory Opinion were intended as examples and should not be considered a definitive list of environmental obligations.[110] In so determining, the Chamber preserved its scope to elaborate on further environmental obligations pertaining to the Area in future proceedings.

* * *

The content of the general provisions in Section 1 of Part XII of UNCLOS has been increasingly clarified, amplified, and articulated in UNCLOS cases and advisory opinions. This practice should serve as a clarion call for other claims of international environmental law violations when maritime activities are challenged between States party to the Convention. When these core obligations are coupled with due regard requirements, the substantive bases to pursue marine environmental law cases are vast. It is worth recalling the *MOX Plant* case and Ireland's efforts to draw in diverse multilateral environmental agreements as part of its challenges to the United Kingdom's actions in commissioning a mixed oxide facility on the shores of the Irish Sea. The United Kingdom opposed 'the wholesale incorporation into and application as part of UNCLOS of every far-flung rule of customary or conventional international law'.[111] Yet it would rather seem that more recent case law has indicated other environmental agreements may be used to assess State conduct when determining whether the core environmental obligations are met.

III. Duty to Cooperate

The principle of cooperation in international environmental law was enshrined in Principle 24 of the Stockholm Declaration and Principle 27 of the Rio Declaration,[112] and the obligation has further been embodied in 'virtually all' international environmental agreements.[113]

[107] *Seabed Advisory Opinion* (n 5) para 138.
[108] ibid para 139.
[109] Sulphides Regulations (n 98) reg 35; Nodules Regulations (n 98) reg 32.
[110] *Seabed Advisory Opinion* (n 5) para 236.
[111] *MOX Plant (Ireland v United Kingdom)* (United Kingdom Rejoinder) PCA Case No 2002-01, para 5.15.
[112] Stockholm Declaration (n 85) Principle 24; 'Rio Declaration on Environment and Development' (adopted 13 June 1992) UN Doc A/Conf.151/26 (Vol. I) Principle 27 (Rio Declaration).
[113] Philippe Sands and Jacqueline Peel, *Principles of International Environmental Law* (3rd edn, CUP 2012) 204.

Within UNCLOS, the duty to cooperate has been included in a large number of provisions,[114] including those concerning the marine environment. In two provisional measures orders, *MOX Plant* and *Land Reclamation*, ITLOS has stated:

> [t]he duty to co-operate is a fundamental principle in the prevention of pollution of the marine environment under Part XII of the Convention and general international law and that rights arise therefrom which the Tribunal may consider appropriate to preserve under Article 290 of the Convention.[115]

Within the context of provisional measures, ITLOS has required the States concerned to cooperate for different purposes, including for the purposes of exchanging information, monitoring or assessing the risks and effects of their activities, and devising measures to prevent pollution.[116] The duty to cooperate in this context forms a procedural requirement for marine environmental protection. The motivations for judges in emphasising the duty to cooperate in this context appear to have varied, as it has been recognised as a procedure that prevents harm to the marine environment, as a principle to reflect community interests as balanced against sovereign interests, a means to prevent aggravation of the dispute and even as a useful contribution to resolve the dispute between the parties.[117]

The *South China Sea* Tribunal addressed the cooperation obligation set out in Article 197 of Part XII of UNCLOS, which requires States to cooperate 'in formulating and elaborating international rules, standards and recommended practices and procedures consistent with this Convention'.[118] In doing so, the Tribunal broadened the obligation to cooperate as a general requirement rather than for the specific act of formulating and elaborating on rules, standards, practices, and procedures. This interpretation was justified by reference to Article 123,[119] which encourages cooperation more generally in relation to enclosed or semi-enclosed seas, and to the above-cited *MOX Plant* provisional measures order of ITLOS.[120] While it may indeed be true that there is a general duty to cooperate, is it possible to hold that a State has violated Article 197 for this broader obligation to cooperate or must there be a finding that aligns with the specific wording of the provision? Scanlon and Beckman are critical of the Tribunal's failure to engage directly with the interpretation of Articles 123 and 197 in its findings on China's conduct.[121] It may be noted that a proposal to replace 'rules, standards and recommended practices and procedures' with 'measures', which may have better aligned with the more wide-ranging obligation to cooperate,

[114] For example, the obligation to cooperate is included in relation to the development and transfer of technology (Article 144), for the conservation and management of living resources (Article 61(2)), in relation to marine scientific research (Articles 143(3) and 242) and search and rescue service (Article 98).

[115] *MOX Plant*, Provisional Measures (n 3) para 82; *Land Reclamation by Singapore in and around the Straits of Johor (Malaysia v Singapore)* (Provisional Measures, Order of 8 October 2003) ITLOS Reports 2003, 10 (*Land Reclamation*, Provisional Measures) para 92.

[116] Boyle, 'Environmental Jurisprudence' (n 4) 378.

[117] See discussion in Gwenaele Rashbrooke, 'The International Tribunal for the Law of the Sea: A Forum for the Development of Principles of International Environmental Law' (2004) 19 IJMCL 515, 529.

[118] UNCLOS (n 1) art 197.

[119] The reference to Article 123 in this way allowed the Tribunal to draw a greater obligation from that provision, which provides the littoral states 'should cooperate' and 'shall endeavour' to coordinate specific activities. See UNCLOS (n 1) art 123. See further Kojima (n 15) 179.

[120] *South China Sea*, Award (n 7) para 946.

[121] See Zoe Scanlon and Robert Beckman, 'Assessing Environmental Impact and the Duty to Cooperate' (2018) 3 Asia-Pacific Journal of Ocean Law and Policy 5, 21–24.

was rejected during UNCLOS negotiations.[122] Rather, these provisions each entail specific forms of cooperation, with the standard to be met in relation to Article 123 very qualified and aspirational.[123]

In relation to the obligation to cooperate, the Tribunal found that there was 'no convincing evidence of China attempting to cooperate or coordinate with the other States bordering the South China Sea'.[124] Presumably, this finding meant there was no attempt to cooperate or coordinate *at all*, let alone for the purposes of formulating standards and practices for the protection and preservation of the marine environment. The award was not clear in this regard, although it still referenced the more general duty to cooperate for environmental protection. Presumably, any customary obligation to cooperate to protect the environment would be encapsulated within the applicable norms that inform the content of Article 192 of the Convention. The *South China Sea* Tribunal nonetheless concluded that Article 197 was also violated.

Boyle has noted that the obligation to cooperate 'in the control of environmental risks is one of the central elements of general international law on environmental protection'.[125] However, as he also observes, the obligation is not clearly articulated in UNCLOS.[126] It has therefore been necessary for different tribunals constituted under UNCLOS to expand on the duty to cooperate as applying under Part XII due to its status in general international law. Boyle supports tribunals doing so, arguing:

> [i]t shows how the Convention can in appropriate cases be interpreted and applied taking general international law into account. The idea that treaties can have a dynamic or living interpretation is an important contribution to the process of evolutionary change in international law. However, in this instance it is arguable that the Tribunal is merely interpreting the Convention in accordance with general international law as it already existed in 1982, rather than incorporating some wholly novel developments.[127]

While it should therefore be expected that the duty to cooperate forms part of the obligation to protect and preserve the marine environment, it should also be incumbent on tribunals constituted under UNCLOS to identify precisely how a specific provision is violated.

IV. Environmental Impact Assessments

The requirement under international law to conduct EIAs has been enshrined in many multilateral treaties,[128] and upheld as an international obligation by the ICJ.[129] Within UNCLOS, Article 206 provides:

[122] *Virginia Commentary* (n 21) vol IV, 81.
[123] See n 119. See further Scanlon and Beckman (n 121) 22–24.
[124] *South China Sea*, Award (n 7) para 986.
[125] Boyle, 'Environmental Jurisprudence' (n 4) 379.
[126] ibid.
[127] ibid (citation omitted).
[128] See eg Convention on Environmental Impact Assessment in a Transboundary Context (adopted 25 February 1991, entered into force 10 September 1997) 1989 UNTS 309, art 2(3); CBD (n 17) art 14(1)(a); Protocol on Environmental Protection to the Antarctic Treaty (adopted 4 October 1991, entered into force 24 January 1998) 2941 UNTS 3, art 8. For further discussion on EIAs in international environmental law see Sands and Peel (n 13) 601–23; Neil Craik, *The International Law of Environmental Impact Assessment: Process, Substance and Integration* (CUP 2008).
[129] *Pulp Mills*, Merits (n 11) para 204; *Construction of a Road* (n 11) para 101.

> When States have reasonable grounds for believing that planned activities under their jurisdiction or control may cause substantial pollution of or significant and harmful changes to the marine environment, they shall, as far as practicable, assess the potential effects of such activities on the marine environment and shall communicate reports of the results of such assessments in the manner provided in article 205.

By reference to Article 205, States are to 'provide such reports at appropriate intervals to the competent international organizations, which should make them available to all States'.

For the conduct of EIAs under UNCLOS, some subjectivity is allowed in judging the State's conduct of that assessment. If a State has 'reasonable grounds' for believing that the proposed activity 'may cause substantial pollution of or significant harm changes to the marine environment', it must 'as far as practicable' assess the effects of such activities.[130] The *MOX Plant* and *South China Sea* cases indicate that large-scale industrial activities with a known risk of potentially serious pollution warrant the conduct of an EIA.[131] It may otherwise seem that the very process of determining whether an activity may cause substantial pollution or significant harm to warrant an EIA is actually part and parcel of an EIA.[132] There are necessarily a number of factual elements to inform the assessment of the applicability of Article 206 and States arguably have a discretion in reaching the decision as to whether an EIA is even needed in the first instance.[133]

Even with the discretionary elements in Article 206 of UNCLOS, the conduct of an EIA has been described as an 'essential part of a comprehensive environmental management system'.[134] Moreover, it supplements the obligation found in Article 194(2) requiring States to take 'all measures necessary' to ensure activities within their jurisdiction or control do not cause damage to other States and their environment.[135] In linking the obligation under Article 206 to Article 194(2), the standards expected of States in conducting EIAs for their maritime activities are arguably raised. A more absolute obligation is entailed in relation to the communication of reports setting out the results of the assessments, which must be done in accordance with Article 205 of UNCLOS.[136]

The importance of EIAs was addressed in the *Seabed Advisory Opinion*. The Chamber had regard to Section 1, paragraph 7 of the Annex to the 1994 Agreement, which provides explicitly for such a requirement,[137] and noted the responsibility fell to the contractor to carry out the EIA. As such, the obligation under the 1994 Agreement is not a direct requirement imposed on the State to conduct an EIA, but is part of the sponsoring State's due diligence obligations.[138] Nonetheless, the direct obligation is established in the Nodules and Sulphides Regulations, which is again transported into UNCLOS obligations as part of the

[130] UNCLOS (n 1) art 206.

[131] In relation to *MOX Plant* see Boyle, 'Environmental Jurisprudence' (n 4) 377 (also referring to *Pulp Mills* as demonstrating this point). In relation to *South China Sea* see *South China Sea*, Award (n 7) para 988. The ICJ has also referred to 'activities carried out within a State's jurisdiction that risk causing significant harm to other States, particularly in areas or regions of shared environmental conditions': *Construction of a Road* (n 11) para 101.

[132] Boyle, 'Environmental Jurisprudence' (n 4) 377.

[133] See Chinese Society of International Law (n 58) para 819; Harrison (n 60) 33. Scanlon and Beckman consider that the *South China Sea* Tribunal injected an objective element into this assessment through their determination. See Scanlon and Beckman (n 121) 13–14.

[134] *South China Sea*, Award (n 7) para 948, citing the *Virginia Commentary* (n 21) vol IV, 121.

[135] *South China Sea*, Award (n 7) para 948.

[136] UNCLOS (n 1) art 206.

[137] *Seabed Advisory Opinion* (n 5) para 141.

[138] See ibid.

State's duty to assist the Authority under Article 153(4) of the Convention.[139] In addition, the Chamber acknowledged the general obligation to conduct an EIA under Article 206, as well as confirming the status of this obligation as customary international law.[140]

In light of this jurisprudence, States therefore appear to be subject to four obligations in relation to EIAs in the Area:

1. a State would need to fulfil its direct obligation to conduct an EIA in relation to activities in the Area consistent with Article 153(4);
2. to the extent there are activities that do not constitute 'activities in the Area', as defined by the Chamber, a direct obligation would still adhere as a result of Article 206;
3. a due diligence obligation to ensure a contractor conducts an EIA in accordance with the 1994 Agreement; and
4. the customary law status of the EIA obligation would further put Article 192 at issue, as well as Article 142.[141]

In articulating the customary law obligation of an EIA, the Chamber considered that the requirements fell within the expectations in Article 142 as part of its system of consultations and prior notifications in relation to resource deposits in the Area that lie across limits of national jurisdiction.[142]

The content of the EIA anticipated under Article 142 is informed by the indicators in Article 206 of the Convention, as well as by the standards articulated in the Nodules and Sulphides Regulations and a set of Recommendations issued by the ISA's Legal and Technical Commission in 2002.[143] These Recommendations specify what activities require a prior EIA.[144] In drawing on these diverse resources, the Chamber concluded, 'the obligations of the contractors and of the sponsoring States concerning EIAs extend beyond the scope of application of specific provisions of the Regulations'.[145] In setting out the expected content of an EIA, the Chamber thus went further than the ICJ in *Pulp Mills*.[146] In the latter case, the ICJ noted:

> [I]t is the view of the Court that it is for each State to determine in its domestic legislation or in the authorization process for the project, the specific content of the environmental impact assessment required in each case, having regard to the nature and magnitude of the proposed development and its likely adverse impact on the environment as well as to the need to exercise due diligence in conducting such an assessment.[147]

139 ibid para 142.

140 ibid para 145.

141 Article 142 of UNCLOS (n 1) provides for the rights and legitimate interests of coastal States where resource deposits cross into areas of national jurisdiction.

142 *Seabed Advisory Opinion* (n 5) para 148.

143 See Legal and Technical Commission of the International Seabed Authority, 'Recommendations for the Guidance of the Contractors for the Assessment of the Possible Environmental Impacts Arising from Exploration for Polymetallic Nodules in the Area' (13 February 2002) ISBA/7/LTC/1/Rev.1**, para 10. See also *Seabed Advisory Opinion* (n 5) para 149.

144 See Legal and Technical Commission of the International Seabed Authority (n 143), para 10. See further Tanaka (n 97) 213.

145 *Seabed Advisory Opinion* (n 5) para 150.

146 Tullio Treves, 'The Jurisprudence of the International Tribunal for the Law of the Sea and Catastrophic Environmental Damage' (2011) 105 ASIL Proc 436, 437 (Treves, 'Catastrophic Environmental Damage').

147 *Pulp Mills*, Merits (n 11) para 205.

Thus, while the ICJ avoided enunciating any international standards for the content of EIAs, the Seabed Chamber was more specific in this regard to provide guidance on what is expected for EIAs at least in relation to activities in the Area.

Whether the standard for conducting an EIA is met remains to be determined in individual cases.[148] For the *South China Sea* Tribunal, Mbengue has suggested that the Tribunal was concerned with the comprehensiveness of the assessment undertaken.[149] In that case, some evidence was available from an administrative agency under the Chinese Ministry of Land and Resources that addressed the environmental impacts of the dredging and construction activities.[150] The Tribunal considered that this evidence fell short of the standards expected for EIAs under China's own national law, as well as not meeting international standards that could be discerned from assessments done in the context of other international cases or from assessments that Chinese scientists referenced in their own reports.[151] This approach suggests objective benchmarking in the quality of the EIA,[152] even though the terms of Article 206 indicate a subjective standard dependent on the activity in question and the capabilities of the State concerned.[153] Nonetheless, the Tribunal was unable to resolve definitively whether China had satisfied the requirements for conducting an environmental assessment prior to its dredging and construction activities at the seven reefs.[154]

By contrast, the requirement to communicate an EIA is clear in Article 206 of the Convention, and the *South China Sea* Tribunal could conclude that China never communicated to a 'relevant international organization' for wider distribution as needed under Article 205. Kojima has commented that this obligation is 'absolute',[155] in that there is no allowance for the varying capacities of States.[156] However, the Tribunal did not engage in any discussion as to which 'relevant international organization' needed to be engaged in this particular situation.[157] Arguably engagement with this issue was unnecessary in light of the determination that there had been no communication whatsoever rather than an issue as to whether the communication to the correct organisation had occurred. As a result, China was still in violation of Article 206 of the Convention, irrespective of the sufficiency of any actual EIA that may have been undertaken in relation to the dredging and construction activities.

[148] 'Determination of the content of the environmental impact assessment should be made in light of the specific circumstances of each case': *Construction of a Road* (n 11) para 104.

[149] Makane Moïse Mbengue, 'The South China Sea Arbitration: Innovations in Marine Environmental Fact-Finding and Due Diligence Obligations' (2016) 110 AJIL Unbound 285, 287.

[150] See *South China Sea*, Award (n 5) para 922.

[151] ibid para 990. See also *Pulp Mills*, Merits (n 11) para 205 and *Construction of a Road* (n 11) para 104.

[152] But see Plakokefalos, who is critical of the Tribunal (as well as the ICJ jurisprudence upon which the Tribunal relied) for not examining the quality of the EIA against prevailing international law standards: Plakokefalos (n 57) 13. Instead, it would be better for judicial recognition of a minimum standard given that State discretion is not unlimited. See Eike Blitza, 'Article 206' in *Proelss Commentary* (n 22) 1376, para 14.

[153] In this regard, Whomersely has raised potential concern that the *South China Sea* Tribunal 'has in effect substituted its own view for that of the coastal State [which is the relevant actor to decide if its activity is consistent with the obligation to protect and preserve the marine environment], and found a breach of international law in respect of activities for which the coastal State considered that it had adequate environmental justification': Chris Whomersley, 'The Award on the Merits in the Case Brought by the Philippines against China Relating to the South China Sea: A Critique' (2017) 16 Chinese JIL 387, 416.

[154] *South China Sea*, Award (n 7) para 991.

[155] As the Tribunal notes. *South China Sea*, Award (n 7) para 948.

[156] Kojima (n 15) 166.

[157] Scanlon and Beckman (n 121) 15–16. Scanlon and Beckman were also critical of the Tribunal's failure to discuss the publication requirement in Article 205: see 16–17.

As with other areas of environmental protection, the UNCLOS jurisprudence on EIAs joins a growing suite of cases that have examined how the international obligation to conduct an EIA is to be implemented. The UNCLOS cases to date have addressed situations where there have been large-scale industrial activities with a known risk of potentially serious pollution. More borderline cases of activities that may or may not cause 'substantial pollution' may test the parameters of this obligation in the future. The communication obligation in Article 205 will be critical as a procedural mechanism by which to notify States of activities and provide an opportunity for them to engage and prevent a dispute from arising in the first instance. Nonetheless, with EIAs being required in an increasing number of international instruments, perhaps the greater challenge for judges will be in assessing the quality of any EIA that has been done by one State but questioned by another, rather than whether an EIA has been done at all. While Article 206 has its own distinct wording, judges deciding cases under UNCLOS may opt to assimilate their approaches to this provision to general international law. Maintaining consistency with general international environmental law could well be seen to align with the broad obligation in Article 192 to protect and preserve the marine environment.

V. Precautionary Approach

Case law under UNCLOS has advanced the international law status and understanding of the precautionary approach. The precautionary approach, as enshrined in Principle 15 of the Rio Declaration, reads:

> In order to protect the environment, the precautionary approach shall be widely applied by States according to their capabilities. Where there are threats of serious or irreversible damage, lack of full scientific certainty shall not be used as a reason for postponing cost-effective measures to prevent environmental degradation.[158]

The precautionary approach has been reflected in multilateral environmental agreements, although its content and status as an international obligation have been extensively debated.[159]

Within the context of UNCLOS, Australia and New Zealand both requested provisional measures in their dispute with Japan in *Southern Bluefin Tuna*, whereby the parties were to act consistently with the precautionary principle pending a final settlement of the dispute.[160] In that case, Australia and New Zealand objected to Japan's initiation of an

[158] Rio Declaration (n 112).

[159] See eg Ling Chen, 'Realizing the Precautionary Principle in Due Diligence' (2016) 25 Dal J Leg Studies 1, 3–11; Rosemary Rayfuse, 'Precaution and the Protection of Marine Biodiversity', in David Freestone (ed), *Areas beyond National Jurisdiction in The 1982 Law of the Sea Convention at 30* (Brill 2013) 99–107; Daniel Kazhdan, 'Precautionary Pulp: Pulp Mills and the Evolving Dispute between International Tribunals over the Reach of the Precautionary Principle' (2011) 38 Ecology LQ 527; Abdullah Al Arif, 'Legal Status of the Precautionary Principle in International Fisheries Law and Its Application in the Marine Fisheries Regime of Bangladesh' (2018) 3 Asia Pac J Ocean L & Pol 95; Ida Lauridsen, 'Precautionary Action: Study on the Status and Implications of the Precautionary Principle in International Environmental Law' (2014) 19 Eastern & Central Eur J Env L 95; Ole W Pedersen, 'From Abundance to Indeterminacy: The Precautionary Principle and Its Two Camps of Custom' (2014) 3 TEL 323; Arie Trouwborst, 'Prevention, Precaution, Logic and Law: The Relationship between the Precautionary Principle and the Preventative Principle in International Law and Associated Questions' (2009) 2 Erasmus L Rev 105.

[160] *Southern Bluefin Tuna*, Provisional Measures (n 76) paras 31–32.

experimental fishing programme that necessitated harvesting southern bluefin tuna in excess of its national allocation. Rayfuse has noted that the case involved a '"clash of precautions" with Australia and New Zealand arguing that scientific uncertainty as to the impact of Japan's proposed experimental fishing programme meant the programme should not proceed, while Japan argued that scientific uncertainty as to stock status and appropriate conservation measures meant that it should'.[161]

At the provisional measures stage, ITLOS stated the parties should act with 'prudence and caution' to ensure effective conservation measures would be taken.[162] No explicit mention of the precautionary approach is otherwise set out in the Tribunal's order. However, as noted by Judge Treves, the precautionary approach is inherent in the notion of provisional measures.[163] Moreover, in each of their separate opinions, Judge Laing[164] and Judge ad hoc Shearer[165] endorsed the use of the precautionary approach by the Tribunal. As Judge ad hoc Shearer rightly noted, given the inherent scientific uncertainty in fisheries management, a precautionary approach was warranted in lieu of a precautionary principle that might have necessitated the cessation of fisheries activities.[166] However, given the majority's limited reference to 'prudence and caution', the legal status and content of the precautionary approach was only slightly advanced in this Order.[167] Although ITLOS has power to prescribe binding measures, the Tribunal only referred to what the parties 'should' do in relation to conservation measures in the management of southern bluefin tuna. The arbitral tribunal constituted to resolve this case on the merits ultimately held that it lacked jurisdiction and consequently did not have an opportunity to consider the content of any obligation in relation to effective conservation measures.

ITLOS further referenced the need for 'prudence and caution' in its provisional measures orders in *MOX Plant*,[168] *Land Reclamation*,[169] *Louisa*,[170] and *Ghana/Côte d'Ivoire*.[171] The orders granted in each instance facilitated steps that supported a precautionary approach (through, for example, exchange of information, conduct of studies and monitoring of activities).[172] The views of ITLOS in the *MOX Plant* provisional measures order arguably established some parameters in asserting that the damage had to be clear and identifiable, rather than general and abstract;[173] the urgency for an order of provisional measures could

[161] Rayfuse (n 159) 101.

[162] *Southern Bluefin Tuna*, Provisional Measures (n 76) para 77. See further *Seabed Advisory Opinion* (n 5) para 132.

[163] See *Southern Bluefin Tuna*, Provisional Measures (n 76) 318 [9] (Separate Opinion of Judge Treves).

[164] ibid 313 [19] (Separate Opinion of Judge Laing).

[165] ibid 327 (Separate Opinion of Judge ad hoc Shearer).

[166] ibid 326 (Separate Opinion of Judge ad hoc Shearer).

[167] For criticism see David L VanderZwaag, 'The ICJ, ITLOS and the Precautionary Approach: Paltry Progressions, Jurisprudential Jousting' (2013) 35 U Haw L Rev 617, 622. See also Rashbrooke (n 117) 523.

[168] *MOX Plant*, Provisional Measures (n 3) para 84 where ITLOS states 'prudence and caution require that Ireland and the United Kingdom cooperate in exchanging information concerning risks or effects of the operation of the MOX Plant and in devising ways to deal with them, as appropriate'.

[169] *Land Reclamation*, Provisional Measures (n 115) para 99.

[170] *M/V Louisa (Saint Vincent and the Grenadines v Spain)* (Provisional Measures, Order of 23 December 2010) ITLOS Reports 2008–2010, 58 (*Louisa*, Provisional Measures) para 77.

[171] *Delimitation of the Maritime Boundary between Ghana and Côte d'Ivoire in the Atlantic Ocean (Ghana/Côte d'Ivoire)* (Provisional Measures Order of 25 April 2015) ITLOS Reports 2015, 146, para 72.

[172] Judge Treves in *Southern Bluefin Tuna*, Provisional Measures (n 76) commented that a precautionary approach was inherent in the very notion of provisional measures: 318 [9] (Separate Opinion of Judge Treves). In light of this perspective, it could be expected that prudence and caution would necessarily feature in all provisional measures orders.

[173] Tiago Vinicius Zanella and Ricardo Pereira Cabral, 'The Application of the Precautionary Principle in International Law: An Analysis of the Contribution of the International Tribunal for the Law of the Sea' (2017) 14 Veredas do Direito 229, 247.

not be established otherwise.[174] Judge Wolfrum went slightly further in *MOX Plant* in acknowledging that the precautionary approach can shift the burden of proof so that it is the State wishing to proceed with the activity that must show lack of harm, rather than the State challenging the activity having to show that harm will result.[175] This aspect of the precautionary approach has not been utilised in any subsequent cases under UNCLOS to date.

In the *Seabed Advisory Opinion*, the Chamber noted that the precautionary approach applied to prospecting and exploratory activities in the Area by virtue of the Nodules and Sulphides Regulations.[176] It was a direct obligation of States, as well as forming part of the due diligence standards associated with a sponsoring State's 'responsibility to ensure' prevention of damage that might result from the activities of its contractors.[177] If States failed to implement the necessary legislative and administrative measures, the implication would be that they were not adopting a precautionary approach.[178]

The Seabed Disputes Chamber's opinion drew on ITLOS's views in the *Southern Bluefin Tuna* provisional measures order.[179] The Chamber still hesitated in describing definitively the precautionary approach as a rule of international law but instead noted the 'trend towards making this approach part of customary international law'.[180] In doing so, the precautionary approach was not explicitly drawn from a provision of UNCLOS but the Chamber read it in as part of its discussion of Article 153(4) and Article 139(2).[181] Rayfuse and French have each argued that in reading precaution into the due diligence standard, the effect is to make precaution part of the general international obligations relating to deep seabed mining.[182] The Seabed Disputes Chamber justified its approach, in part, by reference to the requirement of systemic integration set out in Article 31(3)(c) of the VCLT.[183] However, this approach seems questionable when one takes account of the fact that the various sources of the precautionary approach were not binding rules that applied between the parties.[184]

[174] See *MOX Plant*, Provisional Measures (n 3) (Joint Declaration of Judges Caminos, Yamamoto, Park, Akl, Marsit, Eiriksson, and Jesus).

[175] ibid 134 (Separate Opinion of Judge Wolfrum). This approach was also followed by Judge Gavan Griffith in the *OSPAR Arbitration. Dispute Concerning Access to Information Under Article 9 of the OSPAR Convention (Ireland v United Kingdom)* (2003) 42 ILM 1118, 1173 [90] (Dissenting Opinion of Judge Gavan Griffith).

[176] Nodules Regulations (n 92) reg 31(2); Sulphides Regulations (n 98) reg 33(2). See *Seabed Advisory Opinion* (n 5) paras 125, 127.

[177] *Seabed Advisory Opinion* (n 5) para 131. But see Tanaka's critique of the Chamber reading the precautionary approach and the due diligence obligation together. Tanaka (n 97) 214–15. The point, though seems to relate to whether the precautionary approach applies both as a direct obligation and as an obligation to ensure that private actors follow the precautionary approach. Both would seem feasible depending on which actors are involved in relation to the activity at issue.

[178] *Seabed Advisory Opinion* (n 5) para 131. See also Tim Poisel, 'Deep Seabed Mining: Implications of Seabed Disputes Chamber's Advisory Opinion' (2012) 19 Aust ILJ 213, 223; Zanella and Cabral (n 173) 251.

[179] *Southern Bluefin Tuna*, Provisional Measures (n 76) para 77. See further *Seabed Advisory Opinion* (n 5) para 132.

[180] *Seabed Advisory Opinion* (n 5) para 135.

[181] See also Tullio Treves, 'The International Tribunal for the Law of the Sea and Other Law of the Sea Jurisdictions' (2010) 20 Ital YB Intl L 315, 335 ('ITLOS and Other LOS Jurisdictions').

[182] Rayfuse (n 159) 105–106; Duncan French, 'From the Depths: Rich Pickings of Principles of Sustainable Development and General International Law on the Ocean Floor: the Seabed Disputes Chamber's 2011 Advisory Opinion' (2011) 26 IJMCL 525, 547. See also Aline L Jaeckel, *The International Seabed Authority and the Precautionary Principle: Balancing Deep Seabed Mineral Mining and Marine Environmental Protection* (Brill 2017) 134–35.

[183] *Seabed Advisory Opinion* (n 5) para 135. See also Treves, 'ITLOS and Other LOS Jurisdictions' (n 175) 335; Treves, 'Catastrophic Environmental Damage' (n 146) 437.

[184] For discussion on this form of treaty interpretation to support the incorporation of nascent environmental principles into treaty obligations see Duncan French, 'Treaty Interpretation and the Incorporation of Extraneous Legal Rules' (2006) 55 ICLQ 281, 308–13.

There is clearly scope for greater judicial exposition on the content, applicability and status of the precautionary approach in various situations regulated by UNCLOS.[185] Commentators have responded positively to the Seabed Chamber according a close interrelationship between the precautionary approach and the principle of prevention, arguing the former fills possible gaps left by the latter.[186] Yet VanderZwaag is sceptical of progress, astutely noting:

> [p]rogressive development through further litigation remains doubtful due to various factors. Positivistic thinking continues to dominate among international lawyers and judges. A conservative role for judges in the further development of international law may be an expected practical reality in light of the political background of many judges, the need to bolster judicial legitimacy with sovereign states, and the thinness of consensus that undergirds international law.[187]

VI. Safeguards against Enforcement of Environmental Requirements

Although UNCLOS accorded or reaffirmed a suite of powers to different States for the enforcement of environmental rules and standards, the exercise of these powers has not triggered many disputes that have resulted in judicial resolution. This inaction is particularly true in relation to the prompt release cases under Article 292 of the Convention. All of the applications thus far submitted under Article 292 have concerned the enforcement of fisheries regulations.[188] While Articles 220(6) and (7) and 226(1)(c) anticipate the possibility of a challenge to the exercise of coastal State enforcement powers via Article 292,[189] no such challenge has yet been pursued.

Article 220 was considered briefly in the *Arctic Sunrise* during the Annex VII Tribunal's deliberations on the scope of coastal State law enforcement powers.[190] The Tribunal asked whether Russia's actions arresting Greenpeace activists who attempted to board an oil platform could be justified on the basis of serious violations of its laws related to protection of the marine environment. The Tribunal referred to a coastal State's enforcement powers under Article 220 relating to reduction and control of vessel-source pollution. Article 220 provides, in relevant part:

> 3. Where there are clear grounds for believing that a vessel navigating in the exclusive economic zone or the territorial sea of a State has, in the exclusive economic zone,

[185] A need that has been long recognised. See eg Rashbrooke (n 117) 521.

[186] See Chen (n 159) 21. Chen writes that prevention and precaution 'form part of a continuum in which the precautionary concept may come to play in setting the standard of due diligence in the context of scientific uncertainty. With the emergence of strong scientific evidence, an obligation to take precautionary measures may become an obligation to take preventive action': see 23.

[187] VanderZwaag (n 167) 630 (citations omitted).

[188] For discussion of these cases see ch 3(IV)(B) and ch 8(IV)(E).

[189] St Vincent and the Grenadines initially raised these provisions in relation to prompt release proceedings for the M/V *Saiga* but dropped these submissions and relied only on Article 73: *M/V Saiga (Saint Vincent and the Grenadines v Guinea)* (Prompt Release, Judgment) ITLOS Reports 1997, 16, para 55.

[190] *Arctic Sunrise (Netherlands v Russia)* (Award on the Merits of 14 August 2015) PCA Case No 2014-02, paras 290–92. Other coastal State law enforcement powers are addressed in ch 7(IV).

committed a violation of applicable international rules and standards for the prevention, reduction and control of pollution from vessels or laws and regulations of that State conforming and giving effect to such rules and standards, that State may require the vessel to give information regarding its identity and port of registry, its last and its next port of call and other relevant information required to establish whether a violation has occurred.

...

5. Where there are clear grounds for believing that a vessel navigating in the exclusive economic zone or the territorial sea of a State has, in the exclusive economic zone, committed a violation referred to in paragraph 3 resulting in a substantial discharge causing or threatening significant pollution of the marine environment, that State may undertake physical inspection of the vessel for matters relating to the violation if the vessel has refused to give information or if the information supplied by the vessel is manifestly at variance with the evident factual situation and if the circumstances of the case justify such inspection.
6. Where there is clear objective evidence that a vessel navigating in the exclusive economic zone or the territorial sea of a State has, in the exclusive economic zone, committed a violation referred to in paragraph 3 resulting in a discharge causing major damage or threat of major damage to the coastline or related interests of the coastal State, or to any resources of its territorial sea or exclusive economic zone, that State may, subject to section 7, provided that the evidence so warrants, institute proceedings, including detention of the vessel, in accordance with its laws.

The Tribunal noted that there were no grounds for Russia to believe that the Arctic Sunrise had committed a violation of applicable international rules and standards for the prevention, reduction, or control of vessel-source pollution in the EEZ, and thus considered that Article 220 did not provide a justification for Russia's enforcement measures.[191]

The Tribunal also assessed whether Russia's measures could be justified based on Article 234 of UNCLOS, which permits coastal States to adopt and enforce laws for the prevention, reduction and control of marine pollution from vessels in ice-covered areas within the EEZ. However, the regulations adopted by Russia under Article 234 did not apply to the area where the oil platform, Prirazlomnaya, was located, nor did Russia invoke those laws and regulations as a justification for its actions.[192] The Tribunal therefore concluded that the measures taken by Russia could not be justified on the basis of Article 234.[193]

Finally, the Tribunal considered whether Russia's measures could be justified on the basis of Article 221, which provides for the right of States to take measures beyond the territorial sea in respect of actual or threatened damage from pollution or a threat of pollution following upon a maritime casualty or acts relating to such a casualty. The Tribunal noted that the Russian authorities had made reference to 'a threat of an ecological disaster' and 'activities which may cause damage to the environment'. However, it considered that even if the actions of the Arctic Sunrise fell within Article 221, the threatened damage to Russia's interests could not reasonably have been expected to result in major harmful consequences.

[191] ibid para 291.
[192] ibid para 296.
[193] ibid paras 293–97.

It also noted that at the time of the boarding, seizure, and detention of the Arctic Sunrise, the Russian authorities were aware that the Greenpeace members' protest actions had not resulted in any ecological or environmental adverse consequences, and there had not been any 'maritime casualty' within the meaning of Article 221. It therefore held that Russia's measures could not be justified on the basis of Article 221.[194] The Tribunal's analyses of these provisions reflect a common sense perspective on their scope and helpfully avoided strained interpretations.

Section 7 of Part XII sets out a variety of safeguards against law enforcement actions and while claims have been issued based on these provisions, none have been upheld to date. One of the safeguards against the exercise of enforcement powers was raised in the *Duzgit Integrity*, where Malta argued that São Tomé was in breach of Article 225 in the conduct of a ship-to-ship oil transfer.[195] Article 225 provides: 'In the exercise under this Convention of their powers of enforcement against foreign vessels, States shall not endanger the safety of navigation or otherwise create any hazard to a vessel, or bring it to an unsafe port or anchorage, or expose the marine environment to an unreasonable risk.' Malta also alleged violations of Articles 192 and 194(1) and (4), but the Tribunal did not examine these provisions in its Award.[196]

In relation to Article 225, Malta argued that there was an 'unreasonable or excessive risk of danger' in the transshipment operation.[197] In making this argument, Malta alleged that various international obligations under international shipping treaties had been violated,[198] and provided evidence to support these claims.[199] In assessing this claim, São Tomé proposed that the key question was 'whether the measures taken were reasonable in the circumstances'.[200] The Tribunal agreed that it must focus on the factual circumstances to assess if Article 225 was violated,[201] and deferred to a certain amount of coastal State discretion in allowing for a reasonableness standard.[202] The evidence was thus the critical determinative, rather than any possible violations of national laws.[203] The Tribunal did not consider any violations of the international shipping treaties in this context. The factual predicate was thus decisive even though the Tribunal did not articulate the threshold to be established in applying Article 225 (or Articles 192 or 194 as Malta proposed), beyond noting that Malta had failed to meet its burden of proof to establish its claim.[204]

Panama also argued that Article 225 had been violated in the *Virginia G* case due to the conditions for sailing to which the vessel was subjected following its arrest by officials

[194] ibid Merits, paras 307–13.

[195] *Duzgit Integrity* (n 8) paras 279–85.

[196] Although Articles 192 and 194 were referenced in Malta's arguments on this point, the Tribunal did not consider these provisions in its determination. See ibid para 293.

[197] ibid para 284.

[198] ibid paras 280, 282–83 (referring to *inter alia* International Convention for the Prevention of Pollution from Ships (adopted 2 November 1973, entered into force 2 October 1983) 1340 UNTS 62 (MARPOL Convention) and the International Convention for the Safety of Life at Sea (adopted 1 November 1974, entered into force 25 May 1980) 1184 UNTS 278 (SOLAS Convention)).

[199] ibid para 292.

[200] ibid para 286.

[201] ibid para 293.

[202] Camille Goodman, 'Rights, Obligations, Prohibitions: A Practical Guide to Understanding Judicial Decisions on Coastal State Jurisdiction over Living Resources in the Exclusive Economic Zone' (2018) 33 IJMCL 558, 574.

[203] ibid.

[204] ibid.

from Guinea Bissau.[205] Guinea Bissau disputed the allegation as a factual matter, denying that the safety of navigation was at risk.[206] In considering the scope of Article 225, ITLOS observed that it was not a provision limited in its application to enforcement of environmental laws, even though it was situated in Part XII, but applied to States '[i]n the exercise under this Convention of their powers of enforcement against foreign vessels'.[207] As such, it covered Guinea Bissau's enforcement of fisheries laws under Article 73 of UNCLOS.[208] Nonetheless, the evidence presented was not sufficient to support Panama's claimed breach of Article 225.[209]

The *Louisa* included claims based on Articles 226 and 227 in relation to the detention of the M/V Louisa and its crew. Article 226 relates to the powers of investigation over vessels and Article 227 requires that States not discriminate in form or fact against vessels of any other State in acting under Part XII. Spain challenged the reliance of St Vincent and the Grenadines on these provisions as founding the bases for its claims.[210] ITLOS noted: 'To enable the Tribunal to determine whether it has jurisdiction, it must establish a link between the facts advanced by Saint Vincent and the Grenadines and the provisions of the Convention referred to by it and show that such provisions can sustain the claim or claims submitted by Saint Vincent and the Grenadines.'[211] The Tribunal found that no such link existed as the M/V Louisa had been arrested for criminal proceedings in relation to the possession of weapons of war and in relation to the protection of underwater cultural heritage.[212] In doing so, the Tribunal implicitly agreed with Spain that Articles 226 and 227 were intended to refer to enforcement by coastal states for the protection and preservation of the marine environment, and that they should not be extended beyond that context.[213] If the Tribunal had supported reliance on these provisions in light of the facts of this case, it would have indeed extended them well beyond their plain meaning. Article 226 explicitly refers to investigations 'provided for in Articles 216, 218 and 220', which concern enforcement of environmental laws, and Article 227 sets out the obligation of non-discrimination in the performance of duties 'under this Part', namely Part XII. It would not have been tenable to extend these safeguards in a comparable manner to the approach of ITLOS in *Virginia G*.

VII. Due Diligence Standard

Conceptually, the due diligence standard has two key uses in international law. As Fietta, Saadeh, and Rees-Evans note, '[a]cross all fields of international law, a failure to exercise due diligence can render the acts of a private party legally attributable to the State, or can

[205] *Virginia G* (n 9) para 365.
[206] ibid paras 369–72.
[207] ibid para 373.
[208] ibid para 373. See also ch 8(IV)(D). See also *M/T San Padre Pio (Switzerland v Nigeria)* (Provisional Measures, Order of 6 July 2019) ITLOS Case No 27 (Separate Opinion of Judge ad hoc Petrig) para 4.
[209] The Tribunal stated: 'the Tribunal concludes that it has not been presented with sufficient evidence to establish convincingly that any of the provisions of article 225 of the Convention was violated.' *Virginia G* (n 9) para 374.
[210] *Louisa*, Judgment (n 10) para 93 (arguing that the case did not concern the interpretation or application of UNCLOS).
[211] ibid para 99.
[212] ibid para 113.
[213] ibid para 112.

constitute a breach of a primary obligation'.[214] The latter aspect involves ascertaining the standard of liability to which a State is held in assessing its international responsibility for alleged internationally wrongful acts.[215] The due diligence standard for the preservation and protection of the marine environment is incorporated in a variety of provisions.[216] Most particularly, Article 194(2) of UNCLOS reads: 'States shall take all measures necessary to ensure that activities under their jurisdiction or control are so conducted as not to cause damage by pollution to other States and their environment'.

Second, the due diligence standard is applied to determine the international responsibility of a State in relation to its exercise of control (or lack thereof) over private actors who fall under the State's authority.[217] In the latter context, this standard is articulated as 'a responsibility to ensure' activities do not harm the marine environment.[218] A requirement of due diligence is therefore an obligation of conduct.[219] It requires the adoption of rules as the point of departure. In the operative part of the *Seabed Advisory Opinion*, the Chamber states: 'As regards the protection of the marine environment, the laws and regulations and administrative measures of the sponsoring State cannot be less stringent than those adopted by the Authority, or less effective than international rules, regulations and procedures.'[220] In addition to the establishment of rules, the conduct of the State must evince a 'certain level of vigilance in their enforcement and the exercise of administrative control'.[221] Ultimately, a sponsoring State must 'take measures within its legal system' and the measures must be 'reasonably appropriate'.[222]

The conduct required to meet the due diligence standard will depend on the substantive obligation to be met, as well as any developments that might arise as a result of new technological or scientific knowledge.[223] Changes in relation to the risks involved may also impact upon the relevant standard of due diligence,[224] and the standard may vary depending on the risk involved.[225] For example, when the due diligence standard is applied to the precautionary approach,[226] the assessment would need to take into account that the precautionary approach is applied taking account of the capabilities of the State in question.[227] In such a

[214] Fietta, Saadeh, and Rees-Evans (n 61) 723.

[215] Koivurova describes 'the emergence of primary obligations that require States to exercise due diligence, that is, to endeavour to reach the result set out in the obligation': Timo Koivurova, 'Due Diligence' in Anne Peters (ed), *Max Planck Encyclopedia of Public International Law* (February 2010) para 3. However, the primary obligation is not one of due diligence in and of itself but rather an obligation requiring states to endeavour to reach the result set out in the obligation: see paras 5–8.

[216] See eg UNCLOS (n 1) arts 139(1), 194(2) and 235.

[217] Koivurova (n 215) paras 2–3.

[218] The ICJ has noted that 'the principle of prevention, as a customary rule, has its origins in the due diligence that is required of a State in its territory': *Pulp Mills*, Merits (n 11) para 101. The principle of prevention, sometimes embodied as *sic utere tuo et alienum non laedas*, articulates the responsibility to ensure that activities within a State's jurisdiction or control do not cause damage to the environment of other States or of areas beyond national jurisdiction: see *Legality of the Threat or Use of Nuclear Weapons* (Advisory Opinion) [1996] ICJ Rep 226, para 29. For discussion of the origins of due diligence in international environmental law see Fietta, Saadeh, and Rees-Evans (n 61) 726–31.

[219] *South China Sea*, Award (n 7) para 944.

[220] *Seabed Advisory Opinion* (n 5) para 242. See also para 240.

[221] *SRFC Advisory Opinion* (n 5) para 131, quoting *Pulp Mills*, Merits (n 11) para 197.

[222] *Seabed Advisory Opinion* (n 5) para 120.

[223] ibid para 117. See further Tanaka (n 97) 210.

[224] *Seabed Advisory Opinion* (n 5) para 117. See also Fietta, Saadeh, and Rees-Evans (n 61) 732.

[225] See Poisel (n 178) 219, 225.

[226] As occurred in *Southern Bluefin Tuna*, Provisional Measures (n 76) para 77. Fietta, Saadeh, and Rees-Evans (n 61) 732.

[227] See Rio Declaration (n 112) Principle 15.

situation, the standards as between developing and developed States may be different.[228] By contrast, as discussed further below, the standard of 'best environmental practices' does not entail any comparable differentiation or qualification for developing countries.[229]

As discussed in Chapter 8,[230] the *South China Sea* Tribunal endorsed the due diligence standard that had been applied by the ICJ, ITLOS and the Seabed Disputes Chamber in assessing China's adherence to Articles 192 and 194 with regard to its fishing practices.[231] The *South China Sea* Tribunal determined on the facts that China was aware of the illegal conduct,[232] and had not taken 'any steps to enforce those rules and measures against fishermen engaged in poaching of endangered species'.[233] The latter requirement aligned with the approach of the ICJ in the *Pulp Mills* case,[234] and with the Seabed Disputes Chamber in the *Seabed Advisory Opinion*.[235] In light of these facts, the Tribunal determined that China 'must have known of, and deliberately tolerated, and protected the harmful acts' in relation to harvesting of endangered species and the use of the propeller chopping method.[236]

From the *Seabed Advisory Opinion* and its discussion of Articles 153(4) and 139 of UNCLOS, it has also been elucidated that part of the due diligence requirements for sponsoring States in the Area (as opposed to a direct obligation) is the use of 'best environmental practices', drawing from the standards set out in the Sulphides Regulations.[237] The Chamber remarked that 'member States of the Authority have become convinced of the need for sponsoring States to apply "best environmental practices" in general terms so that they may be seen to have become enshrined in the sponsoring States' obligation of due diligence'.[238] Identifying the best environmental practices will involve benchmarking the conduct in question with what is expected for the activity as well as what information or resources might be available at the time of the determination.[239] Anton and others indicate that 'a survey of ["best environmental practices"] in a variety of international instruments shows that it requires the application of the most appropriate combination of environmental control measures and strategies'.[240] It has also been noted that best environmental practices do

[228] *Seabed Advisory Opinion* (n 5) para 161.

[229] This recognition was important 'to avoid a race to the bottom, to prevent the equivalent of "flag-hopping" by commercial mining enterprises seeking the nationality and sponsorship of developing countries in the hope of less burdensome regulations and controls': Günther Handl, 'Responsibilities and Obligations of States Sponsoring Persons and Entities With Respect to Activities in the Area: The International Tribunal of the Law of the Sea's Recent Contribution to International Environmental Law' (2011) 20 RECIEL 208, 211.

[230] See ch 8(IV)(C).

[231] *South China Sea*, Award (n 7) para 944, citing *Pulp Mills*, Merits (n 11), *SRFC Advisory Opinion* (n 5), and *Seabed Advisory Opinion* (n 5). Mbengue describes the approach of the *South China Sea* Tribunal to due diligence in the law of the sea as 'expansive'. Mbengue (n 149) 285.

[232] *South China Sea*, Award, para 962.

[233] ibid para 963. Commentators have argued that such evidence did in fact exist, but China's non-participation prevented this information from being before the Tribunal. See Jianping Guo and Peng Wang, 'Due Diligence and Overlooked Evidence in the South China Sea Arbitration: A Note' (2019) 50 ODIL 235, 237–38.

[234] *Pulp Mills*, Merits (n 11) para 197.

[235] *Seabed Advisory Opinion* (n 5) para 218.

[236] *South China Sea*, Award (n 7) paras 964–66. There was insufficient evidence before the Tribunal to conclude that Chinese fishers use of cyanide and explosives also violated the Convention: see para 975. See further ch 8(IV)(C).

[237] Sulphides Regulations (n 98) reg 33(2); annex 4, s 5.1. See *Seabed Advisory Opinion* (n 5) para 136. The Chamber considered that the Nodules Regulations (n 98) should be interpreted in light of the more recent Sulphides Regulations in this regard: see para 137. Tanaka describes this as 'an evolutionary interpretation taking subsequent practice into account': Tanaka (n 97) 214.

[238] *Seabed Advisory Opinion* (n 5) para 136.

[239] See further Tanaka (n 97) 211.

[240] Anton, Makgill and Payne (n 106) 63.

not differentiate between State's capabilities.[241] Although the Chamber's view might apply only to activities in the Area, it is possible that future claims will entail demands for best environmental practice as part of the panoply of environmental norms now tucked within Article 192 and, albeit to a lesser extent, Article 194 of UNCLOS.

VIII. Concluding Remarks

The decisions interpreting Part XII and related provisions have undoubtedly contributed to the overall development of international environmental law and will probably be relied upon in multilateral fora tasked with codifying aspects of international environmental law and in other cases decided outside the framework of UNCLOS. This influence arises in respect of both the substantive principles for the protection and preservation of the marine environment and the procedural dimensions for assessing scientific evidence relating to the environment. The *South China Sea* Tribunal's request for an examination of expert reports and evidence is exemplary in this regard, even though it was partially a response to China's refusal to participate in the case.[242]

There are many provisions of Part XII that have not been subject to judicial interpretation, as well as aspects that could still be amplified in future decisions. In relation to the latter, remedies for environmental harm remain to be fully considered. Anton has pointed out that a difficulty with utilising due diligence standards in relation to the protection and preservation of the marine environment is that if a State is found to have exercised due diligence, there is no responsibility to make reparations even though environmental damage has occurred.[243] Such a result is especially problematic for environmental damage to the Area given its legal status as the common heritage, but arguments to support a finding of residual liability were not endorsed by the Seabed Disputes Chamber in the *Seabed Advisory Opinion*.[244]

There are some preliminary indications of remedial orders that might be provided from the provisional measures decisions that ITLOS has issued addressing urgent situations of environmental harm.[245] These orders have established *inter alia* monitoring, consultation and reporting requirements, which could all be viewed as essential to dispute avoidance under international environmental law. In this scenario, judges may rely on the post-adjudicative phase for the further implementation of environmental principles and so the law in this area could be expected to have a socialising effect in State decision-making subsequent to a litigation process.[246]

[241] Poisel (n 178) 224.

[242] For discussion see Plakokefalos (n 57).

[243] See Donald K Anton, 'The Principle of Residual Liability in the Seabed Disputes Chamber of the International Tribunal for the Law of the Sea: The Advisory Opinion on Responsibility and Liability for International Seabed Mining (ITLOS Case No. 17)' (2012) 7 MJSDL 241, 244, 250.

[244] The arguments were raised in statements presented to the Chamber by NGOs. See discussion in ibid 253–56.

[245] See eg *MOX Plant*, Provisional Measures (n 3); *Land Reclamation*, Award (n 4); *Southern Bluefin Tuna*, Provisional Measures (n 76).

[246] Afshin Akhtarkhavari, 'Power, Environmental Principles and the International Court of Justice' (2009) 28 Aust YBIL 91, 103. Akhtarkhavari further observes that '[g]iven the social nature of interactions during the litigation process, post-conflict dialogue can continue in the shadow of the judicial decisions handed down by the institution dealing with an international dispute': see 101.

The only case to date that might have presented an opportunity to provide reparations for violations of provisions relating to the protection and preservation of the marine environment was the *South China Sea* arbitration. However, the Philippines did not seek any compensation or orders of *restitutio in integrum*. Rather, all that was sought were prospective declarations about China's conduct in relation to island-building and respect for the Philippines' rights.[247] The Tribunal was fully cognisant of the environmental harm caused, stating:

> Whatever other States have done within the South China Sea, it pales in comparison to China's recent construction. In practical terms, neither this decision nor any action that either Party may take in response can undo the permanent damage that has been done to the coral reef habitats of the South China Sea.[248]

Yet the Tribunal was still not willing to make any prospective declarations, considering the elucidation of the relevant principles and its findings on the facts before it would be sufficient,[249] especially in light of fundamental obligations of *pacta sunt servanda* and good faith.[250] In such a situation, with no remedial efforts required to restore the situation that existed prior to the commission of the internationally wrongful act, the environment loses out.[251] In this situation, the Tribunal's decision was politically sensible in accepting at face value China's assertions that it adheres to UNCLOS and relies on the principle of good faith. It could not be readily imagined that China would remove the artificial islands now constructed and, based on the scientific evidence, *restitutio in integrum* was not physically possible.[252] There might have been scope for the *South China Sea* Tribunal to contribute to the development of dispute avoidance mechanisms, as ITLOS effectively did in its provisional measures orders, but the opportunity was not pursued.

In endorsing the first ten years of ITLOS's jurisprudence on the marine environment, Boyle writes:

> These are the conclusions we should expect to draw from the jurisprudence of an international court, remembering that the principal purposes of the Convention's provisions on dispute settlement are to provide authoritative mechanisms for determining questions relating to the interpretation or application of the treaty, to guarantee the integrity of the text, and to control its implementation and development by States parties.[253]

Another ten years on, it is worth asking whether these purposes have been met in the subsequent jurisprudence of ITLOS, especially when coupled with the decisions of Annex VII

[247] *South China Sea*, Award (n 7) paras 1185, 1192–94.
[248] ibid para 1178.
[249] ibid para 1198. This position arguably aligns with the view that '[a]s the idea of risk is crucial to the analysis of environmental problems, the sciences and the law must have a position to avoid damage, instead of merely trying to repair it': Zanella and Cabral (n 173) 232.
[250] *South China Sea*, Award (n 7) paras 1195, 1200.
[251] See Joshua Paine, 'Environmental Aspects of the South China Sea Award' *EJIL: Talk!* (21 July 2016) https://www.ejiltalk.org/environmental-aspects-of-the-south-china-sea-award/.
[252] Which prevents the availability of *restitutio in integrum* as a remedy under international law. See International Law Commission, 'Draft Articles on Responsibility of States for Internationally Wrongful Acts with Commentaries' (2001) II(2) UNYBILC 26, commentary to art 35, para 8.
[253] Boyle, 'Environmental Jurisprudence' (n 4) 380.

arbitral tribunals. At this point, it may seem that it is less so the tribunals that 'control . . . the implementation and development by State parties', as Boyle suggested, but rather the judges just controlling implementation and development of the Convention overall. To the extent these advances are considered as guaranteeing the integrity of the text might well depend on the eye of the beholder.

The decisions on the protection and preservation of the marine environment have arguably been the most progressive in developing State obligations under UNCLOS when compared with all the areas of substantive law in UNCLOS that have been subject to judicial scrutiny. This outcome may not be surprising given the framework nature of the obligations on the protection and preservation of the marine environment and the broad reach of those provisions across international environmental law.[254] Indeed, as Fietta, Saadeh, and Rees-Evans have observed:

> In the light of the [*South China Sea*] Award's conclusions as to the nature and scope of the environmental obligations under Part XII of the Convention, it is arguable that *any* State party to UNCLOS has standing to bring an environmental complaint against *any* other State party with respect to the conduct of its nationals or flagged vessels in *any* maritime area.[255]

Judicial contributions may thus be significant in developing and enforcing marine environmental law. Ultimately, the views of a tribunal, and the legal principles articulated in any judgment, can frame subsequent interactions among stakeholders in a way that may not otherwise have occurred without the intervention of the judicial dialogue.[256]

[254] Natalie Klein, *Dispute Settlement in the UN Convention on the Law of the Sea* (CUP 2005) 163. By contrast, Akhtarkhavari (n 246) has argued that the broad scope of some environmental principles has meant it was difficult to apply them in the context of international adjudication: see 101.

[255] Fietta, Saadeh, and Rees-Evans (n 61) 742 (emphasis in original).

[256] Akhtarkhavari (n 246) 102.

10
Judging the Law of the Sea

I. Introduction

At the outset of this book, we noted that there are two models considered that may explain the operation of the UNCLOS dispute settlement procedures.[1] The first, a substantive model, envisages a vigorous role whereby tribunals have a dynamic responsibility through their engagement with the balance of rights and interests between States party to the United Nations Convention on the Law of the Sea (UNCLOS or Convention).[2] This model is 'at the heart of the public order of the oceans',[3] and prioritises judicial intervention under UNCLOS for the resolution of inter-State disputes. The second model, designated as a Westphalian or procedural model, recognises the enduring importance of State consent as a signature feature of inter-State litigation.[4] Without State consent to arbitration or adjudication, these modes of international dispute settlement are simply not available. With this consideration firmly in place, the role for international tribunals may be more circumscribed, or a more circumspect approach to the role of dispute settlement in relation to the dispute at hand may be warranted. The latter model recognises an ongoing role for political or diplomatic processes.

The discussion in this work has tended to eschew this dichotomy when considering judicial activity in resolving UNCLOS disputes.[5] Rather, it has showcased the many instances where UNCLOS tribunals have usefully brought clarity or provided extra details for State party consideration in the implementation of their obligations and assertion of rights under the Convention. Equally, however, the discussion has highlighted some of the difficulties that have emerged as competing opinions have been expressed within one case,[6] or from one case to the next,[7] or where there has been a failure of judicial restraint.[8] There have also been instances where discussion on certain provisions has been very limited, even though UNCLOS provisions have been considered ambiguous or caused controversy in State practice.[9]

[1] See ch 1(III).
[2] United Nations Convention on the Law of the Sea (adopted 10 December 1982, entered into force 16 November 1994) 1833 UNTS 397 (UNCLOS). See Bernard H Oxman, 'Complementary Agreements and Compulsory Jurisdiction' (2001) 95 AJIL 277, 279.
[3] ibid 279. See also Yoshifumi Tanaka, 'Reflections on the Philippines/China Arbitration Award on Jurisdiction and Admissibility' (2016) 15 LPICT 305, 323–24.
[4] Oxman (n 2) 279. See also Tanaka (n 3) 323; Bjørn Kunoy, 'The Scope of Compulsory Jurisdiction and Exceptions Thereto under the United Nations Convention on the Law of the Sea' (2021) 58 Canadian YBIL 78, 82.
[5] Oxman (n 2) also referred to the importance of reconciling the two models: see 312.
[6] Notably in relation flag State authority on the high seas. See ch 7(III)(B)(3).
[7] Notably the decisions on art 281. See ch3(II)(B)(1). See also discussions on art 2(3) and ch 4(V)(B).
[8] This view is not intended to suggest that either a common law adherence to precedent or even the civil law preference for *jurisprudence constante* are essential. Rather, that these divergences are just that and are problematic in their own right.
[9] The most notable example in this regard being in relation to art 7 and straight baselines. See ch V(III).

In this final chapter, we first seek to summarise our key findings from judicial engagement with questions of jurisdiction in UNCLOS dispute settlement and in relation to the substantive law of the sea. We then undertake some final reflections on the role of judges, taking into account the initial discussion in Chapter 2 and what can be gleaned from almost thirty years of UNCLOS jurisprudence. The final section concludes.

II. Key Findings about UNCLOS Dispute Settlement

The inclusion of compulsory procedures entailing binding decisions as Section 2 of Part XV of UNCLOS may be seen in some respects as a 'leap of faith' on the part of the States negotiating the Convention. There was a clear sense that some form of guarantee was needed given the scale of the enterprise in concluding the 'package deal' of UNCLOS.[10] Yet even though the inclusion of compulsory arbitration or adjudication was considered as having a critical role to play,[11] Sections 1 and 3 of Part XV both establish limits and conditions on the operation of compulsory procedures entailing binding decisions.

In Chapter 3, we examined some of the jurisdictional parameters as well as the main objections to admissibility that may arise at the outset of arbitration or adjudication under UNCLOS. The admissibility objections largely aligned with those presented before different international courts, and UNCLOS tribunals are able to draw from that jurisprudence where relevant. We further examined in Chapter 3 what may be conceived of as three conditions precedent in Section 1 of Part XV that are distinct to UNCLOS for resort to compulsory procedures under Section 2. First, there must be an exchange of views as to the means of dispute settlement pursuant to Article 283 of UNCLOS. One important aspect of this obligation is that it underlines that arbitration or adjudication are not the first or primary means of dispute settlement, but that other modes should and would normally be contemplated. That States have objected to jurisdiction, alleging that the applicant State has failed to meet the requirements of Article 283, affirms State expectations as to what is anticipated in resolving disputes through different peaceful means. While States may assume there will be a certain level of engagement about conflicting issues before resort to arbitration or adjudication, the UNCLOS tribunals have largely minimised the significance of this requirement. The threshold to satisfy the requirements in exchanging views under Article 283 has been set very low and has not, as yet, blocked any case from proceeding.

A second possible barrier to arbitration or adjudication under UNCLOS is the availability of alternative dispute settlement procedures. Under Article 281, there may be instances where those alternative procedures should be utilised rather than those available under Section 2 of Part XV of UNCLOS. As discussed in Chapter 3, jurisprudence on the meaning and operation of this provision has evolved, albeit with two Annex VII tribunals reaching different conclusions.[12] In light of the vast number of oceans-related treaties that

[10] Alan E Boyle, 'Dispute Settlement and the Law of the Sea Convention: Problems of Fragmentation and Jurisdiction' (1997) 46 ICLQ 37, 38.

[11] As manifest in Part XV being described as 'the pivot upon which the delicate equilibrium of the compromise must be balanced': HS Amerasinghe, 'Memorandum by the President of the Conference on Document A/CONF.62/WP.10' (22 July 1977) UN Doc A/CONF.62/WP.10/Add. 1, para 6.

[12] See ch 3(II)(B)(1).

may or may not have their own dispute settlement procedures,[13] there remains scope for further judicial intervention on this point.

A similar, third, barrier to jurisdiction is the existence of alternative dispute settlement procedures that have binding outcomes and that are to apply in lieu of UNCLOS procedures by virtue of Article 282. The International Court of Justice (ICJ) in *Maritime Delimitation in the Indian Ocean* prioritised its jurisdiction premised on Article 36(2) of the Court's Statute in light of Article 282 of UNCLOS.[14] Yet in doing so, the Court arguably failed to respect the right of States to preserve the operation of other dispute settlement options in their declarations accepting the ICJ's jurisdiction. Whether an UNCLOS tribunal would similarly favour the Court's jurisdiction over its own in similar circumstances remains to be seen. The *MOX Plant* Tribunal's decision to stay its proceedings on the basis of judicial comity in favour of the European Court of Justice showed unusual deference in this regard.[15] The dominant trend across all judicial scrutiny of Articles 281, 282, and 283 is to favour the exercise of jurisdiction notwithstanding those provisions.

This preference to exercise jurisdiction is also evident in decisions on subject matter jurisdiction, which were assessed in Chapter 4. Section 3 of Part XV of UNCLOS especially highlights the importance of subject matter jurisdiction as some disputes are either necessarily or optionally excluded under Articles 297 and 298, respectively. What the dispute is about—and specifically how claims are formulated—therefore matters. This question is apparent in discussions around the characterisation of the dispute, following from Boyle's early critique: '[E]verything turns in practice not on what each case involves but on how the issues are formulated. Formulate them wrongly and the case falls outside compulsory jurisdiction. Formulate the same case differently and it falls inside.'[16] This task became all the more important as applicant States have sought to find ways to have territorial sovereignty disputes resolved, or at least influenced, through UNCLOS proceedings.[17] Success in this regard was seemingly achieved in *Mauritius/Maldives*,[18] although the jurisprudence otherwise tended to indicate that territorial sovereignty disputes fall outside the jurisdiction of UNCLOS dispute settlement proceedings. There was, however, a small exception allowed for ancillary or incidental questions of territorial sovereignty in the *Chagos Marine Protected Area* arbitration (*Chagos MPA*).[19]

While the precise contours of this exercise of incidental jurisdiction remain to be seen in the context of territorial sovereignty disputes, the potential availability of this basis was

[13] Natalie Klein, 'Law of the Sea Dispute Settlement Outside of the United Nations Convention on the Law of the Sea' in Hélène Ruiz Fabri (ed), *Max Planck Encyclopedia of International Procedural Law* (OUP 2021).

[14] *Maritime Delimitation in the Indian Ocean (Somalia v Kenya)* (Preliminary Objections) [2017] ICJ Rep 3.

[15] *MOX Plant (Ireland v United Kingdom)* (Order No 3 on Suspension of Proceedings on Jurisdiction and Merits, and Request for Further Provisional Measures, Order of 24 June 2003) PCA Case No 2002-01, paras 22–28. The decision to stay was not without difficulties, however. See Natalie Klein, *Dispute Settlement in the UN Convention on the Law of the Sea* (CUP 2005) 50–51.

[16] Boyle (n 10) 38. Harris, on the other hand, has argued that UNCLOS tribunals need not, and should not, follow this process of 'characterising' disputes but simply ask whether the dispute concerns the interpretation or application of UNCLOS or not: Callista Harris, 'Claims with an Ulterior Purpose: Characterising Disputes Concerning the "Interpretation or Application" of a Treaty' (2020) 18(3) LPIT 279, 286–90. Whether that approach entirely resolves the conundrum posed by Boyle is debatable.

[17] See ch 4(II)(A).

[18] *Delimitation of the Maritime Boundary between Mauritius and Maldives in the Indian Ocean (Mauritius/Maldives)* (Preliminary Objections Judgment of 28 January 2021) ITLOS Case No 28 (*Mauritius/Maldives*, Preliminary Objections).

[19] *Chagos Marine Protected Area Arbitration (Mauritius v United Kingdom)* (Award of 18 March 2015) PCA Case No 2011-03 (*Chagos MPA*). See ch 4(II)(B).

realised in *Enrica Lexie* with the decision to consider questions of immunity of State officials.[20] The lack of reasoning for that approach in *Enrica Lexie*, beyond the suggestion that it was 'an incidental question that necessarily presents itself in the application of the Convention in respect of the dispute before it',[21] has been criticised by both dissenting judges and commentators.[22] Jurisdiction was also extended to consider historic rights, as an issue that had 'interaction' with UNCLOS in the *South China Sea* arbitration.[23] Moreover, the applicable law provision, Article 293, has seemingly been used on some occasions as a means of resolving claims relating to the use of force and prompted States to raise a variety of claims from other areas of international law—although the distinction between applicable law and subject matter jurisdiction has been drawn more sharply in more recent cases.[24] UNCLOS does incorporate rules of reference within its overarching frame in different instances: while these provisions may provide the most legitimate means for extending an understanding of what constitutes a dispute concerning the interpretation or application of the Convention, UNCLOS tribunals have taken a relatively modest approach as to what law is encompassed within their terms to date.[25]

For disputes that are explicitly excluded from the scope of compulsory jurisdiction in Articles 297 and 298, the case law to date has largely favoured a narrow perspective so that more rather than less is subject to resolution before an UNCLOS tribunal. This approach has been evident in interpretations relating to fishing in the exclusive economic zone (EEZ), maritime boundary delimitation and historic bays or title.[26] Perhaps one counter-trend was the suggestion from the *Chagos MPA* Tribunal that disputes relating to straddling stocks should be excluded from compulsory procedures by dint of Article 297(3) rather than included, as would be the case with high seas fisheries disputes.[27] What disputes are perceived as 'concerning military activities' has been subject to greater scrutiny in recent case law, and remains pending before an Annex VII Tribunal at the time of writing.[28] What counts as 'military activities' has involved an assessment of diverse actions and the creation of fine distinctions to warrant, in most instances but not all, an assertion of jurisdiction. These judicial views may not only be relevant to determining questions of jurisdiction before UNCLOS tribunals but may also be pertinent for wider debates on the laws relating to the use of force.

On the substantive law of the sea, Chapter 5 considered different judicial assessments relating to the allocation of maritime space and entitlements thereto. As the allocation of

[20] *Enrica Lexie (Italy v India)* (Award of 21 May 2020) PCA Case No 2015-28 (*Enrica Lexie*, Award).

[21] ibid para 811.

[22] *Enrica Lexie*, Award (n 20) (Dissenting Opinion Robinson) paras 30, 37; *Enrica Lexie*, Award (n 20) (Concurring and Dissenting Opinion of Judge Rao) paras 36-39. See also Robin Churchill, 'Dispute Settlement in the Law of the Sea: Survey for 2020' (2021) 36 IJMCL 1, 19; James G Devaney and Christian J Tams, 'In re Arbitration between the Italian Republic and the Republic of India concerning the "Enrica Lexie" Incident' (2021) 115(3) AJIL 513, 518–19.

[23] *South China Sea Arbitration (Philippines v China)* (Award on Jurisdiction and Admissibility of 29 October 2015) PCA Case No 2013-19, para 168.

[24] See ch 4(V)(A). See further Kate Parlett, 'Beyond the Four Corners of the Convention: Expanding the Scope of Jurisdiction of Law of the Sea Tribunals' (2017) 48 Ocean Dev Intl L 284.

[25] As evident in the interpretation of art 2(3) in *Chagos MPA* and in the reliance on the COLREGS in *South China Sea*. See ch 4(V)(B).

[26] See ch 4(III)(A) and (IV)(A) and (B).

[27] *Chagos MPA* (n 19) para 300. See further ch 4(III)(A).

[28] *Dispute Concerning the Detention of Ukrainian Naval Vessels and Servicemen (Ukraine v Russia)* PCA Case No 2019-28.

maritime space is so critical to the assertion of claims to authority in different maritime areas, it is perhaps surprising that there have not been more disputes referred for judicial resolution. Baselines and base points have occasionally featured in questions about the assertion of maritime entitlements, although primarily in the context of maritime boundary delimitation disputes. The distinction as to what features constitute low-tide elevations, rocks, or islands has been very controversial in State practice but the key judicial intervention on this question was the *South China Sea* arbitration. In that case, the Tribunal provided a very detailed and considered interpretation of Article 121(3).[29] It reflected a distinct policy position not to allow States to maximise claims to exclusive rights over maritime space at the expense of any other or all States. However, the salience of the decision may ultimately be undermined by ongoing prioritisation of national interests for the individual States concerned.

Competing rights and duties in different maritime zones have been tested in various ways before UNCLOS tribunals. To date, actions within ports or in internal waters have not been addressed where they do not directly concern the interpretation or application of the Convention.[30] These parameters may be tested in the forthcoming decision on the merits of an Annex VII Tribunal in *Coastal State Rights in the Black Sea*.[31] In the context of the territorial sea, it has been the scope of implicit limitations on coastal State sovereignty under Article 2(3) of UNCLOS that has warranted judicial consideration, rather than the explicit limitations of coastal State authority in relation to passage.[32] Cases concerning the rights and duties of coastal States and those of other States in the EEZ or on the continental shelf have led UNCLOS tribunals to reflect on the appropriate balance to be struck between competing States' interests. The discussions on the possible meaning of 'due regard' have underlined the highly contextual nature of the assessments that judges are called upon to make.

In relation to maritime boundary delimitation, a rich case law has developed, which began prior to the adoption of UNCLOS and has since been undertaken through the UNCLOS dispute settlement procedures, as well as on separate bases of jurisdiction at the ICJ.[33] Chapter 6 captured the core elements of the judicial contributions in relation to maritime boundary delimitations of the territorial sea, the EEZ and the continental shelf. Notable features of the case law in this area have been the emphases on geography, judicial independence in selecting base points, and significant deference accorded to other judicial decisions on maritime boundaries. While the vagaries of coastal geography necessarily inject some unpredictability, the concerted development of an *acquis judiciaire*[34] is the most evident in this area of the law of the sea.

[29] As discussed in ch 5(II).

[30] As was seen in *M/V Louisa (Saint Vincent and the Grenadines v Spain)* (Judgment) ITLOS Reports 2013, 4and *Enrica Lexie*, Award (n 20).

[31] *Dispute Concerning Coastal State Rights in the Black Sea, Sea of Azov, and Kerch Strait (Ukraine v Russia)* PCA Case No 2017-06. The judgment on the merits was pending at time of writing.

[32] See ch 5(IV)(B).

[33] As noted in ch 6, this case law has been the subject of intensive study in the literature, including book-length treatments of the subject. See eg Alex G Oude Elferink, Tore Henriksen, and Signe Veierud Busch (eds), *Maritime Delimitation: The Case Law—Is It Consistent and Predictable?* (CUP 2018); Massimo Lando, *Maritime Delimitation as Judicial Process* (CUP 2019).

[34] *Bay of Bengal Delimitation (Delimitation of the Maritime Boundary in the Bay of Bengal (Bangladesh/Myanmar)* (Judgment) ITLOS Reports 2012, 4, 137 (Declaration of Judge Wolfrum).

Chapter 7 examined different questions pertaining to navigation, including the nationality of vessels, requirements relating to safe navigation and aspects of law enforcement.[35] In relation to the nationality of vessels, challenges to nationality may have implications for standing before an UNCLOS tribunal, which was addressed in Chapter 3, but may also be pertinent in determining what rights might be asserted, when, and by whom. A close factual examination may be warranted in these circumstances and decisions made about adherence to national laws or standards.[36] These discussions have not been used as a judicial opportunity to challenge the phenomenon of 'flags of convenience', leaving questions concerning the effectiveness of flag State authority over vessels to be challenged, or otherwise followed up as needed, to inter-State discourse.

Navigational rights and duties entail a broad range of activities undertaken by State and private vessels and diverse aspects of the 'freedom of navigation' have been presented before UNCLOS tribunals. It may, however, be noted that disputes concerning important rights of passage in the territorial sea, archipelagic waters, or through international straits have largely not been referred to UNCLOS arbitration or adjudication. Instead, matters relating to navigational safety and law enforcement have featured. In relation to navigational safety, the use of International Maritime Organization (IMO) instruments to understand and interpret UNCLOS obligations has demonstrated proper reliance on the UNCLOS rules of reference and may indicate the relevance of UNCLOS dispute settlement as an enforcement mechanism for the varied IMO treaties that otherwise depend on flag State action for their full and proper implementation. With regards to law enforcement, UNCLOS dispute settlement proceedings have reflected varied contemporary understandings of law enforcement operations, as evident in recognising enforcement jurisdiction for continental shelf prescriptions, reading technological developments into the right of hot pursuit, and in reflecting standard rules of engagement in the use of force deployed in the conduct of law enforcement operations. This flexibility may be construed as facilitative of some important State functions in ocean governance. Determining the parameters of State action in law enforcement operations appear to be calibrated by 'considerations of humanity' when individual freedoms are at stake and become salient considerations.

In many respects, the case law relating to navigation is still sparse and in different ways hints at what may emerge as issues in the future. Questions concerning immunity of warships and other government vessels operated on non-commercial service, and most particularly the status of crew, the effect in international law of national confiscation laws, and bunkering of vessels beyond the fishing industry have been subject to some juridical consideration but there are many facets that remain to be fully addressed. That this situation exists is not only understandable but appropriate given that UNCLOS tribunals are tasked with specific legal questions and fact patterns and have not yet been required to deal more fulsomely with these wider concerns. The potential need to resolve these questions instead underlines how UNCLOS does not, and could not, address every ocean matter and, as a result, there remain important roles for both UNCLOS dispute settlement proceedings, as well as other avenues for dispute resolution.

[35] Law enforcement relating to fisheries and the marine environment is also addressed, respectively, in ch 8(IV)(D) and ch 9(VI).

[36] As occurred eg in *Grand Prince (Belize v France)* (Prompt Release, Judgment) ITLOS Reports 2001, 17; and *M/V Saiga (No 2) (Saint Vincent and the Grenadines v Guinea)* (Judgment) ITLOS Reports 1999, 10. See ch 7(II)(A).

Chapter 8 focused on disputes relating to fisheries that have implicated UNCLOS provisions, as well as the *SRFC Advisory Opinion*,[37] which provided an opportunity for the International Tribunal for the Law of the Sea (ITLOS) to engage in important questions relating to conservation and management of fisheries within the EEZ. Although disputes concerning fishing in the EEZ are excluded from compulsory procedures entailing binding decisions under UNCLOS,[38] it is nonetheless notable that a range of provisions in Part V of the Convention have been considered in UNCLOS cases. Especially helpful in this regard has been the affirmation of due diligence obligations that rest with flag States so as to ensure that their vessels adhere to coastal State requirements for conservation and management of marine living resources in the EEZ. The disputes relating to fishing in the EEZ have needed to consider the balance of interests between coastal and flag States, and this dimension has been especially evident in relation to law enforcement and the prompt release of vessels. The *Virginia G* decision tracked through all the requirements for law enforcement under Article 73,[39] and the prompt release decisions of ITLOS have also amplified our understanding of these obligations.[40] How the balance is to be struck has necessarily varied depending on the facts of the specific disputes. Concerns about sustainability and problematic fishing practices were occasionally voiced in individual opinions,[41] and arose in the *South China Sea* arbitration, but the magnitude and complexity of these issues may indicate that bilateral arbitration or adjudication—especially in the narrow confines of Article 292 proceedings—provide only a limited opportunity to contribute to ocean governance on this issue.

While the balance between fishing rights and the freedom of navigation has featured in law enforcement proceedings relating to fishing, what may ultimately be a greater countervailing force in State decisions regarding fishing will be drawn from UNCLOS obligations relating to the protection and preservation of the marine environment. Chapter 9 has highlighted how broad obligations set out in Articles 192 and 194 of the Convention may frame disputes relating to artificial island-building, harmful fishing practices, the operation of marine protected areas, destruction of marine habitats, and transporting or processing activities associated with the exploitation of the Area.[42] Judicial contributions to marine environmental law may also be discerned in the encompassing quality of the duty to co-operate, the enforcement of all requirements associated with environmental impact assessments (such as notification of these assessments) and, albeit perhaps more tentatively, the need for a precautionary approach in State decision-making where there is a risk of harm to the marine environment. States not only have direct obligations to protect the marine environment but must also act with due diligence, especially in efforts to prevent, reduce and control pollution. UNCLOS tribunals have affirmed jurisprudence from the ICJ in this regard.

An over-arching message from the jurisprudence on marine environmental law from UNCLOS proceedings is that accountability before an international tribunal awaits,

[37] *Request for Advisory Opinion Submitted by the Sub-Regional Fisheries Commission* (Advisory Opinion) ITLOS Reports 2015, 4.

[38] As discussed in ch 4(III)(A).

[39] *M/V Virginia G (Panama/Guinea-Bissau)* (Judgment) ITLOS Reports 2014, 4.

[40] The jurisdiction for prompt release cases was discussed in ch 3(IV)(B), with other aspects of these proceedings discussed in ch 8(IV)(E).

[41] See eg *Volga (Russia v Australia)* (Prompt Release, Judgment) ITLOS Reports 2002, 10 (Dissenting Opinion of Judge ad hoc Shearer) para 17 (*Volga*).

[42] See ch 9(II).

provided a State party to UNCLOS is willing to challenge the actions of another State party. That willingness to bring proceedings may not exist. Such an impetus may or may not be stifled in the situations where States seek to justify their decisions by reference to protecting the marine environment even when other goals are equally relevant to their course of action.[43] Yet even where UNCLOS tribunals have found violations of requirements to protect the marine environment in different guises in the cases to date, the remedies have commonly been limited to declarations to that effect. The assumption that a clarification as to State obligations and presumed good faith in fulfilling obligations henceforth may not ultimately prove sufficient in restoring the condition of the marine environment following the illegal acts. More far-reaching remedies may be sought, and may well be needed, in the future.

III. Revisiting the Role of the Judge

Chapter 2 identified some of the people who have been making these decisions.[44] The profile of the judges shifted marginally throughout the time we were writing this book. Slightly more women were appointed to ITLOS, and the composition of that Tribunal has seen more candidates appointed who have served as State legal advisers and fewer judges who were closely involved in the negotiations of UNCLOS (the latter mostly being a function of time passing). Except for the relatively slow inclusion of women in UNCLOS proceedings,[45] the composition of both ITLOS and the Annex VII tribunals is comparable to other international courts and tribunals created for the resolution of inter-State disputes. These judges perform a variety of roles throughout the course of UNCLOS dispute settlement proceedings. We identified these roles in Chapter 2 as: settling the procedure, treaty interpretation, fact-finding, settling the dispute presented, their role in broader dispute settlement, and the provision of advisory opinions.

At the outset, as noted in Chapter 2, questions of procedure will be influential in determining how a dispute will be resolved before an UNCLOS tribunal. In some instances, the decisions on procedure will form an important component of the resolution of the dispute and warrant incidental proceedings. In the latter regard, we considered in particular orders for provisional measures as well as the opportunity to file counter-claims in Chapter 3. Decisions on the bifurcation of the dispute, joining preliminary objections to the merits, or even staying proceedings while allowing another court or dispute settlement process to proceed, including giving the parties additional time to negotiate, may all be instrumental in settling a matter that has arisen under Part XV of UNCLOS and potentially contribute to formative decisions on jurisdiction or on the substance of the law of the sea.

There are other procedural decisions made throughout the course of the proceedings where the significance of those decisions is perhaps best known or understood by the parties to the particular case. These decisions may influence what facts are known or emphasised in any given case. Novel procedural questions may also emerge. For example, the *Mauritius/Maldives* Tribunal had to contemplate the significance of physical attendance of ad hoc

[43] Bunkering and addressing oil theft may well serve as examples in this regard.
[44] ch 2(II). See also Appendix A and Appendix B.
[45] Notably, far fewer women have served on Annex VII tribunals compared to ITLOS. See ch 2(II).

judges for oral proceedings that were held in a hybrid format (on location and virtual). The Tribunal necessarily concluded that no prejudice could result from the different modes of participation of ad hoc judges.[46] The consequences of some procedural decisions for the final resolution of a dispute may remain obscure.

The analysis throughout the book has reflected the essential role that treaty interpretation plays for UNCLOS judges in resolving disputes. That this task is pre-eminent is unsurprising given that the jurisdiction of UNCLOS tribunals is founded on disputes concerning the interpretation or application of the Convention under Article 288. Throughout the cases, the techniques of treaty interpretation set out in Article 31 of the Vienna Convention on the Law of Treaties (VCLT)[47] were frequently used, although judges were not always explicit about their methodology. Further, there was not strict adherence to the hierarchy anticipated as between Articles 31 and 32 of the VCLT whereby recourse to the negotiating history is only to be a supplementary means of interpretation.[48] There are many instances where the negotiating history of UNCLOS has played an important role in understanding the meaning of specific rights and duties in the Convention. That aspect may remain important when recalling the 'package deal' nature of UNCLOS but to ensure the continued relevance of UNCLOS, the contemporary context must also be brought to bear.[49]

When it comes to the function of settling disputes, it is noteworthy that cases arising in UNCLOS dispute settlement procedures are often part of larger, political or diplomatic controversies. This aspect is certainly not unique to UNCLOS.[50] Mauritius has clearly pursued a litigation strategy under UNCLOS as part of its ongoing effort to reclaim the Chagos Archipelago from the United Kingdom. Further, Oral has commented, '[t]here is no doubt that Ukraine is utilising UNCLOS and its compulsory dispute settlement mechanism to gain recognition of its sovereignty, even if implicitly, over Crimea through the international adjudicative process'.[51] Even cases that seemingly involve relatively simple questions concerning the arrest of a vessel may have broader implications: the *Volga* prompt release proceedings emerged among regional efforts to conserve and manage fisheries in Antarctic waters;[52] the *San Padre Pio* dispute reflected Nigeria's efforts to deal with illegal bunkering and oil theft off the coast of western Africa.[53] Even the *Seabed Advisory Opinion*,[54] which addressed a specific set of legal questions, had much at stake for the development goals of the Pacific island States initiating that request. Given this context, we have echoed Judge Feliciano's entreaty that judges recall that '[a] truly humble judge should be able to resist the shimmering vision of an "imperial judiciary" and should come to realize that [s]he has neither the commission nor the competence to solve all the problems of the nation and that there are other "workers in the vineyard" '.[55]

[46] Mauritius/Maldives, Preliminary Objections (n 18) paras 29–34.
[47] Vienna Convention on the Law of Treaties (adopted 23 May 1969, entered into force 27 January 1980) 1155 UNTS 331 (VCLT).
[48] ibid art 32.
[49] Consistent with art 31(1) of the VCLT.
[50] As recognised, for example, by the ICJ in *Tehran Hostages: United States Diplomatic and Consular Staff in Tehran* (Judgment) [1980] ICJ Rep 3, para 36.
[51] Nilüfer Oral, 'Ukraine v The Russian Federation: Navigating Conflict over Sovereignty under UNCLOS' (2021) 97 ILS 478, 507.
[52] *Volga* (n 41).
[53] *M/T San Padre Pio (Switzerland v Nigeria)* (Provisional Measures, Order of 6 July 2019) ITLOS Case No 27.
[54] *Responsibilities and Obligations of States with Respect to Activities in the Area* (Advisory Opinion) ITLOS Reports 2011, 10.
[55] Florentino P Feliciano, 'Qualities of a Good Judge' (1994) 3 The Lawyers Rev 68, 68.

IV. Conclusion

In some respects, this book provides simply a snapshot of the current state of UNCLOS jurisprudence. Compared to the jurisprudence that emerges from the World Trade Organization, which is comparable to UNCLOS in terms of being a treaty of critical and constitutive importance with compulsory jurisdiction, the UNCLOS case law is relatively little. The reasons suggested for the relative paucity of jurisprudence vary.[56] Commentators have recently observed that the selection of specific fora under Article 287 changes the bargaining that occurs between States in resolving certain maritime disputes.[57] In response to that study, Squatrito has emphasised that a tribunal's performance may (instead or additionally) be critical in influencing State decision-making,[58] and de Silva has suggested that an UNCLOS tribunal's non-adjudicative work may be influential.[59] Perhaps most accurately, Ásgeirsdóttir has acknowledged that we just do not know all the reasons as to why States make their decisions in relation to UNCLOS dispute settlement.[60] There are many variables in decisions about instituting proceedings.[61] Consequently, it is hard to demonstrate definitively across all of the UNCLOS arbitrations and adjudications what driving forces are most pertinent when a State party decides to proceed with dispute resolution under Section 2 of Part XV of UNCLOS, whether there are common tendencies as to how a case is run and what States will do following a tribunal's decision.

Throughout this book, we have shown that there are many occasions where tribunal decisions and interpretations of UNCLOS have contributed to the good order of the oceans in resolving the immediate dispute and have potentially contributed to the future conduct of a larger set of stakeholders. This chapter has further indicated that there remains considerable potential for UNCLOS dispute settlement proceedings to canvas an even greater array of issues. We have also on occasions indicated where UNCLOS tribunals have perhaps caused confusion to or risked alienating the varied stakeholders, and not necessarily promoted the public order of the oceans as might have been expected or hoped. However, there may have been good reasons for such results and inevitably different views and priorities will emerge. As we conclude the writing of the book, there are judgments on the merits pending in *Coastal State Rights in the Black Sea* and *Mauritius/Maldives*. There are also several cases pending before the ICJ that will involve the interpretation and/or application of provisions of UNCLOS: a maritime delimitation dispute between Guatemala and Belize,[62] a dispute concerning maritime delimitation and sovereignty over islands between Gabon and Equatorial Guinea,[63] and two cases between Nicaragua and Colombia, concerning

[56] The low number of cases may not be detrimental, however. As Squatrito has suggested that 'more case law can render judicialized dispute settlement less predictable and more costly to states than we might otherwise expect': Theresa Squatrito, 'International Judicial Performance and the Law of the Sea' (2021) 115 AJIL Unbound 399.

[57] See Sara McLaughlin Mitchell and Andrew P Owsiak, 'Judicialization of the Sea: Bargaining in the Shadow of UNCLOS' (2021) 115 AJIL 579.

[58] Squatrito (n 56).

[59] Nicole de Silva, 'International Courts' Shadow Effects and the Aims of Judicialized International Cooperation' (2021) 115 AJIL Unbound 394.

[60] Áslaug Ásgeirsdóttir, 'Explaining State Adjudication Choices: Limits on Focusing on Visible Processes' (2021) 115 AJIL Unbound 384.

[61] Shirley V Scott, 'Litigation Versus Dispute Resolution through Political Processes' in Natalie Klein (ed), *Litigating International Law Disputes: Weighing the Balance* (CUP 2014) 24.

[62] *Guatemala's Territorial, Insular and Maritime Claim (Guatemala/Belize)* (International Court of Justice, General List No 161).

[63] *Land and Maritime Delimitation and Sovereignty over Islands (Gabon/Equatorial Guinea)* (International Court of Justice, General List No 179).

delimitation of the extended continental shelf,[64] and sovereign rights in the contiguous zone and the EEZ.[65] These judgments, and future cases, will elaborate further on the interpretation and application of the Convention in different factual settings.

We anticipate that UNCLOS dispute settlement proceedings may not always be, and do not have to be, 'the pivot upon which the delicate equilibrium of the compromise must be balanced'.[66] States may continue to rely on diverse modes of dispute settlement and opt to respond to perceived violations of the law of the sea in a variety of ways. We have further sought to acknowledge that State parties to UNCLOS are not the only stakeholders when conflicts about ocean governance emerge. In foregrounding the role of judges in UNCLOS dispute settlement, we have sought to underline the relevance of their role in important aspects of ocean governance, including the scope and limits of that role. This perspective should provide further context to our overall understanding of how disputes relating to ocean affairs could or should be resolved.

[64] For the most recent phase in these proceedings, see *Question of the Delimitation of the Continental Shelf between Nicaragua and Colombia beyond 200 Nautical Miles from the Nicaraguan Coast (Nicaragua v Colombia)* (Preliminary Objections) [2016] ICJ Rep 100.

[65] For the most recent phase in these proceedings, see *Alleged Violations of Sovereign Rights and Maritime Spaces in the Caribbean Sea (Nicaragua v Colombia)* (Preliminary Objections) [2016] ICJ Rep 3.

[66] See n 11.

APPENDIX A—BACKGROUND TO ANNEX VII ARBITRATORS

Annex VII Arbitrators as of 1 November 2021*

Name of Arbitrator	DOB	Nationality	ITLOS	Education and Professional Background	Annex VII Arbitrations
HE Judge Awn Shawkat Al-Khasawneh	1950	Jordan	No	**Education:** University of Cambridge **Professional Background**: Academic; Diplomatic appointments; international appointments (ILC, High-Level Panel on Access to Medicines); Judicial appointments (ICJ); National professional appointment (Prime Minister)	*ARA Libertad*, Annex VII Arbitration
HE Judge Boualem Bouguetaia	1946	Algeria	Yes	**Education:** University of Paris; Paris Institute of Political Studies (Sciences Po) **Professional Background**: Academic; Diplomatic appointment; Lawyer; National professional appointments (politician)	*Coastal State Rights in the Black Sea*
Sir Ian Brownlie CBE QC	1932 *(deceased, 2010)*	UK	No	**Education:** Oxford University **Professional Background**: Academic; Arbitrator; Barrister; Judicial appointment (European Nuclear Energy Tribunal); International appointment (ILC)	*Barbados v Trinidad and Tobago*

*The information in Appendix A is drawn from English-language publicly available sources and personal communication with one arbitrator. Best efforts have been undertaken to ensure its accuracy, but errors may remain.

Name of Arbitrator	DOB	Nationality	ITLOS	Education and Professional Background	Annex VII Arbitrations
Mr Henry Burmester AO QC	1949	Australia	No	**Education:** Australian National University; Hague Academy of International Law; University of Virginia **Professional Background**: Academic; Counsel; National professional appointments	*Arctic Sunrise, Merits*
HE Judge P Chandrasekhara Rao	1936 *(deceased, 2018)*	India	Yes	**Education:** University of Madras, India; NALSAR University of Law, Hyderabad, India **Professional Background**: Academic; Counsel; Diplomatic appointments; National professional appointments	*Enrica Lexie*, Annex VII Provisional Measures--*died during proceedings*
Judge Jean-Pierre Cot	1937	France (born Switzerland)	Yes	**Education:** University of Paris **Professional Background**: Academic (Dean); Counsel and Advocate, Judicial appointment; National professional appointment (politician)	*Bay of Bengal Arbitration* *South China Sea*, Award
HE Judge James Crawford AC SC	1948 *(deceased, 2021)*	Australia	No	**Education:** University of Adelaide, Australia; Oxford University **Professional Background**: Academic (Dean); Barrister; International appointments (ILC); Judicial appointments (ICJ); National professional appointments	*MOX Plant*, Termination
Judge Gudmundur Eiriksson	1947	Iceland (born Canada)	Yes –ad hoc	**Education:** Rutgers University; King's College London; Columbia University **Professional Background:** Academic; Arbitrator; Diplomatic appointments; International appointments (Office of Legal Affairs, ILC); National professional appointment	*Detention of Ukrainian Naval Vessels and Servicemen*

HE Judge Florentino Feliciano	1928 *(deceased, 2015)*	Philippines	No	**Education:** University of the Philippines; Yale University **Professional Background**: Academic; Arbitrator; Counsel; Judicial appointments (World Bank Administrative Tribunal; Supreme Court of the Philippines); Negotiator	*Southern Bluefin Tuna*, Jurisdiction and Admissibility
The Hon L Yves Fortier PC CC QQ QC	1935	Canada	No	**Education:** University of Montreal; McGill University; Oxford University **Professional Background**: Arbitrator; Counsel; Diplomatic appointment; Judicial appointment (ICJ); Mediator; National professional appointments	*MOX Plant*, Termination
Professor Francesco Francioni	1942	Italy	Yes – ad hoc	**Education:** University of Florence; Harvard University **Professional Background**: Academic; Associate; Diplomatic appointments; International appointment (UNESCO)	*Enrica Lexie*, Award
Professor Thomas Franck	1931 *(deceased, 2009)*	Germany	No	**Education:** University of British Colombia; Harvard University **Professional Background**: Academic; Counsel; International appointments (consulting and UNITAR)	*Guyana v Suriname*
Judge Vladimir Golitsyn	1947	Russia	Yes	**Education:** Moscow State University; Moscow State Institute of International Relations; Diplomatic Academy of the Ministry of Foreign Affairs of the Russian Federation **Professional Background**: Academic; Diplomatic appointments; International appointments (Office of Legal Affairs); Lawyer; National professional appointment	*Coastal State Rights in the Black Sea* *Enrica Lexie*, Award *Detention of Ukrainian Naval Vessels and Servicemen*

Name of Arbitrator	DOB	Nationality	ITLOS	Education and Professional Background	Annex VII Arbitrations
Judge Alonso Gómez-Robledo	1949	Mexican (born in USA)	Yes	**Education:** Universidad Nacional Autónoma de México; Institute of International Studies, Geneva **Professional Background**: Academic; Diplomatic appointment; National professional appointments	*Coastal State Rights in the Black Sea*
Judge Sir Christopher Greenwood GBE CMG QC	1955	UK	No	**Education:** University of Cambridge **Professional Background**: Academic; Arbitrator; Barrister; Judicial appointments (ICJ, Iran-United States Claims Tribunal)	*Chagos MPA* *Detention of Ukrainian Naval Vessels and Servicemen*
Professor Gerhard Hafner	1943	Austria	No	**Education:** Vienna Law Faculty; University of Paris; The Hague University; University of Moscow. **Professional Background**: Academic; Arbitrator; Conciliator; International appointment (ILC); National professional appointment	*Atlanto-Scandian Herring* *MOX Plant*, Termination
Judge Albert Hoffmann	1955	South Africa	Yes	**Education:** University of Johannesburg; University of Pretoria, South Africa; Columbia University **Professional Background**: Academic; Advocate; Diplomatic appointment; National professional appointment	*Chagos MPA*
Dr Kamal Hossain	1937	Bangladesh	Yes – ad hoc	**Education:** University of Notre Dame, USA; University of Michigan; Oxford University **Professional Background**: Academic; Arbitrator; Barrister; International appointments (UN Compensation Commission; Iran-United States Claims Tribunal; Special Rapporteur on Afghanistan); National professional appointment (politician)	*Land Reclamation*, Award *Guyana v Suriname*

Judge James L Kateka	1945	Tanzania	Yes	**Education:** University of East Africa; Kings College London **Professional Background**: Diplomatic appointment; Judicial appointment (ICJ); Lawyer (Partner); National professional appointment	*Chagos MPA* *Duzgit Integrity*
The Rt Hon Justice Sir Kenneth Keith ONZ KBE QC	1937	New Zealand	No	**Education:** University of Auckland; Victoria University of Wellington; Harvard University **Professional Background**: Academic; Counsel; Judicial appointments (ICJ); National professional appointments	*Southern Bluefin Tuna*, Jurisdiction and Admissibility
Judge Elsa Kelly	1939	Argentina	Yes	**Education:** University of Buenos Aires; Harvard University; Instituto del Servicio Exterior de la Nación **Professional Background**: Academic; Diplomatic appointments; International appointments (UNESCO) Legal adviser; National professional appointments	*ARA Libertad*, Annex VII Arbitration
Professor Vaughan Lowe QC	1952	UK	No	**Education:** University of Wales; University of Cambridge; Oxford University **Professional Background**: Academic; Arbitrator; Barrister	*Barbados v Trinidad and Tobago* *Coastal State Rights in the Black Sea*
Professor Donald M McRae CC ONZM	1944	Canada, New Zealand	No	**Education:** University of Otago; University of Canterbury **Professional Background:** Academic; Arbitrator; Conciliator Counsel; Member of various international trade dispute settlement panels; National professional appointment	*Detention of Ukrainian Naval Vessels and Servicemen*

Name of Arbitrator	DOB	Nationality	ITLOS	Education and Professional Background	Annex VII Arbitrations
Judge Thomas A Mensah	1932 *(deceased, 2020)*	Ghana	Yes	**Education:** University of Ghana; University of London; Yale University **Professional Background**: Academic; Diplomatic appointments; International appointments (IMO, UNEP)	*Atlanto-Scandian Herring* *Bay of Bengal Arbitration* *South China Sea*, Award *ARA Libertad*, Annex VII Arbitration *Arctic Sunrise*, Merits *MOX Plant*, Termination
The Rt Hon Lord Mustill PC QC	1931 *(deceased, 2015)*	UK	No	**Education:** University of Cambridge **Professional Background**: Barrister; Judicial appointment	*MOX Plant*, Termination
Mr L Dolliver M. Nelson	1932 *(deceased, 2016)*	Grenada	Yes	**Education:** University of West Indies; London School of Economics **Professional Background**: Academic; Judicial appointment; International appointments	*Guyana v Suriname*
Professor Francisco Orrego Vicuña	1942 *(deceased, 2018)*	Chile	Yes – ad hoc	**Education:** University of Chile; London School of Economics **Professional Background**: Arbitrator; Diplomatic appointment; Judicial appointments (Administrative Tribunals of the World Bank and of the IMF, ICJ); Lawyer	*Atlanto-Scandian Herring* *Barbados v Trinidad and Tobago*
Professor Bernard H Oxman	1941	USA	Yes – ad hoc	**Education:** Columbia University **Professional Background**: Academic; Diplomatic appointments; Judicial appointment (ICJ); National professional appointment	*Land Reclamation*, Award *ARA Libertad*, Annex VII Arbitration

Judge Jin-Hyun Paik	1958	South Korea	Yes	**Education:** Seoul National University; Columbia University; University of Cambridge **Professional Background**: Academic (Dean); Attorney-at-law; Diplomatic appointments; National professional appointment	*Coastal State Rights in the Black Sea* *Enrica Lexie*, Award
Judge Stanislaw Pawlak	1933	Poland	Yes	**Education:** University of Warsaw **Professional Background**: Academic; Diplomatic appointments; National professional appointment; International appointment (ILC)	*South China Sea*, Award
Dr MCW Pinto	1931	Sri Lanka	No	**Education:** University of Sri Lanka; Sri Lanka Law College; University of Cambridge **Professional Background**: Attorney; Barrister; Diplomatic appointments; International appointments (ILC, Iran-United States Claims Tribunal); National professional appointment	*Atlanto-Scandian Herring* *Land Reclamation*, Award
HE Judge Patrick L Robinson OJ	1944	Jamaica	No	**Education:** University College of the West Indies (London); London University; King's College London; The Hague Academy of International Law **Professional Background**: Academic; Barrister; Diplomatic appointments; International appointments (ILC, UNCITRAL, UNESCO); Judicial appointment (ICTY, ICJ); National professional appointments	*Enrica Lexie*, Award
Judge Stephen M Schwebel	1929	USA	No	**Education:** Harvard University; University of Cambridge; Yale University **Professional Background**: Academic; Attorney; International appointment (ILC); Judicial appointments (ICJ, Administrative Tribunals of the World Bank and of the IMF); National professional appointment;	*Barbados v Trinidad and Tobago* *Southern Bluefin Tuna*, Jurisdiction and Admissibility

Name of Arbitrator	DOB	Nationality	ITLOS	Education and Professional Background	Annex VII Arbitrations
Professor Ivan Shearer AM RFD	1938 *(deceased, 2019)*	Australia	Yes – ad hoc	**Education:** University of Adelaide, Australia; Northwestern University **Professional Background**: Academic (Dean); Barrister; International appointment (UNHRC); Judicial appointment; National professional appointment	*Bay of Bengal Arbitration* *Land Reclamation*, Award *Chagos MPA* *Guyana v Suriname*
HE Judge Bruno Simma	1941	Germany	No	**Education:** University of Innsbruck, Austria **Professional Background**: Academic (Dean); Arbitrator; Co-agent and Counsel; International appointments (ILC, CESCR), Judicial appointments (ICJ, Iran-United States Claims Tribunal); Lawyer	*ARA Libertad*, Annex VII Arbitration
Professor Hans Smit	1927 *(deceased, 2012)*	Netherlands	No	**Education:** University of Amsterdam; Columbia University **Professional Background**: Academic; Arbitrator; International appointments (World Bank and UNCITRAL); National professional appointments	*Guyana v Suriname*
Professor Alfred HA Soons	1948	Netherlands (born Aruba)	No	**Education:** Utrecht University, The Netherlands; University of Washington; University of Cambridge **Professional Background**: Academic; Arbitrator; Counsel; National professional appointments	*Duzgit Integrity* *South China Sea*, Award *Arctic Sunrise*, Merits
Dr Pemmaraju Sreenivasa Rao	1942	India	No	**Education:** Andhra University, India; Yale University **Professional Background**: Academic; International appointments (ILC); Judicial appointment (ICJ); National professional appointment	*Bay of Bengal Arbitration* *Enrica Lexie*, Award

Professor Janusz Symonides	1938 *(deceased, 2020)*	Poland	No	**Education:** Main School of Foreign Service, Warsaw; Nicolaus Copernicus University, Toruń, Poland **Professional Background**: Academic; Diplomatic appointments; Lawyer; International appointment (UNESCO)	*Arctic Sunrise*, Merits
Dr Alberto Székely	1946	Mexico	Yes – ad hoc	**Education:** University of Mexico; Fletcher School – Tufts University, USA; University of London **Professional Background**: Academic; Diplomatic appointments; National professional appointment	*Arctic Sunrise*, Merits
HE Judge Per Tresselt	1937	Norway	No	**Education:** University of Oslo **Professional Background**: Diplomatic appointments; Judicial appointment (EFTA Court); National professional appointment	*Southern Bluefin Tuna*, Jurisdiction and Admissibility
Judge Tullio Treves	1942	Italy	Yes	**Education:** University of Milan **Professional Background**: Academic; Arbitrator; Counsel; Diplomatic appointment; International appointments (consulting and Chairman of the Cairo Regional Centre for International Commercial Arbitration)	*Duzgit Integrity*
Sir Arthur Watts KCMG QC	1931 *(deceased, 2007)*	UK	No	**Education:** University of Cambridge **Professional Background**: Arbitrator; Barrister; Diplomatic appointment; Negotiator	*Barbados v Trinidad and Tobago* *Land Reclamation*, Award *MOX Plant –– died during proceedings*

Name of Arbitrator	DOB	Nationality	ITLOS	Education and Professional Background	Annex VII Arbitrations
Judge Rüdiger Wolfrum	1941	Germany	Yes	**Education:** University of Bonn, University of Tübingen **Professional Background:** Academic (Director – Max Planck Institute); International appointment (CERD); Judicial appointments	*Atlanto-Scandian Herring* *Bay of Bengal Arbitration* *Chagos MPA* *South China Sea*, Award *Detention of Ukrainian Naval Vessels and Servicemen*
Professor Chusei Yamada	1931 *(deceased, 2013)*	Japan	No	**Education:** University of Tokyo; Fletcher School – Tufts University, USA **Professional Background:** Arbitrator; Conciliator; Diplomatic appointments; international appointment (ILC); National professional appointment	*Southern Bluefin Tuna*, Jurisdiction and Admissibility

APPENDIX B—BACKGROUND TO CURRENT ITLOS JUDGES

ITLOS Judges as of 1 November 2021[*]

Name of Judge	DOB	Nationality	Date Joined Tribunal	Education and Professional Background	Cases
Albert J Hoffmann (President)	1955	South Africa	2005	**Education:** University of Johannesburg; University of Pretoria; Programme UNITAR/Columbia University, New York **Professional Background**: Government legal adviser; Academic, Advocate, Diplomatic appointment; National professional appointment	*Hoshinmaru* *Tomimaru* *Bay of Bengal Delimitation* *Seabed Advisory Opinion* *Louisa*, Provisional Measures *Louisa*, Judgment *Virginia G* *ARA Libertad* *SRFC Advisory Opinion* *Arctic* Sunrise, Provisional Measures *Enrica Lexie*, Provisional Measures *Norstar*, Preliminary Objections *Norstar*, Judgment *Detention of Three Ukrainian Naval Vessels*, Provisional Measures *San Padre Pio*, Provisional Measures

[*]The information in Appendix B is primarily drawn from the ITLOS website and other English-language publicly available sources. Best efforts have been undertaken to ensure its accuracy, but errors may remain.

Name of Judge	DOB	Nationality	Date Joined Tribunal	Education and Professional Background	Cases
Tomas Heidar (Vice President)	1962	Iceland	2014	**Education:** University of Iceland; Hague Academy of International Law, The Netherlands; University of Copenhagen, Denmark; Academy of European Law, European University Institute, Fiesole, Italy; Europe Institute, University of Saarland, Saarbrücken, Germany **Professional Background**: Academic; Government legal adviser; Arbitrator; Attorney at Law; Conciliator; Diplomatic appointment; Mediator; National professional appointment	*Enrica Lexie*, Provisional Measures *Norstar*, Preliminary Objections *Norstar*, Judgment *Detention of Three Ukrainian Naval Vessels*, Provisional Measures *San Padre Pio*, Provisional Measures *Mauritius/Maldives*, Preliminary Objections
José Luis Jesus	1950	Cape Verde	1999	**Education:** Classical University of Lisbon; Saint John's University, New York **Professional Background**: Government legal adviser; UNCLOS negotiator; Diplomatic appointments; International appointments (UN Security Council, FAO); National professional appointments (foreign minister)	*Camouco* *Monte Confurco* *Grand Prince* *MOX Plant*, Provisional Measures *Volga* *Land Reclamation*, Provisional Measures *Juno Trader* *Hoshinmaru* *Tomimaru* *Bay of Bengal Delimitation* *Louisa*, Provisional Measures *Louisa*, Judgment *Virginia G*

					ARA Libertad *SRFC Advisory Opinion* *Arctic Sunrise*, Provisional Measures *Enrica Lexie*, Provisional Measures *Norstar*, Preliminary Objections *Norstar*, Judgment *Detention of Three Ukrainian Naval Vessels*, Provisional Measures *San Padre Pio*, Provisional Measures *Mauritius/Maldives*, Preliminary Objections
Stanislaw Pawlak	1933	Poland	2005	**Education:** University of Warsaw **Professional Background**: Government legal adviser; Academic; Diplomatic appointments; National professional appointment	*Hoshinmaru* *Tomimaru* *Bay of Bengal Delimitation* *Louisa*, Provisional Measures *Louisa*, Judgment *Virginia G* *SRFC Advisory Opinion* *ARA Libertad* *Arctic Sunrise*, Provisional Measures *Enrica Lexie*, Provisional Measures *Norstar*, Preliminary Objections *Detention of Three Ukrainian Naval Vessels*, Provisional Measures *San Padre Pio*, Provisional Measures *Mauritius/Maldives*, Preliminary Objections

Name of Judge	DOB	Nationality	Date Joined Tribunal	Education and Professional Background	Cases
Shunji Yanai	1937	Japan	2005	**Education:** University of Tokyo **Professional Background:** Government legal adviser; Academic; Diplomatic appointments; National professional appointment	*Hoshinmaru* *Tomimaru* *Bay of Bengal Delimitation* *Seabed Advisory Opinion* *Louisa*, Provisional Measures *Louisa*, Judgment *Virginia G* *ARA Libertad* *SRFC Advisory Opinion* *Arctic Sunrise*, Provisional Measures *Enrica Lexie*, Provisional Measures *Norstar*, Preliminary Objections *Norstar*, Judgment *Detention of Three Ukrainian Naval Vessels*, Provisional Measures *San Padre Pio*, Provisional Measures *Mauritius/Maldives*, Preliminary Objections
James L Kateka	1945	United Republic of Tanzania	2005	**Education:** Dar-es-Salaam University College; University of East Africa; King's College, University of London **Professional Background:** Government legal adviser; Diplomatic appointment; Judicial appointment (ICJ); Lawyer (Partner); National professional appointment	*Hoshinmaru* *Tomimaru* *Bay of Bengal Delimitation* *Seabed Advisory Opinion* *Louisa*, Provisional Measures *Louisa*, Judgment *Virginia G* *ARA* Libertad *SRFC Advisory Opinion*

					Arctic Sunrise, Provisional Measures *Enrica Lexie*, Provisional Measures *Norstar*, Preliminary Objections *Detention of Three Ukrainian Naval Vessels*, Provisional Measures *San Padre Pio*, Provisional Measures
Boualem Bouguetaia	1946	Algeria	2008	**Education:** University of Paris; Institute of Political Studies of Paris **Professional Background**: Government legal adviser; Academic; UNCLOS negotiator; Diplomatic appointment; Lawyer; National professional appointments (politician)	*Bay of Bengal Delimitation* *Seabed Advisory Opinion* *Louisa*, Provisional Measures *Louisa*, Judgment *Virginia G* *ARA Libertad* *SRFC Advisory Opinion* *Arctic Sunrise*, Provisional Measures *Ghana/Cote d'Ivoire*, Provisional Measures *Ghana/Cote d'Ivoire*, Judgment *Enrica Lexie*, Provisional Measures *Norstar*, Preliminary Objections *Detention of Three Ukrainian Naval Vessels*, Provisional Measures *San Padre Pio*, Provisional Measures *Mauritius/Maldives*, Preliminary Objections

Name of Judge	DOB	Nationality	Date Joined Tribunal	Education and Professional Background	Cases
Jin-Hyun Paik	1958	Republic of Korea	2009	**Education:** Seoul National University; Columbia University School of Law; University of Cambridge **Professional Background**: Academic (Dean); Attorney-at-law; Government legal adviser; Diplomatic appointments; National professional appointment	*Bay of Bengal Delimitation* *Louisa*, Provisional Measures *Louisa*, Judgment *Virginia G* *ARA Libertad* *SRFC Advisory Opinion* *Arctic Sunrise*, Provisional Measures *Ghana/Cote d'Ivoire*, Provisional Measures *Ghana/Cote d'Ivoire*, Judgment *Enrica Lexie*, Provisional Measures *Norstar*, Preliminary Objections *Norstar*, Judgment *Detention of Three Ukrainian Naval Vessels*, Provisional Measures *San Padre Pio*, Provisional Measures *Mauritius/Maldives*, Preliminary Objections *Mauritius/Maldives*, Merits
David Joseph Attard	1953	Malta	2011	**Education:** University of Malta; University of Oxford **Professional Background**: Academic; Government legal adviser; Advocate; Barrister-at-Law, Diplomatic appointments; International appointments (UNEP, IMO, ILA); National professional appointments	*Louisa*, Judgment *Virginia G* *ARA Libertad* *SRFC Advisory Opinion* *Arctic Sunrise*, Provisional Measures *Enrica Lexie*, Provisional Measures *Detention of Three Ukrainian Naval Vessels*, Provisional Measures *San Padre Pio*, Provisional Measures

Markiyan Z Kulyk	1970	Ukraine	2011	**Education:** Moscow Institute for International Relations **Professional Background:** Government legal adviser; Diplomatic appointment; International appointment (Adviser to the President of the UN General Assembly); National professional appointment	*Louisa*, Judgment *Virginia G* *ARA Libertad* *SRFC Advisory Opinion* *Arctic Sunrise*, Provisional Measures *Enrica Lexie*, Provisional Measures *Norstar*, Preliminary Objections *Norstar*, Judgment *Detention of Three Ukrainian Naval Vessels, Provisional Measures* *San Padre Pio*, Provisional Measures
Alonso Gómez-Robledo Verduzco	1949	Mexico (born USA)	2014	**Education:** Universidad Nacional Autónoma de México; Institute of International Studies, Geneva **Professional Background:** Academic; Government legal adviser; UNCLOS negotiator; Diplomatic appointment; National professional appointments	*Enrica Lexie*, Provisional Measures *Norstar*, Preliminary Objections *Detention of Three Ukrainian Naval Vessels*, Provisional Measures *San Padre Pio*, Provisional Measures
Óscar Cabello Sarubbi	1947	Paraguay	2017	**Education:** Universitá degli Studi di Roma; Universitá del Sacro Cuore, Milano; Saint John's University, New York **Professional Background:** Academic; Government legal adviser; UNCLOS negotiator; Diplomatic appointment; National professional appointment	*Norstar*, Judgment *Detention of Three Ukrainian Naval Vessels*, Provisional Measures *San Padre Pio*, Provisional Measures

Name of Judge	DOB	Nationality	Date Joined Tribunal	Education and Professional Background	Cases
Neeru Chadha	1955	India	2017	**Education:** University of Delhi; University of Michigan **Professional Background**: Government legal adviser; Diplomatic appointment (Counsellor and Legal Advisor, Permanent Mission of India to the United Nations); International appointments; National professional appointment	*Norstar*, Judgment *Detention of Three Ukrainian Naval Vessels*, Provisional Measures *San Padre Pio*, Provisional Measures *Mauritius/Maldives*, Preliminary Objections
Kriangsak Kittichaisaree	1958	Thailand	2017	**Education:** Cambridge University **Professional Background**: Government legal adviser; Academic; Arbitrator; Conciliator; Diplomatic appointment; International appointments (UN International Law Commission); Legal Counsel; National professional appointment	*Norstar*, Judgment *Detention of Three Ukrainian Naval Vessels*, Provisional Measures *San Padre Pio*, Provisional Measures
Roman Kolodkin	1960	Russian Federation	2017	**Education:** Moscow State University **Professional Background**: Government legal adviser; Academic; Diplomatic appointments; National professional appointment	*Norstar*, Judgment *Detention of Three Ukrainian Naval Vessels*, Provisional Measures *San Padre Pio*, Provisional Measures

Liesbeth Lijnzaad	1960	The Netherlands	2017	**Education:** University of Amsterdam; T.M.C. Asser Institute, The Hague; Limburg University (now: Maastricht University) **Professional Background**: Government legal adviser; Academic; Arbitrator; Conciliator; Diplomatic appointments; International appointment (PCA and agent in cases before ITLOS, ICJ, PCA); National professional appointment	*Norstar*, Judgment *Detention of Three Ukrainian Naval Vessels*, Provisional Measures *San Padre Pio*, Provisional Measures
Kathy-Ann Brown	1961	Jamaica	2020	**Education:** University of the West Indies; Cambridge University; Norman Manley Law School; York University **Professional Background:** Government legal adviser; Academic; Diplomatic appointment (Permanent Representative of Jamaica to the ISA); National professional appointment; Consultant and legal adviser to international bodies (CRNM, OACPS, Commonwealth Secretariat, CARICOM, OAS, IDB); Solicitor	

Name of Judge	DOB	Nationality	Date Joined Tribunal	Education and Professional Background	Cases
Ida Caracciolo	1961	Italy	2020	**Education:** Sapienza Università di Roma; Hague Academy of International Law; Inter-University Centre of Postgraduate Studies, Dubrovnik. **Professional Background:** Academic; International arbitral and judicial appointments (PCA, European Court of Human Rights (*ad hoc*), OSCE Court of Conciliation and Arbitration); Government legal adviser (of counsel in cases before ITLOS, European Court of Human Rights, ICJ); Barrister	
Jielong Duan	1958	China	2020	**Education:** Southwest University of Political Science and Law; China Foreign Affairs University; Columbia University **Professional Background:** Diplomatic appointments; Government legal adviser; Academic.	
María Teresa Infante Caffi	1949	Chile	2020	**Education:** University of Chile; Graduate Institute of International Studies, Geneva; Hague Academy of International Law **Professional Background:** Academic; Diplomatic appointments; International appointments (PCA and as agent in cases before the ICJ); National professional appointment (National Director of Borders and Limits).	

Maurice K Kamga	1967	Cameroon	2020	**Education:** University of Yaoundé; International Relations Institute of Cameroon; Hague Academy of International Law; Graduate Institute of International Studies, Geneva; Université Paris Nanterre **Professional Background:** Government legal adviser; Diplomatic appointments; Academic; Consultant and legal officer to international bodies (ICTY; ITLOS; FAO; ICJ)

Bibliography

Adede AO, *The System of Settlement of Disputes under the United Nations Convention on the Law the Sea: A Drafting History and Commentary* (Martinus Nijhoff 1987)

Akande D, 'Introduction to the Symposium on Zachary Mollengarden and Noam Zamir "The Monetary Gold Principle: Back to Basics"' (2021) 115 American Journal of International Law Unbound 140

Akhtarkhavari A, 'Power, Environmental Principles and the International Court of Justice' (2009) 28 Australian Yearbook of International Law 91

Al Arif A, 'Exploring the Legal Status and Key Features of Ecosystem-Based Fisheries Management in International Fisheries Law' (2018) 27 Review of European, Comparative and International Environmental Law 320

——— 'Legal Status of the Precautionary Principle in International Fisheries Law and Its Application in the Marine Fisheries Regime of Bangladesh' (2018) 3 Asia-Pacific Journal of Ocean Law and Policy 95

Allen S, 'Article 297 of the United Nations Convention on the Law of the Sea and the Scope of Mandatory Jurisdiction' (2017) 48 Ocean Development and International Law 313

Alter KJ, 'Agents or Trustees? International Courts in Their Political Context' (2008) 14 European Journal of International Relations 33

——— 'The Multiple Roles of International Courts and Tribunals: Enforcement, Dispute Settlement, Constitutional and Administrative Review' in Jeffrey L Dunoff and Mark A Pollack (eds), *International Law and International Relations: Synthesizing Insights from Interdisciplinary Scholarship* (CUP 2013)

Amerasinghe CF, 'Reflections on the Judicial Function in International Law' in Tafsir Malick Ndiaye and Rüdiger Wolfrum (eds), *Law of the Sea, Environmental Law and Settlement of Disputes:* Liber Amicorum *Judge Thomas A Mensah* (Martinus Nijhoff 2007)

Anderson D, 'Coastal State Jurisdiction and High Seas Freedoms in the EEZ in the Light of the Saiga Case' in Clive R Symmons (ed), *Selected Contemporary Issues in the Law of the Sea* (Brill 2011)

Anderson DH, 'Prompt Release of Vessels' in Rüdiger Wolfrum (ed), *Max Planck Encyclopedia of Public International Law* (OUP 2008)

——— 'Some Aspects of the Use of Force in Maritime Law Enforcement' in Nerina Boschiero and others (eds), *International Courts and the Development of International Law* (Springer 2013)

Anton DK, 'The Principle of Residual Liability in the Seabed Disputes Chamber of the International Tribunal for the Law of the Sea: The Advisory Opinion on Responsibility and Liability for International Seabed Mining (ITLOS Case No. 17)' (2012) 7 McGill International Journal of Sustainable Development and Policy 241

——— 'The Timor Sea Treaty Arbitration: Timor-Leste Challenges Australian Espionage and Seizure of Documents' (2014) 18(6) American Society of International Law Insights 1 https://www.asil.org/insights/volume/18/issue/6/timor-sea-treaty-arbitration-timor-leste-challenges-australian-espionage

Anton DK, RA Makgill, and CR Payne, 'Seabed Mining: Advisory Opinion on Responsibility and Liability' (2011) 41 Environmental Policy and Law 60

Bahri A, '"Appellate Body Held Hostage": Is Judicial Activism at Fair Trial?' (2019) 53 Journal of World Trade 293

Bankes N, 'Precluding the Applicability of Section 2 of Part XV of the Law of the Sea Convention' (2017) 48 Ocean Development and International Law 239

Bantz VP, 'Views from Hamburg: The Juno Trader Case or How to Make Sense of the Coastal State's Rights in the Light of Its Duty of Prompt Release' (2005) 24 University of Queensland Law Journal 415

Barnes R, 'Article 2' in Alexander Proelss (ed), *United Nations Convention on the Law of the Sea: A Commentary* (CH Beck, Hart, and Nomos 2017)

Becker MA, 'Request for an Advisory Opinion Submitted by the Sub-Regional Fisheries Commission (SRFC)' (2015) 109 American Journal of International Law 851

Bernard L, 'The Effect of Historic Fishing Rights In Maritime Boundaries Delimitation' in Harry N Scheiber and Moon Sang Kwon (eds), *Securing the Ocean for the Next Generation* (Law of the Sea Institute, UC Berkeley–Korea Institute of Ocean Science and Technology Conference, Seoul, May 2012)

BIICL, 'Report on the Obligations of States under Articles 74(3) and 83(3) of UNCLOS in Respect of Undelimited Maritime Areas' (BIICL 2016)

Blitza E, 'Article 206' in Alexander Proelss (ed), *United Nations Convention on the Law of the Sea: A Commentary* (CH Beck, Hart, and Nomos 2017)

Borgese EM, 'A Constitution for the Oceans' in Elisabeth Mann Borgese and David Krieger (eds), *The Tides of Change: Peace, Pollution and the Potential of the* Oceans (Mason/Charter 1975)

Born G, 'A New Generation of International Adjudication' (2012) 61 Duke Law Journal 775

Bowett DW 'The Second United Nations Conference on the Law of the Sea' (1960) 9 International and Comparative Law Quarterly 415

Boyle A, 'Further Development of the Law of the Sea Convention: Mechanisms for Change' (2005) 54 International and Comparative Law Quarterly 563

——— 'The Environmental Jurisprudence of the International Tribunal for the Law of the Sea' (2007) 22 International Journal of Marine and Coastal Law 369

Boyle AE, 'Dispute Settlement and the Law of the Sea Convention: Problems of Fragmentation and Jurisdiction' (1997) 46 International and Comparative Law Quarterly 37

Brilmayer L and N Klein, 'Land and Sea: Two Sovereignty Regimes in Search of a Common Denominator' (2001) 33 New York University Journal of International Law and Politics 703

Brown C, *A Common Law of International Adjudication* (OUP 2007)

——— 'Inherent Powers in International Adjudication' in Cesare PR Romano, Karen J Alter, and Yuval Shany (eds), *The Oxford Handbook of International Adjudication* (OUP 2014) 828

Burke WT, 'Coastal State Fishery Regulation Under International Law: A Comment on the La Bretagne Award of July 17, 1986' (1988) 25 San Diego Law Review 495

Byers M, 'Policing the High Seas: The Proliferation Security Initiative' (2004) 98 American Journal of International Law 526

Carleton C, 'Problems Relating to Non-Natural and Man-Made Basepoints under UNCLOS' in Clive R Symmons (ed), *Selected Contemporary Issues in the Law of the Sea* (Brill 2011)

Caron DD, 'Towards a Political Theory of International Courts and Tribunals' (2006) 24 Berkeley Journal of International Law 401

——— 'Climate Change, Sea Level Rise and the Coming Uncertainty in Oceanic Boundaries: A Proposal to Avoid Conflict' in Seoung-Yong Hong and Jon M Van Dyke (eds), *Maritime Boundary Disputes, Settlement Processes, and the Law of the Sea* (Brill 2009)

Chan K, 'The ICJ's Judgement in *Somalia v Kenya* and Its Implications for the Law of the Sea' (2019) 34 Utrecht Journal of International & European Law 195

Chandrasekhara Rao P and P Gautier, *The Rules of the International Tribunal for the Law of the Sea: A Commentary* (Martinus Nijhoff 2006)

Charlesworth H, C Chinkin, and S Wright, 'Feminist Approaches to International Law' (1991) 85 American Journal of International Law 613

Chen L, 'Realizing the Precautionary Principle in Due Diligence' (2016) 25 Dalhousie Journal of Legal Studies 1

Cheng B, *General Principles of International Law as Applied by International Courts and Tribunals* (Stevens 1953)

Chinese Society of International Law, 'The South China Sea Arbitration Awards: A Critical Study' (2018) 17 Chinese Journal of International Law 207

Chircop A, 'Obligations of Flag States in the Exclusive Economic Zone' in Øystein Jensen (ed), *The Development of the Law of the Sea Convention: The Role of International Courts and Tribunals* (Edward Elgar Publishing 2020)

Churchill RR, 'Dispute Settlement under the UN Convention on the Law of the Sea: Survey for 2009' (2010) 25 International Journal of Marine and Coastal Law 457

——— 'Dispute Settlement in the Law of the Sea: Survey for 2013' (2015) 30 International Journal of Marine and Coastal Law 1

——— 'Dispute Settlement in the Law of the Sea: Survey for 2015, Part II and 2016' (2017) 32 International Journal of Marine and Coastal Law 379

——— 'Dispute Settlement in the Law of the Sea: Survey for 2020' (2021) 36 International Journal of Marine and Coastal Law 1

——— 'Revealing a Mosaic: International Jurisprudence Concerning the Non-fisheries Elements of the Exclusive Economic Zone Regime' in Øystein Jensen (ed), *The Development of the Law of the Sea Convention: The Role of International Courts and Tribunals* (Edward Elgar Publishing 2020) 69.

——— 'The General Dispute Settlement System of the UN Convention on the Law of the Sea: Overview, Context, and Use' (2017) 48 Ocean Development and International Law 216

——— 'The Jurisprudence of the International Tribunal for the Law of the Sea Relating to Fisheries: Is There Much in the Net?' (2007) 22 International Journal of Marine and Coastal Law 383

——— 'Trends in Dispute Settlement in the Law of the Sea: Towards the Increasing Availability of Compulsory Means' in Duncan French, Matthew Saul, and Nigel D White (eds), *International Law and Dispute Settlement: New Problems and Techniques* (Hart Publishing 2010) 143

Churchill RR and AV Lowe, *The Law of the Sea* (3rd edn, Juris Publishing 1999)

Cogliati-Bantz VP, 'Disentangling the "Genuine Link": Enquiries in Sea, Air and Space Law' (2010) 79 Nordic Journal of International Law 383

——— 'Immune or Not; Warships in Foreign Internal Waters and the UN Convention on the Law of the Sea' (2013) 4 Durham Law Review 1

——— 'International Tribunal for the Law of the Sea, Hoshinmaru (Japan v Russian Federation) and Tomimaru (Japan v Russian Federation), Prompt Release Judgments of 6 August 2007' (2009) 58 International and Comparative Law Quarterly 241

Colson DA and P Hoyle, 'Satisfying the Procedural Prerequisites to the Compulsory Dispute Settlement Mechanisms of the 1982 Law of the Sea Convention: Did the Southern Bluefin Tuna Tribunal Get it Right?' (2003) 34 Ocean Development and International Law 59

Craik N, *The International Law of Environmental Impact Assessment: Process, Substance and Integration* (CUP 2008)

Czybulka D, 'Article 192' in Alexander Proelss (ed), *United Nations Convention on the Law of the Sea: A Commentary* (CH Beck, Hart, and Nomos 2017)

De La Rasilla I and J Viñuales (eds), *Experiments in International Adjudication* (CUP 2018)

Devaney JG and CJ Tams, 'In re Arbitration between the Italian Republic and the Republic of India Concerning the "Enrica Lexie" Incident' (2021) 115(3) American Journal of International Law 513

Djibril M, 'Does a Sovereign State Immunity Say More than We Think: ITLOS's Decisions in ARA Libertad Case' (2015) 37 Journal of Law, Policy and Globalization 6

Driscoll C and M Starik, 'The Primordial Stakeholder: Advancing the Conceptual Consideration of Stakeholder Status for the Natural Environment' (2004) 49 Journal of Business Ethics 55

Dunoff JL and MA Pollack, 'The Judicial Trilemma' (2017) 111 American Journal of International Law 225

Dworkin R, *Taking Rights Seriously* (Harvard University Press 1977)

Dyspriani P, *Traditional Fishing Rights: Analysis of State Practice* (Division for Ocean Affairs and the Law of the Sea, Office of Legal Affairs, UN 2011)

Eesley C and MJ Lennox, 'Firm Responses to Secondary Stakeholder Action' (2006) 27 Strategic Management Journal 765

Einar Fife R, 'Obligations of "Due Regard" in the Exclusive Economic Zone: Their Context, Purpose and State Practice' (2019) 34 International Journal of Marine and Coastal Law 43.

Etzioni A, *Modern Organizations* (Prentice-Hall 1964)

Evans MD, 'Maritime Boundary Delimitation' in Donald R Rothwell and others (eds), *The Oxford Handbook of the Law of the Sea* (OUP 2015)

——— 'Maritime Boundary Delimitation: Whatever Next?' in Jill Barrett and Richard Barnes (eds), *Law of the Sea: UNCLOS as a Living Treaty* (BIICL 2016)

——— 'Maritime Boundary Delimitation: Where Do We Go From Here?' in David Freestone, Richard Barnes, and David Ong (eds), *The Law of the Sea: Progress and Prospects* (OUP 2006)
——— *Relevant Circumstances and Maritime Delimitation* (OUP 1989)
Eveno VB, 'ITLOS Report' (Working Document, ILA Study Group on the Content and Evolution of the Rules of Interpretation, April 2017) https://www.ila-hq.org/index.php/study-groups?study-groupsID=75
Feliciano FP, 'Qualities of a Good Judge' (1994) 3 The Lawyers Review 68
Ferrara P, 'Article 294' in Alexander Proelss (ed), *United Nations Convention on the Law of the Sea: A Commentary* (CH Beck, Hart, and Nomos 2017)
Fietta S and R Cleverly, *A Practitioner's Guide to Maritime Boundary Delimitation* (OUP 2016)
Fietta S, J Saadeh, and L Rees-Evans, 'The South China Sea Award: A Milestone for International Environmental Law, the Duty of Due Diligence and the Litigation of Maritime Environmental Disputes' (2017) 29 Georgetown Environmental Law Review 711
Fitzmaurice G, 'The Law and Procedure of the International Court of Justice, 1951-54: Questions of Jurisdiction, Competence and Procedure' (1958) 34 British Yearbook of International Law 1
Follesdal A, 'To Guide and Guard International Judges' (2014) 46 New York University Journal of International Law and Politics 793
Forteau M, 'Regulating the Competition between International Courts and Tribunals: The Role of Ratione Materiae Jurisdiction under Part XV of UNCLOS' (2016) 15 Law and Practice of International Courts and Tribunals 190
Franck SD and others, 'The Diversity Challenge: Exploring the "Invisible College" of International Arbitration' (2015) 53 Columbia Journal of Transnational Law 429
Franck TM, *Fairness in International Law and Institutions* (OUP 1995)
Franckx E, 'The Arbitral Tribunal's Interpretation of Paragraph 3 in Article 121: A First but Important Step Forward' in S Jayakumar and others (eds), *The South China Sea Arbitration: The Legal Dimension* (Edward Elgar Publishing 2018)
Freeman RE, *Strategic Management: A Stakeholder Approach* (Pitman Publishing 1984)
Freestone D, 'Advisory Opinion of the Seabed Disputes Chamber of the International Tribunal for the Law of the Sea on "Responsibilities and Obligations of States Sponsoring Persons and Entities with Respect to Activities in the Area"' (2011) 15 American Society of International Law Insights 1 https://www.asil.org/insights/volume/15/issue/7/advisory-opinion-seabed-disputes-chamber-international-tribunal-law-sea-
Freestone D, D Vidas, and A Torres Camprubi, 'Sea Level Rise and Impacts on Maritime Zone and Limits: The Work of the ILA Committee on International Law and Sea Level Rise' (2017) 5 Korean Journal of International and Comparative Law 5
French D, 'From the Depths: Rich Pickings of Principles of Sustainable Development and General International Law on the Ocean Floor—the Seabed Disputes Chamber's 2011 Advisory Opinion' (2011) 26 International Journal of Marine and Coastal Law 525
——— 'In the Matter of the South China Sea Arbitration: Republic of Philippines v People's Republic of China, Arbitral Tribunal Constituted under Annex VII to the 1982 United Nations Law of the Sea Convention, Case No. 2013-19, Award of 12 July 2016' (2017) 19 Environmental Law Review 48
——— 'Treaty Interpretation and the Incorporation of Extraneous Legal Rules' (2006) 55 International and Comparative Law Quarterly 281
Gâlea I, 'The Interpretation of "Military Activities" as an Exception to Jurisdiction: The ITLOS Order of 25 May 2019 in the Case Concerning the Detention of Three Ukrainian Naval Vessels' (2019) 21 Romanian Journal of International Law 31
Gao J, 'The ITLOS Advisory Opinion for the SRFC' (2015) 14 Chinese Journal of International Law 735
Gaunce J, 'On the Interpretation of the General Duty of "Due Regard"' (2018) 32(1) Ocean Yearbook 27
Gaver CD, 'Dispute Concerning Delimitation of the Maritime Boundary between Mauritius and Maldives in the Indian Ocean (Mauritius/Maldives)' (2021) 115(3) American Journal of International Law 519

Gavouneli M, 'Request for an Advisory Opinion Submitted by the Sub-Regional Fisheries Commission (SRFC) (ITLOS)' (2015) 54 International Legal Materials 890

Goldsmith JL and EA Posner, *The Limits of International Law* (OUP 2005)

Goodman C, 'Rights, Obligations, Prohibitions: A Practical Guide to Understanding Judicial Decisions on Coastal State Jurisdiction over Living Resources in the Exclusive Economic Zone' (2018) 33 International Journal of Marine and Coastal Law 558

Gray C, 'The 2017 Judicial Activity of the International Court of Justice' (2018) 112 American Journal of International Law 254

Greenwood L, 'Tipping the Balance: Diversity and Inclusion in International Arbitration' (2017) 33 Arbitration International 99

Grossman N, 'Sex on the Bench: Do Women Judges Matter to the Legitimacy of International Courts' (2012) 12 Chicago Journal of International Law 647

—— 'Sex-Representative International Court Benches' (2016) 110 American Journal of International Law 82

—— 'Shattering the Glass Ceiling in International Adjudication' (2016) 56 Virginia Journal of International Law 213

Grossman N and others (eds), *Legitimacy and International Courts* (CUP 2018)

Grotius H, *The Freedom of the Seas or the Right which Belongs to the Dutch to Take Part in the East Indian Trade* (Ralph Van Deman Magoffin tr, OUP 1913)

Guilfoyle D, 'Article 92' in Alexander Proelss (ed), *United Nations Convention on the Law of the Sea: A Commentary* (CH Beck, Hart, and Nomos 2017)

—— 'Article 94' in Alexander Proelss (ed), *United Nations Convention on the Law of the Sea: A Commentary* (CH Beck, Hart and Nomos 2017)

—— 'Governing the Oceans and Dispute Resolution: An Evolving Legal Order?' in Danielle Ireland-Piper and Leon Wolff (eds), *Global Governance and Regulation: Order and Disorder in the 21st Century* (Routledge 2018)

—— 'The High Seas' in Donald R Rothwell and others (eds), *The Oxford Handbook of the Law of the Sea* (OUP 2015)

Gullett W, 'The South China Sea Arbitration's Contribution to the Concept of Juridical Islands' (2018) 47 Questions of International Law 5

Guo J and P Wang, 'Due Diligence and Overlooked Evidence in the South China Sea Arbitration: A Note' (2019) 50 Ocean Development and International Law 235

Habermas J, *Between Facts and Norms: Contributions to a Discourse Theory of Law and Democracy* (MIT Press 1998)

Hamid AG and KM Sein, 'Prompt Release of Vessel and Crew under Article 292 of the UNCLOS: Is It an Adequate Safeguard Against the Powers of Coastal States?' (2011) 7 Journal of Applied Sciences Research 2421

Handl G, 'Flag State Responsibility for Illegal, Unreported and Unregulated Fishing in Foreign EEZs' (2014) 44 Environmental Policy and Law 158

—— 'Responsibilities and Obligations of States Sponsoring Persons and Entities With Respect to Activities in the Area: The International Tribunal of the Law of the Sea's Recent Contribution to International Environmental Law' (2011) 20 Review of European Community and International Environmental Law 208

Harris C, 'Claims with an Ulterior Purpose: Characterising Disputes Concerning the "Interpretation or Application" of a Treaty' (2020) 18(3) Law and Practice of International Courts and Tribunals 279

Harrison J and E Morgera, 'Article 61' in Alexander Proelss (ed), *United Nations Convention on the Law of the Sea: A Commentary* (CH Beck, Hart, and Nomos 2017)

Harrison J, 'Article 73' in Alexander Proelss (ed), *United Nations Convention on the Law of the Sea: A Commentary* (CH Beck, Hart, and Nomos 2017)

—— 'Defining Disputes and Characterizing Claims: Subject-Matter Jurisdiction in Law of the Sea Convention Litigation' (2017) 48 Ocean Development and International Law 269

—— 'Significant International Environmental Law Cases: 2014–15' (2015) 27 Journal of Environmental Law 541

—— *Saving the Oceans Through Law: The International Legal Framework for the Protection of the Marine Environment* (OUP 2017)

Hart HLA, *The Concept of Law* (2nd edn, Clarendon Press 1994)

Hernández G, 'Interpretative Authority and the International Judiciary' in Andrea Bianchi, Daniel Peat, and Matthew Windsor (eds), *Interpretation in International Law* (OUP 2015)

Higgins R, 'Decision-making in International Courts and Tribunals: A Conversation with Leading Judges and Arbitrators' (2011) 105 Proceedings of the American Society of International Law 217

Honniball AN, 'The Exclusive Jurisdiction of Flag States: A Limitation on Pro-active Port States?' (2016) 31 International Journal of Marine and Coastal Law 499

Huang Y and Xuexia Liao, 'Natural Prolongation and Delimitation of the Continental Shelf Beyond 200 nm: Implications of the Bangladesh/Myanmar Case' (2014) 4(2) Asian Journal of International Law 281

ICJ, *The International Court of Justice: Handbook* (5th edn, ICJ 2004)

Insolia A, 'The Law of Maritime Delimitation in the Croatia/Slovenia Final Award' in Angela Del Vecchio and Roberto Virzo (eds), *Interpretations of the United Nations Convention on the Law of the Sea by International Courts and Tribunals* (Springer 2019)

International Law Association, 'Baselines under the International Law of the Sea' (Final Report, 2018) https://www.ila-hq.org/images/ILA/DraftReports/DraftReport_Baselines.pdf

International Union for Conservation of Nature, *ICUN Red List Categories and Criteria* (2nd edn, version 3.1, 2012)

Ishii Y, 'Informal Lawmaking and International Cooperation on Illegal Bunkering at Sea' in Natalie Klein (ed), *Unconventional Lawmaking in the Law of the Sea* (OUP 2022)

Jaeckel AL, *The International Seabed Authority and the Precautionary Principle: Balancing Deep Seabed Mineral Mining and Marine Environmental Protection* (Brill 2017)

Jensen Ø, 'The Delimitation of the Continental Shelf beyond 200 nm: Substantive Issues' in Alex G Oude Elferink, Tore Henriksen, and Signe Veierud Busch (eds), *Maritime Boundary Delimitation: The Case Law—Is It Consistent and Predictable?* (CUP 2018) 372

Jia BB and S Talmon, 'Introduction' in Stefan Talmon and Bing Bing Jia (eds), *The South China Sea Arbitration: A Chinese Perspective* (Hart Publishing 2014)

Jia BB, 'The Curious Case of Article 281: A "Super" Provision within UNCLOS' (2015) 46(4) Ocean Development and International Law 268

Jiang X and J Zhang, 'Marine Environment and the International Tribunal for the Law of the Sea: Twenty Years' Practices and Prospects' (2017) 5 China Legal Science 84

Jimenez Kwast P, 'Maritime Law Enforcement and the Use of Force: Reflections on the Categorisation of Forcible Action at Sea in the Light of the Guyana/Suriname Award' (2008) 13 Journal of Conflict and Security Law 49

Karaman IV, *Dispute Resolution in the Law of the Sea* (Martinus Nijhoff 2012)

Kazhdan D, 'Precautionary Pulp: Pulp Mills and the Evolving Dispute between International Tribunals over the Reach of the Precautionary Principle' (2011) 38 Ecology Law Quarterly 527

Kelsen H, *Pure Theory of Law* (2nd edn, University of California Press 1970)

Klein N, 'International Environmental Law Disputes before International Courts and Tribunals' in Jacqueline Peel and Lavanya Rajamani (eds), *Oxford Handbook of International Environmental Law* (2nd edn, OUP 2021) 1038

—— 'Islands and Rocks after the *South China Sea Arbitration*' (2017) 34 Australian Yearbook of International Law 21

—— 'Land and Sea: Resolving Contested Land and Disappearing Land Disputes under the UN Convention on the Law of the Sea' in Chiara Giorgetti and Natalie Klein (eds), *Resolving Conflicts in the Law: Essays in Honour of Lea Brilmayer* (Brill 2019)

—— 'Law of the Sea Dispute Settlement Outside of the United Nations Convention on the Law of the Sea' in Hélène Ruiz Fabri (ed), *Max Planck Encyclopedia of International Procedural Law* (OUP 2021)

—— 'Provisional Measures and Provisional Arrangements in Maritime Boundary Disputes' (2006) 21 International Journal of Marine and Coastal Law 423

——— 'Provisional Measures and Provisional Arrangements' in Alex G Oude Elferink, Tore Henriksen, and Signe Veierud Busch, *Maritime Boundary Delimitation: The Case Law—Is It Consistent and Predictable?* (CUP 2018)

——— 'Stakeholders in Dispute Settlement under the UN Convention on the Law of the Sea' in Marta Chantal Ribeiro, Fernando Loureiro Bastos, and Tore Henrikson (eds), *Global Challenges and the Law of the Sea* (Springer 2020)

——— 'Strengthening Flag State Performance in Compliance and Enforcement' in Richard Caddell and Erik J Molenaar (eds), *Strengthening International Fisheries Law in an Era of Changing Oceans* (Hart Publishing 2019)

——— 'The Vicissitudes of Dispute Settlement under the Law of the Sea Convention' (2017) 32 International Journal of Marine and Coastal Law 332

——— 'Timor Sea Conciliation: A Harbinger for Dispute Settlement under UNCLOS?' in Hélène Ruiz Fabri and others (eds), *A Bridge Over Troubled Waters: Dispute Resolution in the Law of International Watercourses and the Law of the Sea* (Brill Nijhoff 2021)

——— *Dispute Settlement in the UN Convention on the Law of the Sea* (CUP 2005)

Koh TTB, 'A Constitution for the Oceans: Remarks of the President of the Third United Nations Conference on the Law of the Sea' (Statements Given at the Final Session of the Conference at Montego Bay, 5 and 11 December 1982) https://www.un.org/depts/los/convention_agreements/texts/koh_english.pdf;

Koivurova T, 'Due Diligence' in Anne Peters (ed), *Max Planck Encyclopedia of Public International Law* (OUP 2010)

Kojima C, 'South China Sea Arbitration and the Protection of the Marine Environment: Evolution of UNCLOS Part xii Through Interpretation and the Duty to Cooperate' (2015) 21 Asian Yearbook of International Law 166

Koskenniemi M, *From Apology to Utopia: The Structure of International Legal Argument* (CUP 2005)

Kraska J, 'The "ARA Libertad"' (2013) 107(2) American Journal of International Law 404

———, *Maritime Power and the Law of the Sea: Expeditionary Operations in World Politics* (OUP 2011)

Kunoy B, 'The Admissibility of a Plea to an International Adjudicative Forum to Delimit the Outer Continental Shelf Prior to the Adoption of Final Recommendations by the Commission on the Limits of the Continental Shelf' (2010) 25 International Journal of Marine and Coastal Law 237

——— 'The Scope of Compulsory Jurisdiction and Exceptions Thereto under the United Nations Convention on the Law of the Sea' (2021) Canadian Yearbook of International Law 1

Kwaitkowska B, 'The 2006 Barbados/Trinidad and Tobago Award: A Landmark in Compulsory Jurisdiction and Equitable Maritime Boundary Delimitation' (2007) 22 International Journal of Marine and Coastal Law 7

Lalonde S, 'Evaluating Canada's Position on the Northwest Passage in Light of Two Possible Sources of International Protection' in Clive Schofield, Seokwoo Lee, and Moon-Sang Kwon (eds), *The Limits of Maritime Jurisdiction* (Martinus Nijhoff 2014)

Lando M, 'Delimiting the Continental Shelf Beyond 200 Nautical Miles at the International Court of Justice: The Nicaragua v Colombia Cases' (2017) 16 Chinese Journal of International Law 137

——— 'State Jurisdiction and Immunity of Warships in the ARA Libertad Case' (2015) 58 Japanese Yearbook of International Law 336

——— 'The Advisory Jurisdiction of the International Tribunal for the Law of the Sea: Comments on the Request for an Advisory Opinion Submitted by the Sub-Regional Fisheries Commission' (2016) 29 Leiden Journal of International Law 441

——— 'The Croatia/Slovenia Arbitral Award of 29 June 2017: Is There a Common Method for Delimiting All Maritime Zones under International Law?' (2017) 100(4) Rivista di dirritto internazionale 1184

——— *Maritime Delimitation as Judicial Process* (CUP 2019)

Langford M, D Behn, and R Lie, 'The Revolving Door in International Investment Arbitration' (2017) 20 Journal of International Economic Law 301

Lauridsen I, 'Precautionary Action: Study on the Status and Implications of the Precautionary Principle in International Environmental Law' (2014) 19 Eastern and Central European Journal on Environmental Law 95

Lauterpacht H, *The Development of International Law by the International Court* (CUP 1958)
——— *The Function of Law in the International Community* (Clarendon Press 1933)
Lee S and Lowell Bautista, 'Historic Rights' in Øystein Jensen (ed), *The Development of the Law of the Sea Convention: The Role of International Courts and Tribunals* (Edward Elgar Publishing 2020)
Lima LC, 'The Use of Experts by the International Tribunal for the Law of the Sea and Annex VII Arbitral Tribunals' in Angela Del Vecchio and Roberto Virzo (eds), *Interpretations of the United Nations Convention on the Law of the Sea by International Courts and Tribunals* (Springer 2019)
Linderfalk U, 'The Jan Mayen Case (Iceland/Norway): An Example of Successful Conciliation' in Christian Tomuschat, Riccardo Pisillo Mazzeschi, and Daniel Thürer (eds), *Conciliation in International Law: The OSCE Court of Conciliation and Arbitration* (Brill 2017)
Ma J and Shiyan Sun, 'Restrictions on the Use of Force at Sea: An Environmental Protection Perspective' (2016) 98 International Review of the Red Cross 515
Mackenzie R, and others (eds), *The Manual on International Courts and Tribunals* (2nd edn, OUP 2010)
Magnússon BM, 'Is there a Temporal Relationship between the Delineation and the Delimitation of the Continental Shelf beyond 200 nm?' (2013) 28 International Journal of Marine and Coastal Law 465
——— 'The Grey Areas in the Bay of Bengal' (2016) 56(1) Indian Journal of International Law 41
Mansfield B, 'Peaceful Settlement of International Disputes: Litigation or Negotiation—Some Practical Considerations' (2016) 14 Otago Law Review 329
Marotti L, 'Between Consent and Effectiveness: Incidental Determinations and the Expansion of the Jurisdiction of UNCLOS Tribunals' in Angela Del Vecchio and Roberto Virzo (eds), *Interpretations of the United Nations Convention on the Law of the Sea by International Courts and Tribunals* (Springer 2019)
Martin LH and YB Parkhomenko, 'The Territorial and Maritime Dispute (Nicaragua v. Colombia) and Its Implications for Future Maritime Delimitations in the Caribbean Sea and Elsewhere' in Edgardo Sobrenes Obregon and Benjamin Samson (eds), *Nicaragua Before the International Court of Justice: Impacts on International Law* (Springer 2018)
Mbengue MM, 'The South China Sea Arbitration: Innovations in Marine Environmental Fact-Finding and Due Diligence Obligations' (2016) 110 American Journal of International Law Unbound 285
McDorman TL, 'French Fishing Rights in Canadian Waters: The 1986 La Bretagne Arbitration' (1989) 4 International Journal of Estuarine and Coastal Law 52
McIntyre J, 'Put on Notice: The Role of the Dispute Requirement in Assessing Jurisdiction and Admissibility before the International Court' (2018) 19 Melbourne Journal of International Law 546
Mensah TA, 'The Tribunal and the Prompt Release of Vessels' (2007) 22 International Journal of Marine and Coastal Law 425
Merrills JG, *International Dispute Settlement* (6th edn, CUP 2017)
Miles C, 'The M/V 'Norstar' Case (Panama v Italy)' (2020) 119 American Journal of International Law 116
Miron A, 'The acquis judiciaire, a Tool for Harmonization in a Decentralized System of Litigation? A Case-study in the Law of the Sea' in Chiara Giorgetti and Mark Pollack (eds), *Beyond Fragmentation: Cross-Fertilization, Cooperation and Competition among International Courts and Tribunals* (CUP 2022)
Meron T, 'Decision-making in International Courts and Tribunals: A Conversation with Leading Judges and Arbitrators' (2011) 105 Proceedings of the American Society of International Law 224
Mitchell RK, BR Agle, and DJ Wood, 'Toward a Theory of Stakeholder Identification and Salience: Defining the Principle of Who and What Really Counts' (1997) 22 Academy of Management Review 853
Mitchell RK, JH Lee, and BR Agle, 'Stakeholder Prioritization Work: The Role of Stakeholder Salience in Stakeholder Research' in David M Wasieleski and James Weber (eds), *Stakeholder Management* (Emerald Publishing 2017)
Morgera E, 'Article 62' in Alexander Proelss (ed), *United Nations Convention on the Law of the Sea: A Commentary* (CH Beck, Hart, and Nomos 2017)

Mossop J, 'Can We Make the Oceans Greener: The Successes and Failures of UNCLOS as an Environmental Treaty' (2018) 49 Victoria University of Wellington Law Review 573

——— 'Protests against Oil Exploration at Sea: Lessons from the *Arctic Sunrise* Arbitration' (2016) 31 International Journal of Marine and Coastal Law 60

——— *The Continental Shelf Beyond 200 Nautical Miles: Rights and Responsibilities* (OUP 2016)

Murphy SD, 'International Law Relating to Islands' (2017) 836 Hague Recueil des Cours 5

Nelson LDM, 'The Jurisprudence of the International Tribunal for the Law of the Sea: Some Observations' in Tafsir Malick Ndiaye and Rüdiger Wolfrum (eds), *Law of the Sea, Environmental Law and Settlement of Disputes:* Liber Amicorum *Judge Thomas A Mensah* (Brill 2007)

Nordquist MH (ed), *United Nations Convention on the Law of the Sea 1982: A Commentary* (Martinus Nijhoff 1989–2012)

——— 'UNCLOS Article 121 and Itu Aba in the South China Sea Final Award: A Correct Interpretation?' in S Jayakumar and others (eds), *The South China Sea Arbitration: The Legal Dimension* (Edward Elgar Publishing 2018)

North R, 'Traditional Fishing Rights in International Law: The South China Sea Arbitration' (2017) 36 University of Tasmania Law Review 101

O'Keefe R, 'ITLOS Flags Its Intent' (2000) 59(3) Cambridge Law Journal 428

Oda S, 'Dispute Settlement Prospects in the Law of the Sea' (1995) 44 International and Comparative Law Quarterly 863

——— 'Some Reflections on the Dispute Settlement Clauses in the United Nations Convention on the Law of the Sea' in Jerzy Makarczyk (ed), *Essays in International Law in Honour of Judge Manfred Lachs* (Brill 1984)

Oral N, 'Ukraine v. The Russian Federation: Navigating Conflict over Sovereignty under UNCLOS' (2021) 97 International Law Studies 478

Orellana MA, 'The Law on Highly Migratory Fish Stocks: ITLOS Jurisprudence in Context' (2004) 34 Golden Gate University Law Review 459

Oude Elferink AG, 'Does Undisputed Title to a Maritime Zone Always Exclude its Delimitation: The Grey Area Issue' (1998) 13(2) International Journal of Marine and Coastal Law 143

——— 'The Russian Federation and the Arctic Sunrise Case: Hot Pursuit and Other Issues under the LOSC' (2016) 92 International Law Studies 381, 393

Oude Elferink AG, Tore Henriksen, and Signe Veierud Busch, *Maritime Boundary Delimitation: The Case Law* (CUP 2018)

Oxman BH, 'Courts and Tribunals: The ICJ, ITLOS, and Arbitral Tribunals' in Donald R Rothwell and others (eds), *The Oxford Handbook of the Law of the Sea* (OUP 2015)

——— 'Complementary Agreements and Compulsory Jurisdiction' (2001) 95 American Journal of International Law 277

——— 'The "Tomimaru" (Japan v Russian Federation). Judgment. ITLOS Case No 15' (2008) 102 American Journal of International Law 316

Oxman BH and VP Bantz, 'The "Grand Prince" (Belize v. France) Judgment (2002) 96(1) American Journal of International Law 219

——— 'The M/V Virginia G' (2014) 108 American Journal of International Law 769

Paik JH, 'How Healthy is the Ocean's Constitution? 25 Years of the United Nations Convention on the Law of the Sea' (UNCLOS Conference, 17 October 2019) https://www.itlos.org/fileadmin/itlos/documents/statements_of_president/paik/UNCLOS_25_171019_en.pdf.

Papanicolopulu I, 'The Land Dominates the Sea (Dominates the Land Dominates the Sea)' (2018) 47 Questions of International Law 39

——— 'International Judges and the Protection of Human Rights at Sea' in Nerina Boschiero and others (eds), *International Courts and the Development of International Law: Essays in Honour of Tullio Treves* (Asser Press 2013)

Parent MM and DL Deephouse, 'A Case Study of Stakeholder Identification and Prioritization by Managers' (2007) 75 Journal of Business Ethics 1

Parlett K, 'Beyond the Four Corners of the Convention: Expanding the Scope of Jurisdiction of Law of the Sea Tribunals' (2017) 48 Ocean Development and International Law 284

Parson L, 'Article 76' in Alexander Proelss (ed), *United Nations Convention on the Law of the Sea: A Commentary* (CH Beck, Hart, and Nomos 2017)

Peat D, *Comparative Reasoning in International Courts and Tribunals* (CUP 2019)

Pedersen OW, 'From Abundance to Indeterminacy: The Precautionary Principle and Its Two Camps of Custom' (2014) 3 Transnational Environmental Law 323

Peel J, 'A Paper Umbrella Which Dissolves in the Rain? Implications of the Southern Bluefin Tuna Case for the Compulsory Resolution of Disputes Concerning the Marine Environment under the 1982 LOS Convention' (2001) 6 Asia Pacific Journal of Environmental Law 297

Peiris N, 'Advisory Opinion on Fisheries in the Exclusive Economic Zone from the International Tribunal for the Law of the Sea: The Birth of Regional Treaty-based Advisory Jurisdiction' (2017) 31 Ocean Yearbook 250

—— 'ARA Libertad from ITLOS: How Provisional a Provisional Measure Should Be' (2012) 25 Hague Yearbook of International Law 159

Plakokefalos I, 'Environmental Law Aspects of the Arbitral Tribunal Award in the South China Sea Dispute' (2016) https://papers.ssrn.com/sol3/papers.cfm?abstract_id=2880624

Poisel T, 'Deep Seabed Mining: Implications of Seabed Disputes Chamber's Advisory Opinion' (2012) 19 Australian International Law Journal 213

Posner EA and JC Yoo, 'Judicial Independence in International Tribunals' (2005) 93 California Law Review 1

Proelss A, 'Marine Mammals' in Rüdiger Wolfrum (ed), *Max Planck Encyclopedia of Public International Law* (OUP 2007)

—— 'The Law on the Exclusive Economic Zone in Perspective: Legal Status and Resolution of User Conflicts Revisited' (2012) 26(1) Ocean Yearbook 87

Rajesh Babu R, 'State Responsibility for Illegal, Unreported and Unrelated Fishing and Sustainable Fisheries in the EEZ: Some Reflections on the ITLOS Advisory Opinion of 2015' (2015) 55 Indian Journal of International Law 239

Rao Pemmaraju S, 'The South China Sea Arbitration (the Philippines v. China Case): Assessment of the Award on Jurisdiction and Admissibility' (2016) 15(2) Chinese Journal of International Law 265

Rashbrooke G, 'The International Tribunal for the Law of the Sea: A Forum for the Development of Principles of International Environmental Law' (2004) 19 International Journal of Marine and Coastal Law 515

Rayfuse R, 'Precaution and the Protection of Marine Biodiversity' in David Freestone (ed), *Areas beyond National Jurisdiction in the 1982 Law of the Sea Convention at 30* (Brill 2013)

—— 'Settling Disputes in Regional Fisheries Management Organisations: Dealing with Objections' in Hélène Ruiz Fabri and others (eds), *Dispute Resolution in the Law of International Watercourses and the Law of the Sea: A Bridge Over Troubled Waters* (Brill Nijhoff 2020)

Reisman WM, 'A Judge's Judge: Justice Florentino P Feliciano's Philosophy of the Judicial Function' in Steve Charnovitz, Debra P Steger, and Peter Van den Bossche (eds), *Law in the Service of Human Dignity: Essays in Honour of Florentino Feliciano* (CUP 2005)

—— 'Judge Shigeru Oda: Reflections on the Formation of a Judge' in Misuke Ando, Edward McWhinney, and Rüdiger Wolfrum (eds), *Liber Amicorum Judge Shigeru Oda* (Kluwer Law 2002)

Roberts A, 'Power and Persuasion in Investment Treaty Interpretation: The Dual Role of States' (2010) 104 American Journal of International Law 179

Romano C, 'The Southern Bluefin Tuna Dispute: Hints of a World to Come ... Like It or Not' (2001) 32 Ocean Development and International Law 313

Rose C, 'Justifying Arguments about Selection Procedures for Judges at International Courts and Tribunals: A Response to Nienke Grossman' (2016) 110 American Journal of International Law Unbound 86

Rose GL, 'Arbitration Jurisdiction in Philippines v PRC: Quixotic Judicialisation and Sovereign Resistance in Law of the Sea (2018) 15 Soochow Law Journal 11

Rosenne S, 'International Courts and Tribunals, Jurisdiction and Admissibility of Inter-State Applications' in Rüdiger Wolfrum (ed), *Max Planck Encyclopedia of Public International Law* (OUP 2006)

——— 'The Case-Law of ITLOS (1997-2001): An Overview' in Myron H Nordquist and John Norton Moore (eds), *Current Marine Environmental Issues and the International Tribunal for the Law of the Sea* (Martinus Nijhoff 2001)

——— *The World Court: What It Is and How It Works* (5th edn, Martinus Nijhoff 1995)

Rothwell DR and T Stephens, 'Illegal Southern Ocean Fishing and Prompt Release: Balancing Coastal and Flag State Rights and Interests' (2004) 53 International and Comparative Law Quarterly 171

——— *The International Law of the Sea* (2nd edn, Bloomsbury 2019)

Ruys T and A Soete, '"Creeping" Advisory Jurisdiction of International Courts and Tribunals? The Case of the International Tribunal for the Law of the Sea' (2016) 29 Leiden Journal of International Law 155

Sands P and J Peel, *Principles of International Environmental Law* (3rd edn, CUP 2012)

Scanlon Z and R Beckman, 'Assessing Environmental Impact and the Duty to Cooperate' (2018) 3 Asia-Pacific Journal of Ocean Law and Policy 5

Schachter O, 'The Invisible College of International Lawyers' (1977) 2 Northwest University Law Review 217

Schatz V, 'Fishing for Interpretation: The ITLOS Advisory Opinion on Flag State Responsibility for Illegal Fishing in the EEZ' (2016) 47 Ocean Development and International Law 327

Schatz VJ and D Koval, 'Russia's Annexation of Crimea and the Passage of Ships Through Kerch Strait: A Law of the Sea Perspective' (2019) 50 Ocean Development and International Law 278

Schofield C, 'A Landmark Decision in the South China Sea: The Scope and Implications of the Arbitral Tribunal's Award' 38 (2016) Contemporary Southeast Asia 339

———, 'Climate Change and Changing Coasts: Geophysical and Jurisdictional Implications of Sea Level Rise for Pacific Island States' (2017) 5 Korean Journal of International and Comparative Law 36

Schofield C, A Telesetsky, and S Lee, 'A Tribunal Navigating Complex Waters: Implications of the *Bay of Bengal Case*' (2013) 44 Ocean Development and International Law 363

Scott SV, 'Litigation Versus Dispute Resolution Through Political Processes' in Natalie Klein (ed), *Litigating International Law Disputes* (CUP 2014)

Scovazzi T, '"Due Regard" Obligations, with Particular Emphasis on Fisheries in the Exclusive Economic Zone' (2019) 34 International Journal of Marine and Coastal Law 56

Serdy A, 'Article 280' in Alexander Proelss (ed), *United Nations Convention on the Law of the Sea: A Commentary* (CH Beck, Hart, and Nomos 2017)

——— 'Article 283' in Alexander Proelss (ed), *United Nations Convention on the Law of the Sea: A Commentary* (CH Beck, Hart, and Nomos 2017)

——— 'Article 298' in Alexander Proelss (ed), *United Nations Convention on the Law of the Sea: A Commentary* (CH Beck, Hart, and Nomos 2017)

——— 'Implementing Article 28 of the UN Fish Stocks Agreement: The First Review of a Conservation Measure in the South Pacific Regional Fisheries Management Organisation' (2016) 47 Ocean Development and International Law 1

Shaffer C and MA Pollack, 'Hard vs Soft Law: Alternatives, Complements and Antagonists in International Governance' (2010) 94 Minnesota Law Review 706

Shany Y, *Assessing the Effectiveness of International Courts* (OUP 2014)

Sheehan A, 'Dispute Settlement under UNCLOS: The Exclusion of Maritime Delimitation Disputes' (2005) 24 University of Queensland Law Journal 165

Shelton D, 'Form, Function, and the Powers of International Courts' (2009) 9 Chicago Journal of International Law 537

Song Y, 'The July 2016 Arbitral Award, Interpretation of Article 121(3) of the UNCLOS, and Selecting Examples of Inconsistent State Practice' (2019) 49 Ocean Development and International law 247

Spijkers O, 'Non-Participation in Arbitral Proceedings Under Annex VII United Nations Convention on the Law of the Sea: *Arctic Sunrise* and *South China Sea* Compared' in Angela Del Vecchio and Roberto Virzo (eds), *Interpretations of the United Nations Convention on the Law of the Sea by International Courts and Tribunals* (Springer 2019)

Springer AL, 'The Canadian Turbot War With Spain: Unilateral State Action in Defense of Environmental Interests' (1997) 6 Journal of Environment and Development 26

Squatrito T and others (eds), *The Performance of International Courts and Tribunals* (CUP 2018)

Stephens T, 'The Collateral Damage from China's "Great Wall of Sand": the Environmental Dimensions of the South China Sea Case' (2016) 34 Australian Yearbook of International Law 41

——, *International Courts and Environmental Protection* (CUP 2009)

Suchman MC, 'Managing Legitimacy: Strategic and Institutional Approaches' (1995) 20 Academy of Management Review 571

Sweet AC, 'Constitutional Courts and Parliamentary Democracy' (2002) 25 West European Politics 77

Swigart L and D Terris, 'Who Are International Judges?' in Cesare PR Romano, Karen J Alter, and Yuval Shany (eds), *The Oxford Handbook of International Adjudication* (OUP 2013)

Symmons CR, 'Article 16' in Alexander Proelss (ed), *United Nations Convention on the Law of the Sea: A Commentary* (CH Beck, Hart, and Nomos 2017)

—— 'Historic Rights in the Light of the Award in the South China Sea Arbitration: What Remains of the Doctrine Now?' in S Jayakumar and others (eds), *The South China Sea Arbitration: The Legal Dimension* (Edward Elgar Publishing 2018)

Symmons CR and MW Reed 'Baseline Publicity and Charting Requirements: An Overlooked Issue in the UN Convention on the Law of the Sea' (2010) 41 Ocean Development and International Law 77

Talmon S, 'Article 121' in Alexander Proelss (ed), *United Nations Convention on the Law of the Sea: A Commentary* (CH Beck, Hart, and Nomos 2017)

—— 'The Chagos Marine Protected Area Arbitration: Expansion of the Jurisdiction of UNCLOS Part XV Courts and Tribunals' (2016) 65 International and Comparative Law Quarterly 927

—— 'The South China Sea Arbitration and the Finality of "Final" Awards' (2019) 8 Journal of International Dispute Settlement 338

—— 'The South China Sea Arbitration: Is There a Case to Answer?' in Stefan Talmon and Bing Bing Jia (eds), *The South China Sea Arbitration: A Chinese Perspective* (Hart Publishing 2014)

Tanaka Y, 'Reflections on the Advisory Jurisdiction of ITLOS as a Full Court: The ITLOS Advisory Opinion of 2015' (2015) 14 Law and Practice of International Courts and Tribunals 318

—— 'Obligations and Liability of Sponsoring States Concerning Activities in the Area: Reflections on the ITLOS Advisory Opinion of 1 February 2011' (2013) 60 Netherlands International Law Review 205

—— 'Prompt Release in the United Nations Convention on the Law of the Sea: Some Reflections on the ITLOS Jurisprudence' (2004) 51 Netherlands International Law Review 237

—— 'Reflections on the Philippines/China Arbitration Award on Jurisdiction and Admissibility' (2016) 15 Law and Practice of International Courts and Tribunals 305

—— 'Release of a Detained Warship and Its Crew through Provisional Measures: A Comparative Analysis of the ARA Libertad and Ukraine v Russia Cases' (2020) 96 International Law Studies 223

—— *The International Law of the Sea* (3rd edn, CUP 2019)

—— *The Peaceful Settlement of International Disputes* (CUP 2018)

—— *The South China Sea Arbitration: Toward an International Legal Order in the Oceans* (Hart Publishing 2019)

Techera EJ and N Klein, *International Law of Sharks: Obstacles, Options and Opportunities* (Martinus Nijhoff 2017)

Tondini M, 'The Use of Force in the Course of Maritime Law Enforcement Operations' (2017) 4(2) Journal on the Use of Force and International Law 253

Tran YH, 'The South China Sea Arbitral Award: Legal Implications for Fisheries Management and Cooperation in the South China Sea' (2017) 6 Cambridge International Law Journal 87

Treves T, 'Article 290' in Alexander Proelss (ed), *United Nations Convention on the Law of the Sea: A Commentary* (CH Beck, Hart, and Nomos 2017)

—— 'Article 292' in Alexander Proelss (ed), *United Nations Convention on the Law of the Sea: A Commentary* (CH Beck, Hart, and Nomos 2017)

—— 'The Development of the Law of the Sea Since the Adoption of the UN Convention on the Law of the Sea: Achievements and Challenges for the Future' in Davor Vidas (ed), *Law, Technology and Science for Oceans in Globalisation: IUU Fishing, Oil Pollution, Bioprospecting, Outer Continental Shelf* (Martinus Nijhoff 2010)

—— 'The International Tribunal for the Law of the Sea and Other Law of the Sea Jurisdictions' (2010) 20 Italian Yearbook of International Law 315

——— 'The Jurisprudence of the International Tribunal for the Law of the Sea and Catastrophic Environmental Damage' (2011) 105 American Society of International Law Proceedings 436

Trevisanut S, 'Twenty Years of Prompt Release of Vessels: Admissibility, Jurisdiction, and Recent Trends' (2017) 48 Ocean Development and International Law 300

Trouwborst A, 'Prevention, Precaution, Logic and Law: The Relationship between the Precautionary Principle and the Preventative Principle in International Law and Associated Questions' (2009) 2 Erasmus Law Review 105

Trümpler K, 'Article 5' in Alexander Proelss (ed), *United Nations Convention on the Law of the Sea: A Commentary* (CH Beck, Hart and Nomos 2017)

Tseng H and C Ou, 'The Evolution and Trend of the Traditional Fishing Rights' (2010) 53 Ocean and Coastal Management 270

Tzeng P, 'Jurisdiction and Applicable Law under UNCLOS' (2016) 126 Yale Law Journal 242

——— 'Supplemental Jurisdiction under UNCLOS' (2016) 38(2) Houston Journal of International Law 499

——— 'The Peaceful Non-Settlement of Disputes: Article 4 of *CMATS* in *Timor-Leste v Australia*' (2017) 18 Melbourne Journal of International Law 349

——— 'Ukraine v Russia and Philippines v China: Jurisdiction and Legitimacy' (2017) 46(1) Denver Journal of International Law and Politics 1

Ulfstein G, 'International Courts and Judges: Independence, Interaction, and Legitimacy' (2014) 46 New York University Journal of International Law and Politics 849

UN Office for Ocean Affairs and the Law of the Sea, *Baselines: An Examination of the Relevant Provisions of the United Nations Convention on the Law of the Sea* (UN 1989)

Usuki E, 'China's Three Distinctive Assertions under the 'Nine-dash-line' Claims and the Annex VII Arbitral Tribunal's Interpretation of Article 121 Regarding an Island and Rocks under the 1982 UN Convention on the Law of the Sea' (2014) 21 Asian Yearbook of International Law 141

VanderZwaag DL, 'The ICJ, ITLOS and the Precautionary Approach: Paltry Progressions, Jurisprudential Jousting' (2013) 35 University of Hawai'i Law Review 617

Vega-Barbosa G, 'The Admissibility of Outer Continental Shelf Delimitation Claims Before the ICJ Absent a Recommendation by the CLCS' (2018) 49 Ocean Development and International Law 103

Ventura VAMS, 'Tackling Illegal, Unregulated and Unreported Fishing: The ITLOS Advisory Opinion on Flag State Responsibility for IUU Fishing and the Principle of Due Diligence' (2015) 12 Revista de Direito Internacional 50

Venzke I, 'The Role of International Courts as Interpreters and Developers of the Law: Working Out the Jurisgenerative Practice of Interpretation' (2011) 34 Loyola of Los Angeles International and Comparative Law Journal 99

Vignocchi C, 'ITLOST? The International Tribunal for the Law of the Sea Sounds the Charge to Expand Coastal State Jurisdiction' (2015) 39 Tulane Maritime Law Journal 791

Volterra, RG, GF Mandelli, and Á Nistal, 'The Characterisation of the *Dispute Concerning Coastal State Rights in the Black Sea, Sea of Azov, and Kerch Strait*' (2018) 33 International Journal of Marine and Coastal Law 614

Von Bogdandy A and Ingo Venzke, 'On the Functions of International Courts: An Appraisal in Light of Their Burgeoning Public Authority' (2013) 26 Leiden Journal of International Law 49

Weil, P, *The Law of Maritime Delimitation: Reflections* (CUP 1989)

Wendel P, *State Responsibility for Interferences with the Freedom of Navigation in Public International Law* (Springer 2007)

White M, 'Prompt Release Cases in ITLOS' in Tafsir Malick Ndiaye and Rüdiger Wolfrum (eds), *Law of the Sea, Environmental Law and Settlement of Disputes:* Liber Amicorum *Judge Thomas A. Mensah* (Brill 2007) 1025

Whomersley C, 'The Award on the Merits in the Case Brought by the Philippines against China Relating to the South China Sea: A Critique' (2017) 16 Chinese Journal of International Law 387

Wolfrum R, 'Conciliation under the UN Convention on the Law of the Sea' in Christian Tomuschat, Riccardo Pisillo Mazzeschi, and Daniel Thürer (eds), *Conciliation in International Law: The OSCE Court of Conciliation and Arbitration* (Brill 2016)

Wood M, 'The International Tribunal for the Law of the Sea and General International Law' (2007) 22 International Journal of Marine and Coastal Law 351

Wu X, 'Case Note: Maritime Delimitation in the Indian Ocean (*Somalia v. Kenya*), Judgment on Preliminary Objections' (2018) 17 Chinese Journal of International Law 841

Young MA, 'Maritime Delimitation by the International Court of Justice: Implications of Somalia v Kenya' (ARF Workshop on Dispute Resolution and Law of the Sea, Dili, 27–28 February 2020)

Zanella TV and RP Cabral, 'The Application of the Precautionary Principle in International Law: An Analysis of the Contribution of the International Tribunal for the Law of the Sea' (2017) 14 Veredas do Direito 229

Zarbiyev F, 'Judicial Activism in International Law: A Conceptual Framework for Analysis' (2012) 3 Journal of International Dispute Settlement 247

Zou K and Q Ye, 'Interpretation and Application of Article 298 of the Law of the Sea Convention in Recent Annex VII Arbitrations: An Appraisal' (2017) 48 Ocean Development and International Law 331

Index

For the benefit of digital users, indexed terms that span two pages (e.g., 52–53) may, on occasion, appear on only one of those pages.